George Nugent-Bankes

Memorials of John Hampden

His Party and his Times

George Nugent-Bankes

Memorials of John Hampden
His Party and his Times

ISBN/EAN: 9783743317338

Manufactured in Europe, USA, Canada, Australia, Japa

Cover: Foto ©ninafisch / pixelio.de

Manufactured and distributed by brebook publishing software (www.brebook.com)

George Nugent-Bankes

Memorials of John Hampden

MEMORIALS

OF

JOHN HAMPDEN,

HIS PARTY AND HIS TIMES.

BY LORD NUGENT.

FOURTH EDITION,
WITH A MEMOIR OF THE WRITER, AND A GENERAL INDEX.

ILLUSTRATED WITH TWELVE PORTRAITS ENGRAVED ON STEEL.

LONDON:
HENRY G. BOHN, YORK STREET, COVENT GARDEN.
1860.

CONTENTS.

MEMOIR OF GEORGE GRENVILLE, BARON NUGENT . . ix

THE AUTHOR'S PREFACE TO THE MEMORIALS 1

THE MEMORIALS.

PART THE FIRST.

TO 1625.

Ancestry and Family of Hampden—His Education and early Life—Introductory Matter—Posture of Public Affairs—Advance of general Information and the spirit of Liberty—James the First—Disputes with his first Parliament concerning Privileges and Supply—Disgusts the Nobility, and persecutes the Puritans—Dissolution—Second Parliament—Undertakers—Dissolution—Third Parliament—Hampden takes his Seat—His Mother urges him to seek a Peerage—First Parliamentary Party — Proceedings against Delinquents—Remonstrances — Answers of the King—Protestation — Dissolution—Commitments of Members—Villiers, Duke of Buckingham—His influence over the Prince—Disasters of his Administration—A new Parliament—On better terms with the King—Buckingham's influence declines—Death of the King 5

PART THE SECOND.

FROM 1625 TO 1628.

Accession of Charles the First—His Character—Appearance of a Reformation in the manners of the Court—Renewal of arbitrary Measures—Project of the Popular Party for extending the Representation—Right of Election restored to several Boroughs—Hampden elected for Wendover—Two Subsidies granted—Votes of Censure and Enquiry—

Further Supplies refused—Dissolution—Forced Loans—Ships lent to France to serve against the Huguenots—Failure of the Expedition to Cadiz, and blockade of Dunkirk—Second Parliament—Buckingham impeached—Elected Chancellor of the University of Cambridge—Seizure of Members—Dissolution—Hampden imprisoned—Oppressive Imposts—Members released—A new Parliament—Petition of Right—Further attempts at Redress of Grievances—Activity and industry of Hampden—Prorogation—Merchants' Goods seized—Failure of the Expedition to Rochelle—Death of Buckingham—Failure of a second Expedition—Surrender of Rochelle 32

PART THE THIRD.

FROM 1628 TO 1629.

Eminent Persons of the Country Party won over by the Court—Wentworth—Saville—Noy—A new Session—A Bill proposed to legalise Tonnage and Poundage—The Speaker refuses to put a Resolution of Privilege—The Commons' Protest—Dissolution—Hampden on Divers Committees of the House—Members committed to the Tower—Removed to prevent their Appearance to a Writ of Habeas Corpus—Sir John Eliot—Certain unjust Aspersions on his Memory—Letters to him from Hampden concerning his Sons—Hampden retires into Private Life—Violences of Laud, and Sufferings of the Puritans—Dr. Morley, Dr. Hales, and Dr. Heylin—Star Chamber, and High Commission Court—Hampden's first Wife dies—First Writ for the Levy of the Ship-Money 58

PART THE FOURTH.

FROM 1635 TO 1640.

Ship-Money—The Levy extended to Inland Places—Motives lately imputed to Hampden for his Opposition to it—The Grounds of that imputation examined—Hampden, and Thirty other Freeholders of the Parish of Great Kimble, in Buckinghamshire, refuse Payment—Sir Peter Temple, the High Sheriff, summoned to answer for Arrears—Disconsolate Letter from him to his Mother—Proceedings against Hampden—Judges declare for the Crown—General Discontent of the Country—Emigration of Puritans—Prohibited—Hampden and others detained—Independents and Presbyterians begin to separate—Insurrection in Scotland, and First Episcopal War—Treaty of Berwick—Short Parliament summoned—Hampden quits, for the last time, his retirement in Buckinghamshire 93

CONTENTS. v

PART THE FIFTH.

FROM 1640 TO 1641.

Short Parliament—Industry of Hampden—Hampden marries his second wife—Bishop Williams solicits his assistance in a case of Privilege with the Lords—Vane announces a message from the King concerning Ship-Money and Supply—Opposite Resolutions moved by Hampden and Hyde—Vane's angry declaration—Dissolution—Votes of Convocation, and renewed Resolutions of Grievances—Second Scotch War—Scots pass the Tweed and Tyne—Treaty of Ripon—Meetings of the Country party, and correspondence with the Scots—Opening of the Long Parliament — Committees of Grievances—Prisoners of the Star-Chamber liberated—Strafford, Laud, and others committed — Trial of Strafford — Bill of Attainder — Conduct of Hampden respecting that measure examined—Perfidy of the King . 126

PART THE SIXTH.

1641.

Triennial Bill—Corruptions of the Churchmen—Bill to restrain the Clergy from secular offices—Missions of Panzani and Rosetti—Temporising of the High Church Party in England with the Romish Discipline—Ground of Clarendon's Imputation against Hampden examined—Lord Say—Nathaniel Fiennes—Lord Kimbolton—Lord Digby—Sir Harry Vane, the Younger—Strode—Hazelrigge—Sir Edward Deering—Oliver Cromwell—Pym—Root-and-Branch—Bill for rendering Parliament indissoluble but with its own consent—Proceedings against Finch, Windebanke, and others—Result of the changes in Government—Great Seal given to Sir Edward Littleton—Army Plot . . . 167

PART THE SEVENTH.

FROM 1641 TO 1642.

The King's project of visiting Scotland—Opposed by the Commons—Encouraged by the Scots—The King arrives at Edinburgh — Cultivates Popularity with the Covenanters—Hampden, and others, Commissioners to attend upon the King—Intrigues and Violences of Montrose — The Scottish Incident — Irish Insurrection —The King returns to London—Grand Protestation—Defections from the Country Party—Demand of the King for the Surrender of Kimbolton and the

Five Members—Committee of Privileges retire to the City—Return in Triumph to Westminster—Petition of the Buckinghamshire Men—King leaves London—Departure of the Queen—King goes to York—Summons of Hull—Declaration of his Cause—Is joined by Lords—Raises his Standard—Hampden's motives and Falkland's compared—Breaking out of the Great Civil War 201

PART THE EIGHTH.

1642.

Posture of the two parties—Their motives and objects—Falkland, and others who take part for the King—Sir Bevill Grenvil—His letter to Sir John Trelawney—Formation of the Parliament Armies—Loans, and Contributions of Money and Plate—The Fleet declares for the Parliament—King's conditions from Nottingham rejected—Hampden captures the King's Oxfordshire Commissioners at Ascot—Conflicts in divers parts—Siege and surrender of Portsmouth—Coventry and Northampton attacked by the King's troops—Lord Brook—Brook and Hampden repulse the King's troops at Southam—Conditions of submission proposed to Lord Brook before Warwick—His Answer—He assembles his levies, and harangues his officers, at Warwick Castle 244

PART THE NINTH.

1642.

Defence of Warwick Castle by Sir Edward Peto—Of Caldecot Manor-House by Mrs. Purefoy—Lord Essex advances to Worcester—His Speech to his Army—Skirmish at Powick Bridge—Parliamentarians enter Worcester—Parliament's Petition for Peace—Rejected by the King—Essex advances his Army—Hampden and Holles defeat a party near Aylesbury—and pursue them into Worcestershire—The King puts himself in march towards London—Edge Hill fight—March through the Midland counties—Action between Balfore and Rupert at Aylesbury—Battle of Brentford—Retreat of the King 276

PART THE TENTH.

FROM 1642 TO 1643.

Hampden and Urrie take Reading by assault—Hampden arranges the plan of union of the six associated counties—Parliament's troops press upon the King's quarters at Oxford — Lord Wentworth attacks High Wycombe, and is repulsed—Essex retires—King's successes in divers parts—Queen lands in England—Reading re-entered by the King's troops—Hampden and Mr. Richard Grenvil repulsed from Brill—Sir Bevill Grenvil in Cornwall—Bradock Down, and Stratton Hill—Lansdown—Trelawney's letter to the Lady Grace Grenvil, announcing Sir Bevill's death—Siege of Lichfield—Lord Brook slain—Warder Castle twice taken—Overtures of peace, and cessation of arms—Broken off—Reading besieged by Lord Essex—Surrenders—Defections from the Parliament's cause—Waller's Plot—Rupert's expeditions against the Parliament's quarters—Attacks Chinnor and Postcombe—Chalgrove fight—Hampden wounded—His last moments and death—Conclusion of the Memorials. 315

APPENDIX 367

ERRATA.

Page 173, *for* "Appendix B" *read* "Appendix E."
Page 237, *for* "Appendix C" *read* "Appendix F."
,, *for* "Appendix D" *read* "Appendix G."

LIST OF PORTRAITS.

	PAGE
JOHN HAMPDEN.—*Frontispiece.*	
JOHN PYM	5
GEORGE ABBOTT, ARCHBISHOP OF CANTERBURY	49
WILLIAM FIELDING, EARL OF DENBIGH	55
ARCHIBALD CAMPBELL, MARQUIS OF ARGYLE	118
JAMES GRAHAM, MARQUIS OF MONTROSE	137
OLIVER CROMWELL	182
EDWARD SACKVILLE, EARL OF DORSET	216
ROBERT GREVILLE, LORD BROOKE	273
W. HARVEY, M.D.	303
SIR BEVILL GRENVIL	329
BLANCH SOMERSET, BARONESS ARUNDEL OF WARDOUR	339

GEORGE GRENVILLE, BARON NUGENT.

1789—1850.

THE readers of the *Memorials of Hampden* will perhaps not think it unbecoming that a brief outline of the principal incidents of Lord Nugent's life should be prefixed to a revised edition of the book which he most desired should be connected with his name. Though highly born, endowed with talents and tastes that would have distinguished him in any condition, and devoted to public affairs, Lord Nugent failed to exercise any marked influence in political life ; but he has left behind him the example, always well worthy of being placed on record, of a man faithful to opinions which he believed to be just, displaying them without regard to personal consequences, preferring them to his interests, and always ready to make sacrifices for them. He was a steady, courageous, and consistent politician; and no man was more endeared to his friends by delightful social qualities.

Lord George Grenville, born on the 31st December 1789, at Kilmainham Hospital, Dublin, during his father's Lord-Lieutenancy of Ireland, was the second son of that second Earl Temple who was created Marquis of Buckingham in 1784. But, as he drew the title by which he is now best known, he seems also to have derived his more marked traits of character, from the family of his mother, the Lady Mary Elizabeth Nugent. His maternal grandfather was Goldsmith's friend, Viscount Clare, afterwards Earl Nugent.* His mother in her childhood and girl-

---

* On the dispersion of the contents of Stowe, Lord Nugent was ex-

hood was Goldsmith's playfellow, and one of her harmless practical jokes is given to *Tony Lumpkin*. In right of this lady, whom his father married in 1775, the year after Goldsmith's death, and on whom, at the close of 1800, was conferred the Irish barony of Nugent with remainder to her second son, Lord George Grenville took the title of the barony. His birthright may thus be said to have included something higher than mere rank. He inherited a genial nature and humour, as well as cordial tastes, and most respectable talents in literature. For, Goldsmith's patron and friend, whose reported portliness of person had also descended to his grandson, was a writer not at all of mean mark, and there are verses in his Ode to Pulteney which Akenside or Pope might have written. One of them is quoted by Gibbon to illustrate his character of Brutus.

There was a difference of thirteen years between the eldest and the second son of Lord Buckingham; and when, on the death of the latter in February 1813, Richard became second Marquis, his brother George had been not many months second Lord Nugent, having succeeded to the title on his mother's death, in March 1812.

ceedingly anxious to obtain, for his relative Sir George Nugent, a portrait of his grandfather which had belonged to Lady Buckingham, and on expressing his wish to Lord Lansdowne, who was reported to have given a commission for its purchase at the sale, received the subjoined note.
'Bowood, Sept. 10. Dear Lord Nugent,—You will easily believe that if I
'had given any commission for the purchase of Lord Nugent's portrait at
'Stowe, I should instantly have withdrawn it, on receiving your letter;
'but the fact is that I never had any thought of purchasing it.
  'Your inquiry on the subject recalls to my recollection, that, standing in
'the presence of a great crowd before the picture, I said to Lord Granville,
'who was with me, ".That is an interesting portrait, for I have heard from
'"those who recollected him that he was a person of singular humour and
'"talent for conversation, and the face shows it," which may have reached
'the bystanders, and led to a report, with about as much foundation as
'ninety-nine reports in a hundred have.
  'I sincerely hope Sir George will attain his object.
                'Believe me very faithfully yours,
                                    'LANSDOWNE.'

He had passed with some distinction through his under-graduate course at Oxford, and he left it, as he continued to the close of his life, a fair classical scholar. He was a member of Brazenose, at which College the date of his matriculation was the 25th April 1804;* and in 1807 he contended successfully for the prize in English prose composition, though it was afterwards found that he had not completed the four years' residence necessary to qualify him for receiving the prize awarded. I have not seen this Essay,† but the subject was 'Duelling,' and we may well believe that the feeling of the gentleman, as well as the scholar's accomplishments, were conspicuous in a composition which on such a theme could bear away the palm from many high-spirited competitors. The Principal and Fellows of Brazenose testified their sense of his merit on the occasion, and their sympathy with the accident that diverted its due reward from himself to another member of their college, Mr. Allen, by voting him, out of the college funds, a magnificently bound copy of the three splendid quartos of Musgrave's *Euripides*, which to the last day of his life occupied the most conspicuous place in his little library at Lilies, and from which I copy the following inscription:

'Honoratissimo Domino, GEORGIO GRENVILLE, cui in Cancel-
'larii Oxoniensis certamine Palmam ob ingenii splendorem
'Academia lubenter adjucavit, eam tamen reportandam ob
'Quadriennium nondum exactum victori invita denegavit, hoc
'munusculum ut ejus merita et suam ipsorum comprobationem
'testentur, D.D., Principalis et Socii Collegii Ænei Nasi,
'MDCCCVII.'

* I inferred, from observing among his papers letters addressed to him at Christchurch, that he had afterwards changed his college; but on application to my friend the Rev. Christopher Erle, the Rector of Hardwicke, in Bucks, whose learning and scholarship not less than his generous and kindly nature made him Lord Nugent's valued neighbour and intimate friend in all the latter years of his life, he informs me that he never belonged to Christchurch.

† It was printed in the same year at Buckingham as 'written by Lord 'George Grenville.'

It will further mark the character of Lord George Grenville's pursuits and tastes at this time, to record the fact of his intimacy with Reginald Heber. This distinguished scholar, who was six years his elder, took his Bachelor's degree at Brazenose, in the second year of Lord George's undergraduateship; carried off the Chancellor's prize for the English Essay, the year before Lord George successfully contended for it; and, after an interval of two years' foreign travel, returned to Oxford and graduated Master of Arts in 1808. Among the few letters of his youth which Lord Nugent had preserved, is one from Heber to his 'dear Grenville,' which is dated in the latter year, and the subject of which is the πολιτεια of Aristotle. The composition of a Treatise on the Grecian Republics was now occupying Lord George; and Heber had been 'rummaging that code of slavery and 'prejudice (for such I begin to think it') for anything he could find to assist his friend. 'There is nothing,' he continues, 'which I think can be very useful to you, except 'you may observe, in confirmation of your assertion that the 'Republics of Greece were only a very extended aristocracy, 'that Aristotle always excludes from a well-ordered govern- 'ment, both bourgeois and peasants, whom he does not even 'account *parts* of the REPUBLIC; and though he dissuades from 'the appointment of magistrates from one single family, he 'says their race, however, must be ου το τυχον. You should, 'however, point out the main fault in the Grecian Republics, 'that their nobility or citizens, for they are the same thing, 'were too numerous; which engendered a most intolerable 'bondage of those who were *ordinibus adscripti.* Aristotle 'declares that the peasants should be all attached to the soil, 'and slaves. I think I mentioned to you that he defines the 'authority of a father as monarchical; the situation of his wife 'and children as answering to the aristocracy in a state—and 'the slaves to the subjects, or helots; without such unfortunate 'drudges, neither a state nor a family are perfect.' Another allusion in the letter, in which he recites some authorities for 'the 'black and white bones of the Calmucks,' touches upon the scene of his recent travels, and marks his friend's interest in them.

Some part of the next two years, Lord George Grenville passed with the British army in the Peninsula, where war was raging; and at his return, in 1810, Lord Grenville having meanwhile defeated Lord Eldon and the Duke of Beaufort in a contest for the Chancellorship of Oxford, he received the degree of D.C.L. on the occasion of his uncle's installation. The war of liberation had now let loose as many pens as tongues, in commemoration of the wrongs and struggles of Portugal and Spain; Heber, in the preceding year, had written some graceful verses on that theme; and very early in 1812, Lord George Grenville's *Portugal*, a poem in two parts, was published in a goodly quarto. Youth has had worse sins to answer for, and indulged them in ways less easily forgotten. For though we have more reason to laugh now, than the author of the *Twopenny Post Bag* had then, at the 'patriot monsters from 'Spain' whose decline in popularity he was somewhat prematurely predicting—

> ' Whether the Ministers paw'd them too much
>   (And you know how they spoil whatsoever they touch),
> Or whether Lord George, the young man about town,
>   Has, by dint of bad poetry, written them down,
> One has certainly lost one's *peninsular* rage.'*

—this peninsular rage implied yet a high and manly feeling, of which the 'young man about town' had no call to be ashamed. His poem had no immortal stanzas in it, certainly, and may have had some absurd ones; but without any thoughts that were not generous, and without any sympathies that were not large and just on the side of public principles and national struggles, it expressed such feelings, upon the whole, in no unpleasing or unbecoming form, and still remains, even for

* *Intercepted Letters* of Thomas Brown the Younger, Letter V.

us, a not uninteresting record of that hearty admiration for our great leader in the memorable conflict, which, thus early awakened in Lord Nugent's mind by the lines of Torres Vedras, and the victories of Busaco, Badajoz, and Salamanca, was never afterwards weakened by the party fidelities or political enmities of later life.

The hero himself received it not ungratefully. He was at Nevada, when, towards the end of 1812, the present Duke of Richmond placed it in his hands. 'My dear Lord,' he writes to Lord Nugent, 'many thanks for your letter of the 22nd 'October and your poem, which March delivered to me. I had 'already read the latter with the greatest pleasure; and I am 'highly flattered by your dedication of it to me. You will 'have seen,' continues Lord Wellington, 'that we have had a 'terrible collection of troops upon us; and it was quite 'impossible that we could hold all the ground we had taken 'in consequence of our success in July. The enemy have 'treated us with great respect, and have done us but little 'mischief. The most severe weather, however, that I have 'ever known at this season of the year in any country, has 'done us some.' In the same letter Lord Wellington refers to the death of Lord Nugent's mother. 'I am happy to find,' he says, 'that Lord Buckingham is recovering in some 'degree. I have been always a little anxious respecting his 'return to Stowe. But you will all be about him; and as he 'must return at some time or other, it is best that it should be 'early. Pray present my most affectionate respects to him, 'your brother, and Lady Temple.'

Pretty nearly at the time when this letter was written, Lord Nugent had himself been expressing to his father the same feeling of anxiety and hope in regard to his return to Stowe, and Lord Buckingham was thanking 'his dearest George' for that affectionate sympathy. 'I dread,' he continues, 'the first 'encounter of scenes that will recall so much of what will make 'my wounds bleed afresh; but every delay adds to my 'reluctance, and unless I was determined to abandon the 'struggle, I feel that I ought not to defer it.' The letter may be further quoted for the pleasing way in which it marks Lord Nugent's entrance into public life. The year in which it was written, and in which Lady Buckingham's death* bequeathed him the title by which he was always afterwards known, was also that of the general election which followed within a few months after Mr. Perceval's death, and the reconstruction of his cabinet under the lead of Lord Liverpool.

* In the Second Edition of my *Life of Goldsmith* (ii. 364, 365) I have printed a letter of Lord Nugent's written only a few months before his own death, in which he speaks of his mother, as he recollected her a few weeks before she died, with the grateful affection which to the last accompanied every mention of her name. She divided his thoughts with his wife ('the two highest-minded creatures and the ablest, that I ever 'knew'), and a very delightful crayon sketch of her, by Sir Joshua Reynolds, hung always over the fire-place in the library at Lilies, as happily it does to this day, Lord Nugent's brother-in-law, Doctor Connel, still possessing both. It may not be out of place to subjoin another striking proof of the way in which her virtues lived in the memory of those who had felt their influence, in this letter of the late Field Marshal Sir George Nugent, dated Westhorpe, July 22, 1837, and written to Lord Nugent on the occasion of his contesting Aylesbury in that year. Sir George was the illegitimate son of Lady Buckingham's father. 'My dear Friend,' he writes, 'I thank you for your affectionate letter. 'Although I promised to give my vote to Mr. Praed at the ensuing election 'for Aylesbury, not having the least notion at the time that you were 'likely to become a candidate for the borough, yet as I had determined 'long ago, with my son George, never to oppose you again, I shall not 'attend the election there.—I have passed too many happy days in your 'cheerful society and that of your dear wife, and have too strong an 'affection for you, from various heart-felt recollections, ever to do other- 'wise than love you sincerely. The debt of gratitude I owe to your 'dearest mother, for her affectionate attention to me throughout a long 'and eventful life; and especially for her devotion to my dear children, 'when their parents were at so great a distance from them; and the 'motherly interest she took in acquainting their dearest mother and me 'of their welfare, to the last moment of her existence; affect me deeply, 'whenever I reflect upon her virtues.—I cannot describe what we both felt, 'when we were suddenly informed of her death; it dwelt upon our minds 'during the remainder of our stay in India, and we could never mention 'her name without tears in our eyes.—I have always regretted that we

In this general election Lord Nugent was returned member of parliament for Aylesbury; and,—the failure of the attempt consequent on Mr. Perceval's death, to form a government more favourable to the Roman Catholics by the junction of Lords Grenville and Grey with Lord Wellesley and Mr. Canning, having left the Grenville family in a moderated opposition to the court,—Lord Buckingham thus writes of the elections to the new member for Aylesbury. 'Every one whom I have heard
' speak upon it seems to think that we have certainly gained,
' at least, in the county elections. Canning and Gascoigne
' appear safe at Liverpool' (this was the election in which Canning defeated Brougham), 'and I conclude that he and
' Lord Wellesley's members will oppose government in the
' first divisions. I need not, my dearest George, press most
' earnestly and anxiously on your mind the sanguine and eager
' hopes I entertain that you will apply yourself steadily and
' unremittingly to the duties of parliament, and to constant and
' habitual debate. I never in forty years saw such an opening
' as now presents itself in the House of Commons for a young
' man of talents and application; and I have only to wish that
' you were as decidedly master of the latter indispensable
' quality as you are of the first. But for God's sake do not
' throw away these most valuable years of your life.'

In so strongly implying his belief that the House of Commons now wanted a good debater, Lord Buckingham no doubt purposely overlooked the powers of such men, already in full possession of the house, as Canning, George Ponsonby, Tierney, Romilly, Whitbread, and Wilberforce, and of those

' should have taken so different a line in politics, for your sake, as it has
' been the source of great uneasiness, both to you and other members of
' your family, but I am sure that you have acted throughout conscientiously.
' —I thank you for your kind congratulations on the birth of my dear
' George's son, which has made us all very happy.—God bless you my dear
' friend.—My best love to dear Lady Nugent, who I hope is better.
'Yours most affectionately,
'G. NUGENT.'

younger and more eager spirits, Broughams, Plunkets, Francis Horners, Palmerstons, Huskissons, Peels, and John Russells, whom the elections of 1812 and the succeeding years seated with Lord Nugent in St. Stephen's. For already he understood the defect in his son's character, and his letter was manifestly intended at once to humour and to incite a somewhat sluggish application, by representing as within the easiest possible reach those higher objects of ambition. It was the old lord's honest belief that his second son would make a figure in the House of Commons, and he always steadily resisted his own importunity to be allowed to enter the profession more commonly set apart for younger sons. A letter is before me written nine years after the present date, by Lord Nugent to his brother, in which he reminds him of 'the views ' I was from my earliest boyhood always taught by my father ' to form respecting my objects through life. You know that ' in early days I repeatedly urged my father to give me a ' commission in the army or navy. He uniformly refused, ' desiring me to look to parliament as the object and pursuit ' of my life.'

The Marquis of Buckingham did not long survive his widowed and solitary return to the grandeurs of Stowe. He died on the 11th February, 1813, within a few months after writing the letter above quoted on the elections; and Lord Nugent's marriage with Anne Lucy, the second daughter of Lieutenant General the Hon. Vere Poulett, took place in the following September. The proximity of the seats of Addington and Stowe had led to friendly intercourse between the families; the younger children were playfellows; and the union would have taken place earlier, but that strong family objections arose, which delayed it from time to time. The only issue of the marriage were two infants, which did not survive their birth, and this was the only drawback from its happiness. The most tender affection,—based upon perfect sympathy, and sustained by a confidence in each other, and a mutual esteem, which none of the accidents or disappointments of later life ever sensibly impaired,—subsisted always between Lord and Lady Nugent. Her tastes were in agreement with his; her pencil, with which she drew skilfully, exhibited humourous invention as well as grace of design; she could write with point and ease, both in verse and prose; and it is to be regretted that of such accomplishments of her mind there should not survive even so much in the way of memorial, as the canvas of Lawrence and the marble of Chantrey have preserved of the beauty of her person. Nothing lay so near her husband's heart as the wish to collect materials for such a record, when her death closed suddenly the tender intercourse of thirty-five years: but that event, which made an ineffaceable impression upon him, was speedily followed by his own last illness; and it may perhaps be worthy of mention, that, prominent among the only fragments of her writing which he had then been able to bring together, and which lay near him on his death-bed, were some pathetic stanzas on the infants they had lost in the second and third year of their marriage.

For the first year or two after Lord Nugent's election to the House of Commons, there are not many traces of him in the debates, but he attended to the business of the House, and divided always with the Opposition. The question at the time most prominent in its influence upon parties and cabinets, was that of Catholic Emancipation; its vicissitudes had always most affected the fortunes of his family; its Irish champions and heroes, such as Grattan, Curran,* and others, were among the earliest objects of his admiring sympathy; and such was the

* Among Lord Nugent's papers I find a note from Curran, written shortly before he resigned the Mastership of the Rolls, in one of those intervals of holiday in England which he enjoyed so heartily. 'My dear 'Lord, Accept my very warm and respectful thanks for your kind note. 'Most gladly would I obey your friendly summons, but I am engaged for 'to-morrow under circumstances that cut off all power that my mind might 'exercise over my body. I regret this the more because I myself must set

ardour with which Lord Nugent supported the question in all its bearings, and the zeal and ability he displayed in connection with it, that the English Catholics ultimately singled him out as the member to whom their petition to the Lower House was regularly entrusted. He took also a prominent part in protesting against the treatment of Lord Cochrane, and very ably seconded Lord Ebrington's motion on that subject, in July 1814. In the following year he opposed, in every stage, the bill for a provision for the Duke of Cumberland; and in 1816 he began to speak more frequently, making himself conspicuous for his opposition to the treaties with foreign powers concluded in the previous year. Holding a strong opinion against the expediency, in a constitutional view, of the English army kept up under those treaties in the pay of a foreign monarch and in sight of our own shores, a feeling which was shared by such men as Francis Horner, Tierney, Romilly, Brougham, Lords Milton and Ebrington, and Lord John Russell, he took repeated part in denouncing the ministerial policy, which Lord Grenville was at the same time also opposing in the House of Lords.

But there was all the difference in the world between the

'out and surrender myself, however reluctantly, to the Cimmerian prison
'in three or four days. I hope, however, in a short time to return, and I
'flatter myself with the additional hope that Lord Nugent will not forget
'the tone in which he has permitted our acquaintance to begin. To try
'his memory on that point shall be my first experiment when I come
'hither. Meantime, I shall not fail to remember with great pleasure and
'gratitude what is past.

'I have the honour to be, my dear Lord,
  'Very truly yours,
    'JOHN P. CURRAN.'

Three years after Curran died, Grattan lay on his death-bed, also in London; and a letter from his eldest son to Lord Nugent, written two days before his death (June 2, 1820), and describing his sufferings, lies before me. It concludes thus: 'Mr. Grattan begs me particularly to say 'how much he feels your affectionate enquiries after his health, and to 'assure you how highly he esteems you.'

tone of opposition taken by uncle and nephew, and Lord Buckingham, who had been lately falling off even from Lord Grenville's side, found it of course impossible to keep up with his brother. Nor did matters in this respect improve as time went on, and those political discontents of the manufacturing districts broke forth, which the low wages, high prices, and overstocked markets consequent on the close of the war directly led to; which the ill-advised change in the corn laws, and a series of bad harvests, influenced and aggravated; and which finally spawned such acts as those of Lords Sidmouth and Castlereagh, and such patriots as Mr. Henry Hunt and his associates.

It is difficult to understand what those ten years, from 1816 to 1826, must have seemed to men who were actually looking on, from the House of Commons or elsewhere, on what was passing in the country. To us who look back upon them now, the patriotism and tyranny appear equally shabby. Nothing can exceed the want of dignity on all sides, whether in the consistent and paltry misgovernment that oppressed the people, or the honest and amazing ignorance that resisted it. One of the so-called leaders of sedition, Mr. Samuel Bamford, who appears to have been also one of the simplest, kindliest, and most moderate of God's creatures, had to undergo five examinations before the Privy Council, was brought up in irons from Lancashire as a suspected traitor, was dismissed, was again arrested, and finally was tried upon a charge which had dwindled down from high treason to a common misdemeanour; yet he has written a book of memoirs lately,* in which he very manifestly tells with truth all that was known to him, and makes it clear that, amid all the ignorance,

---

* He has also written poetry, beautiful for its honest and simple unaffectedness, and its earnest advocacy of the poor. A touching little poem of his is quoted in the novel of *Mary Barton*, the author of that remarkable book characterising him as 'a man who illustrates his order, ' and shows what nobility may be in a cottage.'

delusion, and submission to dishonest promptings then prevalent, the masses were really set in motion by nothing more alarming than the wish to redress what they thought to be intolerable wrongs, by what they believed to be legal means. There can be no doubt, in short, that the only infamous projects entertained or discussed, proceeded directly from spies and informers. That kind of gentry were the most active and busily employed people of the day, and their employment shows in what spirit, from the first, the Government proposed and intended to act to the malcontents. Conciliation or concession in the most moderate degree was scouted; Coercion was the only thing thought of, by way of remedy; Suspension of the Habeas Corpus, Six Acts, gaggings alike of the tongue and the pen, were the sole pride of ministerial legislation; everybody suspected was clapped into prison, persecution of the press went on in every conceivable form, and there was a continual stretch and strain upon the treason laws. The truth was, therefore, that though the country had never incurred such infinitesimally small danger from revolutionary doctrines as during the years of Sidmouth and Castlereagh, the danger from anti-revolutionary nostrums was become really very great indeed: and thus may be explained the excitement prevailing against a Government which, at the time, was doing its best to inflame discontent *into* rebellion; which sought to include in the same proscription the Broughams and Henry Hunts, the Lambtons, Burdetts, and Thistlewoods; and under which no independent man could feel himself safe, however loyal.

This feeling broke out very strongly from Lord Nugent in the May of 1817, when he opposed the army estimates moved for by Lord Palmerston, in a speech of sufficient spirit and animation to draw forth characteristic eulogy from Mr. Brougham, who not only sincerely agreed with the member for Aylesbury as to the policy of ruling in the hearts of the people, in preference to lording it over them by military force, but ' con- ' gratulated him on sentiments as much above all despotic views 'and illiberal prejudices, as a truly noble mind was above 'those who looked only to shuffling and sneaking after place.' In the following month Lord Nugent spoke with equal force and boldness against the Habeas Corpus Act Suspension Bill. He opposed the Indemnity Bill in the following year, and his speeches against it were republished with those of Lambton, Brougham, and Romilly. In 1819, the year after Romilly's death, he engaged earnestly with Mackintosh in an attempt to get a Committee on Capital Punishments, with a view to reduce the number (there were even then 156) of separate offences punishable with death, and had the satisfaction to see Government beaten on the occasion by a majority of 19. In the same year he was zealous for the Roman Catholics, active against the Foreign Enlistment Bill, a steady voter in the minorities on Lord John Russell's motions for Reform, and untiring in his opposition to the army votes, mutiny bills, and everything on which battle could be made against the continued existence of a Ministry which he lost no opportunity of denouncing as mischievous and contemptible.

Some example of Lord Nugent's tone and manner in the House of Commons at this time should here perhaps be given, however brief; and the instance may be taken from a speech in the Habeas Corpus Act debates, which, apart from the virulence of ministerial attack immediately provoked by it, exerted a certain influence on the speaker's subsequent career and fortunes. 'The hon. gentleman on the other side,' observed Lord Nugent—

'Has said that the judgment of the people of England is on the
'side of ministers. He has talked of appealing on the subject of
'this suspension to the opinion of the people of England. To the
'opinion of the people of England! Good God, Sir, do we not
'know that the people of England dare not express any free
'opinion at all? We know that we have gagged their speech by
'our Sedition Bills: we know that we have fettered their press
'by our ex-officio informations: we know that we have made

'every magistrate in the country the supreme judge and summary
' punisher of blasphemy and sedition. We have made it sedition
' to talk contemptuously of his Majesty's present government ; and
' lastly, to fill the measure of intolerance and oppression, we add
' insult to it, by appealing to the free opinion of a disfranchised
' people.'

Then, after a bold and uncompromising attack upon 'the
' unfailing profusion and boundless corruption' of Ministers as
having but too well prepared the people for any system that
madness could invent or wickedness could recommend, the
member for Aylesbury continued :

' But were the case a thousand times worse than it is, were it
' capable of being shown (which God forbid!) that we are
' now placed in the dilemma between popular commotion on the
' one hand, and on the other a continued suspension of our rights,
' I think that even at that dreadful issue, even in that dreadful
' alternative, I should be speaking in the spirit, at least, of the
' British Constitution in saying, that I should prefer, as the lesser evil,
' public disquiet to the risk of freedom so long suspended that it
' may never be restored ; that I had rather see my country revolu-
' tionised than see it enslaved (Hear, hear, from Government). I
' repeat it—I had rather see my country revolutionised, than see it
' enslaved. (loud cheers from the Opposition).' *

But loud cheers from the Opposition had lost their charm at
Stowe, Lord Nugent's brother now entertaining what appears to
have been an honest belief that danger was really impending
over the country, and putting faith in those ministerial nostrums,
defences, and precautions against it, which the member for
Aylesbury despised and assailed. Some few months before
the speech was delivered, letters had been interchanged between
the brothers in a spirit highly honourable to both.

Originally, of course, the family influence had returned
Lord Nugent for Aylesbury ; but since his brother's accession

* *Hansard*, xxxvi., 1222-4.

to the title, he had been indebted to him for the means o
cultivating strong personal relations with the borough apart
from the family interests there; and his course in parliament had also, unexpectedly, much strengthened his position
and claims as the independent member for a constituency
with strong liberal leanings, among whom, as owner by his
brother's kindness of the neighbouring little manor house of
Lilies, he was now able to pass several months of residence in
every year. Nevertheless, before the meeting of parliament in
1817, he wrote to Lord Buckingham expressing strongly his
wish to resign his seat. He represented the course which the
questions of the ensuing session appeared likely to take, and
the increased distance at which such questions threatened to
place himself and the Marquis in public life. He said how
irksome it would be to him to feel that he was availing himself of his brother's interest at Aylesbury, while in the House
of Commons he should be voting in direct opposition to his
wishes; and urged him to give effect fairly to his own opinions
by using his interest for the return of some one who could
better represent them in parliament. Whenever such arrangements could be made, therefore, Lord Nugent was to be considered as quite prepared to retire. To this nothing could be
more honourable and affectionate than Lord Buckingham's
reply. He did indeed remind his younger brother that in the
last conversation he held with his poor father, the often-re-
peated saying of the old Marquis had been, that if his two
boys could only stick together they might command what
they pleased; and he also adverted, by way of warning, to an
attack which had been made upon himself by a member of the
more respectable part of the Opposition, a friend of the late
Mr. Fox's ('who permitted himself to tell you that I had sold
'myself for a dukedom, and that you were the only independent
'Grenville now in public life'), as but the revival in his age
of acts practised by the same person in his youth, and the last
effort of a disappointed party to divide a family which it had

not been able to master. But, even on personal grounds, the substance of the letter (which is dated from Stowe in April) was in a high degree honourable to Lord Buckingham, and its remarks on public policy were at least such as to entitle him to his brother's respectful hearing.

'I must in the first place explicitly state, how deeply I feel the
' affectionate and honourable part which you have taken. As ex-
' plicitly and as plainly, I refrain either now or hereafter to discuss
' your seat with you. I never will, directly or indirectly, take any
' step to dissolve the family faggot of sticks, upon the keeping of
' which together, my domestic happiness, my family prospects, my
' private enjoyments, and publick strength depends; and if, instead
' of differing, as I fear we do, upon abstract parts of political
' subjects, I were to form a part of this Government, and you, upon
' mature consideration, should deem it necessary to oppose me, I
' would not accept your seat from you, but content myself with
' lamenting political disunion between two brothers, who never
' could in consequence feel a diminution of affection. *There,*
' *therefore, let the question of your seat rest now and for ever.*
' With respect to political opinions I am free to confess to you,
' that as far as I can venture to look forward into the haze
' of political distance, there seems much more probability of
' disunion increasing between the Opposition and myself, than of
' any approximation taking place. There is but one thing which
' separates opposition from faction, and that is a conscientious
' feeling that by opposition one is doing one's best to bring into
' Government a better system of principles, than those directing
' the actual possessors of the Government. If any thing could
' tend to alarm me more than I am now alarmed by the prevalence
' of bad opinions in the country, it would be the seeing any
' prospect of those bad opinions forcing themselves into the
' government of it. I, therefore, never can be a party to any
' parliamentary exertion to obtain for those opinions the power
' which is, and I in my conscience believe, is all that is, wanting to
' overthrow the country. With respect to the Habeas Corpus
' Suspension Act, it is impossible for me to decide what may or

'may not be the state of the country in July next; but my
'belief is, that it will not be then expedient to repeal the Acts
'passed before Easter. The strongest possible case must be made
'out to me to justify the casting off so soon those guards, which
'as I thought them vitally necessary for our security, I think must
'be continued so long as any danger of the continuance of that
'system which called them forth appears. If I thought, as you do,
'the English law sufficient for the maintenance of the English
'Constitution, I should, as you are, be anxious for the immediate
'reduction of our military establishment. But the experience of
'the last six months has proved to me that powers beyond the
'regular course of our law are necessary for our safety. I must,
'therefore, see the country brought within the pale of the law
'before I would get entirely rid of the excess of numerical military
'force necessary to repel those whose object it is to reduce our
'military force for the purpose of the easier and more effectually
'enslaving the country in revolutionary fetters. I quite, however,
'agree that a military force in the country, in a time of peace,
'beyond that which is necessary to maintain its policy and to
'support its possessions, is most improper and unfitting. What
'now, in my mind, constitutes unfortunately its necessity, is the
'conviction that there is a deep-rooted conspiracy which nothing but
'the strength or fear of the sword can keep down. But with that
'danger, the remedy should cease, and the cessation of the danger
'mainly depends upon those who are the loudest in decrying the
'remedy. With respect to Reform of Parliament I object to it as
'a system, so long as I invariably find that system brought forward
'as a stalking-horse for rebellion. Triennial Parliaments would be
'in my opinion a most dangerous weapon in the hands of the
'people against the crown, just as I think a longer duration than
'that of seven years would be a weapon as dangerous in those of
'the crown against the people. The fact is, that the dissolution of
'a Parliament should not be a weapon of *offence* in the hands of
'either; but has political experience justified the hope that three
'years, or a term within that period, would be a sufficient interval
'within which popular effervescence, upon any popular subject,
'would be likely to subside, so as to make an appeal to the people

'more likely to be one to its sense, than to its nonsense? With
' respect to the remedies you suggest to many evils connected with
' our Parliamentary Establishments, I think them, generally speak-
' ing, good, and that many more may be individually and separately
' brought forward to meet known and acknowledged evils. Those
' remedies you will never find me opposing, if practicable, when
' they are coolly and dispassionately brought forward as individual
' insulated measures; but I will always oppose them, and other
' measures, when brought forward in such a manner and by such
' men as afford me proof or reason to believe that the bringing
' them forward is meant not to reform or amend Parliament, but
' to delude the people and disturb the country. I have now, I
' believe, my dear brother, gone through all your political points;
' and I have discussed them the more freely with you, because, in
' the first part of my letter, I have refused to consider them as in
' any way affecting the question of your seat.'

It seemed just to Lord Buckingham to show, by the evidence of a letter written in the most unreserved confidence five years before he received his Dukedom, that the change in his opinions which was to separate him equally from Lord Grenville and his brother, had begun thus early, and, with whatever view to his own ultimate position, was based, as there appears no reason to doubt, on fair and independent convictions of his own. Nor is there occasion to question the perfect sincerity of his present assurances to Lord Nugent as in any degree incompatible with the misunderstanding that afterwards arose. When a point of departure in opinions is once taken, everything tends to make the severance wider, and the progress in opposite directions more rapid and complete, than either party originally contemplated. The speech which has been quoted appears to have shaken the good understanding between the brothers, and subsequent occurrences had no tendency in any way to contribute to its restoration.

It so fell out that in the short interval of four years between the present date and that of 1822,—when the Marquis received his Dukedom, and a formal adherence of the other members of his family completed that 'coalition with the Grenvilles' which, seeing that Lord Nugent was so strongly committed against it, and Lord Grenville had left public life, need not so mightily have alarmed Chancellor Eldon * for its horrible approximation to Whiggery,—there were no less than two general elections; when the fact of Lord Nugent having carried his return on both occasions, against bitter ministerial opposition, seemed no longer doubtfully to connect the strength of his position at Aylesbury, rather with personal popularity and the approval of political conduct, than with family claims. But what we are not unwilling to concede as a favour, we do not like to see taken as a right; and notwithstanding any former promises, it was really not unnatural that Lord Buckingham, on the eve of his formal junction with the Ministry, and acting only on the ordinary acceptations of political morality both then and since, should have sought to deprive the Opposition of at least that element of strength in his family borough which was supplied by his family name. The subject need not be pursued. Lord Nugent remained the member for Aylesbury, but not without a sacrifice that tested the sincerity of the line he had taken in public life; and by the interference of Lord Grenville, with whose letter to his younger nephew on the close of the family misunderstanding all further allusion to it may most properly cease, cordiality between the brothers was resumed.

'MY DEAR GEORGE,   'Dropmore, Dec. 8, 1822.

' I am too sincerely and affectionately attached to your brother
' and to yourself, not to feel the warmest and most cordial satisfaction
' in what you tell me of your being again together on that footing
' on which brothers ought to live with each other, and which I
' earnestly hope will ever remain unchanged between you. My

---

* 'This coalition, I think, will have consequences very different from 'those expected by the members of administration who brought it about. 'I hate coalitions.' Twiss's *Life*, ii. 446.

'experience enables me to say confidently, that there is nothing
'else in this world that can supply the want of such intercourse
'between persons so connected; it remains to us, when everything
'fails us; and I know you will not mistake the motives which lead
'me earnestly to address the same exhortation to you, as I should
'to him, to beseech you to cultivate and preserve it now it is reco-
'vered, as that, the loss of which nothing else can compensate to you.
'Do not expect to find him faultless; we are none of us so; but
'make allowance for his failings as you hope he will for yours, and
'be assured that the friendship of a brother is a thing of far more
'value than any of those for which it is sometimes too lightly
'hazarded or sacrificed.

'Excuse this preaching, but I feel too earnestly for the happiness
'of both not to say with freedom what I think may contribute to it.

'It will be a very great pleasure to us to receive you and Lady
'Nugent here at the time you mention. She will be here in a
'house where she knows she need put no restraint whatever upon
'herself, but do just as much or as little as her own strength and
'spirits incline her to; and it would be a sincere delight to Lady
'Grenville, as well as to myself, to think that her being here could
'contribute to the restoration of either.

'Ever, my dear George,
'Most affectionately yours,
'G.'

'The year when this letter was written was that in which Canning took the seals of the Foreign Office after the death of Castlereagh, and, upon oppressed peoples and nationalities under the heel of the Holy Alliance, there again broke forth from England gleams of hope and liberation. In the excitement which followed the French invasion of Spain, the withdrawal of the Duke of Wellington from the Congress of Verona, and that expression of sympathy on behalf of the Spanish Constitutionalists to which such noble utterance was given by the English Foreign Secretary, Lord Nugent shared largely; and, as in the former struggle against the French, his personal exertions were not wanting. He repaired, in the summer of 1823, to the scene of conflict,* and took prominent part in such help as an Englishman might afford to Riego, Quiroga, the pure minded and true Arguelles, and their friends. In common with many other members of the opposition, however, his expectations had been lifted too high by the eloquence of the new Foreign Secretary; he too readily supposed that the sympathy for Spanish Constitutionalism which Canning so heartily expressed, would never utterly desert its defenders and heroes in their last extremity; and when, by the sudden withdrawal of the British minister from Seville after the seizure of the person of the King, the fixed neutrality of England was declared, he bitterly felt the disappointment. But he did not quit Spain till near the very last. He was in Cadiz during the last attempt to rally the liberals; and, not many weeks before the final surrender, was suggested as the successor to Sir Robert Wilson when the latter ceased to hold the powers with which the Cortes had entrusted him. 'Knowing no person,' Wilson writes to Lord Nugent, ' more capable than yourself of carrying into execution ' with zeal and effect what in my opinion is more than ever ' important to the Spanish nation, I am very anxious that you ' should propose yourself as my successor, and shall be very ' happy to hear, for the public interest, that the Spanish ' government has accepted you in that character.' Unhappily it was too late. This letter was written in the middle of September: on the 1st of October, Ferdinand was released by the Constitutionalists; on the 3rd they surrendered; and within

* Sir John Hobhouse (Lord Broughton), who took a generous interest in the Spanish struggle, and corresponded with Lord Nugent by cipher, in his absence, thus closes a long letter of friendly and patriotic suggestion written from Brighton before his departure. 'I have no individual 'injunction to pray you to attend to, except the care of yourself, and 'that not only in a military but a medical way; as you will be in Spain ' during the season of pestilence.' In another letter, when the struggle was nearing its close, he says: 'Urge no compromise. All friends of ' liberty here would regard it as a complete surrender. You are authorised ' to say so on the part of all those who have been working for Spain here.'

a month Riego, basely delivered over to his enemies by the Duke of Angoulême, was hanged at Madrid. His brother, the Canon Riego, in his subsequent English exile, found no friendship more affectionate, no hospitality more constant or unwearying, than Lord Nugent's; for that family, and for the Quirogas, his services, in co-operation with those of Lord Holland, were active and incessant; and it was his house which the patriot Arguelles first sought on his arrival in London in November, and where he found afterwards a second home.*

In the middle of October, Lord Nugent had himself reached London, and it would seem, from a letter of his brother's, that even at the time when he left Cadiz, he had not altogether abandoned hope that the patriots might yet hold out. The Duke writes from Wotton.

'My dear George,
    'I received your welcome and affectionate letter this

---

* In the following year Mr. Wilberforce very earnestly sought an introduction to Arguelles, for whose virtues and patriotism he entertained the highest esteem; and, on a particular day fixed by Lord Nugent, came up from Great Missenden, though labouring at the time with severe illness, to meet the Spanish leader. One of the many letters addressed by Arguelles to Lord Nugent, as characteristic of himself as of the meanness of the tyranny he had passed his life in opposing, may perhaps be quoted here. Unlike the majority of his letters, it is in English; and is here printed exactly as it is written. 'Wednesday, April 28. My dear: I am so 'vexed by this confounded cough, particularly in the night, and early in 'the morning, that nothing could be more troublesome and ungovernable 'than such a guest as myself; presantly I am an invalid. Let me get well, 'and, since kind Ferdinand is so much in your interest of detaining me in 'England, I promise to force you to repent of your kind invitation. When 'you will return to Lillies for the season I will stay there a whole fort-'night. Dont be alarmed; something may be substracted if properly 'desired. No more nonsenses.

'From Spain nothing but confirmations of the dreadful state of the 'country. I do not recollect if I told you that a very old, and faithful 'servant of mine, whom I left in Madrid, charged with all my things, after 'having been concealed five months, was at last discovered, and forced to 'deliver all my property. I don't care but for the pictures, half-dozen of 'which were of the first rate. Present my compliment to Lady Nugent, 'and believe me ever truly yours,
    'My Lord Nugent.   A. DE ARGÜELLES.'

'morning at this old place, where we have been rejoicing and
'making merry. Most deeply do I feel the affectionate interest
'which you take in my happiness. I thank God all is going
'on as well as possible. On Tuesday I shall be at the
'Quarter Sessions, on Thursday at Sir George Nugent's at the
'coming of age of young George. Then I return to Stowe, where
'on the 22nd we have beef-eating, and beer-drinking, and ox-
'roasting, in honour of the young John Knox, as Mary calls him;
'and there we shall remain until the first week in November, when
'we go to Avington, where we remain until Christmas, which is
'spent at Stowe. Such is the outline of my plan. Now pray act
'upon it so as to give us as much of your time as you can.

'Your Cadiz speculations are addled by the news which has
'arrived since you left it, so I say nothing thereon, except
'that I sincerely rejoice that you are out of that patriotic city,
'where the Cortez at last dwindled to five individuals, who met
'for safety in a cellar, and sent the king out to negociate for them.
'God bless you, my dear George,
                    'Yours most affectionately,
                                    'B. & C.

'All here join in love to you and joy that you are again in
England.'

The patriotic failure on which the Duke, not perhaps without some hope that it might help to abate his brother's patriotic zeal, jests so pleasantly, but which did not strike graver people, editors of leading journals and such like,* in

* From many letters of public men congratulating Lord Nugent on his safe return, some of them (as Lord Essex's) enquiring with deep anxiety as to the fate of Sir Robert Wilson, I may print the following, which is in the handwriting of Mr. Barnes. '*Times* Office, Sunday, Oct. 12, 1823. 'The Editor of the *Times* presents his respects to Lord Nugent, and with 'many apologies for this intrusion (which he trusts will be ascribed to its 'only cause—the anxiety to furnish the public with accurate information 'from the best sources), hopes his lordship will have the goodness to 'communicate such facts relative to the fall of Cadiz as appear in his 'lordship's judgment to account for that disastrous event.

'If Mr. Brougham, or indeed any of his lordship's parliamentary friends had been in town, the Editor would have had the advantage of an intro-

quite so jocose a light, had nevertheless no perceptible effect on the foreign politics of the Member for Aylesbury. On the reassembling of parliament in February, 1824, in what Mr. Canning afterwards described as 'a most unreasonable and ' untenable proposition, conveyed in a most temperate and ' eloquent speech,'* he characterised as it merited the wickedness of that French invasion; eloquently deplored the fate of the despised leaders at Cadiz; named Ferdinand, amid the cheers of the house, as a 'wretch, the scourge and abhorrence of ' his people, who afforded the most finished specimen that ' perhaps ever existed in human nature, of all that was base ' and grovelling, perfidious, bloody, and tyrannical, and was ' therefore a fit object for the tender sympathy of those powers ' who venerated divine right and adored legitimacy;' and denounced Mr. Canning's policy in sanctioning Sir William A'Court's withdrawal from Seville, as practically an expression of sympathy with Ferdinand, because an irreparable blow dealt against the Constitutionalist cause in its most critical time, and directly leading to the treachery which ultimately betrayed and overthrew it. In the division he was of course defeated, a hundred and forty members voting against him, and only thirty voting on his side: but among the latter will be found the names of Baring, Burdett, Brougham, Cavendish, Denison, Denman, Ellice, Hume, Hobhouse, Mackintosh, John Russell, Wood, and Wilson; and on the whole, perhaps, Canning had not so much reason to be proud of this victory as he professed himself, in replying to a similar motion brought forward in the following month by Lord John Russell.

As this latter was the occasion when some celebrated jokes were fired off against Lord Nugent by the witty and eloquent Secretary, it may be expected that some account should here be given of it. Lord John had made a speech remarkable for

' duction to his lordship, and would not have been compelled to this very
' abrupt application, for which he once more begs to apologise.'

* *Hansard* (Second Series), x. 1266.

the courage with which it denounced the iniquity of the Holy Alliance, the infamy of Ferdinand's government, and the treachery of the French Expedition; characterising the permitted success of the latter as an abandonment of the ancient policy of England in regard to oppressed States,* and invoking

* At a subsequent period, in an ever-famous speech, Canning himself admitted that the French occupation of Spain, thus brought before the house, was in a certain sense a disparagement, an affront to the pride as well as a blow to the feelings of England; but he vindicated himself by declaring, that he had obtained reparation for such disparagement by means better adapted to the present time than any direct interference would have been. He had resolved at the time that France should never be permitted to attack or reconquer the Spanish American colonies, should the latter be able to assert their freedom. 'I sought materials of compensa-
' tion in another hemisphere. Contemplating Spain such as our ancestors
' had known her, I resolved, that if France had Spain, it should not be
' Spain "with the Indies." I called the New World into existence to
' redress the balance of the old.' The comment of Arguelles on this celebrated avowal will doubtless interest the reader. Writing to Lord Nugent on the 1st December, 1826, he says :
' Do not be angry with me, my dear friend; my heart bleeds and is
' half broken since I saw Mr. Canning, after exulting in his sublime con-
' ception of compensating his country with the New World, to which he
' looked at the very moment of the French invasion, assert with a perfect
' serenity, the result of previous deliberation, that you now ought to rivet
' France's chains. He makes it his point of honour to continue the occupa-
' tion of Spain. Good heavens ! a statesman in a public assembly exclaim-
' ing thus, overwhelmed by the very cheerings of the audience, and forcing
' that unfortunate country to curse the moment it was generous enough as
' to contribute to its own ruin ! Buonaparte, it is true, invaded her, but
' delivered her of the Inquisition, the monkish influence, and of all
' the mischievous institutions she laboured under. What a retribution !
' ... My dearest of friends; I have no consolation left; therefore do not
' resent my indiscreet letter. Spain once more condemned to become the
' field of battle between two nations who aim at nobody knows. ... and
' the only object that could be honourable, glorious, even useful in political
' morality, to put an end to that scandal of posterity (I see that it is not
' so, to contemporaries), the butchering one party by another, this, I say,
' is out of the question. The liberal party is never spoken of but to vilify,
' to disgrace, to ruin them in the public opinion of this country. Mr.
' Canning loses all moderation, all circumspection as a stateman whenever
' he alludes to them; is he so certain of his friends as never to be in the
' case of having once more resource to their assistance? The enemies of
' England, are they all, and for ever buried in St. Helena? What are the

the heroes of the short but noble struggle against it, 'the
'virtuous and eloquent Arguelles, the courageous and patriotic
'Mina, the brave and heroic Alava,' as men worthy of the
freedom for which they contended, and whose names would
never be forgotten until patriotism itself should die out of the
world. Sir Robert Wilson had followed Lord John, and made

'means of inspiring the confidence forfeited in every part of the liberal world
'by an uninterrupted series of the most unwarrantable attacks upon the
'friends of rational liberty, on the part of a man who presumes to be the
'abettor and protector of civilisation and enlightened policy? France really
'is now in chains; but I think her present state is transitory; and perhaps
'it will be a great error to rely so much on the Bourbon perpetuity.
'Thousand and thousand events may produce a change of dynasty, or
'destroy the bonds which keep them under your subserviency. And a more
'enlightened policy at the Tuilleries would be sufficient to collect round
'the French in the Peninsula all liberal minds to obtain a rational mode of
'administering the country. Everybody there is tired, oppressed with the
'weight of calamities, disabused, and convinced that no protection is to be
'expected from your cabinet for the planning of a sound and permanent
'government; and the ministry of France must be very stupid if they do
'not profit by the disposition of public mind there. To trust in mere
'efforts of men actuated by desperation, as Mr. Canning seems to do, to
'think that he will always find everywhere powers in sufficient number
'ready to be the tools of ephemeral plans and transitory combinations, is
'an error. I do not presume to tell what may be with respect to other
'countries, but in Spain no honest man, no person of value, will engage
'himself in any enterprise that should not be represented as useful and
'permanently useful to his country, after the cruel lesson of the year 14.
'Even in London, where the horrors of emigration are beyond what any
'think, you may conceive the unfortunate refugees bear testimony to this
'observation. Enough of this sad subject. You see, my dear friend, how
'candidly Mr. Canning has justified what you thought to be merely
'suspicion of mine. Confessing that his political conduct towards Spain
'in the 1823 was regulated by South America, is to say that the
'Peninsula fell a victim to the separation of her colonies. Although I am
'totally ignorant of Parliamentary conservances, I dare say this avowal
'is a triumph to more than one of your enemies in Europe. I hope you
'will take the letter in a favourable sense, and make great allowance to
'my dreadfull situation. My health is so far from mending that I cannot
'have the pleasure of going down to you. I have a very disagreeable
'continual noise in the ear that increases infinitely my indisposition. Tell
'thousand things to Mi lady, and believe me most sincerely yours, Mi lord,
                                            'A. DE ARGÜELLES.'

a striking statement of his personal experiences in Spain, very damning to the government, because proving that their professions of strict neutrality had not been kept. Then, unable to contradict Wilson's facts, Canning had resorted to the argument that if the maintenance of neutrality had been difficult, it was because the most ardent sticklers for it in all its strictness were precisely those who had created the difficulty; and out of this his opportunity arose to weaken the impression made in favour of the Spanish heroes, by humourous comment on the auxiliaries who had gone out from England to their relief. He availed himself of it to the utmost, with undoubted success, and for a considerable time kept the house in such a state of enjoyment as had not been witnessed for many a day.

'Seeing as he did, over the way, a victim who on a former 'night had been completely deserted,' was the allusion with which, indicating Lord Nugent on the opposite bench, he began. Then he insinuated a pleasant contrast between the spare figure of Sir Robert Wilson, and the stout and portly person of Lord Nugent, by remarking that if Sir Robert, by his conduct, 'formed in himself no small breach of neutrality, ' he could assure the house that the noble lord opposite was a ' most enormous breach of neutrality.' Here there were roars of laughter, of course, but nothing to those that followed at the rising of the full tide of his humour. After dwelling for some time on Sir Robert Wilson's participation in the war, he proceeded to say, that while Sir Robert was paying the penalty of his gallantry and courage in one quarter, there arose in another quarter of that country another luminary, who, though he might not have addressed himself to the state of the conflict with as much military effect as Sir Robert had done, certainly did not fall behind him in military intention. He did not wish, Mr. Canning continued, to pry further into matters than was necessary, and by some it might be thought that in what he was about to say he was going too far; but in cases of this nature, it was the duty of government to know what was going on; else, by giving way to too much secrecy in respect to the conduct of individuals, they might, before they could be sufficiently aware of it, become involved in hostilities by the warlike conduct of their own subjects.

All this preparation was in Canning's most exquisite ironical style, and at the words 'warlike conduct,' the house broke into a general laugh, no one yet knew why. But, says Wilberforce,* who was present, Canning was 'invincibly comic' on this occasion, and his drollery of voice and manner were inimitable. There was a lighting up of the features, and a humorous play about the mouth, when the full fun of an approaching witticism struck his own mind, which always prepared his listeners for the burst that was to follow. In this case it soon came. 'Then, sir,' continued Mr. Canning (I quote *Hansard*)—†

'About the middle of the month of last July, the heavy
'Falmouth coach (roars of laughter), yes, sir, the heavy Falmouth
'coach, in the month of last July, was observed to proceed to its
'destination with more than its wonted celerity. The coach con-
'tained two passengers; the one a fair lady of considerable di-
'mensions, the other a gentleman who was about to carry the
'succour of his person to the struggling patriots in Spain. I am
'further informed—and this interesting fact, sir, can also be
'authenticated—that the heavy Falmouth van, which gentlemen,
'doubtless, are aware is constructed for the conveyance of more
'cumbrous articles, was laden on the same memorable occasion
'with a box of most portentous magnitude. Now, sir, whether
'this box, like the flying chest of the conjuror, possessed any
'supernatural properties of locomotion, is a point which I confess
'I am quite unable to determine; but of this I am most credibly
'informed—and I should hesitate long before I stated it to the
'House, if the statement did not rest upon the most unquestion-
'able authority—that this extraordinary box contained a full

---

* *Life,* v. 217. † Second Series, x. 1275.

'uniform of a Spanish general of cavalry, together with a helmet
'of the most curious workmanship; a helmet, allow me to add,
'scarcely inferior in size to the celebrated helmet in the castle of
'Otranto (loud laughter). The idea of going to the relief of a
'fortress blockaded by sea and besieged by land, in a full suit of
'light horseman's equipments, was, perhaps, not strictly consonant
'to modern military operations. However, almost at this time,
'the arrival of the promised force of 10,000 men—which never
'existed except on paper—was hourly expected, and would have
'been most acceptable; and when the gentleman and his box had
'made their appearance, the Cortes no doubt were overwhelmed
'with joy, and rubbed their hands with delight at the approach
'of the long-promised aid. That aid did not come: it came in
'the sense and in no other, which was described by the witty
'Duke of Buckingham, whom the noble lord opposite reckoned
'among his lineal ancestors; when, in the play of *The Rehearsal*,
'there is a scene occupied with the designs of the two kings of
'Brentford, to whom one of their party entering says,

> "The army's at the door, but in disguise,
> Entreats a word of both your majesties."

'How the noble lord was received, or what effects he operated on
'the councils and affairs of the Cortes by his arrival, he (Mr.
'Canning) did not know. Things were at that juncture moving
'rapidly to their final issue. How far the noble lord conduced to
'the termination by throwing his weight into the sinking scale of
'the Cortes, was too nice a question for him just now to settle.
'But it must be evident, that by circumstances like those to which
'he had alluded, the government, if it wished to exercise common
'and necessary caution, was called upon, without any appeal from
'the French government, for disavowal. It was not for him to
'condemn the principles and motives which led the honourable
'gentleman to make that generous sacrifice of himself to the cause
'of Spain; but what he urged was, that if they would have neu-
'trality on the part of the government, they must be content to
'be bound by the feelings, expressions, and determinations of
'government: nor ought they to expect to be allowed individually

'to carry on war against a government with which their own was
'in amity.'

There is not much in all this, as the reader perceives. The heavy coach, the portentous box, the huge helmet, the light horseman's equipments, the succour of the person, and the weight in the sinking scale, are but the repetition of the first witticism; the humouring of a certain comical incongruity, visibly suggested by Lord Nugent's personal appearance, between his desire to give help to the patriots, and the amount of help he had given. But humour relies much upon manner, which, preventing the effect of sameness in a repetition, keeps up in the listener all the effects of novelty and surprise; and there can be no doubt that the House mightily enjoyed this laugh against Lord Nugent. Wilberforce had gone to the debate very unwell, his sons tell us, and not intending to remain, but Canning enchained him. He returned home quite full of what he had heard, and as he repeated the exquisite raillery to his family, was again overpowered with laughter 'as he scarce 'ever was.' * Understanding all this, however, neither is it difficult at the same time to understand and admit the higher spirit in which Sir James Mackintosh rose immediately after Canning had resumed his seat, and, after remarking that the eloquent Secretary had, no doubt, been very facetious in drawing a description of some part of the conduct of his noble friend near him, reminded him and the House that he had passed over other parts which were of a more serious kind, and which redounded to Lord Nugent's honour, evincing as they did those generous feelings which characterised every action of his noble friend's life, and every sentiment of his heart. 'The Right Honourable gentleman would not 'pronounce that the presence of his noble friend in Spain had 'been either unseemly or unimportant, much less inglorious, if 'he considered that during his short residence in Cadiz, his

* *Life*, v. 217.

'noble friend had been instrumental in saving brave and 'unfortunate men, whose only crime was the love of their 'country, from the dungeons and scaffolds of an inexorable 'tyrant. In contributing to the rescue of such men, he had 'done what was worthy of himself and of his illustrious family, 'and he had supported becomingly the English character and 'name.'

And so passed off the pleasant raillery of Mr. Canning. That it had fallen with very small effect on Lord Nugent himself, in so far as regarded his desire and resolve to give what help he could to the oppressed, even by personal sacrifices, was proved in the following year. The Greek cause, which succeeded so closely to the Spanish in the sympathies of Englishmen, had not a warmer or more active supporter, and his presence in the Morea* testified his personal zeal in its behalf.

* On the 24 Sept. 1824, one who has since obtained the highest rank in the Diplomatic Service writes to Lord Nugent from Zante: 'I have had 'a long conversation with the Count de la Decimo, a Cephalonian of great 'credit, and in the closest communication with Mavrocordato and the 'present government. I explained to him the advantage which your 'lordship's presence must bring to those in Greece. This he seemed fully 'to understand, and was of a decided opinion that the condition attached 'to it would most cordially be complied with.

'Indeed, so much were your lordship's views in unison with the idea 'of those to whom you wished me to communicate them, that they 'conceive, as I understand, their chief wants to consist in what you demand, 'and there is a rumour that Mr. Blaquiere has orders thus to supply them. 'I therefore hope to procure a definitive and favourable answer at the seat 'of government, which I shall not fail immediately to forward, and 'Mr. Browne and myself anticipate with the greatest pleasure a meeting 'with your lordship in the Morea.

'Everything we hear is favourable to the Greeks. The government is more 'settled, and the chiefs more submissive to it than at any former time,—the 'loan, from all accounts, has likewise been well employed,—the best proofs 'of which are two splendid victories at Samos and Cos. All seems to 'invite your presence, and no one is more anxious for it, my lord, than

'Yours, very sincerely,
'B.'

'ZANTE, Sept. 24th, 1824.'

In other prominent parliamentary questions, also, he continued to take the same part as of old. Since mention was last made of his exertions in Parliament, he has been active in resisting the proceedings against the Queen; he has won the confidence and thanks of Mr. Wilberforce and Mr. Z. Macaulay for a motion which he handled with much skill, on the oppression of the negroes in Tobago;* he has surprised and propitiated † Jeremy Bentham by his eagerness in law amendments; he has supported every motion, in whatever form submitted to the House, for Catholic Emancipation and Parliamentary Reform; he has introduced, but failed to pass, a bill for the safer independence of colonial judges; he has joined in all humane efforts to obtain counsel for prisoners, and to abate the extreme punishment for forgery; he has voted with every attempt to give greater freedom to industry and commercial exchange; and he has argued strongly for repeal of the Test Acts. It is extremely difficult, looking back from even the limited vantage-ground occupied by the people now, to believe that these, and fifty other such questions, should have remained unsettled as late as 1826. But so it was; and not one of those terse sentences in which Sydney Smith has described the reign of squires, noodles, and jobbers in the first quarter of the century, had yet lost its application. 'The Catholics were not

---

* A letter to Lord Nugent from Mr. Wilberforce, who was then at Bath in very indifferent health, expresses his deep anxiety in the result of the motion, his wish to be present at the debate, and his gratitude for Lord Nugent's offer, if possible, to put it off for some few days.

† I use this word, because the sage and philosopher of Queen's-square had at first taken not so kindly to the Duke of Buckingham's brother. I quote from a letter of his to Lord Nugent, dated at the close of 1824 : ' As ' to *bad company*, what I meant,—and I certainly did as good as tell you,— ' was, company opposite in character to everything I now hear of yours. For ' a man situated as you have been, how can he help himself? He cannot, ' if he would, take himself out of the circle which gave him birth. As to ' your solitude, instead of it I had figured to myself a house brimfull of ' company : of company of that sort with which in former days I got ' surfeited.'

'emancipated; the Corporation and Test Acts were unrepealed;
'the Game Laws were horribly oppressive; steel traps and
'spring guns were set all over the country; Prisoners tried for
'their lives could have no counsel; Lord Eldon and the Court
'of Chancery pressed heavily upon mankind; Libel was
'punished by the most cruel and vindictive imprisonments;
'the principles of Political Economy were little understood; the
'laws of Debt and of Conspiracy were upon the worst possible
'footing; the enormous wickedness of the Slave Trade was
'tolerated;' and to the correction of all these, and many
other evils then fully flourishing, which the talents of good
and able men were devoted to lessening or removing, Lord
Nugent applied whatever energy, influence, or ability he could
command.*

The claims with which he presented himself for the fourth
time to the electors of Aylesbury, at the general election of
1826, have been placed on record by Sir James Mackintosh.
With the latter he had now long been on terms of intimacy,
induced by congeniality of tastes as well as agreement in
opinion; and the letters between them show with what kindly
affection Mackintosh repaid the eager admiration his character

* Sydney Smith will also tell us what was the ordinary penalty of
assailing such wrongs and abuses while yet their upholders basked in
the full sunshine of court favour and support. 'Not only was there no pay,
' but there were many stripes. It is always considered as a piece of imper-
'tinence in England, if a man of less than two or three thousand a-year
' has any opinions at all upon important subjects; and in addition he was
' sure at that time to be assailed with all the Billingsgate of the French
' Revolution—Jacobin, Leveller, Atheist, Deist, Socinian, Incendiary,
' Regicide, were the gentlest appellations used; and the man who breathed
' a syllable against the senseless bigotry of the two Georges, or hinted at
' the abominable tyranny and persecution exercised upon Catholic Ireland,
' was shunned as unfit for the relations of social life. Not a murmur
' against any abuse was permitted; to say a word against the suitorcide
' delays of the Court of Chancery, or the cruel punishments of the Game
' Laws, or against any abuse which a rich man inflicted, or a poor man
' suffered, was treason against the *Plousiocracy*, and was bitterly and steadily
' resented. Lord Grey had not then taken off the bearing rein from the
' English people.'

had inspired in Lord Nugent. Visits were frequently interchanged between Mardocks and Lilies; and I have heard the survivor say that he had been witness more than once, in social intercourse, to what Sydney Smith has so nobly described in Mackintosh, when, after remarking in proof of his genuine love of human happiness, that whatever might assuage the angry passions and arrange the conflicting interests of nations, that whatever could promote peace, increase knowledge, diminish crime, and encourage industry, that whatever could exalt human character and enlarge human understanding, struck at once at his heart and roused all his faculties, he adds, 'I have seen him in a moment when this spirit came 'upon him—like a great ship of war, cut his cable, and spread 'his enormous canvass, and launch into a wide sea of reasoning 'eloquence.' * Lord Nugent would say, that nothing so happily as this expressed what he remembered of the contrast which vivid moments in the eloquence of Mackintosh presented, to the ordinary heaviness and massive immobility of his manner.

Sir James Mackintosh's letter on Lord Nugent's parliamentary services, which is dated the 6th of July 1826, was elicited by an invitation sent to him to attend the dinner at Aylesbury, in celebration of Lord Nugent's return without the expenditure of a shilling, after a very severe contest in which every available ministerial as well as family influence had been exerted against him. Mackintosh was ill at the time, and unable to leave home; but he was very deeply impressed by the result of the election as an example to the other electors of the kingdom, and hence this letter to the chairman of the meeting. 'They have set the example,' he said of his 'former neighbours' at Aylesbury,

'Of a popular election exempt from disorder and expense, from

* Life of Mackintosh by his Son, ii. 504. 'I drew the highest prize in the 'lottery' says Wilberforce, describing a dinner at the Duke of Gloucester's; 'I sat by Sir J. Mackintosh.' Life of Wilberforce by his Sons, v. 213.

'the domineering ascendant of a few, and from the slightest sus-
'picion of corruption. Among them the suffrages of the People
'have neither been disturbed, nor enslaved, nor dishonoured.
'No purse-proud stranger can boast of having bought their votes.
'Without attacking the just influence of property, they have exer-
'cised their own judgment on public men; they have calmly and
'firmly asserted its independence. By returning their member
'without expense, they have deprived great wealth of that mono-
'poly which it may otherwise exercise against the most tried
'integrity, and the most eminent capacity for public service. I do
'not know that an electoral body can render a greater benefit to
'the community than by an example which thus strongly recom-
'mends the most popular institutions of a free government to the
'approbation of all mankind. The electors of Aylesbury have
'bestowed on Lord Nugent the purest honour and the only
'becoming reward which Constituents can confer on an honest
'Representative. It has not been bestowed without long experience
'and abundant time for deliberation. They have had sixteen years
'to observe and consider his parliamentary conduct, before they
'pronounced this their deliberate approbation of it. They have
'approved in him the advocate of a reduced military force, of
'economy in public expense, of liberty in discussing public mea-
'sures, the enemy of slavery, the friend of that right to worship
'God according to the dictates of their conscience without incur-
'ring any legal inconvenience, which the sincere follower of every
'religious community ought to consider as the most valuable and
'sacred of the rights of mankind. The result of the General
'Election now affords them the satisfaction of knowing, that zeal
'for religious liberty comprehending every communion and excepting
'no opinion, is not considered as an objection to candidates for
'seats in Parliament, by the greater and better part of the electors
'of England. They see also that other liberal principles of foreign
'policy and domestic legislation, to the promotion of which Lord
'Nugent and his friends trust that they have contributed by efforts
'at the moment apparently unavailing, are now adopted by those
'of his Majesty's ministers who give most lustre and vigour to
'the government. He will persevere in his efforts to support

'liberal principles, whoever may be their advocates; to lessen the
' burden and shorten the duration of laws against liberty, when he
' cannot defeat them; to complete the removal of restraints on
' industry; to restore freedom in the exchange of its produce, with
' a due regard to established interests; and by rendering religious
' liberty co-extensive with the principle of doing unto others as
' we would that they should do unto us, to justify the tolerant
' spirit of the Protestant religion, as well as to provide for the
' peace and safety of the British empire. It is always an advantage
' that Constituents should be familiarly acquainted with the ordinary
' and daily life of their Representative, which throws the clearest
' light on the true springs of every part of his conduct. In the
' present instance, the electors of Aylesbury derive from that
' familiar acquaintance the means of appreciating the conduct of
' Lord Nugent at those moments when his duty was rendered
' painful by a struggle with feeling, and are well assured that in
' those circumstances (which may now be adverted to without
' pain to any party) his determination arose not from lukewarmness
' in his affections, but from the strength of his public principles.'

From no authority entitled to higher respect could such testimony have fallen, and never was a better merited or more honourable tribute paid. But a very few years were now to pass before the great change of 1830, and in the interval, it may well be supposed, Lord Nugent's exertions to promote the liberal cause in Parliament underwent no abatement. He gave a sincere though qualified support to the Ministries of Canning and Lord Goderich, exulted in the repeal of the Test Acts, and went again into settled opposition when the Wellington Ministry unwisely declared itself against Emancipation and Reform. And if, as a speaker, he held his ground less firmly in the favour of the House than might at one time have been expected,—if in the greater party contests he never attained any marked distinction,—his influence was really considerable on the silent advance of important questions, especially of all that concerned the conscience, or affected in any way great social and human interests. His mere manner of speaking, when bent upon oratorical effect, was in truth not good. At such times there was a certain clumsiness of elaboration, both in his arrangement and delivery of a speech, which did indifferent justice to the clear honesty of purpose, the manly abilities, the excellent common-sense understanding, which, on less formal occasions, seldom failed of their effect in that assembly of which Bobus Smith so happily said that it has more good taste than any man in it.

Concurrently with his work in Parliament, too, he indulged not a few pursuits of literature; and of the shrewdly reasoned, able, and eloquently written pamphlets which Lord Nugent at various times contributed to the illustration or enforcement of those public questions in which he took an active interest, mention, however brief, should not be omitted. There were few more ready pamphleteers, and in this way he did much to promote, by a series of telling and timely arguments, the success of the Test Acts Repeal, the Catholic Question,* Parliamentary Reform, Law Reform, and several branches of administrative improvement. He wrote also some Spanish songs † which had a certain popularity, at the time when public sympathies went strongly with the patriots; he

* In the year before this question was finally settled, Lord Nugent visited Ireland, when O'Connell seized the occasion, claiming him as an Irishman, to invite him to the hospitalities of Derrynane. 'I shall feel 'honoured and pleased to see you in this my mountain hut, where I am 'like the American Squatter endeavouring to make good the settlement. 'The American and I differ, however, in this—*He* cuts down trees to 'improve the land, *I* am endeavouring to rear them for utility and orna-'ment. Amongst these mountains you, my lord, will expect little of those 'accommodations which in a London life are matters of course—we 'endeavour to make compensation by the cordiality with which we treat 'the stranger—and what stranger can bring such claims on our kindliest 'feelings as your lordship?'

† In Moore's *Diary* will be found occasional mention of these songs. I quote one entry of the 24th August 1825. 'Went to meet Lord Nugent 'at the Athenæum. Brought in his words to Spanish songs; *rather* pretty. 'Amused me a little to think of Lord George, the young man about town '(*Vide Twopenny Post Bag*), consulting me friendlily on the subject of his 'poetry.' *Diary*, iv. 308.

published, amid the discussions affecting religious liberty and the rights of conscience in the year 1829, an historical and critical essay on Oxford and Locke; and from this date to the close of his life, contributed many papers to the passing publications of the time, generally entertaining in their character. Among them might be found, though rarely, a grave piece of criticism, more often a capital story told in pointed and humorous verse. Lord Nugent wrote excellent nonsense, which not many people can do.

The first public mention of his being engaged upon a Memoir of Hampden was made in the *Gentleman's Magazine*, in the summer of 1828. From this it appeared that he had taken advantage of some repairs going on in the pavement of the chancel of Hampden Church, to obtain Lord Buckinghamshire's permission for such possible identification of the patriot's remains, supposed to be deposited there, as might clear up the question of the kind of hurt by which he died. The late Chief Justice of England, then Mr. Common Serjeant Denman, was present with Lord Nugent when the attempt was made, and entertained always afterwards the strong belief that they had gazed on what *had been* Hampden;* but the incident is not dwelt upon here, because the contrary persuasion came to be held by Lord Nugent, as I believe more correctly.† No allusion to it appeared in the Memoir, but that version of the patriot's manner of death was silently adopted which the

---

* In a letter of Lord Denman's, hereafter to be quoted, written in 1842 in answer to an invitation from Lord Nugent to be present at the inauguration of a monument to Hampden on the spot where he is supposed to have fallen in Chalgrave field, this expression occurs: 'Yours usque ad 'inferos, I cannot resist your company in attempting to give just honour 'to the great patriot, whose very identical body I am sure we saw.'

† 'I certainly did see' says Lord Nugent, in a letter to the late Mr. Murray, 'in 1828, while the pavement of the chancel of Hampden 'Church was undergoing repair, a skeleton, which I have many reasons for 'believing was not John Hampden's, but that of some gentleman, or lady, 'who probably died a quiet death in bed, certainly with no wound in the 'wrist.'

alleged discovery, as described in the Magazine, if really made with that result,* must have shown to be untrue. Of the book itself, which first appeared in November, 1831, the reader has the means of judgment before him; nor will he need to be told how such a subject had suggested itself to Lord Nugent. The scenes in which the patriot's youth was passed, which saw the power and popularity of his manhood, and witnessed the glory of his death, were the same that had been also familiar to Lord Nugent from his boyhood; nor was the hero less commended to his biographer, by the opinions and the cause for which he died. The biography was in all respects a labour of love with Lord Nugent, and its reception justified his expectations. I will quote what was said of it by

* I ought to add, however, that this description turned out to be anything but correct. The point stated to be in dispute was, whether the patriot died from a shot received in the shoulder, or from the accidental bursting of his pistol in his hand, and of the veracity of the first named statement no one now entertains a doubt; but in what purported to be the result of the opening of Hampden's supposed coffin, as inserted in the *Gentleman's Magazine*, there was a kind of sanction given to the story of the pistol by the alleged discovery of traces that the right hand had been amputated. Southey took part in a discussion on the subject which afterwards arose, and his statement of the result of his inquiries I believe to be the only strictly authentic account of what passed. 'Repairs going on in 'the church at the time, search was made there for the body of Hampden, 'and, as the persons understood, at the instance of Lord Nugent; several 'coffins were inspected, but not opened, because either the date did not 'agree with Hampden's death, or the inscription bore a different name; 'but one coffin was at length found, which had neither date nor inscrip- 'tion, and this was opened, although, from its form, it appears to have 'been older than his time. Mr. Norris, a surgeon of Risborough, examined 'the body, which was that of a very lusty man, the head covered with rich 'auburn hair, reaching beneath the shoulders; it was in high preservation, 'except that one arm had crumbled off, owing to the action of the air, 'which had made its way to that part through a crack in the coffin; but 'there had been no amputation, or operation of any kind.' That the search was made 'at the instance of Lord Nugent' I have no doubt whatever; not simply because of the extract above quoted from the letter of Lord Denman, but because on my mentioning to him an amusing complaint of Mr. Godwin's confided to me, that he had been invited to the disinterment, and, when the day for it was actually fixed, had never been apprised thereof,—Lord Nugent admitted that it was so.

M. de Salvandy, when minister of Louis Philippe, for the judgment of an intelligent foreigner is in some sort as the verdict of posterity. "C'est une production judicieuse, vraie, 'et forte. Un noble cœur, et un bon esprit, l'ont dictée."

Meanwhile the exciting events of 1830 had not passed without their influence on Lord Nugent's political fortunes. The light he had tended so steadily when flickering and low, he was now in every sense to feel the warmth of, as its fierce and burning flame, suddenly blazing forth in France, was caught up and diffused over England. Not the least bitterly contested election of this memorable summer was that of the little borough of Aylesbury, not the least gallantly fought and won. 'There certainly was no election throughout the 'kingdom,' writes Lord Holland to Lord Nugent, in a letter of the 14th of September, 1830, now lying before me, 'in which 'I felt more interested on publick grounds, and none in the 'result of which I more unfeignedly rejoice. If good wishes 'are services, you had as many as you acknowledge from me; 'but all I did was to mention the strength of them to 'Dissenters, who, I believe, whether I had mentioned them or 'not, would have exerted themselves to their utmost, as they 'were bound to do, in your favour.' The same letter is remarkable for what it contains of allusion to the events then passing in France, and may also be quoted for its high and honourable tribute to the zeal and generosity of Lord Nugent's services to the patriots of Spain.

At this time the life of Prince Polignac, whose capture had been effected, was supposed to be in danger; and Lord Holland, for some personal and many public reasons, was anxious to save it. From feelings not only of private regard and compassion, but ('overjoyed as all of us are at the events 'and prospects in France') of public zeal for the character and stability of the new free government, he described himself in this letter to Lord Nugent as most anxious that the commencement of Louis Philippe's reign should not be tarnished

by any vindictive acts of severity towards the ex-ministers
'and Polignac in particular. It has occurred to me,' he
continued, 'that a relation of his conduct and a publication of
'his correspondence in the affair of Riego (which, if I recollect
'rightly, were feeling and generous) would be of some service
'in softening publick indignation (which constitutes his real
'and only danger) against his person just now. Have you a
'copy, or do you know where it can be had, or where our
'friend the Canonigo is. My memory is so bad that I am
'not quite sure whether it was the Riegos or the Quirogas
'about whom we interested ourselves so much; but I recollect
'your warmth, zeal, and generosity well, and I am therefore
'certain that on the present, in some senses similar, and in others
'opposite, occasion, you will, if you can, assist me in softening
'asperity (too natural and too just, it must be owned) against
'Polignac, and his colleagues or accomplices too, if it be practi-
'cable.' Sharing earnestly the feeling thus expressed, Lord
Nugent could hardly have suppressed a smile in contrasting this
letter of Lord Holland's with a dry mention of the same subject
by the Duke of Wellington, in a letter, also to himself, of a
fortnight's earlier date. 'I think,' wrote the Duke, 'that all
'the ministers would have been let off if Prince de Polignac
'had not been taken. But I think they will execute him;
'and probably Peyronnet. The Prince de Polignac, however,
'has adopted the best mode of having his life saved, by proving
'to the world that he is not so able a man as he was believed
'to be. His letter to Mons. Pasquier is a remarkable example
'of weakness.'* As all the world now knows, the latter sup-

---

* In the same letter, which is dated from Walmer Castle on the
27th August 1830, the Duke of Wellington makes a striking and characteristic allusion to the ultra-royalist party. 'I received your note,'
he writes. 'Of course, what you said to me is between ourselves. I have
'already had a different report; and have reason to believe that the Comte
'de Ponthieu is acting prudently, whatever he may say. I know that an
'offer was made to him of services, which I think in former times would
'not have been rejected. This offer was declined; and at the same time

position of the Duke proved to be the correct one, and the poor prince was not thought deserving of the scaffold.

And now followed the overthrow of the Duke's administration, and Lord Grey's accession to power, when Lord Nugent took office as one of the Junior Lords of the Treasury, and in the following spring, after another sharp contest, was again returned member for Aylesbury. The duties of his office received conscientious attention from him, and, during this and the succeeding year, he had charge of several Acts of a useful or necessary kind. Among them he was always glad to remember that he had carried through the House one of the shortest Acts of Parliament contained in the statute book, which nevertheless, in its ten or a dozen lines, abolished not less than forty forms of oaths in the Customs and Excise. For Lord Nugent had faith in the Scriptural precept—swear not at all—and would have given it extensive application in public affairs. He believed that to scatter oaths broadcast was to reap harvests of perjury, and when he found that in the two departments thus brought within his official control nearly fifteen hundred oaths were sworn every year, he justly felt that the interests of morality would be better protected by the substitution of declarations in every case, with the penalty of a heavy fine on discovery of falsehood. Oaths are but fetters on the honest and conscientious, to whom they are also a needless burden. To the dishonest they offer no check whatever. The subjection to them, still rendered compulsory in the highest as in the lowest offices of State, is nothing better than a sheer superstition. There is either no danger, or the remedy is utterly inadequate.

Lord Nugent did not again contest Aylesbury at the dissolution in 1832, having meanwhile, in the July of that year, accepted from Lord Grey the office of Lord High Commis-

‘a declaration made that he would not return if it was in his power; and
‘that even for the Duc de Bourdeaux he would not say a word as long as
‘he should remain in this country.’

sioner of the Ionian Islands. And that this appointment was
not the reward for any indiscriminate support even of the
Ministry under which he held subordinate office, will perhaps
sufficiently appear from the fact, that his name had figured,
not long before, in the minority of 150 liberal members who
voted against the ministerial attempt to save the borough
of Saltash from Schedule A. Lord Nugent left England
while the Reform Bill excitement was still strong, and one of
his last acts before departure was to sit to the ill-fated painter
of the Banquet held in Guildhall to celebrate the passing of
the measure. Mr. Haydon has described this sitting so
cleverly in a diary written at the time, and conveying with
graphic fidelity so manifest an impression of the man, that it
may properly be inserted in this place. The portrait on
Haydon's canvas is less like.*

'26th. Breakfasted with Lord Nugent. Sketched him. Passed
'a very delightful morning. He took down with the grace of high
'birth, a print of Hampden, which hung in an old English frame,
'and presented it to me, writing his name on the back. He said
'some capital things. Talking of the Greeks, he said, "I
'"acknowledge they are liars. But why? It is the arm of slavery
'"against tyranny." He said, "I have as delightful associations
'"about the enclosed country of the civil wars as about Greece or
'"the Troad. I have as much pleasure in standing and thinking
'"I see the whole hedge lined with cuirassiers, as if they were
'"ancient Greeks in the Acropolis," "Yes," said I, "my Lord, and
'"I never think of the civil wars, but I associate the terrific face of
'"Cromwell gleaming—*dira facies*—above the field. He was a
'"grand fellow, my Lord. He died in power." "Yes, he did; but
'"recollect Napoleon," said Lord Nugent, immediately grasping
'my meaning, "what he suffered, with a thief-catcher ferreting his
'"dirty linen, harassed by a hideous complaint, and tortured by
'"insults." He went on; "Do you know who H. B. is?" "No."
'"I think I do." "Who my Lord?" "I think it is Harry
'"Burrard, of the Guards. We went to school together, and he

* Haydon's *Memoirs*, ii. 310. 320.

'"drew capitally." We then went into a long discussion about
'arms; tried rapiers; looked at black-jacks. He ordered up a
'bloodhound and a Scotch greyhound that would honour Abbots-
'ford, and after forty visits, twenty letters, after Joe, and Bill,
'and Dick, and Harry had had their orders, in came the groom.
'"Where's the little mare?" "At Stowe, my Lord." "How
'"came she there?" "My Lord, your own orders." "Get her
'"directly, in time to embark. Who covered her?" "I don't
'"know, my Lord." In came Joe.* "My Lord, the captain of
'"the steamer." "Show him in." "Mr. Haydon, we had better
'"begin." I began, wanting his head to the left; but the captain
'sat on the right, and every instant Lord Nugent jerked his head
'to the right, to discuss the various probabilities of embarkation,
'and there I sat, catching his features as I could, and getting them
'in rapidly.

'After seeing the drawing, he said, "I shall be happy to see
'"you at Corfu. You can be out in three weeks in a steamer.
'"We'll then take a trip to the Troad and Constantinople. Don't
'"forget it. Joe?" "My Lord." "Tell Mr. What's-his-name,
'"Hookham will settle it." "Yes, my Lord. My Lord, here's
'"the silversmith." "Who?" "The silversmith." "Send him
'"to Hookham's too. Then, captain, we must be on board by

* 'Joe,' Joseph Turpin, was Lord Nugent's favourite and attached servant, his friend why should I not call him? He attended him everywhere, travelled over all Europe with him, went with him on his eastern pilgrimage, and was still most at home in the little manor-house of Lilies near which he was born, at which he stood by his master's death-bed, and where he still remains, devoted to his memory. Describing, in his *Lands Classical and Sacred*, an illness which attacked him in Syria, and which gave occasion for the exercise of active and considerate kindness on the part of his friend and fellow traveller, Major Grote, Lord Nugent adds:
'And I should be ungrateful, if, while expressing what I feel of the
'diligent care received from others, I could forget what I owe to the
'intelligence and indefatigable zeal shown on this as on so many other
'occasions, by one whose services, during the many years and various
'scenes we have together passed through, have always been rendered to
'me rather in the spirit of an attached friend than in the mere fulfilment
'of the duty of a trusty servant; I mean my good Joseph Turpin, who
'from his boyhood has been by my side, and whose skill as well as
'attention contributed so much now to set me soon upon my legs again.'

'"three? Can the horses, eh, what do you call it—can the horses
'"—the horses get on board easily?" "As easy as a glove, my
'"Lord." "Well, captain, you had better see Lady Nugent, and
'"talk to her about the baggage." "Yes, my Lord." "Joe."
'"Yes, my Lord." "Ask Lady Nugent for that old painting."
'"Yes, my Lord." "Michel." "*Oui, milord.*"

'In the midst of all this I finished my sketch, and was off. I
'like Lord Nugent very much. He is of race, and looks like a
'noble. His manners are graceful and commanding. He is cul-
'tivated and entertaining, and I dare say will honour his station.

'27th. Finished the head of the chairman. Lord Nugent and
'Sir Matthew Wood called, and liked the picture. Lord Nugent
'made some capital remarks, which I adopted. He embarked at
'three.'

Lord Nugent reached the seat of his government in December 1832, and left in February 1835. But before allusion is made to the circumstances under which he resigned, I will briefly advert to the leading results of his administration.

The subject to which he gave the greatest attention on his arrival in the Islands was that of the financial administration, and the results in this respect of his brief term of power afford the best means of testing the spirit which animated his government, and the value of his services to the country he was called to govern. For they rest upon documents which it is impossible to disprove, and may be verified by any one who consults the Blue Books filed in the Colonial Office. From these it is manifest, that during his residence at Corfu the revenue had considerably increased, while the proportionate expenditure had suffered diminution with each successive year. The account for 1834, for example, shows an increase of nearly £50,000 over that for 1832; and while, in the latter year, the excess of expenditure over revenue amounted to nearly £11,000, the former year showed a balance of revenue over expenditure, of more than £34,000.

In connection with this improvement in revenue, another important change was effected by the new High Commissioner.

In the spring of 1834, he suggested to the Home Government an arrangement to which he had obtained the consent of the Ionian Parliament, that the States should commute, in place of the obligation imposed upon them by the treaty of Paris for the maintenance of the British troops in the Islands and for the repair of fortifications,—an obligation they had never been able to fulfil, and which had always been in arrear,—by annual payment to Great Britain of £35,000 a-year. The English Colonial Minister thought this arrangement equitable to the States, and beneficial to the protecting power. It was therefore duly carried out.

It is not necessary, and would indeed be unbecoming in such a slight sketch as the present, that the other parts of Lord Nugent's government should be here in any manner dwelt upon. It is right to state, however, most emphatically, that his conduct in his office was repeatedly approved by the home authorities; that, on his return, many private and very earnest letters from the Colonial Minister, and other members of the Government, assured him of the undiminished confidence and respect with which they regarded him as a public man; and that, with reference to an enquiry to be mentioned hereafter, Lord Glenelg conveyed to him in an official letter the specific information that no representation or charge of any kind, against any part of his conduct, had been sent to the Colonial Office during his government or afterwards, with one sole exception involving a matter of Ionian law. This latter, I may add, was investigated after Lord Nugent's resignation by the then Colonial Minister, Lord Aberdeen, who decided against the complainant and in favour of Lord Nugent, to whom, with much frankness and courtesy, an official copy of the decision was forwarded at the time.

Nor were the testimonies brought or received by Lord Nugent from the States themselves, less positive and earnest in expression. After his resignation, addresses of regret at his departure were presented him from the various authorities.

The Primary Council of the States, as well as the Archbishop and Clergy of the Greek Church, took part in those addresses. The representatives of Corfu in the Legislative Assembly decreed him a gold tablet, expressive of their high sense of the benefits conferred by his government. A gold medal, a testimony never before given to a Lord High Commissioner, was unanimously voted to him by the Senate. The same feeling of regret and gratitude was expressed publicly by the secretary of the Senate, Sir Edward Baynes, in presence and in the name of all the British civil functionaries of the Ionian government. And finally, there followed him to England addresses from all the seven Islands, signed by the several Regents, the principal proprietors, and numbers of the inhabitants of each.

Yet some of his measures, in dealing with existing monopolies, had exasperated not a little some powerful interests in the Islands; he had also been obliged to dismiss, with the full sanction of the Home Government, an influential officer who had long held an important employment at Corfu; and though it was not from this quarter that anything connected with his resignation proceeded, there can be no doubt that any intriguing ex-treasurer, or any disappointed applicant for employment anxious to vent his spite against the Government House, would find no lack of idle or malignant gossip manufactured to his hand, among the enmities thus provoked.

Nothing could be more honourable to Lord Nugent than the circumstances of his resignation of his High Commissionership, on the sudden fall of the Whig administration, after Lord Spencer's death. At that time he had held the office not more than two years; and any removal of him by the new Administration was quite out of the question, so long as the usual term of colonial governorships remained unexpired. But Lord Nugent conceived himself to stand in peculiar relations to the party with which the elder branch of his family continued to act, and which he had himself so steadily opposed;

and he had already, before his departure from England, so provided that he should not incur in that quarter any obligation that could be avoided, or delay for a moment longer than was necessary his participation in the fortunes of the statesmen with whom he had acted all his life. In the event of any accession of the Conservatives to power, a nobleman connected with the Ministry, and a near relative of Lord Nugent's, had received from him the resignation of his appointment, to be tendered at his discretion.

Upon the unexpected event of 1834, such was the peculiar posture of affairs, and the apparently uncertain issue of any attempt to replace the Whigs, that some doubt occurred to the holder of this resignation as to whether or not it should be tendered at once; but one of the retiring ministers having been consulted, it was thought right so to tender it, and this step received afterwards the cordial approval of Lord Nugent himself. Having mentioned this, however, I ought to add, not less explicitly, that the claim upon his party which he believed himself to have thus established, was not afterwards acknowledged as he held that it ought to have been.

The portion of his administration of which Lord Nugent spoke always with the greatest pride, was that reform of the finances which, with entire approval from home, he was engaged in carrying out, and which already had produced a larger surplus revenue than had ever accrued to those islands, except during the year of Sir Thomas Maitland's Commissionership. His measures in this direction, and in breaking down a very oppressive monopoly in the currant trade, of which the effect was to impoverish the revenue not less than the people, had, as I have shown, secured the approval of the Colonial Ministers in office during his term of power, and of their successor on his recall. But though the fact of these reforms, thus commenced and interrupted, may be said to have strengthened Lord Nugent's claim to be restored to the position he had held so soon as a fair opportunity should present itself, it is to be stated with regret that this met with no recognition, and that almost alone among the lesser members of the Whig Administration of that day, he was left to suffer for having voluntarily linked his fortune to that of his friends. And an incident occurred at the time which, though unconnected with this neglect, or in any degree inducing it, made it in Lord Nugent's case a peculiar wrong, and for some time increased the many painful personal feelings excited by it.

This incident, indeed, which occurred at the close of the year of his return, was in all respects so painful that I would gladly, if possible, have omitted all mention of it here. As it is, I shall touch it very briefly, and only so far as his own generous nature would now have wished, in vindication of his personal honour. For, manifold and great as were the annoyances and irritations connected with the matter at the time, they had long ceased to embitter his recollections of it. In this, as in all things, his mind was one in which as little of the mere spleen of selfish anger continued as in that of any one who ever lived. But he had a natural anxiety that his eagerness to repel a gross calumny should not be forgotten, whatever it might be agreed to forget of the too little sympathy exhibited for a wrong committed, or the too much countenance given to the wrong-doer, by his own political friends and associates; and it is this consideration only which suggests and limits the statement I now permit myself to make.

In November, 1835, there appeared in an evening paper supporting the Government at that time, since extinct, a leading article containing a personal attack on Lord Nugent, stating that he was reported to be a candidate for the Government of Ceylon, hinting at his having committed acts of great impropriety during his residence at Corfu, and asserting that the writer had 'the best grounds for believing 'that representations respecting Lord Nugent's government 'were sent to the Secretary of State, and remain recorded in 'the Colonial Office, which, even if the Administration had not 'been changed in November last, must have led to serious in- 'vestigation, with every probability of the noble lord's recall.'

Upon the appearance of this libel, Lord Nugent lost not an hour in taking steps to vindicate his character; and on a complete and frank retractation being refused, a civil action for damages was commenced against the journal which had published it. On various grounds, and by the interpositions of legal forms and delays always resisted by Lord Nugent, the trial of the case was put off from time to time; but every proposal for a compromise which did not involve an entire withdrawal and disavowal of the libel, was steadily resisted, and even at the last, when, upon the supposed consent of Lord Nugent's representative in these negotiations, a written withdrawal of the charges was printed in the offending journal, Lord Nugent himself at once publicly declared that the apparently modified tone of its disavowal was unsatisfactory to him, and had not received his consent. Upon this, after a few days' delay, the subjoined statement was given in the most prominent part of the paper.

'The Proprietors of the —— regret that the paragraph published 'by them in the —— of Wednesday last, withdrawing imputations 'against the conduct of Lord Nugent in his Administration in the 'Ionian Islands, was not fully satisfactory to his Lordship. They 'now, however, wholly withdraw and disavow those imputations 'and regret their publication. Lord Nugent has discontinued his 'action on this further explanation, and on payment of the expenses 'of the suit.'

If anything could have strengthened Lord Nugent's title to some mark of undiminished confidence from the Government whose employment he had lately quitted, it was this undeserved subjection to calumny from a paper known to be in the Government interest at the time; nor was it a less untoward circumstance that the chief proprietor of this very paper, while its apologies and retractations were in course of preparation, should himself have received a public appointment. But upon this I lay less stress, because I have before me convincing evidence, in a letter of the Cabinet Minister by whom that appointment was conferred, that he knew nothing of the libel when the promise was given, that the libel had been retracted before the gift was confirmed, and that his respect and regard for Lord Nugent continued undiminished. Nor can there be any impropriety in quoting the actual words of a letter written at the time by the late Lord Holland. 'I feel, ' I assure you,' he writes to Lord Nugent,

'That the Government have a debt to discharge to you; and I
' also feel much annoyed that it has been so long deferred. In
' this I really believe we all concur. The appointment of ——
' after libelling you, was certainly unseasonable, but it was inad-
' vertently promised before that circumstance was adverted to;
' and I do believe that ——, with all his offences to Lord
' Brougham and yourself, had some claims of an old date that
' were very strong on the party. The whole transaction has at
' least had this good effect, that it proves to all impartial men, not
' only that —— was not appointed for his recent conduct, but
' that neither the Government which had sent you out, that to
' which you resigned your office, or that which succeeded it, ever in
' the smallest degree implied dissatisfaction, much less censure of
' your administration.'

With this assurance Lord Nugent had to content himself, for the debt which Lord Holland describes remained to the close of his life undischarged. The employment of which he was thus deprived, he never again, in any other form, received. From his first entry into Parliament, at the earliest age at which he could enter it, he had at every conceivable sacrifice of family interest and ambition, given undeviating support to the party whose opinions had so long excluded them from power; and in all fairness it might have been thought that he had established his title to share their better fortunes, as long as his capacity and conduct should remain unimpeached. But it was a wrong done, as well as a debt not paid. In accepting the Ionian Government, he had given up the personal influence of residence which for so many years had secured him his seat at Aylesbury, and by that studied and continued exclusion from office to which he had now to submit, he was affected as much in what are called personal interests, as in those which more especially concern the credit of a position in public life. And though, into the enforced abstinence from affairs to which he was thus sentenced for several years he carried the consciousness that his honour had been publicly and privately acquitted, and that in fidelity to his principles as well as conduct to his party he stood confessedly above reproach, it was not to be expected, however friendly the assurances conveyed to him, that he should accept without repining an exclusion which he felt to be unjust.

He made many attempts to resume his place in the House of Commons. He was named for Marylebone in 1836, but on the result of a ballot to determine the chances of the several candidates proving adverse, he at once actively busied himself in promoting the election of his more fortunate competitor; and he took the same disinterested course in 1838, when a similar incident occurred. In 1837 he contested Aylesbury unsuccessfully against Mr. Praed, and became convinced that the attempt to recover the borough for the liberal party must necessarily fail, where the contest involved only a single seat. He publicly declared therefore, that in future, to protect his friends against sacrifices uncalled for, because useless, he would not ask them for their votes, except where the entire representation was contested; but the reserve thus practised by himself he should also expect from others, and would object to any other Liberal assuming to occupy his place until a majority of the liberal voters should declare themselves dissatisfied with his prior and long-established claim to represent them. When, therefore, on the death of Mr. Praed in the summer of 1839, a liberal candidate unexpectedly presented himself in opposition to Captain Baillie Hamilton, Lord

Nugent was only fulfilling a pledge he was in honour bound to redeem, in actively opposing such an attempt. His conduct was impugned by a section of the popular party unconnected with the borough, and he defended himself with spirit and success. 'If my eager sincerity for the cause of reform,' he said, 'now required any proof or defence, my life would have 'been passed to little purpose. My whole public career has 'been a series of personal sacrifices to the cause.' Certainly, if an always unshrinking disregard of personal interests may be accepted as honourable evidence of a sincerity and earnestness of opinion, the fact of Lord Nugent's could as little be doubted, as that there would often have lain within his reach no small temptations to abandon it, if he had ever allowed himself to consider from what quarter the greater benefit would come.

Shortly after this election, he was engaged in a matter having too direct a connection with the principal subject of the present volume not to receive a brief mention here. The Second Centenary of the Long Parliament, in 1840, brought with it many a memorable anniversary, which the writer of this imperfect sketch had the happiness to enjoy with Lord Nugent; for the author of the Life of Hampden had taken a generous interest in a series of lives illustrating the same great time, and for some years had opened to the writer all the access to original materials he was able to command. One of his many cordial letters now lying before me has reference to one of these anniversaries, when a bottle of wine was to be opened in Hampden's own hall at Great Hampden, in celebration of the 3rd of November, 1640. 'Come,' he wrote, 'and we will explore the whole of this beautiful and 'most interesting country, from the library where John 'Hampden studied Davila, to the field where he received his 'death wound, and the church where he is buried. In the 'rectory of Hampden, there lives a liberal clergyman—on a 'soil sacred to liberty. The *old* parsonage house which stood 'there, until pulled down a few years ago by barbarous hands

'(not my friend's), was inhabited by Lenthal, the Speaker's
' son, to whom John Hampden gave the living; and who died,
' and his whole family, of the *plague* as it was said (perhaps
' of the Restoration of Monarchy) in 1662, and with his whole
' family lies buried at the end of the garden.' At this visit,
the design suggested itself to Lord Nugent of marking, by a
simple memorial of a solid and enduring kind, the spot where
Hampden received his mortal wound, and of erecting it on the
anniversary of the second centenary of the fatal day at Chalgrove.
' Yours usque ad inferos,' said Lord Denman, replying to the
letter inviting his co-operation, with an allusion to the disinterment in Hampden Church, ' I cannot resist your company in
' attempting to give just honour to the great patriot, whose
' very identical body I am sure we saw. You must, however,
' set me down for the smallest subscription (£5), and it must
' be with my initial, for I think there is a serious objection to
' judges volunteering any political profession.' In a like tone,
and to the same effect, Lord Leigh cordially responded, in
defiance of the ghosts of his jacobitical ancestors at Stoneleigh,
who, he said, were grinning at him from his family walls for
his apostasy from the principles of his forefathers. With no
need to apprehend such family terrors, but telling Lord Nugent
that he was still mindful of the old Whig toast, and rejoiced
in the opportunity to declare his continued allegiance to the
'cause for which Hampden bled in the field, and Sidney and
'Russell on the scaffold,' the Duke of Bedford sent £20.
Others as gladly gave their help, and sufficient money was
soon provided for the modest and unpretending design.

It was placed at Chalgrove field on Monday the 19th of June,
1843 (the actual anniversary of the fight, the 18th, falling on a
Sunday), when, as Lord Nugent wrote to me on the day following, ' everything went off admirably well, many thousands on
' the field in the morning, and upwards of two hundred and fifty
' at dinner, gentry, farmers, &c., from all round, and a great
' many more unable to find room in our barn.' The monu-

ment thus raised is a plain and simple record, so durably built as to offer good resistance to attacks of weather, and deriving its sole interest from the inscription it bears. 'Here, 'in this field of Chalgrove, John Hampden, after an able 'and strenuous but unsuccessful resistance in parliament, 'and before the judges of the land, to the measures of an 'arbitrary court, first took arms, assembling the levies of the 'associated counties of Buckingham and Oxford, in 1642; 'and here, within a few paces of this spot, while fighting 'in defence of the free monarchy, and the ancient liberties of 'England, he received a wound of which he died, June 18, '1643. In the two hundredth year from that day, this stone 'was raised in reverence to his memory.' On the south side are the names of those by whose subscriptions it had been erected, and on the west are the arms of Hampden and his deathless motto, Vestigia Nulla Retrorsum. These it was meant to have accompanied by a profile of the patriot, and the intention, though afterwards abandoned, had associated Lady Nugent in the work of honouring her husband's hero. She executed with taste and skill a model in bas-relief founded on the original portrait prefixed to this volume.

Nor should it be omitted that with Lord Nugent she had also shared, some few years earlier than this, in the authorship and publication of two small volumes of Legends of the Library of Lilies;* and that to a quarterly periodical devoted

---

* The delightful little seat in Buckinghamshire from which the book took its title, the home to which Lord Nugent was tenderly attached for more than five-and-thirty years, the scene of all his most cherished recollections, and the place of his death, is described by himself in a preface to the first volume, which may not unfitly be preserved here.

'If you would place yourself just mid-way between the three seas which 'form the boundaries of Southern England, you shall find yourself on a 'small knoll, covered with antique elm, walnut, and sycamore trees, which 'rises out of a vale famous in all time for the natural fertility of its soil, 'and the moral virtues of its people. On this knoll, fitly called by our 'ancestors "the heart of South Britain," stood, distant about half-a-mile from each other, two monasteries, known by the flowery appellatives of

to modern Greek literature, and the illustration of Greek history and antiquities, which ought before to have had mention as published by Lord Nugent at Corfu during his Ionian High Commissionership, she had made some graceful contributions.

' Lilies and Roses; not unaptly setting forth a promise of all that can
' recommend itself as fair and sweet unto the gentler senses. These
' edifices have, for many centuries, been no more; but, on the site of the
' first mentioned of the two, standeth a small mansion, of Tudor architec-
' ture, bearing still its ancient name. Of the monastery little memorial
' beyond the name remains; save only that under a small enclosed space,
' erewhile its cemetery, now a wilderness of flowers, the bones of the monks
' repose. Two lines of artificial slope to the westward mark the boundaries
' of the pleasaunce, where they took their recreation, and cultivated their
' lentils and fruits; and a range of thickly-walled cellar still retains the
' same destination and office as when it furnished to those holy men their
' more generous materials of refection.
    ' What more shall be said of the mansion, or of the domain, full seventy
' statute acres, which surrounds it? of the herds and flocks content to
' thrive in silence on the richness of its fields, and thrive they do in
' wondrous measure of prosperity? Nothing.—Nor much of that more
' gamesome troop of idling steeds, though pleasant to their master's eye,
' who, on its green expanse, frisk and gambol out a sportive colt-hood, or
' gaze and hobble through a tranquil old age, with the active and laborious
' honours of a public life past, but not forgotten. Little shall be said of
' that smooth and narrow pool, scarce visible among the rising shrubs
' which belt in and shroud the grounds from the incurious wayfarer; or
' of such carp and tench as, having 'scaped the treacherous toils of the
' nightly plunderer, gasp and tumble on its surface, delighting to display
' their golden pride in the mid-day sun, before the gaze of lawful posses-
' sion. Nor shall the casual reader be led carelessly and wearily to note
' the many sweet memorials of private friendship, records of the living and
' the dead, which, standing forth from amid the lightsome glades and leafy
' shadows around, make the place sacred to many a strong affection.
' Romantic the scenery without is not, and for spacious halls and gorgeous
' canopies the eye may search in vain within. But for the warm cheer of
' the little oak library, for the quaint carvings, the tracery of other times,
' which abound therein, for the awful note of the blood-hound, baying upon
' his midnight chain, and the pleasing melancholy of the hooting owl from
' his hereditary chamber in the roof, and for the tunefulness of the cooing
' wood-quests, and the morning rooks which bustle and caw, and of the
' high winds that pipe and roar, daily and nightly, through the boughs,
' and for the deep glossy verdure of the pastures stretching forth to the
' brave distant hills which fence the vale,—to those who in such things
' take delight, Lilies hath still its charms.'

It may also seem peculiarly befitting that here, before passing from the subject of Hampden, some reference should be made to an Imaginary Dialogue which Lord Nugent wrote some few years after this date, and published as a *Tract entitled True and Faithful Relation of a Worthy Discourse between Colonel John Hampden and Colonel Oliver Cromwell. Preceded by an explanatory preface.* The discourse is supposed to have been overheard and reported by an Independent divine, and its drift was to exhibit the probable influence which Colonel John might have exerted over Colonel Oliver, if his life had been spared, by contrasting Cromwell's grand but impracticable theories with the more limited but more practicable views of Hampden. It was one of those clever imitations of the political and oratorical literature of the seventeenth century, which could only have been written by one to whom its books and men were familiar; and being put forth (of course anonymously) in the quaint old-faced letter of its period, Lord Nugent took great delight in the success with which he was able, by means of a copy elaborately stained with tobacco-juice, to pass it off upon his uncle, Mr. Thomas Grenville, no indifferent judge of such matters, as a genuine piece of Commonwealth literature.

The six winter and spring months between December 1843 and May 1844 were passed by Lord Nugent in travel through

To complete this description, a brief reference only needs to be added to certain trees scattered over the grounds, each with a stone memorial at its base bearing the name of the friend who planted it, and the date which was to keep that event memorable in the calendar at Lilies; and among the friendly memories thus kept green and fresh in Lord Nugent's country home were those of public and private friends as various as the pursuits and tastes of his life had been, living statesmen, exiled patriots, and distinguished men of letters. Passing through the grounds not many weeks ago, and observing the care with which every association dear to Lord Nugent is still kept and cherished by their present possessor, I saw, among other names attached to goodly trees of various growth, those of the Duke of Sussex, Lord John Russell, Lord Fortescue, Mr. Dickens, Lord Denman, Mr. Landor, Mr. Jerrold, M. Argüelles, some younger members of the Fortescue family, Mr. Ainsworth, Mr. Gleed, the late public orator at Oxford, and Mr. Westmacot the sculptor.

Athens, Egypt, the Holy Land, and Syria; and, both as he went and returned, he made a brief stay at his former seat of government in Corfu, from which he brought a frank and cordial impression of Lord Seaton's policy and success. He afterwards published some results of this journey in a scholarly and agreeable book, *Lands Classical and Sacred*, as full of nice observation as of ingenious suggestion, and from which, in any less limited space than the present, the temptation would be great to quote some of its passages of personal adventure.*

His attention to public affairs suffered no abatement, however, either from literature or travel. He had taken peculiar interest in the wider social direction given to legislative enquiry during the last few years; and politics had never seemed to him so attractive a pursuit, as when they less derived their interest from influencing party struggles than from improving and benefiting great masses of the people. He was never so anxious to enter parliament as when free-

---

* One brief but amusing little picture may at least find insertion in this note, for it quietly expresses Lord Nugent's sense of humour, together with the quick and ready perception which enabled him so often to indulge it. He is describing the principal clown or jester in attendance on a puppet-master and conjuror in the streets of Cairo. 'His principal 'jest was this; Every now and then he would pick a quarrel with the 'puppets, and aim a blow at them with a strap or courbash, apparently 'with intent to kill; but always contriving to make the instrument miss 'his intended victim, and come round with a loud crack on his own 'shoulders. This was always received, happen as often as it would, with 'shrieks of delight by the bystanders, children, women, and men of all ages 'and conditions. There was one very venerable and well-dressed old 'gentleman, in a flowing caftan of yellow silk and ample turban, with a 'large chaplet of beads round his neck, and a long amber-lipped chibouk, 'which he silently and gravely smoked, never disturbing it, save as often 'as this event of the clown's self-castigation occurred. This, however, was 'too much for his gravity, which, from his appearance at all other moments, 'I doubt whether anything else ever did or could affect. This never 'failed. I do not remember ever passing this group without seeing this 'same old gentleman always contemplating this performance, and his pipe 'always alight. He was probably some merchant or agent, who daily set 'forth with intent to cross the Esbekieh on business, but never could 'succeed in passing this spot.'

trade measures came under discussion, and upon the last struggle of the Melbourne Ministry in 1842 he had polled between five and six hundred votes against the Tory candidates at Southampton. A correspondence of some interest on the subject of free-trade passed between himself and the late Lord Grey soon after this contest, in which his own distrust of Sir Robert Peel's sliding-scale proposals somewhat strikingly contrasted with the view of them taken by the veteran statesman. 'To the principles of free-trade,' Lord Grey wrote in one letter (after a deserved compliment to Lord Nugent's 'honest and 'manly spirit'), 'I offer no objection. But in their practical 'application they must be subject to many and various con- 'siderations; and even if I thought as you do, I should have 'acquiesced in Sir Robert Peel's proposition, under whatever 'protest I might have thought necessary as to my own 'opinions. It certainly is a large and important concession, 'and acknowledged by all to be a great improvement of the 'present system. To considering it, had I been a member of 'the House of Commons, I should have added one to the 'majority. It is, at all events, an important step, and if it 'does not practically succeed, as I hope it will, believing the 'country to be by no means so adverse to it as you suppose, it 'would materially strengthen and assist your opinions.'

Lord Nugent had frequent reason to recall those words as he watched the progress of events between 1842 and 1847, when, on the fall of Sir Robert Peel, after the services and sacrifices which have endeared his name and memory to the masses of his countrymen, he contested Aylesbury at the general election in the latter year, and was triumphantly returned. He did not affect to conceal or make light of the exultation and pride with which he received this testimony of continued attachment from the constituency which first returned him to parliament, and in whose service he had now the happiness to think that he should end life as he had begun it, Member for the borough of Aylesbury. 'For 'many, many years,' he told them, 'it has been my fond 'ambition again to serve you in parliament. That strong 'desire has lured me, not coy or reluctant certainly, but with 'every desire and energy engaged in it, from a most pleasant 'retirement, from a happy home, from my darling books 'which, after family and dear friends, of all things I love the 'most; and to the utmost of my power I will serve you 'faithfully. I have no design of looking through parliament 'for official power. When my service may be fulfilled, I 'desire no greater reward, no fairer epitaph in your memory, 'than that I have through life maintained the confidence of my 'friends, and never, by want of courtesy or honesty, deserved 'rancour from my opponents; that I have been, without 'distinction of persons, through good report or evil, the 'opposer of bad government, and the faithful upholder of good, 'the resister of oppression, the advocate of religious freedom, 'and as in the beginning, so to the end, the unflinching 'promoter, according to the best means God may give me, of 'that greatest of His gifts to man, after reason,—Liberty.'

Soon this sense of gladness and satisfaction, however, was to have a dark and melancholy shade drawn over it by a domestic grief, a saddening of that 'happy home,' which no personal success or public acquisition could redeem. The health of Lady Nugent, which had long been extremely delicate, finally gave way in the spring of 1848; and if any of his friends had yet to learn what a manly and true spirit Lord Nugent possessed, they should have seen him at that time. Upon a grief so sacred it would little become even the friendliest speech to intrude, but in his own simple and truthful language some record of it may here find no unfitting place. 'The loss I have sustained,' he wrote to a friend, 'in parting 'from my beloved wife, is indeed irreparable. But I know 'and feel I am not inconsolable. For every kind expression 'which has been addressed to me (and indeed they have come 'in abundant showers upon me), every expression which shows

'me how much and how truly she was valued by all who knew
'her, is a balm of comfort poured upon the deep wound I
'have received. Often and solemnly have she and I promised
'each other, that whichever of us should be the survivor
'would, for duty's sake to the memory of the departed, strive
'to the utmost, by every means which Providence supplies
'(and Providence never intended that the best and most
'dearly cherished affections should be in proportion to their
'intenseness a curse on the survivor), to meet the blow with
'resignation and courage. I renewed the promise to her
'on her death-bed, and, with God's help, I will fulfil it
'thoroughly. I have already drunk the cup, drained it,
'and have not turned my face from it. I saw her die. My
'face' was close to hers, my head on the same pillow with
'hers, during all the process of her departure; and I saw
'her depart in perfect consciousness of all that could
'sweeten it to her, and without one pang, one struggle,
'without almost a change, save the change to tranquil sleep.
'I followed her to her grave; I returned from her grave to
'the home which she had made for more than thirty years
'a paradise to me; and my feelings now assure me I did
'right. I knew all her intentions and wishes, and am
'making it a delightful occupation to carry those inten-
'tions and wishes into effect. A very strong one was that I
'should return as soon as possible, and eagerly, to the duties
'of public life, and I shall do this.'

He kept his word in the latter respect, and, for as much of his life as now remained, public affairs never ceased to interest and occupy him. In particular he made several strenuous efforts to give effect to his views on Capital Punishment, and for much important help rendered in the same direction by Sir Fitzroy Kelly in the House of Commons, and in the press by Mr. Jerrold and other public writers, he felt always peculiarly grateful. But though perhaps no subject during his later years lay nearer to him than this, and he laboured to promote it in every possible way, he left the question much as he found it; abstract reasoning still as decisively carrying it on his side, as practical necessity will continue to carry it on the other. In real truth, the expediency of capital punishment turns altogether upon the efficiency or inefficiency of secondary punishment, and till the latter is in a more satisfactory state, it will be impossible to deal satisfactorily with the former. Another subject that largely occupied Lord Nugent in these years, was the Condition of the Agricultural Labourer; and he originated a discussion in June 1849 by which many valuable truths were elicited on those all-important questions of the necessity of giving freer circulation to labour, and of more effectually contributing to its independence, by abolishing the existing law of settlement and removal, and altering the mode of levying rates, which have since received wise attention from Mr. Baines. In all other liberal directions, too, his exertions were not wanting; and from the position he now took on most questions of progress and reform, several steps in advance of the great mass of the party with whom he had acted in early life, he might seem more directly to challenge the praise which in that earlier time he had drawn from Sydney Smith, in reviewing one of his pamphlets in the *Edinburgh*. 'When ' soldiers exercise, there stands a goodly portly person out of ' the ranks, upon whom all eyes are directed, and whose signs ' and motions in the performance of the manual exercise all ' the soldiers follow. The Germans, we believe, call him a ' flugelman. We propose Lord Nugent as a political flugelman. ' He is always consistent, plain, and honest; steadily and ' straightly pursuing his object without hope or fear, under ' the influence of good feelings and high principles. The ' House of Commons does not contain within its walls a more ' honest upright man.'

To the last moment of Lord Nugent's life this was true. Time and change had impaired nothing of his ardour for 'the good old cause.' The Hungarian war excited his warmest zeal, and for not a little of what was done in behalf of such of that gallant people as found refuge in London after the termination of the struggle, they had to thank his unwearying personal exertions. In this he but repeated his generous services of former years to the refugees from Spain, Portugal, and Greece, many of whom derived almost solely from his limited means the reliefs and consolations of their exile. In truth, a kinder heart, a more genial disposition, a more manly and honorable spirit, never existed than Lord Nugent's; and no man ever excited more affectionate private regards.

His death, which took place at Lilies, in the afternoon of Tuesday the 26th November, 1850, was an unexpected shock to many of his friends, who knew that he had recently and happily recovered from a severe illness. But an imprudent exposure to cold brought on a relapse of rheumatic gout, which ended in low fever and erysipelas. His sufferings were intense for nearly three weeks, but he bore them with the greatest fortitude, and at last died calmly, without pain.

IN the revision of this third edition of the *Memorials of Hampden* now submitted to the reader, care has been taken to make only such brief omissions as Lord Nugent contemplated, and had himself marked, with a view to its appearance in its present form. Nothing of the strictly biographical portion of the work has been touched; but where the historical description too much encumbered or overlaid it, this has been slightly compressed, it is believed with advantage to the general effect of the narrative.

J. F.

58, LINCOLN'S-INN FIELDS,
November, 1854.

AUTHOR'S PREFACE TO THE MEMORIALS.

In the arrangement of these Memorials of the principal passages in the life of John Hampden many difficulties presented themselves, to some of which, as being of mere personal consideration to myself, it is unnecessary to advert. But, besides these, there has been a continually recurring sense of the scantiness of the materials which offered themselves for his early and private history. The undertaking would, I felt, be but idle and presumptuous, unless justified by a consciousness of being able to contribute some material addition to what is generally known of his life and character.

Of his correspondence and conversation less has been preserved than perhaps of any other so remarkable person, living in times so near to our own. Of the papers at Hampden House, to which through the kindness of its present noble proprietor I have had access, there are none of any interest relating to John Hampden. The danger which, about the time of the restoration of the crown, might have accrued to his own family, and probably to many others also, if the correspondence of a chief leader in the transactions which immediately preceded the civil war had been preserved, may abundantly account for the absence of all such matter where we might otherwise the most naturally expect to find it.

The bare outline of the parliamentary life of John Hampden, wherever it has hitherto been attempted in a separate form, has been given with remarkable inaccuracy. Of this a sufficient instance is that, in the articles respecting him in the Biographia Britannica, and in Mr. Chalmers's Biographical Dictionary, and indeed in all the other notices of his life which I have met with, he is described as having first entered the House of Commons in the second parliament of Charles the First: whereas it will be seen that he took his seat in the foregoing reign, and six years before the time at which these writers date his first election; that he had sat in every parliament which was called during that space; and that, although not then filling the station of leader of a party, nor having risen to eminence as a speaker, he was yet of sufficient estimation to be three times appointed to conduct the conferences with the Upper House.

The first, and though scanty, some of the most useful, materials of which I have availed myself I owe to the friendship and confidence of the late Mr. Meadley. The course of reading into which he had fallen while preparing his published Life of Algernon Sidney had directed his enquiries farther back to the origin of those great struggles between privilege and prerogative which render the first half of the seventeenth century, in many respects, the most important portion of the history of our country. After the completion of those memoirs, he had designed to illustrate, with the matter he had collected, the history of some one of the earlier champions of popular rights in England; and he turned his attention to that of Hampden.

With an ardent and steady love of liberty Mr. Meadley joined great industry, perseverance, and accuracy: but, at his death, the documentary part of his undertaking was left with little more than its first foundations laid. That part which related to the execution of the ordinance for raising the militia in Buckinghamshire, and to the first two campaigns of the civil war in the midland counties, he had sent to me, that I might verify, or correct, the local details, and furnish him with any other such matter as is generally most within the reach of a person residing in the district itself. I was, besides, aware of some collections of private papers (a very large one in the possession of my own family), an unrestricted access to which seemed to me to be of the first importance to Mr. Meadley's object.

Of these, Sir Peter Temple's papers concerning the levy of the ship-money, which are preserved at Stowe, and the extensive correspondence, likewise in that collection, of Mr. Richard Grenvil of Wotton Underwood (who, at a later period, was high sheriff of the county, and a commissioner for raising the militia, and some time governor of the town of Aylesbury for the parliament), were evidence proper to be consulted by any person undertaking the work which Mr. Meadley contemplated.

After Mr. Meadley's death, the friendly feeling of his family, and of the Reverend Mr. Tate of Yorkshire, his executor, gave me possession of whatever other matter he had collected, with leave to use it as I might think proper.

I am also under obligation to the Reverend Dr. D'Oyley, and to Mr. Ellis, for the assistances they have given me in consulting the manuscript letters and published tracts in the libraries of Lambeth Palace and the British Museum; and to Mr. W. Staunton of Warwickshire, and to Lord Carteret and Lord Eliot, for their liberal permission to transcribe and make use of such documents as were interesting to me, among the valuable collection of Civil War Tracts in the possession of the former, and among the MS. Family Papers in the hands of the two latter. To my friend Sir Robert Greenhill Russell, of Chequers Court, I am sure that no expression of thanks from me is necessary for the use of his curious and valuable library; which, however, it gives me pleasure to acknowledge among the many tokens I have received of his kindness and regard. These materials, with some other collections of tracts, diurnals, and letters, to which, from time to time, accident, and the liberality of their proprietors, have given me reference, the journals of parliament, the sessional papers, and the contemporary histories, afford the groundwork of these memorials.*

---

* Among the materials for English history which have hitherto been but imperfectly examined, and which require the most careful arrangement, are the early Sessional Papers of the House of Commons. If properly classified, they would form a most valuable body of historical evidence, containing much interesting correspondence, and other matter, which has never yet been published; much, doubtless, that is not known to be in existence. These papers are now in a state which makes all casual reference to them very laborious. The journals alone are not in all cases to be trusted. Of this there is one very remarkable instance, which I do

I have endeavoured, here and there, to illustrate facts well known in history by private letters and other hitherto unpublished documents, giving these sometimes as evidence merely of the style, and sometimes of the characters, of remarkable persons. As such, they may not be unacceptable.

I have also endeavoured to avoid all such comment as did not appear to me necessary to the narrative, in order the better to guard myself against the temptations of a partiality arising out of that deep veneration for the memory of Hampden which I so truly feel to have grown upon enquiry.

not remember to have seen observed upon. In the Commons Journals, April 16, 1641, there is this startling entry:

"3^{tia} vice lecta est Billa   An Act for the Attainder of Tho. Earl of Strafford, of High Treason.

And, upon the Question for the Passing,

The House was divided,

Lord Digby } Tellers for the *Yea* ;   Sir Gilb. Gerard } *Noe* ;
Mr. Lloyd   Sir Tho. Barrington

With the Noe 59
With the Yea 204

Upon Report whereof, the Bill passed."

This was the famous division of the Straffordians, and took place on the same day that Lord Digby made his famous speech *against* the Bill. His name was also published in the list of the fifty-nine Straffordians.

This is not an error in the printing of the Journals only, but in the MS., which may be seen in the Journal Office. And it is the more remarkable, inasmuch as this entry in the Journals was made by Rushworth himself, who, in his Historical Collection, says, ' Upon the Question for the ' passing thereof the house was divided, 59 for the Noes, 204 for the Yeas, ' *the Lord Digby being appointed one of the tellers for the Noes.*'

Engraved by E. Finden.

MEMORIALS OF JOHN HAMPDEN,

HIS PARTY AND HIS TIMES.

Part the First.

TO 1625.

Ancestry and Family of Hampden—His Education and early Life—Introductory Matter—Posture of Public Affairs—Advance of general Information and the spirit of Liberty—James the First—Disputes with his first Parliament concerning Privileges and Supply—Disgusts the Nobility, and persecutes the Puritans—Dissolution—Second Parliament—Undertakers—Dissolution—Third Parliament—Hampden takes his Seat—His Mother urges him to seek a Peerage—First Parliamentary Party—Proceedings against Delinquents—Remonstrances—Answers of the King—Protestation—Dissolution—Commitments of Members—Villiers, Duke of Buckingham—His influence over the Prince—Disasters of his Administration—A new Parliament—On better terms with the King—Buckingham's influence declines—Death of the King.

THE family of Hampden is one of the few which may be traced in an unbroken line from the Saxon times.* It received from Edward the Confessor the grant of the estate and residence in Buckinghamshire from which the name is derived, and which are entered in Doomsday Book as in the possession of Baldwyn de Hampden. Escaping from the rapacity of the Norman princes, and strengthened by rich and powerful alliances, it was continued in direct male succession, increasing in influence and wealth. Mr. Noble and Mr. Lysons state that a local tradition, supported by some quaint, popular verses, represents one of the Hampdens as having forfeited to the Crown the three valuable manors of Tring, Wing, and

* Pedigree in Hampden House.

Ivinghoe, for a blow given to the Black Prince in a dispute at tennis.

> "Tring, Wing, and Ivinghoe
> From the Hampdens did go
> For striking the Black Prince a blow."

But Mr. Lysons very properly throws a doubt over the whole story, believing it to have arisen out of this triplet, expounded by some one who did not remember how common it is for bad rhymes to be made without any meaning at all. I can nowhere find any ground for believing that any one of these manors belonged to the Hampdens. Their property, however, was very large. They were not only rich and flourishing in their own county, but enjoyed considerable possessions in Essex, Berkshire, and Oxfordshire. In Buckinghamshire, they were lords of Great and Little Hampden, Stoke-Mandeville, Kimble, Prestwood, Dunton, Hoggestone, and Hartwell, and had lands in many other parishes. They appear to have been distinguished in chivalry; they were often entrusted with civil authority, and represented their native county in several parliaments. We find, in the Rolls of Parliament, that some lands were escheated from the family, on account of their adherence to the party of Henry VI., and that they were excepted from the general act of restitution, in the first Edward IV. Edmund Hampden * was one of the Esquires of the Body, and Privy Councillor to Henry VII. And, in the succeeding reign, we find 'Sir John Hampden of the Hill,'† appointed, with others, to attend upon the English Queen at the interview of the Sovereigns in the Champ du Drap d'Or. It is to his daughter, Sybel Hampden, who was nurse to the Prince of Wales, afterwards Edward VI., and ancestress to Willam Penn, of Pennsylvania, that the monument is raised in Hampton Church, Middlesex, which records so many virtues and so much wisdom. During the reign of Elizabeth, Griffith Hampden, having served as High Sheriff of the county of Buckingham, represented it in the Parliament of 1585. By him the Queen was received with great magnificence at his mansion at Hampden, which he had in part rebuilt, and much enlarged. An extensive avenue was cut for her passage through the woods to the house; and a part of that opening is still to be seen on the brow of the Chilterns from many

---

* Wood, Fasti Oxon. † Du Carel, Ang. Norm. Antiquities.

miles round, retaining the name of 'The Queen's Gap,' in commemoration of that visit. His eldest son, William, who succeeded him in 1591, was member, in 1593, for East Looe, then a considerable borough. He married Elizabeth, second daughter of Sir Henry Cromwell,* of Hinchinbrooke in Huntingdonshire, and aunt to the Protector; and died in 1597, leaving two sons, John and Richard, the latter of whom, in after times, resided at Emmington, in Oxfordshire.

John Hampden was born in 1594,† and, as the general concurrence of writers has determined, in London. Divers stories, however, there are, which fix his birthplace elsewhere. By some he is reported to have been born at a manor-house, long in the possession of his family, at Hoggestone, in the hundred of Cottesloe, in Buckinghamshire. But registers, at that time very imperfectly kept, give no information on this point, and leave us to determine between the vagueness of tradition, and the doubtful testimony of modern memoirs, which do not state their authority, and the first of which probably was used as authority by all the rest.

Succeeding to his father's estate in his infancy, Hampden remained for some years under the care of Richard Bouchier, master of the free-grammar-school at Thame, in Oxfordshire.‡ In 1609, he was entered as commoner at Magdalen College, Oxford,§ where it may be supposed that his attainments gained him some reputation; for he was chosen, with a few others, among whom was Laud, then master of St. John's, to write the Oxford gratulations on the marriage of the Elector Palatine with the Princess Elizabeth.|| As a student of the Inner Temple, to which he was admitted 1613,¶ he made considerable progress in the study of the common law. He

---

* Pedigree at Hampden House.
† Wood's Ath. Oxon., Bliss. Do. Life.   ‡ Anthony Wood.
§ Lib. Matric. Oxon. 108.
|| These verses, published at Oxford, 1613, in a volume entitled "Lusus Palatini,' contain little worth remark, unless it be the last three lines:

> 'Ut surgat inde proles,
> Cui nulla terra, nulla
> Gens, sit parem datura.'

Remarkable when it is remembered that from this marriage Rupert was born, who led, at Chalgrove, the troops by whom Hampden was slain; but also that from it sprang the succession to which stands limited the guardianship of the free monarchy of England.
¶ Books of the Inner Temple.

was married in the church of Pyrton, in Oxfordshire,* 1619, to Elizabeth, only daughter of Edmund Symeon, Esq., lord of that manor and estate. To this lady he was tenderly attached; and in several parts of his correspondence, he pays tribute to her virtues, talents, and affection. For some years, he seemed to addict himself mainly to the pursuits and enjoyments of a country life; and, from great natural cheerfulness, joined with qualities of mind and address which recommended him generally to society, he was induced, according to his own confession,† to enter freely into the amusements and dissipations of his age. By disposition, however, active, accurate, and laborious,‡ even from the earliest days of his manhood he allowed himself these indulgences as exercises only of recreation and relief, during the intervals of those literary habits to which his taste always powerfully inclined him.§

At the period of life when the attention of a reflecting person usually begins to direct itself to the public affairs of his country, Hampden found those of England in a new and interesting posture, to which, and to the causes which produced it, it is fit for a while that our attention should be turned. A remarkable era had already commenced in her moral and political history, some particulars of which demand our notice, as leading to that great crisis in which he and the party with whom he acted were afterwards seen bearing so distinguished a part. Some of these causes had been long and steadily, though not uninterruptedly, in progress, and require, in order to be understood, to be traced back through more than a century before their appearance in the shape of open disputes between royal prerogative and popular privilege. The power of the crown, raised and strengthened in proportion to the depression of that of the nobles, had been increased by the jealousies of the first Tudor sovereign, by the violences of the three next, and by the glories of the last, to an amount beyond what the temper of the times was disposed long to endure. The great civil war of the two Roses, which had begun with separating the aristocracy into factions, had, in the havoc of its course, nearly extinguished the oldest and greatest names, and rendered their houses powerless. A counterpoise to the

* Register of Pyrton, June 24, 1619. He died on the anniversary of that day. † Clarendon's Hist. Reb.
‡ Sir Philip Warwick. Perfect Diurnall, July 1, 1643.
§ Yearly Chron. 1761, 8vo., 127, 189.

accession of influence which thus accrued to the sovereign was nowhere to be found but in the improving genius of the people. The rising importance of the commonalty, and their own consciousness of it, may be traced to a variety of events, all tending one way, and some of them with great force and rapidity. Among these undoubtedly were the new impulse which maritime discovery had begun to give to our commerce, which had been formerly very much limited to the trade with Italy and the Hanse towns; the increased demand for manufactures which that extended commerce had begun to create; and the consequent increase of mercantile wealth, and the gradual investment of it in the purchase of the sequestered estates. Add to this that the revival of letters had produced, in an almost equal degree, a spirit of free inquiry in the minds of the people. The origin and ends of civil government had been boldly treated of; particularly, and with the greatest freedom, by Poynet, Bishop of Winchester, in his 'Politick Power,' a treatise which alone would have entitled him to a high station among the early patrons of what are called the popular doctrines. The reformation of the National Church, though, in casting off the spiritual bonds of Rome, it pointed to religious liberty, very little advanced the establishment of it in England. Still, the principles on which that reformation recommended itself to men's minds gave a habit of bold speculation, probably beyond what its first doctors intended or foresaw; and this, their successors soon found it impossible to extinguish, and difficult to control. The advance of public information, and of the spirit of liberty, and the decay of the feudal principle, have, by some writers, been attributed to the increasing number of large towns. But, besides the error of ascribing to one favourite cause a great event, which, like most other great events, arises out of the concurrence of many, the rapid increase of large towns must surely be rather classed among the effects than the causes of this spirit. It is unquestionably so in all the most remarkable examples, from the most ancient to the later instances of the republican towns of Italy and the Netherlands. In truth, the habit of associating in cities cannot be considered as a primary cause of the spirit of liberty, although doubtless tending to strengthen and diffuse that love of a government of known laws, which is so obviously one of the first moral advantages of a state of civil freedom, and in so especial a degree to men assembled to enrich themselves in such situations as are the most exempt from all feudal control.

Meantime, the rapidly prevailing influence of letters over the actions of men and the affairs of states forbade that the advances of liberty should keep a tranquil and even pace. Wit and learning, which had begun to flourish high under the sway of Elizabeth (so liberal in its character when compared with the factious violence of Edward's reign, or the dark intolerance of Mary's), did not always array themselves on the side of that fostering principle under which they had found protection. The court of her successor had its writers and its preachers, and powerful ones too, for the doctrines of divine right and unconditional obedience; but indirectly and unconsciously they helped to prepare the public mind for the overthrow of the very principle which they laboured to uphold. Even the vanity which led King James to range himself among the metaphysical dogmatists with whom that age abounded, engaged him, and encouraged others, in a taste for speculative inquiry, which always in the end works for liberty.* At the same time that these elements were thus forming and disposing themselves, the successful struggles of the reformers in Scotland, the gallant triumph of the Low Countries over their Spanish tyrants, and the desperate efforts of the Huguenots in France, which subsided but for a time in the union of parties under the healing government of Henry IV., had combined to raise new and more practical views among a people, like the English, always fond of a reputation for liberty, and now contemplating the principle in its progress abroad.

---

* The poets of Elizabeth's time (and poets understand better than philosophers how to make their addresses acceptable to sovereigns), even the poets and 'writers of the presence,' would speak of the throne rather as founded on the people's love than on any other title. Fulke Greville, though one of the most adroit of courtiers and of ministers, 'servant of Queen Elizabeth, and counsellor to King James,' and receiving Warwick Castle as a royal grant from a monarch who, unlike his predecessor, objected not to be complimented on his divine right, yet put forth some strong opinions as to the origin and duties of kingship in his poems of 'Monarchy and Religion,' in which there are several passages written in a spirit of this sort:

'Princes again, o'errack not your creation,
   Lest power return to that whence it began ;
But keep up sceptres by that reputation
   Which raiseth one to rule this world of man.'
The Beginning of Monarchy. Lord BROOKE's *Works.*

Thus was a great moral revolution at work, checked and delayed for a time by the power, the address, and the popularity of Qneen Elizabeth, but still tending forwards, when the sceptre of this mighty princess passed into the hands of her kinsman. Such a spirit it required a sovereign of more than ordinary qualities so to direct, as that the reform should advance by steady and controllable degrees, and in such a manner as might carry with it the appearance rather of a wise agreement between prerogative and liberty, than of a forcible abridgment of the one, and a contested triumph of the other. In the later reigns, all the recorded precedents had leaned towards the claims of prerogative; but all the feelings of the people strengthened those of liberty. The feudal dues and tenures, although not abolished by statute till near a century afterwards, had one by one faded away; and with them had ceased all the protection which, during times when law was weak, and civil rights imperfectly understood, the feudal power had afforded to the people. The feudal lords had, in their jealousy, established certain securities for themselves, and had maintained them by their power. These became incidentally a protection to other classes also. Upon the decay of this power, therefore, it was necessary that some new barrier should be raised against the crown, or additional strength and effect given to some old one. By the common law of Parliaments, Magna Charta, the Forest Charter, the Statute de Tallagio, and the Statute of Provisors, severally, the monarchy of England had been declared to be a limited one; and, so long as the military force of the country remained in the hands of the nobles, it did not concern them to look further than to military force for means whereby the limitations might be preserved. But that power had lately been withdrawn from them by the policy of Henry VII., who had provided for the maintenance of peace and the succession by rigorous edicts, limiting suit and service. The army, such as it was, had become now, for the first time, the king's army; for personal service had been commuted for rent, and those who had once been vassals had now become tenants. A little later, in France, and under the able government of Ximenes in Spain, the influence of the nobles had been in like manner weakened. Then the commercial spirit arose and extended rapidly, and the luxuries which it introduced gradually increased the expenses and wants of the great families which had outlasted the wars. But it was imperfectly and ill-directed. Wealth changed hands, and, among the labouring classes (as is often the case upon the sudden introduction of any new system for applying capital), there was a grievous want of the means of subsistence. Public begging, and the unappeasable tumults of starving men, ensued. It is true that, in the cities and sea-ports, the third estate was becoming enlightened and rich. But it had not yet power. All saw the means of power increasing in their hands, but few saw the manner of giving them direction or effect. The popular influences could be permanently secured, and usefully administered, only by a Parliament more freely representing and more intimately connected with a people, particularly the citizens, who were so manifestly increasing their share in the general stock of wealth and intelligence. The control over the revenue had been repeatedly contested, and finally acknowledged as an undoubted privilege of parliament; but, under different names, the means of supply were still left by usage in the sovereign's hands, and the sovereign had never been reduced to the necessity of making terms on this matter with his people. Mr. Hume, however inconclusive the argument which he founds upon it, is surely right in this position—that, of the two great contending principles of these times, it was the popular spirit which first encroached upon the prerogative, and not the prerogative on liberty. It is clear that, in exact proportion to the improvement in the intelligence, and consequently in the manners of a people, their influence in government will, and ought to, increase. A wise prince would have perceived that this tendency was not to be rudely thwarted, and would have bent his policy to meet with grace the growing genius and demands of the times. Not so King James. His understanding, though shrewd, busy, and cautious, was yet by nature capable of little more than the narrowest artifices of dissimulation and intrigue. The vices of his heart have been too mildly dealt with in general history; nor has there been wanting of late a class of writers who appear strangely to consider it good service to monarchy, and to the memory of the Stuarts, to endeavour, by perverting all documentary testimony and all moral reasoning, to do the work of apology for him who did more to bring that institution to hazard, and that family to ruin, than any other sovereign who ever filled the English throne. To enumerate evil qualities, particularly such as denote a base and perverse nature, and to show their influence over the public, as well as private, acts of men, is an occupation neither adding to the pleasures of history, nor generally among its duties; but it is indeed no exaggerated measure of censure to say that, of all the kings of that unhappy race of which he was the first in England, he was the most absolutely destitute of all that could win the affections or command the esteem of men who desire any higher motive for reverencing a sovereign than the mere feeling of homage due to his office. Insincere, like Charles I., — mean, profligate, and unprincipled, like Charles II.,—vindictive, prejudiced, and irresolute, like James II., — he had not the amiable or respectable qualities of any. Without the dignity or courage of the first, the pliant and popular temper of the second, — or even the obstinate and perverse conscientiousness of the last, —he went near to unite in his character the worst vices of each, with others in addition which belonged to none. Amongst the latter was great inconstancy in friendship, joined with a degree of personal pusillanimity, which seldom fails, in public life, to make men implacable and cruel. For the rest, his honour, and even his partialities, were ever ready to be sacrificed to his fears. His fears had surrendered Raleigh to the jealousies of Cecil and the menaces of Spain; and the fickleness of his temper, which had already triumphed over his shameful fondness for three successive favourites, transferred to a fourth, upon his first appearance at court, the undivided stewardship of the prerogative; thus proving equally to his courtiers and to the country that their only sure defence against the inconstancy of his character was what might be maintained by an appeal to its timidity. Even in Somerset's case, it appears to have been the awe in which that great criminal held the king bound, rather than any pity or fondness, which saved him from the just punishment which James had solemnly, and in the presence of the judges and of his whole court, sworn, under a dreadful condition of the curse of the Almighty on himself and his posterity, to execute impartially upon the murderers of Overbury, whosoever they might be, against whom that act should be proved.*

---

* The baseness of James's mind, and the corruption of his habits, are not subjects of an inviting sort. To such as can find amusement in the loathsome infirmities of the king, and the shameless insolence of his favourites, it has been already afforded elsewhere in abundant measure.

Nor does his reputation stand better for steadiness in religion than for constancy in friendship. Educated in the bosom of the Kirk, he was afterwards won over to defend, in the famous controversy at Hampton Court, that Arminian discipline, and those remains of Popish ceremonial, which (contrary to the Articles, as the Calvinists contended) were maintained by the prelatical party in England. So that, in the end, it may be doubted whether he was ever sincerely attached to the religion of either of his kingdoms. We find him, on the one hand, secretly favouring the Roman Catholics at court, from dread of private conspiracy; while, on the other, to humour the popular inveteracy against them, he openly authorised the most violent persecutions, and ostentatiously took God to witness before his Parliament that he never harboured the thought of extending to them even toleration.* Having entered the lists of public controversy against Bellarmine, he, at the same time (as is shown by many original papers, some published), was secretly corresponding with him in terms of confidence on those very dogmas which were the matter of their apparently fierce encounter.† Thus did he, alternately, and with as much impartiality as the spirit of the times would permit, show favour to the churches of England and of Rome, in order to strengthen, at all events, episcopacy, as a useful state engine against the democratic tendency of the Presbyterian discipline.

It is truly remarked by Lord Bolingbroke,‡ that the causes of the Parliamentary war were laid in the conduct of James as early as his accession to the throne of England. At that period, opportunities of the utmost value to a good prince, but full of difficulty and peril to a bad one, surrounded him on every side. Nor did they ever quite desert him throughout his shameful reign. The strength and glory of this kingdom had already reached the consummation to which Elizabeth's long and brilliant administration had tended to raise them. Not only had foreign states been compelled, by the wisdom of her councils, and the power of her arms, to leave her in the enjoyment of triumphant peace; not only had she with-

---

* Burnet gives, in proof of James's early bias to Popery, a curious account of his overtures to the court of Rome made through Elphinstone, Lord Balmerinoch, and Seaton, Earl of Dumferling, with which Bellarmine afterwards reproaches him.—Hist. Own Times, 8vo. i. 13, 14.
† Holkham Papers. ‡ Remarks on English History.

stood the assaults of the mightiest prince in Europe, and unallied, and alone, baffled his projects of universal monarchy; not only were the maritime rights of England secured, her public credit redeemed, the independence of her church established, the French Protestants protected from persecution, and Holland placed, by her generous aid, in a condition to break the Spanish yoke; but faction at home had yielded to the strength, the prudence, and the popularity of her sway. Whatever there remained of hostile spirit among the Scots, after the death of their Queen, was now reconciled by the union of claims in James's person. England and Scotland, each powerful to disturb, though unable to subdue, the other,— *mutuo metu, et montibus, divisi*, — had, in effect, fallen under the rule of one sceptre; and the English jealousy of a Scottish King was merged in the general goodwill which the memory of Elizabeth bespoke for her appointed successor. Thus favoured by every circumstance that could promise stability to a throne, James had, in addition, received the legacy of her example, and had before him her experience in the art of controlling the English people.

If any further elements of public prosperity remained to be desired by James, they were to be found in the great weakness of every power in Europe, whose enmity was to be apprehended, or whose friendship was doubtful. Spain, the proud, the warlike, and the ambitious, was slumbering under the feeble sway of Philip III., a prince of small abilities and no application, and entirely governed by the Cardinal Duke of Lerma, who was labouring to repair, by the improvement of her colonial resources, the loss of power and reputation which she had sustained in the Netherlands. For, though the independence of those provinces had not yet been established by treaty, the inability of Spain to continue the war had been acknowledged in the truce. This sovereign, shortly after James's accession, was succeeded by his son, a boy of sixteen, governed as absolutely by the favourite Olivarez, as his father had been by Lerma. The defeat of Tyrone, and of Don John d'Aguila, in Ireland, had terminated the hopes of the Spaniards in that quarter; and, in four years after, the United Provinces were treated with at Antwerp as an independent power,—a fresh and important triumph to the Protestant cause.

Meanwhile, France, stunned and dismayed by the blow

which had deprived her of the best of her kings, was left under the rule of an infant, and perplexed by the disquieting prospects of all she might have to endure, throughout a long minority of the Crown, from a turbulent nobility, inflamed at the same time by both civil and religious animosities. Poland and Sweden were at war with each other, and the tranquillity of the German Empire seemed secured by the weak and indolent character of Rudolph. Nothing threatened to disturb this general repose abroad, or to distract King James from the business of improving all these mighty advantages, till the war of 1618, concerning the claims of the Protestant Elector Palatine, his own son-in-law, to the throne of Bohemia.

But scarcely was the first year of James's reign completed when he became involved in disputes with his Parliament. He assumed by proclamation a direct control over returns of elections, all of which he commanded should be filed in Chancery: and, charging the electors to avoid choosing persons 'noted for their superstitious blindness one way, or 'for their turbulent humour other ways,' he threatened with fine all places that should make returns contrary to such proclamation; and with fine and imprisonment all persons who should be so returned.* These monstrous pretensions were instantly resisted, in the case of Sir Francis Goodwin,† who had been elected by the county of Buckingham, in opposition to Sir John Fortescue. After a dispute of nearly three weeks, the matter of privilege was compromised, upon the proposal of the King, but not without an expression of strong dissatisfaction from the Commons. The house, however, had thus in some sort gained an admission of its right of final judgment.‡

James had begun his reign with a plain declaration of absolute authority, founded on divine commission. With an

---

* Parliamentary History.   † Carte. Parliamentary History.

‡ 'Concerning our refusing conference with the Lords, there was none 'desired till after our sentence passed. And then we thought that, in a 'matter private to our own House, which, by rules of order, might not be 'by us revoked, we might, without any imputation, refuse to confer. Yet, 'understanding that your Majesty had been informed against us, we made 'haste (as in all duty we were bound) to lay open to your Majesty the 'whole manner of our proceeding. *Not doubting, though we were but part of* '*a body, as to make new laws, yet, for any matter of privileges of our House, we* '*are, and ever have been, a court, of ourselves of sufficient power to discern and* '*determine, without their lordships, as their lordships have used always to do* '*for theirs without us.*'—Comm. Journ., 3rd April, 1604.

extremely imperfect title by descent, he was foolish enough to dispute the power of Parliament to confer or confirm one. Unfurnished with troops, or money to enable him to support them, and untaught by his early experience in Scotland to deal wisely with the mounting spirit of party, he proceeded to form new projects of arbitrary taxation, and to lavish the greater part of the treasure so raised in grants to unworthy favourites. The laws were set at nought by the Scottish and English courtiers in the course of the quarrels, arising out of their national jealousies. Frequent duels arose between them, the deadliest feuds, the bitterest machinations of private intrigue, and not unfrequent attempts at assassination both secret and open.* The influence of the prelates increased; the Established Church was discredited by the servility of the court divines; and the ancient nobility were insulted by the vulgar sale of public honours by the King, to feed the vanity of his creatures, and to meet the demands of his own cupidity and of their corruption. Though betaking himself freely to those expedients for revenue, he, nevertheless, does not appear to have deceived himself as to the disgrace which they brought upon his person and government. James had discernment; he had, moreover, some powers of drollery, which, however, generally broke forth in such sallies as are easiest to all men when they are not controlled by feelings of honourable shame. It is given as one of his sharp and ingenious sayings, that, when conferring a purchased knighthood on a country gentleman, who was receiving it bashfully and in confusion, he exclaimed—' What! hold up thy head, man; I have more ' reason to be ashamed than thou.' †

The examples of profusion, debauchery, and riot, given by the court, spread their baneful influence throughout the country; all sort of shameful vices, according to Lord Brooke, abounding among the higher orders, and even the ladies of the nobility dishonouring themselves and their names to support the luxury of their families; ' there being,' says he, ' as much ' extortion for sinne as racking for rentes. So our ancient ' customes were abandoned, and that strictness and severity ' that had wont to be amongst us, the English, scorned and ' contemned, every one applauding strange or new things, ' though never so costly, and, for the attaining of them,

---

* Fulke Lord Brooke's Five Years of King James.   † Miss Aikin.

'neither sparing purse nor credit.'* Then began that love of excess, and that tyranny of private manners, so simply but eloquently described by Mrs. Hutchinson in one of the most striking passages in her Memoirs. Men of sober habits, particularly those who combined with a dislike of the dissolute manners of the court a leaning in favour of popular rights, were reviled as puritans; and those who ventured to uphold the authority of the laws for the protection of the subject were marked out for calumny and oppression. 'Pollutæ ' cæremoniæ, magna adulteria, plenum exsiliis mare, infecti ' cædibus scopuli, atrociùs in urbe sævitum. Nobilitas, opes, ' omissi gestique honores pro crimine, et ob virtutes certis- ' simum exitium. Nec minus præmia delatorum invisa quam ' scelera. Cum alii sacerdotia et consulatus ut spolia adepti, ' procurationes alii et interiorem potentiam . . . . Non ' tamen adeò virtutum sterile sæculum ut non et bona exempla ' prodiderit.' †

The natural consequence of an unjust proscription ensued. The friends of liberty were all drawn together to make common cause with the oppressed sectarians;—and the oppressed sectarians all learned to be friends of liberty.

The sturdy opposition excited in the first Parliament of 1603-4 increased and spread; it produced in the King's mind a feeling of violent and deep resentment; and, after six years of almost unremitting conflict, came a sudden and angry dissolution, December 31, 1610.

A second Parliament was convened in a little more than three years after. Of this House of Commons, Mr. Hume says, that they discovered 'an extraordinary alarm on account ' of the rumours spread abroad concerning Undertakers. It ' was reported that several persons attached to the King had ' entered into a confederacy, and, having laid a regular plan ' for the new elections, had distributed their interest all over ' England, and had undertaken to secure a majority for the ' court. So ignorant,' continues he, 'were the Commons, ' that they knew not this incident to be the first infallible ' symptom of any regular or established liberty.'

All attempts to manage returns are unquestionably symptoms of the advance of liberty, inasmuch as they shew how great is the value which those who would manage them attach to the

---

* Fulke Lord Brooke's Five Years of King James.
* Tacitus, Hist., lib. i.

support of Parliament, and to the influence of the public voice. Yet surely it is a singular conclusion, that the alarm manifested by the Commons shewed their ignorance of this obvious truth. On the contrary, the jealousy of such influence cannot but be considered a proof, on the part of the Commons (as the use of such influence was on the part of the court), of a quick sense of the importance of popular representation, as an engine of public liberty. The purpose, however, of Mr. Hume becomes tolerably clear, where he insinuates that the resolution of the House was founded on nothing better than a 'rumour 'spread abroad concerning Undertakers.' The Journals shew that it was not mere rumour; evidence had been taken before several committees on this matter; and the words of the resolution itself, alluded to but not quoted by Mr. Hume, set forth the evidence in detail.

This Parliament also, manifesting a spirit of resistance to monopolies, and to grants illegally charged on the revenue, and, moreover, questioning sharply certain words alleged to have been spoken against its privileges by Neile, Bishop of Lincoln, who had already commenced his career of court favour, was dissolved after a session of two months;* and James, not caring to submit his measures again to such control, forbore for many years from calling another.

In the meanwhile the demands upon the Treasury became more urgent, the revenue was falling off and in arrears, and the general state of public affairs was disastrous and discreditable to England. Nor was there anything in prospect that promised better. The period of her strength and glory had been suffered to pass fruitlessly away; while her ancient rivals, improving their means, and practising upon the pusillanimity of James, had gradually assumed a new tone of boldness; and her honour was tarnished at a great political crisis, by a display alike of feebleness and bad faith.

Such was the position of this country, when the King, having governed for near seven years without a Parliament, and being pressed by absolute want of money for the public service to summon a new one, January 30, 1620-1, Hampden

---

* The Speaker, on one occasion, left the chair without consent of the House, and was rebuked for it by several members. Mallory, opening the debate, says, 'his mouth open, and his heart free,—will spare none, though 'they sit in chairs, — whereof Mr. Speaker is likely to have a share.' Commons' Journals.

first took his seat in the House of Commons. It was for a borough which has become in our day a byword in the ears of such as love the sound of public virtue and popular representation. Grampound, which was then a place, as we shall hereafter have occasion to see, of no inconsiderable wealth and importance, had the glory of first sending John Hampden to Parliament. It appears that about this time certain of his friends were desirous that he should seek other means of advancement. His mother was very urgent with him to look to adding a peerage to the dignity of his family. 'If ever,' says this lady, in a letter preserved in the British Museum,— 'if ever my sonn will seek for his honor, tell him nowe 'to come; for heare is multitudes of lords a makinge— 'Vicount Mandvile Lo. Thresorer, Vicount Dunbar, which 'was Sr. Ha. Constable, Vicount Faukland which was Sr. 'Harry Carew. These two last of Scotland, of Ireland divers, 'the deputy a vicount, and one Mr. Fitzwilliams a Barron of 'Ingland, Mr. Villers a Vicount, and Sr. Will. Filding a 'Barron. . . . . I am ambitious of my sonn's honor, which I 'wish were nowe conferred upon hime, that he mighte not 'come after so many new creations.' * But this counsel was not followed. In whatever course of public service her son may, thus early, have thought that the path of his honour lay, it is most certain that he did not seek it in the presence-chamber of James I. It might, not improbably, hence occur to some persons who have made themselves commentators on the secret motives of Hampden, and who profess to see in his acts no nobler aim than to advance the ends of his private ambition, to ascribe his active patriotism in after life to early disappointment in a negotiation for a peerage. This would, however, be the reverse of truth. He never sought one. On the contrary, he declined both the means and the object suggested; and when it is recollected how titles were at this time obtained, it will not be thought that such an object, if desired, could have been difficult of attainment to a young man at the head of so ancient, and powerful, and, above all, so wealthy a family. When it is remembered, also, that it was by advancement of this sort that the court afterwards reconciled several of its most powerful opponents, it will not seem probable that James or his successor would have neglected

---

* Harl. Coll. Brit. Mus.; Mrs. Eliz. Hampden to Mr. Anthony Knyvett.

to win over, if it had been possible, at such a rate, so powerful a foe as Hampden.

During the first year he took no very forward part in public business, except by serving upon the Committee on the Bill of Informers,* and managing, at the age of twenty-seven, a conference with the Lords on the same matter.† Though not a frequent speaker, he was diligent and eager in discharge of the more ordinary and less inviting duties of a parliamentary life. We find him concurring in the general measures for restraining abuses, and joining in the remonstrances against the marriage of Prince Charles with the Infanta, and in favour of the Protestant cause in Germany, over-matched, as it was, by the power and connexion of the House of Austria.

The perseverance of the leading members in detecting delinquencies among some of the highest officers in the state, and their boldness and eagerness in exposing them, had inflamed the indignation of the King. But this Parliament was also famous as having been the first to discover and apply the only true means possessed by a deliberative body for controlling a bad government. It is to this period, and to these men, that we trace the formation of the system of Parliamentary Party, and the first workings of that spirit of political union on which it depends; a spirit plainly, and in the highest degree important to liberty, and which it has therefore been ever since the great business of arbitrary politicians to discredit in the estimation of the country. A system of association, founded not upon the surrender of principles, but upon the compromise of extreme opinions, and which, while it affords to the people the only effectual defence against the corrupt influences of a government, raises up for the sovereign the only lasting security against those violent enterprises which, where parliamentary party is unknown, are the ordinary and only effectual checks upon regal power.‡

To this first party, thus formed, and considerable as it was in the wealth, talents, and reputation of most of its principal

---

* Martis, 5 Feb. 18 Jac. An Act against certain troublesome persons, relators, informers, and promoters.—Commons' Journals.

† Commons' Journals.

‡ The following definition, profoundly conceived and wittily expressed, was given of the mightiest arbitrary Government in the North of Europe, by a very celebrated person of our own times, and may be generally predicated of all sovereignties under which there is no spirit of popular party—' C'est une monarchie, presque absolue, limitée par l'assassinât.'

members, Hampden early and closely attached himself. Among them were Selden and Pym: the first eminent above all others for prudence and deep learning to direct and temper the efforts of his public virtue; the latter almost his equal in parliamentary lore—fully his equal in shrewdness, courage, and perseverance. With these was St. John, crafty, enterprising, inveterate, and indefatigable; with a zeal uncompromising in the pursuit of its objects, and an inscrutable reserve in his manner of pursuing them,—and a disgust to the court, confirmed by his having been the first person marked out to pay, by fine and imprisonment, under a Star Chamber decree, the penalty of his former opposition. Of this party, entering Parliament in the same year with Hampden, was Wentworth, who, with the most brilliant qualities of a vigorous mind, a commanding eloquence, and a lofty and dauntless spirit, in due season betrayed his willingness to bend to the terms insinuated by the court; and at last surrendered his constancy to the love of power and to the allurements of a bad ambition, with as much ease as other men made sacrifice of their smaller reputation in barter for the mere rewards of title and subordinate office. Of Sir Edward Coke, also prominent in this party, it must be suspected, notwithstanding his immortal services to his profession and to his country, that much of his opposition was attributable to his jealousy of the Chancellor and of Villiers, the latter of whom he had, beforetime, vainly endeavoured to propitiate by the most base and impious adulation. To these may be added the eminent name of Eliot, and with it are to be reckoned many, such as Mallory, Saville, Sir Dudley Digges, and Sir Robert Phillips, who, though not considered in any respect as leaders in that memorable association, yet, from their station in their respective counties, and from the acknowledged reputation of some of them for highmindedness and integrity, were of great importance to the public cause. Admitted to an intimate share in their councils, with such as were not in after times detached by the court, Hampden maintained through life the closest personal friendship.

This Parliament, soon feeling its own strength, pursued, but with increased energy, the same course as the preceding one; and the King, anxious to relieve himself from all further importunity, dissolved it by proclamation, January 6, 1621-2, after rather less than a year's duration. Within that short time, however, much had been done towards effecting a system of reformation of abuses, and a control of the expenditure, which had been attempted with less success by the former Parliaments of this reign. Sir Giles Mompesson, and Sir Henry Yelverton, Attorney-General, with some other offenders of less note, were sentenced to fine and imprisonment; some for malversation in office, and others for private pecuniary frauds upon the revenue. But the storm, as it swept on, assailed higher places in the court and state.* Among others convicted of peculation was Sir Edward Villiers, brother to the favourite whose rapid rise and boundless influence had already become so distasteful to the country. Nor could the high station nor the matchless renown of Lord Bacon himself save from the even-handed severity of the Parliament this illustrious victim to the temptations of a corrupt time. Mompesson fled from judgment,† and Villiers obtained also, through his brother's influence, the means of retiring beyond seas. But Bacon was doomed, after a long and melancholy exposure, to expiate in poverty and dishonour what it is fit to observe never amounted to a perversion of justice for personal emolument. It is no defence, and but a poor palliation; and yet the load of this great man's disgrace is somewhat lightened by describing his offence truly. He accepted gratuities from suitors to hasten the decision of their causes in chancery; a sale, as he himself pleaded, 'of justice, but not of injustice:' aggravated doubtless by the facilities which his indolence afforded to the frauds of others, and countenanced only by long-prevailing practice in that court, and by such examples as it would be shameful to urge in excuse of such a man. He was forbidden by the King to defend himself;—a condition to which his wounded spirit easily bowed itself; and his unqualified submission was presented by Prince Charles to the Lords, in order that, wholly occupied with so great a sacrifice, the Parliament might be led from pursuing the much deeper corruptions of others nearer to the person and the partialities of the King. Of this motive no doubt can remain

---

* 'Funditus expellant monopolos et nomopolos,' said Sir Edward Coke.—Commons' Journals.

† Sir Edward Coke reports, March 27, from the conference with the Lords on Mompesson's case, that the Lord Treasurer said that—'As the Jews' hearts brent when they spake with Him going to Emmaus, so they to hear the King yesterday in His Royal Seat.'—Commons' Journals.

since the publication of his correspondence with Buckingham. We are left, however, to mourn over what is too plainly admitted by himself, where he confesses, with an eloquence so touching, his abject sense of his own degradation, concluding with these sad words to the commissioners appointed to receive his confession and humble submission: 'My Lords, 'it is my act, my hand, and my heart. I beseech your Lord- 'ships to be merciful to a broken reed.' *

The great and salutary works, achieved by the boldness of the popular party, were strengthened by the vigour of their remonstrances. They strenuously insisted upon the danger of the growing power of Austria to the liberties of Europe, and to the Protestant interest; they spoke of the surrender which had been made of the cause of the Elector; they represented the growth of Popery in England, and complained of the countenance which would be afforded to it by the projected marriage of Prince Charles.† The King's reply, in which he plainly told the Commons that these matters were 'beyond 'their reach and capacity,' and sharply warned them against 'meddling in future with what concerned his honour and 'government alone,'‡ was of a sound ill calculated to reconcile the high spirit of a body which was not to be subdued. In the resolution which followed, upon Sir Edward Sandys's commitment by the privy council for words spoken in the House, they asserted their privilege to advise on all matters of state, and claimed liberty of speech, for the use of which they contended that each member was answerable to the House alone.§ So new to James was this doctrine, and so unexpected the tone in which it was propounded, that upon hearing of the vote which directed that a committee of twelve members should present the remonstrance to him, he straightway commanded that as many chairs should be brought into the presence-chamber, 'Chairs!' cried he, 'chairs!—a' God's name, here be twelve kings a coming!'|| But his answer to them was in very serious earnestness. He disallowed their phrase of 'undoubted right and inheritance,' and told them that their

---

* Parliamentary History—Lords' Journals.
† Parliamentary History.   ‡ Ibid.
§ The debate on this memorable resolution appears to have been the first occasion on which candles were brought into the House of Commons, 'they having sat late, even to six of the clock in that evening.'—Parliamentary History. || Kennet, Rapin, Wilson.

privileges were derived to them 'from the grace and permission 'of his ancestors,' and 'rested rather on toleration than in- 'heritance.' Then passed unanimously that renowned protestation, called by Selden the second Magna Charta, declaring that the 'liberties, franchises, privileges, and jurisdictions of ' Parliament are the ancient and undoubted birthright and ' inheritance of the subjects of England; and that the arduous ' and urgent affairs concerning the King, state, and defence of ' the realm, and Church of England, and the maintenance and ' making of laws and redress of mischiefs and grievances which ' daily happen within this realm, are proper subject and matter ' of counsel and debate in Parliament; and that in the ' handling and proceeding of those businesses every member of ' the House of Parliament hath, and of right ought to have, ' freedom of speech to propound, treat, reason, and bring to ' conclusion the same; and that the Commons in Parliament ' have like liberty and freedom to treat of these matters in ' such order as in their judgments shall seem fittest. And ' that every member of the said House hath like freedom from ' all impeachment, imprisonment, and molestation, (otherwise ' than by censure of the House itself,) for or concerning any ' speaking, reasoning, or declaring any matter or matters ' touching the Parliament or parliament business. And that ' if any of the said members be complained of and questioned ' for anything done or said in Parliament, the same is to be ' shewed to the King by the advice and assent of all the ' Commons assembled in Parliament before the King give ' credence to any private information.'*

A House of Commons breathing such a spirit was not to be expected long to survive this protestation. The King dissolved it, and with his own hand struck the entry off the Journals. But his vengeance pursued its members even beyond its dissolution; Coke, Phillips, Selden, Pym, and Mallory, Sir Dudley Digges, Sir Thomas Crew, Sir Nathaniel Rich, and Sir James Perrott, were all committed under one warrant to prison; the four last (for a lighter punishment, as Rushworth oddly phrases it) being afterwards put upon a commission in Ireland. A desperate measure;—ensuring, whenever again a Parliament should meet, the confirmation of the very doctrine in dispute, which no king could hope to see formally ceded to

---

* Parliamentary History.

him, but which a wiser one might have contrived to leave for some time longer in doubt between himself and his people. Nature had not designed James to act the part of a tyrant with dignity. His passion for absolute authority, when opposed, was restless and querulous;—powerless when indulged. Unable to rule but by first enslaving himself to some unworthy minion, he had substituted for the influence of Somerset one of much greater public mischief. The power of Somerset had been felt in the disgraceful advancement and burthensome charge of his creatures and dependants, and by three foolish, corrupt, and ineffective projects of finance,* Villiers at once grasped the helm of the whole state, and adventured the newest and most dangerous courses, at a more difficult crisis than till then had ever befallen England in her domestic policy. As a statesman, he displayed neither genius nor moderation; but, as a courtier, he had every quality for distinction and advancement. To an admirable person and address he joined an unwearied spirit of intrigue, and a boundless ambition. The first introduction of Villiers at court is an imputation upon the otherwise blameless memory of the upright and venerable Archbishop Abbott. He placed him near the King's person; he urged his promotion; he reconciled the Queen to it. Of this misuse of a well-deserved influence the only apology is, that it was to break down the shameful power of Somerset; and the penalty was soon suffered by the good archbishop in the jealousy and ingratitude of the favourite, advanced with a ceaseless rapidity to the highest rank which a subject can attain, and to offices for the duties of which he was totally unfit.

At the head of a government at open variance with the Parliament, and of a court which spared nothing to a beggared treasury, and denied nothing to its own profuse magnificence, this minister displayed a character full of strange vanities and vices, yet shrouded in a blaze of shewy qualities. Without eloquence in Parliament or knowledge in diplomacy, he yet had a certain quickness of perception and decision, assisted by

---

* His schemes were, 1st, creating the new order of baronets and selling the dignity; 2d, raising the price of English coined gold ten per cent., having before prohibited the exporting of it, so that the Unity, which before passed at 20*s*, was raised to 22*s*. 'Yet this,' says Stow, 'was no 'more than what English coin was valued at abroad, so that much of it was 'exported;' and 3rd, the establishment of the first State Lottery, which was for royal grants in Virginia; but all failed as means of revenue.

a loftiness of carriage, which often gave him an undue ascendancy in both. He had, besides, a high and dauntless courage which recommended him for command. But, even in the most eager pursuits of ambition or policy, his personal vanity was always sufficient to divert him to any trifling project for mortifying a rival or gaining a woman's favour, and would lead him into enterprizes of difficulty from which he had not resources of mind to extricate him with glory, or even with credit. In addition to these failings, he early fell into the error, so common among arbitrary politicians, of not adapting his measures to the improving character of the times. His shrewdness in judging of men was employed only to enable him to found his influence upon their weaknesses and vices: so that, when opposed to men of capacity, or thwarted by what remained of public virtue in the country, he found himself in conflict with weapons of which he knew not the use; and his counsels were dangerous, and his administration unprosperous. His only wisdom was the craft with which he managed weak or bad men; and his only virtue the courage with which he overawed timid ones.

His government, however, in some important passages of this reign was not altogether unpopular. The project of the Spanish match was throughout fruitful to him in the means of greatness. Long the subject of King James's eager wishes, that negotiation first afforded to Buckingham the opportunities which he desired of access to the Prince of Wales; nor did he fail to improve these, until by administering to the romantic sallies of the young Prince, and by obsequiously forwarding all his objects with the King his father, he had succeeded in changing the aversion, which, according to Lord Clarendon, had been felt and declared by Charles, into the most devoted and lasting partiality. When the expedition to Spain was proposed by Charles to his father, his father remonstrated, stormed, and refused;—when urged by the favourite, he wept, swore he was undone, and consented. After the departure, he revoked his consent, remonstrated by letter, and wept again. But again urged by the favourite, he supplied the Prince and his followers in almost boundless measure with the means of outshining Philip and his court in the Escurial itself. Finally, Buckingham, when, to gratify his own wounded pride, he determined that the match should be broken off, managed that intrigue also in a manner which flattered the feelings of the Prince, and, at the same time, gave satisfaction to the country, and a triumph to the popular party. A war with Spain followed, which Buckingham never could put upon justifiable grounds, and which, by his ill management, was made to arise out of a breach of treaty on the part of England. But its recommendation in men's opinions was the experience which they had had that James could not remain at peace with Spain without being her slave; and, therefore, by the declaration of war, the minister still further addressed himself to public favour. But a popularity thus acquired by the accidental agreement of his own passions with the general desire of the nation, was not of very durable materials; and he saw that he had no sure protection against the hostility of Parliament or the inconstancy of the King, but in the general support which Charles was now prepared to give him. To confirm this bond upon the heir apparent by a measure which might also be agreeable to the country, he next engaged the Prince to favour the project of a treaty with Louis XIII. against Austria, by the tempting proposal of a marriage with Henrietta, whom Charles, while on his way to Spain, had, by Buckingham's contrivance, seen in all her beauty and sprightliness; but this scheme was not yet to meet with success.

Meanwhile the Austrian government, ever ambitious, crafty, and well served in its diplomacy, neither lost sight of its design upon Bohemia, nor relaxed its activity in the pursuit; and the assistances on which the cause of Frederick entirely depended were delayed until that wretched prince, the Protestant husband of his daughter Elizabeth, had been forced to surrender his last fortress, and, with it, all hopes of gaining the crown to which he had aspired, or recovering the electorate which he had lost.

Amused and thwarted in turn by keen-witted diplomatists, whom he thought keenly to outwit, James vainly endeavoured to obtain leave from France for his army under Count Mansfeldt to pass, according to articles, into the Palatinate; and, feebly and without success, urged on Spain the cession of Frankendahl, to which she also stood bound to him by treaty. Thus baffled and insulted, and mortified in his most sensitive point, the failure of that king-craft of which he made his boast, he gradually became aware of the extent of Buckingham's oversights, not only in his foreign policy, but in the whole, also, of his fatal plan of administration at home. He found the government become too weak to protect its own honour, the nation embroiled in a quarrel, which from the outset, though popular, was one of very doubtful promise, and which he could now neither pursue with any hope of success, nor retire from with any show of dignity; and the Commons too jealous to grant any supplies without a previous redress of grievances.

Such was the state to which the King was now, when entering on the last year of his life, reduced. Embarrassed with an enormous debt of his own creating, though discredited by the surrender of the Dutch cautionary towns for money; embarrassed by the expenses of an increased navy, though discredited by the indignities everywhere offered to its before untarnished and triumphant flag; and the Parliament and the people crying out for war as the only means of avenging the wronged reputation of their country. And yet Lord Clarendon pronounces these to have been 'excellent times, *sua si bona 'norint;*' and Mr. Hume asserts that 'Mansfeldt's expedition 'was the only disaster which happened during this prosperous 'and pacific reign;*—a reign,' he continues, 'than which it 'would be difficult to find one in all history less illustrious, yet 'more unspotted and unblemished.' † Upon this reign, besides the foul sacrifice of Raleigh, and the equally foul pardon of the highest actors in the murder of Overbury, remain the spot and blemish of a general dissolution of manners, a government whose measures were notoriously bid for and purchased by foreign gold, titles of honour publicly put to sale, ministers of state convicted of peculation, and a Lord Chancellor degraded for countenancing bribes in his court and office.

The Parliament, which was convened February 12, 1623-4, gratified with the Spanish quarrel, and with the prospects which it opened, was of a more placable temper than those which had preceded it; and the Commons readily consented to make good the first expenses of the war, although stipulating for the abolition of all the most unpopular and burthensome monopolies, and remonstrating against the favour shown to Papists. It may be truly said to have been the most practically useful Parliament which met during this reign. Its

---

* Hume's History of England, chap. xlix.   † Ibid.

proceedings against the Lord Treasurer Middlesex for gross and open bribery in the Treasury, and corruption in the Court of Wards, and the conclusion to which that trial was brought, were acts creditable to its industry and spirit; though it cannot fail to be seen that these proceedings were encouraged by Buckingham to increase his own influence, and not improbably too, as Middlesex himself insinuates in his defence, to punish him for standing in the way of some no less corrupt practices of his own. How prophetic had been Lord Bacon's warning to the Treasurer on his appointment, to 'remember ever that a Parliament will come!'

After passing more acts than ever a Parliament before had passed in one session, it came to a close on the 29th of May. The King prorogued it in good-humour, looking, as he expressed himself, to a meeting in the following year, 'which should make him greater and happier than any king ever was.'

The influence of the Duke of Buckingham over the Royal mind was now evidently on the decline, and charges were in preparation by many hands for the ensuing session; when, on the 27th of March, 1625, James closed by death his inglorious and oppressive reign.

The surmises concerning the manner of his death, vague as they were, and imperfectly supported by facts or probability, would be scarcely deserving of mention, had they not been urged in the three next Parliaments, and had they not in some sort influenced the measures which were, in consequence, pursued by Charles. The charge of poisoning was, in those times, a very ordinary way of accounting for so great a mystery as the unexpected death of any sovereign or other great person. That the death of James was caused by these means soon became the creed of a party, and was supported by heated and uncandid reasonings. Nor, on the other hand, has it been more fairly dealt with by Lord Clarendon, who describes it as being 'without the least colour or ground, as appeared upon the strictest and most malicious examination that could be made.' It was early matter of parliamentary inquiry; but this inquiry was in every way impeded by the court. The story, indeed, vouched by Lilly, of the old Countess of Buckingham's poisoned plaister, requires a faith in the power of chemistry, as then understood, about as reasonable as that which the same learned writer exacts in behalf of dæmonology and the influence of the stars. Still there were circumstances which tended to strengthen the popular belief in the guilt of a favourite, whom some of his opponents might, at the renewal of his career of greatness, have thought it easier to destroy than to appease.

All, however, that remains certain is this. After evidence taken by a committee of the Commons, one of the articles against Buckingham is, that he officiously administered to the King certain drugs which had been prepared by the countess in the absence of the physicians; and the doing so was with great propriety declared 'a transcendant presumption of a dangerous consequence.' *

To this no answer was made, but a passionate protestation of the duke's; and, on three several occasions, the Commons, declaring that they were 'ready to prove their 'charges against him, unless prevented,' were prevented by a dissolution.

* Echard.

PART THE SECOND.

FROM 1625 TO 1628.

Accession of Charles the First—His Character—Appearance of a Reformation in the Manners of the Court—Renewal of arbitrary Measures—Project of the Popular Party for extending the Representation—Right of Election restored to several Boroughs—Hampden elected for Wendover—Two Subsidies granted—Votes of Censure and Enquiry—Further Supplies refused—Dissolution—Forced Loans—Ships lent to France to serve against the Huguenots—Failure of the Expedition to Cadiz, and Blockade of Dunkirk—Second Parliament—Buckingham impeached—Elected Chancellor of the University of Cambridge—Seizure of Members—Dissolution—Hampden imprisoned—Oppressive Imposts—Members released—A new Parliament—Petition of Right—Further attempts at Redress of Grievances — Activity and industry of Hampden—Prorogation—Merchants' Goods seized—Failure of the Expedition to Rochelle—Death of Buckingham—Failure of a second Expedition—Surrender of Rochelle.

KING CHARLES's accession was hailed with all those tokens of affection and joy which seldom fail to accompany such an event, whatever may be the motives of hope in the prospect of the opening reign, or the recollections of that which has immediately preceded it.

Nor can this enthusiasm be always with justice referred to an unreflecting or a servile feeling. For, though sometimes, and to a certain extent, attributable to that sanguine love of change which is no uncommon vice in popular bodies, it may surely derive strength from another, and a far more reasonable, desire in the people, to place the new King upon good terms with themselves, by a spontaneous offer of good will and confidence, on their part, to begin the account. On this occasion many things seemed to justify favourable expectations. There were doubtless in Charles eminent parts of disposition and address, such as could not but secure the affections of those whose office placed them near his person. If it be difficult to form a just estimate of his character, it is owing, certainly, in some measure to the singularly-blended good and bad qualities which composed it, but still more to the opposite and raging passions of those writers, who, having lived through his stormy time, could not, in becoming its historians, cease to be partisans. Measured by the standard of either of the conflicting principles, which, for two centuries, have distinguished in this country those persons who are specially lovers of the monarchical, from those whose leaning is towards the more popular, elements of the constitution,—by the one class he has been canonised as a martyr, and recommended as a model and mirror for sovereigns; and by the other, with as little truth, concluded to have been an unprincipled and heartless tyrant, without a virtue, and without an excuse.

This was inevitable. But surely it would be weakness to be deterred by any fear of the advantages which intemperate persons may unfairly take of such admissions as truth and justice demand, from coming to a candid acknowledgment of the many high qualities, as of the one great vice and fatal error, of this unhappy sovereign. His education had been of a mixed and dangerous sort. From the days of his preceptor Murray's rigid discipline, to those of the demoralising influence of Villiers, he had ever been in the hands of successive factions; each busy to mould to its own purposes a prince, whose views of the intent and duties of his office do not appear to have extended further than to the obligation of maintaining, in full integrity for himself and his successors, a power for the exercise of which he heartily believed that he was answerable only to heaven. Favourably to Charles's memory, his errors have been often entirely imputed to what in themselves are virtues; love for his wife, and tenacity of purpose in matters of public duty. But the former seems never to have influenced him in state-matters, further than by exciting and confirming him in courses to which, independently of her counsels, he was ever too much inclined; nor the latter to have placed him above occasional recourse to unworthy compromises. The Queen's known aversion to Strafford did not deter Charles from adopting him for an adviser; nor a sense of personal or private duty from surrendering him to the scaffold. His fondness for the Queen did not prevent him from making occasional concessions to a people whom she disliked, and to whom she would have fain persuaded him to concede nothing; nor did his tenacity of purpose check him from breaking engagements which every moral bond would have made inviolable. Resolute in danger, and temperate in his personal habits amidst the excesses of a luxurious nobility, his chief infirmity was an obstinacy of temper which expostulation could not persuade, nor experience correct, but which generally, as obstinacy often does, made him the dupe of some one favourite who knew how to practise adroitly upon it. His chief vice was an insincerity, and distrust of his people, in which he had been confirmed by the evil counsels of Buckingham.

When the Spanish match was broken off, the Duke had, in a conference of the two Houses, made a long exposition, for which, says Lord Clarendon, 'he had not the least directions 'from the King, and a great part of which he knew to be 'untrue.' 'But yet,' says Rushworth, 'the Prince not only 'gave the testimony of his silence to these untruths, but, on 'its being reported to the House the same day, approved 'thereof there also.' And this in a matter not only tending to an untrue vindication of Buckingham, but also to an unjust impeachment of Bristol, and a general deception upon the country. The accusation of hardness of heart, urged against him by Lilly and Whitelocke, and grounded upon an allegation of his having remained an unmoved spectator of the sufferings of Prince Rupert's prisoners brought from Cirencester, 'many 'wounded, bound with cords, and in great misery;' on which occasion, according to the former of these writers, 'it was 'noted of some there present he rejoiced in their sad affliction;' is a charge single of its kind, and hinging upon minute and doubtful interpretations of his comportment on an occasion where, obviously, it was most liable to misrepresentation. There appears to be no other instance to countenance the notion that wanton cruelty ever stained a character strongly marked as his was by warm and tender feelings in private life. These in Charles are qualities so generally acknowledged as to lead at once to what appears to be the fair conclusion—that whenever he departed, as it must be admitted he often did, from the plainest laws of moderation and public honesty (sometimes even entering upon negotiations, as may be shown, with a previous purpose to deceive), it was owing to the mastery which the superstition of Divine Right had obtained over a judgment which, if not the most vigorous, was at least not swayed, like his father's, by any base or vulgar passions. Without any great depth of learning or research, his attainments as a scholar were above the ordinary rate, and he was well stored with general information. He was gifted with eloquence and dignity, both in speaking and writing. We are told that he took great pains in amending with his own hand the wording of such state-papers as his ministers laid before him for approbation, many of which, drawn up by the masterly pens of Falkland and of Hyde, received the corrections of his accurate taste, and the infusions of his flowing style. Accomplished as well in bodily graces and exercises as in those of his mind, and with a spirit strongly imbued with something chivalrous and heroic, he appears to have possessed every requisite of a perfect gentleman, except the most important,—Truth, and Good Faith. And he failed in these, because he had persuaded himself that they are not among the public duties of a Sovereign whose prerogative is in dispute.

As Charles's temperance formed a favourable contrast with the shameful vices of his predecessor, it was regarded as a presage of better times. A rapid change was wrought in the manners of the courtiers. Arts, and the more liberal sort of Literature, were protected and advanced. And, although Lord Sunderland, a few years after, in a well-known letter to his wife, gives a somewhat astounding description of the topics which were still allowed to prevail in the presence-chamber, Mrs. Hutchinson (no indulgent judge of kings and courts) bears her testimony to the discountenance which, for a time, was given to licentiousness within the precincts of the royal palace. But Charles and his people began by mistaking each other. The people, long used to see arbitrary sovereignty in a shape which could inspire only mockery and disgust, expected, from the grave and imposing demeanour of their new King, a disposition to respect the rights of the Commons, and support them. Charles on his part hoped, from the general piety of the people, that they would be easily led to recognise and revere an extent of authority, for which he thought that he found unquestionable warranty in the Word of God; 'since,' as his father early stated it, 'Kings are in 'the Word of God itself called Gods, as being His lieutenants 'and vicegerents on earth, and so adorned and furnished with 'some sparkles of the Divinity.'* The people knew not the despotic temper of their King, and the King knew not the mounting spirit of his people; and each was soon resolved to put to trial a power of which neither had ascertained the exact and due limits.

Pretensions, the most unpromising to liberty and to general concord, had already shown themselves; and, at the coronation, an attempt was made by Laud, then Bishop of Bath and Wells, officiating as Dean of Westminster, to alter the form of engagement pronounced by the King. Endeavours were made to reconcile the country to the omission of a phrase, 'quas 'vulgus elegerit (leges),' † acknowledging the legislative power of Parliaments, and to the insertion of another which hinted at a dispensing power in the Crown, 'salvo prerogativo 'regali.'‡ During the issuing of the writs for the first Parliament, money was raised through a compulsory purchase of knighthoods; and a levy of three thousand soldiers was ordered by royal warrant and proclamation. Coat and conduct-money was at the same time required from the counties; and martial law was enforced among the new troops, who thus were separated from the body of the people, and taken from under the control of the common law of the realm. Certain prelates, and other clergymen, were advanced into favour and promoted, who had been censured by former Parliaments for preaching in favour of the late King's arbitrary measures, and for maintaining that his will had the force and virtue of law. The obnoxious favourite was retained in the chief administration of affairs; and, in defiance of the wishes of the nation, the King concluded a marriage with a Princess bred up in the persecuting doctrines of the French court, and, as was soon believed, too little scrupulous in all matters of conduct, except those which related to the rites of a religion to which she was bigoted and the English people deeply and passionately opposed. The impolicy of this match was aggravated by this circumstance—that every indulgence in her religious observances, so justly the right of all, but so peculiarly due to the wife and daughter of a King, was in direct breach of the law. According to the secret article in the marriage-treaty, to which, in order to obtain the Pope's dispensation

---

* James I.'s speech on opening his Parliament, 1604.—Parliamentary Hist.
   † Rushworth.   ‡ Rapin.

for Henrietta, Charles had bound himself by oath, it was stipulated that her household should be composed entirely of Roman Catholics. Such of these as were French, it was provided, should be irremovable; and such as were English, were, contrary to law, to be protected in the ostentatious profession and exercise of their faith.* A singular instance of an article in which one state bargained for the suspension of statutes affecting the condition of the subjects of another. Several of these persons were raised to offices of high authority and trust; and, at great charge, and with still greater public scandal, a splendid chapel was fitted up at Somerset House. Then, for the first time since the reign of Mary, an English Queen was seen passing in pomp through the streets of London to the abomination, as it was termed, of the mass. Thus, proscribed equally by public opinion and by the law, but advanced and favoured at Court in opposition to both, it is not to be wondered at that the Roman Catholics of England openly boasted that their religion was, through the influence of the Queen, to be re-established; or that Bossuet should have recorded that intention, and the view which was taken of its final success, amongst the topics of his immortal panegyric pronounced upon her memory.†

As for the politics of the Roman Catholics, it was natural that they should be undividedly for absolute monarchy. They had nothing but oppression to expect from Parliament or people. Their only hope was from the Court; and the only chance for that Court becoming strong enough to befriend their cause, consisted in its power being rendered absolute. Charles began, on his part, openly to countenance the revival of the terms 'courtier' and 'precisian,' as signifying the being in his favour or opposed to his government.

By such unwise and unwarrantable affronts to public feeling, the favourable expectations at first so eagerly indulged were gradually dispelled. The people were dismayed. Their affections, so willingly and warmly tendered to the young King, were chilled; and, even before his first Parliament was opened, they saw, with mortification and disgust, the system of his subsequent government revealed. His foreign policy, however, at the outset promised better. He began his reign by entirely occupying the public attention with the cause of the

---

* Bassompierre.—Rushworth. † Oraison Funèbre.

Elector Palatine, to which the country had been always so well affected; thereby involving the Parliament in engagements of supply upon a large scale, which he might have calculated upon its afterwards finding some difficulty in reducing. Although it is unquestionable that war is the position in which a nation is the most easily familiarised with arbitrary measures and a suspension of its free customs and privileges, it is, notwithstanding, no less true that war affords to the people increased means of obtaining terms for public liberty by making their own conditions of supply. It appears as if the English Court, well aware of the first of these obvious truths, had been altogether inattentive to the second; until taught by an experience which came too late to warn the obstinacy of Charles, or control the violence of his Minister.

In the first Parliament of this reign, which met in June, 1625, Hampden again took his seat. He was now elected for the borough of Wendover, a town in the neighbourhood of his paternal estates, which had, just before, recovered from the Crown its custom of returning members. This privilege had lately been restored to certain boroughs, which in early times had claimed and exercised it, but to which, for several reigns, writs had ceased to be directed. The immediate motives of those persons, by whose efforts a series of measures of this sort was undertaken for extending a share of the representation to such classes of the people as might be the least likely to fall under the influence of the Court, and the most disposed to favour the interest and strengthen the hands of the country party,—the manner in which these measures were accomplished, and the success which followed them,—form an interesting part of the history of those times, and of the party with which Hampden had connected himself. If not the projector of this scheme for the furtherance of the public cause, in Parliament, he was one of the first, by his sagacity to become aware of its importance, and, by his industry and address, to bring it to a successful issue. And this was the earliest of those measures which he had the power (according to Lord Clarendon's words) to 'contrive,' to 'persuade,' and to 'execute,' in the great struggle for liberty. It was his fortune also to adorn this triumph in his own person, as representative of one of the places for which he had obtained the restoration of the privilege of popular election; thus fulfilling, in all its parts, a metaphor quaintly applied by an old English writer to an achievement, in its consequences, much less important: 'Primus inter eos qui communi prælio in 'libertatem spiraverint, hoc, quasi præsidium libertatis, 'sopitum excitavit, excitatum reparavit, reparatum decoravit.'*

We have already seen how, under the reign of James, the Court had become aware that, through a necessity imposed by the course of events, the epoch of simple, undisguised despotism was drawing near to its end in England; and that, thenceforward, the Sovereign could hope to be absolute only by influencing the elections and managing the Parliament. We have seen that expedients for influencing elections had been attempted by King James, through the instrumentality of persons then known by the name of Undertakers, who, having possessed themselves of means of local influence, offered their services to the Court to procure favourable returns. It being plain, then, that the House of Commons was the contested ground on which Liberty or Absolute Prerogative was ultimately to prevail, the first step for the friends of freedom (necessarily the first in order, and manifestly the first in importance), was to gain a hold, stronger than that which the Court possessed, over so powerful an engine. And this could only be done by securing an additional infusion of popular representation. But the object of such a measure was likely to be so soon detected by some of those persons who had lately attached themselves to the Court, that it was essential to its success that its progress should be discreetly urged, and effectually disguised. It was determined, then, that several boroughs, by which returns had anciently been made to Parliament, should petition for the restitution of that right, which had fallen into disuse. The practice of restoring old rights of election, and of creating new ones, had been exercised by the Crown on particular occasions, ever since the reign of Henry VIII. That Monarch had, in several instances, restored the privilege, or rather reimposed the charge, of representation. For, in old times, when members received their wages for service, we often find boroughs petitioning against the obligation of sending representatives to Parliament.† Indeed, the writs being, in all cases, so worded as to require the sheriffs to

---

* W. de Malmsbury—De Gest. Reg. Angliæ.
† Willis's Notitia Parliamentaria.

cause members to be returned for all the cities and boroughs within their bailiwick, it was in a great degree left to the discretion of the sheriff to confer that right, or impose that burthen, upon whichever of such cities and boroughs he might choose. It appearing to Henry VIII. that several elections had terminated unfavourably to the views of the Court, he resolved to strengthen his hands in Parliament; and, in a spirit of moderation unusual with a sovereign by whom the most direct and summary course to the fulfilment of his pleasure was generally esteemed the best, he, for the time, contented himself with ordering that writs should be addressed to twenty boroughs, nineteen of which had never before returned members, and in the twentieth of which the practice had fallen into disuse. But now when the extension of the representation became likely, from a change in the spirit of the times, to be favourable to liberty, the country party conceived the project of retaliating this expedient upon the Crown, and of endeavouring, for the sake of increasing their influence in the House of Commons, to increase the number of popular elections. During the reign of Elizabeth, the journals furnish several instances of the Commons having begun, of their own authority, to decide upon disputed elections. The number of controverted returns had now vastly increased; and, at the instance of the country party, it came to pass that the decision was referred to a grand committee of privileges. This was the famous committee generally known since by the name of Serjeant Glanville's Committee, that eminent person having been its chairman. Among its members were some of the ablest and most learned of that age of able and learned men, such as Selden, St. John, Pym, Coke, &c. The cases first presented were those of returns made by boroughs which did not bear any connexion with persons of the country party, and the names of which gave little alarm to the jealousies of the Court. Nor were such persons seen as movers in any of the petitions. The committee first decided on some unsuspected cases of contested returns for the counties of Norfolk and Cambridge, and the boroughs of Southwark, Stafford, Arundel, Winchelsea, Chippenham, Dover, and Newcastle-under-Line.* In the last four cases the question had turned upon the rights of voting. It was then felt that some system or outline of the legal right of

* Glanville's Reports.

voting ought to be laid down; and in this spirit was drawn up the report of that renowned committee. But, in the course of its labours, another and a separate class of cases arose, and was to be decided upon by the committee — namely, cases in which the custom of returning members had fallen into disuse. In this latter class were those of Marlow, Amersham, and Wendover, whose petitions were argued and managed by Hakewill, of Lincoln's Inn, a shrewd and industrious lawyer, who had served in the last Parliament, but, till then, with no very eminent reputation for ability. These places set forth, in their prayer to the House, that 'they were ancient par-'liamentary boroughs by prescription, and ought thereby 'and of right to send burgesses to Parliament;' and Sir Edwin Sandys, say the Journals, 'speaketh for Pomfret.'*
In all these cases, of both the classes, it is to be observed that the tendency was to enlarge the basis of the representation. In the first class, in which the rights of the rated inhabitants had been usurped by the select corporators, and in the second, in which the custom of making returns had entirely lapsed, the restored franchise was equally to be vested in the hands of the 'Populacy.' The cases of the three Buckinghamshire boroughs, there is little reason to doubt, were in reality drawn up and put forward by Hampden, although ostensibly managed by Hakewill. This is all the more probable from its appearing, from Hampden's correspondence, that Hakewill had before been frequently employed by him to conduct suits and arbitrations for him, respecting his property in that county. In consequence of these petitions, Noy and Selden were ordered to make search in the records, and the committee reported that all four had the right, and ought to be admitted accordingly; furthermore declaring it to be 'the ancient 'privilege and power of the Commons in Parliament to examine 'the validity of elections and returns concerning this House ' and Assembly;' in opposition to the former decision of James, that they should be judged in Chancery. Whether Hakewill was aware or not of the full extent of the object for which he was working, does not appear. It seems, at all events, probable, that the greater number of the opposite party were not; and that those who were, did not at the beginning think it prudent to give the alarm. King James, however, had

* Commons Journals.

shrewdness enough to detect the tendency of this measure; and, accordingly, notice thereof being given to him, he stated his unwillingness to have the number of the burgesses increased, 'declaring,' says Glanville, 'he was troubled with too great a 'number already, and commanded his then solicitor, Sir 'Robert Heath, being of the House of Commons, to oppose it 'what he might; and most of the courtiers then of the House, 'understanding the King's inclinations, did their utmost 'endeavours to cross it.'* The report nevertheless was, in the end, confirmed by the House. 'Whereupon,' says Glanville, a 'warrant under the Speaker's hand was made to the clerk of the 'Crown in the Chancery, for the making of such a writ, which 'was issued out accordingly. And therefore were elected and 'returned to serve in the same Parliament, for Amersham, Mr. 'Hakewill and Mr. John Crew; for Wendover, Mr. John 'Hampden (who beareth the charge) and Sir Alexander Denton; 'for Marlow, Mr. H. Burlace and Mr. Cotton.'† The last of these was nephew of the famous Sir Robert Cotton, one of the members of the Committee; and all of them, besides a very great majority of those persons who came into Parliament for the other places to which the new writs were directed, were of the same principles and opinions.

This was the first decisive and notable advantage gained by this party against the power of the Crown. But a long and difficult course lay before them: beset with dangers, obstructed by difficulties of all sorts, and requiring the utmost discretion both as to the manner and order in which the different parts of the great scheme should be made to go forward.

In February, 1625-6, upon a repetition of the King's demand for supplies, the House went up with an address, respectfully and cautiously worded, promising supplies, but pointing to redress of grievances. To this the King's answer was intemperate and threatening. The House, however, kept its engagement; but, after a ready grant of two subsidies, was proceeding to votes of inquiry and censure, when, the plague having broke out in London, the session was removed to Oxford. Again the illegal loans and imposts levied by the Privy Council, and by the inferior courts, became matter of remonstrance; and the House, refusing, notwithstanding the

* Glanville's Reports. † Ibid.

most urgent instances, to grant any further supply until after the grievances should be redressed, and passing to the charges against Buckingham, was hastily dissolved by commission, on the 12th of August, before any measure of public relief had been accomplished for the country, or the Act of Subsidies carried through for the Crown.*

Besides the two modes, already mentioned, of raising money without the counsel or consent of Parliament, there was that of Monopolies, which were suddenly and vastly extended. They had been instituted by our early kings to protect the subject from combinations in trade; a scheme weak and ineffectual for that purpose, as giving to one person a control over prices which would have been more safely left to be regulated by the conflicting interests of many. Elizabeth had, in some instances, made it a provision for favourites, and this abuse had been greatly increased by James. It was Charles who first made it a project for public revenue also.

Relieved by this dissolution from all parliamentary control, the King now first openly assumed the power of dispensing with the laws. Letters were issued, by order of council, under the privy seal, requiring loans from private persons, generally those who were connected by blood or interest with the leaders of the popular party, who, on refusal or delay, were struck out of the commissions of Lieutenancy and of the peace.†

In furtherance of the confederacy which had been ratified with France, Denmark, and the United Provinces, against the House of Austria, a ship of the line, and seven other armed ships borrowed from merchants, were lent by the English Government to the French, under pretence of investing Genoa, then the bank of Spain. The country watched this process

---

* Rapin.—Parliamentary History.—Rushworth.—May.—Ludlow's Letters.—Willis' Not. Parl.

† One of these requisitions formed part of the manuscript collection at Stowe. It is addressed to Sir William Andrews of Lathbury in Buckinghamshire, then a tenant of John Hampden's, and afterwards one of the Deputy Lieutenants for that country under the Parliament, and requires a loan of twenty pounds, ' for divers publique services, which, without manifold incon-' veniences to us and our kingdomes, cannot be deferred.' It appears that for these contributions, exacted with the utmost severity and injustice, collectors were appointed, whose acquittance should be a sufficient warrant for repayment in eighteen months. But it appears also (unless Sir William Andrews's case were an exception), that these loans were never repaid; for his acquittance remains appended to the requisition.

with suspicion. And soon were its suspicions justified, when its ships were seen joining in the siege of the Protestant town of Rochelle.* In the mean while, the main fleet of England was defeated in an ill-conducted enterprise against Cadiz, and the allied squadron, employed in blockading Dunkirk, was dispersed by a storm. Whilst the impression of these disasters was fresh, the King called another parliament, but not till after he had endeavoured to render some of his prominent opponents, Sir Edward Coke, Sir T. Wentworth, and others ineligible, by suddenly appointing them sheriffs in their several counties.

In this Parliament, which met at Westminster on the 6th of February, Hampden was again returned for Wendover; and, on the 28th of March, we find him named on various committees. No time was lost in renewing the consideration of grievances, and again a resolution of supply was passed, on the condition of speedy and effectual redress.† In vain did the King use every means of personal remonstrance and intimidation to deter the members from proceeding to arraign the Duke of Buckingham. It was not without reason that they pointed to the Duke as to the high delinquent whose credit at court stood between the King and his Parliament. Nor had the Duke on his part less cause to feel that his objects, not only of ambition, but of safety also, demanded an entire surrender by the House of Commons of all its inquisitorial power. This he endeavoured to effect by the utmost contumacy to the House and to its privileges, in the person of Serjeant Glanville, who had been appointed to draw up the articles of charge against him, and whom he openly insulted in his place.‡ To bring this struggle to an issue, the

---

* Admiral Pennington, who commanded this squadron, with true English feeling remonstrated. His was a hard position. He commanded the ship and led the fleet of his sovereign. But he had been sent forth, amid the acclamations of his country, to give effect to a generous treaty with the oppressed and the besieged. He had no sooner arrived at his destination, than he found himself under secret orders to put himself at the disposal of a foreign command, in a murderous warfare against English honour and the Protestant religion. A copy of his high-minded protest, and the original orders from Buckingham and from Charles himself, still remain among Lord St. Germain's papers. They were probably sent to Sir John Eliot by Pennington as his vindication before the Parliament of his offended country. (See Appendix A.)

† Commons Journals.—Rushworth.—May.—Ludlow's Letters.
‡ Ellis's Original Letters.

Commons, on the 8th of May, impeached the Duke, at the bar of the Lords, of high crimes and misdemeanours; and, having first prayed that he be removed from the royal presence, pending impeachment, proceeded to support their prayer by a spirited remonstrance: when the King, alarmed at their increasing boldness, hastily dissolved them by commission, June 15th, in little more than four months from their first meeting, and again before any one of their acts was complete.

In the early part of the proceedings against the Duke, Sir Dudley Digges, and Sir John Eliot (of whose incorruptible patriotism and steady friendship for Hampden we shall hereafter have occasion to make mention), having delivered some sharp speeches in favour of the impeachment, were called out of the House by a message to attend his Majesty, and were then forthwith taken into custody and conveyed by water to the Tower under a charge of treason.* It is doubtful whether the immediate cause of this monstrous outrage is to be referred to their having supported the impeachment (as stated by Rushworth), or to some phrases of very small importance charged against them in the original informations which are preserved in the manuscript library at Lambeth Palace. But, notice of the proceeding having been given to the House, there was an instant and tumultuous cry to adjourn. In vain did Pym endeavour to restore temper and moderation. The House broke up in confusion and did not sit next day. Some days after, the subject was renewed in both houses, in the shape of a motion for an address of remonstrance; and the Commons protesting that the words charged against their members had not been used, Charles made a speech to the Lords, in which he declared that, touching the matters against the Duke of Buckingham, 'he could himself be a witness to clear him in every one of them:"—thus endeavouring to force the Lords into a dilemma; either to acquit Buckingham, or to convict against the King's proffered evidence. A new proof was now given of the headstrong obstinacy of the King, and of his determination at all hazards to support his favourite. The Chancellorship of the University of Cambridge having fallen vacant, the King, by message, through Bishop Laud and Bishop Neile, desired the convocation to elect the Duke.

* Parl. Hist.—Willis' Not. Parl.—Commons Journals.—Rushworth.

Every entreaty to postpone the election, at least until after the event of the impeachment should be known, was resisted. 'My Lord Bishop,' says Mr. Mead, in a letter describing that election, 'labours. Mr. Madon (my Lord Duke's secretary) 'labours for his Lord. Mr. Cosins for the most true patron 'of the clergy and of scholars. Masters belabour their fellows. 'Dr. Maw sends for his, one by one, to persuade them, some 'twice over. . . . Divers in town got hackneys, and fled, to 'avoid importunity. Many, some whole colleges, were 'gotten, by their fearful masters, the bishop, and others, to 'suspend, who otherwise were resolved against the Duke, and 'kept awaye with much indignation.'* In the end he was elected by a majority of three votes, over Lord Andover (afterwards Berkshire), who had been hastily set up to contest it with him. The exasperation produced in Parliament by this proceeding was rendered still more violent by a formal letter of approbation addressed, under the royal signet, to the university, 'for that, upon our pleasure intimated unto you 'by the Bishop of Durham, for the choice of your chancellor, 'you have, with such a duty as We expected, highly satisfied 'Us in your election,'† &c. To complete this desperate measure of irritation, when the House of Commons, after a stormy debate, sent to crave audience of his Majesty, 'about 'serious business concerning all the Commons of the land,' the King returned for answer that they should hear from him on the next day; and, on the next day they were indeed summoned,—not for audience, but for dissolution.

During the last week of this parliament, besides the seizure of Digges and Eliot, other arrests had taken place, and commitments *per ipsum Regem*. Among the persons who were committed to close custody was Sir Thomas Wentworth—a man ever remarkable for his large share in the toils, the fame, and the sufferings, of the troubled times through which he lived; but far more renowned for his zeal, ability, and courage, when enlisted in the battle against liberty, than while those qualities were employed in her defence; and, lastly and most, for the way in which he met his fate at the hands of the party among which his name now stood prominent and high. Sir Thomas Darnall, Sir John Corbett, Sir Walter Earl, Sir John Heveringham, and Sir Edward Hampden, having been

---

* Ellis's Original Letters. † Id. Appendix III.

brought by writ of Habeas Corpus into the Court of King's Bench, took exceptions by counsel to the return, as not declaring the cause of commitment, and prayed to be discharged. But the Court 'maintaining,' says Whitelocke, 'in opposition to 'Magna Charta and six statutes, the validity of the return,' they were remanded to prison.

The selection of certain eminent persons at the close of each Parliament, to expiate to the Court their opposition to its measures, had been a course adopted, though with doubtful success, three times before. Now, for the first time, John Hampden was considered to be of sufficient public importance to be ranked among its victims. When the King, in pursuance of his threat to resort to new modes of raising supplies, required a general loan equal to the last assessment for a subsidy (in the raising of which it was announced that persuasion, if ineffectual, was to be only the forerunner of force), Hampden resolutely refused his part; and on being asked why he would not contribute to the King's necessities, made this bold and remarkable reply.*—'That he could be 'content to lend, as well as others, but feared to draw upon 'himself that curse in Magna Charta which should be read 'twice a year against those who infringe it.' The privy council, not being satisfied with his own recognisance to appear at the board, although answerable with a landed property nearly the largest possessed by any commoner in England, committed him to a close and rigorous imprisonment in the Gate-house. Being again brought before the council, and persisting in his first refusal, he was sent in custody, although a mitigated one, into Hampshire.

The war, which about this time was suddenly declared against France, is one of those great public events for which history, in recording them, fails to assign any sufficient cause or motive. By it this country, which for nearly twenty years had been engaged in an active struggle with the great Catholic power of Europe, a war justified only by the objects of the Protestant league, at the very crisis of failure and distress broke up that league; and not for the purpose of peace, which she so much needed, but, remaining at war with the one great state, simply to embroil herself ruinously, and as it would seem without provocation, with the other. It is difficult to

* Rushworth.—Whitelocke.

feel satisfied with the ordinary solution of this question, namely that this war arose from the resentment with which Buckingham is said to have menaced the French Queen in consequence of her repelling his presumptuous proposals of love. And yet it is not very easy for one who would refer the acts of men to their ordinary motives to assign any other. It had been the unvarying policy of Henry IV. to balance France and the Protestant North of Germany against the gigantic force of Austria joined with Spain, as it was afterwards the endeavour of Retz in the thirty years' war to restore that connexion by treaty with Sweden. The reformation, out of which all the great events of the preceding half century in Germany, Spain, France, and Holland, may be said to have arisen, had bound up Sweden and Denmark with the Protestant league of Europe. So strangely had the previous dissensions of the world, beginning in spiritual hate, yet tended to cement the political relations of states which differed in their religious creeds.

This rupture was not caused nor hastened by the French King's persecution of his Protestant subjects : for in that object, as we have seen, he was assisted by a fleet furnished by Protestant England. Nor does it appear that France had failed in her part of the engagement with the combined powers against Spain. Richelieu was too crafty to furnish this pretext for war. The motives of this double contest, so manifestly destructive of what, through so many years and so many disasters, had been held to be English policy, is a problem with which no historian has fairly grappled, and which Mr. Hume has entirely passed over ; apparently because he found himself incapable of solving it in any way that would not necessarily involve Charles in the heavy charge which this act leaves upon the memory of Buckingham's administration.

As the court proceeded, at home, with less reserve to violate the law, it evinced more ingenuity in varying its modes. The duties of tonnage and poundage (the revenue of the customs), were raised by order of council. The sea-ports and maritime counties were required to furnish ships duly manned and equipped, and benevolences were unsparingly exacted. Commissions were issued to the lieutenants of counties, on pretence of an expected attempt at invasion, to muster and array the people, and to put the country at discretion under

GEORGE ABBOT,
ARCHBISHOP OF CANTERBURY.

Martial Law.* Soldiers were billeted on the houses of such persons as had expressed opinions against the Court, and the greatest disorders were countenanced among the troops. Those proprietors in the maritime districts who, to escape these excesses, had retired into the interior, were required to return and reside on their estates. Nor was any class low enough to avoid the sweeping hardships of this tyranny. Those of the poorer sort, who exclaimed against the impositions, or had rendered themselves obnoxious on private grounds to any of the local authorities, were impressed for the navy, or sent to join the army abroad. The people were taunted under these oppressions by the preachings of the Court Divines. Bishop Williams, learned, and benevolent, but one of the worst of politicians, had been driven by the jealousy and ingratitude of Laud to abandon in disgust the courtly game which he had long played with great assiduity but without success. He now begun to find himself classed among the marked victims of persecution, but without reverence or even credit. The venerable George Abbott, Archbishop of Canterbury, who, alone among the prelates since the death of Bishop Andrews, endeavoured, though bred at Court and attached to the person of the Sovereign, to stem the tide down which others were content to glide into favour and promotion, was suspended from his functions for refusing to license a sermon in support of unqualified prerogative.†

But, after the failure of the Duke of Buckingham's second expedition against the Isle of Rhé, when the revenue was still found failing, a new Parliament was summoned, and an attempt at temporary conciliation was unskilfully and ineffectually made by Charles.‡ Warrants were issued for the release of those persons who had been imprisoned for refusing to contribute to the last loan. Seventy-seven persons of various conditions, of whom Hampden was one, were set at liberty under one order of the council board.§ No submission was required on the one hand to satisfy the lofty claims of the Crown; on the other, no indemnity or explanation was offered to reconcile the sufferers, who now, upon their enlargement, were hailed by the country as the champions of triumphant

---

* Rushworth—Ludlow's Letters.—Weekly Account, No. I., July 3-4, 1643. Dugdale.—Noble's Memoirs of the House of Cromwell.
† Rushworth.—Whitelocke. ‡ Rushworth. § See Appendix B.

privilege. Being, for the most part, men of fortune and local importance, they were almost unanimously returned, upon the writs for new elections.

The Court, having thus added to the popularity of its opponents, and restored them to their functions, now renewed the ill-advised course which, during the former Parliament, had united both Houses in opposition to it. Former supplies had been raised during the suspension of Parliament. New ones were now attempted against its consent. A commission was made out under the great seal for the levying of money, by way of excise; and, to provide, as it appeared, against all further resistance, thirty thousand pounds were sent into the low countries for the raising of a body of one thousand foreign cavalry, and for the purchasing of arms and accoutrements for horse and foot.* At the opening of the session, March 17, 1627-8, not only the state of public affairs, but the feelings with which Parliament was known to have met, rendered its first step subject of very anxious and fearful expectation. Nor was that assembly composed of materials easy to be dealt with. Many of its principal members had been imprisoned under the King's own commitment. They had in their persons protested, and they had been supported by the joint protest of both Houses, against the imprisonment which they had suffered; and now, by the manner of their liberation, they were left with the two most important matters, control over the supplies, and liberty of speech itself, undecided, and in flagrant dispute between themselves and the sovereign. It was absolutely necessary to the co-existence of a Parliament with monarchy that these matters should be brought to a final and immediate settlement. If the remembrance of recent persecution made it difficult for the popular party, it was no less than impossible for Charles, with Buckingham as his minister, to come to such a settlement with a disposition to render it effectual. To what Charles's views really tended, or on what calculation he could have built his hopes of final triumph, is not easy to comprehend. Yet the first measures of the Parliament, considering the temper in which they met, and their determination to maintain the ground which the last Parliament had taken, were conceived in a spirit of moderation. They passed over,

* Rushworth.—Whitelocke.—Warwick's Memoirs.

without discussion (because they could not have discussed without violence), the King's menace of 'resorting to those 'other means which God had placed in his hands, if the 'House of Commons should not afford a speedy relief to his 'necessities.' They resumed the old questions of grievances, aggravated by the late transactions; and, after much discussion in the House and in committees, their complaints were embodied by Sir Edward Coke and Selden, in the renowned Petition of Right. Sir Robert Heath the Attorney-General, having, on the first discussion, treated some of their precedents for the ancient liberties of England slightingly, Coke replied, restating them, and declaring in the full confidence of his powers and his cause, that ' it was not under Mr. Attorney's 'cap to answer any one of these arguments.' By many artifices, and abundant assurances, such as before he had never condescended to, did Charles now endeavour to divert them from the completion of this great work. Nor were the Houses themselves at first agreed. The Lords had sent down propositions to justify imprisonments during pleasure by warrant of the Council, under pretence of state necessity. To soften this to the Commons, the new Lord Keeper assured them that his Majesty held the statute of Magna Charta, and the six others passed for the liberty of the subject, to be all in force; that he would maintain all his subjects in the just freedom of their persons, and safety of their estates; that he would govern them according to the laws and statutes of the realm; and that they should find as much security in his Majesty's royal word as in the strength of any law they could make.* The Commons, however, persisting, Mr. Secretary Cook, the feeblest old man that ever was employed as an instrument of violent designs, brought down a message, desiring to know whether the House would rest on the royal word as declared to them by the Lord Keeper. Pym's answer was conceived with great presence of mind, and consummate address and moderation. 'We have his Majesty's coronation 'oath to maintain the laws of England. What need we then 'to take his word?' The Commons, however, being pressed to return a reply through their Speaker, answered that, 'as 'there had been a public violation of the laws and the subject's 'liberties, they would have a public remedy.' The King then

---

* Rushworth.—Parliamentary History.—Whitelocke.

declared by letter to the House of Lords, that 'without the 'overthrow of sovereignty, he could not suffer the power of 'general commitment to be questioned;' and the Lords were for adding to the bill a saving clause in general terms for the sovereign power. Again, however, the Commons, declining to discuss the value of those promises (which they could not have questioned without insult to the person of the King), pressed the measure steadily forward. To recede or to pause, would have been to surrender the only barrier that remained in defence of public liberty.

Accordingly, after a conference with the Lords, June 2, 1628, the Petition of Right was read a third time in that House, and agreed to. The King's answer was irresolute and evasive. At length the royal assent was given. But the Commons, not satisfied with this reluctant concession, though they instantly passed the bill of five subsidies, the largest grant ever, till then, given by Parliament to an English sovereign, and which they had held out as a lure for his compliance, persevered in their purpose of complete redress. They had already impeached Dr. Mainwaring for preaching against the authority of Parliament and asserting the vested right of the crown over the property of its subjects; and they now obliged the King to cancel the illegal commission of excise.* They also returned to their charges against the Duke of Buckingham, earnestly requiring that he should be removed from his Majesty's counsels.† But as they were entering on a second remonstrance against the claim of tonnage and poundage, which had continued to be exacted in defiance of the Petition of Right, the King went hastily to the House of Lords, June 26, and, after giving the royal assent in person to the bill of subsidies, prorogued the Parliament to the 20th of October. On the next day, he ordered all the proceedings which, to propitiate Parliament, he had instituted in the Star Chamber against the Duke of Buckingham, to be struck off the file.

By the part which Hampden had taken in resisting these arbitrary measures, and particularly the forced loan, and by his sufferings in consequence of it, he had now become more generally known and more prominently advanced in the House of Commons, in which he again sat as member for Wendover

* Rushworth.—Whitelocke. † Parl. Hist.

during this important session. Accordingly, from this time forward, scarcely was a bill prepared, or an inquiry begun, upon any subject, however remotely or incidentally affecting any one of the three great matters at issue—privilege, religion, or the supplies—but he was thought fit to be associated with St. John, Selden, Coke, and Pym, on the committee. On the 21st of March, a few days after the meeting of Parliament, he was placed upon the committee on 'an act to restrain the ' sending away persons to be popishly bred beyond seas,' and, on the 28th, on one ' to examine the warrants for billeting ' soldiers, or levying money, in the county of Surrey.'* On the 3rd of April, he was on the committee on a bill 'to regu- ' late the pressing men as ambassadors, or on other foreign ' service, so as to promote the good of the people as well as ' the service of the state;' and, during the course of the same month, he was engaged in others ' for the better continuance ' of peace and unity in the church and commonwealth,' 'on ' the foundation of the Charter House,' on acts 'against scan- ' dalous and unworthy ministers,' † ' concerning subscription, ' or against procuring judicial appointments for money or ' other rewards,' and, ' on the presentments of recusants made ' by the knights of the several shires.' On the 10th of May, he was put upon the committee ' on the case of the Turkey ' merchants,' whose goods were detained till they should pay the tonnage and poundage; and, afterwards on the com- mittees for ' redressing the neglect of preaching and cate- ' chising,' ' on the petitions of Burgesse and Sparke,' who had been persecuted by the Bishop of Durham, ' to search for ' records and precedents,'—' to consider the two commissions ' for compounding with recusants,' and, ' for explaining a ' branch of the statute 3rd of James.' On the 13th of June, he closed, for the session, his laborious share in this sort of business with two committees, the one ' to take the certificates ' of the Trinity House merchants for the loss of ships,' and the other, ' to meet that afternoon on the Exchequer business.'

In a curious manuscript volume of Parliamentary Cases, and other Papers, preserved at Sir Robert Greenhill Russell's

---

* Commons Journals.—Willis, Not. Parl.
† This committee, afterwards popularly known by the name of the 'Scandalous Ministers committee,' lasted for many years, and became a powerful instrument in the proceedings for new-modelling the church establishment.

at Chequers Court, is abundant evidence of the pains which Hampden took to fortify himself in the science of precedent and privilege. A great part of that volume is filled with extracts from what are called 'Mr. Hampden's notes,' the originals of which however, in his own hand, I believe no longer to be in existence.

No sooner was the Parliament prorogued, than Montague, who had published two violent tracts, the one called 'A Gag to Puritans,' the other called 'An Appeal to Cæsar,' which he addressed to the King, and for which he had been censured by the Commons, was promoted to the see of Chichester;[*] and Mainwaring, who had been sentenced to imprisonment by the Lords, and declared disabled from preaching, was preferred to the Crown rectory of Stamford Rivers. The goods of several merchants were seized for non-compliance with the levy of tonnage and poundage which still continued to be exacted contrary to law; and such owners as endeavoured to remove their property were summoned before the council and committed.[†]

In the meanwhile the hopes of the country were defeated by the failure of the long-prepared and vaunted expeditions to Rochelle, and its sympathies shocked by the almost unconditional surrender to which, in consequence, the persecuted Protestants of France were reduced. This was the final blow to the wishes and to the pride of the English nation, under the personal administration of the Duke of Buckingham. The event of the armament, in the preceding summer, had been signally disgraceful. To endeavour to repair it, Buckingham had landed his forces on the Isle of Rhé. Thoryas, the French commander, had defended the fortress of St. Martin with great courage and activity, until the arrival of Count Schomberg, who landed, and obliged the English to raise the siege precipitately, and to re-embark with great loss of men and honour. In this enterprise, the English lost about fifty officers, nearly two thousand soldiers, thirty-five prisoners of note, and forty-four stand of colours, which were carried in triumph to Notre Dame.[‡]

---

[*] Petty's Miscellanea Parliamentaria.
[†] Rolls, Chambers, and Vassal were imprisoned for refusing to pay a new duty, imposed by the King, without consent of Parliament, on warrants.—See Parliamentary History.
[‡] Burchett's Naval Hist.—Strafford's Letters.—Mémoires de Rohan.

VISCOUNT FIELDING,
EARL OF DENBIGH.
OB. 1643.

In the early part of this year, another powerful fleet of fifty sail, under the Earl of Denbigh, had anchored in the roads of Rochelle. Finding twenty sail of French ships before the harbour's mouth, the Earl sent word into the town that he would sink them as soon as the winds and tide should permit. But, on the 8th of May, though favoured by both the one and the other, he, without attempting the fulfilment of his large promise, returned to Plymouth, which, says Burchett, caused no small murmurings and jealousies in England. A third fleet was prepared, to be led by the Duke in person, and of which he was proceeding to take the command when he fell by the knife of Felton.

So ended the career of a minister who, under two Sovereigns, had held greater power than perhaps any other man ever acquired from the personal favour of his master, unsupported by any great qualities of mind, and undistinguished by any successful enterprise for his country. He fell by the private hand of an enthusiast, and was carried secretly and by night to his grave, for fear of the people.*

The expedition, however, sailed under the Earl of Lindsay, who found a bar across the harbour, which he made two weak attempts to force, and then abandoned; although the Marquis de Soubize volunteered to pass it with some few ill-appointed French ships, if the English would promise to follow. The Rochellers, now reduced to the last extremity of famine, and despairing of relief, surrendered. An inglorious peace soon followed; and the Protestants of France, more unfortunate from the support proffered by England than even those of Germany had been in the last reign, were fain to submit to any terms, obtaining in the end but a bare and precarious toleration for their religion. It is difficult indeed to imagine grounds of complaint more grievous than those of the gallant and unhappy Rochellers against England. They had maintained themselves and their glorious cause with a valour which had been animated by the example of Rohan the governor and Guiton the mayor of their city, and fatally encouraged by the false promises of Charles. Rohan, himself the commander and historian of that heroic garrison, accuses him of the utmost treachery, and says that all the blood which was shed in Dauphiny is fairly to be laid to his account. Nor can this be

* Ellis's Original Letters.

deemed an unjustly aggravated reproach, though cast upon him with all the bitterness of a man who had lost all, and had seen his brave companions, after one of the noblest defences that history records, given up to the pleasure of a merciless enemy. He had trusted to that sort of encouragement so often offered by one large state for its own purposes to the insurgent subjects of an enemy, but of which there are so few examples that have not ended in the insurgents being sacrificed as victims to a treaty of peace between the two great powers. The letter delivered to Rohan by Sir William Beecher from King Charles promised him that he would 'assist the French 'Protestants to the utmost against their Sovereign for the 'liberty of their religion, on condition that they would not 'make peace,' and Montague had also been sent by Charles to assure him that 30,000 men and three fleets should be sent to his assistance; one to land at Rhé, one in the Garonne, and the third in Normandy.* Thus, however, not only in Rochelle, but in Languedoc, Piedmont, and Dauphiny, were the French Protestants left to surrender at discretion to a vain and tyrannical prince, now taking his first lesson of blood from Richelieu, whom they had been incited, by the proffered support of England, to defy; England never after having struck one effective blow in their behalf, and, according to Rohan, having sent only a few useless troops into their garrison, who consumed their provisions, and hastened their surrender.† Thus shamed and discomfited was our flag, both by land and sea, at the close of this powerful and enterprising minister's career;—baffled at Cadiz, defied at Rochelle, beaten at Rhé, threatened off our own coasts, and insulted by the pirates from the Channel to the Mediterranean. Yet a very late writer, whimsically enough, but, as it should seem, not in irony, makes it matter of much praise to Charles that he 're-established the sovereignty of the seas.'

Remarkable as is the inferiority into which the English navy had fallen during the last two reigns, it is not, on the whole, difficult to be accounted for. All history shows that, for maintaining a superiority at sea, the Government at home must be, if not a free, at least a popular one. From the example of Carthage down to that of Holland and of Venice in her best times, this remark holds good. Venice, while her

---

* Discourse on the Troubles of France. † Mémoires de Rohan.

government was supported by the spirit of her people, was great in her commercial navy, and formidable in her warlike. But, when reduced by her vices to the condition of a corrupt oligarchy, she was beaten on her own waters, her flag became tributary to the galleys of the Levant, and at length subsided into a mere quartering in the heraldry of the German empire. The same moral may be traced through our own history. Our naval power, which arose with the dawn of free institutions under Alfred, slept under the dull and chilling despotism of the Plantagenets and of the first Tudors. Its reign was triumphant and undisputed under Elizabeth, when, as Raleigh tells us, 'one ship of her Majesty would have made forty 'Hollanders (the subjects of arbitrary Spain) strike sail.' It languished, was disgraced, and overthrown, under the two first Stuarts; was restored, confirmed and victorious, under the Commonwealth; under the second Charles and James, it hardly defended our own shores against the United Provinces; and since the revolution, has been the first maritime influence of Europe.

It is not necessary to this view to dispute concerning the substantial freedom enjoyed by the people under these governments. It is enough to show that they were popular governments, and that their naval prosperity kept an exact pace with the popularity of their civil institutions. Yet an Englishman, whose 'first love,' that of the naval fame of his country, is a strong passion, may rejoice if he find reason for believing it to be closely connected with the love and enjoyment of liberty. The people who feel an interest in their governments have many motives and many advantages for cultivating that maritime spirit which a despotism always tends to depress. A sense of security in property is essential to manufacturing enterprise, and to the carrying trade; and foreign commerce makes seamen. But commerce also creates a necessity for a warlike navy to protect it. If maritime power depended solely on situation, extent of sea-coast, rivers, or population, France should have always been more than a match for England. If on military genius, she should, at the least, have equalled us. But it depends on circumstances that change: in a word, on popularity of government. In this view the writer of what is called the Political Testament of Cardinal Richelieu says truly, that 'The empire of the sea was never ' well secured to any.'

PART THE THIRD.

FROM 1628 TO 1629.

Eminent Persons of the Country Party won over by the Court — Wentworth — Saville—Noy—A new Session—A Bill proposed to legalise Tonnage and Poundage—The Speaker refuses to put a Resolution of Privilege—The Commons' Protest—Dissolution—Hampden on divers Committees of the House—Members committed to the Tower— Removed to prevent their Appearance to a Writ of Habeas Corpus—Sir John Eliot—Certain unjust Aspersions on his Memory — Letters to him from Hampden concerning his Sons — Hampden retires into Private Life — Violences of Laud, and Sufferings of the Puritans —Dr. Morley, Dr. Hales, and Dr. Heylin — Star Chamber, and High Commission Court — Hampden's first Wife dies—First Writ for the Levy of the Ship-Money.

The troops, returning from the second expedition, were again billeted on the people; and their excesses now surpassed those of which the country had so lately and so loudly complained. The King's first, and unfavourable, answer to the Petition of Right, and his speech on closing the session, were by his command entered, with the petition itself, on the Rolls of Parliament, and of the courts below; and, next, as if it were likely that those persons by whose activity and address such an Act of Parliament had been carried through, would suffer it to be reversed by so poor an artifice as that of a fraudulent record, 15,000 copies were circulated, in which that answer was substituted for the final words of assent.* No means were left untried by the Court to weaken the impression of so great a triumph of privilege, and to frustrate the purpose of an Act, the provisions of which it was intended so soon to overthrow. 'Till now, the frontier lines of royal prerogative and Parliamentary privilege, like the borders of

---

* Rushworth.—Whitelocke.—Parliamentary History.

two neighbouring and warlike nations, had remained undefined and confounded in many parts, and had been many times contested with various success. But Charles himself had now ratified a boundary treaty. It left nothing open for justifiable dispute. He had made it the law of the land. That law he had promised to observe; and, in return, had obtained from his Parliament their thanks, and a subsidy. He kept the subsidy, but broke the promise; and the Parliament was thus left without any security from the King, and the King without any credit with the Parliament. For his first assault upon the conditions of the Petition of Right, Charles most imprudently selected the very point on which his former differences with the Commons had arisen; namely, the control over the supplies. Thenceforward did he redouble the number of his exactions, and increase their severity; as if it were to revenge on Parliament and on the people their having gained from him a renunciation of all power to do so legally. He had, before, taught his Parliament that he would part with no ancient claim of prerogative but after a struggle and a bargain; and he now showed that the struggle was no warning to his violence, and the bargain no bond upon his fidelity. Even the death of Buckingham brought no beneficial change to the people, except the termination of a wanton, disastrous, and inglorious war with two crowns. But the services of a far abler man were now engaged by the Court.

Certain eminent persons of the country party, who had long affected popularity, and some of whom had severely suffered for it, were won over about the same time. Those whose motives were the most suspected were soon made to earn the wages of their defection, and to drink the cup of their dishonour to the very dregs; for upon them was imposed the shameful distinction of becoming the prime instruments in forwarding those arbitrary fines and imprisonments, and those other invasions of parliamentary privilege, of which they had, before, been the opposers and the victims. Of these persons the most remarkable were Wentworth, Saville, and Noy.

Wentworth and Saville had long been rivals in their native county of York, and had been always opposed to each other as candidates to represent it in the Commons. Under the management of the Lord Treasurer Weston, it was contrived, notwithstanding their agreement in general politics, to keep them rivals still, in order afterwards the more easily to detach both from the cause of the people. Saville's constancy was first assailed; and he was raised to the privy council, and to the office of Comptroller of the King's household. This promotion, though it secured the services of Saville, was thought by many to have rendered Wentworth irreconcilable. But, in good time, Weston reconciled him also. By the Lord Treasurer's advice, the King removed Saville out of the path of Wentworth's local ambition, to a peerage; and Wentworth was, in his turn, advanced to the council board. The Presidency of the North was soon added to Wentworth's dignities. The largest absolute powers under the crown were thus conferred on him who the most loved absolute power, and was the most capable of extending it; and he became supreme in his own great county. Nor was it long before the vastness of the general authority which this office gave him, made him the greatest subject in the kingdom.* As the importance of Wentworth's accession began to be more felt, and his talents and zeal to be more manifest, he also was raised to the peerage,—victorious over his former competitor, as well in the Court as in their native province. But his triumph did not stop here; for Saville (whom public contempt had now, for a time at least, rendered useless) was deprived of his office, from which he retired into Yorkshire, abject and disconsolate, with the prospect of spending his age in the very centre of his great rival's connection and power †—restless still, though hopeless of redeeming either credit or station; crushed beneath the wreck of his own character, and unsupported by any such qualities of mind as enabled Wentworth to live feared and courted, and to meet his ruin at last without degradation. What the feelings towards Wentworth were of the party whom he had abandoned appears in the bitter reply of one of the most eminent persons of that body. When the new-made Viscount, coming out of the House of Lords, said to some of his former friends, in a tone of familiarity unusual with him, and unsuited to the temper of those whom he was addressing, 'Well, you see I have left you.'—'Yes, my Lord,' replied Pym, whose demeanour was not less proud or resolute than his own, 'Yes, my Lord, but we will never leave you

---

* Heylin's Life of Laud.—Hardwicke Papers.—Hacket's Life of Archbishop Williams.
† Strafford's Letters.—Radcliffe's Life of Strafford.

'while that head is on your shoulders;'—a prediction rigidly fulfilled.

Of Noy,—of his qualities and motives, and of the means by which he was wrought upon to barter reputation and connection for the office of Attorney-General,—Lord Clarendon speaks in a spirit of shrewd and severe animadversion, separating him from the rest of those who (before the measures of the country party had afforded any justification to the alarms of such as qualified their support of popular rights with a paramount attachment to the monarchy) had deserted the cause of struggling privilege to strengthen that of a powerful and persecuting court. 'He suffered himself to be 'made the King's Attorney-General,' says Clarendon.

Weak and trifling, though with much exact learning, Noy, in pursuit of his objects of ambition and vanity, could but ill disguise the meanness of his nature; and, when he had succeeded in obtaining office and influence, knew not how to make the one respected, or the other feared.

To try the firmness of parliament respecting those illegal levies of tonnage and poundage which had been raised for the King's use, by order of council, during the recess, a bill was now prepared, by command from the King, granting them absolutely to the crown from the commencement of the reign: and a dissolution was resolved upon, in case the Commons should delay the bill in its progress, or resume their former habits of inquiry and censure.* Upon this determination, rashly announced by message, the King paused before putting it into execution. Meanwhile the Commons pursued their course. Resenting the prepared bill as an attempt to obtain an indemnity for former inroads upon their privileges, they resolved, in a committee of their whole body, to examine the grievances in liberty and property, and then to proceed to the innovations in religion. But this Parliament was not of longer duration than the former, and it terminated in a more tumultuous manner. In one of the messages of explanation and importunity from the King, an admission was made that the goods of a member † had been seized. Upon a resolution being moved that this seizure was a breach of privilege, the Speaker, Finch, refused to put the question, and, after a fiery protest from Selden, of his own motion, adjourned the House.

* May's History.—Whitelocke. † Mr. Rolls.

At its next meeting, a few days after, when the matter was resumed, he pleaded that the King had commanded him, in the event of such a question being again proposed, again to leave the chair, and thus evade the duty of putting it to the vote. But, upon his rising to do so, a tumult ensued, the like of which has seldom been seen in any assembly engaged in maintaining its privileges. The spirit of the country party rose to the level of the emergency which called it forth. 'It was,' says Sir Symonds D'Ewes, 'the most gloomy, sad, and dismal 'day for England that has happened for five hundred years.' Sir John Eliot, the mover of the resolution, in the confusion, unable to prevail on the trembling Speaker to put his question, dashed the paper which contained it on the floor of the House. In a short, vehement harangue, he claimed that it should be read. Finch was forcibly detained in the chair, while his own kinsman, Peter Hayman, reviled him as 'the 'disgrace and blot of a noble family, and one whom all 'posterity would remember with scorn and disdain.' The question, now read by Holles and Valentine, was echoed back with shouts. The Usher of the Black Rod demanded admittance in the King's name, in vain: the door was locked and the key on the table. But when the Captain of the Guard arrived with orders from the King to force his entrance and bring away the mace, he found the door wide open. The resolution, and a general protestation against illegal imposts and innovations in religion, had passed, by acclamation, and unanimously.* The House then adjourned for eight days; and, on its next day of meeting, the 10th of May, the King went to the Lords, and without calling the Commons to the bar, after a threatening speech, caused the Parliament to be dissolved by proclamation.

> 'Moche discoursed, and little amended,
> 'The Treasury in pawne, and the Parliament ended.'†

In the meanwhile Hampden had laboured with great diligence in the public business of these two sessions, and already the subject of church reform appears to have particularly recommended itself to his attention and his industry. He had been on the committees for preparing bills 'for 'enlarging the liberty of hearing the word of God,' and

---

* Sir Symonds D'Ewes.—Carte.   † Black Tom's owne Garland.

'against bribery, and procuring places for money and other
'rewards;' and on the committee to prepare a bill to explain
the statute 3rd James, 'concerning the appropriation of
'vicarages.' He was also put upon committees 'to view the
'entries in the clerk's book, and to search the entry of the
'Petition of Right;' and 'to examine a person who had
'petitioned the King with articles against Dr. Williams,
'Bishop of Lincoln, the keeper;' and again, 'concerning the
'differences in the several impressions of the thirty-nine
'articles.' Again, 'to examine the matter and the information
'in the Star Chamber,' and 'concerning the particulars of
'Sir Joseph Eppesley, and all others where commissioners are
'drawn to answer before the Lords;' and 'to search the
'course and precedents in the Exchequer concerning the
'injunction against merchants' goods detained for the non-
'payment of duties;' and, lastly, 'to prevent corruption in
'the presentation and collation to benefices, headships, fellow-
'ships, and scholarships, in colleges.'*

This Parliament thus persisting in the same jealous course
with those which had gone just before, the King on his part
clung with no less obstinacy to those hostile measures which
now sufficiently justified the distrust of the Parliament. The
nature of the matters in dispute had rendered the breach
nearly irreparable, and in truth the temper of the contending parties was not now favourable to repairing it.
Each had by this time begun to look rather to a triumph than
to an accommodation.

Before the dissolution, Charles again summoned several
members to appear at the council board; and on their refusal
to answer for their conduct in Parliament elsewhere than
before the House itself, committed them to close imprisonment in the Tower. Holles desired before the council that
he might be the subject rather of his Majesty's mercy than
of his power. 'You mean,' said the Lord Treasurer Weston,
'rather of his Majesty's mercy than of his justice.'—'I say,
'my Lord,' replied Holles, 'of his Majesty's power.'

With the purpose of proceeding against them in the Star
Chamber, Charles now resolved to fortify himself against the
plea of privilege by what he hoped to find a more manageable
authority,—that of judges holding their offices at the pleasure

* Rushworth.—Whitelocke.—Parliamentary Hist.—Commons' Journals.

of the crown. He therefore propounded to them certain questions as to the manner of proceeding in such cases by common law, and also as to the privileges of Parliament generally.

When the members were brought up by Habeas Corpus to the King's Bench, demanding to be admitted to bail, and to be heard by counsel on the illegality of the proceedings against them, they were remanded; and, it being represented that the judges were bound by their oaths of office to take bail on sufficient recognisances, commitments were made out, under the King's own warrant, to other prisons. This desperate step was soon sought to be retraced; but unsuccessfully. It was indeed now proposed by the Attorney-General that bail should be taken; but bail was refused unanimously by the prisoners themselves, on the ground, taken by Selden, that it would be an acknowledgment of the legality of the commitment;* and in the same spirit, and for the same reason, they refused to petition the King for their liberty. A new information being exhibited in the Court of King's Bench, they demurred generally to the jurisdiction of the Courts below in their case;† and, this plea coming to be argued, it was thrown upon the judges to find some middle course between disputing the privilege, as it affected every member of a resolute and incensed Parliament, and forcing the King to a public and shameful retreat.‡ The expedient was adopted of giving judgment against the prisoners on a 'nihil dicit;' and they were accordingly sentenced to a heavy fine, and to imprisonment during the King's pleasure, in failure of giving security for their good behaviour. The majority of the imprisoned members, refusing to make this admission against their own case, continued thenceforth for many years in a very rigorous and painful confinement.§

Among these unbending victims to Charles's disappointed and desperate policy, remained, and at last perished in captivity, the brave and, I believe, blameless, Sir John Eliot; who during his eager and faithful struggle in behalf of public

---

* Rushworth.   † Whitelocke.—May.   ‡ Warwick's Memoirs.

§ Besides Sir John Eliot, at the beginning of Trinity Term, 1629, were brought up, by writ of Habeas Corpus, Selden, Stroud, Sir Miles Hubbard, Mr. Long, Mr. Valentine, and Denzil Holles. These were all removed by warrant *per ipsum regem* to different prisons and fortresses.

liberty, was distinguished, in an equal degree, by the hatred of the Court, and the confidence of the country party.

Against the memory of this renowned person some monstrous and improbable charges, not believed, as it appears, at the time, (for they were never objected to him by his opponents in Parliament, nor used by his persecutors for their own justification,) have been revived in a late publication, with a degree of passionate credulity, not inferior to that with which, in the same work, imputations, equally void of foundation and probability, (and of which, in the course of these memorials, some notice shall be taken,) are cast upon Hampden himself. The author of a book, entitled 'Commentaries on the Life of 'Charles the First,' concludes a passage of very zealous invective against the conduct and supposed motives of the country party, with no less a charge against Sir John Eliot, than that of a cruel and treacherous attempt at murder; 'a story,' says he, 'too well authenticated to be omitted.' He, moreover, states that Sir John escaped the punishment due to such a crime, only by assiduous application to the favour of the Duke of Buckingham; whose protection he is likewise accused of having repaid by becoming his most vehement public enemy.* It appeared improbable, at first sight, that an unpunished assassin should ever after dare to show himself ungrateful to so powerful a minister, and so arbitrary a court; and such a charge seemed to demand an inquiry, which, however, was rendered the more difficult by the absence of any marginal reference to any better authority for the facts cited than that of Eachard. And Eachard's unsupported testimony, in matters criminatory of the leading persons of that party, is notoriously not to be relied on. It appears, however, from certain original papers in the possession of the Earl of St. Germains, that the person himself, Mr. Moyle of Bake, whom Sir John Eliot is accused of having 'treacherously stabbed in the back,' did not take the same view of the character of that transaction as Mr. Eachard and the author of the 'Commentaries' have done; inasmuch as he corresponds with Sir John Eliot afterwards, in terms of friendship, and moreover, solicits his favour and assistance.† The truth of the story upon which

---

* Mr. D'Israeli's 'Commentaries on the Life of Charles I.' vol. ii. p. 268, et seq.
† Since these remarks were written, two additional volumes have proceeded from the pen of the same author. In the last of these are some

F

Mr. Eachard founded this preposterous calumny has now come to light. In a letter in the possession of Miss Aikin, written by explanations of his former passage concerning Sir John Eliot; in which, however, there is little amended in respect of the manner in which facts are given, or inferences drawn. Soon after the two first volumes appeared, Lord Eliot addressed to the author of the 'Commentaries' a remonstrance in behalf of his ancestor, written in a spirit of mildness, modesty, and good sense, such as anybody acquainted with the noble writer of it might well have expected from him, and which he accompanied with the loan of a volume of the Eliot family papers, and with a copy of an apology made by Sir John to Mr. Moyle for this pretended 'assassination.' The apology is witnessed by Coryton, Bevill Grenvil, Tremayne, and four others. It is in these words:

'MR. MOYLE,—I doe acknowledge I have done you a greate injury, which
'I wish I had never done, and doe desire you to remitt it; and I desire
'that all unkindnesse may be forgiven and forgotten betwixt us, and hence-
'forwarde I shall desire and deserve your love in all frendly offices, as I
'hope you will mine.   Jº. ELYOTTE.'

Lord Eliot's is a natural and obvious inference. 'The language in 'which it is couched would hardly lead one to suppose that it was 'addressed by an assassin to his victim. It appears to me to be an 'acknowledgement of a hasty and unpremeditated act of violence, but not 'one which precluded, in the writer's opinion, the possibility of a restora-'tion of friendly feeling between him and the injured party.' Mr. D'Israeli, however, sees nothing in this but ground for thus renewing his accusation. 'I perfectly agree with his Lordship,' says the immoveable author of the Commentaries, 'that this extraordinary apology was not written by a man 'who had stabbed his companion in the back; nor can I imagine that 'after such a revolting incident, any approximation to a renewal of inter-'course would have been possible. It is *therefore* evident to me, that this 'apology was drawn up for some *former* great injury, whatever it might 'be,—*but it surely confirms the recorded tale*.' The apology was accepted; 'and it was in the hour of reconciliation, with wine before them,' that the 'treacherous blow was struck.' Mr. D'Israeli neglects to cite any authority for any part of this latter statement.

But one word more in taking leave of this strange accusation against Sir John Eliot. What shall be said, when we find that, from some extraordinary oversight, (for no man would be justified in suspecting such extraordinary disingenuity,) Mr. D'Israeli entirely discards the conclusive evidence of two letters contained in the very volume of the Eliot papers, with which he was intrusted by Lord Eliot? For conclusive they must be in the opinion of any one who, like Mr. D'Israeli, declares that 'he 'cannot imagine, after such a revolting incident, any approximation to a 'renewal of intercourse to be possible;' and yet he does not notice even the existence of these two letters! They are marked No. 63 and No. 98 in the volume. They are addressed by Sir John to the very Mr. Moyle in question, and dated many years after the pretended 'assassination,' in answer to solicitations for favours.

SIR JOHN ELIOT TO MR. MOYLE.

'SIR,—According to your desire I have used my best endeavour with 'the proctor to obtain your satisfaction for the choice of a minister at

an ancestor of one of the most respectable families in Devonshire, the cause and course of the quarrel are given, as described by the daughter of Mr. Moyle himself, a witness not likely to be unjustly partial to Sir John Eliot. Her statement is this:

Mr. Moyle, having acquainted Sir John Eliot's father with some extravagancies in his son's expenses, and this being reported with some aggravating circumstances, young Eliot went hastily to Mr. Moyle's house and remonstrated. What words passed she knew not; but Eliot drew his sword, and wounded Mr. Moyle in the side. 'On reflection,' continues Mr. Moyle's daughter, 'he soon detested the fact; and, from 'thenceforward, became as remarkable for his private deport-'ment, in every view of it, as his publick conduct. Mr. Moyle 'was so entirely reconciled to him, that no person in his time 'held him in higher esteem.'

'St. Germains, and something by way of preparation I had done before the 'receipt of your letters, upon the intelligence of Luke's death, to incline 'him therein; but the effect is little to answer the merit of the suit, though 'as much in respect of favour as I looked for. This is not a denial, but 'that which really may prove so; he seems to refer it wholly to the 'House, yet if they elect his kinsman, I presume his expectation is not 'lost. I am sorry this return is not better to the occasion you have given 'me; it may serve for an expression of my power, though my affection be 'beyond it. I can command corruption out of no man, but in mine own 'heart have a clear will to serve you, and shall faithfully remain

'*Tower*, 22 *April*, 1630.   Your true friend.
   'Mr. Moyle.'

'Sir John Eliot to Mr. Moyle.'

'Sir,
'I am sorry my tenant Rodd should be an occasion of your trouble for 'the reparation of his fault. I confess to me he does but what we 'expected in the non-performance of his bargain, the doubt of which has 'made me always unwilling to deal with him, and the composition which 'he had was granted in my absence, wherefore without prejudice to justice I 'might now insist upon the advantages, if your respect prevailed not, but 'that has a greater power in me therein to secure him; and notwith-'standing the improvidence of the man to estate him where he was, to 'which end, in answer to your love, I will give order to my servant Hill, 'at his return into the country, to repay him the money that's received, 'and so to leave him to his old interest for the tenement, in which he 'must acknowledge your courtesy and favor, for whose satisfaction it is 'done by   Your most affectionate friend,   J. E.

'7 *December*, 1631.
   'Mr. Moyle.'

These letters, unnoticed by Mr. D'Israeli, cannot fail, upon the grounds of his own former admission to Lord Eliot, to set the question at rest.

Nor does the accusation of subserviency and adulation towards the Duke of Buckingham rest on any better grounds. It is attempted to be inferred, from an unconnected phrase or two in a certain letter given by Mr. D'Israeli (he does not state on what authority), which are written in only the style of compliment then universally in use, and which refer, as Mr. D'Israeli himself observes, to his official character as Vice-admiral of Devonshire, and Chairman to the committee of Stannaries. The circumstance, however, which renders it impossible to ascertain the ground on which the author of the 'Commentaries' rests the gravamen of this charge is, that some of his references themselves, are erroneous. For a part of his case, he refers to the Harl. MSS. 7050. Throughout the whole of that volume there is not one word respecting Sir John Eliot, or his property, as cited in the 'Commentaries.' The passage referred to as in the same collection, 7000, contains the story of two very dignified petitions of Eliot's to the King for a temporary release, till he should have recovered his health; and a very spirited and touching refusal, although in the last stage of illness, to purchase liberty by admitting the justice of the sentence against him.*

But it would be wrong to fall into the tediousness of a further defence of this eminent person against a discursive attack, for which, indeed, there appears no justification. In one of the few cases in which a reference is given that can be

---

* Harl. MSS. 7000, fol. 186.

'A gentleman, not unknown to Sir Thomas *Lucy*, tolde mee from my
' Lord Cottington's mouth, that Sir John Elyotts late maner of proceeding
' was this. Hee first presented a petition to his Ma^{ty} by the hand of the
' Lieutenant his keeper, to this effect. "Sir, your Judges have co͂mitted
' mee to prison here in yor Tower of London, where, by reason of the
' quality of the ayer, I am fallen into a dangerous disease. I humbly
' beseech your Ma^{ty} you will co͂maund your Judges to set me at liberty,
' that for recovery of my health I may take some fresh ayer," &c. &c.
' Whereunto his Matie's answere was, it was not humble enough. Then
' Sir John sent another petition by his own sonne to the effect following.
' "Sir, I am heartily sory I have displeased your Ma^{ty}, and, having soe
' said, doe humbly beseech you, once againe, to sett me at liberty, that,
' when I have recovered my health, I may returne back to my prison, there
' to undergoe suche punishment as God hath allotted unto me," &c. &c.
' Upon this the Lieu^t came and expostulated with him, saying it was proper
' to him, and co͂mon to none else, to doe that office of delivering petitions
' for his prisoners. And if Sir John, in a third petition, would humble
' himselfe to his Ma^{tye} in acknowledging his fault and craving pardon, hee
' would willingly deliver it, and made no doubt but he should obtaine his
' liberty. Unto this, Sir John's answer was,—" I thanke you (Sir) for

traced, it is done in so ambiguous a phrase as to leave an impression that the author, quoted by Mr. D'Israeli, agrees with him in opinion as to the character of Sir John Eliot; which in truth he does not, but directly the reverse. 'Eliot,' says the author of the 'Commentaries,' 'like Sir Dudley Digges, 'was, in fact, a great servant of the Duke's.'* And, for this, a marginal reference is made to Rushworth, vol. i., p. 450, from which it would naturally be supposed that Rushworth had given this character of Eliot as well as of Digges; whereas the passage in Rushworth, which occurs in a transcript of Archbishop Abbott's defence of himself, says of Sir Dudley Digges, 'That man, now so hated (Digges), was a great 'servant of the Duke's.' In that passage, Eliot is not mentioned nor alluded to. It is only the author of the 'Commen-'taries' who makes the epithet carry double, by coupling Eliot's name with that of Digges. It cannot be supposed that Mr. D'Israeli intended to convey a wrong impression of Rushworth's words; but it is unfortunate that he should have used a phrase which was likely to do so.

Of the estimation in which Eliot's private as well as public character was held, little more need be said, but that he is spoken of by Hampden, in several letters, with the utmost esteem and admiration, as of one 'whose affections he accounts 'a noble purchase.'† Nor is it less in his favour, that he was the intimate friend of the gallant and virtuous Sir Bevill Grenvil, who was never a factious enemy of the Court, although, throughout his early career, an opposer of its measures; and whose death, when at last he fell, fighting on the King's part at Landsdowne, 'would,' says Lord Clarendon, 'have 'clouded any victory, and made the loss of others less 'spoken of.'

Eliot was chosen by Sir Bevill to be godfather to his second

'your friendly advise : but my spirits are growen feeble & faint, wch when 'it shall please God to restore unto their former vigour, I will take it 'farther into my consideration." Sir John dying not long after, his sonne 'petitioned his Ma^{tye} once more, he would be pleased to permit his body 'to be carried into Cornwall, there to be buried. Whereto was answered 'at the foot of the petition, " Lett Sir John Eliot's body be buried in the 'Churche of that parish where he dyed." And, so it was buried in the 'Tower.'

The letter is dated in the handwriting of Dr. Birch—'December 13, 1632.'

* Commentaries on the Life of Charles I., vol. i., p. 272.
† Hampden's Letter, No. 126, Eliot Collection.

son; and is mentioned by him, in letters to his wife, the Lady Grace Grenvil, in terms of warm affection. Eliot's attachments seem to have been strong and lasting; his enmities, bold, open, and vehement; his public virtue indefatigable and unstained. His eloquence was ardent and flowing, and his mind deeply imbued with a love of philosophy and a confidence in religion, both of which gave a lofty solemnity of tone to his letters, many of which are written under the hardships of captivity and the rapid approaches of death.

During the last few months of Eliot's sufferings, the remonstrances of his physicians warned the Privy Council of the advancing issue of his disorder, which could only be relieved by releasing him from his imprisonment, or, at the least, by relaxing its severities.* But all indulgence was refused; and his liberty offered only upon conditions which his proud spirit, having already rejected them on grounds of public duty, would never stoop to accept for personal ease or safety.† It is stated by May, that in his sickness, he was strictly debarred from the society of his friends and family. This appears, from Eliot's correspondence, to have been quite true of the latter period of his imprisonment; but May is misled in asserting that he was also refused all means of communication with them by letter.‡ His hours of solitary misery in the Tower, he still dedicated to the defence of his views of civil government, in a treatise entitled 'The Monarchy of Man.' He also had the consolation of a correspondence with his friend, John Hampden,—a copy of one letter from whom I here give from the original in the British Museum.§ Although containing as little information of any importance as a letter written to a prisoner in close and jealous custody was like to do, and though consisting of absolutely nothing but an apology for not writing more, it is, nevertheless, not uninteresting, from the neatness of its style, and from the warm affection which it manifests to the unhappy friend to whom it is addressed:

'SIR,—You shall receave ye booke I promised by this bearer's
' immediate hand; for ye other papers I presume to take a little,
' and but little, respitt. I have looked upon y^t rare piece ownly
' with a superficiall view; as at first sight to take ye aspect and
' proportion in ye whole; after, with a more accurate eye, to take

---

* Grand Remonstrance.   † Ludlow's Letters.
‡ May, Appendix.   § Donat. MSS. No. 2228.

'out y⁶ linaments of every part. 'Twere rashnesse in mee, there-
'fore, to discover any iudgment before I have ground to make one.
'This I discerne, that 'tis as compleate an image of y⁶ patterne as
'can be drawne by lines; a lively character of a large minde; the
'subject, method, and expressions, excellent and homogeniall, and,
'to say truth (sweete heart) somewhat exceeding my commenda-
'tions. My words cannot render them to the life; yet (to show
'my ingenuity rather than witt), would not a lesse modell have
'given a full representation of that subject? not by diminution,
'but by contraction, of parts? I desire to learn; I dare not say.
'The variations upon each particular seem many; all, I confesse,
'excellent. The fountaine was full; y⁶ channel narrow; yᵗ may
'be y⁶ cause; or that the author imitated Virgill, who made more
'verses by many than he intended to write. To extract a iust
'number, had I seen all his, I could easily have bidd him make
'fewer; but if he had badd mee tell which he should have spared,
'I had been apposed. So say I of these expressions; and that to
'satisfy you, not myselfe, but that, by obeying you in a command
'so contrary to my own disposition, you may measure how large a
'power you have ouer   'Jo. HAMPDEN.

'HAMPDEN, *June* 29*th*, 1631.

'Recomend my seruice to Mr. Long, and if Sʳ Ol. Luke be in
'toune, expresse my affection to him in these words; y⁶ first part
'of y⁶ papers you had by y⁶ hands of B. Valentine long since. If
'you heare of yoʳ sonnes, or can send to yᵐ, let me know.'

Eliot's correspondence shows that he consulted Hampden
upon the literary work in which he was employing himself.
Several of his letters refer also to the education and characters
of his two sons, whom, during his long captivity, he intrusted
to the care of his friend. To Hampden's faithful and valuable
counsel he seems to have mainly applied himself for direction
in the government and advancement of them. Towards the
younger of the two, Mr. Richard Eliot, the 'souldier'
alluded to in the postscript of the fac-simile letter, Hampden
seems to have borne a strong and almost parental affection.
In one of his letters to his father he describes him as one 'of
'whome, if ever you live to see a fruite answerable to the
'promise of the present blossomes, it will be a blessing of yᵗ
'weight as will turne the scale against all worldly afflictions
'and denominate yoʳ life happy.'* Both, however, of these

* Eliot Papers, No. 23.

young men (the elder by some idle and riotous habits which brought him into difficulties with his superiors at Oxford, the younger by a vivacious and unsteady humour, which was considered as fitting him rather for the activity of a military life than for a course of literary study), it is plain gave no small trouble and solicitude to their father's friend in the discharge of the duties which he had undertaken towards them. But so natural and amiable are the expressions of an indulgent heart, particularly when pleading in extenuation of some of these youthful irregularities, that I have been led to transcribe some passages of a correspondence which has nothing of historical importance to recommend it. Where it is possible in any part to make such a man as Hampden his own biographer, who would substitute any other words for those in which he tells the story of his own feelings and opinions? Some of the letters which follow I cannot content myself with merely making extracts from.

'SIR,—I hope you will receave yor sonnes both safe, and that
' God will direct you to dispose of them as they may be trained up
' for his service and to yor comfort. Some words I have had wth
' yor younger sonne, and given him a tast of those apprehensions he
' is like to find wth you; wch I tell hime future obedience to yor
' pleasure, rather than iustification of past passages, must remove.
' He professeth faire; and ye ingenuity of his nature doth it
' without words; but you know vertuous actions flow not infallibly
' fro: the flexiblest dispositions: there's ownly a fit subiect for
' admonition and government to worke on, especially that wch is
' paternall I confesse my shallownesse to resolve, and therefore
' unwillingnesse to say anything concerning his course; yet will I
' not give over the consideration; because I much desire to see y^t
' spiritt rightly managed. But, for yor elder, I thinke you may
' with security return him in conuenient time; for certainly there
' was nothing to administer from of a plott, and, in another action
' y^t concerned himself, wch he'll tell you of, he receaved good satis-
' faction of the Vice Chancellor's faire carriage towards hime. I
' searched my study this morning for a booke to send you of a like
' subiect to y^t of the papers I had of you, but find it not. As
' soone as I recouer it I'll recommend it to yor view. When you
' haue finished ye other part, I pray thinke mee as worthy of y^e
' sight of it as ye former; and in both together I'll betray my
' weaknesse to my friend by declaring my sense of them. That I
' did see is an exquisite nosegay, composed of curious flowers,
' bound together with as fine a thredd. But I must in the end

'expect hony fro: my friend. Somewhat out of those flowers
'digested, made his owne, and givinge a true tast of his owne
'sweetnesse; though for that I shall awaite a fitter time and
'place. The Lord sanctify unto you ye sowrenesse of yor present
'estate, and ye comforts of yor posterity.

'Yo^r ever ye same assured friend,
'Jo. HAMPDEN.
'*April 4th*, 1631.'

Sir John Eliot in his answer, dated from the Tower, proposes to send his younger son, Richard, as a soldier, to the Netherlands, to learn the art of war in the train of Sir Horace Vere. He states also his elder son's (John's) desire to go to France, but his own wish that he should remain at Oxford till he should have obtained his 'licence,' or degree, at that university. To this the following is the reply:

'SIR,—I am so perfectly acquainted with your cleare insight
'into the dispositions of men, and ability to fitt them with courses
'suitable, that, had you bestowed sonnes of mine as you have done
'yor owne, my iudgement durst hardly haue called it into question;
'especially when, in laying the design, you haue prevented y^e
'obiections to be made against it. For if Mr. Rich. Eliot will, in
'the intermissions of action, adde study to practise, and adorn that
'liuely spiritt with flowers of contemplation, he'll raise our
'expectations of another Sr Edw.* Veere, that had this character;
'"All summer in the field, all winter in his study;" in whose fall
'fame makes this kingdome a great looser; and, having taken this
'resolution from counsaile with ye highest wisdome (as I doubt
'not you haue), I hope and praye ye same power will crown it with
'a blessing answerable to our wish.

'The way you take with my other friend declares you to be none
'of ye B^p of Exeter's converts,† of whose minde neither am I super-
'stitiously; but, had my opinion bine asked, I should, (as vulgar
'conceipts use to do,) haue shewed my power rather to raise
'obiections than to answer them. A temper ‡ between France

---
* Francis.
† I had imagined the allusion here to have been to Dr. Hall's, Bishop of Exeter's, Letter to the House of Commons, during the discussions between the two Houses on the Petition of Right, in which he says, 'If you love yourselves and your country, remit something of your own terms.' But I have now no doubt that the Edinburgh Review, in its criticism on this supposition, is quite right, and that Hampden referred to Hall's Tract on Education, recommending foreign travel.
‡ A middle course, a compromise.

'and Oxford might have taken away his scruple, with more advan-
' tage to his yeares; to visit Cambridge as a free man for variety
' and delight, and there entertained himself till ye next spring,
' when University studyes and peace had bine better settled than I
' learn it is. For, although he be one of those that, if his age were
' looked for in no other booke but that of the minde, would be
' found no ward if you should dy to-morrow; yet 'tis a great
' hazard, meethinkes, to see so sweet a disposition guarded with no
' more amongst a people whereof many make it their religion to be
' superstitious in impiety, and their behaviour to be affected in ill
' manners. But God, who ownly knows ye periods of life, and
' opportunities to come, hath designed hime (I hope) for his owne
' seruice betime, and stirred up yor providence to husband hime so
' early for great affaires. Then shall hee be sure to finde him in
' Fraunce that Abraham did in Sichem, and Joseph in Egypt, under
' whose wing alone is perfect safety. Concerning that Lord,* who
' is now reported to be as deepe in repentance as he was profound
' in sinne, the papers, &c., I shall take leave fro: your favour, and
' my streight of time, to be silent, till the next weeke, when I hope
' for the happinesse to kisse your handes, and present you with my
' most humble thankes for yor letters, wch confirm ye observation I
' have made in the progresse of affections: that it is easier much to
' winne upon ingenuous natures then to meritt it. This, they tell
' mee, I have done of your's: and I account it a noble purchas, w^{ch}
' to improve with the best services you can command, and I performe,
' shall be ye care of   ' Your affectionate friend and servant,

'HAMPDEN, *May* 11*th*, 1631.   'JO. HAMPDEN.

' Present my seruices to Mr. Long, Mr. Valentine, &c.
' Do not thinke by what I say y^t I am fully satisfyed of your
' younger sonne's course intended, for I have a crotchett out of y^e
' ordinary way, wch I had acquainted you wth if I had spoken wth
' you before he had gone, but ame almost ashamed to communicate.'

The next letter is from Hampden to one of the sons, his
' young friends.'

'SIR,—I receaved yor commaunds by ye hands of Mr. Wian,
' and was glad to know by them that another's word had power to
' commaund yor faith in my readinesse to obey you, wch mine it

---

* Merven Touchet, Lord Audley, the infamous Earl of Castlehaven, of whose removal from the Tower, and trial and sentence, Eliot had spoken in the letter to which this is the answer.

'seems had not. If you yet lack an experience, I wish you had
'put mee upon yᵉ test of a workè more difficult and important, yᵗ
'yᵒʳ opinion might be changed into beliefe. That man you wrote
'for I will unfainedly receave into my good opinion, and declare it
'really when he shall have occasion to putt me to yᵉ proofe. I
'cannot trouble you with many words this time. Make good use
'of the booke you shall receave fro: mee, and of yoʳ time. Be sure
'you shall render a strict account of both to

'Yoʳ ever assured friend and seruant,

'Jo. Hampden.

'Present my seruice to Mr. Long. I would faine heare of his
'health.

'Hampden, *June 8th*, 1631.'

The rest are to Sir John Eliot.

'Deare Sir,—I receaued a letter from you the last weeke, for
'wᶜʰ I owe you ten, to countervaile those lines by excesse in number,
'that I cannot equall in weight. But time is not mine now, nor
'hath bine since that came to my hands; in your favour, therefore,
'hold mee excused. This bearer is appointed to present you wᵗʰ a
'buck out of my paddock, wᶜʰ must be a small one to hold propor-
'tion with yᵉ place and soyle it was bred in. Shortly I hope, (if I
'do well to hope,) to see you; yet durst I not prolong yᵉ expecta-
'tion of yoʳ papers. You have concerning them layde comaundes
'upon mee beyond my ability to give you satisfaction in; but, if
'my apology will not serve when wee meete, I will not decline yᵉ
'seruice to yᵉ betraying of my owne ignorance, which yet I hope
'yoʳ love will couer.

'Yoʳ ever assured friend and seruant,

'Hampden, *July 27*. 'Jo. Hampden.

'I am heartily glad to learne my friend is well in Fraunce.
'Captaine Waller hath bine in these parts, who I have seene, but
'could not entertaine; to my shame and sorrow I speake it.'

'Sir,—In the end of my travailes, I meate yᵉ messengers of yoʳ
'loue, wᶜʰ bring mee a most gratefull wellcome. Yoʳ intentions
'outfly mine, that thought to have prevented yoʳˢ, and convince mee
'of my disability to keepe pace with you or the times. My imploi-
'ment of late in interrogatory with like affaires hath deprived mee
'of leisure to compliment; and yᵉ frame of dispositions is able to

'iustle the estyle of a letter. You were farre enough above my
'emulation before; but, breathing now the same ayre wth an ambas-
'sador, you are out of all ayme. I beleive well of his negociation
'for ye large testimony you have given of his parts; and I beleive
'ye king of Sweden's sword will be ye best of his topicks to persuade
'a peace. 'Tis a powerfull one nowe, if I heare aright; fame
'giving Tilly a late defeate in Saxony wth 20,000 losse; the truth
'whereof will facilitate o^r worke; the Spaniard's curtesy being
'knowne to be no lesse then willingly to render that which he cannot
'hold. The notion of these effects interrupts not o^r quiett, though
'ye reasons by wch they are gouerned do transcend o^r pitch. Yo^r
'apprehensions, y^t ascend a region above those clouds wch shadow
'us, are fitt to pierce such heights; and o^{rs} to receave such notions
'as descend from thence; which while you are pleased to impart,
'you make ye demonstrations of yor favour to become ye rich
'possessions of   Yo^r ever faithful friend and seruant,

'Jo. HAMPDEN.

'Present my seruice to Mr. Long.

'HAMPDEN, Oct. 3.

'God, I thanke him, hath made me father of another sonne.'

'NOBLE SIR,—I hope this letter is conveyed to you by so safe
'a hand y^t yo^{rs} will be ye first y^t shall open it; or, if not, yet, since
'you inioy, as much as without contradiction you may, ye liberty of
'a prison, it shall be no offence to wish you to make ye best use
'ont, and y^t God may find you as much his, now you inioy y^e
'benefitt of secondary helpes, as you found hime yo^{rs} while, by
'deprivation of all others, you were cast upon his immediate
'support. This is all I have, or am willing, to say; but y^t y^e
'paper of considerations concerning ye plantation * might be very
'safely conueyed to mee by this hand, and, after transcribing,
'should be as safely returned, if you vouchsafe to send it mee. I
'beseech you present my seruice to Mr. Valentine, and Mr. Long
'my countryman, if with you, and let me be honoured with the
'stile of

'Yo^r faithful friend and seruant,   Jo. HAMPDEN.

'HAMPDEN, *December* 8.'

This is the last of his letters to Sir John Eliot. The

---

* Referring to the project of emigration to the plantation founded by the Puritans in Connecticut, of which further notice will be taken hereafter.

rigours of the imprisonment had been abated by reason of the representation of the physicians. But too late. Disease, aggravated by hardships already suffered, was advancing with a pace which was not to be arrested, and in the following November Eliot expired; leaving testimony of a hardihood of purpose and a resolute endurance of all the sufferings it brought upon him, which, if we consider the length and fatal termination of them, and, above all, the repeated occasions offered to him to escape them by compromising public duty and private honour, were unparalleled even in those days of patient and obstinate courage under persecution. I hope that I stand excused for making so copious extracts of letters on matters which throw so little light on general history. Of Hampden's correspondence, probably for the reasons already mentioned in the preface, the remains are very rare. It is difficult to conceive that any letters of his would be quite unworthy of attention: certainly not those which make so touching a display of the affectionate feelings of his heart.

Before the dissolution of the Parliament of 1628-9, Hampden, although retaining his seat for Wendover, had retired to his estate in Buckinghamshire, to live in entire privacy; without display, but not inactive; contemplating from a distance the madness of the Government, the luxury and insolence of the courtiers, and the portentous apathy of the people, who, amazed by the late measures, and by the prospect of uninterruptedly increasing violence, saw no hope from petition or complaint, and watched, in confusion and silence, the inevitable advance of an open rupture between the King and the Parliament. The literary acquirements of his youth he now carefully improved; increasing that stock of general knowledge which had already gained him the reputation of being one of the most learned and accomplished men of his age; and directing his attention chiefly to writers on history and politics.* Davila's 'History of the Civil Wars of 'France' became his favourite study; his *Vade Mecum*, as Sir Philip Warwick styles it; as if, forecasting from afar the course of the storm which hung over his own country, he already saw the sad parallel it was likely to afford to the story of that work. In his retirement, he bent the whole force of his capacious mind to the most effectual means by which the

---

* Clarendon—Hist. Reb.

abuses of ecclesiastical authority were to be corrected, and the tide of headlong prerogative checked, whenever the slumbering spirit of the country should be roused to deal with those duties to which he was preparing to devote himself.

Meanwhile the raising of a revenue, without consent of Parliament, so often declared illegal, both by resolution and by statute, was more and more actively pursued, and new imposts laid, in some cases to an amount exceeding the prime cost of the goods on which they were charged. Coat and conduct money for the militia was still levied upon the counties, and the names of all who resisted were reported to the Council Board. Patents of monopoly on articles of the most ordinary and necessary use, as in the former reign, were sold to companies, and granted to favoured individuals. Heavy fines were inflicted on all such persons as, being possessed of forty pounds a-year, had declined to submit themselves to the honour of knighthood at the coronation; and payment was enforced by Exchequer process. Contrary to statute, the old forest laws were revived, and the royalties of chase, and timber, and pasturage, extended at will, in order that recoveries or annual rents might be extorted by way of composition. Proclamations were issued from the Privy Council, claiming for these encroachments the force of law.* And yet from all these extraordinary means the Crown derived but a scanty revenue, the chief profit of the exactions being swallowed up in the collecting of them.†

Then began Wentworth to fill up the measure of his qualifications for the highest pitch of favour and power at which his ambition could aim, or his great abilities, inferior only to his ambition, help him to arrive. Then began, too, the more cruel violences of Laud, who had early directed the attention of the Court towards Wentworth, and had prepared him for the overtures made by Weston. At the beginning of this reign, Laud had been noted as a zealous champion of the new forms and ceremonies. A wiser courtier than Williams, and a more subtle and effective labourer for the claims of the high church than Bancroft, or Neale, he had early recommended himself by his success in advancing the power and revenues of the Crown, jointly with the temporalities of the clergy; and now he had become no less distinguished for the

---

* May.—Appendix.—Rushworth.   † Clarendon.—Hist. Reb.

relentless severity with which he pursued those persons who endeavoured a reformation of their excesses. Crafty in pursuit of the means of his influence, Laud was bold and sincere in the ends to which he applied them. Rash, cruel, and tyrannical in the exercise of power, and vain and trifling in his display of an ambition which aimed at the greatest objects, his lofty courage and fervent piety threw a deep interest round his latter days. He was a learned, and an enterprising, but not a wise, man; ever aspiring to eminence in the state, and showing, when he had attained it, that his nature had not qualified him to fill it with prudence or dignity. He was not without generosity, although his inveterate hate of Williams made him use unfairly the advantages which his better fortune gave him over his rival in the conflict of intrigue. Laud, for a space, prevailed. But for the superior magnanimity of Williams (with all his faults), it must be said, that, in after times, when he was in favour, and Laud in danger, he laboured harder to save his fallen enemy's life than he had ever done to check or destroy his power.

Under the masterly genius and authority of Wentworth, who was preparing to graft for himself upon the great office of President of the North the yet higher dignity of Lord Deputy of Ireland, and under the implacable vigilance of Laud (joined with Cottington and Coventry in the Treasury Commission, and only detained from the Primacy by the spark of life which still lingered in the good old Archbishop Abbott), the united power of the court and clergy was now at its noon, and prospered. Parliamentary privilege, no longer a barrier in its path, had become its plaything and its scorn; and ministers of state, courtiers, and divines, each in their several office and vocation, openly counselled the King against ever recalling into activity the vexatious control of a Parliament.* The personal liberty of such of the gentry of the country party as had never been sufficiently forward in its ranks to afford a pretext for seizure and imprisonment, was next assailed. Many were ordered home to their country-seats, and forbidden to return to the capital; and the Statute of Improvements was occasionally used for the confiscation of large portions of their land. Merchants were prohibited from landing cargoes at convenient ports, whenever the interests of favoured monopolists

* Clarendon—Life.

chanced to require their unloading at others.* Families were impoverished, some ruined, by excessive fines to the Court of Wards for compounding wardships. But the power of the court, the treasury, and the clergy, fell with its heaviest visitation on the Puritans; and this designation was accordingly fixed on all such as it was intended to provoke to the indiscretion of complaint, and then to dignify by a persecution, which the enthusiasm of many inclined them rather to invite than, by a prudent silence, to avoid. Among the various means which have been at different times adopted for forcibly extinguishing religious sects, none, short of extermination, have ever, in the whole history of the world, been successful. Mere persecution has always, on the contrary, been found to unite sects by a closer bond, and warm them with a more fervent zeal. Vanity, indignation, and piety, are impulses too strong for its control; it sometimes kindles, often illumines, but never can consume, them.

Tyranny, however, in the selection of its early victims, rarely fixes its choice upon persons whose discretion and mildness of deportment are likely to leave the oppressor without some show of justification. Passions heated by controversy, and tempers soured by unjust obloquy, have been the ordinary subjects of its most violent and cruel experiments. This was the case with Leighton, who, moved by a litigious and not very orderly zeal, had, in a book called 'Sion's Plea,' lectured the prelates, and railed against the Queen as a 'Canaanitish woman and idolatress.' He was also convicted, contrary to the evidence of the book itself, in which no such passage is to be found, of having, on the ground of Scripture precedent, recommended to 'smite the bishops under the fifth rib.' In like manner Prynne. He had devoted his industry and learning to make manifest, in another book, 'God's wrath against Stage-players;' and his misfortune it was, that a few days after the publication, it pleased the Queen's highness to act a part in a masque at court; in consequence of which, by a simple inversion of the order of dates, it was set forth, in the proceedings against him, that the ill-mannered epithets against actresses, with which his book abounded, were levelled

---

* The monopolies were not limited to licenses for importation. The excise paid its share liberally to the demands of the Court. Soap, oats, wine, publicans' licenses, leather, glass, iron, tin, and lead, were successively charged with duty to great persons, for favour or for composition.

at her Majesty.* Of the same class of victims, also, were Bastwick and Burton; and the year afterwards, John Lilburne, whose remarkable fate it was, (ever engaged in controversy,) to be ever the victim of some powerful and vindictive enemy, and to be made the martyr of his zeal by the Parliament in later times, as he now was by the court; by Presbyterians in the end, as he was by prelates at the beginning. Of him, and of his polemical spirit, it was once sharply said, that, if John Lilburne were left alone on the earth, John would quarrel with Lilburne, and Lilburne with John. His honesty, however, is scarcely less clear than the courage which, as a controversialist and as a soldier, he so eminently displayed; and of the eloquence and vigour of his speaking and writing some splendid proofs are given among his defences, as well before the Star Chamber in 1637, and before the Court of King's Bench at Oxford, on his trial for treason in 1642, as before the Parliament, on a charge of libel brought against him by Prynne and the Presbyterians in 1645. He now began his sufferings in the pillory at the early age of nineteen, for having undertaken the publication of the works of Burton and Bastwick.

The security of the prelates was taken, jointly with the honour of the Queen and of the stage, under the powerful protection of the Star Chamber; and were jointly avenged upon the persons of the victims, by a censure of fine and imprisonment, by the scourge inflicted with extraordinary cruelty, and by the pillory, with the loss of their ears. These inhuman penalties were inflicted on all four in their entire and utmost severity.† Upon Prynne, who had returned after his former mutilations to prison only to launch forth from thence fresh thunders against his proud tormentors, the punishment was renewed,‡ the stumps of his ears being rooted out with the knife, and his cheeks branded with a glowing iron. Lastly, to remove him and his fellow-sufferers to a distance, at which the spectacle and sound of their woes should be unmarked and forgotten, the sentence against all was extended to the term of their lives in fortresses beyond seas.§ The bloody cruelty of the

---

* 'Ungrateful author!' exclaims a Roman Catholick writer, (Mayolino Bisaccioni, Guerre Civile d'Inghilterra,) 'did he not remember that it was 'a dance of a Queen (Anna Bullen) which first introduced schism and 'heresy into England)'

† Whitelocke.—Rushworth.   ‡ State Trials.

§ The Earl of Dorset, in declaring to Prynne the censure of the Star

lash and the shears, and the torment of the hot iron dwelling on the flesh, failed to extort any expression of terror or of pain. All suffered with a spirit of constancy and lofty cheerfulness deriveable only from their unmixed devotion to a cause now rendered dearer and holier to them by the example of courage which they vied with each other in giving.

This enthusiasm had not only mounted above all fear of torture or of death, but had risen to an entire contempt of mercy at the hands of men. Acting—

'As ever in their great Task-master's eye,'

from Him only would they solicit, and from Him only accept, either direction or pardon. This may be a disposition ill suited to discipline men for the ordinary duties of subjects under a good government; but it makes them glorious foes to a bad one. Nothing was there in the aspect of affairs to inspire a hope of what a few years afterwards accomplished for them;— that they should all return in triumph from their banishment, restored and rewarded by a vote of Parliament. To Prynne, whose sufferings had not taught him moderation, was reserved a yet stranger fortune;—to be selected to conduct the impeachment which took away the life of the very prelate of whose relentless power he was now the victim.

Meanwhile nothing was spared to insult in their observances the whole party nicknamed Puritans, and to further provoke that captiousness of feeling on all religious matters which had now extended itself over a large portion of the country. After the example of his father, the king renewed the proclamation for the encouragement of those sports and pastimes on the Lord's day, which had been stigmatised by Parliament as popish, lax, and ungodly; and the practice of which, (innocent under proper limitations, and important to promote the cheerfulness of the labouring classes,) became, at this time, a license for irregularities most offensive to the sober and jealous feelings of those whom it was the purpose of the Government to oppress. Nor should it be overlooked that, in opposing the proclamation for sports and pastimes, the Puritans were not actuated solely, as it has often been most unfairly represented, by an intolerant aversion from such harmless indulgences. A much more

Chamber, is merry upon the operation of cutting off his ears, as tending to the use of 'those unlovely love-locks on both sides, which he hath 'inveighed against.'—Rushworth.

reasonable motive is discoverable to readers who may be persuaded to look into the proclamation itself before judging of the motives of its opposers.* By the words and by the effect of that proclamation these sports were permitted only to such persons as had attended at the service of the Church of England: all being excepted who might, from disgust at the courtly doctrines then preached by that church, have preferred a discipline of their own; and a vexatious and insulting line of separation being thus drawn between the high-church conformists and the followers of a simpler mode of worship. This feature of the proclamation, and of the resistance made to it, is kept entirely out of sight by Hume and others. On these points, however, and in their general conduct in politics, the established clergy themselves were not united; although, undoubtedly, the great majority of that body, as has generally been the case with the priesthood of every state religion, clove to the Court, and therefore at this time favoured that ecclesiastical discipline which was represented, and not unjustly, as popish, with only the qualification of a domestic supremacy. It was described by Lord Falkland as being 'an English, ' though not a Roman, popery; so it seemed,' says he, ' their ' work was to try how much of a papist might be brought in ' without popery, and to destroy as much as they could of the ' Gospel, without bringing themselves into danger of being ' destroyed by the law.' †

Chief among that small body of the clergy who, after the death of Abbott, stood stoutly against the innovations of the high-church faction, was Dr. Morley, Bishop of Winchester, the intimate friend and companion of Hampden and of Arthur Goodwyn. With him, inferior in rank, but not in abilities or integrity, was Dr. Hales, the Greek Professor of the University of Oxford, well known by the appellation of the ' ever memor- ' able;' who has been singularly represented by a late biographer as having been reclaimed from some heterodox opinions by Laud. Reclaimed he certainly seems to have been from heterodox opinions at one time held by him; but as certainly not reclaimed by Laud, whose zeal, it is true, he respected, but whose theological acquirements, on the contrary, he appears to have rated extremely low; and whose formalities, and violences, and thirst of power, he held in extreme distaste. He, with

* Rushworth. † Speech concerning Episcopacy.—1641.

Bishop Morley, was often found among that party of distinguished men who frequented Lord Falkland's house at Tew, that 'college,' as Lord Clarendon terms it, 'situate in a purer air.'* He was a man of great piety, and a singular simplicity of manners, and had refused from Laud and others many offers of advancement in the Church. Nothing, we are told by Lord Clarendon, troubled him more than religious brawls; and his detestation of Romish tyranny arose more from the bonds it imposed upon free conscience than from the errors of its creed.† He would often say that 'he would 'renounce the Church of England to-morrow if it obliged him to 'believe that any other Christians should be damned;' and that nobody would conclude another man to be damned who did 'not wish him so.' No man was more severe to himself: while to other men he was so charitable, that he thought those who were otherwise to be more in fault for their severity, than those whom they impugned were for their errors; and that pride and passion, more than conscience, were the cause of all difference of communion; no doctrinal points on which men differed being fit to hold a place in any liturgy.

But far different in spirit was the more powerful party which had arisen in the Church, and, for a time, prevailed; which not only lay under the much abhorred imputations of 'for- 'mality and popery,' but openly avowed a tendency to Arminianism. It is clear that a mere speculative difference concerning the tenet of Absolute Decrees could not have influenced political principle or conduct. Indeed the proof, if proof were wanting, is, that, in Holland, the Arminian sect, which, opposing the Calvinists, rejected the doctrine of preordination, was that from the bosom of which Barnevelt and Grotius arose to resist the power of the House of Orange; and that the sect of the Gomarists, who professed those doctrines in their most unqualified extent, was established and privileged by the Court. In England they had in these respects changed places, and the Arminians were the supporters of arbitrary power, the Calvinists of liberty. A leaning to this or that belief was then, according to a mode of conclusion too common in all times, held to be a test of political opinions. This must always be the case where the principles of civil government are so ill understood as to be made to interfere with free conscience, and where religion has been so warped in its

---

* Clarendon—Hist. Reb.   † Clarendon—Life.

character as to have become an engine of civil government. In this fault undoubtedly a large party of the nonconformists shared equally with their persecutors. All that can be said for them is, that, in England at least, they were not the first aggressors. Like many other persecuted sects of which there are examples in history, their intolerance grew with that under which they suffered. As the persecutors made conformity to a particular creed the passport to favour and privilege, so the persecuted made the adoption of its opposite the test of a love of liberty, and the condition of being admitted to the honours of a fellowship in suffering. Such a spirit of religious uncharitableness can live only by persecution; by inflicting, or by enduring, it.

To such an extent had the Arminian doctrines won their way in Court favour, that Bishop Morley, being once asked by a grave gentleman who was desirous to be informed of their tenets and opinions, 'what the Arminians held?' pleasantly answered that 'They held all the best bishoprics and 'deaneries in England.' 'Which,' says Lord Clarendon,* 'with other like harmless and jocular sayings, brought upon 'him the displeasure of Laud.'

Of the class generally described as Arminians was Dr. Peter Heylin, afterwards well known as the principal instrument by whose means the King obtained, under the name of a benevolence, a large vote of money from Convocation, which Parliament had refused. He was engaged, as one of the King's chaplains, to answer Bishop Williams on the 'Discipline of the 'Church;' as also to publish an argument praying for punishment upon Prynne, Burton, and Bastwick; for which service he obtained the treasurership of the Cathedral of Westminster, and the living of Islip. He first recommended himself in 1633, by attacking, in a bitter sermon, and in the name of the whole church, the law of Feoffees for the purchase of impropriations. 'This sermon,' says his biographer, Vernon, 'he 'delivered to his endeared friend, Mr. Noye, (Attorney-'General,) who undertook their suppression in the King's 'name; and they were accordingly suppressed, in a judicial 'way of proceeding, in the Exchequer Chamber:' a measure which, contrary to law, threw nearly all presentations at once into the hands of the bishops and the council.†

---
* Clarendon—Life. † Vernon's Life of Heylin.

In this conflict between the high and low Church of England, Popery, which was not tolerated by law, yet throve by connivance. Though its professors were not sheltered by a legal indemnity, yet the privileges which were secured to the Queen's household by treaty, and the countenance which, in consequence, the English Roman Catholics did not fail to share, inspired them with confidence to look for better times. Meanwhile, they were abetted by the King himself, not, as it appeared, so much from a spirit of favour towards them, as from the wish to strengthen a party who, in common with him, saw their interest in further discountenancing the Puritans.

With the dissolution of Convocation (and, even before the dissolution of it, on the defeat of its assumed power to collect revenue), ceased the importance of Dr. Heylin. In later times, indeed, charges were preferred against him in the Long Parliament, as a public delinquent. Such an intimation, at such a crisis, did not pass unheeded by the approved servant of Laud. Warned by the storm which was gathering round his master, but uninspired by the example of his master's courage, Heylin fled;* and thenceforward throughout the troubles, was only known as the conductor and publisher of the 'Mercurius Aulicus,' at the head quarters of the King's army. He died, after the Restoration, Sub-dean of Westminster.

It was not, however, in the ambition and corruption of the clergy alone that the pretensions of prerogative sought support. The administration of civil justice was corrupted at its source, by the removal of such judges and petty magistrates as refused to decide, contrary to their oaths of office, against persons disobeying the illegal requisitions of the several boards. Some country gentlemen who were the most obnoxious to the Government (but in much greater numbers, those who were the most devoted to it) were named to serve as sheriffs;† the former in order to disqualify them from Parliament, or to harass them with ruinous fines; the latter to make them instruments of extortion against others who were thus placed under their jurisdiction. Barristers were checked, and solicitors threatened and sometimes punished, for fidelity to their clients. Orders were issued from the Council Board, interfering with the settlement of

* Evelyn's Memoirs.   † May.

private property; and, in all suits of the Crown, undue practices prevailed for obtaining verdicts.* The grossest venality was countenanced in all the departments of the law; promotion publicly sold, and the buyers repaid by authorised extortion from suitors; and above all other courts, those of Star Chamber and High Commission were distinguished for their power, and for the unscrupulous manner in which they exercised it.

The situation and prospects of the country were now, therefore, becoming daily more portentous.† The distaste to Parliaments in which the King had been so fatally encouraged by all who had access to his person, was about this time expressed in that often-quoted letter of his to the Lord Deputy Wentworth.‡ Luxury, impiety, and excess, prevailed amongst the higher orders; and the pompous ceremonial and fiery intolerance of the clergy opposed but a feeble barrier, if any, to their increase. The sober minded, and of these the far greater proportion amongst the yeomanry and the country gentry, by habit and example endeavoured to stem the torrent which threatened alike the morals and the freedom of their country. Even those among them who were indolent or unskilful to watch the advances of prerogative still clove with reverence to the reviled customs and scruples of their simple life, and sadly, but irresolutely, saw all the ties loosening which bind a free and reflecting people to a government of law. Nor did the crisis they deprecated appear distant. Many foresaw that slavery must either be fixed upon themselves and their posterity, or shaken off by an effort such as no good man could but dread and deplore. Deprived of all prospect of relief from Parliament, forbidden by proclamation, forbidden from the bench, the pulpit, and the throne, to speak of asserting their ancient privileges in a parliamentary way, they looked forward to the alternative with affliction and dismay; whilst

---

* Appendix.—Commons Remonstrance.—Parl. Hist.
† May.
‡ 'For the first,' (the not continuing the Parliament of Ireland,) 'my 'reasons are grounded upon my experience of them here. They are of the 'nature of cats; they ever grow curst with age; so that, if you will have 'good of them, put them off handsomely when they come to any age; for 'young ones are ever more tractable. And, in earnest, you will find that 'nothing can more conduce to the beginning of the new than the well 'ending of the former Parliament. Wherefore, now that we are well, let 'us content ourselves therewith.'—Strafford's Letters.

the manners of a great part were so corrupt, that, unable to bear patiently the pressure of mis-government, they were ill-prepared to remonstrate with dignity.*

Although to Hampden's shrewd and cautious mind, deeply pondering these melancholy signs, the time seemed distant at which he might stir himself with effect, still he continued to bend all his views, studies, and pursuits, to that end. The passage in his favourite author, Davila, describing the retirement to which for a while the virtuous Coligny withdrew himself in Chatillon, and from which he saw the approaches of that civil war which he could not prevent, and in which his duty to his religion and his country pointed out to him a forward station, affords a striking parallel to the position of Hampden at this juncture of his life.†

These painful prognostics of public calamity were embittered by the severe wound which the death of his first wife had inflicted on his domestic happiness. She lies buried in the chancel of Great Hampden Church, where an epitaph on a plain black stone records her merits, and her

---

* Whitelock.—Sir Philip Warwick.—Mrs. Hutchinson.—Clarendon.

† 'L' Ammiraglio, con la solita sagacità, quasi che volesse riserbarsi 'neutrale, per poter in ogni caso tanto maggiormente giovare al suo partito, 'retiratosi a casa sua nella terra di Ciatiglione, fingeva d'attendere al 'commodo della vita privata, senza pensiero alcuno delle cose publiche 'appartenenti al governo; il che non tanto faceva per potere occultamente 'favorire, con i consigli, e con l' opera, l' impresa commune; quanto che, 'stimando la troppo temeraria, e troppo pericolosa, dubitava di travaglioso 'incontro, ed' infelice fin.'—Davila, Guerre Civ., lib. i.

From this retirement when Coligny came forth, it was, like Hampden, to further measures for religious liberty. Indeed there is a very marked coincidence between some of the principal circumstances which Davila enumerates as the causes of the civil war in France, and those that afterwards led to the scenes in England in which Hampden bore so large a part. The court of France, like that of England, was ill enough advised in its persecution of sectarians to confound the love of liberty with an imputed aversion to the doctrines of the established Church, and in its proclamations, most unwisely used the terms 'Huguenot' and 'Royalist,' to express the two great conflicting parties in the state. In the French struggle, as in the Episcopal war of Scotland, it was the bishops who began the contest; and the Huguenots asked assistance, on the stipulations of a treaty, from Elizabeth, as the Scots were afterwards fain to do from France. 'Ma,' says Davila of the Huguenot preachers, and the words might be well applied to the preachers of the Covenant, 'i predicanti, che in tutte le 'deliberationi ottenevano grandissima autorità, ed erano a guisa d' oracoli 'venerati, allegavano non doversi tener conto di queste cose terrene, ove si 'tratta della dottrina celeste, e della propagatione della parola di Dio, e 'però convenirsi vilipendere ogn' altra consideratione, pur che fosse 'protetta la religione, e confermata la libertà della Fede.'—Davila, lib. iii.

husband's affectionate regrets.* She left him three sons, John, Richard, and William; and six daughters. Of these, Elizabeth, the eldest, was married soon after to Richard Knightley, of Fawsley Court, in Northamptonshire, the son of an eager and distinguished fellow-labourer with Hampden in the cause of liberty. The second, Anne, was married to Sir Robert Pye, of Farringdon, in Berkshire. Besides these alliances, thus formed, Hampden had other connexions of kindred with persons prominent in the country party. Edmund Waller was, by his mother's side, Hampden's first cousin, and Oliver Cromwell was related to him in the same degree. Thus connected with families of influence in his own and neighbouring counties, he diligently improved his other resources. His mind richly stored with all the materials which are lent in aid by the examples of other times, his genius never more active than when taking counsel with itself in retirement, and his spirit never more resolved than when fitting on the armour which his wisdom had prepared, he awaited the time at which the public indignation, already aroused, might gain a strength and constancy befitting the struggle whose approaches he foresaw.

Meanwhile Charles's policy, as weak and inglorious abroad as at home it was violent and rapacious, neglected all the opportunities which offered themselves, unsought, for forming alliances the most important to England. Peace being con-

---

* TO THE ETERNALL MEMORY
OF THE TRUELY VIRTUOUS AND PIOUS
ELIZABETH HAMPDEN,
WIFE OF JOHN HAMPDEN, OF GREAT HAMPDEN, ESQUIRE.
SOLE DAUGHTER AND HEIRE OF EDMUND SYMEON
OF PYRTON, IN THE COUNTY OF OXON, ESQUIRE.
THE TENDER MOTHER OF A HAPPY OFFSPRING
IN 9 HOPEFULL CHILDREN.

In her pilgrimage,
The staie and comfort of her neighbours,
The love and glory of a well-ordered family,
The delight and happines of tender parents—
But a crown of Blessings to a husband.
In a wife, to all an eternall paterne of goodnes
And cause of love, while she was.
In her dissolution
A losse invaluable to each,
Yet herselfe blest, and they fully recompenced
In her translation, from a Tabernacle of Claye
And Fellowship with Mortalls, to a celestiall Mansion
And communion with a Deity.

20 DAY OF AUGUST 1634.
JOHN HAMPDEN, HER SORROWFULL HUSBAND,
IN PERPETUALL TESTIMONY OF HIS CONIUGAL LOUE,
HATH DEDICATED THIS MONUMENT.

cluded with the two crowns of France and Spain, on terms by which England was foiled in both the great objects which had led her into the war, the favourable occasion was lost, which the successes of Gustavus Adolphus and the consequent embarrassments of the Austrian empire had afforded, for assisting the Protestant cause in Germany, and for securing the restoration of Charles Lewis, the young Elector;—an object which Charles had always described as being dear to his heart. The English Court, though triumphant over the laws and liberties of the country, had little influence or reputation with foreign states. Our commerce was clogged with tributes on the high seas, and monopolies at home; and the British channel was vexed with the depredations of the corsairs of Tunis and Algiers. A dispute also had arisen with the Dutch, concerning the right of fishery, in which the talents of Selden and Grotius were opposed to each other upon the question of the dominion or freedom of the seas. But the reasonings of the British jurist remained unsupported by any show of power on the part of his country; and thus the 'Mare Clausum' was open to the unmolested trade of every state but that one which claimed the undivided empire of the maritime world.

Every proof, however, of its helplessness abroad was used by the English Government as a pretext for some new enterprize at home against law and public right. The want of money to support the Dutch controversy by force was urged as the motive of a fresh attempt to levy it without authority of Parliament.* The sale of knighthoods and of other public honours ('the envy and reproach of which,' according to Lord Clarendon, 'came to the King, the profit to other men,') had already reached its utmost limits; and the duties imposed upon merchandise, in many cases amounted to prohibition; but, in many more, were evaded without difficulty or disguise. At length, by the advice of the Attorney-General Noy,† and of

---

* Clarendon—Hist. Reb.—May—Parl. Hist.

† Lloyd, in his State Worthies, gives a character of Noy which is very remarkable for this singular contradiction; the first sentence praises him for honesty, and the next but one describes him, in very caustic terms, as having changed the principles of his public conduct for advancement at court. 'William Noy was a man passing humourous, but very honest— 'clownish, but knowing; a most indefatigable plodder and searcher of ' ancient records; verifying his anagram—I moyl in law. He was for ' many years the stoutest champion for the subjects' liberty, until King

Chief Justice Finch, ('the one,' says Lord Clarendon, 'knowing 'nothing of, nor caring for, the Court, the other knowing, or 'caring for, nothing else,') a writ was issued, October 20, 1634, addressed to the sheriffs of the city of London, requiring a supply of ships duly manned and otherwise equipped, under pretence of providing for the safety of the kingdom, and for guarding the dominion of the seas.

This was the impost of the ship-money; 'A word,' says Lord Clarendon, 'of a lasting sound in the memory of this 'kingdom;' a project which, in its progress, made the divisions between the King and Parliament irreparable, and, in its consequences, led to the misery of eleven years of almost uninterrupted civil war.* To the project of the ship-money may be justly traced, as to the proximate and special cause, the dispute which, directing the whole enmity of the Court against the most able and resolute and popular person in the country, inflamed a spirit fierce and powerful enough in the end, for the entire overthrow of this ancient and mighty monarchy.

There are certain passages at which the mind naturally pauses, as at landmarks and resting places, in its progress through the history of mankind, which seem as though they had been designed to establish some great axiom in morals and in government. These are strongly marked in the English history. The attempts of King John to load the country with new feudal exactions, to invade the rights of property in general, and to surrender the independence of the Crown to the papal see, — united, for the first time, in one bond of interest, nobility, clergy, and commonalty; and produced the Great Charter. Thus, also, the abuses, corruptions, and extortions of the popes, Julius II. and Leo X., forced forward our separation from the Church of Rome. Thus, also, in more modern times, it was the senseless bigotry of James II. which, (not content with re-establishing popery, but aiming at absolute tyranny also,) by the very act of attempting at one encounter the overthrow of religion and freedom, confirmed both, and caused it to be first declared by Act of Parliament, that the

'Charles entertained him to be his attorney. No sooner did the King 'show him the line of advancement, but quitting his former inclinations, 'he wheeled about to the prerogative, and made amends with his future 'service for all his former disobligements.'

* From the first Episcopal War in Scotland, in 1640, to the 'crowning victory' of Oliver at Worcester.

sovereign power is held on conditions which may be regulated and enforced by the estates of the realm.

All these revolutions have been successful and permanent, because produced, not by a mere appeal to abstract principles or speculations, but by the pressure of practical and weighty grievances. Nor can we fail to recognise, in the event upon which we are now entering, one of the four great passages in our history, out of which has gradually arisen and been compacted a system of liberty which we may hope will endure, without further struggle, through every succeeding age. The first ship-money writ may be considered as the foundation, though laid by no friendly hand, on which was afterwards to be reared the stoutest buttress of our English constitution, the entire and undisputed control of Parliament over the supplies.

PART THE FOURTH.

FROM 1635 TO 1640.

Ship-Money—The Levy extended to Inland Places—Motives lately imputed to Hampden for his Opposition to it. The Grounds of that Imputation examined—Hampden, and Thirty other Freeholders of the Parish of Great Kimble, in Buckinghamshire, refuse Payment—Sir Peter Temple, the High Sheriff, summoned to answer for Arrears—Disconsolate Letter from him to his Mother—Proceedings against Hampden—Judges declare for the Crown—General Discontent of the Country—Emigration of Puritans—Prohibited—Hampden and others detained—Independents and Presbyterians begin to separate—Insurrection in Scotland, and First Episcopal War—Treaty of Berwick—Short Parliament summoned—Hampden quits, for the last time, his Retirement in Buckinghamshire.

No sooner was the ship-money project made known than it met with a firm and open opposition. Although it had very probably been calculated by the authors of that measure that a certain feeling of national vanity on the part of the country generally, and even of remote interest on the part of the merchants, whose cargoes were in constant danger of capture at sea, might command a ready consent to the declared purpose of the contribution, still it encountered, even at the outset, much murmuring, and some active resistance. For, after the common council of London had in vain pleaded by address their ancient privileges, payment was refused (on the Act De Tallagio Non Concedendo, and other public statutes,) by Richard Chambers, a merchant who had before been honourably distinguished for his courage and his sufferings. At first the requisition, although extended beyond the city of London, was limited to the maritime towns, and thus attempted to be justified upon the alleged precedent of that made by Queen Elizabeth at the period of the Spanish Armada, when her appeal to her people had been promptly and liberally answered.

At that time every seaport had supplied armed vessels, one or more, each; and the citizens of London had furnished thirty, although only fifteen were required of them; and between forty and fifty had been fitted out by the voluntary subscriptions of the nobility and gentry throughout the kingdom.

A fleet, however, of sixty ships of war being at length collected, upon the strength of contributions paid in principally by the small towns along the coast, for the purpose of securing the trade in the narrow seas, Charles was advised to disregard the tokens of increasing discontent, and to urge still further this ill-omened design. It was now determined to extend the tax to inland places, which, notwithstanding the appearance of an option to contribute, either in money or in ships properly manned and victualled for six months, would, from their situation, be under the necessity of making their contribution in money, applicable by the King to general objects of revenue. In the following year, therefore (1636), the charge was laid, by order of Council, generally on all counties, cities, and corporate towns; and all sheriffs were required, in case of refusal or delay, to proceed by distress. To clothe this process with a better appearance of formality, the judges were directed by the Lord Keeper Coventry, in the Star Chamber, at the close of Midsummer Term,* to promote it throughout their circuits, by laying it down as law in their charges, and by every other means of persuasion.† But, though some of that body acted with great zeal and alacrity in this particular, their success was small. Letters of instruction were addressed from the Council Board to the several sheriffs, exhorting them to proceed with the greatest precision and dispatch, and with the strictest regard to equality in the levy. With this intent, schedules were sent to each sheriff, containing the list of all counties, cities, and corporate towns, together with the proportions in which each was rated, to the end that each district and community might be made aware that the contribution was enforced impartially. These schedules present a view of the comparative wealth and importance of these places, which is remarkable for the contrast it affords with their condition in the present times. It will appear that the towns of Lancaster, Liverpool, and Preston, which (taken with Manchester) now contain more than half the commercial and

---

* Rushworth.   † Strafford's Letters.

manufacturing capital of our country,* were then rated at an amount below that which was charged on several of the smallest of those western boroughs, whose names have in later times been barely known beyond the limits of their county, but as places furnishing representatives to the British empire. It seems as if the general influence of these small places, and perhaps their privileges of election also, had arisen partly from their proximity to the Royal stannaries; but partly too, and principally, from their having been, for ages, the places of refuge from the elements and from the enemy, for the trade with Spain and the West Indies in its passage up channel. It is probable that the privileges enjoyed by the Cinque Ports, and by the other boroughs near the French coast, were granted on account of the importance which those places derived from their nearness to the possessions anciently held in fee by the Crown in Normandy and Aquitaine.†

It is a slight and imperfect view of this impost to consider it only as one levied without and against the consent of Parliament, and, therefore, against law. It proclaimed a principle of confiscation, and established a machinery, for the purpose of giving effect to it, which was quite incompatible with all the rights of property. This principle had been hinted at, and approached by, the Crown on many former occasions, and in divers ways, by benevolences, and under other names; but never till now had it been introduced into any regular system of taxation. Yet, odious as the assessment was throughout the country, and imperfectly collected even from the beginning, it early became a productive means of revenue. In the first year, upwards of £200,000, clear of all charges of collection, were paid into the treasury on the ship-money account.‡

It was against this project that, in the spring of 1636, Hampden resolved to make a decisive stand. He accordingly took counsel with Bulstrode Whitelocke, Oliver St. John, Holborne, and others of his immediate friends, concerning the means of trying the issue at law.§ The writ, which

---

* In 1827 the number of ships unloading at the port of Liverpool exceeded, by three or four, that of the merchant ships that entered the Thames during the same year.

† For a copy of one of these schedules, addressed to Sir Peter Temple, and among his papers at Stowe, and differing a little from that in Rushworth, see Appendix C.

‡ Whitelocke—Rushworth. § Whitelocke.

was directed in the autumn of 1635 to Sir Peter Temple of Stowe, then High Sheriff of Buckinghamshire, required that county to supply a ship of war of 450 tons burthen, and 150 men, fitted out with cordage, munition, and other necessaries, before the first of the then ensuing March, and from that time, to provide mariners' wages and provisions for twenty-six weeks; or, in lieu thereof, a sum of £4500, to be levied upon the inhabitants, and returned to the Treasurer of the Navy for the King's use.* As might have been expected from a county which, by reason of its central position and the high public spirit which prevailed amongst its gentry, was well disposed to be forward in resisting so arbitrary a demand, the return proved most unsatisfactory to the Court. The defaulters were numerous; and some stated boldly, publicly, and peremptorily, the ground of their refusal. But, no sooner was the name of Hampden seen among this number, than, as if by one common desire that the combat should be decided in the person of a single champion, the eyes of the court and of the people were alike turned on him. He stood the high and forward mark against whom the concen-

* To all persons recollecting that, of all places in England, the centre of Buckinghamshire is the most nearly equi-distant from the four seas which surround the island, but especially to such persons as are locally acquainted with the parishes mentioned in the writ, and with the habits of the people, so little cognizant of maritime affairs, the requisition tells the story of its own preposterous injustice rather whimsically. It runs thus:—'To the 'sheriff of our county of Bucks, the bailiff and burgesses of the 'borough and parish of Buckingham, the mayor, bailiff, and burgesses of 'Chipping Wiccombe, and the good men in the said boroughs, parishes, 'and their members; and in the towns of Agmondesham, Wendover, and 'Great Marlow, and in all other boroughs, villages, hamlets, and other 'places in the s^d county of Bucks, greeting:—Because we are given to 'understand that certain thieves, pirates, and sea robbers, as well Turks as 'others, confederated together, wickedly take away and despoil the ships, 'goods, and merchandizes, &c. . . . We firmly enjoin you, as you love 'us and our honour, as also under the forfeiture of all things you can 'possibly forfeit to us, that you cause to be fitted out one ship of war, of 'the burden of 450 tons, with men, as well skilful officers, as able and 'experienced mariners, a hundred and fourscore at least; as also with a 'sufficient quantity of cannon, muskets, gunpowder, pikes, and spears, and 'other arms necessary for war, with double tackling, &c. &c. . . . And 'that you cause the same to be brought into the port of Portsmouth before 'the s^d 1st day of March, so that they may be there that day at furthest; 'thence to proceed with our ships, &c. . . . And moreover to assess 'every man in the aforesaid towns, and in the members thereof, &c. . . . 'not having the ship aforesaid, or any part thereof, or not serving in the 'same, to contribute to the expenses about the provision of the necessary 'premises, &c. . . . every one of them according to their estate, and 'goods, or employment,' &c. &c.

trated wrath of all the penalties was to be directed. The condition of his fortune, and the small amount of the sum in which he was assessed, sufficiently established his case as the best for determining the principle of a demand, important to the court, not only as a fruitful source of revenue, but as supplying a precedent entirely decisive against the popular cause. Upon a rate, therefore, of thirty-one shillings and sixpence, he resolutely proceeded to rest for himself, for his country, and for posterity, this great and signal act of resistance to arbitrary taxation.

And here it becomes necessary again, in a few words, to take notice (as a sample of the imperfect evidence on which historical impressions are sometimes received) of another passage in Mr. D'Israeli's 'Commentaries on the Life of 'Charles the First.' ' I have been informed,' says that gentleman (speaking of the ship-money), ' of papers, in the ' possession of a family of the highest respectability, which ' will show that Hampden had long lived in a state of civil ' warfare with his neighbour, the sheriff of the county. They ' mutually harassed each other. It is probable that these ' papers may relate to quarrels about levying the sixpence in ' the pound on Hampden's estate, for which he was assessed. ' It is from the jealousy of Truth that we are anxious to ' learn whether the sixpence was refused out of pique to his ' old enemy and neighbour, the sheriff, or from the purest, ' unmixed patriotism.'* Disputes concerning the private motives which may influence the public acts of men are difficult to undertake, and hazardous to decide upon; and it is a bold inquest to institute, even ' from the jealousy of ' Truth.' We are invited, however, to try whether Hampden be justly chargeable with the deep guilt of having been moved by a base private pique (concerning an assessment of sixpence in the pound, as Mr. D'Israeli incorrectly states) to a resistance in which, according to the same writer, ' he afterwards ' drew his sword to shed the blood of half the nation!' It is not often that to imputations so insinuated a negative can be proved; but in this case it may. Sir Peter Temple was the sheriff whose official act it was to enforce this ill-founded demand, and to whom, in this matter, Hampden was opposed, and on whose writ the issue was tried. His papers and cor-

---

* Commentaries on the Life and Reign of Charles the First, vol. ii. p. 290, *et seq.*

respondence are at Stowe, and I have carefully examined them. There is not, in that collection, the shadow of evidence of any private pique or quarrel; nor does the sheriff, nor do those before whom the case came to trial, nor does Lord Clarendon, or any other writer equally unfavourably disposed towards Hampden, impute or appear to suspect any such motive. If it be to the papers of any other sheriff than Sir Peter Temple that Mr. D'Israeli alludes, he has been deceived as to the person with whom that great question was contested by Hampden. It may also in this place be observed that, where the same writer represents Hampden at a subsequent period of his life as 'to be viewed at the head of his Buckinghamshire ' men, inciting thousands to present petitions,'* he says that for which he adduces no authority. There is no ground for asserting that Hampden 'incited' the famous petitions from Buckinghamshire to the King and to both Houses; and there is this reason, at least, for concluding that he was not at the head of the petitioners, that he was then, and had been ever since the occurrence which occasioned those petitions, concealed in the city of London, and guarded by the citizens against the search made for him and for the other four members by Charles.

On the 25th of January, 1635-6, new sheriffs having been in the interval appointed, a writ was issued, directed 'To Sir ' Peter Temple, baronet, late High Sheriff, and Heneage ' Proby, Esq., now appointed High Sheriff for the county of

---

* Commentaries on the Life and Reign of Charles the First, vol. ii. p. 292. But Mr. D'Israeli, as we have already seen, is not always careful in his references. At the close of the same passage, he says of Pym, 'one 'would have wished that the man whose character has incurred the taint 'of a suspicion of having taken a heavy bribe from a French minister, had 'been graced with purer hands.' He says, in a note, 'I write this down 'from recollection, and cannot immediately recover my authority.' It might be superfluous to offer any remarks on the propriety of making such a charge as that of corruption on authority which he who makes it 'cannot 'immediately recover.' The authority on the recollection of which it is made, (for there is no other,) is Lord Clarendon's, who thus states the grounds of the imputation. 'And some said boldly, and (*an obscure person 'or two*) have since affirmed it, as upon their knowledge, that Mr. Pym 'received five thousand pounds from that French minister to hinder that 'supply to Spain.' The words inserted in Italics, and which bear so importantly on the credibility of the charge, had been suppressed by the committee who first published Lord Clarendon's History, but were restored from the manuscript, in the ungarbled edition which, much to the credit of the University of Oxford, was published by that body in 1826.

' Bucks,'* directing the one to deliver, and the other to receive, the original warrant, as well as all accompts and returns concerning the levy of the former year. This return was accordingly made by the assessors of the different parishes; and, among others where payment had been delayed, by those of the parish of Great Kimble, a village at the foot of the Chiltern Hills, round which the principal property of John Hampden lay, and in the immediate neighbourhood of his house. The return † contains the names of those who, with him, had tendered their refusal to the constables and assessors, together with an account of the sums charged upon each person. Among the names of the protestors it is to be observed that the constables and assessors have the courage to return their own; and, at the head of the list, stands that of John Hampden, as a passport for the rest to an honourable memory, so long as the love of liberty shall retain a place in the hearts of the British nation.

A protest thus made by a private gentleman, although backed by the concurrent conduct of the Lord Say and Sele, and some others of lesser note, was not likely to be an effectual warning to a temper like Charles's, or to deter him from pursuing an enterprise so long and so maturely arranged. By a warrant, therefore, from Hampton Court (dated June 24, and signed by Laud, Coventry, Juxon, Manchester, Wentworth, Vane, Cottington, and Windebank), the late High Sheriff was summoned to answer for default of arrears; and it appears that, he being unable, from ill health, to give his personal attendance on the appointed day, such were the jealousy and rage of the Court, that he was kept for a considerable time in custody of a messenger, at his own house at Stowe. A letter, written by Sir Peter to his mother, while he was suffering under this grievance, and expecting worse, gives a lively picture of his disconsolate condition, and of the relentless rigour with which the Government proceeded against its own helpless and unoffending officer.

'DEARE MOTHER,—In haste I write to you. I, hauinge my
'handes full, cannot write to you with my owne handes, I hauinge
'byne latelye ill at London, and takeing physicke. Yet muste I

---

* See Appendix D.
† The original of this interesting document was preserved among the papers of Sir Peter Temple at Stowe.

'leaue the means of my health to doe the Kinge seruice. I was sente
'for on the 30th of June, by a messenger, to attend the Kinge on
'Sundaye the 3d of July, about the shippe-moneye; wherein I am
'blamed for the Sherriffe's actions that nowe is, and am compelled
'wth a messenger, nowe wayteing on me, with all the distresses and
'imprisoneings that maye be imposed on the countrye. But the
'Sherriffe muste answere what is done by me in the future tyme.
'I am to attende the Kinge at Theobaldes, on the 17th daye of
'July, to giue an accompte to him what I haue done in the seruice,
'and as he likes my proceedinges, I am to continue in the messenger's
'hande, or be releassed, or worsse. My lyfe is nothing but toyle,
'and hath byne for many yeares, to the Commonwealth, and nowe
'to the Kinge. The change is somethinge amended for the pressent,
'but yet released of neither. Not soe much tyme as to doe my
'dutye to my deere parentes, nor to sende to them. Yett I hoped
'that they wolde haue sente for a bucke or what Stowe wolde
'afforde, before thys tyme. But seeinge they will not, I will spare
'myselfe soe much tyme as to presente nowe unto them one by thys
'bearer.

'Although I am debarred from father, mother, wife, and chilldren,
'and state,—though some of them farre absente,—wyth thys I
'presente my dutye, wyth these unhappye lynes, and remayne

'Yo^r Sonne, that loues and honoures
'my father and you, PETER TEMPLE.

'STOWE, *thys 8th of July*, 1636.

'To his deere mother, the Lady Hester Temple, at Dorsett, theis
'pressente.'

By advice of Chief Justice Finch, the King now required
the opinion of the twelve judges. The queries were propounded in a form not unusual with those who, in putting
their case, desire only to strengthen their own preconceived
opinions or determinations with the sanction of a learned
authority. There is a mode in which Kings may so propose
their questions to lawyers as clearly to show what is the
answer that will best meet the Royal purpose. It was
demanded, 'Whether, when the general safety was concerned,
'and the whole state in danger, he might not, by writ under
'the great seal, legally compel his subjects to furnish as large
'a number of ships for its defence, and for as long a period,
'as he might think necessary; and whether, in such a case,
'he were not the sole judge of the danger, as well as of the

'means of preventing it?'* Thus assuming not only this vast prerogative, but also the whole discretionary power of declaring its limits, and of determining the occasions on which it should have the force of law;—a compendious definition of purely arbitrary power.

After much solicitation, and not without certain hopes of preferment held out to some, and threats to others, an answer was obtained, February 14, 1636-7, in favour of these propositions in every particular.† But, although this opinion was signed by all the judges, they were not unanimous in their decision. Croke and Hutton, who had strongly opposed it in a long and solemn argument, had the weakness to be at last prevailed upon to sign it, as the opinion of the majority; an assurance being given by their brethren that they should not be held bounden thereby in giving judgment, whenever such a question might be tried by them in Court.‡ A plain inconsistency. On whatever principle they were bound to subscribe to the opinion of the majority as law, they would in like manner have been bound to lay it down as law upon trial also. But, notwithstanding the assurance which had been given them, the opinion was instantly enrolled in all the courts of Westminster Hall as an unanimous one, and directed to be so published throughout the realm.

Whilst this proceeding was distasteful to many, both lawyers and others, as being new in principle and of evil tendency in respect of precedent, it was loudly applauded by the Court party, who cared not to dissemble their joy. 'It is 'plain indeed,' said Lord Wentworth, 'that the judges, 'declaring the lawfulness of the assignment for the shipping, 'is the greatest service that profession hath done the Crown 'in my time. But, unless his Majesty hath the like power 'declared to raise a land army upon the same exigent of state, 'the Crown seems to me to stand but upon one leg at home, 'and to be considerable but by halves to foreign princes 'abroad.'§ And, again, after some pregnant advice respecting the foreign policy, he adds, 'and hereby also insensibly gain a 'precedent, and settle an authority and right in the Crown to 'levies of that nature; which thread draws after it many huge 'and great advantages, more proper to be thought on at some 'other seasons than now.'

* Rushworth.   † Whitelocke.
‡ Rushworth.   § Strafford's Letters.

But, although this impure and collusive decision of the judges was thus regarded with complacency by Wentworth, and hailed by him as the forerunner of further 'huge and 'great advantages,' it increased the uneasiness of the country. The exaction of the ship-money, after this declaration of its legality, was even more generally and systematically opposed than before.* With whatever joy the courtiers received this 'rescue,' as they termed it, of the prerogative royal, and re-establishment of the power and glory of the Crown, the indignation of the country party was not slow in manifesting what was, on their side, felt respecting the part taken by the lawyers in efforts so clearly tending to bring the Monarchy itself into weakness and jeopardy. A sovereign more calmly observant of the course of the times than Charles was, would sooner have taken warning of the great danger of tainting the administration of justice, and thus diminishing the honour and reverence of the bench. For, as a corrupt judicature is the most formidable engine of arbitrary sovereignty, so long as the judicial authority is still owned and obeyed through the realm, fearful indeed, when its moral influence has been thoroughly impaired, becomes the condition of the sovereign through whose wicked and short-sighted policy it was corrupted.

No sooner was this decision recorded than directions were given to the crown lawyers to proceed against Hampden as the principal defaulter. He had cast himself behind the defences of the law. The lines were still entire; the watch-towers and ramparts stood, but dismantled; and the garrison, for the most part, were corrupted or dismayed. A writ of Certiorari was, on the 9th of March, directed from Chancery to Sir Heneage Proby; and, on the 5th of May, a writ of Mittimus was sent into the Court of Exchequer, commanding that proceedings should be commenced there. In consequence, on the 20th of the same month, a writ of Scire Facias was awarded against Hampden, requiring him to show cause why the sum assessed upon him by the late sheriff of Bucks should not be satisfied; and further, enjoining him to abide the order of the court. The case selected for trial was an assessment of twenty shillings, charged upon him in respect of his lands in the parish of Stoke Mandeville, adjoining to Great Kimble. To this he appeared in Trinity Term, and prayed oyer of the

---

* Clarendon—Hist. Reb.

original writ, and of each subsequent proceeding. On their being read to him, he demurred generally in law, complaining that, by such proceedings, he had been unjustly and grievously disquieted, and that the matters contained in the divers writs and returns were not sufficient to legally oblige his complying with them, or his accounting in any other way for his refusal to do so. The Attorney-General having joined issue on the demurrer, the record was made up, and the barons, adjourning the argument to the Exchequer Chamber, desired the assistance and judgment of the whole bench.

The point of law was argued in Michaelmas Term, from the 6th of November to the 18th of December;* on the part of Hampden, by Oliver St. John and Robert Holbourne; and, for the Crown, by the Attorney-General, Sir John Bankes, of Corfe Castle, and the Solicitor, Sir Edward Littleton.† The crown lawyers insisted on precedents of ancient writs, from the Saxon times downwards, which required ships for the defence of the nation, sometimes at the charge of a county, sometimes of a port only. They cited precedents from the rolls of the early Parliaments of Edward I. and Richard II. to show that the Commons had acknowledged the right in the King not only to impress men, but to levy money in aid ‘as ‘belonging to the wars.’ They put the argument, ‘ad ‘absurdum,’ thus : ‘Is the King to direct the war, and yet ‘shall he have neither men nor money without asking his ‘subjects’ leave ?’ They argued the fairness and equality of the levy, and the wealth and station of Mr. Hampden, contrasting it with the insignificant amount of the sum charged upon him in respect of each of his estates. ‘If he be too ‘highly assessed,’ it was urged, ‘he might call the sheriff in ‘question. But the sheriff of Bucks is rather to be fined for ‘setting him at so low a rate as twenty shillings. We know ‘what house Mr. Hampden is of, and his estate too. For ‘anything I know, it might as well be twenty pounds. But, ‘to the legal part, some one must be trusted with it, and who ‘should be but the sheriff ? and the parties not without ‘remedy, if over-rated.’‡ These, with accumulated precedents

---

* Rushworth.
† St. John and Bankes each took three days, and Holbourne four, for his argument. Their speeches alone occupy one hundred and seventeen pages in Rushworth. Important as they are, I do a better part by the reader in referring to them than I should by quoting them at length.
‡ State Trials.

of taillage, benevolences, and other such imposts, as well as of impressments of men, and ships too, by warrant, in cases of emergency, were the principal topics used in the case for the Crown; enforced always by strong appeals to the court on the necessity of giving the King free use of such means as might be necessary to vindicate the national honour, and protect the trade, at sea, and particularly when they were insulted by the pirates of the Barbary States, and menaced by the navies of other nations. St. John, on the other part, well justifying his already established reputation for learning and boldness, supported his argument with great weight of authorities; resting his case against the whole proceeding upon the fundamental principles of the constitution, upon the terms of the Great Charter, upon the statute de Tallagio, and upon the declaratory matter of the Petition of Right, so lately passed, and so stoutly contested in all its clauses, confirmatory of preceding acts. Holbourne followed, and argued on wider grounds of history, law, and civil policy. He rejected precedents of emergency in remote times as explanatory of statutes which had, in those extreme instances, been violated or set aside; and turned against the crown lawyers their cases of illegal practices of ancient memory, now urged to take away the force of Acts of Parliament. But, when he distinctly pointed towards the general principles of free government, and towards the danger of these violent acts of power to the Crown itself, he was, more than once, checked from the bench. At length, the judges prepared to deliver their opinions in court; and, to give the greater solemnity to their judgment, they argued the matter largely in the three succeeding Terms. Weston, Crawley, Berkeley, and Vernon, who gave judgment, two in a day, in Hilary Term, were unanimous in favour of the Crown. But when, in Easter Term, the matter was resumed, a great diversity of opinion arose. Trevor spoke for the legality of the writ, but Croke concluded as directly against it. According to Whitelocke, Croke was preparing, against his own conscience and conviction, to give judgment for the King. But he was reproached for his baseness by his wife. This noble lady cast the shield of her feminine virtue before the honour of her husband, to guard it from the assaults equally of interest and fear; and, with that moral bravery which is so often found the purest and brightest in her sex, she exhorted him to do his duty, at any risk to himself, to her, or to their children;—and she prevailed.

A few days after, when Judge Jones, treating the case somewhat doubtfully, decided for the King, but with the condition that no part of the money should go in aid of the privy purse, Hutton strenuously denied the validity of all claim on pretence of the prerogative; and, maintaining that the scire facias could not lie, advised that judgment should be given in all respects for Hampden.* The deliberate opposition thus made by two judges, whose expressed opinions from the first had never varied, was productive of a very great effect. The opposers of the ship-money everywhere took heart. It proceeded slowly and laboriously in the collection. The assessments were made with hesitation and reluctance, and the arrears were daily increasing. In Trinity Term, the two remaining judges gave sentence. Denham, absent on two certificates of ill health, declared, in writing, for Hampden; and the Chief Baron Davenport in his argument followed the same course. But the Chief Justices, Finch and Bramston, having on the 9th of June, concluded against him, the sentence of the majority was for the King. On the 11th, therefore, the Attorney-General moved that the decision should be entered and prayed judgment on the record the following day.†

While this conflict of opinion among the Judges left the result in doubt, the attention of the country was steadily at a gaze. The great principle at issue was never lost sight of, and, as the judgments proceeded in succession, the pervading sense of a common interest, which the court might not have been without hopes of wearying out by the great length and slow pace of the discussion, became more and more intense. Once declared, the award excited an equally general and deep disgust. The Lord Say, who had begun the same contest in Warwickshire, (where, under his influence, and that of the Lord Brook, the popular principles had spread almost as widely as they had in Buckinghamshire, under Hampden,) now attempted, but in vain, to procure a trial in his own case. 'By 'the choice of the King's counsel,' says Lord Clarendon, 'Hampden had brought his cause to be first heard and argued; 'and with that judgment it was intended that the whole right

---

* Rushworth.—Append. to Rushworth.—State Trials.—Whitelocke.—Clarendon—Hist. Reb. † Strafford's Letters.

'of the matter should be concluded, and all other cases over-
'ruled.'* The record already obtained on this memorable
occasion, (on which, says a court writer, 'Monarchy and
'Liberty were permitted to plead at the same bar,' †
had been much too valuable to the pretensions of the
King to be put to the hazard of a fresh and doubtful
issue. But the question could not be thus set at rest, nor the
strong excitement which it had occasioned subdued. It is
seldom the inclination of a multitude to support one man in
resisting a grievance which they have collectively been forced
or persuaded to endure. Nay more. There is sometimes in
our nature a sense of personal triumph, a very base one, which
is gratified by seeing others fail in an attempt to withstand that
to which we before have tamely submitted. Thus it is, that
the first enterprises of this sort are usually rather regarded
with jealousy than accompanied by any lively demonstrations
of countenance or applause; and this is a vice of which a
crafty government is seldom slow in availing itself to its own
advantage. But, on this occasion, the minds of men reasoned
more largely, and their hearts were influenced by a purer feeling. It was fortunate for freedom that, after all particular
precedent set up on the King's part had been shown ‡ to fail
him, his case was argued on general principles easy to be
weighed and understood, and upon lapsed notions of prerogative royal which a succession of numerous statutes, from
Henry the Third's time downwards, had been framed to cancel
and supersede.§ Every low and unworthy sentiment of
personal jealousy, every short-sighted calculation of more or
less personal grievance or advantage, gave place to a conviction that, together with the doctrines of which Hampden had
now become the champion, and by dint of those with which
Finch had so wantonly overlaid the case of the King, the
dearest rights of all were placed in jeopardy. This feeling, as
one which had been gravely adopted, and which had gradually
and deliberately advanced among the people, was not likely
to be lightly abandoned, or irresolutely pursued. Nor did
those persons with whose concurrence the first stand was
made, (after a successful resistance on the broader ground had
become no longer practicable,) fail to oppose and thwart the
measure in its details by all the means which exhortation,

* Hist. Reb.
‡ Clarendon—Hist. Reb.
† Royal Martyr.
§ Rushworth, App.

example, and the influence of character or station, could supply. St. John, although renowned for prodigious parts and industry among his own party in Parliament, had not risen to any extensive practice in Westminster Hall until after the fame of his argument in Hampden's case. This, however, gained him so much reputation, that he was afterwards engaged in all the different courts and causes in which the claims of the royal prerogative were contested.* Meanwhile, with the increasing disaffection towards the measures of the King and his advisers, did the conduct of Hampden daily advance in public admiration and honour. 'The eyes of all 'men,' according to Lord Clarendon, 'were fixed upon him as 'their Pater Patriæ, and the pilot who must steer the vessel 'through the tempests and rocks that threatened it.' With qualities of heart and mind well matched to do service and honour to each other, the modesty, discretion, and composure, with which, (always bearing onwards in his steady course,) he mastered in himself every allurement of personal vanity, are parts of his character more admirable even than the courage which all contemporary testimony agrees in so eminently ascribing to him. It has been well observed, that the highest praise which has been bestowed on Hampden is to be found in the acknowledgment of one of his most jealous enemies. Lord Clarendon, who had known him both as a colleague and as a competitor, and, in each position, had learned to respect his deportment, admits that he behaved himself with a temper and modesty such as marvellously to win the hearts of men, and to deprive his adversaries of all occasion, which they diligently sought, of impeaching the conduct, while they blamed the motive, of his opposition. Far different, however, was the spirit of the inveterate Wentworth. His zeal was overflowing against those who still stood for the principles and party which he had, without any assignable motive or excuse, but the basest, betrayed. 'Mr. Hampden,' says he in a letter to Archbishop Laud, 'is a great Brother;' (Puritan;) 'and 'the very genius of that nation of people leads them always 'to oppose, both civilly and ecclesiastically, all that ever 'Authority ordains for them. But, in good faith, were they 'rightly served, they should be whipped home into their right 'wits; and much beholden they should be to any that would 'thoroughly take pains with them in that sort.' Again, with

* Clarendon—Hist. Reb. Weekly Account, July 3—10, 1643.

the same soberness and propriety of metaphor, he says, 'In 'truth I still wish Mr. Hampden, and others to his likeness, 'were well whipped into their right senses. And, if the rod be 'so used that it smart not, I am the more sorry.'* Such is the language of one who well knew the person and the party of whom he spoke. For he once had shared deeply in their councils, and, 'whether' (as his friend and biographer Ratcliffe says of him) 'animated by patriotism, or led by a skilful 'ambition,' had also shared with them their sufferings and their fame, in resisting those very schemes of taxation of which he had now become an active and forward instrument. † The bitterness of such a man,—'odisse quos læserit,' (who, accomplished as he was, both in statesmanship and letters, illustrious for his abilities, his station, and afterwards for his misfortunes, yet felt that, in deserting his party, he was abandoning the dearest possession of his public life, his reputation for honesty,)— carries with it its moral to posterity, and, for the moral's sake, ought to be recorded. The verdict of many generations has been passed upon the memory of Hampden, and upon that of his reviler; and they must indeed be very sanguine enemies to the liberties of their country who can now hope to see that judgment reversed.

It was but a short time before this that those bloody scenes of human agony and mutilation, which formed a part of the ordinary punishment of the pillory, had been revived by Laud. It was in the summer of 1637 that the sentence, of which we have before spoken, was executed upon Burton and Bastwick, and renewed, with horrible circumstances of further cruelty, upon Prynne; and it was in the next winter that Lilburne also suffered the same punishment, under an order signed by Laud; the whipping being inflicted with a rigour which endangered his life. This was, in all probability, the very instance, because it had been the most recent, which prompted Wentworth's jest.

---

* Strafford's Letters.

† I know that Mr. Brodie believes that, in many of the early votes of the country party, the name of Sir Thomas Wentworth has been confounded with that of Mr. Thomas Wentworth, member for Oxford. But that Sir Thomas Wentworth was imprisoned for his opposition to the Court, that he joined in the impeachment of the Duke of Buckingham, in the protestations against illegal imposts, and moved one of the most important clauses in the Petition of Right, is certain, from the testimony of Ratcliffe, as well as of Rushworth and the Journals.

Again, the hopes of the country party almost died within them. Had it not been for a fresh act of cruel and unwise compulsion, which bereft the persecuted Puritans of the power of leaving to Charles, by their flight, an undisputed triumph over law and liberty, the whole struggle in this country would have been abandoned, at least by that generation, in despair. Many eminent persons were induced, by their sufferings, or by their fears, to sell their estates at a great loss, in order to seek a shelter, which, by its distance from home, promised at least security from the vindictive spirit of the government, and from the stormy threatenings of the times. The plantations of New England, held under royal patents granted by James, offered a place of refuge to such as might be driven by hatred of the great tyranny that reigned in their own country to look for peace and freedom among the wildernesses of another hemisphere. Such a retreat had been prepared there by the foresight of the Lord Say and the Lord Brook, by whose directions a little town, now the capital of the flourishing province of Connecticut, had been built, in 1635, under the name of Saybrook. They had from their boyhood, lived together as brothers, and the ties of their affection had been strengthened by a close and constant agreement in public life. To this wild and distant settlement they had determined to retreat, in failure of their efforts for justice and peace at home, and there they were jointly to become the founders of a patriarchal community. Of this new settlement liberty of conscience was to be the first law, and it was afterwards to be governed according to their darling scheme of a free commonwealth. Thither several persons of rank and fortune had already led the way.

The Crown had laid claim to the power of taxing, in whatever measure, and on whatever exigents of state, it should please to determine; and this had been confirmed by the ship-money judgment, which had given up to the discretion of the King the whole property of the country. All cases of libel against the Government, or any of the great officers of state, were taken out of the courts below, to be tried and punished by the offended parties themselves, in the Star Chamber; and, of the Puritans, or Precisians, as they now began to be called, those who withstood these powers were pursued by all manner of penalties, and those who were patient by mockery and insult no less intolerable. The spirit of emigration spread daily among the Puritans; the views of the greater number of that party were entirely directed to that object; thus leaving their leaders without any further hope to cherish, and, indeed, without any further duties to fulfil, in England. But even this refuge from a persecution which appeared irresistible, and from which there remained no other means of escape, was refused them.* This project, which would also have relieved the Government from the embarrassment of their presence, and of all their further plans, was defeated by an order of the King in council, dated April 6, 1638, by which all masters and owners of ships were restrained from setting forth any vessel with passengers for America, without special licence.†

The immediate effect of this monstrous edict is rendered remarkable by an event, which has thrown over the whole an air of strange fatality. Eight ships, with respectable emigrants on board, were, at this time, lying in the Thames, bound for the new colony. In one of these had actually embarked, for their voyage across the Atlantic, two no less considerable persons than John Hampden and his kinsman Oliver Cromwell: the latter then little distinguished, except for an opposition which he had conducted with great spirit and ability, in his native county of Huntingdon, against the project of the Bedford level; a work which, like all the other great schemes of improvement, had been converted into a monopoly which was to give new means of influence to the Crown.

But the Court was unwilling that its opponents should, anywhere, enjoy or communicate the systems of freedom which they sought, or should peaceably withdraw themselves, even at the hazard of the total confiscation of their estates at home, from a contest of whose success they despaired, and from a country which they deemed to be hopelessly enslaved. A special order was therefore issued that these vessels, by name, should be detained, and the provisions landed which had been shipped for the voyage.‡ Thus, in the alternative between flight and resistance, the Government, as it were, bound down these eminent men to an opposite condition to that which they had

---

* Rushworth.—Neale's Hist. of the Puritans.
† Bancroft, in his early persecution of the Puritans, under James, seeing that great numbers of them were emigrating to Virginia, obtained a proclamation enjoining them not to depart without the King's license.
‡ Neale's Hist. of Puritans.—Rushworth.—Dugdale's Troubles.

chosen for themselves. Pride, character, and obligation to party and to principle, pledged them, so long as they should inhabit the country of their birth, to pursue the course they had begun.—Hampden and Cromwell remained;—to act, probably with very different views, certainly in very different circumstances;—the one to be the first mover of resistance in arms against the power of the King, the other to finally defeat and ruin that power in the field, to overthrow the monarchy, and to bring the Sovereign, by whom he was now arbitrarily detained, to a public scaffold.*

Mr. Hume avers that Hampden, and the rest, were going to New England for the privilege of hearing sermons of seven hours long. No vindication this for detaining them from that enjoyment, if such were their sober and innocent taste. But, unfortunately for a jest at any rate ill-suited to the character of just and impartial history, it appears, first, that the total infraction of all the conditions of the Petition of Right, and the hazard to which the persons and property of these men had been brought, were motives sufficient to account for the desire of emigration, without the necessity of imputing it to a mere passion for long sermons. Secondly, the Presbyterians were the long preachers, and not the Independents; and Hampden and Cromwell, and their followers, were Independents, and not Presbyterians.

The real separation between these two sects had begun to show itself as early even as the conference at Hampton Court, and had, for some time before that of which we are now treating, been distinctly marked; although, as is well known, they did not form themselves into opposite parties in the state, till after the assembly of divines on Church Government, and the publishing of the 'Apologetical Narration,' in 1644. In truth, nothing can have tended more to give an unfair view of the different motives of those who were acting together to resist the encroachment of monarchy and prelacy, than the mode, introduced by the Court of James I., and since carelessly adopted by writers on these times, of classing all the opposers of the Hierarchy under the general, undistinguishing denomination of Puritans. From the earliest days of their

---

* [This alleged incident has been shown to rest on no reliable authority. See Mr. Forster's *Statesmen of the Commonwealth*, vol. ii., p. 81. But against the passage in the text Lord Nugent affixed no mark for modification or erasure, and it is therefore left as first written.]

common sufferings and resistance, no two codes of civil conduct on religious matters could be more opposite to each other than that of the Independents from that of the Presbyterians. At the beginning, the Presbyterians were much the more powerful, and, indeed, the only recognised, sect; for they possessed those two vast elements of power, unity of discipline, and original establishment by law in a very important portion of this island. With that establishment, they had cherished a spirit thoroughly intolerant of all other sects. Not content without an entire uniformity of church government throughout the land, they claimed for their synod a power, as absolute as that which the Episcopalians claimed for the Bishops, over the pulpit and the press:

'New Presbyter was but Old Priest writ large.'

Far from setting up for their intolerance the excuse which the Papists have claimed, they had founded their religious tenets on the assumed right of free inquiry, and yet became as unwilling as the Papists of the worst times to admit either the freedom of discussion or the innocence of error. They had rejected human infallibility, and yet they persecuted dissent. When brought into conflict with the Church of England, by the monstrous attempt to establish Episcopalian Ascendency and the Liturgy in Scotland, the spirit of intolerance grew warmer in the followers of both modes of discipline. The Independents rose between them. They stood between the Convocation and the Synod; not for Ascendency, but for Freedom. Neither the Episcopalians nor the Presbyterians had yet advanced so far as to consider religious toleration a duty. The Independents began by proclaiming religious liberty to be a right. In this doctrine, and in this practice, the Independents of England have ever continued. In the American settlements, towards the end of the seventeenth century, they unhappily followed the example of others in endeavouring to reform spiritual error by force; and by their persecution of the Anabaptists there, have sealed the melancholy truth, that no large sect has ever been uniformly and thoroughly innocent of the great folly and great crime of religious persecution. But, as far as English history goes, the proud exception may be claimed for them. The Erastians had no church government at all, but 'reduced the pastoral 'functions to exhortation and prayer,' 'considering the office 'as only persuasive, without any power of censures.'* The Independents established their church government on the basis of a free Commonwealth; but it was a government still; regular and strict, though mild. The Erastians and the Independents, with the sect then called Antipædobaptists,† a small society, differing from the latter only with respect to infant baptism, acted together in civil matters without difficulty or dispute. They had struggled together for liberty; and, above all, for liberty of conscience and of worship.

The assembling of a Parliament, which might interpose its authority to stay the dreadful extremities towards which the measures of the Court were clearly and rapidly advancing, was now the only prospect of deliverance to the people from the miseries which they suffered, and from those greater calamities which they dreaded. On the other hand, the King and his advisers, availing themselves of the apparent calm, and not content unless the means as well as the spirit of resistance were effectually subdued, continued to prosecute, without stop or intermission, their dangerous career.

But the attention of the nation was unexpectedly called to another quarter, by the course of a struggle which had begun, during the year before, in a remote part of the island, where Discontent had already ripened into open Insurrection. The pretensions and persecutions of the prelatical faction in Scotland had long kept that country in a state of unceasing religious feud, and, of late, the furious elements of the Episcopalian and Presbyterian warfare had broken forth, from many magazines of confederacy and cabal, into alarming civil broils. The religious disputes between England and Scotland, which were afterwards, with little intermission, for about sixty years, and through four successive reigns, contested in arms, (until a wise and healing policy, at length conciliating the jealous spirit which it had been before in vain attempted to subdue, re-established in Scotland by law the religion of the people), had begun as early as the junction of the two crowns. The memorable assembly of Perth had introduced and established the High Commission Court, the book of Canons, and Rites and Ceremonies, offensive on many accounts to the Scots. King Charles, soon after his accession, following

---

* Laing's Hist. of Scotland.—Neale's Hist. of Puritans.
† Now called, generally, Baptists.

up the project conceived by his father, had endeavoured, by order of that commission, to introduce the English service-book of Common Prayer. But the main cause of grievance was the establishment of the Commission of Superiority and Tythes, under the pretext of a revocation, as it was called, of certain rights and dues of the Crown, which, during the late minorities of the Scottish Kings, had been alienated into the hands of several opulent families. The powers of this commission were exercised far from the reach of appeal, and entrusted to violent and rapacious favourites, whose chief recommendations were attachment to the forms of a church of which the people were jealous, and feudal enmity towards those influential persons, the means of whose wealth they now became the ready instruments to abridge.* While the prelates were violently and indiscreetly putting themselves into conflict with the great lay proprietors, the high church ceremonials, advancing at an equal pace with these temporal innovations, shocked the feelings and habits of the lower orders. All the smaller matters of controversy between the parties were forgotten in the great division of Covenant on the one hand, and Liturgy and Diocesan Episcopacy on the other. New levies of men and money, more than ever oppressive upon the English part of the King's dominions, were raised to enforce obedience to ordinances more than ever hateful to the Scotch.† To Scotland the discipline of John Knox was dear, not only as a memorial of her religious reformation, but also as one of the few remaining badges of her independent sovereignty. From Charles she had conceived the best hopes of protection for both; for she had given him birth; her ancient palace had been his cradle, and that of his ancestors; and she had received from him the oath to defend the Presbyterian rites, when, (four years before,) she placed her ancient crown upon his head. On Sunday, the 23rd of July, 1637, these jealousies first broke out into open resistance. The service-book was publicly read in the great church at Edinburgh. 'What!' exclaimed an old woman, provoked beyond measure at the portentous sound of prayers and canticles, translated from the missal, and issuing from what had been the pulpit of the first apostle of the Scottish reformation, 'What, ye villain! do you say mass in ' my lug?' and, hurling the stool on which she had been

---

* Burnet—Own Times.   † Heath's Chronicle.

sitting at the head of the reader, she gave the signal of uproar. The Bishop of Edinburgh, who officiated, the Archbishop of St. Andrews, the Lord Chancellor, and the Provost, and City Council, were driven from the church by the enraged populace, and, among the cries of 'A pape! a pape!—stane him; 'stane him!' narrowly escaped the martyrdom which was threatened by these fearful words. In consequence of this commotion, by a proclamation of the English Privy Council, with Archbishop Laud at its head, all concourses of people were prohibited within the city of Edinburgh, under pain of death. So irritating a measure only produced corresponding violences on the part of the people in the Scottish metropolis. The City Council was forcibly dissolved, the members of it obliged to crave protection from the leaders of the insurgent party, and in 1638, under the auspices of the Earls of Hume and Lindsey, the 'National Covenant' was published and subscribed to by great masses of the people throughout the whole kingdom of Scotland.* The Marquis of Hamilton was now commissioned by the King to act with full powers to allay these growing distempers.† Under the more moderate councils of this eminent person, a declaration was put forth, dated June 30, 1638, dispensing with the service-books and canons, promising a parliament, and calling back the King's subjects to their allegiance. But the tyranny and bad faith of the English Government had already produced an impression which it was difficult to counteract. All confidence in the royal promise had been shaken. At length, through the

* Laing's History of Scotland.—Heath's Chron.
† Hamilton was a Presbyterian, and descended from one of the early martyrs of the Reformation. Nor was his personal popularity among his countrymen impaired even by the recollection that it was his father who published the obnoxious Articles of Perth. It is, indeed, sadly difficult to find among the rest of the political leaders, on either side, in Scotland, during this period of her history, a character unstained by cruelty or treachery. But Hamilton seems, on the whole, to have been a sincere and faithful servant to the King, and an ardent well-wisher to his country; but prudent, and perhaps timid, as a statesman, to a degree which, in violent times, brought upon him misrepresentation and obloquy, and caused some dishonourable imputations, such as the having purloined, and transmitted to the Covenanters, Montrose's letter of offers to the King, for which shameful slander there seems not to have been the smallest foundation. No man could, at the crisis of which we are now treating, have more honestly done his duty between an incensed King and an aroused people, nor could, afterwards, in the great civil war, have more faithfully stood by the royal cause to which he attached himself; more courageously encountered danger in the field, or gone with greater firmness to the scaffold.

mediation of Hamilton, after many harassing journeys and negotiations, a reconciliation seemed to be approaching, and an Assembly, elected by the people, from which Bishops were excluded, was held, November, 1638, at Glasgow. The demands, however, of this body, which assumed to itself the right of spiritual excommunication, as well as very effectual temporal securities for the preservation of Kirk and Covenant, were of a nature little likely to be tolerated by the Privy Council in London. At the end of a session of only seven days, it was dissolved by a proclamation which the Lord Commissioner was directed to issue; and this proclamation was met by a protestation from the members, declaring the assembly undissolved, and indissoluble, until such satisfaction as had been demanded should have been fully attained. Meanwhile, the Earl of Argyle having declared for the Covenant, negotiations were opened by the Scotch with the Court of France for assistance, which was readily promised. Nor was Richelieu, probably, an unapproving spectator of a quarrel which promised to enable him the more easily to obtain vengeance or reparation for the part which Charles had, in the early part of his reign, taken in behalf of the Rochellers, and for the opposition which he had lately given to the joint efforts of the French and Dutch in the Spanish Netherlands. About the beginning of 1639, in consequence of this encouragement, the Scotch had proceeded, by ordinance of the Assembly, to get together a competent army; and the cooperation of the friends of religious liberty in England was anxiously sought, not only by the Presbyterians, but by others also, who, on more general grounds of displeasure with the Court, had joined the malcontents. But many considerations deterred that party in England, notwithstanding all solicitations from without and provocations at home, from yet countenancing any project of open insurrection. Nor does it appear that any hopes were held out from England, or any pains taken at that time, to excite the feelings of the Scotch, or even to enter into communication with them.* The

---

* Anthony Wood states that Hampden had made more than one journey into Scotland, about this time, in order to ascertain the feelings of the Covenanters, and to negotiate with them on the part of the Country party in England. It does not appear on what authority he states this, and it seems to refer to a later period. For it is probable that, otherwise, it would have been specially made matter of charge against him at the time of the accusation of the five members.

parliamentary leaders of this country may have felt that things were not yet sufficiently ripe for such an enterprise; and that, immaturely undertaken, it might endanger or destroy the hopes of successful resistance at last;—that, although the intention of their adversaries to destroy public right, to its very foundations, might be sufficiently manifest, still it had not yet been displayed in such a manner as to establish a clear moral case for recourse to those last means which remain to the oppressed for the recovery of freedom. They may have felt that, even after resistance shall have been morally justified by the tyranny of a government, there are still many considerations, not affecting themselves only, which it is the duty of good men very scrupulously to balance; and that complete success should, upon calculation, appear at the least probable, before it can behove those who love their country, or mankind, to commit the fortunes and lives of thousands to the fearful issue of arms. Moreover, the intentions of France were very doubtful, and her resentment against the English Court had been excited by a set of feelings and principles bearing no sympathy with those of the Puritans in Scotland; while it clearly was not the part of the leaders in England to raise the standard of civil war for the hazardous chance of giving liberty to the English people, the great body of whom, perhaps, had not the spirit of liberty, or, at least, might not be prepared to join in the only means by which liberty was to be attained.

In the meanwhile, the King had equipped a large armament by dint of forced loans under a precept of the Privy Council. In this he was assisted, also, by the voluntary contributions of many of the nobility, of the clergy, influenced by Laud, and of the Roman Catholics, instigated by the Queen.* He then proclaimed the Scotch insurgents rebels, marched upon York, and, at the beginning of May, arrived at Berwick. The Earl of Arundel he appointed General in Chief of his forces in the north, the Earl of Essex Lieutenant-General of the foot, and the Earl of Holland of the horse. The Scotch Assembly, on their part, replied from Glasgow by an ordinance repeating their demands for a parliament, and liberty of conscience, and protesting against Episcopacy: then, putting their powers in motion, they disclaimed, under the penalties of a solemn curse, any intentions of a hostile incursion upon England, and

---

* Père d'Orleans.—Laing's Hist. Scot.

concluded by describing their cause as being strictly a defensive one, and founded upon natural and civil right.

Thus arose that war, known under the name of the Bellum Episcopale. A conflict provoked on the one side without any apparent motive of policy or justice, but in which (as is the case in almost all civil wars) it is difficult to say by which party the first hostile movement was made,—since each, however eager to engage, was desirous, even to the last, that the other should seem the aggressor, and thus be answerable for all the calamities that might ensue. Yet both had advanced to a point at which it became inglorious to retreat and impossible to stand still. Apparent, however, as were the motives under which it was begun, those which could cause it so suddenly to subside into a treaty, almost without a battle, and by the yielding of the stronger power, are not so easily to be accounted for or understood.

On the approach of the King to the Border, a general enthusiasm spread itself among the Covenanters, who were joined by not a few of the Episcopal Church. This spirit was confirmed, not dismayed, by the greatness of the danger. The spectacle was one not often paralleled in history. A people unused to arms, not inspired by any of the feelings which animate aggressive war, (for these were not only disclaimed, but carefully repressed,) excited to resistance, not by the influence of any popular leader, but by a deep and pervading sense of the illegality of what was threatened to be imposed upon them, and of the sacredness of the cause to which, in consequence, they had set their hands; and thus preparing to cope with all the perplexing perils of an invasion headed by their sovereign, and the attacks of domestic enemies rising on their rear.

A military committee was instantly established in Edinburgh. A band of Scottish officers, trained to war in the school of Gustavus, on the first intelligence returned, with Alexander Lesly, to the defence of their country. Levies were raised in the several districts, marshalled by their captains, and exhorted and disciplined by their clergy; so that, in less than two months from the first movement of the King, an army of above twenty-four thousand men-at-arms were in the field against him. The Highland frontier was guarded by Montrose and Argyle against the descent of the Gordons and Macdonalds; the southern border manned and fortified under Lesly and

Monro; and Edinburgh, Dumbarton, and Dalkeith, garrisoned by troops entering to the sound of psalms and prayers, and under banners inscribed with the Crown and Covenant of Christ. To the eastward, the shores of the Firth were lined with batteries, and the hills to the south bristling with powers variously trained and accoutred: some drilled to the scientific and precise forms of the Swedish and German strategy; many called fresh from the peaceful occupations of trade and husbandry; most of them inured to danger, fatigue, and hardship, by the wild habits of the chase and the sheep-walk in their mountain forests; and all filled with a spirit that scorned any terms but such as should begin with establishing the independence of their country, and the integrity of its religion. The armies of the King and of the Covenant thus remained for several days,—the outposts in view of each other, and the lines and reserves, on both sides, formed in array of battle, and the royal fleet, with troops on board, commanded by Hamilton, in the Firth, flanking Leith, the guns of whose batteries were loaded and ready for the expected signal of the enemy's assault. While these things were in suspense, and only one slight and unsuccessful attack had been made by Lord Holland, with part of the King's cavalry, the Earl of Roxburgh was dispatched to the royal camp to endeavour once more to treat on the original grounds of demand.

It was at this sudden and momentous juncture that a change of purpose was wrought in Charles. No longer accompanied by Wentworth or Laud, and obliged to act under the influence of his own judgment, or of some milder counsels, he consented to a truce, and soon afterwards a peace was concluded, and the long wished for Scottish Parliament summoned for the 15th of May.

To whatever it may be attributed that the King was thus suddenly induced to accept terms so different in spirit from the demands contained in his late proclamation, a general satisfaction prevailed, and, for a while, hopes arose of a permanent accommodation. But whether this short-lived disposition to peace on Charles's part ceased upon his returning to counsel with his customary advisers, or whether he had at first acceded to the treaty of Berwick only for the purpose of masking some object of less gentle and less honourable policy, the pacification lasted only long enough to give him time to complete in England his projects of supply. Ground, indeed, was afforded to him for complaint of non-performance of the articles by the Scots. The treaty had stipulated for the disbanding of both armies.* The King withdrew his accordingly, and sent his Irish levies home again. The Scots retired also from their frontier, restored the fortresses to the King, but kept the greater part of their levies entire. It would be difficult, with what we know of the policy of Charles on many occasions, to pronounce that this act of the Scots may not have been justified by some intelligence of a stratagem in preparation against them. Still, in ignorance of any such design having been discovered or entertained, it would be unjust not to avow that there was a case against the Scots of manifest invasion of the articles. This treaty was not faithfully observed on either part. The Covenanters were too distrustful of the King to disarm themselves first, and the King assuredly did not set them the example; and the article which provided for the abolition of Episcopacy in Scotland was shamefully evaded by Charles. The probability is that neither party expected the treaty of Berwick to last long; that little more was hoped for by the Scots than the occasion of putting forth, under cover of the articles, a solemn and public statement, which might represent their demands favourably to the English people; and that nothing more was intended by Charles than to gain time for improving those powers which he now saw were entirely inadequate to command success against so formidable a resistance.

As it seemed dangerous to awaken the jealousy of the English people by fresh impositions for maintaining a standing army in the south, Charles determined to issue writs for a Parliament at Westminster, which might enable him to renew hostilities with Scotland. To supply his immediate wants, a new subscription was promoted among the courtiers, the clergy, and the Catholics. Wentworth returned, as Lord Lieutenant, to Ireland, with the title of Earl of Strafford; and, that an example might not be wanting of the liberality and obedience of a Parliament, he summoned the houses there, and proposed four subsidies, which were immediately granted. Active and undisguised preparations were now made on both sides for war. Meanwhile the Scottish Parliament, proceeding to remonstrances concerning Episcopacy, was, contrary to promise, prorogued. The Earl of

* See articles in Rushworth.

Dumferling and Lord Loudon were dispatched to London by the Covenanters, as their Commissioners, to justify them to the King, and to complain of the prorogation. They had frequent opportunities for consultation there with the party who had so long opposed the arbitrary measures of the English court; and Lord Say, Pym, Hampden, Holles, and a few other of the principal members of that body, then (for the first time, as it appears) put themselves into communication with the Covenanters. With them they were thenceforward in constant and intimate conference upon the means of averting or opposing the incursion which was in open preparation, and which, if once successful, would have left Charles at full leisure to overrun and extinguish all remains of public freedom in England. If it were treasonable in the English puritans to conspire with the malcontents of another country, in order to try the last chance for the liberties of their own, from this time began their treasons.

During these negotiations, the Earl of Traquair, Lord Treasurer of Scotland, whose influence at court was on the wane, sought to restore it by treacherously producing a letter of Loudon's, written to the French King before the pacification, soliciting aids for the Scottish army. This unhappy instrument, which, as it appears, had never been sent to its destination, was signed by seven of the chief nobles of Scotland; among others, by Montrose, who so soon after became a pattern of faithful loyalty in the estimation of the court writers. The indignation of Charles blinded him equally to the impolicy of breaking with the Scots by so unjustifiable an act as the seizure of one of their Commissioners, and to the unfairness of visiting upon a man, after a treaty, a letter written by him while at open war. Loudon was instantly sent to the Tower; and thus ended, in the way the least likely to promote an amicable issue, this short-lived commission.*
The expectation of a Parliament in England having now become general, every exertion was made by the country party to secure the election of persons well affected to their cause. Nor when, at length, the writs were issued, were the people

---

* Dr. Birch, in the Appendix to his Enquiry concerning the Transactions of Glamorgan, gives the grounds on which he believes the story of Loudon's having been saved, (only by the entreaties and even menaces of Hamilton), from assassination in prison. But the testimony is not direct enough to justify so black a charge against the memory of Charles.

found to be unmindful of the high duties which they had to discharge, or of the deserts of those persons who, during the interval which had elapsed since the last Parliament, had stood by the wreck of their cause with such patient, though almost hopeless, fidelity. Hampden, whose bold and judicious conduct in the great ship-money contest had signally won the confidence of that party, and made him 'the argument of all 'tongues,' was elected, in conjunction with his friend, Arthur Goodwin, of Upper Winchenden, to serve for the county of Bucks.

Still the levy of the ship-money was enforced with unrelenting pertinacity, under the management, principally, of Chief Justice Finch, on whom the court writers of later times have been too prone to cast the whole blame of that disastrous project,—the greater share of which, in truth, is much more fairly chargeable on the Archbishop and on Strafford. Finch was but their ready agent. He was now entrusted with the custody of the Great Seal. By him the judges were again directed to promote the 'business of the 'shipping' in their several circuits; and, on a demurrer to a bill authorised by the council, he declared, that, 'whilst he 'was keeper, no man should be so saucy as to dispute those 'orders, but that the wisdom of that board should be always 'ground for him to make a decree.' * It is remarkable, however, that there is no appearance of an assessment of ship-money having been made on the county of Buckingham after the trial in the case of Hampden.

In the practice of this short but stormy Parliament is found established, more distinctly than at any former time, the general doctrine of the precedence of questions of grievance over supply. Its whole existence, indeed, was spent in a memorable struggle to assert this privilege and custom. Instantly after the meeting, on the 13th of April, the Commons, in compliance with the petitions of various counties, proceeded to the consideration of grievances affecting the freedom of Parliament, the preservation of religion, and the common liberties of the realm,—appointing a grand committee of enquiry upon each.† Upon Pym's recapitulation, Edward Hyde, then member for Wotton Basset, began the attack on the 'tribunals of censure,' by complaining of the Earl Marshall's court, as 'erected without colour or shadow of law,'

---

* Parliamentary History.   † Commons Journals.

and as having assumed a power to fine the King's subjects in great damages, for matters in which the law gave none.

And now began the practice of convening assemblies of the people to petition Parliament;—a course which had never before been systematically resorted to, to manifest the feelings of the country on the conduct of its representatives.

During the first week, minutes of the proceedings and judgment in Hampden's case were laid on the table of the Commons by St. John and Holborne, and were reported upon by the Grand Committee as matter of grievance. The King, in the meanwhile, as early, urged the hastening of the supplies. But the report of the Grand Committee could not remain unnoticed. He therefore qualified his message by a verbal renunciation of all claims to tonnage and poundage, except such as should be given by Parliamentary grant, and of all intention to establish a permanent revenue of ship-money; declaring that, having levied it upon the exigent of the public safety, he should have remitted it, if the pressing demands of the war had allowed him;—and so required the concurrence of the two Houses in such modes of raising it in future as might secure the proper application of it. This was considered by the Commons as no satisfaction for the former illegal proceedings in this matter: Viewing it only as an endeavour, by a plausible concession, to avoid a decision on the principle, they continued steadily to pursue their object; and, on the 30th, with a view of proceeding against the advisers and instruments in that proceeding, they required, by address, a copy of the record as made up by the judges themselves.*

During this conflict, Hampden was strenuously engaged in the various business of the House. No question of principle or detail, whether affecting the most important interests of the commonwealth and posterity, or the smaller concerns to be adjusted for his own county in the assembly to which she had sent him, none were too mighty for his capacity and courage, or too minute for his indefatigable industry. To all he applied those natural gifts of a ready understanding and a winning persuasion, as well as those acquired habits of arrangement, which fitted him to meet the necessities of the times and the demands of his electors.

During the whole of the three last eventful years of his life, which were now beginning, his mind, which before had been

* Parliamentary History.

occasionally applied to unconnected pursuits, was, without intermission, employed in that uniform course of public service to which his great duties, and his own deep sense of them, now wholly bound him. Never inactive, he had hitherto divided his time between the business of Parliament, the study of books, and the amusements, as well as the useful occupations, of a country life. As a magistrate, he had borne a diligent share in the local affairs of his county;* but he had also found leisure for indulging himself in 'an exceeding pre-'penseness to field sports,' and in the embellishment of his paternal estate, of which he was very fond. When, therefore, he finally abandoned all those pursuits and habits of social ease, which his temper, and talents, and the mild virtues of his domestic character, so much inclined and fitted him to enjoy, the motive must have been powerful, and the sacrifice great.

From this time till his death, except at some few hasty intervals, when business of public concern called him from the Parliament, from the council, or from the camp, he never again returned to that home to which the remembrances of his youth, his studies, his pleasures, and the blameless happiness of tranquil hours, had so strongly attached him.

His mansion still remains. It stands, away from both the principal roads which pass through Buckinghamshire, at the back of that chalky range of the Chilterns which bounds, on one side, the vale of Aylesbury. The scenery which immediately surrounds it, from its seclusion little known, is of singular beauty; opening upon a ridge which commands a very extensive view over several counties, and diversified by dells, clothed with a natural growth of box, juniper, and beech.† What has once been the abode of such a man can

---

* Of his industry in these particulars I found abundant traces in the MS. Collection at Stowe.

† The woods of Hampden terminate to the North upon the bare brow of a lofty hill, called Green Haly, on the side of which is cut, in the chalk, the form of a cross, which is seen from all the country round. This monument, of a very remote antiquity, is known by the name of the White Leaf Cross, and is supposed by Mr. Wise (in a learned letter to Browne Willis on the subject of Saxon antiquities) to have been designed in commemoration of a victory gained by Edward, King of the West Saxons, over the Danes, early in the tenth century. It appears, however, with more probability, to have been intended as a memorial of the last battle of Hengist and Horsa with the Britons, which was fought over the extensive plain of Risborough and Saunderton, when on this height, and on the Bledlow Ridge which adjoins it, the Saxon princes planted their victorious standards to recall their troops from the pursuit.

never but be interesting from the associations which belong to it. But, even forgetting these, no one surely who has heart or taste for the charm of high breezy hills, and green glades enclosed within the shadowy stillness of ancient woods, and avenues leading to a house on whose walls the remains of the different styles of architecture, from the early Norman to the Tudor, are still partly traced through the deforming innovations of the eighteenth century,—no one, surely, can visit the residence of Hampden, and not do justice to the love which its master bore it, and to that stronger feeling which could lead him from such a retirement to the toils and perils to which, thenceforth, he entirely devoted himself.

PART THE FIFTH.

FROM 1640 TO 1641.

Short Parliament—Industry of Hampden—Hampden marries his second wife—Bishop Williams solicits his assistance in a case of Privilege with the Lords—Vane announces a message from the King concerning Ship-Money and Supply—Opposite Resolutions moved by Hampden and Hyde—Vane's angry declaration—Dissolution—Votes of Convocation, and renewed Resolutions of Grievances—Second Scotch War—Scots pass the Tweed and Tyne—Treaty of Rippon—Meetings of the Country party, and correspondence with the Scots—Opening of the Long Parliament—Committees of Grievances—Prisoners of the Star-Chamber liberated—Strafford, Laud, and others committed—Trial of Strafford—Bill of Attainder—Conduct of Hampden respecting that measure examined—Perfidy of the King.

TWELVE years had now elapsed, during which England had been governed without a Parliament. The Commons of this Parliament began their course in a manner which gave promise of great and lasting benefit to the public cause; and the courage, the tenacity, the moderation and singleness of purpose, which marked every proceeding throughout their short career, justified the expectations they had raised. Though thwarted and baffled by the King in every project of redress, and dissolved angrily before they had passed any one complete act, still, sitting as they had done from day to day without longer adjournment, and always in conflict with the Crown on the highest matters of popular right and parliamentary privilege, their journals are not dishonoured by any trace of irregularity or passion. Considering the temper which had now shewn itself in both parties through the country, this distinction, which they so well deserve, was perhaps owing in part to their existence having been brought to a close before any of those extreme violences had begun on the King's part, which, if not fully justifying all the acts to which the Long Parliament afterwards proceeded, at least rendered it impossible for that body, with safety to itself, to abide within the boundaries which the constitution of England assigns. A more choice selection of all the master spirits of a country in an age remarkable for deep thinking and resolute acting, was never sent to take its part within the walls of any representative assembly. The court, as well as the country party, had busied itself to secure favourable returns; and though with less success, had formed within the House of Commons a small phalanx of learning and ability sufficient to make shew of coping at once with the shrewdness of St. John, the experience of Pym, the learning of Selden, the sagacity of Hampden, and the uncompromising resoluteness of each. The strength of the Crown in the Lower House consisted principally of lawyers. A few of those on the popular side already shewed a disposition to waver. Hyde, though still, as we have seen, and even for some time after this, concurring in some of the strongest measures of opposition to the Court, had nevertheless given token of a willingness to recommend himself to its favour by occasional subtleties, which embarrassed his own party and were of service to the objects of the King. Sir Dudley Digges had been propitiated and silenced by the Mastership of the Rolls; but the virtuous Falkland and Sir Bevill Grenvil, and even the faithless Digby, Mallory, Philips, and Holborne, were still forward in their support of the motions of inquiry and crimination.

It has been already seen that, during this period, Hampden was studiously and eagerly employed in those details which are no small part of the duties of a faithful member of Parliament. To these, in truth, he devoted almost every day from the meeting to the dissolution. On the 16th, three days after the meeting, he was on a committee to examine all questions relating to election returns and other privileges, and, on the 17th, on one to report upon the state of the journals and records.* On the 18th, on one concerning the violation of privilege at the close of the last Parliament; and, on the 20th, on another to prepare an address to the King, praying ' that ' the like infringement of their liberties might not be practised ' in future to their prejudice and his own.' On the 21st, he

---

* Commons Journals.

was on the committee appointed to inquire into the effect of the commission lately granted to Convocation, and, on the 22d, on two others—one upon the case of Smart, a prebendary of Durham, who had petitioned as a prisoner against Bishop Neile, and the other to prepare the heads of a conference with the Lords concerning the petitions from the country. On the 23rd, he was on one to expedite the matter of this conference by stating the reasons for postponing the supplies until effectual means should have been taken to prevent innovations in religion, to secure the property of the subject, and the privileges of Parliament, and to prepare an answer on these heads to the King. On the 24th, he was a manager of that conference; on the 25th, he reported it to the House; and, on the 1st of May, we find him reporting a second conference, touching some matters which had occurred in the first. The journals of the House, indeed, and the minutes of its committees throughout, are ample vouchers of his unwearied assiduity.

In this patient and industrious course of public service did he justify the character which circumstances, in themselves accidental, and over which he had no control, had first enabled him to establish; proving himself worthy to attract the confidence and lead the efforts of this assembly of able, bold, and diligent men.

Hampden had very lately married his second wife, Letitia, the daughter of —— Vachell, of Coley,* near Reading, who survived him a great many years, and lived to a very advanced age; but, after his second marriage, he never resided in Buckinghamshire. The demands of the times had altered the habits of his domestic life; and, during that part of it which was passed in London, this lady lived with him at his lodgings, near the house which was occupied by Pym, in Gray's Inn Lane.

About this time, Bishop Williams, who had long suffered under the inveterate persecution of Laud and the personal anger of Charles, was endeavouring, by bringing a case of privilege before the Lords, to regain his liberty, and, by petitions to the King, to obtain his summons to Parliament, and a composition for the enormous fine to which he had been sentenced by the Star Chamber. During his trial before that tribunal, he had defended himself with great spirit, and with

* Parish Register, Coley.

an ability which baffled the craft of Noy, and the mercenary zeal of Lamb and Sibthorp, who were employed by the Archbishop to prepare and prosecute the informations against him.* But, after the death of Noy, the matter had been brought to a judgment by the exertions of Kilvert, a wily solicitor, and, accordingly, a sentence was passed, suspending the Bishop from all his offices and dignities, and imposing upon him a fine of 10,000*l.* and imprisonment during the King's pleasure. But Williams, by habit a courtier, and only, from his failure in this pursuit, an occasional patriot, was not of a character long to suffer persecution with patience. Finding the Lords not disposed to assert with spirit the question of privilege in his behalf, he endeavoured to engage Hampden, during this session, to make his case one of parliamentary grievance. Among the manuscripts at Lambeth is a sheet of notes in his handwriting, under the title of 'Remembrances to 'Mr. Hampden,' dated April 27th, to which the answer is found appended. The style of cold civility in which Hampden declines this business is that of a man who already suspected that the public virtue of the Bishop was wavering, and that he was preparing to embark again in the course of court favour into which, on his enlargement and elevation to the Archbishopric of York, he soon after was content to relapse. Hampden's answer was as follows:

'My Lord,—I should be very ready to serve you in anything I
'conceaved good for you and fitt for mee; but in your L^{d}p's
'present commands I doubt that to make overture of yor intentions,
'and be prevented by a suddaine conclusion of ye Parl^t. wch many
'feare, may render y^{or} condition worse than now it is. To begin in
'o^r house is not ye right place; the most important businesses of
'the King and king^d. are pressd on with such expedition y^t any of
'a more particular nature will be but unwellcome, and hardly
'prosecuted wth effect; besides that, there is at this instant a
'tendernesse betweene ye Lords and us about priviledge; and for
'my owne unfitnesse, I neede mention no more but my disability to
'carry through a businesse of this nature, though yor L^p may easily
'conceave another incompetency in my person. In these regards I
'humbly desire yor L^p to excuse mee, and thereby to lay a newe
'obligation upon mee of being

'Your L^{dps} most humble servant,

'*Westm^r. Ap^r. 29, 1640.*'   'Jo. Hampden.†

---

* Hacket's Life of Williams.   † Lambeth Lib., No, 1030, 108.

Yet Williams was not without some great and high virtues. It is but justice to the memory of this learned prelate to mention, together with his faults, the noble and contemptuous generosity with which, after his restoration to power, he forbore to take vengeance on his former persecutors. Some of these being sent to try how he was affected towards them, he told them that 'if they had no worse foes than him they might 'fear no harm, and that he saluted them with the charity of 'a bishop.' And, when Kilvert had the meanness to crave his pardon for the wrongs he had done him—'I assure you,' answered Williams, 'pardon for what you have done before; 'but this is a new fault, that you take me to be of so base a 'spirit as to defile myself with treading on so mean a creature: 'live still by pettyfogging and impeaching, and think that I 'have forgotten you.' *

This Parliament, as has been already observed, although it was not suffered to complete a single act, may yet be justly considered one of the most useful that ever sat; because, without show of violence or passion, it first reduced to system those resources which are in the hands of every Parliament for its own defence, but which, before, had been viewed only at a distance, and in speculation. The landmarks of the Constitution, for centuries set up, had of late years been pointed out anew by Coke and Selden in many a glorious precedent. It was not the purpose of the leaders of the House of Commons to frame a new theory of government. They did not amuse themselves or the country with vain abstract declarations that the origin of government is from the people. They did much better. They contented themselves with maintaining the inherent right of the people to be well governed. And thus they left it on record that a House of Commons, representing the opinions, generally, of the country, and enjoying its confidence, and acting resolutely up to its own faculties, may successfully begin the work which, according to Lord Bolingbroke, it is always in the power of any House of Commons to achieve. He says, but, as is the case with some of his other political generalities, in terms not sufficiently qualified, 'that 'a Parliament, nay one House of Parliament, is able, at any 'time, and at once, to destroy any corrupt plan of power.' One obvious condition, with which this predicate must always

* Hacket's Life of Williams.

be taken, is, that such a Parliament, or House of Parliament, be supported by the Spirit of the People.

The King had desired, by message to the Lords, their good offices with the Commons on the matter of supply, and the peers represented their opinion that, 'in reason and decency,' supply should precede remonstrance. Such advice given on such a matter was well calculated to produce 'a tenderness' between the Houses; and the Commons instantly voted it a breach of privilege.

The conference, however, which ensued, was conducted with great spirit and discretion, to an accommodation, by the managers for the Lower House; and, on the 4th of May, the elder Sir Henry Vane, Secretary of State and Treasurer of the Household, brought down a message from the King. In essentials it differed but little from that which, at the beginning of the session, had been voted unsatisfactory. Its purport was, that his Majesty would forbear from any further levy of the ship-money for the present, and give up all future claims to it, upon the condition of a grant of twelve subsidies, to be paid in three years; promising full time afterwards for the redress of grievances; but requiring an immediate answer, his affairs in Scotland being too urgent to admit of delay: a condition, say the writers of the Court party, unauthorised by the King.

Mr. Hume so far agrees with Père d'Orleans,* (who comes to an absurd conclusion through an evident mistake between the two Sir Harry Vanes,) as to insinuate that Vane's motive was to provoke a spirit of resistance in the House. To those who can discover in the elder Vane any motive of interest in thus thwarting the designs of his master, or who think that such a declaration as his, if unauthorised by the King, would have remained, for several hours, subject of debate and remonstrance, without one word of question from any others of the

---

* Père d'Orleans, whose learning as an English historian was not sufficiently accurate to justify the violent conclusions at which he often arrives, gravely lays the whole of this transaction to the charge of Sir Harry Vane the younger. Hard upon an enthusiastic republican, who innocently suffered death as a regicide, that he should also be made innocently to suffer in his memory for the faults of his courtly father. 'Henri Vane,' says the Père, '*traître fameux*, étoit Secrétaire d'Etat.' . . . . 'Vane, ' dis-je, avoit dans son instruction de demander douze subsides, mais de ' se relacher jusqu' à six, pour peu qu'on lui disputât le terrain. Le perfide, ' *déjà vendu aux ennemis du Roi son maître*, tint ferme sur douze, pour ' aigrir les esprits, et y réussit si bien que le Parlement refusa le Roi, et le ' Roi cassa le Parlement.'—Liv. ix.

Court party, it may be credible that a violent and arbitrary minister would suddenly become a secret partisan of an opposing faction, against a sovereign on whose favour his own public fortunes entirely depended. Even so, the artifice would have been a shallow one on the part of Vane; for Charles, for the purpose of gaining the desired supplies, would scarcely have failed to expose the fraud of his minister, and so to reconcile the Parliament.

Charles had, more than once, in the early part of his reign, obtained votes of money by assurances of prospective redress, and had always dissolved his Parliament as soon as it came to seriously press the terms of that engagement upon him. His royal word had been too often pledged, and was now no security. The house, however, having resolved itself into a Committee of Supply, a great difference of opinion arose. Several members spoke against voting any grant in a spirit of compromise for the discontinuance of an illegal impost; and another party objected to it only with reference to the amount of the sum. To those who took the plain high ground of 'redress before supply,' it became, of course, desirable to unite in one vote all who objected to the grant, either in respect of the principle or of the amount. With this view, Hampden moved that the question should be put broadly thus,— 'Whether the House would agree to the proposal contained in 'the King's message?' which motion was strongly supported. But, in the course of the debate, the Speaker, Glanville, who, says Whitelocke, 'had engaged to be a better 'servant to the King than formerly, and was very active to 'promote his Majesty's desires, whereof he gave a sufficient 'testimony, and of the change of his former opinion,' condemning as illegal the imposition of the ship-money, nevertheless urged the House, on account of the low state of the revenue, to comply with the message. Hyde, taking advantage of this to thwart the design of Hampden, objected to the form of the question as being captious, and stated his opinion that such only as were disposed to reject the King's message altogether, and not such as objected only to the manner or to the amount of the grant, could give a clear vote with Hampden on this proposition. He moved, therefore, that the question might be confined to the proposal that 'a supply be granted;' thus effectually drawing off many who, on account of the proposed amount of the grant, objected to the message, and artfully leading them to a first vote in concurrence with it. But Hampden's motion had been already put, and was in discussion. Herbert, the Solicitor-General, a more moderate and crafty man than Vane, fruitlessly endeavoured a compromise. And now a confused clamour arose in the committee, and cries, from different quarters, for the question as framed by Hampden or by Hyde.* But, while the House was thus in an uproar, Vane declared, as from authority, that a supply, unless voted as required, would not be accepted; and this warning being seconded by the Solicitor-General, Herbert, the matter was no further pressed. The House, desiring Sir Henry Vane to acquaint his Majesty that they hoped to return him an answer to his message on the following day, adjourned.

The King now came to the rash and passionate determination of putting an end to this Parliament, and, with it, to that truce of public feeling, which had lasted so long as the people could look to an assembly which might make their complaints heard, and, peradventure, also, procure redress. Like the countryman with Jupiter, in Lucian's fable,—while the monarch reasoned, the people thought him wrong; but when, from reasoning, he betook himself again to his thunder, they knew him to be wrong. The contemporary writers, even such as are the most favourable to Charles, leave this act without a vindication, and confess it to have done irreparable harm to his cause.† Lord Clarendon lays the blame on Vane, Whitelocke on Laud, Ludlow on Strafford, and Rushworth on the Queen. There was but one class of persons, according to Lord Clarendon, who had reason, and felt that they had reason, to rejoice at it, as a measure favourable to their views;—those who wish not to control the King by constitutional means, but to see liberty vindicated by a tumultuous triumph over Royalty itself. He says that, within an hour after the King's angry speech to the Commons at the bar of the Upper House, he met St. John, who, addressing him with a most unusually cheerful aspect, asked him, 'what 'troubled him?' To which Hyde replying 'that the same 'that troubled him he believed troubled most good men;— 'that, in such a time of confusion, so wise a Parliament, which 'alone could have found a remedy for it, was so unseasonably 'dismissed;'—the other said, with some warmth, 'that all was

---

* Rushworth, Parl. Hist.—Clarendon, Hist. Reb. May.
† Warwick's Memoirs.—Sir Hugh Cholmondeley's Memoirs.—Clarendon, Hist. Reb.—Whitelocke.—Rushworth.

'well, and that it must be worse before it could be better; 'and that this Parliament could never have done what was 'necessary to be done.' The conclusion was a just one. It was then but too plain, that all 'must be worse before it could 'be better;' and that, with Charles, no Parliament could be safe, or useful to the country, that did not begin by taking the whole power of the government into its own hands.*

Contrary to all usage, and in spite of the protest of thirty-six of its own members, the Convocation was, by Laud's advice, continued under a new Commission, until they had voted certain new Canons, and a benevolence of four shillings in the pound for six years; and attached to the new Canons was the famous *et cætera* oath.† It was, besides, directed as part of the discipline of the Church, that four times a year the clergy should instruct their parishioners of the divine right of kings, and the damnable sin of resistance. And, the more to mark the spirit in which this proceeding was conceived, the Book of Canons was put forth at once by the High Church party under the name of the Anti-Covenant.‡

Scarcely had the Parliament been dissolved, when the King sought to repair an act which he saw had caused the greatest alarm among the more prudent of his advisers, by a Declaration which was no better suited to the temper of the times. It seems as if the same passions, which had prompted the mischief he had done, became again excited, even while he was in the act of preparing what he meant to be a healing instrument; for, with great inconsistency, he laid down in his declaration, to its utmost extent, the doctrine of his being 'accountable to God alone,' at the very instant while he was employed in giving an account to his people;§ and, on the next day, he had again recourse to his old unhappy practice of committing several members under his own warrant to prison.‖ This he accompanied with the new outrage of ordering that the lodgings, and even the pockets, of two of the Lords, the Earl of Warwick, and the Lord Brooke, should be searched for treasonable papers; but without effect.¶

---

* Clarendon, Hist. Reb.—Whitelocke.—Rushworth.—Mrs. Hutchinson's Memoirs.

† This oath, to be imposed, not on the clergy only, but on many of the laity also, contained an obligation to 'maintain the government of the 'church by archbishops, bishops, deans, chapters, *et cætera*.' ‡ Fuller.

§ Whitelocke. ‖ Rushworth. ¶ May.

On the other hand the peace of the metropolis was assailed by numerous and turbulent assemblages of the populace. Placards of violent invective against Laud for some days appeared on the walls of Westminster; and an attempt was made by some thousands of people, chiefly apprentices, collected and marching by sound of drum, to force the gates of Lambeth Palace. The Archbishop on their approach had removed himself, by timely flight, to Croydon. It was not without bloodshed that the mob were at length dispersed by the Train Bands. Several were killed; and one of the rioters was, under a very forced construction of the Statute of Treasons, executed as having levied war against the King.

Now, again, coat and conduct, and ship-money, were levied with the greatest rigour and despatch, and in larger proportions than before; and several sheriffs of counties, and the Lord Mayor of London, were prosecuted in the Star Chamber for forbearing to distrain. A return of the names and incomes of the richest citizens was required; magistrates were ordered to apprehend all defaulters; and a sum of £40,000 was borrowed from certain merchants, under a threat of seizing the bullion which they had sent to the Mint to be assayed. At the same time all the pepper in the East India warehouses was bought from the company on trust, and sold, at a great discount, for ready money; and a scheme was proposed for coining two or three hundred thousand pounds of base-money.*

At length the King was enabled to proceed northward, August 20th, having already despatched a fleet to the eastern coast of Scotland, and ordered his army to rendezvous at York. The general result of this second Scotch war is well known. It terminated as rapidly as the former, and in a manner more disastrous to Charles. For the treaty was even more inglorious than that of Berwick, and preceded by the capture of a large fortified city within the English border, and a decisive advantage gained by the insurgents in the field. The Scots, with their accustomed activity, had passed the Tweed, and instantly advanced upon Newbourn, fording the Tyne with infantry and cavalry, in the face of Lord Conway, who in vain disputed it with them after haughtily rejecting a requisition that a few hundreds might be allowed to pass over with a petition to the King. His works, hastily constructed, crumbled from before the well-directed fire of the Scottish guns, which had

---

* Laud's Diary.—Laud's Troubles.—Lilly.—Mrs. Hutchinson.

been prepared for little more than that day's service, being formed of leather, hooped round with iron, and carried to the river's bank on the backs of horses. Lesly had filled up the intervals between the squadrons of his dragoons with companies of fleet-footed Highlanders, who, running by their sides, and sometimes hanging on the manes of their chargers, kept pace with them to cover their movements, or act in line with them either with the musket or the broad-sword. The advance guard of Conway's cavalry, after a momentary success, was demolished in the ford, and the first and second line of the Covenanters instantly crossed under cover of their batteries, leaving nothing behind them but their reserves, with their left thrown back to guard against the event of that flank being threatened from the eastward. The body of the English army, that defended the ford was forced to retire ' with such pre-' cipitation,' says Burnet, ' that Sir Thomas Fairfax, who had ' a command in it, did not stick to own that, till he passed ' the Tees, his legs trembled under him.' The next day the Scots took possession of Newcastle, making themselves masters of Northumberland, the Bishoprick of Durham, and the collieries, with a force of 23,000 infantry and 3000 cavalry.*

Whether by misconduct or misfortune, in this affair Lord Conway lost much reputation; some accusing him of cowardice, and some of treachery. Lord Strafford, who had been in vain struggling with the gout and stone, and endeavouring to reach the army in time to take the field before a battle, writes to him from York two days before the passage of the Tyne, and says, ' I find all men in this place extream ill satisfied with the ' guiding of our horse, and publish it infinitely to your dis-' advantage, that, having with you a thousand horse and five ' hundred foot, you should suffer an enemy to march so long a ' way without one skirmish, nay without once looking upon ' him. And it imports you most extreamly, by some noble ' action, to put yourself from under the weight of ill tongues.'†
Neither Lord Conway nor his troops at all expected that power of artillery which Lesly brought against them, and had mounted in battery, masked by brushwood, to open on their flank.‡

---

* Burnet—Own Times. † Strafford's Letters.
‡ The annexed letter from Sir Jacob Astley to Lord Strafford, describing the ill-appointed and destitute state in which the army took the field in this second war, which had been begun by the King himself, at his own

MARQUIS OF MONTROSE

Montrose, who, on the former outbreak of the Episcopal war, had been posted on the Highland frontier to keep the Roman Catholic clans in check, on the passing of the Tweed took a forward station. The chieftains having drawn lots for the honour of first entering England, the chance fell on him, and he instantly plunged into the river, and crossed it at the head of his infantry. According to his biographer, (who is singularly eager to redeem him from the suspicion of ever having been faithful to the Covenant, to which he had sworn,) he had, even before the treaty of Berwick, put himself into secret communication with the King.* This is also said by Burnet. At all events, almost immediately after the invasion of England, the great discovery of his treachery was made, and thenceforward he was the most eager agent for the King in every enterprize, political or military, which was to be undertaken in Scotland. In truth there never was a man who owed more of his fame in the estimation of posterity to his only virtue, dauntless and romantic courage, than Montrose.

How far it may have been under the advice of the leaders of the popular party in London that the Scottish army was now advanced into England, will probably always remain matter of doubt. Nor is the question one of much import-time, so long prepared, and provided for by means so arbitrary and oppressive, goes some way to exculpate Lord Conway from his share in the blame of the failure.

'Right Honourable, and my singular good Lord,—I reseiued y^{rs} of the '27th of this month. Yesterday the Scotes army passed the Tyne at 'Newbrenc, as I leave the manner of it to my Lord Devereaux relation. I, 'upon this occasion, assembled all the colloneles, and by a generall consent 'it was found fittinge to quitt Newcastell. It was not to bee held they 'havinge passed the Tweede. This night all our foot ar to moue to Durham, 'and to-morrow wee shall march to. . . . Wee are in an ill casse, 'wantinge vitualles and amunitie and spades. Wee could bringe none. 'I humbly pray y^r Lordeship that I may reseiue y^r directions how I shall 'governe myselfe. If his Ma^{ty} will have good of this army, there must bee 'a speatiall car had to furnishe itt as itt ought to bee. Otherwise whosoever 'shall have anie chardge in itt will suffer in his reputation. Theur muste 'bee a speedy course taken to supply us wth vitualles, cannon, and 'amunitie, and severall other thinges. I wish we weare mad able to fight, 'or the occation taken away. More I have not for the present to give y^r 'Lordeship troubell, but doe rest ever,

'Most nobell Lorde,
'Y^r Lordeship's humble servant,
'JACOB ASTELEY.'†

---

* Life of Montrose, 1640. † Orig. Letter, MS. Coll. Stowe.

ance. That a constant communication was kept up between them by letters and by messengers is certain; certain, too, that the Puritans of England now looked to the success of the Covenanters, as the best hope for reducing the King to the necessity of dependence on his Parliament for supplies, and, through this necessity, to a compromise in favour of public liberty. The community of political feeling and objects between them has never been doubted or denied. True it is that the letter laid before the assembly by Lord Saville, (who had now emerged from his obscurity to do an act consistent with a character which no new baseness could more deeply stain,) and subscribed by him with the forged names of six English noblemen, has been always believed to have been the invitation on which the Scots changed their plan from the defence of their own frontier to the invasion of the English border. But probably this unprincipled artifice, (intended to lead the Scots into jeopardy, and to involve the English Puritans in the penalties of treason,) contributed, contrary to the intention of its author, mainly to the success of their common cause, by transmitting and giving effect to the counsels which the parliamentary leaders were in reality most desirous should be adopted. The principle of resistance had, doubtless, long before this, received its justification in the minds of Hampden and the other principal men of that party; and the delay can be attributed only to that strong motive of duty which, after resistance shall have been otherwise morally justified, will always deter good men from engaging themselves and others in a hopeless conflict. No justice, no protection, was to be derived to them, or to the country, from the courts of law. All means of redress in a parliamentary way were denied them. Every barrier with which the ancient constitution had fenced the rights of the people had been destroyed or removed; and the stream of the law was tainted to the fountain head. The vindication of the cabal which was sitting in London must rest, not on any single act of persecution then flagrant, but on the whole system and character of Charles's government; on all that had preceded this crisis, and all that was then threatened.

Moreover there are no grounds to presume that, even under these provocations, the cabal in London had yet determined on the last sad hazard of a civil war. But it would be weakness to suppose that their minds were not prepared for it. Still we have no right to conclude that their designs had, as yet, gone farther than to countenance such operations, on the frontier of the country, as might force the King to fair and equitable terms with his Parliament. In a word, the justification of Hampden and the rest, for their correspondence with the Scots, was the same that we shall hereafter have to discuss as the justification of their conduct when driven in their own persons to an appeal to arms; with this exception, that the King had not yet declared a war of force against the Parliament. He had only determined to govern without Parliament, and in spite of Parliament. Against the people of England he had long been working the two great and formidable engines of the Exchequer and the Church; and taxation and religious persecution are provocations powerful exactly in proportion to the importance of the several interests which they affect. Religious persecution is odious to all: to those who do not value religion, as interposing in the affairs of men a restraint, and a mode of discipline, which they hold to be superstitious; —to those who do value it, as interposing a human power in things divine, which they hold to be a profanation. This last is, doubtless, the stronger feeling, because it concerns a higher and a deeper interest. And this feeling, partly from the nature of their tenets and disposition, and partly from the insults they had already suffered, was peculiarly strong with the Puritans. By the Independents, in particular, who acknowledge no head of their church under Christ, it is not to be wondered at that tests, imposed by a temporal power, and backed by persecution, should have been felt grievous in no ordinary degree. Their position was peculiarly irksome. They were the only large sect of Christians who were then of opinion that the granting of entire religious liberty is not only one of the most unfailing proofs of increasing wisdom in a state, but is one of the most important of its moral obligations; and that the injunction, under penalties, of a peculiar mode of worship, is not only a tyrannical usurpation of the liberties of the creature who worships, but an impious inroad on the privilege of the Creator to whose acceptance the worship is addressed. The discipline of every other large sect was at that time founded on penal tests. *Nisi placuerit hominibus Deus, Deus non erit.* And how lately have states begun to discover that this is as foolish and vain as it is wicked! Fortunate it is, that no human language can frame a penal test which may not be evaded by craft, or baffled by simplicity. Because, if penal tests could be made generally efficient for their purpose, such is the spirit of intolerance in man, there would be no limit to persecution.

The country-houses of such of the leading persons among the malcontents as were admitted into their most secret counsels alternately became the places of consultation with the Scottish Commissioners. Broughton Castle, in Oxfordshire, which belonged to the Lord Say, and Fawsley, in Northamptonshire, the house of Sir Richard Knightley, (whose son had married Hampden's daughter,) were, from their position with reference to the north road, and their easy distance from London, convenient for these interviews.* Here did Pym, Hampden, St. John, Lord Say, and Lord Brook, and, later in this year, the Earls of Bedford, Warwick, and Essex, Lord Holland, Nathaniel Fiennes, and the younger Vane, hold their sittings, which were sometimes attended by other persons of great rank and property, who were as deeply involved in the general plan of resistance.† Their meetings in London were usually in Gray's-inn-lane, whither the reports from their council-tables in the country were addressed; and from whence, after these had been considered, advices were communicated to the friends of the country party in the city.‡

Another great national disgrace at this time befel England in her navy; and it was all the more intolerable, since the main pretext for all the King's heaviest impositions of late years had been to strengthen his power at sea. Such, indeed, had been the display of naval means, that it was observed by

---

* Nalson.

† The old printing press, established at Fawsley by Sir Richard's father, is said to have been at this time again brought into use for the purposes of the London cabal; and at Broughton Castle there is a room, so contrived, by being surrounded with thick stone walls and casemated, that no sound from within can be heard. This room appears to have been built about the time of King John, and is reported, on very doubtful grounds of tradition, to have been the room used for the sittings of the Puritans. It seems an odd fancy, although a very prevailing one, to suppose that wise men, employed in capital matters of state, must needs choose the most mysterious and suspicious retirements for consultation, instead of the safer and less remarkable expedient of a walk into the open fields. The story of the use made by the Puritans of the stone room in Broughton Castle probably rests on the same sort of authority which lays the venue of the Revolution of 1688 in the subterraneous vaults of the Lord Lovelace's house, at Lady Place, in Berkshire.

‡ Clarendon Papers.—Windebank's Despatch.—Warwick's Memoirs.—D'Estrades.—Whitelocke.

some, that the troops which, during the last year, were sent round to the Firth, might have been more easily transported by land; but that the King's ships of war were lying idle. Scarcely two months after this, was fought in the Downs the great battle between the Spaniards under Ocqueda, and the combined fleets of the Dutch, under Van Tromp and De Witt. In addition to the disgrace of permitting a battle to be fought in a British roadstead, in sight of a powerful British fleet, Charles had incurred the greater, of having endeavoured to make a pecuniary bargain, offering to the court at Brussels, for £150,000, first to take the Spanish ships under his protection, (which he was bound, at any rate, to do by the law of nations, so long as they should remain in his port,) and then to convoy them to their destination in Spain, which he was bound by treaty with Holland not to do.

The Scots, meanwhile, masters of four English counties, had intrenched themselves in positions connecting the line of the fortified cities which were in their hands, and, having entered England ill provided with stores of any kind, levied large contributions for the supply of their army.* The King, dismayed, rather as it appears by certain symptoms of disaffection among his own troops, than by the temporary success of the enemy, had retired to Northallerton, and thence to York.† Here a great petition was brought up from the Londoners, who were deprived of their supplies of coals and cattle from the north. Other addresses also, signed by the nobility and greater part of the gentry of Yorkshire, to the number of one hundred and forty,‡ and from the inhabitants of other counties, who were in instant peril of their estates from the pressure of contributions to the two armies, were presented to the King.§ Not only were these rejected, but the gentlemen who brought them were threatened with the Star Chamber. Strafford, who had at length sufficiently recovered from a painful and dangerous disease to be able to take the command and bring off the rear of the retreating army to York, went so far in a council of war, says Burnet, as to propose that the Lords Wharton and Howard, for having undertaken to present some of these, should be shot at the head of the army, as sowers of sedition.‖ Hamilton, after the

---

* Sydney Papers.
† Clarendon, Hist. Reb.   ‡ Whitelocke.   § May.
‖ Burnet's own Times.

council, rose and asked him, if he were sure of the army? Startled at the question, Strafford made such inquiries as satisfied him that a general mutiny would probably have followed, had any such execution been attempted.* And now a strong and urgent address, procured, say the court writers, by Hampden and Pym, and signed by twelve English Peers,† most of them already distinguished on the popular side, gave the King the opportunity, which, probably, by this time he was not indisposed to embrace, of calling a council to consider of the means, by treaty or otherwise, of clearing the English Border from the invaders. The Covenanters met this advantage with prudence, and resumed the ground of petition; and, as on the former occasion at Berwick, a treaty was proposed. A parliament was promised, to be convened on the 3rd of November, and a commission of sixteen noblemen, the most popular of those who were still esteemed the King's friends, was appointed to negociate terms with the committee of the Scotch Estates.‡ The treaty of Rippon, which ensued, led to a discussion of terms, prolonged by the Scots, probably not without the willing consent of the English commissioners, until the expected meeting of a parliament should be secured beyond the risk of any duplicity or change of purpose in the King. During the cessation of arms, and the settlement of the treaty, the condition to which Charles's rashness had reduced him was severe and mortifying in the extreme. Unable to advance or to retire, obliged to keep his own forces collected to check any farther advance of the Scots, and pressed to relieve the northern counties from the contributions, he was driven to the necessity of maintaining the levies of the Covenanters at the stipulated charge of £850 a day; himself, the Sovereign, supporting at once two armies of his own subjects, opposed to each other, in the field. The English council, as a test of their sincerity, now assisted the King in raising a loan of £200,000 from the city of London, by adding their

---

* Whitelocke says that divers of the officers and private soldiers 'in 'their march to their rendezvous, spared not to declare their judgments 'against the war, and that they would not fight to maintain the pride and 'power of the Bishops. And this resolution seemed not to be feigned by 'the ill success afterwards.' (Memorials.) Laud, says Dr. Lingard, but I have not been able to trace his authority, had argued against Strafford in favour of a peace with Scotland, but was silenced by him, and by the known sentiments of the King.—See *Sydney Papers*, ii. 614, 615, 618, 621; *Clarendon Papers*, ii. 81, 82.   † Rushworth.
‡ Laing's Hist. of Scotland.

personal security to his.* But, by an ill-judged fancy of his own that he could better dictate terms at Westminster, he was soon after led into the most perplexing error of all, that of transferring the negotiations thither; thus bringing the Commissioners of the Covenanters into personal and daily communication with that party whose object it was, by dint of such difficulties as might by concert with the Commissioners be thrown in the way of an accommodation, to force him to a redress of English grievances.†

Thus the negotiation continued to subsist through the whole of October into November. Rothes, Loudon, Johnstone of Waristoune, and others of the Commission, resided in the city. A church was assigned for their religious observances, whither Henderson, one of the most able and zealous ministers of the Kirk, attracted crowds of all classes and sects to catch the excitement of his vehement eloquence. With a caution derived from the failure of a pacification at Berwick,‡ the Commissioners rejected all verbal negotiation, and required written minutes to be made of every proceeding, grounding upon a respectful formality towards the King their absolute refusal to stipulate in his presence.§

They demanded, first, that the King should sanction with his consent the proceedings of the last Scottish Parliament; secondly, that their fortresses should be placed in the hands of countrymen of their own, appointed by the King, but approved by the Estates; thirdly, that all Scotch subjects should be released from all oaths inconsistent with the Covenant; fourthly that the authors of the hostilities should be subject to the sentence of the respective parliaments; fifthly, that their ships and goods should be restored; sixthly, that Scotland should be indemnified for the charges and losses of the war; seventhly, that all hostile proclamations should be recalled; and, eighthly, that the religion and liberties of the country should be recognised and secured. The fourth article, it will be seen, implied the surrender of the Ministers of State to public justice; and the sixth called for a supply, which the King would be able to raise only by granting all that the English parliament could desire in the way of enquiry and redress of grievances.—Hard terms, and containing a conclusive security against any sudden dissolution or assault upon the privileges of the Houses.

---

* Heylin's Life of Laud.   † Clarendon, Hist. Reb.—May.
‡ Clarendon, Hist. Reb.   § Rushworth.

The first and most important object of the popular leaders was to strengthen their own party in the ensuing parliament; not only for the general reformation of abuses, but also for the more urgent purpose of removing from the King's counsels those persons whose influence with him was a barrier against any measures favourable to liberty, and a source of personal danger to those members through whose efforts such measures were now, or never more, to be successful. Of the delinquent ministers Strafford and Laud were the foremost. The vast abilities and courage of Lord Strafford made him, beyond comparison, the most formidable enemy to the principles and persons of the country party; while the destruction of that party was of an importance to him proportionate to the detestation and alarm in which powerful principles and powerful men must ever be held by one who has openly deserted and betrayed them. Laud, who shared none of the great qualities of his colleague, and who was, says Baillie, considered as 'a mere pendicle at the Lieutenant's ear,' could never, on account of his vanity and rashness, have been an antagonist to be feared, but that his station, his intolerance, and his boldness, had given the whole political power of the Church into his hands, and that his services in managing the contributions of the clergy had secured for him an influence with the King for which it would otherwise be difficult to account.*

As soon as the resolution of summoning a new parliament was announced, and before the writs were issued, the friends of liberty proceeded with the utmost skill and diligence to canvass the country through for the returns of persons of their party and connexion to the lower House. The Earl of Warwick, Lord Brook, and the Earl of Bedford took an active share in these preparations; and Lord Kimbolton, the eldest son of the Earl of Manchester, Nathaniel Fiennes, second son of the Lord Say, and Henry Vane, the eldest son of the Secretary, now became forward persons in the party. Pym and Hampden rode through various counties,† using the utmost exertions, by every appeal to public spirit, to rouse the electors to the support of candidates of known courage and fidelity in their cause. The result was at once so hopeful that the Earl of Warwick wrote from York,‡ although that county had so lately been occupied by the King's court and army, and

---

* Baillie's Letters.—Guthrie.
† Wood's Athenæ. ‡ Clarendon—Hist. Reb.

threatened with invasion by the Covenanters, that 'the game 'was well begun.'* We have it on the very doubtful authority of Eachard that one of the leaders, intemperate in his zeal and his success, openly boasted that 'they were strong 'enough to pull the King's crown from his head, but the 'Gospel would not let them.' †

Nor was the Court inactive in its canvass. But its means were ill concerted, its purposes ill disguised, and the minds of the people ill disposed to yield to its menaces or receive its tardy addresses with favour; and a comparatively small proportion of the candidates so recommended were chosen.

Undoubtedly, of all the abuses of the Royal Prerogative, none had so much contributed to this general disgust as the innovations in religion. And these were the most general topics of excitement used by the popular canvassers, as affecting feelings the deepest and the most earnest, and as concerning matters much more generally embraced by the mind of the people than the mere duty of resisting taxes when imposed by the single will of the King, and of submitting to them when voted by the authority of parliament. Eachard states that when Hampden, about this time, was asked by a friend, apparently not very high in the confidence of the party, 'why they pretended religion, when liberty, property, 'and temporal matters, were the chief end of their proceedings?' He replied, 'Should we not use the pretence of religion, the 'people would not listen to us.' This is a tale very likely to catch the fancy of Eachard, but a sentiment very unlikely to have been avowed by Hampden. The sincerity of Hampden's motives has often been doubted by a certain class of political writers; and these are doubts which may always be safely objected to the memory of all great men by the base ones who succeed them, since, with the means which this world affords, they must be always incapable of a decisive solution. But that Hampden should have confessed to a questioning and traditional friend that the show of religion was, with his party, a mere politic pretence, would surely be much derogatory from his, otherwise universal, reputation for wisdom. Hampden it has been the general fashion of the courtiers of that and subsequent times to describe as a discreet and shrewd dissembler. Something more is required than the authority of Eachard to make us believe him to have been a shallow babbler.

* Whitelocke.   † Eachard's Hist.

Charles, before consenting to the issue of the writs, demanded from his council, 'If this Parliament should prove as 'untoward as some have lately been, will you then assist me 'in such extraordinary ways as in that extremity shall be 'thought fit?' The Council gave this assurance, and the Parliament was called.

When the returns of the members were made up, many names of old renown in the struggles of former parliaments reappeared, and many new ones were added, which at once gave an earnest of popular principles. Hampden's was a double return for the borough of Wendover and for the county of Buckingham; and he made his election for the county. Pym was chosen for Tavistock, and Lord Russell was his colleague; St. John for Totness, Holbourne for St. Michael's, Fiennes for Banbury, and the younger Vane for Kingston-upon-Hull. Several persons nearly connected in blood with Hampden were also returned. His cousins, Oliver Cromwell, Sir John Trevor, and Edmund Waller, were elected for Cambridge, Grampound, and St. Ives; and his two sons-in-law, the younger Knightley and Sir Robert Pye, for Northampton and Woodstock.*

On the 3rd of November, 1640, Charles opened in person a Parliament, which, whether the more to be remembered for its later acts (as having abolished an inseparable part of the ancient constitution of England by razing her monarchy to the ground and destroying even its ruins), or for its earlier (as having redeemed another inseparable part of it by restoring the privileges and power of her free legislature), must by all men be confessed to have been the mightiest assembly that ever brought rare abilities and inflexible courage to grapple for liberty or empire. The time appears scarcely yet to have arrived, but it surely cannot be far distant, when the zeal of writers on this part of our history may be sufficiently cooled

---

* Clarendon accuses the leaders of having packed the House;—no unusual accusation from a disappointed faction who find a great majority returned on the opposite side to their own by the people. He says that this was done by resolving, upon cases of contested elections, their own friends to be duly returned, and declaring that regard should not be had to the merits of the cases but to the fitness of the persons. There is no foundation for this charge. There are on the journals but eight controverted returns. In five of these, the grounds of the determination are stated, and seem to rest entirely on the merits of the cases; and no declaration like that cited by Lord Clarendon is any where to be found but in his History. On this point, see Guthrie's History; on the whole one of the most impartial narratives of these transactions and times.

to allow them to treat of the conduct of the Long Parliament without the inclination to pronounce any but a fair and equal judgment on its acts. Summoned, as it was, to strengthen the military power of one despot, whom it overthrew; and at last destroyed, as it was, by that of another far more powerful; that the acts of this Parliament were always in conformity with one undeviating set of principles, its most zealous admirers cannot contend. But that the tyranny which it undertook to control could have been dealt with on a mere defensive plan, working within the limits of the constitution, the most bitter revilers of its memory will scarcely maintain. Nor, surely, do our general conclusions in favour of a cause require that everything which was done to support it shall be capable of a full moral vindication; least of all that we should be able to show, throughout the conduct of a popular assembly in tumultuous times, that uniformity of virtuous purpose which can rarely be predicated but by an advocate of his unerring client, or by a romancer of his faultless hero. Legislative inconsistencies, and judicial offences may be owned to have been committed on both sides, without materially weakening the just case for either; nor perhaps would it be reasonable, under all the circumstances, to expect to find a course demanding unmixed praise, until some clear examples shall have been shown, in some other age or country, of princes without a vice, and parliaments without a passion. Comparatively easy, meanwhile, is his task who has to consider the conduct and objects of the Long Parliament only with reference to its three first years,—that portion of its existence which closed with the life of Hampden.

Immediately on the meeting, the table of the Commons was loaded with petitions from the counties complaining of the general sufferings of the country, and from individuals setting forth cases of particular hardship. These were strongly urged, on their several grounds, by most of the county members. Committees were formed to consider of the several grievances, and of the means of redress. These were divided by Pym, on the fourth day of the session, into three classes,—privilege, religion, and the liberty of the subject; and, two days after, a grand committee was appointed on each, and out of these a select one, to frame upon their reports a general remonstrance on the state of the nation. The Crown also was addressed that those persons who were still suffering imprisonment by censure of the Star Chamber might be brought to the bar of the House. Nor was this a crisis at which it was possible for the King to pause;—his treasury drained by the expenses of two wasteful expeditions, his credit exhausted, two armies to be maintained, a treaty pending, and the murmurs of a distracted country becoming daily louder and more significant. No means were left to him to restore the finances or conclude a pacification, but by addressing himself to the favour of a party whom he saw determined, before supply, to dispose thoroughly of those questions of grievance on which so many former parliaments had suffered wreck. The Commons perceived their advantage, and pursued it.* Leighton and Lilburne were brought up from the Fleet Prison, and Prynne, Burton, and Bastwick from their solitary captivity in different fortresses; and, by a solemn, and not hasty judgment, obtained a reversal of their sentences, and an award of heavy damages against their persecutors. These were the substantial parts of their triumph. The more ornamental were furnished by the enthusiasm of the people out of doors. The three who had been banished were accompanied by an escort of many thousands, from the place of their re-landing, with banners and music, in gaudy and tumultuous procession. The spectacle, in some respects, was a singularly touching one. Their very different conditions, habits, and ages;—the green and ardent youth of Lilburne; the infirmity of the hoary Leighton, who had lost in captivity both sight and hearing, and nearly the use of his limbs; and the deep and sullen energy of the rest;—equals in their fortitude and their sufferings, and restored, under circumstances of such excitement, from a lengthened penance, during which, though withdrawn from sight, they had never been forgotten, and the traces of which remained in the wasted forms of the elder, and in the scars and brands still visible on all.

But there was one privilege which it was necessary for the parliament at the outset to secure beyond reach of dispute, and without which the struggle for any other would have been premature, abortive, and dangerous. Its first efforts were bent against the Star Chamber, High Commission, and those other courts by which the liberty of speech within its walls had been so often checked and punished.

And now, notice was given of a great judicial act which was

* Rushworth.—Whitelocke.—May.

to put its strength to proof;—to arraign, before the highest tribunal of the realm, one whose very existence in the state was declared by an unanimous vote of the Commons to be incompatible with the public safety. On the 11th of November, the Earl of Strafford was impeached of high treason at the Bar of the Lords, and immediately sequestered from his seat in their House, and committed. In Strafford's case, it is almost unnecessary to state, though very important to be remembered, that the two different courses adopted to further the charges against him were totally independent of, and almost at variance with, each other in principle as well as in form. It would be quite superfluous to bespeak attention to what thus lies on the surface of the history of this great transaction, but that both the Impeachment and the Bill of Attainder, having been founded on the same evidence, and equally directed against the life of this powerful person, have been too often confounded in one common measure of blame or vindication. A select and secret committee was appointed, consisting of twelve persons,—Pym, Hampden, Holles,* Lord Digby, Strode, Sir Walter Earle, Selden, St. John, Maynard, Palmer, Glynne, and Whitelocke.† These were to consider the information against the Earl, to arrange the evidence, and, with the occasional assistance of Lord Falkland, Colepepper, and Hyde, to manage the conferences with the Lords, and conduct to its close this solemn and long-protracted trial.

Hampden was also one of the Committee appointed, December 18th, to expedite the charges against Laud, which were severally agreed to on the 24th of February, and, two days after, accompanied by Pym and Maynard, to deliver them at the Bar of the Lords. On Monday, the 1st of March, the Archbishop was finally committed by the Lords to the Tower, and debarred all intercourse with the Earl of Strafford. In this imprisonment he remained for two years, without putting in his answer or petitioning for trial.‡

About the same time with the preparation of articles against Strafford and Laud, several other Officers of State, Judges, and Bishops, who had been concerned in the different illegal

---

* The appointment of Denzil Holles on the secret committee was a singular one, connected as he was with Strafford by the nearest bond of family alliance. It appears, however, that, acting faithfully with the popular party in all its other enterprizes, he was excused from taking any share in this. † Whitelocke's Memorials.

‡ Rushworth.—Neale's History of the Puritans.

sentences, were arraigned.* Of these, after Finch and Secretary Windebank, the chief were Sir George Ratcliffe (the friend and biographer of Strafford), Wren, Bishop of Ely, and Judge Berkeley.† But the attention of Parliament was principally fixed on the case against the Earl, as that without the successful prosecution of which no proceedings against less important delinquents could afford any security to public liberty, and after the pursuing of which to legal judgment public liberty would require no further atonement.‡

The speed with which Parliament now gave effect to its determination to proceed capitally against Lord Strafford, was proportionate to the secrecy with which the country party had conducted and arranged their councils. The fourth article of the Treaty of Rippon, which was still in discussion, and which referred only to the 'incendiaries' in Scotland, required to be countenanced by a corresponding proceeding in England. But there is little doubt that, even if the leaders of the House of Commons had had no other motive, there was a close and urgent one, of personal safety, which made it absolutely necessary that the blow aimed at Strafford should be struck without delay. The courtiers, and even some of the ministers, had already spoken of charges of high treason against Pym, and Hampden, and the rest; Pym, and Hampden, and the rest, were more discreet and as much in earnest as they, and anticipated the arraignment which Strafford was actually preparing, by a sudden and unanimous resolution of the House, and twenty-eight charges of high treason against himself.

During the course of this great impeachment, which lasted, from the presentation of the Articles at the Bar of the Lords, just five months, so far was it from absorbing the attention of those men who had thus engaged no less than their lives in the enterprise, that two of the most important measures that ever occupied the attention of any legislative assembly were proceeding, separately and independently, at an equal pace with it; the curtailment of the political power of the Bishops, and the securing of meetings of parliaments at short and regular intervals. Important, however, as these objects were, they formed but episodes in the history of the winter of 1640, and of the ensuing spring, the great act of which was the trial of Lord Strafford. The general outline of the facts charged is well known, and the grounds on which it was endeavoured to

* Rushworth.   † Whitelocke.—May.   ‡ Somers's Tracts.

bring them within the Statute of Treasons. The arrangement of the evidence, and afterwards the pleadings before the Lords, occupied a space of time, and led to a complication of detail, through which it would be as needless to travel, in order to obtain a just view of the nature of the process, as it would be a course, to most people, uninviting and tedious. Nor is this prolixity to be wondered at in a work so new and difficult as was the attempt to convict a Minister of high treason, in conspiring with his Sovereign to accomplish an unexecuted plan to destroy parliaments and introduce an arbitrary power by means of an army; in levying, of his own power, taxes on divers merchandises; in establishing, of his own power, a criminal jurisdiction beyond the law; and all this by acts spread over a series of years, and out of which, taken together, the offence against the statute was to be compounded. The long suspense in which, during the early part of these proceedings, the Earl was kept, on a matter affecting his life, has been by some enumerated among the cruelties of this transaction;—by others, the haste with which, after a certain period, it was urged on to its close. In whatever manner the proofs of the treason may be considered, surely nothing can be less just than to impute to the parliament either the delay at first or the haste at last, as a charge of unnecessary severity. If Lord Strafford were to be impeached of high treason at all, surely the suspense, and afterwards the great length, of the trial, are not truly to be made matter of accusation against the prosecutors. From the beginning, it was their interest to proceed more summarily, and thus to baffle the intrigues of Charles, the address and eloquence of the Earl repeatedly displayed, and the conspiracies among the leaders of the northern army to save him. The frequent endeavours of the Commons to urge forward the proceedings, resisted as often by the Earl on the ground of his ill-health and the difficulties of his defence, as well as the eagerness of the Court party to hasten the Scottish Treaty (by the conclusion of which the King would fain have put himself in possession of the services of his army before the Lords should be in a condition to pass judgment upon his Minister), equally tend to show that delay was the policy of those who would have saved Strafford, while that of the parliament, from the beginning, would have been to proceed with that haste which was at last imputed to them as indecent and inhuman.

Overbearing and tyrannical as was the temper of Strafford, no one can refuse admiration to that commanding ability and haughty courage of demeanour which forsook him not at any time in this great trial. The energies of his mind increased in vigour and capacity, his natural spirit broke forth into greater fervour and brightness, as he beheld himself more and more closely encompassed by the toils of his bold and indefatigable prosecutors. From the hour when the first proceedings against him were announced, he must have seen that his danger was great, and his defences, at the best, precarious. The popular powers of three countries were against him; and he knew too well the faithlessness of his master to look with any confidence for that support which, by every conceivable obligation, the closest and most sacred, of feeling, honour, conscience, and renewed and written promise, Charles had bound himself in the sight of God and man, at every hazard, to give him. Scarcely had the measure taken root in the House of Commons, when all who felt, in person or in property, the grievances of the late war; all who had suffered from the arbitrary courts, from illegal taxes, or quarterings of troops; all who resented the usurped supremacy of the presidency of the North, or who had groaned under the absolute government of the Irish Lieutenancy;—saw in Strafford a public enemy put upon his deliverance, and in the success of the impeachment their only chance of relief and retribution. The Scottish Commissioners petitioned for justice against him on the ground of his inveterate counsels for war against their country and their religion;—the Irish Parliament, now relieved both from his presence and from that of his army,* revoked the subsidies which they had voted, and sent Deputies also to London, to join with the Scots in arraigning their proud and dauntless victim.†

The first order for his attendance found him at York. Several of his friends would have persuaded him to avoid the storm, or at least not to meet it until its fury might have been spent. But it was not in Strafford's temper to shrink from a conflict which his ambition had provoked. He instantly came up to London; and, on the day when the Articles were read by the managers to the Lords, attempted by a sudden display of pride and passion, to frown down, as he had been wont, the assaults of his enemies. But Pym, and Hampden, and

---

* Commons' Journals.   † Carte's Life of Ormond.—Rushworth.

St. John, had now, for the first time, come fairly to the conflict with him; and it was in the name of the Commons of England. They maintained the station which was assigned them; and Strafford was forbidden to speak until the appointed time should arrive for his defence against each separate charge.

Of all the accounts of this most memorable transaction, that by Baillie, who was present with the Scotch Commissioners, is given with the greatest power and minuteness, and he proceeds, through his compressed journal of the trial, with a shrewdness of observation and a liveliness of description which lighten details otherwise varied only by the almost endless niceties of legal ingenuity. Strafford's tyrannies during his presidency of the North, the general course of his government in Ireland, his arbitrarily raising duties on articles of trade for purposes of secret service or private profit, his illegal attempts to ruin the Earl of Cork and to destroy the Lord Mountnorris, his advice as to the Scotch war, and as to using the Irish army to reduce *this* kingdom, (a phrase, the ambiguity of which was not removed either by the paper furnished by the younger Vane, or the unwilling evidence of his father,) were the main points insisted on by the managers. The inference as to the treasonable intentions respecting the army was surely justified by the propositions for 'the bridling of parliaments and for the 'encrease of the revenue,' and has been since proved, beyond doubt, by the published correspondence of Strafford. But the evidence at the trial was clearly defective on this point; and the 'intent to subvert the fundamental laws' is no treason by statute. It is impossible, besides, not to observe the vagueness and generality of two or three of the charges, and the strained and quibbling conclusions by which the lawyers of the committee of management endeavoured to maintain such a proposition, for instance, as that the establishing of a private monopoly in the duties on tobacco, and on the exportation of hides and wool, is high treason, as 'depriving the King of his revenue, 'and so depriving him of his government.' * It would be a very poor vindication of such reasoning as this in such men as St. John and Maynard to say, however truly, that the practice of the courts in these times was fertile in judgments of constructive treason, and that by none had the intent of penal statutes been more distorted than by Strafford himself.†

---

* For observations on the evidence on these charges, see Phillips's State Trials. † Lords' Journals.

Strafford, before his great speech in defence,* had spoken at the close of each separate charge, and had lost no occasion to challenge the support of the peers by the shrewdness and vigour of his reasoning, or to enlist on his side the sympathies of an assembled audience of almost all the first persons in the land by his forcible and sometimes deeply pathetic eloquence.† With such as are swayed in their judgment of guilt by their admiration of a courageous heart, and a nobly gifted mind struggling against danger and dishonour, Strafford's acquittal is always sure. And to these feelings he frequently and powerfully appealed.

After a long and hard-fought argument upon evidence, in which he had singly and with great energy encountered St. John, Maynard, and a host of their witnesses, on charges relating to his Irish government, and had disputed the ground step by step, sometimes involving the managers in great difficulties, on their proceeding to another article, Lord Strafford declared himself unable to endure more fatigue. 'Turn your ' eye inwards,' said he, ' look into the recesses of your own ' hearts, and then judge whether you will not allow a respite ' for a few short hours in so weighty a cause, which involves ' my life, my honour, the fate of my children, and all I have!' Upon this the court adjourned.

Upon the treasonable words deposed to by Bristol, Northumberland, Holland, and Newburgh, he thus declaimed: —' Shall words,' said he, ' spoken by way of argument in com- ' mon discourse between man and man, when nothing has been ' done upon them, shall such bare words be brought against a ' man, and charged on him as high treason? God forbid that ' we should ever live to see such an example in this kingdom. ' If words spoken to friends in familiar discourse, spoken in ' one's chamber, spoken at one's table, spoken in one's sick- ' bed, spoken perhaps to gain clearer light and judgment by ' reasoning, if these can be brought against a man as treason, ' all intercourse, all confidence, all the comfort of human ' society, are destroyed. Let no man henceforth venture to ' impart his solitary thoughts to his friend or neighbour.' Never, it must be confessed, was an ordinary artifice managed with more masterly address than in the construction of this noble appeal to the highest and most generous passions of a

---

* Parliamentary History. † Phillips's State Trials.

noble audience. Nothing can be more different from the supposed situations or circumstances described, (the chamber, the table, or the sick-bed,) than those which were in evidence; phrases used by a minister in deliberation with officers and statesmen on acts of state to be done by them. And yet, manifest as is the fallacy, it is an appeal against which the heart is with difficulty guarded.

Upon the words alleged by Vane to have been spoken at the Council Board, 'These words,' said he, 'were not wantonly or
' unnecessarily spoken, or whispered in a corner; but they
' were spoken in full council, where, by the duty of my oath, I
' was obliged to speak, according to my heart and conscience,
' in all things concerning the King's service. If I had forborne
' to speak what I conceived to be for the benefit of the King
' and the people, I had been perjured towards Almighty God.
' And for delivering my mind openly and freely, shall I be in
' danger of my life as a traitor? If that necessity be put upon
' me, I thank God by his blessing I have learned not to stand
' in fear of him who can only kill the body. If the question be
' whether I must be traitor to man, or perjured to God, I will
' be faithful to my Creator. And whatsoever shall befall me
' from popular rage or from my own weakness, I must leave it
' to that Almighty Being, and to the justice and honour of my
' judges. My Lords, I conjure you not to make yourselves
' so unhappy as to disable yourselves and your children from
' undertaking the great charge and trust of the Common-
' wealth. You inherit that trust from your fathers; you are
' born to great thought; you are nursed up for the great and
' weighty employments of the kingdom. But if it be once
' admitted that a counsellor, delivering his opinion with
' others at the council table, candidè et castè, under an oath
' of secrecy and faithfulness, shall be brought into question
' upon some misapprehension or ignorance of law, if every
' word that he speaks from a sincere and noble intention
' shall be drawn against him, for the attainting of him, his
' children, and posterity, I know not (under favour I speak
' it) any wise or noble person of fortune who will, upon
' such perilous and unsafe terms, adventure to be counsellor
' to the King. Therefore I beseech your lordships so to look
' on me, that my misfortune may not bring an inconvenience
' upon yourselves. And, though my words were not so advised
' and discreet, or so well weighed, as they ought to be, yet, I

'trust, your lordships are too honourable and just to lay them
'to my charge as high treason.'

On one occasion his naturally impetuous and arrogant temper broke forth, and he charged the parliaments of England and Ireland with conspiring against him. For this he was instantly rebuked by Maynard, and he apologised. But by this, and by the reading of the Irish Remonstrance, (which he objected to as if it had been offered in evidence, when in fact it was not offered in evidence, but read as part of the charge,) 'he lost,' says Baillie, 'much reputation.'

What, however, prejudiced him the most in the eyes of his judges, on the first day, was the personal interference which was attempted on the part of the King, who, though prevented from sitting on his throne to influence the lords or managers by his presence, sat, with the Queen and Court, 'full in the eyes of all,' having with his own hands removed the 'tirlie' (curtain) which concealed the Royal Party.*

It is now fit to consider the second course of proceedings against him. What was the immediate motive for the change from the judicial to the legislative mode has never yet appeared. The charges were closed, and the lords had voted the facts. The judges were preparing to declare them treason by law. It is not true, therefore, that the Bill of Attainder arose out of any failure of the impeachment, or out of any misunderstanding between the Houses. For, in the end, it must be remembered, the bill declaring the treason required the consent of the Lords; and the Lords were as competent to conclude against it legislatively as they had been to acquit judicially on the evidence; besides the increased moral difficulties in the way of their doing by means so questionable what it appears that they were prepared to do by the ordinary course of trial and judgment. Nor, if it be supposed that the Lords were influenced in passing that bill by the fear of popular tumult, can that be alleged as having been a motive with the Commons for forcing the Lords with a bill. For the cries of 'Justice! Justice!' from the populace would have sounded as fearfully to the Lords proceeding to judgment in Westminster Hall as when they were proceeding with the bill in their house of parliament, and thus the same conclusions would have been obtained from them without the indelible and just odium attached to an ex post facto declara-

---

* Baillie.

tion of a highly penal law. Some reason beyond any which has hitherto been imputed, some supposed necessity arising out of the discovered intrigue for the escape of the prisoner and for the bringing up of the army, is wanting to account for the determination by such means to hasten in so small a degree the issue of this long-protracted trial.

For this and for every other reason, the view of all the circumstances under which this change of the proceedings took place ought to be approached with the utmost coolness and candour. The act is not to be dealt with, for a moment, in the profligate terms in which Macpherson half apologises for the illegality of the trial of Argyle under the restored government, when he says that 'the informality of the proceedings against ' him could scarce be justified by his crimes.'* All departure from the substantial rules of justice to procure judgment against a man for his crimes is in itself one of the worst of crimes, and admits neither of justification nor apology. But, on the other hand, it would be no less shameful to speak of that proceeding, as Evelyn does, as being 'the ' greatest malice and greatest innocency that ever met before ' so illustrious an assembly.' Let the case be put fairly. We may assume, (without the sort of palliation insinuated to qualify the murder of Argyle), that the only ground on which, in this case, an attempt at justification can be rested, is that very dangerous one of state necessity, and this state necessity arising out of the peculiar position as well as character of the person himself. For the imminent danger to the state arose out of the peculiarities of his position as well as character. And these, taken together, were doubtless dangerous to it in the highest degree. His apostacy had been of the most execrable sort, and took effect at a time when any apostacy from the popular cause was the most execrable. For it was not to be palliated by any reason of alarm, nor even by the temptation of a great revenge upon political antagonists. His only political antagonists were those into whose ranks he was proceeding to desert with all the arms about him which he had borne in the cause of liberty. The cause of liberty was not then triumphant, nor had its pretensions, nor the demands of the popular party, risen beyond the level of that Petition of Right of which Strafford had been one of the foremost

* Macpherson—Hist. Great Britain.

champions.* His power had soon become fully commensurate with his daring. Like Buckingham a stranger equally to moderation and to fear, his capacities were immeasurably greater; and, at the time of his fall, he was meditating a blow at the constitution such as Buckingham had never contemplated, nor probably could ever have obtained the means to attempt. It is difficult to admit that the act which threw Strafford into the hands of his prosecutors had of itself dissolved the spell of his power. Charles had promised to banish him for ever from his presence and councils, and even from the land. But slender indeed would have been the security of this engagement, if ever the state of those negotiations which the King was then carrying on with the army had given the means to restore and avenge him; and to avenge him the more signally in proportion to the power which had been shown by his adversaries. If it were a doctrine admissible that laws may be framed ex post facto to fit particular cases, the whole argument on the justice of this act would be as complete as the argument on the injustice of the principle is now complete the other way. If, on the other hand, it be said that charges of accumulative treason may be held to be proved in cases where it is doubtful whether any one act taken singly can be made treasonable within the law of the land, no man is safe, and especially when he is to be tried by a council of many, where each judge separately may be satisfied on some one separate charge, and so all be found to condemn on the charges taken in the aggregate, while on each particular the majority of the judges might have acquitted.

Those who voted on the Bill of Attainder had to determine whether they would allow a criminal to escape death because his crime was so great and so complicated that it was difficult to bring it within the bounds of a statute, and thus show future ministers a way to baffle justice; or whether, in order to destroy a powerful enemy to their country, they should for a time cast loose from the anchorage ground of law, and on a capital matter too. Be it remembered, these prosecutors were charged with no ordinary duties, they were fighting against no

---

* It was Wentworth who moved this clause to be added to the Petition of Right, 'That, for the comfort and safety of his subjects, his Majesty 'would be pleased to declare his will and pleasure that all his Ministers 'should serve him according to the laws and statutes of the realm.'

ordinary man, and with inferior means; and, above all, they were fighting a great battle for the liberties of their country.

Thus much for their motives, and for the difficulties and dangers with which on every side they were surrounded.

On the whole, however, it must be admitted that the proceeding by bill is not capable of any complete vindication. Mercy is never the attribute of great assemblies, and justice not always. And, in this case, much was owed to precedent as well as to justice; for good precedent is justice due to after times. It has often been observed that the strongest practical admission on the part of the promoters of this measure, that they knew the principle to be wrong, was their proviso that it should not be drawn into precedent. This has been generally argued upon as if it had been a proviso against all future bills of attainder, which would be an absurd supposition. The precedent against which in all probability they meant to guard was that of an act of attainder brought in pending a trial at law. But the strongest proof that their principle was wrong was this; that, in spite of that proviso, their act was pleaded as precedent, three years after, for the taking off of Laud;—a measure still more repugnant to all notions of legal principle.

To treat of it as a legal act would be an idle misuse of terms. The apology for it is that, while Strafford lived, there was no security against Charles's restoring him to power; and that, while he was in power, there was no law in England for the protection of the subject. The phrase in Oliver St. John's speech, that 'there is no law for wolves and 'beasts of prey,' it would be a solecism in language to call an argument in law. Taken as such, it would have been but insolent and cruel mockery. But it was a fit declaration of the character of an act which was to demolish an authority stronger than the law, and an authority which it was difficult, without demolishing, to abate. It was, on the whole, the case of the most dangerous minister that England ever knew, destroyed by the most dangerous precedent that an English Parliament ever established.

The conduct of Lord Digby in this matter would have entitled him to praise, if it had not been stained by his baseness in secretly purloining a material piece of evidence from the Committee, and afterwards vehemently, impiously, and falsely, protesting his innocence before God and the Parliament on oath.* His speech in the House of Commons was eloquent and powerful. It states the whole of the argument against the Bill, and states it in the best manner; nor is the reasoning of it materially shaken by that of St. John, which, however, is very superior to Pym's, and is, in every respect, the best vindication of that measure which has ever been put forth. Lord Digby's opposition to the Bill was the more effective, so long as his motives were regarded as pure and honourable, on account of the unceasing vehemence with which he had before urged the impeachment.

Then followed that great last speech of the Earl himself before the Lords, the peroration of which has been so often and so deservedly celebrated as one of the finest specimens of pathetic eloquence in our language. It is so generally known, that the transcribing of it here would hardly be justified. And, indeed, so beautiful are several of the passages which precede it, that it would be difficult to determine where the quotation ought to commence. No reader, who is not familiar with the conclusion of that speech, will repent the having searched for it in the report of the trial; and if, in the course of that search, he should be led to read through the whole of that memorable defence, he will be well repaid for the time which it will have cost him.

We have already remarked how necessary it is for any man who would do fair justice to the leaders in this prosecution to keep his mind free to judge between the two modes of proceeding adopted during its course. Of this we shall presently adduce a remarkable proof. Those writers who discuss this matter in a mere spirit of political controversy, and who would therefore include that whole party and that whole prosecution in one undistinguishing measure of either approbation or blame, have endeavoured to veil the great barrier of principle which separates the trial upon the impeachment from the ex post facto law of pains and penalties. This course has been lately taken in an eminent critical work, in its observations on Mr. Hallam's history.† The Impeachment and Bill of Attainder are there treated of but as parts of one great measure, and then pronounced upon together as being an

---

* His treachery in this matter, and the falsehood of his protestations, which at the time deceived many, were afterwards proved by the purloined document found, copied in his own handwriting, among papers taken at Naseby. † Quarterly Review, No. lxxiii. Article 7.

'extra legal murder.' They are said to have originated in the failure of the proposal for giving office to some of the leaders of that party who 'wanted places and power, and being 'disappointed in their expectations, determined upon shedding 'the blood of the man with whom, if they had been taken 'into office, they were willing to have coalesced.' This imputation must have been made without due inquiry into the history of that transaction. None of those persons who were named for office appear to have been privy to any compromise in favour of Lord Strafford, except the Earl of Bedford,* with whom the negotiation originated, by whom it was secretly conducted, and by whose death it was abruptly closed. There is, consequently, no reason for imputing to them a folly so gross as the having been willing to coalesce with one who would not have lost much time after such a coalition in effectually working their ruin and that of their cause. Besides, the impeachment had preceded that negotiation; and, consequently, the remarks of this writer upon those who, 'being disappointed in their expectations, were 'thereby determined upon shedding blood,' must be strictly limited to the promoters of the bill of pains and penalties, among whom he strangely classes Hampden with the Earl of Bedford, who was working to defeat it, and died before it reached the Upper House,† and with Lord Say, who counselled, spoke, and voted against it.‡ 'This fact alone,' concludes the passage in question, 'might suffice to reclaim an ingenuous 'mind from the worship of Pym and Hampden.' It is pleasing to a mind which would contemplate with unqualified admiration the high and blameless character of Hampden to be able, without disingenuousness, to satisfy itself that the premises on which this censure rests are likewise destitute of foundation. Throughout the progress of the attainder, the memory of Hampden is not stained by any appearance of his having been concerned in it. That he was a manager of the impeachment, and an active one, we have seen. The remarkable fact, therefore, of his name not appearing in any of the proceedings on the Bill, whether it afford a more or less strong presumption

---

* Perhaps also the Marquis of Hamilton, who, according to Clarendon, early engaged with Bedford in recommending the project of popularising the King's government by the introduction of some of the leaders of the country party. † Clarendon, Hist. Reb.
‡ Collection of Speeches, published 1648.—Parl. Hist.

of his having disapproved of that course, is at least a sufficient answer to an accusation which ought not to have been made unless accompanied by direct affirmative proof.

But the case does not stop here. Hampden's steady abstinence from any participation in the act of attainder, and in the proceedings which led to it, is not inferred from such circumstances only as might have been accidental or undesigned. From the opening of the charges, to the last free conference 'touching the matter of law in the case of the trial,' (the heads of which he was appointed, together with Pym, Pierrepoint, Colepepper, and others, to prepare,) in almost every step of the impeachment he is conspicuous.* To 'the further proceedings' he is no party, although they are at different times countenanced by all his colleagues in the Lower House except Digby and Selden. This is the more fit to be observed on account of the unfavourable contrast in which it is sometimes attempted to place the conduct of Hampden with that of Falkland and of Hyde. Now, Hyde at best did no more to mark his disapproval of the Bill than Hampden did. On the contrary, on the 24th of April, when Glyn and Hill were appointed to manage a conference 'for the expediting of the 'bill of attainder,' Hyde went up with a message 'to acquaint 'their Lordships that the House hath received information 'that the Earl may have a design to escape, &c., &c., and 'therefore to desire their Lordships that he may be close 'prisoner, and the guard strengthened.' †

Falkland, it appears clearly from Sir Ralph Verney's notes, on the 15th of April, spoke in answer to Digby and in favour of the Bill; Hampden never.‡ And, on the 16th, while Hampden was on one committee to prepare heads for a conference 'concerning their Lordships' resolution to hear counsel 'in matter of law, and to desire that their Lordships would

---

* See Commons Journals, January 4, April 15, 16, 22, 23, and 24, 1640-1 et passim.

† Clarendon, with remarkable disingenuousness, passes over, in his History, the whole of his own conduct on the prosecution of Strafford, and particularly the fact of his having taken up this message, which arose out of the apprehension entertained by the House of the project of 'bringing 'up the army,' afterwards strangely called by him 'the pretended plot.' In his account of the progress of the Bill against Episcopacy, he states that, until then, Falkland and he had never differed in a vote. This, if taken strictly, is an admission that he (Hyde) had voted for Strafford's attainder; for Falkland unquestionably did.

‡ Sir Ralph Verney's MS. notes, in the possession of Sir Harry Verney.

'use all expedition to give an end to this trial as much as in
'justice may be,' Falkland was on another which was appointed
to prepare heads for a conference ' concerning the *further*
' proceedings,' on the report of which committee it was that
the Bill was passed.*

In debate, Hampden never alluded to the proceeding by bill
but once. On the 16th of April, when it was discussed,
pending the attainder, whether the Commons should continue
to hear the Earl's counsel at the bar of the Lords, or proceed
with the Bill, St. John, having said that ' being possessed of
' a bill, they had made themselves judges, and being so, it were
' a dishonour to hear counsel any where but at their own bar;'
and Colepepper having said, ' if we reply to Lord Strafford's
' counsel before the Lords, we prejudice our cause in taking
' away the power of declaring treason,' Hampden, according to
Sir Ralph Verney's notes, in opposition to his fellow managers,
urged that they should proceed, not by bill, but by trial at the
Lords' bar. ' The Bill now depending doth not tie us to goe
' by bill. Our counsel hath been heard. Ergo, in justice we
' must heare his. Noe more prejudice to goe to heare matter
' of law, than to heare counsel to matter of fact.' †

I may have been too prolix in these details. But I have
undertaken these memorials with a desire to do justice; and
the injustice of general imputations, made without foundation
of authority, cannot be met but by reference to particulars.

Then why, it may be asked, if Hampden disapproved of the
Bill, did he not take the part of actively opposing it? and why
do we not find his name in the list of Straffordians? First,
it might, in reply, be asked, why do we not find Edward
Hyde's? It is not necessary to rest anything on the fact of
several of the strongest opposers of that Bill not having voted
in that minority of fifty-six members afterwards called the
Straffordians. Let it be admitted that it is most improbable
indeed that Hampden took any further part against the Bill.
I am decidedly of opinion that he did not. I only mention
this fact as a singular one; I know not why it was so; that
some of the boldest and most active opponents of the attainder
are not to be found in that list. Heath says that ' at the time

---

* Commons Journals.

† Sir Ralph Verney's Notes. Glyn supports Pym's argument against
hearing Strafford's counsel as to the point of law. Sir Benjamin Rudyerd
agrees with Hampden.

'of passing the Bill of Attainder in the House of Commons,
'Sir Bevill Grenvil and Sir Alexander Carew sitting together,
'they both serving for the same county of Cornwall, Sir Bevill
'bespoke Sir Alexander in such like words :—" Pray, Sir, let
'it not be said that any member of our county should have
'a hand in this ominous business, and, therefore, pray give
'your vote against this Bill." To whom the other instantly
'replied, " If I were sure to be the next man that should suffer
'upon the same scaffold with the same axe, I would give my
'consent to the passing of it."' * And yet, plain as it is that
Sir Bevill very thoroughly opposed the Bill, he does not appear
among the Straffordians.

But why then, it is again asked, if Hampden disapproved
of the precedent of a bill of attainder, did he not make head
against it as manfully as he had before supported the impeachment? Plainly, because in a case doubtful to him only as
matter of precedent but clear to him in respect of the guilt of
the accused person, in a case in which the accused person, in
his estimation, deserved death, and in which all law but that of
the sceptre and the sword was at an end if he had escaped it,
when all the ordinary protection of law to the subject throughout the country was suspended, and suspended mainly by the
counsels of Strafford himself, Hampden was not prepared to
heroically immolate the liberties of England in order to save
the life of him who would have destroyed them. Hampden
probably considered the bill which took away Strafford's life
(and indeed it must in fairness be so considered) as a revolutionary act undertaken for the defence of the Commonwealth.
That in his conscience he believed it to be an act of substantial
injustice to the person arraigned, no man has any right to
conclude. I moreover aver that there is not more ground for
imputing a participation in that measure to him than to Lord
Clarendon, and not near so much as to Lord Falkland.†

* Brief Chronicle.
† [The Editor of the present edition of this biography has reason to
believe that had its author lived himself to superintend it, he would at least
have modified many expressions in the above argument as to Hampden's
supposed opposition to the bill of attainder. Lord Nugent felt latterly
that he had given more importance to the entry in Sir Harry Verney's
Notes than it ought legitimately to bear, seeing that the strict alternative
presented in the discussion on which he spoke does not appear to have
been whether Strafford's counsel should be heard, *or* the bill proceeded with,
for the very obvious and satisfactory reason that both were ultimately
done. Hampden's opinion prevailed, and the bill nevertheless went
forward.]

The conduct of Hampden in this matter has been unjustly dealt with. It has been (designedly, as it appears) confounded with that of others, by Lord Clarendon, by the Commonwealth writers, and by the inflamed Tory writers of modern times. Lord Clarendon never did justice to any opponent, and there were many feelings which specially interfered with his doing justice to Hampden. The Commonwealth writers are, of course, partial to Hampden's memory; but they are generally defenders also of the proceedings against Strafford, and would not willingly disconnect a name which they revered from a measure which they approved. And the modern Tory writers are well content to assume, without any authority for it, that Hampden's reputation is involved in a measure which they represent as an ' extra legal murder,' blackening every reputation which can be connected with it.

But, in whatever light the conduct of the Managers is to be viewed, upon that of the King there can be but one judgment formed by any man who respects the clear boundaries which divide the most obvious duty from the most unmitigated injustice and perfidy. It may be said to have been an unnecessary severity in the Parliament to adopt a course by which it was proposed to him to become a party to the destruction of his favourite, for acts many of which he had enjoined, and to all of which he had consented. But nothing can palliate the falsehood and cruelty of Charles, who, rather than have sent Lord Strafford to his fate, ought to have prepared himself to meet any result, even that, if need had been, of sharing it. The merely sacrificing his Minister for acts to which he had been himself a party, was an infamous baseness; the sacrificing him after a letter of assurance that not a hair of his head should suffer, but that he (the King) would risk all and suffer all first, was shameful treachery. The postscript to his letter to the Lords, pleading for Strafford at the beginning, and at the end delivering him up to death, with an ' if he must die, ' 'twere charity to reprieve him till Saturday,' was unfeeling and cruel. But more base, more treacherous, and more cruel still, was the permitting St. John, in consequence of a half-executed design for conciliating the country party, to continue to lead the prosecution and bring up the Bill as Solicitor-General to the King. Who, seeing this, can believe the King to have been at any time in conscience irreconcileable to the project of destroying Strafford? who, seeing this, but would admit that it gave countenance to the declared purpose of the Commons, and encouragement to them to proceed? Though Strafford knew his master's duplicity, still, when he wrote to him his famous letter urging him to pass the Bill, he seems to have thoroughly expected that he would resist. This was shown by his exclamation of surprise, and grief, and reproach, when he was told that the King had given way.

Next in guilt to the conduct of Charles was that of Williams and the other Bishops, with whom was performed the mockery of a consultation on a point of plain and absolute duty. From this hypocrisy Juxon alone was free. To his honour be it remembered that, scorning the sophistry of divided conscience, he told the King that he was bound before God and man to refuse his assent.

Thus fell Lord Strafford; in the circumstances of his death giving to his enemies no advantage over his character. It is truly said of him in the 'Eikon,' 'I looked upon him as 'a gentleman whose abilities might well make a Prince rather 'afraid than ashamed in the greatest affairs of State.'

PART THE SIXTH.

1641.

Triennial Bill—Corruptions of the Churchmen—Bill to restrain the Clergy from secular offices—Missions of Panzani and Rosetti—Temporising of the High Church Party in England with the Romish Discipline—Ground of Clarendon's Imputation against Hampden examined—Lord Say—Nathaniel Fiennes—Lord Kimbolton—Lord Digby—Sir Harry Vane, the Younger—Strode—Hazelrigge—Sir Edward Deering—Oliver Cromwell—Pym—Root-and-Branch Bill for rendering Parliament indissoluble but with it's own consent—Proceedings against Finch, Windebanke, and others—Result of the changes in Government—Great Seal given to Sir Edward Littleton—Army Plot.

It has been already remarked that two other very important measures were proceeding, separately and independently, at an equal pace with the impeachment of Lord Strafford. These were to deprive the Bishops of votes in Parliament, by a bill prohibiting the exercise of any civil office by clergymen; and to provide, by what was called the Triennial Bill, that parliaments should be holden at intervals of not longer than three years. By the Triennial Bill it was endeavoured to secure the country from the arbitrary courses which the King had been enabled to pursue during the long intermission of parliaments. But precarious and ineffectual would such an enactment be as a security against any King who might resolve to govern without parliaments and in opposition to law. For the provisions of the bill itself could only be guarded by the parliamentary power of impeaching the minister under whose advice the King should infringe them; and the very act of infringing them by governing without parliaments would be the minister's protection against impeachment. This law provided, indeed, that if the king should refuse to summon a parliament within the time prescribed, the Chancellor or Keeper of the Great Seal might issue writs for summoning the Peers, and for the election of the Commons; and that, if the Chancellor or Keeper should neglect to do it, any twelve of the Peers might summon the parliament, and that if the Peers should neglect to issue the necessary summons, the sheriffs of the counties and other magistrates respectively might proceed to the election; and should they refuse, then that the freeholders of each county might elect their members; and that the members so chosen should be obliged under severe penalties to attend.*

The passing of this bill was received with public rejoicings, and the thanks of both houses were solemnly tendered to the King as soon as he had pronounced the Royal assent. It, doubtless, was giving a large power to the people. But it was at best a law which, in extreme cases, (and it was a law intended to meet extreme cases only,) would have failed before a tyrannical King, and a resolute minister, with an army to back them. For in those times during a cessation of parliaments, the public voice spoke through but imperfect organs. The press had not influence to assist it either by calling public meetings of the people or by directing their deliberations when called.

The Bill affecting the Bishops' votes was, even separately considered, a measure of primary importance in the eyes of the country party. Apart from every vindictive feeling, which could not but have had its influence against an order under whose intolerance the separatists of England and the churchmen of Scotland had so severely suffered, and apart from all considerations of the character and deportment of the persons then composing the Hierarchy, the political functions of churchmen were regarded by the Puritans generally as founded on an abuse, and tending to a profanation, of the Ecclesiastical Institution. It was so considered, doubtless, by the Presbyterians, in whose estimation the temporalities of the prelates were, like their spiritual powers, an ample remnant of the abhorred discipline of Rome. It was considered so, in an equal degree, by the Independents, who had grafted their love of civil liberty on the profession of a religion 'whose kingdom is not of this world.'

* Parl. Hist.—Guthrie.

There was no country, except the papal dominions themselves, where an alliance with the state had led the Churchmen into such shameless servility as in England. The established Church of England had, although possessing some of the ablest ministers of any time, become exceedingly corrupt. In proportion to what she felt to be the growing distaste in which her corruptions were held by the people did she seek support from the Crown, by making her sacred functions subservient to its arbitrary purposes, and by offering to the person of the Sovereign the basest and most impious measure of adulation. Pluralities, also, had long been matter of grievous and very general complaint. 'For the Bill,' says Archbishop Bancroft, in a letter to James the First, in 1610, 'that is in hand against ' pluralities, it is the same that, for above forty years, from ' parliament to parliament, hath been rejected; and that very ' worthily.' 'Religio peperit Divitias, et Filia devoravit Matrem,' said Lord Falkland in his speech concerning episcopacy. And in no history has the truth of this saying been oftener or more strikingly shown than in that of England both before and since the Reformation. Even the Reformation was rendered popular, not so much by the pressure of the Church revenues on the wealth and industry of the country, as by the laxity of habits among the Churchmen, which it was believed that the overgrown amount of those revenues had tended to promote. The reforming of long established canons of faith and discipline is an enterprise too bold for the generality of men to contemplate with cheerfulness, unless under the excitement of some practical grievance which is seen and felt. Few undertake to decide on controversial points of belief; all can judge of the accordance or discrepancy of the manners of the clergy with true religion. Indeed no hierarchy, and no creed, has ever been overthrown by the people, on account only of its theoretical dogmas, so long as the practice of the clergy was incorrupt and conformable with their professions.

Soon after the first settlement of the Reformation, at all events from the beginning of James's reign, the prelates had adopted a mistaken view not only of the duties but of the interests also of the body which they represented. They were startled at the natural and inevitable workings of the spirit which their immediate predecessors had evoked to assist them in their great work. They looked back instead of forward, and neglected to cultivate to advantage those improving resources which the disenthralled genius of free discussion now opened before them and before the people. Though willing, from time to time, to call in the vices of popular enthusiasm, to abet them in persecuting the religion over which the virtuous energies of the people had helped the reformers to triumph, they yet looked back to the pomp and power which the unreformed church had possessed, and occasionally took not only the persons of the Roman Catholics under their protection, but their ceremonies also into observance. Above all, finding that the principles of the Reformation had tended to bring matters of civil right also into debate, they had unwisely persisted in siding with the Crown in the controversy. With the doctrine of 'a divine right of Kings to their prerogative, they combined that of a divine right of Bishops to their temporalities; plainly incompatible with the King's supremacy as recognised at the head of the first enacting clause of every act of Parliament, and incompatible equally with the tenure by which every Bishop admits in the form of homage that he holds his temporalities of the King. They had openly asserted their divine origin in their sermons and charges, and had significantly glanced at it in the new canon of 1640. It was boldly and well remarked in Parliament that ' even a Pope at ' Rome was more tolerable than a Pope at Lambeth.' *

The Roman Catholics, on their part, had been scarcely less improvident. They were elated with the protection and connivance which they received. 'They were not,' says Lord Clarendon, ' prudent managers of their prosperity;' but, putting themselves forward to make and to boast their converts, and to show their zeal, as a body, for the King, when it was dangerous for them to be seen as a body at all, they became conspicuous opponents of the leading party in the House of Commons who were backed by a merciless penal code and urged forward by the cherished intolerance of the people. Thus the Roman Catholics brought increasing hatred and danger on themselves, and, by implication, on their friends also. Meanwhile the Court of Rome could not be expected to adopt a wiser policy. Its views were formed upon the sanguine representation of its English adherents. The approaching downfall of the Arch Heresy of the west was openly proclaimed. The name and

* Sir Benjamin Rudyerd's speech, Collection of Speeches, published 1648.

influence of the Queen were rendered still more odious to the Protestants by an exaggerated estimate of her power in religious matters over the mind of her husband. Charles was announced to the Roman Catholics of Europe as favourable to their faith, and it is said that a Cardinal's hat was more than once offered to Laud himself. If this be true, credulous indeed was the Court of Rome to suppose that the time was ripe for engaging the Primate of England to bow his ambition before that of a foreign church, and ill indeed informed not to know that Henrietta Maria was to the full as jealous of Laud as she was of Strafford, and had been of Buckingham; and for the same reason; a natural antipathy to any Minister who might be powerful enough to interfere with her influence over the King. Panzani and Rosetti were successively received, contrary to the law of England, as Nuncios from Rome, and another Priest, a Scotchman, was deputed to be the Queen's confessor. It was, besides, known as a secret to the friends of the court, and, therefore, as such secrets usually are, to its opponents also, that Brett was, likewise, contrary to law, residing at Rome as an envoy and agent from Charles.*

To a spirit and ambition hereditary in a daughter of Henry the Fourth, the Queen joined none of her father's prudence or moderation. In vain was she warned by the advice of her mother, who, during a visit of more than a year in England, had by the modesty of her demeanour, particularly with reference to religious observances, called forth, in spite of popular animadversion, a willing testimony of approbation from some of the country party.† Mary of Medicis, it is true, has been represented by many writers as having been deeply engaged in the popish intrigues; but, as it appears, without sufficient evidence. She was on one occasion assaulted by a mob as she returned from mass, and was finally driven out of England by popular clamour; but these insults were brought upon her rather by her daughter's imprudence than by any act of her own. Resolutions were passed complaining of the encroachments of Henrietta upon law and treaty; and these remonstrances were made all the more significant by the warm and lavish support given by the leaders of the country party to an increase of her civil establishment, in return for her promise

---

* Clarendon Papers.
† Journals, 12th May.—See Lord Holland's Speech. Collection of Speeches, published 1648.

of being more cautious in future not to give scandal by an ostentatious and illegal display of the pomps of her religion.

The committees on religion, and the resolutions concerning copes and crosses, bowings and genuflexions, and tables put altar-wise, and pictures in churches, were by no means idle or capricious assaults upon the innocent forms under which particular congregations sought to worship God. These things were not harmless, as innovations on the discipline of the reformed religion, or as symptoms of relapse into the discipline of the old; they were the symbols under which the high church, compromising with popery, was proceeding to scandalise, discredit, and persecute, the Puritans. And he is but a careless observer of the affairs of men and states who fails to see that such are the means by which great passions are often set at work, and great moral effects not unfrequently produced. Political symbols are often of too much importance to be neglected by practical statesmen. But how formidable are they when they assume a religious shape, and appeal, through the outward senses of men, to things above the limits of this world?

Mr. Hume says that the different appellations of 'Sunday, 'which the Puritans affected to call the Sabbath,* were at that 'time known symbols of the different parties,' and he treats the opposition to the innovations of the Court clergy as only a 'poisonous infusion of theological hatred.' 'On account of 'these,' says he, 'were the popular leaders content to throw 'the government into such violent convulsions; and to the 'disgrace of that age and of this island, it must be acknow- 'ledged that the disorders in Scotland entirely, and those in 'England mostly, proceeded from so mean and contemptible 'an origin.'† What has been already said of the opposition raised to certain compliances with popish discipline, may be urged with equal fairness to justify the jealousy with which all the relics of its ceremonial were regarded by a party still sore from oppression and insult.

It is idle to contend that the means of persecution which the high church had exercised were now destroyed by the Puritans having become the dominant party in the House of Commons, and by the House of Commons having become, in some respects, the ruling power of the Parliament, and by the

* History of England, chap. i.   † Hist. of England, chap. liv.

Parliament having become strong enough to overawe the Court. All this, doubtless, is true in part; but, granting that it were entirely so, how had this popular influence been secured? By calling in the reforming principle to act against church abuses. These abuses were only checked, not crushed, while any political power remained with a hierarchy whose intemperance had been inflamed by successful resistance, and whose reign of active persecution was so recent, and still ready, upon any opportunity, to be renewed by the same hands. Hampden had, from the beginning of his public life, opposed these innovations as a pure and zealous Christian. But, on the principles of civil liberty only, he would have been bound to guard against the revival of the high church ascendancy, now half subdued in its attempts to force free conscience. Archbishop Neile, fortunately for himself, was now dead. Pierce, bishop of Bath and Wells, and Dr. Cozens, dean of Durham, had boldly proceeded to make levies of public money in those dioceses for the building of high altars, where they had established boys with tapers to serve at the communion, a consecrated knife to cut the sacramental bread, and almost all those outward appearances of a mass which had some years before been introduced with so much scandal at the consecration of St. Paul's, by Laud. Cozens, indeed, had gone so far as to declare that the reformers, 'when they took away the mass, had instead of a reformed, 'made a deformed religion.' He had denied the King's supremacy over the church, saying that 'the King had no more 'power over the church than the boy who rubbed his horse's 'heels.' And all these doctrines he had made practical by his violent persecution of Smart the prebendary, whose case was just now beginning to be subject of a Parliamentary inquiry, conducted by Hampden.* Hampden also undertook the case against Wren, bishop of Ely; and served on the committee of thirty which had been appointed, February 10, to consider the matter of church government.†

On these questions Selden's was a singular course. His great mind, stored with profound learning, and guided by a pure and lofty integrity, was not unfrequently capricious and impracticable in the affairs of a party; sometimes, in spite of

---

* Parl. Hist.—Rushworth.

† For Sir Ralph Verney's account of the proceedings of this Committee, as given in his MS. notes in the possession of Sir Harry Verney, see Appendix B.

his mild and humble temper, sanctioning extreme propositions, and sometimes deviating into scrupulous debates on points of mere form and nicety, little suited to a time when a rapid and determined spirit was so important to the popular cause. On the examinations and report of this committee he took a decided part, denying the sole power of ordination in the bishops, and concurring in the report against their civil jurisdiction. Yet, in the debates on the question of whether the bishops sat in Parliament as barons or as prelates, he gave it as his opinion that they sat as neither, but as representatives of the clergy. This, opening up again the whole question of separate jurisdiction, led to the reply, that the clergy were already represented out of Parliament in convocation, and in the end, tended powerfully to the exclusion of the spiritual Lords from Parliament. Selden afterwards concurred with the leaders in framing the Grand Protestation to maintain the Doctrine of the Church, and the person and authority of the King, privileges of Parliament, and rights of the Subject.

It is not true, as has been insinuated, that the bill to restrain the clergy from the administration of secular affairs had the purpose of debarring Strafford from the assistance of the votes of persons favourable to his cause; for, astounded at the commitment of Laud, and at the proceedings announced against certain of the judges, and willing to compound with the popular party, the bishops had spontaneously declared that, as spiritual persons, they could take no part in a matter of blood. Besides, Pym, the great author and conductor of the proceedings against the Earl, was but a faint supporter of the bill to restrain the bishops from voting; and, on the further measures for abolishing Episcopacy, he was openly opposed to Hampden, Vane, Hazelrigge, Fiennes, Sir Edward Deering, Harry Martin, and Lord Say, by whom that course was urged in the two houses. Nor can it be at all true, as Lord Clarendon would have it believed upon the alleged authority of Lord Falkland, that some persons, well-wishers to the church establishment, were betrayed into voting for the first Bill against the Bishops by false assurances as to the limits at which the attack upon the temporal powers of the church was to stop.

According to Clarendon, Hampden's engagement to Lord Falkland was, that he would proceed no further against the clergy, if the bill respecting their votes in Parliament and their holding of civil offices should pass. But the two universities petitioned; and the whole high church party, with Williams at their head, whose notions of ecclesiastical prerogative had risen with his elevation to the archbishopric of York, determined to abandon the wiser policy to which, for a short space, some of them had inclined, and in their speeches declared that the claims of the bishops to vote in Parliament rested on the foundations of divine right. The wise and moderate compromise, proposed by Archbishop Usher, was scouted by his brethren; and that bill was accordingly rejected in the Lords by a great majority. How, then, did Hampden depart from his engagement to Falkland? On the contrary, Hampden seems, by Clarendon's showing, to have proceeded in conformity with the very condition which he had proposed. Of the many instances in which the grave and searching mind of Lord Clarendon has blinded itself by looking at facts through the heated glare of its own resentments, there is none more remarkable than this violent and self-contradicting charge, insinuated, as is not unusual with him, on the words of another person, loosely quoted. It is clear that, for some time, Hyde had viewed, with the jealousy of a rival, Hampden's influence over the mind of Falkland; and this accounts for the uncontrollable bitterness with which he always speaks of Hampden.

But, from the time of the rejection of that bill by the Lords, it appears that Hampden, quitting the more moderate course, was considered to be of the party who supported the London Petition for the abolishing of Episcopacy, 'root and branch.' To say merely that an extreme resistance to a more moderate proposition generally provokes to those which are more violent, is not enough;—it is not putting this case fairly or truly. If, as Falkland maintained, it were really necessary for the well being of both Church and State that the temporal power of the clergy should be curtailed, it is difficult to see what other course was left, after the determination of the Lords, but to proceed by 'root and branch.' If, with Lord Falkland, we admit the first position, we cannot easily avoid the conclusion to which, under altered circumstances, Hampden came with respect to the second.

Among those by whom, in conjunction with Hampden, the abolition of Episcopacy now began to be urged in the two houses, Lord Say, Lord Kimbolton, Nathaniel Fiennes, and the younger Vane, were prominent.

Lord Say is generally described as of a shrewd mind, and

a persevering and resolute temper. It is difficult to come to a true conclusion as to the moral character of a man whose motives it was the business of the contending writers of those times to extol or vilify in an almost equally exaggerated measure. And, by even the writers in these times in which we live, the history of Charles and of his Parliaments seems as though it were fated never to be approached but as a contested field on which the battles of liberty and prerogative are to be in dispute still and for ever. Nor is this all : each particular character is considered as it were a vantage ground to be fiercely assailed or obstinately maintained ; and as each, in its turn, surrenders to the assault, or repels it, the victorious party sends up a cry of triumph as though the flag of a great cause were planted upon the outwork of an enemy. The lapse of almost two centuries has scarcely mitigated this spirit ; and every historian who will deal truly, must own, as he proceeds, how hard it is to quell this spirit in himself, and how doubtful he must be, in the end, whether he have succeeded in the first moral duty which he has deliberately undertaken, that of being, to the utmost of his power, impartial. The safest way to form his judgment of disputed facts, and especially of disputed characters, is to rely rather on the admissions of adverse than on the assertions of friendly parties ; and, above all, he must remember, in his endeavour to unravel the truth, that many more passions were at work in those times unfairly to break down reputations than undeservedly to extol them.

Clarendon suggests a doubt of the sincerity of Lord Say's advice to Charles to urge the Lords in person to spare the life of Strafford; but without stating a reason to support the doubt, or to justify the suggestion. The noble historian, in like manner, insinuates against Lord Say a charge of avarice and corruption in his acceptance of the Mastership of the Court of Wards ; confessing, however, that that high office was afterwards thrown up by him, under an impulse of party zeal, when refusing to obey the summons to attend the King at Oxford. Clarendon also admits that he was of 'good 'reputation with many who were not discontented.' May and Viccars speak of his great abilities and unimpeached honour, in terms which show that the party to which they belonged considered him as one with whom it might be proud to associate its own character and that of its cause ; and Whitelocke, writing after the Restoration, represents him as ' a person of 'great parts, wisdom, and integrity,' imbued with the loftiest spirit of patriotism. His appointment to the privy seal, under Charles the Second, he obtained and held without taint or suspicion of change of principle, and as far as can be traced, without any of those unworthy compliances which have cast a shade over the memories of many who only transferred their services from the Commonwealth to thrive in office under the restored King; and whose inconstancy, 'under change of 'times,' it was ever the inclination of their new master rather to display than to assist them in disguising.

We are left then to conclude that a man so praised and so blackened was one with qualities of mind and courage sufficient to make him deeply revered and violently hated.

Nathaniel Fiennes, his son, who had already risen, at an early age, to great consideration and eminence in the country party, was, in the common admission of all, a person of abilities at least equal to his father's. Like his father, after a youth spent in an active and uncompromising support of the popular cause, he enjoyed favour under the restored government, without any imputation of dishonourable compliance with the altered spirit of the times. Clarendon says of him that, 'besides the credit and reputation of his father, he had 'a very good stock of estimation in the House of Commons 'upon his own score; for truly he had very good parts of 'learning and nature, and was privy to, and a great manager 'in, the most secret designs from the beginning; and, if he 'had not encumbered himself with command in the army, to 'which men thought his nature not so well disposed, he had sure 'been second to none in those counsels, after Mr. Hampden's 'death.' His education at Geneva, and perhaps also the connexions into which, after his return, he was early thrown, had tended to excite in an ambitious and generous mind a thorough abhorrence of the course of church government in England. Wiser than Hazelrigge, and as much disposed to be forward in supporting or proposing the strongest measures, he and the younger Vane had, from the beginning of this Parliament, become useful and powerful leaders.

With these also must be mentioned Lord Kimbolton, now rising high in esteem among those whom Clarendon calls 'the 'select junto.' He was a well-bred man, of popular manners and address, and generally beloved, not only on his own account, but on that of his father and uncle, both of whom had lived to a venerable age with honour and reputation; the former for many years holding the office of Lord Privy Seal. Early separating himself from their politics, and becoming intimate with some of the leaders of the popular party by his marriage with the daughter of the Earl of Warwick, Kimbolton had, says Lord Clarendon, as 'full power in the House of Commons 'as any man.' *

A stock table was kept at Pym's lodgings in Gray's-inn-lane, where these and a few others the most in each other's confidence, transacted business. Thither Hyde was often invited, until, perceiving in conversation with Fiennes and Marten the lengths to which they were prepared to go, he withdrew himself, and Colepepper, from their society. Colepepper and Hyde were soon after sent for by the King, and commanded by him to meet from time to time in council upon his affairs.†

With less show of justification, Digby, too, having now entirely changed his course, was received into open favour by the Queen, and more strangely, (when it is considered how little he was fitted for it by any qualities of probity or discretion,) into the closest confidence by the King. He was a man of a brilliant eloquence, an active spirit, and eminent address as a courtier. He had received, says Carte, 'a most 'elaborate education from his father, and had improved his 'natural parts by travel.' He was an ingenious and accurate proficient in the exact sciences, and had, in his early youth, distinguished himself not a little in theological controversy. But his restless and overweening vanity made him careless of all the essentials of a good fame, and as unsafe a counsellor to his master as he was an improvident guardian of his own reputation. His speech on the bill against Strafford had gained him, and not unreasonably, great applause. But the eagerness with which, as if unable to hold any even way of conduct or opinions, he rushed into the direct opposite of his former course, discrediting his former opinions, and denouncing his former connexions, leaves him on record, if not as one of the most perfidious, as one of the most absurd men of showy abilities, whom that or any other age has produced.

The adventurous character of the career upon which the events of each successive day were now hurrying the country

* Clarendon—Life. † Ibid.

party, the perils which menaced the foremost, and the temptations with which all were from time to time assailed, had introduced a very temporising spirit into many. It is generally the case during the period when the elements of any great change are beginning to work, that the popular counsels are encumbered by the presence of some suspected persons, and often damaged by the treachery of others. It was so now in an eminent degree. Several, profiting by the experience of Strafford's life but neglecting the moral of his death, had deserted from the popular side; others were wavering; and many more appeared plainly to have attached themselves to it, for the mere purpose of exhibiting themselves to the King for purchase. The impolicy of at once forcing such persons, in such times, from a hollow neutrality into active enmity, did not occur to the country party as soon as it ought. The trimmers were discarded and insulted in council and debate. They were treated with a contumely which took away from such base minds all desire to further dissemble their baseness. It has been well observed, that men's real qualities are very apt to rise or fall to the level of their reputation: so was it now with the trimmers. And it may well be doubted whether Hampden's phrase was in this respect well timed, or chosen with his usual prudence, when he said that the trouble which had lately befallen the party 'had been attended with this 'benefit, that they knew who were their friends.' *

The largest number of all, though honest in their intentions for liberty, endeavoured to keep the means of retreat still open. In such a state of things, men of the rank, virtue, and courage of Fiennes and the younger Vane were eminently valuable to the leaders. Yet the courage of Fiennes was given to him in an unequal measure; and his is one of the instances, not unfrequently met with, which show that courage is a faculty which may materially depend upon the different positions of responsibility in which the man is placed. There is no reason for imputing personal timidity to Nathaniel Fiennes. On the contrary, his valour was often and eminently displayed; nor was there ever, in the most hazardous moments, a bolder politician. Yet there never was a man whose timidity under a great military charge, such as that in which it was his misfortune to find himself when he commanded at the defence

* Clarendon—Life.

of Bristol, gave stronger proof of his consciousness that for such duties he was entirely unfit.

Vane's principles were of a more unmixed sort; and he had, in his early life, many great difficulties and allurements to struggle with. The son of a trading courtier, who had been the ready minister of two arbitrary Sovereigns, the younger Sir Harry Vane maintained and avowed, through every change of affairs, the most uncompromising attachment to the republican doctrines. This was expressed by him, to his father's great displeasure, upon his return from Geneva; from which place, as from its seminary, the spirit of popular liberty has so often gone forth to other nations, and in which it has so often found again an asylum when driven back and discomfited. He sought to cultivate these principles, in their utmost speculative purity, in New England, where he was instantly raised, by acclamation, to the government of Massachusetts. In this office he openly countenanced antinomian opinions, too absolutely exempt from all human control both in church and state for even the settlers there. And so terminated his short career as a president and lawgiver; which, when considered as the aspiring effort of a man of twenty-three years old, at the head of an infant society, in a new world, cannot but be thought to be too severely dealt with by both Neal and Baxter. Appointed, soon after his return, at his father's instance, to the treasurership of the Navy, he nevertheless took deep disgust at the measures of the court, and, throwing up his office, attached himself to the cause and fortunes of the country party;—a course sufficiently explained by the earliest and uniform dispositions of his mind; but which has been lightly and injuriously impugned by some who have imputed it, without any probability of truth, to resentment on account of the mortified ambition and disappointed intrigues of his father. Unlike Hampden, whose professions and views may be shown to have been uniformly bounded to the establishment of a freedom guarded by limited monarchy, Vane's darling scheme throughout was a Platonic republic; from the avowal of which he never swerved, even from the hour of his first appearance in the Long Parliament, to that at which he bravely met the fate to which he was unjustly doomed, for an act not only in which he had taken no part, but from which he had signally abstained. In religion and politics equally an enthusiast, he was as stern and incorruptible in opposition to the sovereignty of Cromwell as he had been to that of Charles. His genius was shrewd and ardent, his judgment penetrating, his eloquence glowing, and chastened by a better taste than was common among the orators of that time.

Strode was scarcely of sufficient importance, or Hazelrigge or Deering of sufficient discretion, to hold a place in the secret councils of the leading men. Dauntless and persevering in his course, whether selected by his party to post, in disguise, from Fawsley to the Scottish border, or, in his place in Parliament, to move the bringing in of the Triennial Act, Hazelrigge was ever ready and faithful to sustain his allotted share of an action in the previous arranging of which he neither took nor desired to take a part. It was sufficient for him that it had the consent of Hampden, whose directing genius he held in the deepest veneration, and that it should be manifestly in furtherance of that great cause to which he was so entirely devoted. Deering, also a subordinate actor, had neither the courage nor fidelity of Hazelrigge;—his name and station in an important county appear to have been, from the beginning, his only recommendation in the eyes of those under whose direction he moved. Turbulent and selfish, and ever ambitious to concur in the strongest measures, when they seemed likely to advance him along the road of his personal interest, he had none of that careless purity of purpose which, aiming at generous ends, pursues the most direct and rigorous means; nor had he that discretion in the choice of his objects, or uniformity in his pursuit of them, which sometimes gives to even a bad or foolish consistency a false semblance of public virtue. Devoted to the most sordid aims of private advantage, he never rose higher than to be an instrument, working and controlled by the direction of others; and, at length, baffled in his speculations of unjust profit to be derived from Parliamentary confiscations, he found himself sunk at once in fortune and reputation.

One person, and one only, was there in this confederacy whose powers seem to have long remained unknown and unmeasured by all but by the searching sagacity of his kinsman Hampden; and this was Oliver Cromwell, burgess for Cambridge; who, with an ill-favoured countenance, a sharp untunable voice, an ungraceful address, a 'plain cloth suit 'which seemed to have been made by an ill country taylor, 'and a little band, none of the cleanest,' * had never yet risen to notice in debate, but by some occasional disjointed proposition, coarse in itself, and not recommended by the mode of the delivery. Yet this was he concerning whom, when Lord Digby asked, 'Pray, Mr. Hampden, who is that man? for I see he is on our side by his speaking so warmly to-day:' Hampden answered, 'That sloven whom you see before you 'hath no ornament in his speech; but that sloven, I say, if 'we should ever come to a breach with the King, (which God 'forbid!) in such a case, I say, that sloven will be the greatest man in England!'†

The prophecy was more than accomplished. He lived not only to be the first man in England, but to fill the most extraordinary station to which any man in England was ever raised by the most extraordinary fortune and abilities. Dishonoured by one great over-mastering vice, he had not one weakness. And, perhaps, it is but truth to say of Cromwell, that the deep inscrutable dissimulation which, in the later days of his career, he summoned to his aid against both foreign and domestic machination, to baffle the assaults at once of the despotic powers of Europe and the democratic spirits of England, was a vice rather called forth by the difficulties of his position than forming an original or natural part among his wondrous qualities. Flattered and magnified by the praises of those who had grown under the shadow of his greatness, he has also been the subject of more vulgar and savage malignity than, perhaps, ever assailed the memory of any other human creature. He was pursued by the hatred of those who opposed his usurpation or were the open enemies of his tyranny; and it has been likewise the trade of many who had crouched before his footstool, with corresponding baseness, to insult over his grave. The courtiers and statesmen of Europe, for one generation at least, were all leagued in this work. For the statesmen of foreign nations were those whom he had discomfited, and upon whose disgrace, or with whose enforced assistance, he had raised the glory of England to no second rank of fame among empires; and the statesmen of England forgot, after the Restoration, the greatness he had achieved for their country, or remembered it too well ever to forgive the contrast in which it stood to her degradation under the sway of their restored

---

* Sir Philip Warwick's Memoirs.   † Sir Richard Bulstrode's Memoirs.

master. The courtiers of all nations hated the memory of one who had showed that a nation could be governed gloriously without a court. Those of France were eager to revile the memory of him to whom their greatest minister had yielded the palm of his continental policy; whom their vain and arrogant prince had been forced to address as his 'brother;' who, with 6000 Englishmen, had eclipsed the glories of their nation at Dunkirk; and who had brought the ablest of their negotiators to confess an attempted and baffled fraud. He had shamed Kings,—himself at the head of a people whom he governed only through a sense that he was the fittest man in the country to govern them; and, at that hour when it may be believed that, with all men, dissimulation is at an end, he breathed his last words forth in a prayer of simple but affecting resignation, commending his own soul to mercy, but, with it, the never-neglected fortunes of a country whose gratitude had not kept pace with his immortal services.

Cromwell, at the beginning, probably sincere, was doubtless a dissembler from the hour at which he aspired to rule; but he had to deal with many bad men; and dissimulation was the weapon which they used. Cromwell took it up and vanquished them. Cromwell was a tyrant; but, of his personal ambition, this is truly to be said, that it was never seen but directed to the promotion of his country's greatness.

Nor has the unfairness of party zeal been much less actively employed to defame as well as to extol the reputation of Pym, who may be called the colleague of Hampden in the government of the country party. For eight and twenty successive years after the Restoration, powerful pens were incessantly employed to desecrate the ashes of the great men of the generation which had just gone by; and, as their descriptions have not unnaturally been taken as models upon which most of the later historians have formed their own, the character of Pym is not likely to have received favourable measure. With a courage that never quailed, a vigilance that never slept, a severity, sharp as the sunbeam to penetrate, and rapid as the thunderbolt to consume, Pym was the undaunted, indefatigable, implacable foe, of every measure, and of every man, that threatened to assail the power of the Parliament, or to destroy the great work which was in hand for the people and posterity.

When the citadel of public liberty was menaced, Pym defended it as one who thought in such a battle all arms lawful.

That his parts were, according to Mr. Hume's phrase, 'more 'fitted for use than ornament,' is little to say of those abilities which, after the Earl of Bedford's death, and when Pym was unsupported by any other influence, raised him to the rank in the estimation of his opponents of being one of the 'Parlia-'mentary drivers,'* and gave to him in their phraseology the nickname of 'King Pym.' His great experience in the practice of Parliament, on which his authority was hardly inferior to that of Selden himself, gave to Pym the greatest advantages of preparedness in debate. His efforts were mainly directed to maintain the privileges and power of the Commons. His ruling maxim was that which he expressed on Strafford's impeachment.—' Parliaments, without parliamentary power, '' are but a fair and plausible way into bondage.' Nor was he less well versed in the business of the Treasury than of the House. A man so forward and powerful, and by the court so hated and so feared, was sure to be assailed with calumnies the most virulent and the most improbable. Accordingly, the almost repulsive austerity of Pym's habits and demeanour could not protect him against the foolish imputation of having won over the beauteous Countess of Carlisle, by a softer influence than that of political agreement, to the interests of the country party; and a modern author, to whom it has been necessary to advert more than once in these memorials, after a fanciful picture of Pym's system of secret intelligence, ends with discovering a close resemblance between his stern unbending course and the occupation and office of a 'French 'Lieutenant of Police.' Nor are such extravagances very surprising or unpardonable in writers of small account, when we see the grave and lofty Clarendon himself recording the disproved statement, so industriously circulated by some of the Royalists, that the death of Pym was caused by a loathsome disease; and then condescending to countenance a superstitious belief that it was the wrath of heaven manifesting itself against the public acts of the old man's life: thus leaving us to conclude between the probabilities of a miracle and a calumny. In either case, how injudicious in the adherents of the unhappy family of the Stuarts to insist upon accounting the worldly misfortunes of men as visible judgments upon their political offences! On the other hand, Baxter gives to Pym, with

* Wood's Athenæ.—Persecutio Undecima.

Hampden and with Vane, an assured place among the highest mansions of the blessed.* And, if there ever was a man who would have been less likely than another to assign such praise to one whom in his heart he thought justly chargeable with blame, that man was the pious and honest Baxter.

Hampden's powers, which were now vigorously exerting themselves in parliamentary debate, were of a different sort from those of the other popular leaders. He was not a frequent speaker; nor, when the course of a discussion called upon him to take his part in it, did he sacrifice anything to a vain display of words and figures, which was so general a vice in the rhetoric of those days; nor did he indulge himself in those violences of invective, or exaggerations of illustration, of which so many instances are found in the published speeches of the rest. His practice was usually to reserve himself until near the close of a debate; and, then, having watched its progress, to endeavour to moderate the redundances of his friends, to weaken the impression produced by his opponents, to confirm the timid, and to reconcile the reluctant. And this he did, according to the testimony of his opponents themselves, with a modesty, gentleness, and apparent diffidence in his own judgment, which usually brought men round to his conclusions. It is natural that Clarendon, in his unmitigated hatred of Hampden, and of the cause in which he successfully directed the spirits and minds of others, should give to that triumphant genius, tempered by modesty, and guided by discretion, the name of craft; and that, labouring to represent him as a bad man whom all outward evidence had raised high in public affection and esteem, he should pronounce that, from the time when Hampden and Hyde were opposed to each other, ' there ' never was a man less what he seemed to be than Mr. ' Hampden.'

About this time, a difference arose in the party, with respect to the course of public affairs, between those who were called the religious, and the political, Puritans. Of those who were called the religious Puritans, the less considerable of the two classes both as to number and influence, Pym was accounted the leader. Of this schism in the junto the King tried to avail himself; but in vain. For, no sooner did any question of state grievance, apart from that on which they were divided,

---

* " Saint's Rest.'

appear, but they were again found closely and eagerly united. Yet the bill for abolishing episcopacy was a prominent and practical question, concerning which, not only the party was at issue within itself, but Pym and Hampden, the 'Parliament drivers,' were opposed to each other. To the first proposal touching 'root and branch' the rashness of Archbishop Williams had much contributed. The grounds on which the protest of the bishops against the bill restraining the clergy from civil office was placed, were doubtless a high breach of the privileges of the Lords, and a denial of the power of an act of Parliament. For, not content with defending the parliamentary and other franchises of their own order, they went in effect the monstrous length of resisting the legality of all votes of the Lords at the passing of which they and their brethren should not assist. Into this ill-advised course they were betrayed by the hasty temper of the Archbishop, kindling at the violence of a mob which had impeded his passage through Palace Yard. It led at once to the impeachment of those who subscribed their names to it, as having questioned the power of Acts of Parliament; an offence which, if it did not amount to fit matter of committment for treason, was evidence at least of a madness sufficient, (as Lord Clarendon says was remarked at the time) to justify their being placed in a confinement of another and scarcely a milder sort.

But, among these struggles, the foundations of the constitution were broken up, and its elements in conflict. The efforts of the Court to regain the lost ground of arbitrary prerogative, and those of the Parliament to strengthen its own defences, became more frequent and less disguised. In nothing does the deep feeling which the Parliament had of its own strength appear more remarkably than in its conduct towards the Scots, when we remember that it was to renew his enterprise against them that Charles had called the Parliament together. With as little good discretion as good faith, and choosing rather to put his trust in the force of national jealousies than in the popularity of his own government, he had, in his speech at the opening of the session, gone the length of calling the Scottish army rebels; and this too during a treaty. The Parliament seemed for a while to disregard this phrase. But, in exactly three months after, the disposition of Parliament was plainly shown by voting, under the name of a 'brotherly assistance,' upon a petition from the

Scots, a grant of three hundred thousand pounds, ' as a fit
' proportion towards the supply of the losses and necessities of
' our brethren of Scotland.' *

In such a conflict it was clear that the system of government itself must dissolve, or that, of its two great powers thus put in action against each other, one must effectually and signally prevail, and thus the balance be destroyed.

The Triennial bill, alone, as we have seen, was but a poor defence against any King who might be disposed to look to his army as a resource against his Parliament, and who had still the prerogative of dissolution in his hands, so often before abused in practice, and lately again appealed to as a menace. Another Act had therefore been passed, which in truth rendered the two Houses entirely independent of the crown;—and two Houses entirely independent of the Crown must soon become the sovereign authority of the state. This was the famous Act by which the Parliament declared itself indissoluble but with its own consent. What rendered this necessary was the state of the treaty with the Scots; which, if hastily concluded, would have placed at Charles's disposal a great army, the leaders of which he was at the least countenancing in plots against the Parliament.† But, that it was establishing a power which could be justified only upon necessity, no man can deny.

It was not in ignorance that Charles had thus hung the fate of his prerogative on the verge of the slippery precipice on which he now stood. But he had disguised the danger to himself, still looking forward to those false hopes with which the ambitious boldness of Strafford and the wanton violence of Laud had so long deceived him. His astonishment at the threatened inroad on his darling prerogative (and he now saw his difficulties in their full extent) deprived him of the power of meeting it with prudence or with firmness. It was besides a part of his character, as it is with many obstinate persons, when driven to retract or qualify his course, to rush for a while into the opposite extreme, as if it were to shame and spite the fortune which had checked him.

In addition to these infirmities of temper and purpose, a sanguine, but not very distinct, calculation of relief from his army influenced him even in these concessions. They thus became part of a temporary policy by which he expected to

* Commons' Journals,—Feb. 3. † Guthrie.

amuse his parliament until the Scots army might be disbanded, and his own left free for him to deal with.

Rapin believes that the King's compliances were furthermore occasioned by a belief that the Parliament might be tempted by them into demands so plainly unreasonable as to materially strengthen his case in the public opinion; and M. Guizot inclines to the same notion. But this is surely searching too deep for the solution of a conduct sufficiently to be accounted for in a more obvious way. It is seldom the custom with arbitrary princes to make any surrender of substantial power for the less important object of enlisting an additional argument on their side. On the contrary, instead of being led out of their way to strengthen their case in public opinion, their mistake has usually been, when meditating an assault upon liberty, rather to undervalue public opinion and therefore too much to neglect all appeals to it. Nor should we be justified in lightly supposing Charles guilty of so foul a crime as, among other compliances, to surrender his servant to death, in order to decoy his opponents into demands which might afterwards give him the means of destroying them also.

Whatever may have been the motives of Charles, this at least is certain; the plan of his opponents was more prudent and more prosperous. Both King and Parliament were now paying court to the Scots. Whatever the Scots might have thought of the King, they were wise enough to see that it was the interest of the Parliament to be sincere with them. On the side of the Parliament then lay their safety. The Parliament, on their part, were more and more convinced that the motives of the King's compliances were not sincere. They therefore fortified themselves against his insincerity, in the meanwhile by availing themselves of these compliances, and extorting others; until the King, when his blow was to have been struck, found the weapon in his hands rendered powerless by his own act, and new means of incalculable strength placed in those of the bold and wary adversaries with whom he had been dealing. He had not been prepared for the consequences of the first assault. It had not only deprived him of the counsels of his two chief advisers, Strafford and Laud, but it had made wreck of their whole system, and had involved in the same ruin almost all the inferior agents, striking speechless, motionless, and hopeless, the few and insignificant that remained. The greater number were permitted to escape from personal arrest. Ratcliffe was released, but retired beyond sea, and the Lord Keeper Finch, and Secretary Sir Francis Windebanke, fled.

Against Windebanke divers petitions had been presented, complaining of illegal warrants issued by him, particularly for the discharge of prosecutions against Roman Catholic Seminary Priests. It was also known, that the Secretary had been, for a while covertly, and afterwards openly, in communion with their Church. Finch was brought to the bar of the Commons, and there arraigned of his practices against privilege and law, in articles setting forth his refusal, while Speaker, to put certain resolutions of the House to the vote, and his advice to the Crown, and his charges on the Circuit, while Chief Justice, in the matter of the ship-money. He was admitted to speak in reply. On his knees he pleaded to the jurisdiction of the House, and, in a speech of eloquent but piteous apology, professed his devotion to the privileges of Parliament, and his sorrow if in any sort he had offended against them. The triumph of the popular party thus far was complete. Finch was impeached by an unanimous vote. It was moved by Lord Falkland, with an asperity, says Lord Clarendon, 'contrary to the usual gentleness of his nature,' calling him 'a 'silent speaker, an unjust judge, and an unconscionable 'keeper; bringing all law from His Majesty's courts into His 'Majesty's breast, and giving our goods to the King, and our 'liberties to the sheriffs; so that there was no way by which 'we had not been oppressed and destroyed, if the power of 'this person had been equal to his will, or the will of the 'King equal to his power.' *

Windebanke did not even face his accusers with any answer to their charge. Holland was chosen by him as a place of refuge, and France by Finch. The letters which, from their exile, they both addressed to the Parliament, were in accordance with their deportment under accusation; Finch excusing himself, as he had done in his speech, by humble expressions of submission, and Windebanke by laying the whole blame on the King.

M. Guizot concludes that their escape was countenanced by the 'Junto;'—and with good reason. To pardon them, and to proceed to the utmost extent of penalty against Strafford,

---

* Falkland's Speech on the articles brought up by him to the Lords.— Jan. 14th.

would have been impracticable; yet, on the other hand, much more was to be gained for the popular cause by the abject submission and pusillanimous flight of its enemies than by the shedding of their blood. The event justified the policy; nor can there be a doubt that the court was as much discredited in the eyes of all men by the self-degradation of the keeper and secretary, as was the popular cause by the courageous bearing of Strafford, and, afterwards, of Laud. It would have been better for the Parliament if the lieutenant and the archbishop had also been of a temper to barter reputation for life.

Chief Justice Bramston, Chief Baron Davenport, and Judge Crawley, were held to bail for their appearance to answer to charges, principally on ship-money; and Judge Berkeley was apprehended upon Speaker Lenthall's warrant while sitting in his own court of King's Bench;* such was the pervading and irresistible power of the House. Smart, prebendary of Durham, and Alexander Jennings, a gentleman of Buckinghamshire, the latter of whom had been imprisoned for resisting payment of ship-money, and whose bail had been refused, had now reparation made to them of all costs and damages; and the Chief Justice of the Common Pleas, Sir Edward Littleton, was entrusted with the great seal. This was probably not an improper, and certainly not an unpopular, appointment. With the single exception of Selden, with whom he had lived and studied long, Littleton was, perhaps, the greatest lawyer in England. Without the energy or firmness of St. John, and, perhaps, with less of natural ability, he was a man of more moderation, and better qualified by rank in his profession, as well as by his political character, to be a mediating minister; in such times, between King and people. His early bias, like that of most lawyers, had been to the side of liberty; but his tone in defence of it had been qualified and subdued by the nearer prospect of professional advancement. Littleton had, during two eventful sessions, sided vehemently with the country party in Parliament. He had, with Sir John Eliot, undertaken to manage the charge against the Duke of Buckingham of poisoning the late King, and was appointed, with Coke and Sir Dudley Digges, to carry the Petition of Right to the Lords. But he was saved, by preferment, from continuing to render himself conspicuous in a course which brought upon several

* Whitelocke.—Parliamentary History.

of those with whom he had been associated such frequent and severe persecutions. On his father's death, he was rapidly advanced, through a Welch judgeship, to the office of Solicitor-general, and, in 1639, to the chief justiceship of the Common Pleas.

Though Littleton cannot with truth be accused of having changed his politics, they were of an undefined and temporising sort. It required a lofty sense of public duty, in those days, to save a lawyer from corruption; and Littleton never was corrupt. He never was prevailed upon, for the sake of acquiring office or retaining it, to devote himself to the purposes of the court; and, when Chief Justice, he was selected by both Houses to lay before the King their Address of Thanks for the passing of the Triennial Bill. Nor, even after he had placed himself by the King's side at Oxford with the great seal, did he ever entirely abandon the cause for which the Parliament were contending, or ever acquire the entire favour of his master.

In pursuing the story of the proceedings against Strafford, it was necessary to pass by several transactions of great importance, concurrent with it in respect of time. Among these was the negotiation, slightly alluded to before, for admitting the principal leaders of the country party into prominent and responsible office. The design, as is well known, was broken off by the death of the Earl of Bedford, who seems to have indulged the notion that Strafford might have been saved by the compromise;—a weak and groundless expectation, to provide for Strafford's safety by raising to power men who knew that their own safety, as well as that of the cause for which they had risked everything, depended upon bringing him to public execution. Pym was to have been Chancellor of the Exchequer in the room of Cottington; Holles Secretary of State; and Lord Essex Governor, and John Hampden tutor, to the Prince of Wales.

It must be always an unprofitable and an endless occupation to speculate upon what might have been the event of an arrangement which never took place, and which, if it had taken place, must have given a totally different course to public affairs. The enquiry with which some writers have amused themselves, as to how far the vices of a character so mean and so depraved as that of Charles the Second were vices of nature, or how far of education, is of small consequence either to the historian or philosopher. None of the facts or lessons of history are affected by such an enquiry. We have already seen, faintly shadowed out by Hampden himself, in his letters to Eliot, his own views of the fit education of a young man of quality destined for public occupations. This, then, may be safely predicated, nor is it worth while to go further; that, by the failure of an arrangement, by which Hampden would have been appointed to form the habits of the future Sovereign of his country, one of the worst of pupils was taken from one of the greatest of masters. The difficulty must be spared to posterity of determining whether or not Charles the Second could have come forth, such as he afterwards was, from the hands of John Hampden.

The object of such of the country party as had any views or interests in these projects was to effect a great change in the administration, not only about the person and court of the King, but principally in the revenue. The King perceived this design, and thwarted it, even before Bedford's death; and this was seen in the result,—in the arrangements that failed, and in those that were effected. The Treasurership was only transferred to one of the court party, the Earl of Middleton;* the Chancellorship of the Exchequer remained in the hands which before had held it; the Privy Council was increased; the Court of Wards and the Solicitor-generalship were made peace-offerings to the people. The King had no violent repugnance to admitting persons from the popular side to his presence; but he kept the responsible offices of the revenue in hands which he could control.

Thus a negotiation, supposed by the Tory writers to have been begun for the purpose of saving Lord Strafford, and according to the insinuations of some, to have nearly triumphed over the virtue of the country party, ended, not in conciliating that party,—not in delaying them from their object, but in giving them the additional power of pursuing it with the agency of a crown lawyer. All levies of ship-money were declared for the future to be illegal; the Star Chamber was utterly abolished; its judgments were struck off the file; and above all, the levying of the revenue of Customs placed by

---

* Juxon desired leave to resign the treasurership. With the utmost fidelity to his master throughout, even to that master's last moments, Juxon never intermeddled in politics or faction; and, says Sir Philip Warwick, during all the troubles was never questioned or molested.

law for evermore under the control of Parliament. Nor did the Commons stop here. But the event which, falling out at this time, went the furthest to colour, if not to justify, the assumption of the whole power of the state by Parliament, was the conduct and discovery of the Army Plot. How far Charles was a party in the main design of then marching a portion of the northern army upon London to dissolve the Parliament, is doubtful. That, at one time, he deterred the conspirators from the attempt to put it into execution is certain; but it is equally so that he countersigned, with his own initials, the 'Army Officers' Petition.' That he corresponded with the principal conspirators, and continued his countenance to them during a great part of the action of the plot, appears under his own hand; and Newcastle's papers sufficiently show that it had been part of his original project, a very short time before, to bring up the army, and that he now maintained a secret communication with it through the dangerous agency of these wild and desperate intriguers. The royalist writers, indeed, generally do not deny this, but content themselves with justifying it; and of the Queen's active participation in the whole plot there is no doubt.* The evidence of it, which appeared before Parliament, unquestionably assisted the objects of the country party, and continued to keep the public mind in a state of alarm which, though perhaps oftenest found serviceable to the purposes of a government, is sometimes of no small use to a party in opposition to a government. But the imputation of fable and of artifice, with which Lord Clarendon endeavours to dissemble the realities of the whole transaction (confounding it with others less genuine, and entirely passing by all that was important in the confessions of Percy and Goring), is most disingenuous; the more so in him, since he had, a short time before, himself been eagerly employed in pursuing the evidence of another design to be executed by the soldiery, and had, in consequence, taken up the message of the Lords concerning the expected attempt to rescue Lord Strafford from the Tower;† both of which facts he keeps out of sight in his history.

There was abundant evidence of a spirit in the army, in the courtiers and in the King, jointly, which rendered some very extraordinary and lasting measures necessary for providing for

* Madame de Motteville. † Commons' Journals, April 28.

the safety of the House. Accordingly, great pains have been taken by the court party, in their writings, to draw attention away from those outrages of which there was undeniable evidence, in order to expose the over-coloured statements of fanciful and groundless panic, of which, in such times, and in such a conflict of passions, there was not a little felt, and perhaps not a little feigned. That many false alarms were excited and many false plots bruited about, is unquestionably true. True also, that the mind of the Parliament was so harassed by the informations it was constantly receiving, that, on one occasion, the breaking down of a bench in the gallery under two corpulent gentlemen, Mr. Moyle and Mr. Chamberlayne, threw the House, for a moment, into such a sudden amazement, that a cry arose of a second gunpowder plot.* In truth, the fair way of looking at the question of the reality of the dangers, at different times and from different quarters apprehended, is to rest the cases mainly on the testimony of those who could not have been parties with the Parliament in any exaggeration of them, and which show, beyond question, the existence of a rash but deep-laid scheme to destroy the Parliament by military force. The Marchioness of Newcastle cannot be suspected of becoming intentionally a favourable witness; yet, in the 'Life of her Husband,' written by her, we have the comment on the evidence which his own correspondence affords of the King's settled intention being already formed of ' securing his interests in the North,' against his Parliament, by which he was ' unjustly and unmannerly treated.'

The information, it appears, had long been in the possession of Pym. The principal agents in it were known; but, because they were known (and a knowledge of the chieftains accounted for the unscrupulous character of the enterprise), it was difficult to make men believe in the real importance of it. Charles's Presence Chamber and Council Board had been for some time beset with soldiers of fortune and men of pleasure, who, from the Queen's favour, soon found their way, if not into the entire confidence of the King, at least into his good graces, which they believed to be his entire confidence. And they acted accordingly. The conspiracy was guided by two amatory poets, two mere profligates, and two young men of family who

* Carte.

were only known to the country, the one as being a Roman Catholic, whose uncle had been engaged in the Gunpowder Treason, the other as having received his education amid the morals and politics of the French court. Suckling and Davenant, Jermyn and Goring, Percy and Wilmot, with the rash Jack Ashburnham, and a few subordinate agents, were the actors in a plot which was to move a great army upon London, capture the Parliament, secure the seaports, negotiate foreign succours, and turn back from the footstool of the Throne that flowing tide of popular power before which Strafford, at the head of the councils of England and of the government of Ireland, had stood in vain and had been overwhelmed.

For the Parliamentary leaders to allow the King to see that they were aware of the desperate nature of the scheme, before they might be able to bring it to public proof, would have been perilous in the highest degree. Still no time was to be lost in deranging its machinery, and at all events in providing for the Scots being kept together and on good terms with the Parliament. A middle course therefore was adopted.

As early as the 7th of January a committee had been established, 'Concerning the Public Safety,' of which Hampden was a member and manager. And now it was that the vote of 'a brotherly assistance' of 300,000*l.* to the Scots was passed;* the King was addressed in general terms on the subject of plots and dangers; on the Irish army; on the public discontents, and against the introduction of foreign troops; and, at length, on the 9th of May, an unanimous Declaration was obtained, signed and sworn to by all the members of the Commons, and by all the Lords but two, for the defence of religion, privilege, and liberty. At one blow the army plot

---

* Clarendon, in his account of these transactions, complains much of this vote, saying that 'foreigners were paid, and the English not.' What can be thought of the honesty or the value of Clarendon's animadversions, when it is seen that, in this case, as in that of the conference with the Lords concerning the plot to rescue Strafford from the Tower, Clarendon has kept back in his History the whole fact of his having himself borne a very considerable part in it ? It was Hyde himself who brought up the report of the Committee recommending the 'brotherly assistance,' and managed the conference upon it.—Comm. Journ. 20 Martii, post merid. He was afterwards on the Committee, with Hampden and others, to negotiate with the City the loan of 120,000*l.* in part of this 'assistance.'— Comm. Journ. 25 Martii, post merid.

was ruined. The King saw that it was known to the Junto; that they were preparing to make it known to the country; that the Scottish army, which he hoped would disband for want of money, was supplied with means to keep itself entire; and that his own army, which he hoped to have at his disposal, was still to be occupied for a renewed period in watching it. The conspirators took the alarm. Jermyn fled to France, and Percy to concealment in the house of his brother the Duke of Northumberland; Wilmot and Pollard were committed to the Gate-house, together with Ashburnham, who never undertook any design that he did not help to ruin by his indiscretion; and the infamous Goring, who never joined in any cause that he did not help to ruin by his treachery, saved himself by giving early intimation to Pym of his willingness to divulge all.* Lord Kimbolton and two others were accordingly sent to Portsmouth, where Goring commanded, to take his information; and Hampden and Holles to Alnwick, to examine the Duke of Northumberland touching his brother's correspondence: directions were despatched by the Speaker's warrant to secure the other ports in Hants, Dorsetshire, Guernsey, and Jersey, and to put the train bands in readiness; Sir John Hotham and Sir Hugh Cholmley were sent to the north, Sir Walter Earle to the West, and the King was addressed to appoint the Earl of Essex Lieutenant of York, ' in this time of 'danger.' † A letter was moreover directed by the Speaker to Sir John Coniers and Sir Jacob Asteley, commanding the army in the north. It was prepared by Hampden, as Chairman of the Committee of Seven. It set forth the general ' causes of 'jealousy that there have been some secret attempts and 'practices' with the army; that the House intends to inquire into the conspiracy, ' for the purpose of proceeding especially 'against the principal actors therein,' promising freedom from all punishment to such as had been worked upon by such conspirators, ' if they shall testify their fidelity to the State ' by 'a timely discovery of what they know, and can certify 'therein;' engaging to 'satisfy all such arrears as this 'House hath formerly promised to discharge,' and directing

---

* 'Goring,' says Sir Philip Warwick, 'is said to have betrayed them all, 'as he did; but he swore to me (which was no great assurance), that he 'never revealed it till he certainly knew that the chief members of both 'houses were before acquainted with it.'
  † Sir Ralph Verney's Notes.

the generals to communicate these things to all under their command.*

To whatever extent the connexion of Charles with the rash scheme of the Army Plot had gone, it affords a clue to all the concessions that he was now making to his Parliament. Without his army, all attempts to recover his lost ground were hopeless, except by casting himself frankly upon his Parliament and people, which was the only course he never could bring himself to adopt, and which in truth would now have been received by them with a degree of suspicion too well justified by all his former conduct. Without money he could not maintain his army; and without the Royal assent being previously given to the concessions which the Parliament demanded, the Parliament would not give the money. A poll tax meanwhile was in progress, for the payment of both armies, of five per cent. on all expended income, and an additional tax on all patents and titles.

But the tone and attitude of the Commons had undergone a material change. The forms of petition were studiously, it is true, and punctiliously observed, but in such a manner as to show the King that the House was aware of the violence he meditated against its privileges and its existence. It recognised the power of the sword as in him; but pointed distantly at the limitations under which that power was to be exercised, and even at the circumstances under which the public safety might demand that the control of Parliament should extend over his use of that power. He was told that, in a free state, it is given to the Sovereign for the defence of the people and of that form of government of which the House of Commons is a part. He was told that his officers were in a conspiracy against the State, and he was told moreover to whom the chief command in one of the largest provinces of his kingdom ought, for the public safety, to be entrusted. These doubtless were extraordinary powers assumed by the Parliament; and it is equally true that, by degrees, these demands were rising to an amount quite irreconcilable with any just notion of a form of government in which the monarchical principle was to have its due influence upon the balance. It had not, as yet, made any claim of power over the army. But it was laying ground for this claim, in case that future circumstances should render

* Comm. Journ. 8 May.

the exercise of it necessary. And this is not the English Constitution. Still there is the constantly recurring question: by what other means was any balanced form of government to be protected against Charles the First? How could the power and authority of Parliament have been otherwise preserved, to be again reduced within their proper dimensions under the sway of some succeeding Prince? Short of having these powers in its hands, could the House of Commons have reasonably hoped to survive one week, with the supplies voted, Scotland tranquillised, a standing army of soldiers and a standing army of lawyers at the disposal of the King, and those who had destroyed his friend and minister cast powerless at his discretion? The Parliament knew, by experience often repeated, the whole political and moral scheme of Charles's government. His policy was the restoration of the absolute prerogative royal, such as it had been claimed by the Plantagenets and the Tudors, —and his moral creed was such as to justify the effecting of this restoration by all and any means of fraud or force. His conduct, from as far back as the time of giving the royal assent to the Petition of Right, to that of his correspondence with the army plotters, was an ineffaceable and renewed proof that no bond of treaty or accommodation with him, of which Parliament did not hold the security in its own hands, was of any value. The true way of judging of the conduct of the Long Parliament in these transactions, is to compare it with the conduct of the Convention Parliament in 1688; under circumstances not identical,—not similar in all their parts,— but so nearly analogous, that the only very marked difference in Charles's favour is, that James had an example in memory which his father had not; and this, though mitigating the case for Charles, in no way lowers, in the comparison, the justification of his Parliament. James II. once endeavoured to govern for three years without Parliaments. Charles had done so five times, in violation of personal engagements such as James had never entered into, and had governed without a Parliament for a period of nearly twelve years. James II. assumed a power to dispense with the known laws of the land, and threatened and began a transfer of church property, and the restoration of popery. Charles had actually dispensed with the known laws of the land, in cases of confiscation, taxation, billeting, imprisonment, banishment, pillory, and mutilation. He, indeed, may fairly be supposed never to have meditated the restoration of popery; but he had effected the establishment of a sort of popery in Protestant clothing, a discipline more at variance with the spirit of the age than any which had ever been endured by the English nation from the time of King John to that of Henry the Eighth, when England boasted, and the world believed, that the shackles of priestly tyranny had been broken for ever. In Scotland, he had striven to establish the rites of the Church of England, contrary to law and to his oath. In England, he had not only cast off, but made war upon, the old reforming principle of the English Church, leaning for support upon that limb of her discipline which was of the nature of that ecclesiastical government which she had broken, and was therefore most distasteful generally to the people. Yet the Long Parliament had not, like that of the Convention, voted these acts to be a virtual abdication of the throne, nor had it proceeded, by its own authority, to dispossess the Sovereign of his title and bestow it elsewhere. Probably it may be answered, because it had not yet the power;—perhaps so; but, be that as it may, surely it is not just to blame the Parliament of Charles, not having the power, because it did not take the direct course of power which was taken by the Parliament of James. The time for taking the pledge of the royal word was passed. The ruling party had learned the lesson that it is no part of the moral law of arbitrary Sovereigns to keep faith with such of their subjects as have resisted them. History abounds with instances of engagements solemnly ratified between arbitrary Kings and their people, after advantages gained on the popular side: it affords not one of an arbitrary King who has ever observed any such engagements, when the power of breaking them has returned to him. The question of whether Charles was to be resisted at all is a separate one; but, if to be resisted, surely it would have been madness in the Parliament to trust to his faith without the security of an hostage.

The Parliament proceeded, therefore, gradually and warily, in a defensive course, towards an assumption of power which could alone protect it against the assaults which it was in evidence before them that the King had in his immediate contemplation. It proceeded gradually to withdraw from the Crown all means of violence, until the Crown might be found on the head of some prince who might be trusted with such prerogative as is compatible with liberty, and is an essential part of a free monarchy.

It was in this spirit that Hampden, when, at a more advanced period of the dispute, he was asked, 'what he would 'require that the King should do?' answered, 'That he place 'himself, with his children, and all that he hath, in our 'hands.'

PART THE SEVENTH.

FROM 1641 TO 1642.

The King's project of visiting Scotland—Opposed by the Commons—Encouraged by the Scots—The King arrives at Edinburgh — Cultivates Popularity with the Covenanters — Hampden, and others, Commissioners to attend upon the King—Intrigues and Violences of Montrose—The Scottish Incident—Irish Insurrection—The King returns to London—Grand Protestation—Defections from the Country Party—Demand of the King for the Surrender of Kimbolton and the Five Members—Committee of Privileges retire to the City—Return in Triumph to Westminster—Petition of the Buckinghamshire Men—King leaves London—Departure of the Queen —King goes to York—Summons of Hull—Declaration of his Cause—Is joined by Lords—Raises his Standard—Hampden's motives and Falkland's compared—Breaking out of the Great Civil War.

WHETHER, in Charles's judgment, the time had now become ripe for the blow which he had so long contemplated, or whether, a part of the machinery having failed him, the crisis was thus hastened, it is certain that he began to look impatiently for the means of redeeming himself from that temporising course which he had lately pursued with so much disadvantage. The policy with which he had endeavoured to lull the suspicions of the Commons lay bare before them and the country;—the discovery of the Army Plot, and his ill-disguised eagerness to keep together the levies of Roman Catholics in Ireland (useless, since the pacification with the Scots, for any purpose which would bear the avowal), were strong and public evidence of some dangerous design. But other considerations there were, besides the difficulty of longer keeping his motives secret, which determined him to hasten their accomplishment. Some circumstances, of late, had threatened to raise jealousies among the English people, and to sow differences between a portion of them and the Houses. May admits that, for a short time, the popularity of the Parliament had been on the decline: 'Bishops,' says he, 'had been 'much lifted at, though not taken away; whereby a great 'party whose livelihood and fortune depended upon them, and 'far more, whose hopes of preferment looked that way, most of 'the clergy, and both the Universities, began to be daily more 'disaffected to the Parliament, complaining that all rewards of 'learning must be taken away, which wrought deeply in the 'hearts of the young and more ambitious of that coat.' The populace also had, on many occasions, committed great excesses in interruption of the Church service, while the Common Prayer was reading; and the Parliament, taunted by the Court with being the abettors of them (and unsupported by the Crown), had not, in truth, the power to control them; unless by having recourse to means which would have impaired their own credit with a strong party among the people. And such means they could not, while unsupported by the Crown, be expected to adopt.

To these causes of disgust were added the public preachings of illiterate persons, mostly of the lowest order of tradesmen. 'This, however,' says May, 'some, in a merry way, would put 'off; considering the precedent times, and saying that these 'tradesmen did but take up that duty which the Prelates and 'great Doctors had let fall,—the preaching of the Gospel; 'and that it was but a reciprocal invasion of each other's 'callings; that chandlers, salters, weavers, and the like, 'preached while the Archbishop himself, instead of preaching, 'was busied in projects about leather, salt, soap, and such 'commodities as belonged to those tradesmen.'

These distempers are almost inseparable from a state in which a country party is endeavouring by popular means to diminish the power of the King, and the King is well pleased, at any risk, to discredit the popular party, by casting them on the support of a tumultuous multitude, for whose acts they are unfairly made answerable. Besides, the House of Commons had been obliged to substitute new imposts for those which they had abolished; and now, first for many years, the people felt themselves taxed by votes of Parliament. It was, for many reasons, the King's desire at this juncture that the Parliament should adjourn; the more so, because the bill against Episcopacy was yet pending, and the Houses were also engaged in other committees, for reparation to those who had suffered under the ship-money and other illegal taxes, for settling permanently the revenue of the customs in the hands of Parliament, and for taking into consideration, generally, the state of the kingdom. Charles suddenly announced to them that the visit which he had promised to his friends at Edinburgh must now be paid, and the Scottish Parliament opened by him in person. In vain did the Commons represent to him the charge of such a journey, at a time when the beggared condition of the exchequer, and the embarrassments of the public credit, made it very difficult to carry on the public service at all, and almost hopeless to meet the demands of arrears due to both armies. And with what propriety was he to expose himself in person to the complaints and excesses of troops, some flushed with their late receipt of pay, some clamouring for what was due to them,—and all thirsting to be set free from a military restraint which was at once irksome and inglorious? The King changed his pretext, and now announced his journey as for the purpose of softening these difficulties and allaying these disorders, and of preparing the armies to disband in peace. The Houses scarcely required this proof that the motive was a treacherous one, and that, foiled in his attempt to bring up the English soldiers to London, he wished to join them on their own ground, and put himself at their head. The object of going northward was to further a double intrigue,—with the English officers, and with the Scottish Covenanters. It is also probable that he was not without hopes of finding evidence to set up the authenticity of the letter which Saville had forged, and thus to establish a case of treason against the Parliamentary leaders.

On the other hand, it appeared that the Scottish Commissioners (having, as long as the Puritans of England could assist them, pursued the objects so important to their own country in conjunction with that party) were disposed to push forward the interests of Scotland, separately from that general cause in which they had met with such cordial assistance. They lent themselves readily and eagerly to the project of the King's journey, in order that they might in Edinburgh receive his ratification of the terms for which they had stipulated by treaty in London. Of this difference between the Parliamentary ' Grandees ' and their ' Brethren of Scotland,' Charles was not slow to take note; nor was the advantage small which he promised himself in further separating their interests and feelings by personal negotiation in the metropolis of the North. There was a point beyond which it was not prudent for the English leaders to urge their remonstrances, for fear of irritating the Scots, and of perchance assisting by opposition the disunion which the King was endeavouring to effect by intrigue. The Commons took, therefore, a middle course;— they addressed him, praying that he would defer his journey for a fortnight, in order that the two armies on the frontier might be paid off, and the road be left unoccupied by which he and his train should pass. This address it was not easy to find stateable reasons for declining to comply with. The Earl of Holland was sent down with a commission to disband the armies; yet to avoid falling in with the English troops, already discontented with the irregularity of the supplies voted for their pay, does not appear to have suited the King's main design;—nor could he, in the end, be prevailed upon to delay his departure beyond two days. The public display which he made, passing on horseback with the Duke of Richmond, the Marquis of Hamilton, Lord Willoughby, his heralds, and a numerous retinue, in sight of the disbanding armies, and his early endeavours (if Baillie be to be believed) to engage the Scots with the Cavaliers of the English army in the forcible dissolution of the English Parliament, show that what was urged by the Commons as a motive for delaying his journey was, in truth, one of his main incentives to undertake and to hasten it.* He lost no time in addressing himself to the Covenanters. He raised Hamilton to the highest rank in the peerage of his country; Argyle he made a Marquis; and he created old Leslie, who had for the greater part of his life been a soldier of fortune, Earl of Leven; Loudon and Almond were also made Earls; and on the Earl of Dunfermline he bestowed a large grant of crown lands, and a pension out of the public revenue. Hamilton accepted the dukedom, but retained his attachment to the Covenant; and Leslie, in the overflowing of a short-lived gratitude, protested that he never

---

* Ludlow, who does not appear to have ever been led by party feelings into mis-stating such facts as he avers on his own knowledge, says that Charles offered to surrender to the Scots four English counties in pledge for the performance of his terms with them if they would assist him in this object.

again would bear arms against so good a King. But the English Parliament would have been blind indeed not to see the approaching confirmation of what they had apprehended from Charles's obstinate adherence to the project of moving northwards. He had, in the last days of his stay in London, evaded giving any direct answer to them; but, when pressed on that point, had, like one importuned on a secret which troubled him, changed the subject, and spoken on the Dutch treaty, and the depredations of the pirates from Tangier and Sallee. The Parliament was not of materials or of a temper thus to be dealt with. If, indeed, the King had not had good reason to know the suspicions of his Parliament, or the Parliament to know the designs of the King, either party might, in these transactions, have easily been made the dupe of the other. But both were playing an exceeding deep game; and each understood every move of the other as it was made. The Scottish Presbyterians were troubled with no interest but their own; and both parties were bidding for their assistance. One course alone remained to the Parliament, as a check upon the objects which the King now so actively pursued. And that course was adopted. It was to depute commissioners, nominally to treat with the Scots concerning the ratification of the treaty, and to obtain security for the debt due from them to the northern counties of England, but really to thwart the King's negotiations with the Covenanters, and to report upon them to the Parliament. For this Committee, openly appointed by votes of both Houses, and openly proceeding to where the King held his Court, Lord Clarendon can find no less violent name than that of spies; which designation is eagerly adopted by Mr. Hume. In order that the jealousy of the Parliament and the true purpose of this Committee might be no secret to the King, the Commissioners named to attend him were, for the Lords, the Earl of Bedford, and Lord Howard of Escricke; and, for the Commons, Hampden and Fiennes; and afterwards were added Sir Philip Stapleton and Sir William Armyne.

They presented themselves to the King at Holyrood; and, with whatever distaste Charles was likely to view the presence and conduct of a Parliamentary Committee appointed for these acknowledged purposes, his communications with the members of it were conducted with all show of graciousness on his side, and of duty and respect on theirs. Hampden and Fiennes were the active and responsible chiefs of that Committee,—

the soul of its counsels, and the conductors of its correspondence with the Parliament. The latter of these two, on account of the rising importance which his abilities and his powerful connexions had given him; the former on account of his boldness, temper, discretion, and wisdom; of his being the man of 'the most absolute spirit of popularity' in both kingdoms; and because, moreover, he had, of all men of that party, been in the most constant communication with the Scots, and was best acquainted with the means of keeping them in awe of their former engagements and of their future interests with the English Parliament. Nor was it long before the duties of that commission were called into activity. The leaders of the Scottish Presbyterians, as we have seen, and several also of their principal preachers, were taken into high favour and close counsel by the King. Henderson was always at his side, and had a grant of the rents of the Chapel Royal. He lived at his palace, advising with him in his closet, and ministering to his popularity with the multitude by accompanying him on every occasion of representation and display. Charles publicly accepted, and swore to, the terms of the Covenant; and one of the earliest acts of the Scottish Parliament which received the royal assent was the act of pacification, declaring that the commotions had arisen from the innovations in religion, and corruption of church government.* Argyle, Hamilton, and Lanerick his brother, were at first to be used for the purpose of bringing over the affections of the powerful families of Scotland. But Charles had always failed in this important object of his Scottish policy. A body of nobility so divided by old feudal recollections as that of Scotland, and so distrustful of Hamilton in consequence of his having openly sided with the King in his late wars on the southern frontier of that country, was not to be bound to the King's interests through his means. Above all, Argyle and Hamilton had been ever the marked and personal foes of Montrose. And he was one whose restless spirit was never stayed by any considerations from pursuing by any means of violence or fraud the destruction of any man who thwarted his objects of intrigue, or obstructed the views of his high-reaching ambition. Montrose, of whom Clarendon, forgetful of the crimes which he imputes to him in the early part of his history, says, in the latter part

* Rushworth.

of it, that 'he was not without vanity, but his virtues were 'much superiour,' had been thrown into confinement by the Parliament of Scotland for a complication of proved offences of the highest sort. He had, the year before, engaged himself in a plot to betray the Covenanters' army with whom he was serving, because he had failed in an attempt to procure the chief command; and prudential motives alone prevented the Scots from publicly arraigning him for the act.* But all the circumstances of his treachery were known to the Committee of Estates,—their knowledge of it communicated to him,— and his conduct from thenceforth closely watched. And it was not long before his restless spirit threw him upon another design, of which he was openly convicted. He had incited one Stewart to accuse Argyle, Hamilton, and Rothes, of a treasonable intent to depose Charles. On the proceedings, Stewart, ill-qualified to be the agent of so bold an intriguer as Montrose, confessed his crime. Nothing then remained for Montrose but to denounce Stewart as having been suborned by Argyle to forge this confession; and thus, embroiling the charge, he left his wretched accomplice in the dilemma of a capital accusation of leasing-making against one, at least, of the nobles, and to be consequently put to an ignominious death.†

But the turbulent genius of Montrose was not subdued by the failure of this enterprise;—he well knew how to feed the suspicious temper of Charles, and, even from prison, secretly corresponded with him, through the means of a page of the Bed Chamber. ‡ He indulged him with assurances of being able to furnish proof against the Hamiltons and Argyle; but, as Clarendon assures us, advised the simpler mode of disposing of them by assassination, which, says the noble writer, he 'frankly undertook himself to manage.' 'The King,' says Clarendon, 'abhorred that expedient, though, for his own 'security, he advised that proofs might be prepared for the 'Parliament.' Yet still had not he the virtue or courage to free himself from the agency of so unprincipled an adviser.

---

* Burnet's Hist. Own Times.—Nalson.—Clarendon, Hist. Reb.—Hardwicke's State Papers.—Sidney Papers.
† Brodie.—Baillie's and Woodrow's MS. Letters in the Advocates' Library, as quoted by Brodie.—Baillie's published Letters.—Guthrie's Memoirs.—Appendix to Scottish Acts for 1641.
‡ Hailes's Letters.—Laing's History.

But Montrose established a stronger hold over the passions of Charles; he flattered him with the assurance of full evidence to convict the leaders of the English Parliament of treasonable correspondence with the Scottish army.

To cut off at one blow, by course of law, Pym, Hampden, Fiennes, and the rest, before whose courage and skill he stood in bonds, and from whose strong grasp he despaired of wresting the power he had lost, unless by getting a pretext for at once destroying them, was a tempting proposal. Charles was intoxicated with the hope,—threw off all discretion and reserve with this rash bad man,—and committed his conduct at once to his dangerous guidance.

What evidence Montrose may have suborned, prepared, or only promised, will probably never be known. According to some writers, the wretched Saville was implicated in this plot with a second forgery.* Ready as he always was to betray any party or person who might be misled into trusting him, he has left his character answerable, perhaps, for some acts of guilt of which it was morally clear. Saville must have been a man of no inconsiderable abilities; for, universally suspected, he was yet always employed as the busy agent of alternate factions for their several purposes, though never far enough in the confidence of any to be able to make his perfidy profitable to himself.

The immediate result of these intrigues was the event so well known to all readers of Scottish history under the name of the 'Incident.' In itself, probably, little more than one of those sudden enterprises of feudal treachery and violence with which the Scottish history of the seventeenth century abounds, it has been covered by the actors and writers on both sides with a veil of pompous mystery, through which only occasional glimpses have been given, which have tended rather to confound than discover the truth.

Suddenly, in the midst of Montrose's darker designs, Lord Henry Kerr, a generous-spirited rash young man, son to the Earl of Roxburgh, sent his defiance to Hamilton, proclaiming him a traitor to God, his King, and his country, and saying that he would make good 'his charge against him with his 'life.' Of this outrage Hamilton complained in his place in the Parliament the same day; and Kerr, being ordered by his

* Laing's History of Scotland.

father to go to the Parliament House to make submission, went with the inappropriate accompaniment of six hundred officers and soldiers under arms. The Parliament, in consternation, raised the city guard, and, by proclamation, ordered Kerr's followers, and the multitude who were flocking from all parts, to disperse. For two days, peace seemed to be restored; but, on the third night Argyle and the two Hamiltons fled to Kinneil. The alarm of an assassination plot instantly flew from mouth to mouth through Edinburgh. What afterwards appeared on evidence was that a band of desperadoes, most of them men of noble family, with the Earl of Crawford at their head, and with a following of some hundreds, had undertaken to arrest Argyle and the Hamiltons, and to hurry them off to a frigate stationed in Leith Roads, where they were to remain for trial on Montrose's charges; and that Crawford was to assassinate them in case of resistance. Thus much was communicated to them on the information of Colonel Urrie, afterwards so well known in the civil wars of both countries, to whom the plot had been laid open by a Colonel Stewart, who had obtained his knowledge through an identity of name with one of the conspirators.* Popular belief assigned to the enterprise a much wider range. It was said that Cochrane, one of Crawford's party, who commanded a regiment stationed near Edinburgh, was to march upon the city, to break into the Parliament House, to seize certain suspected members there, to liberate Montrose, and with the assistance of the Kerrs, Humes, Johnstones, and some other borderers, to place Scotland entirely within the power of the King;—furthermore, that Montrose was to procure evidence against the Covenanting Lords on their trials, the other insurgents to furnish troops, and, after this first blow had been struck, to accompany the King to England, and, with the remnants of the disbanded English army, to secure the means for dissolving the Parliament, and destroying the leaders of the country party there. To whatever length the intention had in fact gone, the Scottish Parliament forthwith called on Leslie to take command of the city guard and such other troops as could be collected and relied on, and to remain under arms for its protection. The fugitive Lords, after some

---

* Lanerick's Relation.—Baillie's MS. Letters, quoted by Brodie.—Baillie's published Letters.—Clarendon's Hist. Reb.—Laing.—Evidence in Balfour's Diurnal.—MS. Papers in Advocates' Library, as quoted by Brodie.

negotiation, returned. The King, on his part, loudly complained of what he represented as a plot forged by the leaders of the Covenant to excite dissensions between him and his Scottish subjects. But what the most tended to throw suspicion upon the King, and to discredit his remonstrance against Argyle and the Hamiltons, was his sudden attempt to raise a large sum of money in Holland; and above all, his going down on the very evening of the discovery to the Parliament House, with all the persons who had been named by Urrie, and with five hundred or six hundred soldiers.*

That a violent seizure of the persons of the three Covenanting Lords was intended there appears to be no reasonable doubt; nor is it very improbable, on the other hand, that the Covenanting Lords were eager to act in public upon the impulse of their fears, and so to expose the machinations of the plotters, and the double-dealing of Charles, instead of thwarting the design and providing for their own safety, which perhaps they might have done secretly, and without noise. After all, it is likely that this plot, like many other state plots, odious and dangerous in its intention, was exaggerated by those whose safety had been threatened, partly from passionate resentment, and partly for further political objects. Certain it is that the news was instantly dispatched to London express by the English Commissioners, and that it arrived there with extraordinary speed, spreading consternation and panic in the Standing Committee, and in the two Houses, who had just reassembled after the adjournment. It was, doubtless, in many respects, a fortunate discovery for the country party in England. It gave manifest warning of a new course of designs on the part of the King. It opened also to both countries the whole secret of his dealings with Montrose; and it hastened the steps which the English Parliament had, before the recess, been inclined to adopt for its own safety, but for which it still wanted a signal and stateable justification. The Commissioners now set out for London, to resume their seats and report to the Houses. But, before they left Edinburgh, they addressed the King, praying him to return with them to Parliament as he had promised. Nor did many days elapse before he followed them; but, before his departure from Edinburgh, again receiving the Covenanting Lords into

* Evelyn's Memoirs.—Appendix.—Correspondence between King Charles and Secretary Nicholas.

seeming favour, he gave a great feast to the Parliament. Once more Scotland saw her ancient palace glittering with the emblems of her independent sovereignty, and the descendant of her kings, the origin of whose race she traced amid the clouds of dim antiquity, now again 'encompassed with his 'kingdom's pearl,' and courting and receiving the favour of his people. For the time, the Scots forgot all but that Charles was their countryman and their King, and that he was soon to leave them; and he left Scotland with more applause, (notwithstanding their belief that he had so lately borne part in a plot against their Parliament,) than met him when he came to confirm their Civil Constitution and Ecclesiastical Liberties. 'His Majesty departed,' says Heath, 'a 'contented King from a contented people.' *

But in the Sister Island a fearful storm at this time broke forth, soon to rage with a fury that threatened the total and bloody dismemberment of the Empire. It went near to effect, at once, the extermination of the whole Protestant population of Ireland.

The amount of the massacre actually perpetrated is variously stated; the fears of all the Protestants, the passions of many, and the interests of not a few, tending to exaggerate the number of the slain; the exaggerations, of course, increasing with the efforts of the Popish writers afterwards to underrate it. The slaughter was not limited to the towns and villages. It pursued its victims among the bogs, the mountains, and the woods, to which they fled for refuge. All calculation, therefore, of its amount must be, to a great degree, fanciful. Thus much only is certain; that the purpose of the insurgents extended to the entire rooting out of the Protestant settlers, by an indiscriminate butchery of both sexes and of all ages; and that, for several weeks, it proceeded almost unchecked. Dublin itself was saved by a mere accident. For a short space, the rebels had made some show of humanity, until they secured the co-operation of the Lords of the Pale, who, in their detestation of the Puritans, and their remembrance of the persecutions which for near a century had been endured by themselves and their forefathers of their own faith and country, joined interests and forces with the Irish of the ancient stock, to crush the power of the English Parliament.

* Heath's Chronicle.

The next day after this union beheld the whole province of Ulster in carnage and conflagration, traversed by columns of armed men who were intoxicated with religious hate, and deaf to every plea for mercy, marching upon points, and carrying to all quarters at once devastation and death. Modes of torture too horrible for the human mind to contemplate, and too detestable for description, were invented and executed. The havock spread southward, abating only where it had consumed the materials on which its fury had been exercised. The Shannon became choked with the bodies of the slain. The generous though turbulent nature of Roger Moore, the chief who had first excited the rebellion, recoiled from the barbarities which marked its course; and, at last, finding his authority unable to control the spirit which it had been powerful to evoke, he, after a gallant protest, quitted the blood-stained and dishonoured cause which he had undertaken in the hope to give liberty to his country; and he fled to Flanders. The principal leaders of this hideous warfare were, of the ancient Irish, Sir Phelim O'Neale, Macguire, and Macmahon, and of those of the Pale, Lord Gormanstown. They pleaded a Royal Commission under a seal, surreptitiously obtained, as some writers state (but this Mr. Godwin satisfactorily disproves), from the foot of an ancient monastic charter; and putting forth as their justification the intention to assist the King against his Scottish and English enemies, and assured of assistance from the Roman Catholic powers of the Continent, they assumed the ill-omened appellation of the Queen's Army.*

No candid person, who has well examined the evidence, now imputes to Charles that he connived at this atrocious insurrection; though, unhappily for him, his consent was proclaimed by the insurgents themselves, and, not very unreasonably, suspected by the English Parliament. On the other hand, it cannot be disguised that countenance and facilities had been afforded to them by his unjustifiable obstinacy in so long persisting, contrary to promise, and in defiance of repeated remonstrance, in keeping Strafford's Roman Catholic army together. His communications with it had been detected and published to the whole English and Scottish nations, with great care, and some exaggeration; and it had been disbanded;

* Whitelocke.—Birch's Relation of Glamorgan's Transactions.

after an ineffectual attempt on his part to transport it into Flanders, there to remain, within call, in the hands of the King of Spain. But, after so much tampering with so wild and dangerous a body, the formal act of disbanding did not disunite its elements. They instantly reassembled for the most tremendous outbreak which has ravaged any country in modern times, and which continued in Ireland, with various and seldom abated rage, for upwards of two years.

On Charles's return to London, he found the state in the greatest disorder, and men's minds in the utmost alarm. During the whole adjournment, the Standing Committee, with Pym in the chair, had been collecting the materials for a solemn appeal to the country. Parliament had met on the 20th of October. The country was beset with danger and distraction, external and domestic. The Scottish intrigues, the Irish insurrection, France taking a part in each, Holland and Denmark in secret negotiation with the King to furnish him with military means against his subjects,* the Exchequer of England in pledge for an unprecedented amount of debt, and the public credit nearly exhausted. To finish the sum of calamity and dismay, the plague was again breaking out in several parts of Middlesex, and even of Westminster itself.†

The two Houses had, before the King's return, gone no small way towards assuming the powers of an independent government. Just before the adjournment, they had, for the first time, entered on their Journals a resolution under the name of an Ordinance against ' the raising and transporting of ' forces of horse or foot out of his Majesty's dominions of ' England and Ireland ; ' ‡ which, whether intended or not, by its framers, to furnish a convenient precedent for afterwards enacting laws on the mere vote of the two Houses, had been in this case rendered almost unavoidable by the attempt of the King to establish his Irish army in Flanders. To this, however, the royal assent was afterwards given; and it is remarkable only as the first instrument bearing a name which, not long after, began to signify an Act of Parliament passed without the consent or authority of the Crown.

Charles, on his arrival in London, proceeded as he had done in Edinburgh. He applied himself first to pay court to the

---

* Newcastle's Letters.—Duchess of Newcastle's Memoirs.
† Commons' Journals, Sept. 6.   ‡ Ibid., Sept. 9.

City. As in Edinburgh, he met with extraordinary testimonies of affection in return; but, as in Edinburgh, he mistook both the motive of these demonstrations and the nature of his own popularity. He had never been personally disliked by his people. On the contrary, they were anxious to mark their affection towards him,—perhaps also towards the due prerogatives of the Crown; but they were equally eager, in all they did and said, to separate him from his evil counsellors. He believed his evil counsellors, and not his people, and weakly and passionately concluded that the City would proceed to support him to the utmost against his Parliament. He knew not—he would not be convinced—that silently, slowly, but irresistibly, was growing up and spreading a jealousy of all the institutions of the country, except the courts of common law. These had never been seen as instruments of tyranny, except in the great case of the Ship-Money decision; and that decision had been struck off the Rolls, the Judges who had concurred in it disgraced and punished, the precedent reversed, and the patents of the Judges declared to be no longer held at the pleasure of the Crown.

Charles was received as one who had power to act a great part at a crisis of great danger and difficulty; and, at such a crisis, public bodies are always inclined to form sanguine expectations of those who come with great power of doing good. He was gloriously feasted in the City. In return, he feasted the citizens gloriously at Hampton Court; but, scarcely had they time to proffer their love and duty before it was made matter of general discourse among the Court party that the City was weary of the Parliament, and was prepared to support the King alone. 'Whether,' says May, ' it begat the same
' opinion in the King or not, I cannot tell; but certainly some
' conceived so by actions which immediately followed, expressing
' a greater confidence against the Parliament than before;
' displacing some from such trusts as they had conferred upon
' them;—insomuch that the City, presently after, finding what
' ill use was made of those expressions, were enforced to declare
' themselves, in a petition to both Houses, that, since some
' ill affected people had interpreted their loyal and affectionate
' attachment to the King as a sign that they would wholly
' adhere to him and desert the Parliament, they openly pro-
' fessed the contrary; and that they would live and die with
' them for the good of the Commonwealth. After which, the

'City, no less than the Parliament, did seem to be distasted
'both by the King and Queen.'

Most men agree that the crisis of the Grand Remonstrance
was that at which all shallow truce, all insidious compromise,
ceased between King and Parliament; and when secret jealousy,
intrigue, and machination were changed into manifest and
avowed enmity. There was no longer a chance left of restoring
the balance of the Constitution. All that remained was to
make choice between rendering up to the King, without further
dispute, the whole of that arbitrary prerogative which he had
claimed, or giving the sovereign power of the Commonwealth
in trust to the Parliament during the remainder of his reign,
in the hope of its being surrendered back whenever the purposes
of the trust should be at an end;—and that were to know
little of the nature of popular assemblies, once invested with
such a power.

It is a difficult question to determine at what period, after
the meeting of the Long Parliament, it might have been
possible for Charles, even if he could have been persuaded to
act sincerely, and under good counsel, to preserve the due
prerogatives of his crown by a course consistent at once with
his own dignity and with the spirit of wise concession befitting
the temper of the times and of the men with whom he had to
act. This only is clear, that, at the beginning, such a course
was practicable, and that now it was no longer so. No form
of constitution of which monarchy is a part, can preserve
liberty, nor can a free monarchy stand, where the separate
powers of king and people are employed to invade each other's
lawful authority. This, however, is to be observed of the
testimony of Clarendon: up to the time of the Long Parliament, the whole course of his narrative and reasoning
are against the King; afterwards uniformly in his favour.
Upon the evidence then of him, who, of all men, wrote on
these matters with his affections the most strongly bound to
the cause of Charles, it is clear, with respect to the often
agitated question of 'Which party gave the provocation?' that
the course of aggression was begun by Charles.

The King having refused, when he left England, to appoint
any lawful commission for administering the sovereign power
in his name, the Parliament, in his absence, and under the
urgent alarm of the Irish rebellion, was not loth to issue an
ordinance for the raising of troops in that country. Charles,

on his return to his English metropolis, removed the guard which the two Houses had by address obtained from him to be placed in Palace Yard for their protection under command of the Earl of Essex; thus leaving them no better pledge than his promise for their security, when appearances justified every suspicion that one of those violent enterprises might be repeated from which they had so lately and so narrowly escaped. He appointed other troops to quarter at their doors under the orders of the Earl of Dorset, an intemperate man, devoted to the court, and known, most unfavourably, to the Parliament, as a prime promoter of some of those cruel censures in the Star Chamber, so lately denounced by resolution and reversed by statute. In this difficulty, the Commons proceeded with moderation and dignity. They directed the Speaker, by his authority, to remove the guard, and required that, instead of it, the High Constable should provide 'a strong and sufficient watch.'* They moreover voted a conference with the Lords, touching the tumultuous assembly of people about the Houses of Parliament. But here the Lords deserted them. And at best, this precaution was but temporary. Their permanent safety remained to be provided for; for, at the same time, the King had placed the Tower of London, with the charge of the Mint, in the hands of Colonel Lunsford, an unprincipled desperado, who had signalised himself by many acts of outrageous violence, one of which had nearly brought him to the gibbet, and who was believed to be a ready instrument for any lawless enterprise. Lunsford was in a few days removed from this command, in consequence of an unanimous address; but, on the morrow of his dismissal, he began to take vengeance on the Parliament, and justify their opinion of him, by marching down to Westminster Hall with an armed mob, assaulting and wounding several persons, and threatening to drag the members out by force. It was on the 7th of January that both Houses prayed the King's consent to a bill for placing the militia, both by sea and land, in the hands of commissioners to be appointed by the Parliament.

The Lord Keeper Littleton supported this bill.† Selden, the highest constitutional authority in the House, opposed it. In truth, it was not capable of any defence but that of the overwhelming danger and necessity of the time. But, with

---

* Commons' Journal, Dec. 30, Jan. 1. † Clarendon—Hist. Reb.

RICHARD SACKVILLE,
FOURTH EARL OF DORSET
OB. 1652.

equal vehemence, he resisted the King's commission of array; and, afterwards, to sanction by his example the expedient which the danger and necessity of the time had imposed, he accepted a commission of lieutenancy under the Parliament for raising the militia in their behalf. To that clause in the bill for pressing soldiers which denied the power of the crown to press, save under the authority of a bill, he gave his entire and eager consent. To this check upon an unlawfully assumed power the King made furious and obstinate opposition, sending a message, pending the discussion of the bill, to declare that he would never pass it. A declaration which only produced a remonstrance against the King's interference with bills in their passage through Parliament.

In the Correspondence appended to the diary of Evelyn is a letter from the Queen to Secretary Nicholas, November 12, which shows that both she and the King were well aware of the tendency of such a precedent as that of the first Ordinance, even though justified by such an emergency as that in Ireland. ' I send you,' says she, ' a lettre for Milord Keeper, that the ' King ded send to me, to deliver it if I thought fit. The ' subject of it is to make a declaration against the ordres of ' Parliament which ar made without the King.'

Meanwhile, on the 1st of December, the Grand Remonstrance was presented to the King. At great length, and with great power, it summed up all the grievances under which the Parliament and people had suffered throughout his whole reign. Illegal imposts, monopolies, fines, and arbitrary imprisonments, denials of justice by some courts, and oppressive jurisdiction of others, Popish Lords in Parliament, and favour shown to evil counsellors,—all were presented at one view; and it concluded with a general petition that the prelates should be deprived of their votes, that none should be entrusted with the public affairs whom the Parliament might not approve of, and that the escheated lands of the Irish rebels might not be alienated, but reserved for the support of the Crown and the payment of the expenses of the war.

On the different clauses a great and violent debate had arisen. On the 22nd of November, the House had continued sitting till three in the morning, having met at ten on the preceding day, and having begun the debate on the remonstrance at three in the afternoon. Some of the members, struck with alarm, and many, says Clarendon, worn out with fatigue, had retired from the House.* At length, the resolutions were carried, after two divisions, by a majority of only 159 to 148, and of 124 to 101. And now a desperate stand was attempted to be made by Hyde. It was to the effect of a protest, to be entered by the minority against the decision of the House. The conflict of passions and voices was tremendous, and bloodshed, says Sir Philip Warwick, would probably have ensued; 'we had catched at each other's locks, and sheathed our 'swords in each other's bowels, had not the sagacity and great 'calmness of Mr. Hampden, by a short speech, prevented it, 'and led us to defer our angry debate until the next morning.' He rose amidst the uproar, and, with that commanding influence, which, though rarely exerted, he possessed above all men in the House, he subdued for a moment the rage of the contending parties, sufficiently to gain their consent to an adjournment; by which, at once, he saved them from a less appeasable conflict, and effectually baffled Hyde's project, which could only have succeeded by some compromise, forced on in the confusion, for striking the former proceedings from the journals. Cromwell declared next day to Lord Falkland, that, had the Remonstrance not been carried, 'he would 'instantly have sold all that he had, and gone to America; 'and that he knew there were many other honest men of the 'same resolution.'† The opposition, thus vanquished, was not renewed, and the Remonstrance passed peaceably through its next and final stage.

Thus far, however, since the King's breach with the City, some of these events over which he had no control had, indirectly, worked benefit to his cause. The Grand Remonstrance had given a motive to some, and a pretext to others, who heretofore had opposed him, for now devoting themselves entirely to his interests. Hyde had thrown off all disguise with the Country Party, and Colepeper, though occasionally serving with them in committees, in cases of privilege, and even

---

* Clarendon and Dugdale endeavour to show, that so many of the old members had left the House, that the votes were passed by a packed committee. Mr. Brodie very properly observes, that this falling off in the members of the House, towards the end of the debate, would affect both parties. But the proportionate numbers of the two divisions upon the remonstrance, and of the third, on Hyde's motion, show that the comparative strength of the minority had not decreased.—See Sir Philip Warwick's account of the same transaction. See also Appendix to Evelyn.

† Clarendon—Hist. Reb.

on the defence of the kingdom and the levying of soldiers, was now acknowledged by all as one of the selected council of the King. Falkland was shaken by late events, and, looking forward with dismay, wavered in his course; yet his veneration for Parliaments and their privileges, and his strong and jealous love of liberty, still attached him to the persons, and made him reluctant to quit the party, with which he had so long and cordially served. Sir Ralph Hopton was still as eager as ever in support of the strongest votes against the Court. That Falkland had not yet, nor till after the affair of the five members, quitted the country party is clear, from reference to the journals; and to suppose that his association with them, during the short time which passed between the Remonstrance and that event, was insidious or insincere, 'in tanto viro,' to use the words of his friend, 'in tanto viro injuria virtutum fuerit.'

But the time unquestionably was now come at which the most honourable and constant spirit might fairly justify itself in a direct and open change of politics. It was not that the terms of the Grand Remonstrance had put forth any new doctrines, or made any new claim for the Commons; but it was clearly intended as a public justification of claims already made, and which had now daily become more frequent and decisive. And many an honest and high mind, which had acquiesced in the necessity of some of the earlier assumptions of power by the Parliament, thought that the time had arrived at which, at length, to make a stand for Monarchy.

Besides the advantage which Charles derived from the late adhesion of so many honourable men to his interests, and from the example which it held forth to others, his own published answer to the Remonstrance was calculated to strengthen it. Hyde drew up this answer for his master, with an ability worthy of that pen which has since commended to posterity the recital of his troubles and his fate. Charles's impatience, however, would never long suffer favourable events or good counsel to work for his advantage; but would always embroil his case, at the very moment when the greatest circumspection was wanted to improve it. The attempt to seize the five members was the decisive act of his rashness and perfidy:— perfidious, because, on the very day before, he had remonstrated with the House on its renewed demand for a guard of soldiers, and had assured its members, 'on the word of a king,' that he should be as tender of their persons as of those of his children;*—decisive, as rendering it no longer possible, from that fatal day, for the House to set up for itself any security but that of absolute force. Votes and resolutions, which are the lawful weapons of a Parliament while the Constitution stands, are powerless when it is suspended. The 'power ' of the purse' is popularly said to be the security of Parliaments against sovereigns; but against a tyrant, with the power of the sword in his hands, it is none. It would be as reasonable for the unarmed man to console himself with his fancied power of the purse, in presence of the spoiler who has that of the sword.

On the 4th of January this frantic enterprise was undertaken;—whether solely of Charles's own motion, or whether under the advice of Digby, against whom the House had, a few days before, complained to the Lords on account of his declaration 'that this was no free Parliament,' or whether at the instance of the Queen, who is said to have bid him 'pull ' those rogues out by the ears, or never see her face again,' is unnecessary here to inquire. The boundary which separates the empire of absolute violence from that of law and privilege was now passed; and, as if to make the act more signal, and to deprive himself of all hope of retreat or shelter under the responsibility of others, Charles did it in person. From that hour, all reserve and scruple on the other side was at an end, except so far as related to the still disclaiming all violence to his person or to his 'lawful power.'

Charles, relying on the information, more or less authentic, which he had received in Scotland, respecting the English leaders, and assuming as proveable, what does not appear ever to have existed, some correspondence between them and Richelieu, on the 3rd sent down his Attorney-General, Sir Edward Herbert, to the bar of the House of Lords, to accuse in his name the Lord Kimbolton, and five gentlemen of the House of Commons, of high treason, desiring that a Secret Committee might examine witnesses, and that the accused persons should be placed in custody. The Lord Kimbolton, who was in his place, with strong professions of his innocence, submitted himself to whatever order the House should make, but prayed that he might be cleared as publicly as he had

---

* Rushworth.

been charged.* A Committee being immediately appointed to examine precedents as to the regularity of proceedings, and the Commons being informed of the accusation against its members, the Lords adjourned till the following day, no man moving for the commitment of Kimbolton on the King's behalf.† The Commons, meanwhile, having received inforformation that the lodgings and trunks of Mr. Strode, Hazelrigge, Pym, Hampden and Holles, had in their absence been sealed up by the King's command, ordered, by resolution, that the Serjeant-at-Arms attending the House should break the seals, and that the Speaker's warrant should be issued for the apprehension of the persons who had affixed them. The House further declared, in conformity with the unanimous protestation which they had signed four months before, that any hindrance or molestation to the persons of any of their members, until the House should have been first made acquainted with the grounds of such proceedings, was a high breach of privilege, and might be resisted by force. The House then desired an immediate conference with the Lords: but, before the Lords' answer came down, a serjeant-at-arms appeared at the table, and required the persons of the five members. The Commons unanimously stood upon their privilege, and, desiring the serjeant to retire, sent a message by a Committee of their own body, that they should take the premises into their serious consideration, and that the members should be ready to answer any legal charge. The Lords, next day, took a similar course. The Commons, however, instantly went into committee; and Strode and Holles spoke, repelling the charge of treason, demanding trial, and professing their willingness to submit themselves and their case, without any further preparation, to any legal process of inquisition and judgment.‡

On the 4th, the accused members attending according to order in their places, Lord Falkland, in the name of the Committee who had taken the message to the King, stated for answer that he was desired to inform the House that the serjeant had done nothing but what he had it in command to do. Upon this Hampden arose, and, on grounds distinctly

---

* See his published speech, King's Collection, Brit. Mus.
† Rushworth, Whitelocke, Clarendon, Hist. Reb.
‡ Rushworth, Commons' Journals, Jan. 3. Somers's Tracts. Published Speeches, Brit. Mus.

and powerfully stated, laid down the tests by which he desired, with respect to the matter of accusation, that his conduct might be tried. He entered not on the particulars of the charges; for the evidence to support them had not yet been opened to the House; but, as was necessary when the terms loyalty, obedience, and resistance, had been so loosely employed, he particularised upon these several duties as constituting the difference between a good and a bad subject. He divided them under the heads of ' Religion towards God, loyalty and due ' submission to the lawful commands of the Sovereign, and ' good affection towards the safety and just rights of the ' people, according to the ancient and fundamental laws of the ' realm.' Concerning religion, he claimed the right of determining, by searching the sacred writings, in which ' are con- ' tained all things necessary to salvation ;' he contrasted this law with the doctrine and discipline of the Church of Rome, and averred that ' all other sects and schisms that lean not ' only on the Scriptures, though never so contrary to the ' Church of Rome, are a false worshipping of God, and not ' the true religion.' He then proceeded to define the limits and extent of ' lawful obedience' to the Sovereign, ' acting ' with the free consent of his great council of state, assembled ' in Parliament. For the first, to deny a willing and dutiful ' obedience to a lawful sovereign and his privy council, (for, as ' Camden truly saith, the commands of the Lords Privy Coun- ' sellors, and the edict of the prince is one, they are inseparable, ' the one never without the other,) to deny to defend his royal ' person and kingdoms against the enemies of the same, either ' public or private, or to deny to defend the ancient privileges ' and prerogatives of the King, as pertinent and belonging of ' right to his royal Crown, and the maintenance of his honour ' and dignity, or to deny to defend and maintain true religion ' in the land, according to the truth of God, is one sign of an ' evil subject. Secondly, to yield obedience to the commands ' of a King, if against the true religion, and the ancient and ' fundamental laws of the land, is another sign of an ill ' subject. Thirdly, to resist the lawful power of the King, to ' raise insurrection against the King, admit him averse in his ' religion, to conspire or in any way to rebel against his sacred ' person, though commanding things against our consciences ' in exercising religion, or against the rights and privileges of ' the subject, is an absolute sign of a disaffected and trayterous 'subject.' Of the means to know the difference between a good subject and a bad, 'by their obedience to the laws, statutes, 'and ordinances made by the King, with the whole consent of 'his Parliament,' he spoke thus :—' First, I conceive, if any 'particular Member of a Parliament, although his judgment and 'vote be contrary, do not willingly submit to the rest, he is an 'ill subject to his king and country; and, secondly, to resist 'the ordinance of the whole state of the kingdom, either by 'the stirring up a dislike in the hearts of his Majesty's 'subjects of the proceedings of the Parliament, to endeavour, 'by levying arms, to compel the King and Parliament to make 'such laws as seem best to them, to deny the power, authority, 'and privileges, of Parliament, to cast aspersions upon the 'same and its proceedings, thereby inducing the King to think 'ill of the same, and to be incensed against the same, to 'procure the untimely breaking up and dissolution of a Parlia-'ment, before all things be settled by the same, for the safety 'and tranquillity both of King and state, these are apparent 'signs of a treacherous and disloyal subject against his King 'and country. I humbly desire my actions may be compared 'with either; and both as a subject, a Protestant, as a native 'of this my country, and as I am a Member of this present 'and happy Parliament, that I be esteemed, as I shall be found 'guilty upon these articles exhibited against myself and the 'other gentlemen, to be a bad or a good subject to my sove-'reign and native country : and to receive such sentence upon 'the same as by this honourable House shall be conceived to 'agree with law and justice.' *

Hazelrigge followed, approaching the specific charges in the articles rather nearer than Hampden had done. He took the phrase, ' to subvert the fundamental laws,' under which head he classed privilege of Parliament. Treason could consist only of words or acts. His speeches in that House were in their recollection, and, in his votes, he had generally concurred with the majority. His acts, and those of the gentlemen with him, particularly with reference to Scotland, had been in accordance with votes and resolutions of that House ; and the levying of war, and promoting of tumults and seditions, could only refer to their concurrence with the rest of the House in the ordinance for troops in Ireland to stay the

---

* A learned and discreet Speech of Master John Hampden, &c. &c. &c. —London, 1642.

progress of the rebellion, or to the raising of the militia, and placing the city guard of Westminster before the doors of the House, to suppress the tumults of the people, and to protect the House from a military force unlawfully menacing the freedom of its debates. Hazelrigge's speech was not destitute of ingenuity or force; but, as men generally do who defend themselves by anticipation, he fell into the error of imputing some motives for the accusation which could not have had any place in the minds of the accusing party. The supposition that Charles undertook the prosecution of the five members for the purpose of stopping the further proceedings of the bill against episcopacy, cannot be true. That bill had only very lately been resumed by a portion of the Country Party, and had not yet recovered the check which, through the successful artifice of Hyde, it had received during the preceding session.* It was a matter more likely to divide than strengthen the power of the Country Party. And, above all, if it had been Charles's object, by impeachment, to remove from the House the principal promoters of that bill, he would not have included in that impeachment two, who, by their position, were the most important opposers of it, Pym and Holles. The single and simple object of Charles was to at once destroy six of the most active and popular opponents of his Government. What evidence he may have supposed himself to be possessed of for this purpose has never appeared. By his rashness he put it beyond his own power to proceed further with it; and, if there were any documents in his possession on which he could have proceeded, these he kept out of sight, in order to keep out of sight also all means of detecting the source from which he derived them. Unless, by the valuable and indefatigable labours of Mr. Lemon, in arranging the stores of the State Paper Office, some evidence, now unknown, should arise, it will in all probability remain for ever an unsolved question, upon what testimony Charles was urged to this ill-fated and disastrous enterprise. The evening before had been passed by him in active preparations. Arms were moved from the Tower to Whitehall, and a band of rash young men were assembled, for whom a table was prepared at the palace, and who, the next morning, from the violent expres-

---

* See Clarendon's account (Hist. Reb.) of his own conduct in the Chair of the Committee on the Bill against Episcopacy, whereby for a time it was defeated.

sions which they used against the Houses, seemed prepared for any deed of desperate violence.

Scarcely had the House reassembled, after the dinner hour's adjournment, for the renewal of the debate, when intelligence was brought by a Captain Langrish, who had passed the party in their way down the street, that the King, escorted by a guard of some hundreds of officers, soldiers, and other armed attendants, was advancing upon Westminster Hall. Private information had been received of this design by Lord Holland from Lady Carlisle, who was in the Queen's household; and by him it was communicated to Pym. To avoid the bloodshed which must probably have ensued, if the House, which had so lately pledged itself to its privileges, had been forced to defend them against armed men with the King in person at their head, the five members were ordered to withdraw, which, after some expostulation and resistance from Strode, they did. The King, meanwhile, entered New Palace Yard, and, proceeding through Westminster Hall, where his attendants ranged themselves on both sides, he ascended the stairs, and knocked at the door of the House of Commons.* Entering, with his nephew, Charles, the Prince Palatine of the Rhine,† at his side, he glanced his eye towards the place where Pym was wont to sit, and then walked directly to the chair. The Speaker, though commanded by the House to sit still with the mace before him, rose, with the rest of the members, at the King's approach, and, leaving the steps of the chair to which the King ascended, flung himself on his knee before him. In vain did the King look round for the objects of his search. The members stood, with their heads uncovered, in stern respectful silence, while the King addressed the Speaker, Lenthall, in words which are well known as being the cause of this memorable reply:—' May it please your Majesty, I
' have neither eyes to see, nor tongue to speak, in this place,
' but as the House is pleased to direct me, whose servant I am
' here; and I humbly beg your Majesty's pardon that I cannot
' give any other answer than this to what your Majesty is
' pleased to demand of me.' ‡

---

* Rushworth. Warwick. Whitelocke. Clarendon—Hist. Rebellion. May.

† Prince Rupert, whom some historians mistakenly represent to have accompanied him, did not arrive in England till two months afterwards.

‡ Rushworth. Whitelocke. Clarendon—Hist. Rebellion. Hatsell's Precedents.

The King's speech, in answer, sufficiently shows how little, before he entered on this strange proceeding, he had foreseen the chance of any part of his plan failing him. All the difficulties of his position now at once rushed to his mind. He saw no means of honourable or dignified retreat. He looked around from the chair, and he saw all eyes bent upon him; every countenance expressive of amazement at his rashness, but all men determined to act the great part he had imposed upon them, as became their position, their engagements, and their duties. He looked down, and he saw the Speaker, in the posture which denoted an awful sense of what was demanded of him by the presence before which he knelt, but to which he would not surrender the trust with which the Commons had invested him. At the table sat Rushworth taking down the words which alone broke that portentous silence, and which, on the morrow, must sound in every ear in the metropolis, to spread alarm through the Empire, and to be delivered down to all posterity with the story of that day. The King's reply was weak and confused, and it bore not on the question. 'There is no privilege in cases of treason.' ... 'I intend nothing but to proceed against them in a fair and 'legal way.'* The breach of privilege was his entering the House;—the breach of law was his endeavouring to execute a committal for treason without examination and without warrant. 'I tell you I do expect that, as soon as they come to the 'House, you will send them to me, otherwise I must take my 'own course to find them.' He must have known that the House could not, after the unanimous declaration for the defence of its privileges, suffer its members to be surrendered at this illegal bidding: and thus he retired, amid loud and repeated cries of 'Privilege, privilege!' The House instantly adjourned.

On the following day, a resolution was passed, expressing the sense of the House concerning the violence which had been committed. A Committee of Privileges was voted to sit in the City, and to confer with the Lords. To the City the King repaired before the Committee had assembled. He went there for the double purpose of requiring from the Common Council their assistance in apprehending the five members, and of ascertaining how far he might, by his presence, secure

* See Commons' Journals, Jan. 4.

the support of the magistrates and of the people. The spirit, however, which had shown itself in the House of Commons, had been already eagerly seconded by the citizens of London. The cries of 'Privilege!' which he had left sounding from so many voices in the House of Commons, met and pursued him in his progress through the streets; and a letter of fearful purport was thrown into his carriage as he passed along, containing the words of the Ten Tribes of Judah when they forsook the weak and tyrannical Rehoboam, — 'To your tents, O Israel!' In the Guildhall his speech was received without one responsive cheer; and, though he was that day nobly feasted, and, though he returned unimpeded and uninsulted to Whitehall, he clearly saw that, except within the walls of his own palace, and among his devoted courtiers and the dissolute levies which had followed him the day before, it was vain to look in his metropolis for support against the Parliament.*

The five accused members meanwhile were received into a house in Coleman Street, from which place of refuge, notwithstanding a proclamation issued to apprehend them and to forbid the harbouring of them, the King was unable to dislodge them. From thence they maintained an uninterrupted communication with the Committee of Privileges, which, after its first meeting, sat, day by day, alternately, in the Grocers', Goldsmiths' and Merchant Tailors', Halls. To make a powerful appeal to the citizens upon Parliamentary privilege invaded, and public liberty menaced, to prepare and confirm them for the times that were at hand, and to ensure their protection to the secluded members, was the first work of this Committee. This was managed principally by Serjeants Glyn and Maynard. The next few days were spent in preparing to resume the sittings of Parliament at Westminster. The Committee declined, with thanks, the offer of the City apprentices to conduct them back to the House, alleging that the guard of the train bands was sufficient for their protection; but it was at last determined that the services of the mariners should be accepted to convoy them by water. They ordered a ship, which had arrived from Berwick with arms and ammunition, to fall down the river, out of the reach of the Tower guns, and

---

* Rushworth. Clarendon — Hist. Reb. Micro Chronicon. Lilly's Observations.

moor herself midway, to assist, in the event of any sudden attack; and, on a report that the King proposed to come again to the House with a purpose of reconciliation, they ordered that he and the nobles in his train should be received with all duty and respect. Till the 10th, daily remonstrances and petitions were tendered. On the 11th, the five members returned by water, with the Committee, to attend the first meeting of the House. Lord Kimbolton was with them. The Thames was covered with boats, and the bridge and banks were lined with spectators. The Sheriffs embarked with a part of the city guard, attended by armed boats and barges manned by sailors and carrying ordnance with matches lighted; and the rest of the train bands marched by land to secure the avenues to the House. The procession was doubtless to the full as much for triumph as for security. The members, who had, a week before, with difficulty escaped a doubtful, perhaps a bloody, conflict with the followers of the King, were now borne along upon their return under the gaudy flashing of arms and standards, to the sounds of martial music, and of 'guns and sakers,' and to the acclamations of the people of both cities.

On the following day the famous Buckinghamshire Petition was presented to the Houses by about four thousand freeholders, who had ridden up from their county, each with a copy of the late protestation worn in his hat, to show their affection to the cause of the Parliament, and to the person of Hampden, their representative.* They complained of 'a 'malignant faction, whereby the perfecting of a reformation is 'hindered; the endeavours of the House of Commons in great 'part successless; our dangers grown upon us by reiterated 'plots; and priests and other delinquents unpunished, to the 'encouragement of others; Ireland lost by protracted counsels; 'and, to cut off all hopes of future reformation, the very being 'of Parliaments endangered by a desperate and unexampled 'breach of privileges, which, by our protestation lately taken, 'we are bound with our lives and estates to maintain. And, 'in respect of that latter attempt upon the honourable House 'of Commons, we are now come to offer our service to that 'end, and resolved in their just defence to live and die.'

They were dismissed, with a vote of thanks, and informed

* Rushworth. Clarendon—Hist. Reb.

that, as the Parliament was sufficiently guarded by the great care of the City, they might return home, till further occasion; of which they should be duly informed.*

Meanwhile, the King had suddenly retired to Hampton Court, from that metropolis to which he never more returned but as a prisoner.

The Buckinghamshire men had told the House of Commons that they had also a petition to the King, and desired the directions of that House as to the best way of delivering it, who advised them, that ' if they selected eight or ten of their ' number to wait upon his Majesty with it, that course would ' be most acceptable.' †

To Windsor, therefore, this deputation repaired, where the King now held his court, having stayed but a few days at his palace at Hampton. This petition limited itself to the case of their representative, and of five other impeached persons.

' That having, by virtue of your Highness's writ, chosen John
' Hampden Knight for our shire, in whose loyalty we, his
' countrymen and neighbours, have ever had good cause to
' confide, of late we, to our no less amazement than grief, find
' him, with other members of parliament, accused of treason;
' and, having taken into our serious consideration the manner
' of their impeachment, we cannot but, under your Majesty's
' favour, conceive that it doth so oppugn the rights of par-
' liament, (to the maintenance whereof our protestation binds
' us,) that we believe it is the malice which their zeal to your
' Majesty's service and of the State hath contracted in the
' enemies to your Majesty, the Church, and the Common-
' wealth, that hath occasioned this foul accusation, rather than
' any deserts of their's who do likewise, through their sides,
' wound us, your petitioners, and others by whose choice they
' were presented to the House. We, therefore, most humbly
' pray that Mr. Hampden, and the rest that lie under the
' burthen of that accusation, may enjoy the just privileges of
' Parliament.'

The King's answer was conceived in a mild and prudent tone. That ' being graciously pleased to let all his subjects
' understand his care not knowingly to violate any of the
' privileges of Parliament, he had signified, through the Lord

---

* Rushworth.—Commons' Journals.
† Commons' Journals.

'Keeper, that, because of the doubt that hath been raised of the manner, he would waive his former proceedings, and proceed in an unquestionable way. That then it will appear that he had so sufficient grounds, as he might not, in justice to the kingdom and honour to himself, have foreborne. And yet that he had much rather that the said persons should prove innocent than be found guilty. However, he could not conceive that their crimes could in any sort reflect upon those, his good subjects, who elected them to serve in Parliament.'*

This reply, as well as the form of message which had been sent to the Lords, engaging, 'as some doubts had arisen concerning the manner,' to proceed by due course of law, were probably advised and drawn up by Falkland. Falkland, it will be remembered, had been deputed by the Commons on that unsuccessful mission of remonstrance against Herbert's articles of impeachment, and against the conduct of the serjeant-at-arms. Loyally and affectionately zealous for the interests of his master, he had spared no pains to advise an answer very different in spirit from that which he had, on that occasion, been obliged to return.

In three days after, the King sent for Falkland, and gave him the seals of office of Chief Secretary of State, Colepeper having, the day before, been made Chancellor of the Exchequer.†

Falkland did not, because his advice had been rejected, feel it the less his duty to give his best services when Charles's returning prudence inclined him, in danger and alarm, to seek them. And yet, embroiled as the King's cause had now been by the petulance of Digby, and the ferocity of Lunsford, he had not firmness enough to disembarrass himself of their fatal presence and advice. They pushed their dangerous course to still further extremities. They appeared openly in arms against the Parliament; yet were they not disclaimed or rebuked by Charles. They put themselves at the head of a small turbulent body of some two or three hundred men, at Kingston-on-

---

* Rushworth.

† Colepeper's appointment was a very strange one. He was made Chancellor of the Exchequer for life, by patent dated January 6. Another instance of the unwise and unconstitutional modes in which Charles undertook to baffle the power of the Commons to obtain the removal of public servants by address.—*Parl. Hist.*

Thames, avowing a wild and impracticable scheme for investing the metropolis, and cutting off the supplies.* A proclamation was instantly issued against them by both Houses. The train bands of the midland counties were ordered to march. Again the county of Buckingham offered to raise troops to defend the Parliament; and again it received the thanks of Parliament through its representatives; and a committee of public safety was formed, of which Hampden was a member. From this time forward a struggle was inevitable. Bodies of troops appeared, in divers parts, for the King. The Marquis of Newcastle, not long after, raised the people of the north, and, in the beginning of the spring, coined money, under royal warrant, to pay his levies.†

On the other hand, the Houses, on a report presented by Sir Harry Vane, passed a vote to put the kingdom in a posture of defence; ‡ and Goring, at Portsmouth, and Sir John Hotham, at Hull, were directed, by ordinance, to hold those magazines 'for King and Parliament,' and to surrender their trust to none but under the same authority.

The votes, too, relating to the civil affairs of the state, assumed daily a more decisive aspect. Former resolutions became declarations and ordinances; and the bill for taking away the bishops' votes was resumed, and passed into a law, receiving (at the instance of the queen, says Clarendon) the royal assent, when it was too late for even that great concession to be made with grace, or to be received with any more than a cold and formal acknowledgment.

But the period from which the Parliament dated the commencement of hostilities by the King, was that of the Queen's departure for Holland. Her pretext was to accompany her daughter, lately married to the Prince of Orange; her object was to procure supplies, and negotiate for the aid of foreign regiments. And she carried with her a large part of the Crown jewels to pledge for a loan of money.§ Here, again, Digby was the evil genius that worked mischief to the fortunes

---

* Clarendon states this transaction very untruly, representing it as if Digby had come alone to Kingston from Hampton Court in a coach and six, whereas the evidence shows, that he and Lunsford were there with three troops of horse, making proclamation for recruits, and thanking in the King's name those who joined them.
† Duchess of Newcastle's Memoirs.
‡ Commons' Journals,—January 25.
§ Clarendon.—Hist. Reb. Heath's Chron.

of the King and Queen. It was in a letter of his that the full discovery of this negotiation was made. Whether or no it was his rashness that counselled this correspondence is doubtful, but it was his incaution that betrayed it.

From Dover, her place of embarkation, Charles repaired to Greenwich, and, from thence, with the two young princes, and Lord Hertford their governor, and a train of some forty or fifty gentlemen, and a troop of horse, he began his journey to York. Thither he went, to secure the magazine of Hull, and to put himself at the head of Newcastle's levies. This province presented to him great and commanding advantages. It was powerful for the raising of troops; it was fertile in the means for supporting them; its distance from London gave time for completing his preparations, unmolested; the local interests and feelings of its inhabitants were distinct from those of the Londoners and of the people of the midland counties. Besides all this, the influence of the Cavendishes and Wentworths, backed by that of Lord Derby in Lancashire, gave him vast support; and Hyde himself had obtained a large share of popularity with the gentry and middle classes by his successful efforts in the abolition of that odious and oppressive tyranny the Presidency of the North. This journey, says Sir Philip Warwick, the King never could have performed, but that 'the Houses thought it would conduce more to their 'victory to fetch him back in triumph than to stop him in 'the way.' Surely, the Houses had a stronger, and much more obvious, motive. Conscious that the crisis which must bring against them a force raised in his name was now near at hand, conscious that a main part of the strength of their own cause depended on their being able to maintain in public the profession they had so often made, that no show of violence should be offered against his person, it was matter with them equally of principle and indubitable policy, that the first aggressive act should be allowed to proceed from him.

Nor was it long before he gave them the opportunity which they awaited. His first movement towards ascertaining the firmness of the Parliament's officers to fulfil their trust, and of the Parliament itself to maintain its ground, was the summoning of Hull. Besides its containing all the arms, ammunition, and artillery of the disbanded army of the north, Hull was of great importance to Charles, as affording a place of shelter and support to any force which he might collect; and it commanded the entrance of the Humber, where, as it afterwards appeared, the King's intention was to collect a fleet of war, and receive the supplies thrown in from Denmark and from Holland. The young Duke of York and Prince Rupert, who were upon a visit to Sir John Hotham, were dining with him when he received intelligence of the King being, with a body of three hundred horse, in full march upon the city.* Hotham had barely time to see the drawbridges up before Charles appeared at the Beverley Gate, and demanded admittance for himself and his followers. With protestations of all humility, Hotham on his knees offered to receive his Majesty and his household, but refused to admit a military force to occupy the city with which he had been entrusted. The King's determination thus to present himself under the walls, without any previous communication with the Governor, or knowledge of his probable intentions, was rash and ill-advised. It was, as in the attempt to arrest the five members, a deliberate risk of ungraceful discomfiture, strange in a person possessed of so high a sense of dignity as Charles. Moreover, the failure of this demand, which he might at least with more propriety have deputed to another to make in his behalf, threw him at once on the necessity of proclaiming Hotham a traitor, and on making, shortly after, a feeble and ineffectual attempt to enter by force, with three thousand foot and one thousand horse, which led to an unsuccessful siege of some days, by sea and land, and cost many lives.† Thus he gave notice of war, when he had not a garrisoned town, no regular army in the field, small store of ammunition, few ships, and little money to supply any of these wants: while the Parliament had all the public revenue and magazines of the country in their hands.

Which of the two parties began the Civil War has always since been matter of strenuous dispute. It is incapable of being satisfactorily determined; nor in truth is it of the least importance to the justification of either. The one class of writers insist on the Ordinance for the Militia, which preceded the Commissions of Array, as having been a levying of war by the Parliament. The other, with as much truth, impute to the King his negotiations with foreign powers for aid, his attempt upon Hull, his commission to Newcastle, and his declaration

---

* Heath's Chronicle.
† Viccars—Parliamentary Chronicle.

from York, which may be said to have put him in the field before the Parliament, as having been a beginning of the war on his part. The preparations on each side went on together, and the approaches of the war were so gradual, (but after a certain time so rapid,) that it must remain with historians to adopt whichever of these acts it may suit their fancies or passions to assign, as the point from which to date the actual commencement of hostilities;—a point which, when determined, decides nothing with respect to the moral argument either way. In truth, the war had been for some time determined on by both parties, and (on whichever side the better justification lies) it is rather matter of wonder that it was deferred so long.

Charles now pursued, with the utmost activity, the course which he had begun in Yorkshire,—availing himself of the interest and zeal of his friends, not only in the districts well affected to his cause, but in some, also, where the Parliament had its main strength. Worsted in his first summons of Hull, he returned to York; but, on his way, a large body of gentry met him at Beverley, with a tender of their utmost services, and accompanied him to the metropolis of their province. At York, he summoned the country round, and issued his first Commission of Array. It was a few days after, that both Houses voted that 'It appears that the King, seduced by wicked 'counsel, intends to make war against the Parliament; that, 'whensoever the King maketh war upon the Parliament, it is 'a high breach of the trust reposed in him by his people, 'contrary to his oath, and tending to the dissolution of the 'Government; and that whosoever shall serve or assist him in 'such wars are traitors by the fundamental laws of this King-'dom.'* Next day, they sent him a petition praying him to disband his forces. On the 1st of June, (the same day that the Commission of Array was published by the Commissioners through Yorkshire,) were voted the nineteen propositions to the King.† These, it is clear, though put forth in expressions of the humblest duty to the King's person, and breathing the most urgent desire of peace, were not propounded with any hope of being able to engage the royal assent, or prevent the evils they deprecated; but rather as a manifestation of the terms on which the two Houses were anxious to rest their justification in the struggle which was then to begin.

* Commons' Journals, May 20.   † Ibid., June 1.

They urged upon the King, to make the appointment of his great officers of state, his principal ministers, and the commanders of his guards and garrisons, subject to the approbation of the two Houses;—the taking away of the votes of the Popish Lords, who, indeed, had long been found, as a party in the Upper House, supporting all the most unreasonable claims of prerogative, and, in many cases of privilege, going near to put the Houses in conflict with each other;—the reformation of Church government;—the settlement of the militia in Commissioners approved by the Parliament;—the swearing of the Privy Councillors and Judges to maintain the Petition of Right, and all other statutes hereafter to be made;—that all public officers should hold their places *quamdiu se bene gesserint*; —that the King should disband his newly raised levies;—that Lord Kimbolton and the five members should be cleared by statute;—and that no peer thereafter to be made should sit without consent of Parliament. Large, doubtless, and before unheard-of, claims of power; and described by the King, in his answer, ' as a profession of peace which, joined to such pro- ' positions, did appear a mockery and a scorn.' Yet it is hard to say that to make the choice of the public servants of the state subject to the consent of Parliament, (which, in truth, was the point which the King rejected as contrary to the essentials of the English Constitution,) was, under all the circumstances of outrage which had occurred, a much more violent power than that which, according to the Constitution in happier times, Parliaments possess, as of unquestionable right and practice, to secure the removal of them by impeachment or address.*

The King now put forth the famous declaration of his cause; on which the Peers and principal gentry who had joined him made an engagement for the defence of the King, and against obedience to any ordinance concerning the militia that hath not the royal assent. It was subscribed by the Lord Keeper, the Duke of Richmond, the Marquis of Hertford; the Earls of Lindsey, Cumberland, Huntingdon, Bath, Southampton, Dorset, Salisbury, Northampton, Devon-

---

* Sir Philip Warwick gives a somewhat unfair appearance to the nineteen propositions, by putting them forth in his Memoirs as if they had preceded the drawing up of the King's first Commission of Array, and his summoning of Hull; when, in fact, they followed, and may be truly said to have been in consequence of, these acts.

shire, Bristol, Westmoreland, Berkshire, Monmouth, Rivers, Newcastle, Dover, Carnarvon, and Newport; the Lords Mowbray and Maltravers, Willoughby of Eresby, Rich, Charles Howard, Newark, Paget, Chandoys, Falconbridge, Poulett, Lovelace, Coventry, Dunsmore, Seymour, Gray of Ruthen, and Falkland; the Comptroller, Secretary Nicholas, Sir John Colepeper, the Lord Chief Justice Banks, and a number of gentry.

The Lord Keeper Littleton, too, on the requisition of the King, sent the Great Seal of England to York, and, the next day, followed it himself. Lord Salisbury's course cannot easily be accounted for. Within a few days after he had signed the engagement, he left the King, and escaped back to London.* His motive for thus deserting his pledged faith does not appear: his baseness only is clear. Lord Paget, appointed by the Parliament Lord Lieutenant of Buckinghamshire, had fled from his county to the King, about the first week in June. Mr. Tyrill, one of his Deputy-Lieutenants, in a letter, dated Inner Temple, June 15, to his son-in-law, Mr. Richard Grenvil, of Wotton, then High Sheriff, says—'I suppose you heare of ye flight of yor cosen 'the Lord Lieutenant, whoe is gone for Yorke, wth the Lord 'Bristol; ye Lord Fawkland and Sir John Colepeper are 'gone alsoe: and nowe, all theire intelligences beinge gone, it 'is to be thought some suddayne storme will falle upon y^e 'kingdome; ye citizens bringe in theire mony and plate 'roundly, according to ye expositions. Notwithstandinge y^e 'Lord Lieutenant is gone, ye meeting holds at Aylesbury on 'Friday; the deputies are armed wth ye power of his Lo^p, by 'a newe order of Parliament.†' His flight was caused by the almost unanimous determination of the gentry of that county not to give up into his hands the powder which the Committee of public safety had sent down to store at Aylesbury. At the meeting on that Friday were assembled the whole lieutenancy of the county, thirty-two in number, with the Lord Wharton, who was shortly after invested with the office of Lord Lieutenant, by ordinance. They were appointed to collect the money of the county, and vest it in the hands of a treasurer, to levy and train the militia, to form a garrison at

---

* Warwick's Memoirs. Whitelocke.

† Mr. Richard Grenvil's Papers, at Stowe.

Aylesbury, and manage generally the public affairs of the district.*

The King, meanwhile, had proceeded southward. He fixed his head-quarters at Nottingham, the largest town near the borders of that division of England where the Parliament interest was the strongest, and through which he knew that he must pass, as through an enemy's country, by force. Here it was that, on the 22nd of August, with great pomp, he raised and planted his royal standard, inviting the people of the country round to join it. Many slight encounters had already taken place. The Parliament had several regiments in Northamptonshire and Warwickshire, and Prince Rupert had pushed forward with a strong body of horse to Leicester; the Earl of Newcastle was moving with about five thousand men to the eastward, and the advanced posts had met and skirmished. But now the war began.†

By such as had looked forward through passing events to consequences, an appeal to arms must, for a long time, have been deemed unavoidable. Yet, to most, even of those who took part in the preparations and watched their progress, the Great Civil War came at last as matter of surprise. Many, of both parties, who had fanned the hidden and infant spark into life, saw with dismay the flames as they burst forth from either side, soon to meet in one general and mingling blaze. Thus it must ever be in civil war. By most men, however long it has threatened in its approach, it is not seen to be imminent until it is upon them; nor can it be comprehended in all its dreadful particulars until they are to be dealt with face to face. The images of extreme and unnatural strife, so often pictured by the poet,—brother battling against

---

* For a list of the Deputy-Lieutenants of Buckinghamshire, see Appendix C. It is curious to those who know that county well, and take interest in it, to observe from that return how many of the families of the first gentry in it have become extinct, while several of the names in the list are now to be found among the yeomen and farmers residing where the manor-houses of their ancestors stood.

† For Charles's final and eloquent proclamation announcing his intention to raise the standard, see Appendix D. It is a singular circumstance that Clarendon, who must have been present at that memorable ceremony, states it to have occurred on the 25th, whereas the proclamation itself dates it three days before. This is the more remarkable, as this misstatement of dates is calculated to lead to an inference that the Parliament's order to Lord Essex to take command of the army preceded this act of the King's; whereas it was voted on the 24th, when the news had reached London of the standard being actually raised.

brother,—the arm of the son raised against the parent,—are not among those which the most commonly present themselves to afflict society in civil war. But it is that many of those ties of habit and affection which bind men the most closely to life are loosened:—severed by public enmity, or, what is less tolerable still than public enmity, suspicion and distrust. These are unhappinesses which, in civil war, may be the lot even of those whose condition leads them into the dispute only as the attached and obedient followers of the standard raised by some neighbouring influence, and among whom the connexions of friendship and of kindred are, generally, the least liable to be disturbed. But, with those on whom their station imposes loftier callings, and who are answerable in the highest degree for the course which they assign to themselves and others, much more fearful are the trials which must hourly occur;—duties in conflict,—every private affection opposed to every public obligation,—and every plea, the strongest, for sympathy and protection, which cannot be answered.

Even things inanimate, which appeal to remembrance only, crowd in with their numberless associations, to tell us how unnatural a state of man is civil war. The village street barricaded;—the house deserted by all its social charities, perhaps occupied as the stronghold of a foe;—the church, where lie our parents' bones, become a battery of cannon, an hospital for wounded, a stable for horses, or a keep for captives;—the accustomed paths of our early youth beset with open menace or hidden danger;—its fields made foul with carnage;—and the imprecations of furious hate, or the supplications of mortal agony, coming to us in our own language, haply in the very dialect of our peculiar province;—these are among the familiar and frequent griefs of civil war.

The family of Hampden did not escape those divisions which so unhappily distracted some of the noble houses at this time. Mr. Alexander Hampden had not only formed opinions which separated him entirely from his illustrious kinsman, but, about a year after the commencement of the war, he gave testimony of them by an act dishonouring to the name and station which he bore. He engaged himself in Edmund Waller's plot; two first cousins of John Hampden thus joining in a conspiracy against the persons of the principal members of the Parliament, which, if not originally a scheme of assassination, was one which could have succeeded only by bloodshed, and for which two of the subordinate agents suffered justly an ignominious death. The first year of the civil war, grievous in so many ways for public considerations to Hampden, was a time also of great domestic affliction to him. Soon after the outbreak his eldest son died. But the severest blow was the loss of his favourite and beloved daughter, Mrs. Knightley. This was a sad visitation, the memory of which hung gloomily over his spirit during the short remainder of his life.*

It will not be improper here to direct our attention to the system by which Hampden's conduct from this period seems to have been governed. From the time of Charles's violent entry into the House of Commons, Hampden's carriage in public, which, we are told by Clarendon and others, had been ever marked by modesty and mildness, 'became fiercer; and 'he threw away the scabbard when he drew the sword.' Mr. Guthrie, a fair and candid writer, says that 'if Hampden, in 'any part of his great plan, fell short of his usual sagacity, it 'was in thinking Charles to be more weak and wicked than 'he really was.' Perhaps this observation may have proceeded from a rather inconsiderate acquiescence in the hasty conclusion that, at such a crisis, the severest and most active course of conduct necessarily betokens the most inveterate and irreconcilable feelings. The contrary is often the case; and an attentive consideration makes it probable that it was so with Hampden. It is true that, henceforward, we shall always find him foremost to urge the strongest and most decisive measures. To believe that he, whom all agree in accounting the most sagacious and considerate of his party, was changed, in an hour of resentment, to be the most intemperate and impracticable, would be a supposition at variance with all moral probability. This personal antipathy to Charles does not appear; nor, if it did, could it afford the just solution of his change of demeanour now. One, more probable, may be found in some remarkable passages of what remains of his history. It is sufficient, for the present, to bespeak attention to this fact, that, in the execution of a great plan to which the mind has with difficulty reconciled itself, the fiercest and most decisive course is perfectly in unison with the soberest motives, and may often be the wisest way of accomplishing the most moderate ends. Lord Clarendon says of Falkland, that he was 'one of

* Sir Philip Warwick.

'those who believed that one great battle would end all differences.' Others there were, who resolutely ventured all for themselves and for the country, without laying down in their own minds any definite term to the war, or probable occasion for a treaty. Thus, as was afterwards said, 'a summer's triumph proved but a winter's story; and the game, however it seemed won in autumn, was to be played over again in the spring.'*

But as, of all the King's advisers, Lord Falkland was the most reluctant to begin the contest, and the most anxiously thirsting for any probable overtures of a lasting peace, so, among the parliamentary leaders, till the disputes had risen so high as to preclude mediation, Hampden's conduct had been the most conciliatory, the most 'public minded,' and the least influenced by animosity or passion. But, from the taking up of arms, as Lord Falkland was, thenceforward, of those on the King's side, the most in favour of bold and rapid enterprises, so was Hampden, in the Council of War and Committee of Public Safety; and, as he was the first to see how impracticable was the hope of accommodation, till grounded upon some decisive advantage, so was he unremitting to push for that advantage, and to urge upon his tardier chiefs and compeers such undertakings as might shorten the conflict, and hasten on the treaty. Thus, if it had come to pass that fortune had plainly declared for the King's side, Falkland would have been the fittest of his counsellors to restrain his demands within such bounds as a conqueror might be persuaded to respect; and, if the event had been favourable to the Parliament's cause, Hampden would have had the best means of controlling that party in success within or near those limits of privilege beyond which they had not proceeded, until it became at least questionable whether they could any longer defend privilege without invading prerogative. In the wisdom and influence of these two men lay the best hope of such a settlement, which, to be permanent, must have been matter of compromise, and which, to become matter of compromise, must have been founded upon great power of dictation placed in prudent hands like theirs. But of this more hereafter.

It was under the woody brows of his own beauteous Chilterns that Hampden first published the ordinance to

---

* See Rush. vi. pp. 3, 4.

marshal the militia of his native county. The parishes and hundreds, often with their preachers at the head, mustered at their market-houses to march forth to training. In the dearth of all the ordinary implements of war, arms and accoutrements of the most grotesque fashion now left the walls where, from the times of the civil wars of the two Roses, they had hung as hereditary trophies in the manor-houses, the churches, and the cottages of the yeomen. In the returns of arms, particularly of the levies of the northern parts, at the first outbreak, the long-bow, the brown bill, and the cross-bow, resumed their place among the equipments of a man-at-arms.* It was not till some months after, when the stores of Hull, and Newcastle, and Plymouth, and of the Tower of London, were distributed, that the match-lock and pistol found their way into the hands of the 'ordered musqueteers and dragooners' in the country parts; and, even to the end of the civil wars, large bodies of men, besides the regular pike-men, were furnished only with rude lances; and, on the King's part, many thousands, particularly of the Welshmen, went to the battle with staves and Danish clubs.

The conflicts which arose out of the meetings of parties, acting under warrant to raise troops and collect the other materials of war, gradually assumed the character of military skirmishes; and the towns, the high roads, and woods, through which the supplies had to pass, became daily, and in almost all parts of England, the scenes of encounters more or less obstinate and bloody. By degrees, as these parties grew larger in their numbers, and more confident in their strength, they issued out from the fortified towns to try their arms and spirit against bodies which they knew to be collecting in the neighbourhood, and to drive in cattle for the magazines which, in all parts, were in progress of being formed. As the summer advanced, the corn, still green, was reaped by working parties on each side, whether to swell with its unripe produce their own guarded granaries, or, as was oftener the case, for forage for their horses, or oftenest, in order to take it from the reach of their enemies. This course had also the effect, in the neighbourhood of the cities, of obliging the country people to follow their food, and thus to enlist themselves and increase the garrisons.

The history of these wars, as they proceeded, casts a

* Mr. R. Grenvil's Returns.

peculiar interest on places, the names of which, as connected with the events of later times, carry with them no very lofty recollections. Even the small scale on which, throughout the civil wars, operations, insignificant in themselves but mighty in their consequences, were carried on, gives, at first hearing, a homely and contracted sound to the story of the contest. Thus, some men have made it matter of complaint, while traversing the plains and passes of Greece, that they have found that land, which has been made immortal by the warrior's sword, by the poet's song, by the gown of the orator the statesman and the philosopher, confined within such petty limits as those between the Egean Sea and the mountain boundary of her States. But this is an ill-considered feeling. What can more sustain the glory of that famous history than the reflection, how narrow the space in which the spirit of freedom made good for ages her cause against the world? No trifling cause of admiration is it, that the powerful lessons of liberty have sprung up into ripeness, and been reaped, and stored up, even by other nations, from a germ like that of the Grecian Republics, or the Commonwealth of England. He who contemplates, without emotion, the victorious progress of mighty empires, may yet feel some enthusiasm, when, standing in a rocky pass, dark with pine and plane trees, or on a small sandy plain broken only by a few rude and shapeless hillocks, he is told,—' Here Grecian freedom bled, to die but not to be ' subdued,—this is Thermopylæ;—here she triumphed, you ' are among the graves of Marathon.' Then, though but the ploughman be seen on Chalgrove now,—though the names of Birmingham, and Coventry, and Gloucester be no more known but by the peaceful contests of busy trade, with all its powers and all its enterprise,—though a few hours of journey suffice to carry us from the opening to the concluding scene,—from Oxford where Charles held his court, to where last he grappled with his subjects at Naseby,—we may acknowledge, in even these names of familiar sound, the feelings which must ever attach themselves to places made memorable by bold endeavour or great achievement, by the acts, or by the fall of men, who have contributed to the fame of their native land.

Once aroused to the fearful necessity of taking arms, and of using them, the principal leaders of the Puritans were rapid, resolute, and unwearied, in all the various business of the approaching war. They had matured their secret and sturdy plan, and now worked with an energy which at first was wanting among the greater part of the adherents to the Royalist cause. They had added to their rigid morals a noble and simple vigour;—'they had put on,' says Sidney, 'the 'athletic habit of liberty for the contest;'—they had made the laws of God the study of their lives;—they found them often in conflict with those of their rulers;—they made their choice, and solemnly appealed to the issue of battle, as men who thoroughly believed themselves especially designed

> 'To some great work, His glory,
> And people's safety.' *—

And many who had before looked with doubt and fear upon the very name of liberty, now made proclamation of it with their lips, inscribed it, and 'God with us,' upon their banners, to challenge lawless prerogative: and, having drawn their swords in its behalf, sheathed them not, until they had made what long had been a bye-word and a grievous jest, their leading cry to victory.

* Samson Agonistes.

PART THE EIGHTH.

1642.

Posture of the two parties—Their motives and objects—Falkland, and others who take part for the King—Sir Bevill Grenvil—His letter to Sir John Trelawney—Formation of the Parliament Armies—Loans, and Contributions of Money and Plate—The Fleet declares for the Parliament—King's conditions from Nottingham rejected—Hampden captures the King's Oxfordshire Commissioners at Ascot—Conflicts in divers parts—Siege and surrender of Portsmouth—Coventry and Northampton attacked by the King's troops —Lord Brook—Brook and Hampden repulse the King's troops at Southam —Conditions of submission proposed to Lord Brook before Warwick—His Answer—He assembles his levies, and harangues his officers, at Warwick Castle.

AT the time of raising the standard, the King's affairs wore but a discouraging aspect: and they continued to do so for some weeks after. He had been led into too sanguine a calculation both of his actual strength and of the rapidity with which it might be increased. His standard floated over the rising ground on which it had been planted, daily and nightly guarded, and graced with all the ceremony and splendour befitting so majestic a symbol of war; the royal pavilion and the tents of the nobles and the gentry were pitched around it, and the household and body-guard formed a brave encampment in the rear; each morning, soon after sunrise, the heralds assembled, by sound of trumpet, at its foot, and then dispersed themselves through the towns and country adjacent, making proclamation and summons in the King's name. Bands of military music played throughout the day, and in the course of it the King himself frequently appeared. But the people of the country did not flock in from around to enlist themselves in the cause;—and even the spectacle soon ceased to attract. In truth, the King had not husbanded wisely his means of display. He had been too much seen among the ordinary and not very popular preparations for the war; and, above all, he had taken the field, and unsuccessfully, before he raised his standard. He had at that time not above three or four hundred regular troops with him in and about Nottingham. It is true that he knew the greater part of the gentry of England to be in his favour;—true also that he knew how great an advantage he possessed in having the choice of his own time, and of his own terms too, for beginning the war. For still the Parliament could not, with any show of regard to its own repeated declarations, nor consistently with what was still its undoubted policy, make any hostile movement in advance of him. He was also at liberty to hold a much more unreserved and decisive tone than theirs. His published statements were more calculated to address themselves to the feelings of all classes: they abounded in topics to be dealt with much more freely than those of the Parliament; and the language of a King, casting himself and his royal cause upon the sympathies of his people, had a charm which did not belong to the colder reasonings of the opposing party. The Parliament were fain, in their replies, to use his name, jointly with their own, as the sanction and vindication of their quarrel, professing 'that the separation of the King from the Parlia-' ment could not be without a destruction of the Government, ' and that the dividers were enemies to the State.' The King had no measures to keep. In phrases more quickly intelligible, and more easily communicable through the country, he called them 'rebels and traitors to God and the King, who raised a ' hand against the ancient monarchy of the land and against ' the Lord's anointed.' The Parliament represented him as in the thraldom of a malignant faction. He protested that his acts and his cause were his own. They proposed to 'redeem ' him from those that took him a voluntary captive, and would ' separate him from his Parliament; they professed to fight ' against his will only, not against his person, which they ' desired to rescue and preserve, nor against his authority, ' which was with them.' The King ' disowned their service ' as a scorn, that they should say they fought for King and ' Parliament when their armies were ready to charge him in ' the field.' *

* Baxter's Life.

These were mighty advantages, of which Charles well knew the value, and to which he frequently and powerfully appealed. There was no class or description of his subjects to whom he did not separately apply himself, and very generally with success. To the unreflecting the cause which bore the King's name singly had a sound at once brilliant and holy; to the vain-glorious it appeared bedecked with decorations and titles, and hopes of reward springing fresh from the fountain, so called, of honour; to the dissolute it recommended itself as contrasted with the sway of a party, the severity of whose personal observances, and whose system of moral government over others, were distasteful and irksome. Besides, there were some, not a few, of those soldiers of fortune, whose experience in the art of war was brought to market, and considered of high value, in a country inexperienced in that science, to whom the cavalier's side showed in prospect more occasions of preferment and of plunder. London herself, with all her spoil, was in view.

The gaiety—the splendour—the inlaid armour—the braided love-lock—the glittering badge of a sovereign's, or, more precious still, of a court lady's favour—dazzled the eyes and warmed the fancies of the young; the venerable sacrednesss of antique institutions, the hazardous indistinctness of new, and a proneness to seek shelter under the edifice of power even after its foundations had been shaken, fixed the hearts of the old: while, to the gentry and the nobles, the lofty associations of chivalry, and the generous recollections of hereditary and personal fealty, gave a powerful bias in a quarrel where neutrality was seldom practicable, and never honourable. These were interests and passions likely all to lead men to the party of the King. Meanwhile, public principle and a sense of duty may be admitted to have equally guided both ways in this great dispute. And, doubtless, on both sides these influences had equal power. So long as subsidies—so long as quarterings of troops—so long as Bishops' tyrannies and Popish innovations—so long as outrages on the privileges of the Parliament and the liberties of the people, were uppermost in men's minds —while grievances met their eyes at every turn, and the alternative of resistance was only contemplated distantly and in principle, the popular voice was loud against the King; but, loud in its outcry against the grievance, the popular voice must not always be expected to be equally firm in support of the remedy, when the time for applying the remedy shall have arrived. The Londoners and the counties had, with a wonderful accordance of feeling, acknowledged that their liberties were inseparably involved in the independence of Parliament. They had gone along with Parliament, not only in the grand remonstrance, but even in its claim upon the power over the militia, and confessed it to be founded purely and simply on the necessity of self-defence. Even the King's standard displayed at Nottingham at first failed as a talisman on the minds of the people. As yet, they had seen only preparations for hostilities which they thought the King had provoked, and had been weak enough to suppose that mere preparations and a display of power on the other side might produce concessions and give security. Sanguine in their hopes of avoiding the extremity of war, they had still to learn that, until forced by defeat, it is not in the nature of a King who has been nursed in notions of divine right to treat in good faith with a once revolted people, or of a once revolted people to have any confidence in the good faith of a King. But when the menace ceased, and its accomplishment arrived, resolutions began to waver and to change.

It is said by a court writer, after the Restoration, that Sir Benjamin Rudyard, who died about this time, declared on his death-bed that Pym and Hampden told him ' that they thought ' the King so ill-beloved by his subjects, that he could never ' be able to raise an army to oppose them.' * If this be believed, it needs not to be remarked in what an error Pym and Hampden had indulged themselves. But it is not very like truth. The difficulties which both had met with, during their unremitting exertions to execute the ordinances for the militia, and to hinder the success of the commission of array, must, to men of their sagacity, have sooner brought conviction of their error. It is however certain that the party, generally, confident in their own strength, and hoping to the last that a protracted civil war might be avoided, very much underrated the influence of the royalist spirit.

Many who had, through danger and disrepute, proved themselves friends of liberty, and whose names, so long as the memory of good men is safe, are a sufficient answer to any scandal on their motives, now took arms for the King. They had opposed prerogative, when liberty was oppressed and in

---

* See Brief Chron. of the Civil Wars.

peril; they offered themselves to support what they conceived to be the essentials of monarchy, when the Parliament leaders began to feel their power and to be the rulers of the state. At a crisis of this sort, decisive as each man's conduct must be on his own fortunes, and, perhaps, on those too of his country, and fierce as is the conflict on which he is entering, it is, with reflecting persons, generally the result of the most nicely balanced considerations. One, who, at the first outbreak of civil dissensions, can take his part without hesitation, must generally take it without any very grave or fixed view of the principles which have governed his decision. There never yet was a civil war in which either side had a clear case of unqualified right against a clear case of unmitigated wrong. It is the wisely moderate and the scrupulously good who have usually the greatest difficulty in deciding for themselves. It is they therefore who have the greatest risk to run of differing from each other in their decisions. And if this were remembered in reviewing the conduct of men and parties in difficult times, there would be more charity and more truth in the conclusions both of those who act in public affairs and of those who write about them.

At the head of those who,—friends of liberty,—when the contest became irreconcilable between King and people, took part, for the sake of the monarchy, with the King, and who, having taken that part, clove to it with eagerness and fidelity, —at the head of these Lord Falkland may not improperly be placed. On the motives of his conduct, at a crisis to him of such unhappiness, there seems to be no stain; nor is there any cause assigned for his change of parties, at the time and in the manner in which it happened, that can be a dishonour to his memory. It was not, like Colepeper's, to be suspected of having arisen from any appetite for office; for dates and facts show that he abstained from serving the King, in place, until he ran the risk, by further refusal, of encouraging a supposition that he declined to render himself answerable for the advice he gave. And then he eagerly embraced the office for the sake of the responsibility it imposed. It was not, like Hyde's, mixed up with any jealousies or resentments; for he long resisted the persuasions of Hyde to think ill of the intentions of those against whose acts he thought it necessary to protest. Least of all was it from a spirit of intrigue, or of self-advancement by unworthy artifices, such as suited the minds and morals of many factious men; for we have other testimony corroborative of that of Clarendon, that the scrupulous virtue of Falkland forbade him generally from recurring to such means of information or assistance as could not be given without violation of morality and honour.* Indeed we may well believe his friend's eloquent tribute to be but little exaggerated, and that it was but the truth to say that he took more pains to avoid office than most men do to gain it; and that he used no means to persuade the King to bestow office upon him, but deserving it.

Unqualified and unsuspected praise may also be given to some others who followed in his course: high-minded and steady friends of liberty, who yet, to use the metaphor of one of them, 'had they seen the Crown of England on a hedge 'stake,' would have remained with it to the death to defend it. Among these we may fairly class Lord Hertford, Lord Dunsmore, Lord Capel, Lord Paget, and Sir Ralph Hopton. Of others, who subscribed high and honourable names to the Declaration which was drawn out under the shadow of the King's standard, such as Newcastle, Paulet, Northampton, Derby, and Lindsey, the first of whom was appointed General of the King's Northern Army, and the last Lieutenant General in Chief of the forces which he himself commanded in person, little need be said but that, from the beginning, and to the utmost extent, supporters of the policy of the King, they were bold, uncompromising, and faithful to him, in his need. Some there were, on that side, such as Saville, and Salisbury, and some who began by taking the field with the parliamentary party, such as Goring, Clare, Northumberland, Holland (and unhappily we must add, afterwards, Bedford too), who changed more than once in the course of the war, concerning whom the less enquiry is made with reference to the purity of their apparent motives the more charitably will their memories be

---

* The only exception I can find is in the correspondence, which he conducted for the King, with the conspirators in Waller's plot. It would be most unjust to impeach the honour of a public man, because, in the furtherance of a great cause, he may be obliged, on occasions, to accept the services of unworthy agents. Nor does this cast any blame on Falkland. But Clarendon was not justified, with all that he must have known of the missions of Mr. Alexander Hampden and of the Lady Aubigny, in saying that Falkland 'could never bring himself to give any 'countenance or entertainment' to such as 'by communication of guilt or 'dissimulation of manners, wind themselves into such trusts and secrets 'as enable them to make discoveries.'

dealt with. Such there must be at all times, who, to the great damage of public liberty, join the popular cause on account of private disgusts, of personal expectations, or for the sake of becoming important, in the only way open to them, by tampering alternately with both parties.

Sir Edmund Verney was appointed Standard-bearer to the King. He had no taste for courts, had ever sided with the country party in Parliament, and not only felt, but expressed, doubts of the justice of the cause on which he was entering.* He stated, as his sole motive, a soldier-like reason, showing more anxiety not to do wrong than reflection to guide him in doing right,—of the sincerity of which, however, from the hour when he reluctantly raised the standard to that at which he bravely died defending it, there is no ground of doubt. He said 'he had eaten the King's bread,' and was therefore bound to his service in personal honour; otherwise he disapproved of the cause in which he was engaged:† a sentiment fit only for a feudal vassal, which had carelessly been allowed a place in the heart of a high-minded gentleman.

It was at this unpromising period of the King's affairs that the brave Sir Bevill Grenvil declared himself in the field, and in a moment of general doubt and dismay, first published the commission of array and raised troops and occupied a line of posts in the West. In his native county of Cornwall, which he had long represented in Parliament, he took his part, as one who, having weighed and resolved with caution, was now ready to act with determination and effect. There was no man who had more faithfully done his duty in the House of Commons against the arbitrary measures of the King. He had early associated himself with the reformers of abuses, and, personally and politically attached to Sir John Eliot, had joined in the remonstrances upon his commitment. In one of his letters to his wife, his 'best friend the Lady Grace Grenvil,' many of which give so amiable a view of his private virtues and gentleness of disposition, he speaks of Eliot as being 'resolved to have him out of his imprisonment.' He had also, much later, put himself at the head of a local opposition to the ship-money, and in 1640, presented to the House of Commons the petition and remonstrance of Watford and of other

---

* Sir P. Warwick's Memoirs.—Clarendon, Life.
† Clarendon, Life.—Ludlow's Memoirs.

towns in Hertfordshire.* But Sir Bevill seems never to have contemplated the possibility of any justification in any case for a subject resisting a sovereign in arms, and to have considered the weapons of war as to be used by a good man at the bidding of his sovereign only, and then that such bidding always makes the use just and glorious. Such was his feeling even as early as the first Scottish war, though undertaken by the insurgents in defence of those very principles of personal and religious liberty which he had always manfully supported in parliament. In a letter to Morice, dated Newcastle, May 13, 1639,† he says—' For my part, I go with joy ' and comfort to venture my life in as good a cause, and with ' as good company, as ever Englishman did; and I do take God ' to witness, if I were to choose a death, it should be no other ' but this.' He appears to have always indulged himself in a melancholy foreboding,—strange in so brave and fixed a mind, —of the fate which really befell him early in the civil wars. In the following letter he justifies to an affectionate and anxious friend his quitting his home, his children, and that amiable and high-minded woman by whom his strong love was so well deserved, for the purpose of entering on a service in which he was, ever after, in life and death, among the foremost. It so well lays open his pure and gallant heart, that it deserves insertion:

To Sir Jo. Trelawny.

' Mo. Hon. S^r,—I have in many kindes had tryall of y^r noblenes,
' but in none more than in this singular expression of y^r kind care
' and love. I give also y^r excell^t Lady humble thankes for respect
' unto my poore woman, who hath been long a faithfull much obliged
' servant of your Ladyes. But, S^r, for my journey, it is fixt.
' I cannot containe myself wthin my doores when the K^g of Eng^s
' standard waves in the field upon so just occasion—the cause being
' such as must make all those that dye in it little inferiour to
' martyrs. And, for myne owne, I desire to acquire an honest
' name, or an hon^{ble} grave. I never loved my life or ease so much
' as to shunn such an occasion, wch if I should, I were unworthy of
' the profession I have held, or to succede those ances. of mine, who
' have so many of them, in severall ages, sacrificed their lives for
' their country.

' S^r, the barbarous and implacable enemy, (notwithstanding His

---

* Commons' Journals. † Hardwick Papers.

'Majesty's gracious proceedings wth them,) do continue their insolencies and rebellion in the highest degree, and are united in a body of great strength; so as you must expect, if they be not prevented and mastered neer their own homes, they will be troublesome in y^rs, and in the remotest pl^s ere long.

'I am not w^thout the consideration, (as you lovingly advise,) of my wife and family; and as for her, I must acknowledge she hath ever drawne so evenly in her yoke with me as she hath never prest before or hung behinde me, nor ever opposed or resisted my will. And yet truly I have not, in this or any thing else, endeavoured to walke in the way of power wth her, but of reason; and though her love will submit to either, yet truly my respect will not suffer me to urge her with power, unless I can convince with reason. So much for that, whereof I am willing to be accomptable unto so good a friend.

'I have no suite unto you in mine owne behalfe, but for y^r prayers and good wishes, and that, if I live to come home againe, you would please to continue me in the number of your servants.

'I shall give a true relation unto my very nob. friend Mr. Mo. (Moyle) of y^r and his aunt's loving respects to him, which he hath good reason to be thankfull for; and so, I beseech God to send you and your nob. family all health and happiness; and, while I live,

'I am, Sir,

'Y^r unfay. lov. and fai. serv.

'B. G.' *

To one of the proudest spirits that ever rose up against the King in his injustice and tyranny was joined one of the most generous that ever lent him its aid in his need and peril. Sir Bevill had an almost romantic appetite for danger, which is sometimes apt, unknown to its possessor, to form a powerful quantity in the scale in which he balances his resolves at a moment like that of which we are now treating. The generosity of his nature was such as to make him, at such a time, almost suspect his own former conduct, and put himself more forward than perhaps otherwise he would have done, when anything was to be achieved in a cause which he now thought in its turn to be oppressed. 'His temper and affections,' says Lord Clarendon, 'were so public, that no accident which happened could make any impressions in him; and his example kept others from taking anything ill, or at least, seeming to do so. In a word,

---

* Among Lord Carteret's papers, discovered and lent to me by the Lord Bishop of Llandaff.

'a brighter courage and a gentler disposition were never
'married together, to make the most cheerful and innocent
'conversation.'*

The King being now actually in the field, no time was lost in the Parliament in displaying and putting into activity all the various preparations which it had already made for the war. The raising of troops, and the garrisoning and fortifying of towns, proceeded with great and increasing rapidity. The new levies were formed into regiments and brigades. Sir Thomas Fairfax, who had been sent down to assist Sir John Hotham, began, but with small success, to collect a force, which was destined to make head against the Marquis of Newcastle in the north. On Sir William Waller, who had commanded at Exeter, devolved a like charge in the west, where Sir Ralph Hopton, Slanning, and Grenvil, occupied the greater part of the country, and some of the small sea-ports, for the King. Lord Brook in Warwickshire, Lord Say and his sons in Northamptonshire, the Earl of Bedford in Bedfordshire, Lord Kimbolton and Cromwell in Huntingdon and Cambridgeshire, and Lord Wharton, Arthur Goodwyn, Mr. West, Mr. Bulstrode, Mr. Tirrell, and Mr. Richard Grenvil the High Sheriff, in Buckinghamshire, Skippon, and Holles, and Stapleton, in Middlesex, and the Sheriffs of Essex, Surrey, and Berkshire, in their respective counties, formed the militia reinforcements for the army, which was placed under the chief direction of the Earl of Essex. This became soon the main army of the Parliament; and, in the course of less than a month after the raising of the King's standard, the parliamentarian force throughout England amounted to about 25,000 men. The whole was at the disposal of the Committee of Public Safety. The divisions were generally placed under the command of such of the chiefs as had served in the wars of Gustavus Adolphus; and a few French and German engineers were engaged to superintend the fortifications, and the drilling of the artillery. The brigades and single regiments were raised and led by such of the noblemen and country gentlemen as were found combining with their local influence activity, courage, and genius enough for military affairs to be entrusted with commands. The regiments of infantry, as their clothing became more complete, assumed the colours of their respective

* Hist. Reb.

leaders,—generally such as had been worn by the serving men of the families. Holles's were the London red-coats; Lord Brook's the purple; Hampden's the green-coats; Lord Say's and Lord Mandeville's the blue. The orange, which had long been the colour of Lord Essex's household, and now that of his body-guard, was worn in a scarf over the armour of all the officers of the Parliament army, as the distinguishing symbol of their cause. Each regiment also carried a small standard, or cornet, with, on one side, the device and motto of its colonel, and, on the other, the watchword of the Parliament— 'God With Us.' The Earl of Essex's bore the inscription, 'Cave, Adsum,'—words not well chosen, as, in the course of the wars, they sometimes afforded occasion for jest among the Cavaliers, when his regiment chanced to be seen in retreat, or engaged in levying contributions, or in some such other duties which were distasteful to the parts of the country over which it was moving, and which thus gave a somewhat whimsical air to the warning. Some of these mottos were better chosen, and better justified. In the third year of the war, when the second son of the Earl of Leicester, Algernon Sidney, drew his youthful sword in that cause to which, in his old age, he gave testimony with his blood, he inscribed his standard with these words—'Sanctus Amor Patriæ Dat Animum.' The motto which was borne at the head of Hampden's regiment marked well its leader's public course,—'Vestigia Nulla 'Retrorsum.'

The infantry, on account of the scarcity of the weapons of war, during the first campaign, were variously armed, but the greater number carried matchlocks, pikes, or pole-axes. The cavalry were better appointed. The dragoon wore his steel cap and gorget, back and breast plates, with tassets descending to the knees, and he carried his long sword, and carbine and pistols; and some of the horsemen were armed, like the German Cravats, with long lances. Hazelrigge's regiment of horse, from the completeness of their defensive armour, obtained the name of the Lobsters, and Cromwell's that of the Ironsides. Hampden's green regiment was composed entirely of Buckinghamshire men; and his colleague, Arthur Goodwyn of Upper Winchenden, raised a regiment of cavalry in the same county.

It appears from the returns of Lord Essex's army, that soon after the outbreak of the war it must have consisted of, in the whole, nearly fifteen thousand infantry, and four thousand five hundred horse. Of the former there were twenty regiments. The Lord General's Body Guard, and the regiments of the Earl of Peterborough, the Earl of Stamford, Viscount Say, Viscount Rochford, Viscount St. John, Lord Kimbolton, Lord Brook, Lord Roberts, Lord Wharton, John Hampden, Denzil Holles, Sir John Merrick, Sir Henry Cholmely, Sir William Constable, Sir William Fairfax, Charles Essex, Thomas Grantham, Thomas Ballard, and William Bamfield. The cavalry were in seventy-five troops. These were all raised, as were many of the infantry regiments, at the charge of their commanders. They were the Lord General's Life Guard of Gentlemen, and the troops of the Earls of Bedford, Peterborough, and Stamford, Viscounts Say, St. John, and Fielding, Lords Brook, Wharton, Willoughby of Parham, Hastings, Grey of Groby, Sir William Balfour, Sir William Waller, Sir Arthur Hazelrigge, Sir Walter Erle, Sir Faithful Fortescue, Nathaniel Francis and John Fiennes, Oliver Cromwell, Valentine Waughton, Henry Ireton, Arthur Goodwyn, John Dalbier, Adrian Scroope, Thomas Hatcher, John Hotham, Sir Robert Pye, Sir William Wray, Sir John Saunders, John Alured, Edwyn Sandys, John and Thomas Hammond, Alexander Pym, Anthony and Henry Mildmay, James and Thomas Temple, Arthur Evelyn, Robert Vivers, Hercules Langrishe, William Pretty, James Sheffield, John Gunter, Robert and Francis Dowett, John Bird, Mathew Draper, —— Dimmocke, Horatio Carey, John Neale, Edward Ayscough, John and Francis Thompson, Edward Keighley, Alexander Douglas, Thomas Lydcot, John Fleming, Richard Grenvil, Thomas Tyrill, John Hale, William Balfour, George Austin, Edward Wingate, Edward Bayntun, Charles Chichester, Walter Long, Edward West, William Anselm, Robert Kirle, and Simon Rudgeley.* Sir John Merrick was, according to the military phrase then in use, Serjeant-Major-General of this army, the Earl of Peterborough General of the Ordnance, and the Earl of Bedford of the Horse.

Divers loans of money had at various times been advanced in aid of the Parliament. In these offers the City of London and the Associated Company of Merchant Adventurers had taken the lead, as early as in January—the former with an advance of fifty thousand, the latter of thirty thousand pounds,

* List of the Army raised under the command of Robert, Earl of Essex, 1642.

and a promise of twenty thousand more for the service of Ireland;* and the City advanced an additional loan of a hundred thousand. This had been assisted by voluntary subscriptions to a great amount throughout the country. There is, in Rushworth, a list consisting of the names of all the principal persons of the parliamentary party, affixed to large sums subscribed for the public service, in which it appears that John Hampden advanced two sums of a thousand pounds each. These payments, however, were inadequate to the double purpose of suppressing the rebellion in Ireland, and of putting England in a posture of defence. Scotland had been applied to for a 'brotherly assistance' in the Irish affairs. Fiennes, Stapleton, and Hampden, had been appointed by Parliament to treat with her Commissioners for the transporting of two thousand five hundred men from Scotland into Ireland; and the Scots sold this assistance at the rate of sixteen thousand pounds, and the delivery of the town and castle of Carrickfergus to them in pledge.† But application was now made in vain by the Parliament to their 'brethren of Scotland' for support in the work of placing the country in a state of defence. The midland counties of England, however, undertook with great alacrity to bear this charge. They voluntarily subscribed their money and their plate. The cities of London and Westminster were forward and liberal in their contributions. The women brought in their rings and jewels, the goldsmiths and silversmiths their stock, and the train bands mustered daily to exercise in Moorfields, amid the acclamations of their fellow-citizens, who, to the no small annoyance of the old Serjeant-Major-General of the London army, General Skippon, crowded in to 'pledge healths and gratulations, not without 'prayers and thanksgivings, that the Lord had put it into the 'hearts of those brave defenders to stand so stoutly for his 'cause, and for the liberties of the land.'‡

Propositions for further loans of money, at an interest of eight per cent., were now made, and, for a time, freely answered. Buckinghamshire was foremost among the counties with a tender of thirty thousand pounds for the public service, for which aid it received the thanks of Parliament, through its representatives, Hampden and Goodwyn. The arrival of

* Commons' Journals, January 15 and 24.
† Commons' Journals, January 25.
‡ City and Country Intelligencer, August 24 to 30.

supplies of troops and money to the King, from the Dutch and Danes, had been a main cause of alarm to the Parliament. The sea line of defence became an object of primary importance on this account, and also for cheap and easy transport of troops and stores to the remoter parts of the island.

The fleet had been entrusted to the Earl of Northumberland, as Lord High Admiral, by the Parliament, to whom his conduct had been most acceptable in the case of the army plot, in which his brother had been so deeply engaged. But Northumberland was not a man to be confided in by any party. It was not, perhaps, that he was treacherous by design; but he was naturally timid; and his high station in the country, and the overwrought estimate which he had formed of his own importance, and perhaps of his own abilities too, made him reluctant to bind himself to the fortunes of any party, and gave him a tendency to a course of trimming and intrigue, in times when no man's interest or reputation could stand but in close and faithful connexion with one of the two great parties in the State. He had put himself, with the Navy of England, at the disposal of Parliament; but, when called upon to join the rendezvous of the fleet, he fell sick, and retired to Alnwick. The Earl of Warwick was instantly named by ordinance to succeed him; and the sailors and officers of the fleet, who had, ever since the business of the ship money, as a body, taken part with the merchants in favour of the popular interest, saluted his flag, and almost unanimously declaring for King and Parliament, placed themselves and their ships under his command. A large detachment instantly sailed under Warwick for the Humber.

It was now that the King, at Nottingham, made overtures of treaty, sending the Earls of Southampton and Dorset, Sir John Colepeper, and Sir William Udall, to present them to the Parliament. Clarendon admits that the King was persuaded to this by a belief that the Parliament would refuse to treat, and thereby disgust the country, and that, during the interval, he might gain time to forward his levies and other preparations; aggravating the proofs of the insincere spirit in which this was done, by citing the very words in which the proposal was made. 'We assure you, nothing but our Christian and 'pious care to prevent the effusion of blood hath begot this 'motion; our provision of men, arms, and money, being such 'as may secure us from further violence, till it pleases God to 'open the eyes of our people.'* An effort of duplicity, superfluous, and quite ineffectual, since the Parliament well knew the real state of his affairs, and had had frequent experience of his unhappy habit of making such professions with a disguised and contrary intention. He stated also, in his message, his determination that nothing should be wanting on his part 'to advance the True Protestant Religion, and confirm all just 'power and privileges of Parliament.' Under these words, so often employed by him on similar occasions, it is but too evident that he always veiled a double meaning. By 'True 'Protestant Religion' it is to be shown that he reserved to himself this interpretation,—'the ancient immunities of the 'Episcopal order;' and by 'just power and privileges of 'Parliament,'—his own notions of the limits which, from the beginning of his reign, he had endeavoured unlawfully to assign to them. One of Charles's great vices was a constant desire to gain an advantage in treaties by betraying his Parliament into acquiescing in some doubtful phrase; and one of his remarkable weaknesses was the being usually too hasty to do this successfully.† Yet Clarendon, ascribing these overtures to a mere wish to gain time, makes it matter of charge against Hampden that he persuaded the Parliament to reject them.

After two days, this answer was returned by both Houses. That they had 'endeavoured to prevent, by several advices and 'petitions, the dangerous and distracted state of this kingdom, 'not only without success, but that there have followed those 'several proclamations and declarations against both the 'Houses of Parliament, whereby their actions are declared 'treasonable and their persons traitors; and, thereupon, your 'Majesty hath set up your standard against them, whereby 'you have put them, and in them the whole kingdom, out 'of your protection. So that, untill your Majesty shall re-'call those proclamations and declarations, whereby the Earl 'of Essex and both Houses of Parliament are declared traitors 'or otherwise delinquents, and untill the standard set up in 'pursuance of the said proclamation be taken down, your 'Majesty hath put us into such a condition, that, while we so 'remain, we cannot, by the fundamental privileges of Parlia-'ment, the publick trust reposed in us, or with the general

---

* Hist. Reb.
† Of his intention in using these ambiguous generalities there is abundant proof in his letters taken at Naseby. See 'King's Cabinet opened.'

'good and safety of this kingdom, give your Majesty any other answer to this message.' *

The King returned a further reply, to the end, Clarendon says, 'that he might make further use of their pride and passion.' In this he offered, that if they would appoint a day for the revoking of their declarations against all persons as traitors or otherwise for assisting him, he would, on the same day, recall his proclamations and declarations, and take down his standard; the noble historian confessing that, when he took this resolution, all means of resisting them were hopeless, and that some advised him to appear at once in London; 'conceiving there would be more likelihood for him to prevail 'that way than by any army he was like to raise.' Lord Falkland was received by Parliament in his place to deliver this message; but Charles, in the interval, and pending the treaty, as if to prepare ground for departing from any terms which might after be arranged, repeated, in fresh instructions to his Commissioners of Array, his proclamation of treason. Of this the Houses complained in their rejoinder; but again promised that, if his standard be taken down, and the proclamation recalled, and if he would return to his Parliament, 'your Majesty shall find such expressions of our fidelities and 'duties, as shall assure you that your safety, honour, and great- 'ness, can only be found in the affections of your people, and 'the sincere counsels of your Parliament.' What hope could there be of the result of negotiations so begun and continued; while the King persisted in calling those with whom he was treating traitors, and while they felt that no terms would be kept with them, but such as should be first ensured by his placing himself entirely and unreservedly in their hands?

At length, wearied with what they saw were only artifices to gain time, the Houses, on the 9th of September, published a declaration to the whole kingdom, and sent down again Hampden and some of their other principal officers to Northampton, to put their regiments and brigades in readiness to march.

On the same day the Earl of Essex, with great pomp, at the head of the London train-bands and the levies from the adjacent counties which had come in the night before, proceeded to join the grand army. He was accompanied for

* Collection of Remonstrances.

several miles along the Barnet road by the Members of both Houses, and the several guilds and companies of merchants, and greeted by the acclamations and prayers of the populace of both cities, who had poured forth to line the way as he passed.

In the midland counties, the King's Commission of Array had been published only partially, and with little success; and, on several occasions, the Commissioners had been taken by the country people, or by detachments of the Parliament's troops, and sent up under escort to London.

About a month before, while Hampden and Goodwyn were mustering the Buckinghamshire and Oxfordshire levies on Chalgrove, information had been sent to them, by Whitelocke, that a party of gentlemen, with the Earl of Berkshire at their head, were assembling at Watlington, to make proclamation for troops, in the King's name, under the Commission of Array. With that quick spirit of decision which so strongly marked his character on so many greater occasions, Hampden seized the opportunity; and, without dissolving the meeting on Chalgrove, departed with a troop of Goodwyn's horse, and a company of his own regiment, for Watlington. But the Commissioners, hearing of the muster at Chalgrove, had hastened with the soldiers whom they had brought down with them, and some who had joined them, to Sir Robert Dormer's house at Ascot, where they raised the drawbridge on the moat, and stood upon their defence. Finding that they had been pursued, and that the house was invested, they fired a few shots from within; but, the besiegers making ready for an assault, they yielded upon quarter, and the Earl, and Sir John Curzon, and three others, the principal Commissioners, were sent prisoners to London.* From thence Hampden proceeded towards Oxford, in company with Lord Say, who joined him with some forces from the neighbourhood of Banbury, and entered it, after three days' preparation for a siege; the King's party retiring into Gloucestershire. This enterprise very much discomposed and angered the Cavaliers, and delayed the progress of the array in those parts, leaving to Hampden the power of completing the business of the Buckinghamshire muster unmolested.† But more active and more urgent business soon called him in another direction.

* Whitelocke's Memorials.—Rushworth.—Perfect Diurnal, August 15.
† Harl. MSS., Brit. Mus.

The several Ordinances which followed each other rapidly for 'putting the kingdom in a posture of defence' had been before the arrival of Essex's main army, enforced with the greatest zeal in the district lying between Nottingham and London, along which it was reasonable to suppose that the King's first great enterprize would be directed. It was important for the Parliament that the counties and principal towns along this line should receive the strongest marks of its trust,—should be inspired with confidence while declaring themselves in its behalf,—and that they should be protected and provisioned at the least charge to themselves. It was fortunate for the Parliament, that in those counties and principal towns its cause was, at the outset, eminently popular. Warwickshire, Bedfordshire, and Buckinghamshire, under the influence of their principal gentry, had declared themselves, almost unanimously, on that side, and were in the most diligent preparation. In Hertfordshire also, the spirit, though divided, was generally favourable to the Parliament. In Northamptonshire alone, nearly one-half of the strength of the county inclined towards the party of the King. The interest of the Earl of Manchester, the Lord Lieutenant, was divided with that of Lord Kimbolton, his son. Lord Northampton had great power: he was proud, active, and resolute; but, on account of his reputation for courage and high honour, was beloved as well as powerful. He was indefatigable in thwarting the Parliamentary levies, and in proceeding with the Commission of Array; yet the town of Northampton declared for the Parliament, and was made a place of arms. Cirencester took the same part, in spite of the influence of the Lord Chandoys, who lived at Sudely Castle in great magnificence. The Mayor and principal inhabitants answered his requisition with a protestation against the illegality of any commission under the Great Seal to raise troops without consent of parliament; and moreover desired him to prepare himself for going up to London, under a guard of the townsmen, to answer before Parliament for the act. He fled that night, and rejoined the King.*

Besides Northampton and Cirencester, Warwick, Aylesbury, and St. Albans, began to be strengthened with batteries, and received the magazines for the supply of the country along the two great London roads.

* Viccars's Parliamentary Chronicle.

Gradually this spirit spread itself through other parts of England, but not with the same unity of action. It had been endeavoured by both parties to secure the towns along the western coast. The Marquis of Hertford had dispatched from Sherborne Castle a requisition to the town of Poole; but Poole had declared for the Parliament, and begun to fortify itself. Lord Hertford then summoned the town by virtue of his new commission as Lieutenant-General of Dorset, Somerset, Hants, Wilts, and all Wales. It was at Poole that he purposed to fix his head quarters; but the Mayor, in the name of the whole town, replied that 'no commission under the 'Broad Seal could make law; that the commission to raise 'troops, without consent of the Houses, was against law; and 'that, instead of obeying, they trusted to be able, before long, 'to bring him up to the Parliament to answer for that illegal 'act.' *

Shortly after the raising of the Royal standard, the Earl of Bedford, Denzil Holles, and Sir Walter Erle, marched with an army (according to Clarendon, of at least seven thousand foot, and eight troops of horse), raised by Charles Essex, from Wells to Sherborne, where they were kept in check by Lord Hertford, with a very inferior force.

Portsmouth was, at the time of the raising of the Standard, held for the King, by one whose course,—from first to last, devious, uncertain, and unprincipled,—shed disgrace upon the nobleness of his name, and upon the honourable profession of a soldier. This man was Goring; than whom, on account of his private vices of drunkennesss, cruelty, and rapacity, and of his political timidity and treachery, scarcely any one was more unworthy to be trusted with any important matters for counsel or execution. The King, forgetful of how Goring, by formerly betraying his associates in the army plot, had saved himself from the Parliament's wrath, and for a time had won his way into popular favour, was cajoled by his apparent devotedness to the Royal cause, now that, in turn, he deceived the expectations of the Parliament, and held against them the charge they had given him. Goring continued, therefore, in command of the most important fortified town on the sea-board of England; and that at a time when (the state of the whole west of the island and of the fleet being considered), the most brave and

* Viccars—Parl. Chron.

faithful hand should surely have been selected to hold the keys of Portsmouth.

Goring, however, seemed to prepare for a bold and obstinate defence. He raised a powerful battery at Portbridge, which commanded the only pass into the island of Portsea, and he strengthened all the works of the town to the land-side. Towards the end of August, the Parliament's troops, which had been collected under Sir John Merrick, appearing on Portsdown, took possession of the London road; and, forcing Portbridge, invested the town to the northward and eastward of Southsea, which was defended by the castle and a line of outworks. On this quarter the siege commenced, and was continued for several days with no advantage gained against the garrison, till a two-gun battery was thrown up on the other side of the town, across the water, at Gosport. By this small work was that great and powerful place of arms, fortified according to the best rules of art in those days known, bristling with cannon, and its beach lined with boats, so annoyed as, in the course of a few days more, to be brought near to a surrender. On the night of the third of September, the Parliamentarians took Southsea Castle by escalade; and on the next morning, 'the Governor seeing,' says Viccars, 'through perspective glasses, that a good and 'fair platform was erected at Gosport for ten pieces of 'ordnance,' proposed terms, and was allowed to march out with the garrison. Upon this inconsiderable menace and shameful capitulation (whether moved by treachery or cowardice, or both), did Goring quit the town which he had boasted should never be taken until he should have blown up the magazine, which would have laid it in ruins; and, leaving his garrison to effect a difficult and hazardous march to the King's quarters in the west, he, on the same night, took boat for Holland.*

Meanwhile, the King, having quitted Nottingham, proceeded to Leicester, and, moving on the main London road, menaced Coventry and Warwick. He desired the attendance of the Mayor and Sheriffs of Coventry, and announced to them his intention of occupying their town in person. But the greater number of the inhabitants, putting on Lord Brook's colours, in spite of the presence of the Earl of Northampton,

---

* Viccars—Parl. Chron. Clarendon—Hist. Reb.

their recorder, instructed the Mayor, in conjunction with the principal citizens, to return for answer, that 'his Majesty's 'Royal person should be most respectfully welcome to them, 'but that they humbly besought his Majesty to pardon 'them if they could not with safety permit his cavaliers 'to enter with him.'* By a subsequent message they limited the number of such attendants as might be permitted to enter with the King to two hundred. The Earl in vain endeavoured to collect an adverse party; but failing, with his utmost efforts, to muster more than four hundred, was obliged to leave the town, escaping, with great difficulty, through the back door of an inn. Disappointed and incensed at the obstacle which Coventry presented to his advance, the King brought up his battering train, and, sitting down with a large force, opened his fire upon the city.† Then began a fierce assault and a gallant defence. The condition of Coventry had been considered by Lord Brook as so little promising, opposed to so large a force as was marched against it, that he had removed the greater part of the ammunition to Warwick Castle for security. But the brave townsmen undertook to endure the siege. Unsupported by soldiers, unassisted by engineers, and very scantily supplied with the materials of war, they prepared for one of those defences which, in later years, and on a larger scale, unfortified towns in the hands of the people have sometimes successfully made against the regular operations of war. Having barricaded the streets with harrows, carts, and spars, they first endeavoured to man the breach which the king's guns had made in their walls. Driven from thence, they rallied in the streets, and several times forced back his troops beyond their broken gates. At length, having, on one occasion, thrown the cavaliers into utter confusion, they pursued the advantage, and, rushing out of the town, stormed the King's nearest lines, and, taking several guns, turned them on the retreating enemy with no small execution. The Lord Brook, with Hampden, Lord Say, Lord Grey, Holles, and Cholmley, who had joined from several parts, were now advancing to the relief of this gallant town; on intelligence of which, all further attack on Coventry was abandoned, and the King, drawing off his forces, returned to Leicester.

* Viccars—Parl. Chron.
† Collections for History of Coventry. Dugdale's Warwickshire.

Hampden had been dispatched out of Buckinghamshire to take the command at Northampton, with a small brigade of infantry and some guns,—his colleague, Arthur Goodwyn, accompanying him with his regiment of cavalry. On the alarm, however, of the King's activity in Warwickshire, he hastened, with all he could collect, to join Lord Brook for the support of that county.* Some weeks before, Lord Brook had been threatened with a siege in his own castle.

On the night of the 28th of August, the Earl of Newcastle, the Earl of Lindsey, the Earl of Northampton, the Earl of Rivers, the Lord Rich, the Lord Mowbray, and the Lord Capel, with five regiments of foot and ten troops of horse, had marched from Nottingham towards Warwick, where Lord Brook lay with his new levies, but in greater force than they expected, the gentry of the county having flocked thither with their men at arms, forming altogether a body of nearly seven thousand men. Brook, having received intelligence in the morning of the approach of the Royalist Lords with their army, met them moving upon the town from Grove Park, where they had been entertained by Mr. Dormer, a Roman Catholic gentleman. The two powers met in the fields about a mile from Warwick, when a trumpet was sent forward by the Lords to demand a parley. Their propositions were, that Lord Brook should lay down his arms, a royal pardon being offered to him, that he should resign Warwick Castle into such hands as the King should think fit, that he should disavow the Ordinance of the Militia, endeavour the execution of the Commission of Array, deliver the magazine of the county into the hands of the Earl of Northampton, and make submission to the King.

To these conditions the Lords added, that if they were refused by Lord Brook, he must expect no less than signal and instant punishment. Lord Brook was of a temper not quick to anger, and a mind deeply imbued with the stern and patient reserve which partly the externals of their religion, and partly the pressure of political necessity, had imposed upon the Puritan party. But the spirit of a gallant gentleman, in whose veins flowed the blood of many generations of proud and valiant ancestors, rose up against terms so unworthy to be

---

* True and Remarkable Passages, from Monday, 5th Sept., to Saturday, 10th, 1642.

proposed to him, and against a tone and bearing so unbecoming to the noble persons who addressed him in the confidence of fancied power. Incensed, he wheeled his horse about, to leave them without reply; but, after a moment's consideration, he returned, and, fronting them, thus spoke:

' MY LORDS,

'I much wonder that men of judgment, in whose breasts
' true honour should hold her seat, should so much wrong their
' noble predecessors as to seek the ruin of those high and noble
' thoughts they should endeavour to support. Doth fond ambition,
' or your self-willed pride, so much bewitch you that you cannot
' see the crown of this your act? When the great council of
' the Parliament was first assembled, you then were members,—
' honourable members. Why did you not continue? Was it
' because your actions were so bad you were ashamed to own
' them? Had you done evil in some petty kind, a better course
' might have quitted you from that, and you had been still
' honoured, loved, and feared. As for these propositions, take this
' in answer—When that his Majesty, his posterity, and the peace
' of the kingdom, shall be secured from you, I gladly shall lay down
' my arms and power. As for the castle, it was delivered to my
' trust by the High Court of Parliament, who reserve it for the
' King's good use, and I dare boldly say will so employ it. As for
' the Commission of Array, you know it is unlawful. For the
' magazine of the county, it was delivered to me also by the
' Parliament, and, as a faithful servant to the country, I am
' resolved to continue it, till Northampton can show me greater
' authority for the delivery of the same. As touching his Majesty's
' pardon, as I am confident I have not given any occasion of offence
' to his Majesty, so I need not his pardon; and I doubt not in a
' short time his Majesty will find who are his best friends. As for
' your fury, I wholly disdain it; and answer it but by hoping that
' Northampton may be translated to Warwick, to stand sentry
' upon Warwick castle, to fright crows and kites.'

These words being thus spoken, the Lords rode back to their party, and Lord Brook to his; and it was not till the King's troops, seeing those of the Parliament more numerous than they had expected, had fairly left the field, that Lord Brook returned with his men to Warwick, where, with thanks for their support, he read to them the resolution of approbation which had been passed by the Lords and Commons for a further incitement.*

Meanwhile intelligence was received at Warwick that Northampton's army had passed to the eastward, and was in full march towards Northamptonshire; upon which Lord Brook set forth with a small part of his army, about three thousand, for Southam, where he was joined by Hampden's brigade, which was then moving towards Banbury, Warwick, and Coventry, to his support. These, together, formed a corps of near six thousand infantry, with three hundred horse, and nine guns. The chief officers who commanded this force with Brook and Hampden, were Lord Say, Lord Grey, Denzil Holles, and Cholmley. Thus, raised and led by chiefs to whom the profession of arms was new, and who had only their zeal, reputation, and general abilities, to contribute in aid of the cause, these regiments, particularly those of Brook, Hampden, and Holles, early in the war became distinguished for discipline as well as courage. Gradually ridding themselves of some officers whose skill was unequal to the task they had undertaken, deserted by some, and joined by others, they formed the right wing of Essex's army, of which they were now the first division in the field.

In the middle of the night, this little army being quartered in Southam, and the powder and other stores found in the town being secured, the men had retired to their billets, wearied with the harassing and rapid march which both brigades had that day made, when news came in from the patrols that the Earl of Northampton had pushed on to within two miles of the town with all his force. The drums instantly beat to arms throughout the town, 'upon hearing whereof, of 'such magnanimous spirits were the soldiers, and possessed 'with such a sudden passion of joy, that their enemies, the 'Cavaliers, were so near, that they gave a great shout, with 'flinging up of their hats and clattering their arms, till the 'town rang again with the sound thereof, and, casting aside 'all desire of meat and lodging provided for them, went 'immediately into the fields adjoining to the town, ready for 'battle, where they continued till the morning.'† At daybreak, the enemy, who had been checked overnight by the

---

* Narrative of Propositions, &c.; with Lord Brook's Answer. Published by authority of Parliament, August 20. In Mr. Staunton's Collection.
† 'A True and Perfect Relation.'—Mr. Staunton's Coll. of Tracts.

sounds which told them that the town was on the alert, appeared on the Dunsmore road and lanes adjoining, and formed opposite. Hampden's brigade, with the guns, being in the first line, had taken post on some rising ground; and Lord Brook, with the second line, and the cavalry in reserve, was covered by the brow of the hill. Thus the two bodies remained, each in silence, awaiting the attack, till about eight o'clock, when the soldiers of the Parliament becoming impatient, began shouting, and setting up their hats on their pikes and musket-rests, to draw on the enemy. Lord Brook then moved up his cavalry on Hampden's right, to extend his line, the enemy being observed to bring up some fresh troops, with some pieces of ordnance, on that flank. Hampden began the fight, charging with his infantry, under cover of the guns, and supported by the horse. After a sharp skirmish, the King's troops gave way, and were pursued to the river, leaving their guns behind them, which they had scarcely brought into action; but beyond this, Lord Brook, with his cavalry, could not follow them, the enemy showing in position behind the river a body of dragoons of at least four times his number. This success against a superior force seems to have been owing to the Parliament having more cannon, and using them with effect at the beginning of the affair, the whole of the first line advancing at the moment when the artillery of the King had taken up their ground to answer their fire. Two of Lord Northampton's officers fell into their hands; one of these, Captain Legge, mistaking the green regiment of the enemy for his own (no uncommon disaster in the commencement of these ill-disciplined campaigns), was made prisoner in the very midst of the opposite lines. The King and Prince Rupert were said to have been on the field as spectators, and to have retired before the rout to Nottingham, and from thence again to Leicestershire. Towards the close of the skirmish, Hampden and Brook were joined by fresh levies of volunteers out of Northamptonshire, Warwickshire, and Buckinghamshire; the country bringing in provisions from every part, and the peasantry of the district, through which the King's troops retired, rising upon the stragglers in the rear of his retreating masses with cudgels and staves.*

Meanwhile, the town of Northampton began to fortify.

* Viccars - Parl. Chron.

On the 5th of September, letters, we find, were received by the Parliament from Withers, the Mayor, stating that Hampden and Goodwyn had marched for Leicester, by which the town of Northampton had been left without assistance to resist the adverse party in that neighbourhood, and praying for troops from London to supply the place of the former garrison.*
With this requisition the Parliament had not the means of complying. And now, left to their own resources, the citizens began to emulate the late example of those of Coventry, and to prepare for defence. The women worked with the men, day and night, throwing up earth from the ditch, and forming ramparts.

But the King, mortified at the slowness with which his levies proceeded throughout the midland counties, and the delays which in consequence befel his cause, resolved to put himself at the head of the forces which were assembling in Shropshire and in Wales. Sending orders to the Earl of Newcastle to move his army southward, to support Lord Northampton and keep Lord Essex's advanced guard in check, he repaired to Derby, and thence to Wellington. Here, halting, he issued his orders of war, to be spread through the country wherever troops were collecting in his behalf; and he published a protestation, again declaring the Earl of Essex and his adherents to be traitors, and his troops an army of Brownists, Anabaptists, and Atheists. From thence he proceeded to Shrewsbury. Here all was favourable and cheering to his cause. Above ten thousand men had, within a week, marched in brigade to join him, well armed, and already disciplined by bodies of old soldiers mixed up in their ranks to the amount of full one-half of the whole number. These powers were daily increasing, and supported by crowds of Welshmen, ill-armed and undisciplined, but still formidable on account of their wild spirit, and of the vast accession which they gave to an army in a fertile country, where an abundant harvest had just been reaped, and which was well able to support them. It was here, too, that he received the encouraging news from the north, of the arrival of a second supply from Holland, of arms, ammunition, and money, which had escaped the vigilance of Warwick's cruisers.

* True and Remarkable Passages, &c., from Monday, 5th of September, to Saturday, 10th, 1642.

Clarendon expresses his surprise that during this period, and even before the King left Nottingham, Lord Essex did not advance upon the line which was before him. A week before the King began his journey, no assurance (to use the phrase quoted by Lord Clarendon as Sir Jacob Astley's) could have been given to the King against his being taken out of his bed, if a brisk attempt had been made to that purpose. But, short of any extremity which these words are meant to describe, Rupert might have been driven back, the King obliged to place himself in the hands of the Parliament, or to quit the island, and the war thus brought to an end.* This was the first grand display of Lord Essex's overmastering faults of dilatoriness and indecision. By those who confound these qualities in war or politics with a spirit of moderation, Essex is praised for not pressing upon the King; but even Clarendon, with all his feelings on these subjects, treats this only as matter of oversight on the one part, and of wonder on the other. It was not what Hampden meant when he advised refusing the offer of treaty from Nottingham. No delay, in truth, occasioned during a treaty, could have given the King greater advantage than Essex now voluntarily afforded him. Essex had experience in the details of war: he was a good general in the day of battle; but, beyond the science of operations in the field, he had no qualities for command. His recommendation for the office of General-in-Chief consisted, indeed, only in his possessing to an eminent degree the love and confidence of his soldiers, and in his high birth and Presbyterian tenets, which made his appointment a compromise agreeable to a large party in the Upper House, who, though faithful in the cause, were yet well pleased to see in the Lord-General a person qualified by position and by religion to neutralise the ascendancy of the Root and Branch men, and of the Independents. Accordingly, with good motives and great means, he conducted himself throughout as one acting for a party rather than for a cause; and his timid and temporising policy inclined him always (as Cromwell afterwards said of Kimbolton) to 'such a peace to which victory would have been 'an obstacle.' He entered upon the business of the Civil War, having by his side Dalbier, and other soldiers of fortune, who had long served abroad in foreign pay. In a war of great

* Clarendon—Hist. Reb.

principles, mercenaries may be good agents, but are bad advisers. Hampden saw this; and his penetration was afterwards done justice to by Cromwell. In the field Cromwell pursued the system which Hampden had in vain recommended. The technical rules of war were easily to be learnt; but the successful application of them in great affairs required more than mere soldiership. Dalbier and Lesley failed before Oliver, who had studied the lessons of their experience, but had, in addition, higher gifts,—the knowledge of how the spirits of men were to be dealt with. He cultivated the enthusiasm of the young troops; and he conquered. Hampden from the beginning kept the cause, and the object of it, straight in view. He knew that to begin with displaying a spirit of compromise renders an advantageous compromise in the end impracticable. It was those who knew little of his real ends, or were little disposed to do them justice, who said, that 'when he drew the sword, he threw away the scabbard.' Such a metaphor describes a feeling seldom known in any higher grade of an army than among its ranks.

But from this time began that conflict of system between Hampden and the Lord-General, of which the history of the next year gives so many instances.

A party in Yorkshire began now to form and arm for the Parliament, under Sir John Hotham and his son, who, by the departure of the Earl of Newcastle, were enabled to move out of Hull, and occupy a line of country to the north of the Humber. These levies increasing gradually in numbers, the leaders chose Ferdinando Lord Fairfax to be their Commander-in-Chief; and their choice was confirmed by Ordinance. They then proceeded to garrison some other fortified places in the county, and forced Sir William Saville, and the other Cavaliers who had been left in weak and detached parties, to throw themselves into Pomfret Castle. On the other bank of the river, the Lord Willoughby of Parham, the Earl of Lincoln, and other persons of influence in Lincolnshire, raised troops of horse, and proceeded to form a junction with Fairfax's northern army.*

Meanwhile, a division of the King's troops, moving southward, began to take in towns upon their line of advance. The Earl of Derby, with Lord Molineux, marching with a

---

* Viccars—Parl. Chron.

large force to the westward of the course which the Earl of Newcastle had taken, traversed Cheshire; and, in order to place themselves on the flank of Fairfax, summoned the town of Manchester, establishing their batteries in Salford; but the citizens, assisted by a German engineer, stood a close and hot siege for some days, and obliged the Earl to retire. The state of Yorkshire, however,—its inclinations strongly favourable to the King's cause, and supported by the presence of this well-appointed and numerous army on its western frontier,—presented such difficulties in the way of any active operations for the Parliament in those parts, that Lord Fairfax, and many of the gentry who had joined him, showed a disposition to propose a treaty of neutrality;—a measure evidently fraught with the most serious injury to the Parliamentary cause in the midland counties. For, the King's object being to collect all his disposable force nearer the metropolis, he would have been thus enabled to leave the whole north, with the Parliament's levies there, such as they were, neutralised, and put out of a condition to act; while he might have carried on the great objects of the war undisturbed, until it should have suited his convenience to return northwards in force.

This negotiation, however, was stopped by peremptory instructions from Westminster. But to the same instrument the Houses, inflamed by the King's denunciations against Lord Essex and their other leaders, were persuaded to enter exceptions, charging treason against eleven of the ministers and principal officers of the household, who had first declared against their authority. These were the Earls of Bristol, Cumberland, Rivers, and Newcastle, Lord Newark, and Endymion Porter; and, besides these, some of the wisest and best of the advisers of the King,—the Duke of Richmond, the Earl of Carnarvon, Lord Falkland, Hyde, and Secretary Nicholas,—who, if there had been a chance of moderating the King's temper and counsels, so as to bring him to any hopeful terms of treaty, would probably have been the most inclined, and certainly the most able, to do so. This was a violent and ill-advised act of the Parliament, and is hardly to be accounted for but by a degree of passion unworthy of their accustomed sagacity and prudence.

But, upon this proclamation, their army in the north ceased from its inactivity. Hotham put himself in march, with a brigade, to the support of the western towns; and took

ROBERT GREVILLE,

LORD BROOKE.

OB: 1643.

Doncaster, and Selby, and Cawood Castle, where the Archbishop of York had established a place of arms.*

On the first show of the King's intention to move southward with his main army, London and Westminster completed their fortifications, and increased their train-bands to a great amount. Batteries were thrown up in the suburbs, at Mile End, Islington, and the approaches to Westminster; bars and chains were drawn across the entrances of the main streets, and lines constructed on the heights towards Hampstead and Harrow; and armed boats, with ordnance, were sent up the river to Maidenhead and Windsor.† To supply the expenses of this defence, votes of sequestration were passed against the revenues of bishoprics and deaneries, and against the rents of those who had been declared delinquents.

It was now that Bishops were voted down, root and branch; on which occasion great illuminations and bonfires were kindled in London, and an ordinance was passed, (a singular accompaniment to a general rejoicing,) putting down stage plays, and directing monthly fasts; and the people, animated at once by resentment and by danger, loaded the tables of both Houses with unqualified tenders of fidelity and service for life or death.

The Parliament, having ceased to treat, now set forth, in a long and eloquent proclamation, the provocations under which they had taken arms, and that the end for which they did so was ' to procure and establish the safety of religion ' and fruition of our laws and liberties in this and all other his ' Majesty's dominions, which we do here again protest before ' the Almighty God to be the chief end of all our counsels ' and resolutions, without any intention or desire to hurt or ' injure his Majesty, either in his person or just power.'

The virtuous and brave Lord Brook, to whose high qualities even his enemies paid their reluctant tribute, had been placed by vote at the head of the Lieutenancy of the County of Warwick.‡ He assembled at his castle the commanders and captains who had been elected to take charge of that county, to deliver to them their commissions. There, in the hall of

---

* Continuation of certain Special and Remarkable Passages, from Monday, 10th October, to Friday, 14th.
† Special Passages and Certain Informations, from Tuesday, 11th October, to Tuesday, 18th. Perfect Diurnal, Tuesday, 18th October.
‡ Clarendon—Hist. Reb.

that noble fortress, threatened with an instant siege, and his troops newly mustered, and unprepared for war, save by the spirit which they had already caught from their dauntless leader, he harangued his officers, in a speech abounding in high and manly feeling. He enlarged upon the miseries of a civil war, and the unprovoked courses which compelled them to engage in it.* 'Persuasions,' said he, 'to valiant men, as 'I know you to be, are useless; and if I thought there were 'any of you that was not to be incited more by the justice of 'the quarrel than any oratory to fight in this cause, surely 'I would rather wish his room than his company; for, if the 'nobility and bravery of the cause be not sufficient to animate 'even cowards, and make even the meanest spirits courageous, 'I know not what possibly can stir up mortal men to put on 'undaunted resolutions.' He then appealed to them as husbands and brothers, who would save their houses, their wives, and sisters, from the lawless fury of soldiers, hired and incensed to insult and to outrage. He described the conduct of the royal troops, on free quarter, where they had been admitted or faintly opposed. He appealed to them by their religion,—by that 'freedom of conscience which invokes you 'to stand up its champions against those Papistical malignants 'who would strike at God through the very heart of his 'known truth so long practised among us.' He vindicated their cause from the aspersion of its having been undertaken against the King. 'They were to fight,' said he, 'to keep 'the crown and kingdom for the sovereign and his posterity, 'to maintain his known rights and privileges, which are only 'relative with the people's liberties.' He concluded thus:—

'Touching those gentlemen who, being strangers, are come 'hither to proffer to us their services, and, in testimonial of their 'abilities, and that they have been commanders in the German 'wars, have here produced their several certificates. I must needs 'thank the gentlemen for their kind proffer, and yet desire license 'to be plain with them, hoping they will not take it as a disparage-'ment of their valours if I tell them we have now too woful 'experience in this kingdom of the German wars, and therefore 'cannot so well approve of the aid of foreign and mercenary 'auxiliaries. In Germany, they fought only for spoil, rapine, and 'destruction; merely money it was, and hope of gain, that

* In Mr. Staunton's Collection.

'excited the soldier to that service. It is not here so required,
' as the cause stands with us. We must rather employ men
' who will fight merely for the cause sake, and bear their own
' charge, than those who expect rewards and salaries; for by such
' means we shall never have a conclusion of these wars. For
' mercenaries, whose end is merely their pay, as for their sub-
' sistence, rather covet to spin out the wars to a prodigious length,
' as they have done in other countries, than to see them brought to
' a happy period. We must dispatch this great work in a short
' time, or be all liable to inevitable ruin. I shall, therefore, speak
' my conscience. I had rather have a thousand honest citizens that
' can handle their arms, whose hearts go with their hands, than
' thousands of mercenary soldiers that boast of their foreign
' experience.' * * ' And so I shall conclude my speech, and turn
' it into prayer, that God Almighty will arise and maintain his own
' cause, scattering and confounding the devices of his enemies, not
' suffering the ungodly to prevail over his flock. Lord, we are but
' a handful in consideration of thine and our enemies. Therefore,
' O Lord, fight thou our battles: go out as thou didst in the time
' of David before the hosts of thy servants; and strengthen and
' give us hearts, that we may show ourselves men, for the defence
' of thy true religion, and our own and the King and Kingdom's
' safety.'

PART THE NINTH.

1642.

Defence of Warwick Castle by Sir Edward Peto—Of Caldecot Manor-House by Mrs. Purefoy—Lord Essex advances to Worcester—His Speech to his Army—Skirmish at Powick Bridge—Parliamentarians enter Worcester—Parliament's Petition for Peace—Rejected by the King—Essex advances his Army—Hampden and Holles defeat a party near Aylesbury—and pursue them into Worcestershire—The King puts himself in march towards London—Edge Hill fight—March through the midland counties—Action between Balfore and Rupert at Aylesbury—Battle of Brentford—Retreat of the King.

BEFORE the arrival of the main army, the Parliament's quarters round Northampton and Daventry had been harassed by sharp and frequent attacks, and Lord Brook had quitted his castle, and hastened to their relief. Warwick had for a while ceased to be threatened; yet it was not safe to materially weaken its defences. He therefore took only his troop of horse, and a few companies of pikemen, leaving Sir John Peto in command, with a part of the infantry, mostly of the new levies, and despatching the rest to the neighbourhood of Coventry and Birmingham. On the same day, his departure was made known to Lord Northampton, who instantly put a large body of troops in march for Warwick; but making a circuit to the southward, he first entered Banbury, where, little prepared for such an incursion, the townsmen held a large store of ammunition, with some pieces of ordnance. Of these supplies the Earl possessed himself, meeting with little, if any, opposition; and then proceeded rapidly to his destination. Early in the morning of the next day but one, he entered Warwick with all his forces, and summoned the castle.

Sir Edward Peto without hesitation returned an absolute refusal to treat. After a pause of two hours, another summons was sent in, and terms offered, which were met by an indignant reply, that the Earl might at first have taken the word of a gentleman who would not surrender his trust. Lord Compton, the Earl's son, began the attack with a few guns from the town, while his father and Lord Dunsmore threw up a battery on some rising ground in the park, on the other side of the castle. Sir Edward then sent a trumpet, desiring that 'all friends should leave the town, but, for the rest, he bid 'them look to themselves;' and, upon the return of the officer, hung out a red flag of defiance from Guy's Tower. Well furnished with ammunition, but with no heavier ordnance than a few drakes and some large wall-pieces, he now began to return the fire, which continued, though without much effect on either side, for three days. The castle's strength was security enough against any attempt by storm, nor had it anything to fear from the effect of the few guns which had been brought from Banbury; while the assailants on the town side were covered by the houses, which the garrison were loth to batter or burn down. On the third day, Lord Compton planted some cannon on the church tower, from which the fire of the castle soon dislodged him, knocking down one of the pinnacles, and making his position too dangerous to be held. The besiegers then trusted to starving out the garrison, and, thenceforward, remained under shelter of the town; those on the other side never having unmasked their battery, but keeping the trees still standing for their protection. The castle being thus invested, Sir Edward hoisted on the flagstaff of the tower a Bible and a winding-sheet, the one as a testimony of his cause, and the other of his determination to maintain it to the last.

Nothing seemed likely to be gained to the opposite party by protracting the siege. The King was advancing to relieve Worcester. He required the whole strength of his army; and Lord Northampton, therefore, drew off his troops to join him.*

Scarcely had the siege of Warwick Castle been raised, when Prince Rupert, with from five to six hundred cavalry, marched

---

* Tracts in the possession of Mr. Staunton. Collection for a History of Warwickshire.

upon Caldecot Manor-house, in the north of the county, with intent to take it by surprise. It belonged to Mr. William Purefoy, a gentleman of ancient family, a member of the House of Commons, and colonel of a regiment in garrison at Warwick Castle. When Rupert summoned Caldecot, there were none within but Mrs. Purefoy, her two daughters, Mr. Abbott, her son-in-law, eight serving men, and a few maid-servants.* This brave little garrison refused to surrender, inspired by the example of a woman's courage and fidelity to maintain the charge for her absent husband. The history of the civil wars affords several such instances. The stories of Lathom Hall, held by the Countess of Derby, and of Warder Castle, by Blanch Lady Arundell, have added lustre to those noble names. The holding of Caldecot was not less heroic, nor its capitulation less honourable. The assailants broke down the main gate of the outer court; but the men, stationed at the windows, received them with so well-directed a fire, that, at the first onset, three of Rupert's officers, and several of his soldiers, were slain. There were twelve muskets in the house; the women loading them, as the men continued the execution with rapid and deadly aim. The attack continued for several hours, with repeated assaults, in the intervals between which, as the bullets were expended, the women ran the pewter of their kitchen dishes into moulds for a fresh supply. At length, towards nightfall, mortified with the obstinate resistance, and with the loss he had already sustained, Rupert drew off his party, but, as he retired, set fire to the barns and outhouses. The wind blowing fresh upon the main building, he again advanced under cover of the smoke and darkness. And now,—the ammunition within failing, the house threatened with instant conflagration, and no hope of succour remaining,—the brave lady went forth, and claimed protection from the Prince, stipulating for the lives of her garrison.

It was then first that he was made aware of the smallness of the force which had so gallantly withstood so fierce and protracted an assault. He granted her condition; and, to his honour, as Viccars confesses, ' being much taken with their ' most notable valour, saved their lives and house from plun- ' dering, saying to Mr. Abbott that he was worthy to be a chief

* Gibson's Additions to Camden.

'commander in an army, and proffered him such a place in
'his army, if he would go with him; but he modestly refused
'it. However, the said Prince fairly performed his promise,
'and would not suffer a pennyworth of the goods in the
'house to be taken from them; and so departed.' *

Prince Rupert rejoined the King at Shrewsbury, where he remained till the preparations were completed for taking the field with the whole army. He now returned with the advanced guard. Worcester was held for the King, and Rupert was moving along the Severn in the direction of that city, in order to relieve the garrison, which was threatened by the Earl of Essex.

On the 19th of September, he sent a flag of truce, with a message, to the Lord-General, who was then at Northampton preparing to march upon Worcester. He reproached him with his treasons, questioned him as to his intended line of march, whether on Worcester or Coventry, and offered to give him the meeting, with the best army each could provide, on Dunsmore Heath. Essex was not tempted by this proposal of the Prince's to allow the King's army to advance in front of Birmingham, Coventry, and Warwick, (thus effectually cutting off these towns from all relief,) nor to allow an enemy, superior to him in the numbers and equipment of his cavalry,† to choose the place of meeting on an open heath, and in the midst of a country abounding with forage, of which the Prince stood much in need.‡ The offer was such as might have been expected from a chieftain of twenty-three, with a brilliant division of above five thousand newly raised horse; but not such as was likely to be accepted by an experienced general, whose advantage consisted in infantry, in artillery (which, in those days, was a cumbrous weapon, not easily to be wielded in the open field against cavalry,) and in the extent of friendly district in his rear. Nor, probably, was he without his suspicions that the time expended in arranging the terms of this challenge, might be employed by the King in strengthening and relieving Worcester. 'Whereupon, his Excellency
'returned answer, that the manner of his raising those forces
'that were then with him ready to march under his command

---

* Viccars—Parl. Chron.—Continuation of Special and Remarkable Passages—Gibson's Additions to Camden.—Monument of Mr. Abbott in Caldecot Church.

† Clarendon—Hist. Reb. ‡ Ibid.

'was a thing not now to be disputed on between them, the
'occasions and legality thereof being already determined by
'both Houses of Parliament; neither had he undertaken that
'command with any intent for to levy forces or to make war
'against his Majesty's Royal person; but to obtain a peace
'between his Sacred Majesty and his Great Council of Parlia-
'ment, and all the rest of his Majesty's faithful, dutiful, and
'most loyal subjects, against any persons whatsoever that
'should oppose and resist the same; and that he feared not to
'meet the prince in any place that he should appoint or make
'choice of.' *   But, meanwhile, he put his army in march for
Worcester. He was again accompanied from Northampton,
as he had been from London, along several miles of road, by
the principal gentry of the neighbourhood, and by crowds
of people, with great rejoicings, and loud expressions of
good-will.

The Lord-General now established himself in Worcester;
and he lost no time in issuing his orders of war in the form of
a speech at the head of his army. He desired them to take
notice of what on his honour he promised to perform, and
what he should expect from them.

'I do promise, in the sight of Almighty God, to undertake
'nothing but what shall tend to the advancement of the true
'Protestant religion, the securing of his Majesty's Royal person,
'the maintenance of the just privileges of Parliament, and the
'liberty and property of the subject. Neither will I engage any
'of you into any danger, but I will, in my own person, run an
'equal hazard with you, and either bring you off with honour, or,
'(if God have so decreed) fall with you, and willingly become a
'sacrifice for the preservation of my country. Likewise I do pro-
'mise that my ear shall be open to hear the complaint of the poorest
'of my soldiers, though against the chiefest of my officers, neither
'shall his greatness (if justly taxed) gain any privilege; but I shall
'be ready to execute justice against all, from the greatest to the
'least. Your pay shall be constantly delivered to your commanders,
'and, if default be made by any officer, give me timely notice, and
'you shall find speedy redress. I shall now declare what is your
'duty towards me, which I must likewise expect to be carefully
'performed by you. I shall desire all and every officer to endeavour

---

* Prince Robert's Speech to the Earl of Essex, and his Excellency's
Answer thereunto from Northampton, on Monday, Sept. 19. King's Coll.,
Brit. Mus.

'by love and affable carriage to command his soldiers; since what
'is done for fear is done unwillingly, and what is unwillingly
'attempted can never prosper. Likewise 'tis my request that you
'be very careful in the exercising of your men, and bring them to
'use their arms readily and expertly, and not busy them in prac-
'tising the ceremonious forms of military discipline; only let them
'be well instructed in the necessary rudiments of war; that they
'may fall on with discretion, and retreat with care; how maintain
'their order, and make good their ground. Also I do expect that
'all those which voluntarily engaged themselves in this service
'should answer my expectation in the performance of these ensuing
'articles.

'1. That you willingly and cheerfully obey such as by your own
'election you have made commanders over you.

'2. That you take especial care to keep your arms at all times
'fit for service, that upon all occasions you may be ready, when the
'signal shall be given by the sound of drum or trumpet, to repair
'to your colours, and so to march upon any service, where and when
'occasion shall require.

'3. That you bear yourselves like soldiers, without doing any
'spoil to the inhabitants of the country; so doing you shall obtain
'love and friendship, where, otherwise, you will be hated and com-
'plained of, and I, that should protect you, shall be forced to punish
'you according to the severity of law.

'4. That you accept, and rest satisfied with, such quarters as
'shall fall to your lot, or be appointed you by your quarter-master.

'5. That you shall, if appointed for sentries or perdues, faith-
'fully discharge that duty; for, upon fail thereof, you shall be sure
'to undergo a very severe censure.

'6. You shall forbear to prophane the sabbath, either by being
'drunk, or by unlawful games; for whosoever shall be found
'faulty must not expect to pass unpunished.

'7. Whosoever shall be known to neglect the feeding of his
'horse with necessary provender, to the end that his horse be
'disabled or unfit for service, the party for the said default shall
'suffer a month's imprisonment, and afterwards be cashiered, as
'unworthy the name of a soldier.

'8. That no trooper, or other of our soldiers, shall suffer his
'paddee to feed his horse in the corn, or to steal men's hay, but
'shall pay, every man, for hay 6d. day and night, and for oats
'2s. the bushel.

'Lastly, that you avoid cruelty. For it is my desire rather to
'save the lives of thousands than to kill one; so that it may be
'done without prejudice. These things faithfully performed, and
'the justice of our cause truly considered, let us advance with a

'religious courage, and willingly adventure our lives in the defence
'of the King and Parliament.' *

On the 22nd of September, while the army was on its
march, a skirmish was fought, which both parties agreed in
calling the battle of Worcester. Improperly so named; for it
was but an affair of outposts in which a few hundred men were
engaged, and it was not fought at Worcester, but about four
miles from that city, at Powick Bridge, upon the river Team.
But both parties were equally eager to announce to the country
that a battle had been fought, and equally well determined to
claim the result of it as a victory to themselves; each giving
very inflated accounts of their enemy's superiority in numbers,
and of the decisiveness of their own success. All the diurnals,
proclamations, and intelligencers, which issued from either side
to spread the news, were remarkably unscrupulous on this
point. The exaggerations seem to be very evenly balanced.
The real issue of the engagement was, (no very uncommon
event in the beginning of these wars,) that the one party was
beaten back in the field, and the other, immediately after,
retired in a panic, leaving the post which they had to defend
to an adversary who had given no proof of being able to take
it. Ludlow, however, in his memoirs, appears to give the
most honest and credible evidence, inasmuch as he speaks very
frankly of the misconduct on his own side, and owns the
defeat. This, compared with Clarendon's, and correcting the
misrepresentations of other more detailed accounts, gives
a tolerably intelligible view of the affair.

About ten troops of the Parliament's regular horse, and six
of dragoons,† under the command of Colonel Browne and
Colonel Sandys, being in all about five hundred, made good
their passage of the bridge, and, drawing up in a meadow on
the left of the road, established themselves there till the next
day, waiting the support of the main body, and, apparently,
little expecting to be attacked; for they had placed themselves

---

* King's Pamphlets—British Mus.

† The dragoons are, in these accounts, always distinguished from the
horse. They were troops who acted with the regular cavalry, but often
on foot, and sometimes mounted behind the horsemen in advance or
retreat. They were armed with long swords, like the troopers; but they
also carried matchlocks, and are supposed by Dr. Meyrick to have derived
their name from the locks of the carbines of the first dragoons having the
representation of a dragon's head, with the lighted match borne in its jaws.

with a narrow bridge and an unfordable river behind them. To lead them into further disadvantage, the enemy dispatched a messenger, disguised, with a false report that Sir William Balfore, lieutenant-general in chief of the Parliament's cavalry, was in force on the other side of the city. The messenger delivered orders, as from Balfore, that, upon the firing of a cannon, which was to be his signal of onset, they were to advance upon the lanes nearer the city, to stop and capture the flying garrison. Soon after this, some of the enemy's dragoons shewed themselves on the road, and, Colonel Sandys having mounted for the attack, the whole body, contrary to Nathaniel Fiennes's and Captain Wingate's advice, (who would, at all events, have waited for the signal,) pushed forward. But, though they had not given time for the enemy's ambush to be thoroughly formed, they soon discovered that they had been mistaken in supposing those in front to be beaten men leaving the town. For, while engaged with the dragoons, they suddenly found themselves attacked on both flanks by infantry, who opened a severe fire, and then charged them with their pole-axes. Nathaniel Fiennes, on whose reputation for personal courage there never was a just stain, (however unfurnished he was with the firmness befitting the higher responsibilities of the military profession), behaved with great valour. He instantly supported the advanced party, and, with his own hand, pistolled the officer commanding the enemy's horse. Then, breaking through them, he forced them over the hedges among their own infantry. But Sandys was mortally wounded, and taken. At length, pressed by fresh troops, (Rupert and Maurice being both in the field with about 1600 men,) the Parliamentarians retired in confusion across the bridge, hotly pursued, and with great loss.* Edmund Ludlow was with the advanced guard of the main army, being then in the Lord-General's body-guard of gentlemen, at Parshot, on the way from Northamptonshire. 'The ' body of our routed party,' says he, ' returned in great ' disorder to Parshot, at which place our life-guard was ' appointed to quarter that night; where, as we were marching ' into the town, we discovered horsemen riding very hard ' towards us, with drawn swords, and many of them without

---

* Viccars's Parl. Chron. Ludlow's Memoirs.—Clarendon—Hist. Reb. Kingdome's Weekly Intelligencer. Continuation of Special and Remarkable Passages, from Monday the 3rd, till the 5th of October.

' hats, from whom we understood the particulars of our loss,
' not without improvement, by reason of the fear with which
' they were possessed, telling us that the enemy was hard by
' in pursuit of them; whereas, it afterwards appeared, they
' came not within four miles of that place. Our life-guard
' being, for the most part, strangers to things of this nature,
' were much alarmed with this report; yet some of us,
' unwilling to give credit to it till we were better informed,
' offered ourselves to go out upon a further discovery of the
' matter; but our captain, Sir Philip Stapylton, not being
' then with us, his lieutenant, one Bainham, an old soldier
' (a generation of men much cried up at that time), drawing
' us into a field, where he pretended we might more advantage-
' ously charge if there should be occasion, commanded us to
' wheel about. But our gentlemen, not yet well understanding
' the difference between "wheeling-about" and " shifting for
' " themselves," their backs being now towards the enemy whom
' they thought to be close in the rear, retired to the army in a
' very dishonourable manner, and the next morning rallied at
' the head-quarters, where we received but cold welcome from
' the General, as we well deserved.'

The next day the garrison of Worcester retired on its way to Shrewsbury, though the King was advancing to their relief, with a force, which, together with theirs, outnumbered Essex's whole army. They took with them Wingate, whom they had made prisoner in the fight, and (as Viccars says), ' it was
' credibly reported, most barbarously and basely made him ride
' naked, though a Member of Parliament, and a pious worthy
' gentleman.' How far this special case may be true, with its somewhat whimsical aggravations, is not perhaps very much worth serious inquiry.* Rupert, generally known at that time under the name of the Prince Robert, and among the Parliamentarians, by no very forced conceit, under that of ' the
' Prince Robber,' had not served at the head of a regiment in Germany, without acquiring, and encouraging very abund- antly and freely among his horsemen, the insolent and cruel

* A very different account is given of the subsequent treatment which he received. ' Captaine Wingate is used like a gentleman by the Cavaliers;
' and the printed pamphlets doe much injury that expresse any hard usage
' of him by them. Give the devill his due, and doe soe to the Cavaliers in this thing.' Special Passages. From the 11th to the 18th of October.

spirit of partisan warfare. Particular instances of this sort, it is true, were treasured up by the Parliamentary chroniclers, to serve as general examples of the conduct of the opposite party; but it is equally true, that Rupert's general conduct in these respects subjected him, more than once, to a check in the published orders of the King, and that, wherever he appeared, the war was usually marked with great ferocity and excess. His generous conduct to Mrs. Purefoy, after the surrender of Caldecot House, appears, indeed, as a solitary exception.

Lord Essex now took possession of Worcester.

On the 29th of September, a struggle took place in the Guildhall, on the election of the Lord Mayor of London; those of the Livery who were secretly attached to the Court proposing Sir John Cordwell, but the Parliamentarians carrying the election of Alderman Pennington by a very large majority; an event as injurious to what remained of the King's interest in the city, as the attempt had been unwise. It exasperated, if possible still more, the already inflamed spirits of the citizens; and it did so in a manner which only gave them a public triumph, and exposed to danger the opposing minority, who had thus displayed themselves as a party, and proved at once their own weakness and the utter hopelessness of their further progress there.

The Parliament, however, resumed a tone of moderation. Though their cause was already in arms throughout the country, it had not yet been committed in open field against the King in person. While a hope remained of avoiding this extremity, every effort to delay it was a duty. And this justice, at least, must be done to the Parliament's motives in this delay, that every day was increasing the King's means in men, in military stores from abroad, and in the influence of his name and of those of his supporters; while the preparations made by the Houses, and by their generals, were complete, and not likely to be further extended. They, however, instantly dispatched another petition for peace, setting forth the distractions of the country, protesting against the machinations of the secret cabinet, particularly in respect of the dreadful massacres still flagrant in Ireland, and of the open menace of an incursion of the Irish rebels, and of troops from Germany and Denmark; and ending with what Viccars terms a ' most 'just redargution of the malignants' foul and false slanders 'on the Parliament.'

To this proposition forwarded by Essex to the King, and praying also safe conduct and free access for himself to his Majesty, this brief and haughty answer was returned:—'That his Majesty 'would receive any petition that should be presented to him 'from his Parliament, and give free access to those that should 'bring the same; but that he would not receive any petition 'from the hands of any traitor.' In one short intemperate sentence thus casting back at once every approach to a treaty, and rendering all further proposition, as affairs then stood, entirely hopeless. For, besides the unnecessary violence of recalling, at such a moment, to the Parliament's remembrance that the person in whom they had voted their chief confidence had been proclaimed a traitor, it showed them the impossibility of procuring access to the King for any other person entrusted with a similar project of accommodation; almost every one of those leading members of either House to whom such project or petition could be with benefit confided, being precluded under the same proscription from appearing in the Royal presence.

On this a resolution was passed, that 'for his Majesty to 'make such a distinction of his Parliament, that he would 'receive no petition from the hands of such whom he accounts 'traitors, he did therein abridge them of the greatest privilege 'of Parliament that can be, and in effect refuse to receive any 'petition from them at all. For that his Majesty, by pro- 'claiming the Earl of Essex and his adherents to be traitors, 'hath, in these words, comprehended both the Houses of 'Parliament, which is not only against the privileges of 'Parliament, but also against the fundamental laws of the 'land.' It was therefore also voted, 'that the Earl of Essex 'should go forward in raising forces according to his instruc- 'tions, and lay by the said petition which was to have been 'presented to his Majesty; and that the Lord-General should 'advance his army.'

Nor did the mischief rest here. The Lord Mohun and the Earl of Bath had returned their summonses to the Parliament, denying it to be a free Parliament, and alleging that they had the King's warrant for not obeying its commands. The Lord Capel had also, at the same time, given commission to the

Marquis of Hertford to apply all his rents in the west to the maintaining of the war against the Parliament. Again, then, the Parliament proceeded with these three Lords as it had done with the eleven who had first left Westminster for York; and, in order to retaliate upon the King a petulant course which showed no better in the imitation, voted them to be capital delinquents, and that their estates should be placed in commission for the public service of the Commonwealth. The lands and estates, also, of all convicted Papists, and Popish recusants, (the common unjust resource of the English Government on all such occasions of need,) were voted to be sequestered, and their persons to be secured.*

Meanwhile, it appears that Hampden was incessantly and variously occupied in all the affairs of the war. We find him in Northampton, at the head-quarters of the Earl of Essex, and leading his brigade in the general advance of the army upon Worcester; but, several times was he journeying to and fro between Northampton and London, to hold counsel with the Parliament, and to assist at the Committee of Public Safety; and, a very few days before the advance, he was dispatched to take the command at Aylesbury, where the magazines of the county lay, and towards which, it seems, that parties of the Earl of Northampton's division were moving by circuitous routes, occasionally laying waste the country round, and threatening to force the new raised and unconnected bodies of volunteers who guarded the London road in Essex's rear. On the 16th, supported by Holles, he commanded in a severe skirmish at a short distance from the town of Aylesbury, in which many were slain, and the cavaliers were repulsed and pursued, the prisoners being sent to Buckingham and Wycombe jails. A requisition was instantly sent to London for troops to reinforce the garrison of Aylesbury. Hampden and Holles, however, did not pause upon their advantage, but pursued the beaten party in the direction of Oxford, from which city they dislodged the Lord Byron, and followed him into the Vale of Evesham, where, on the 21st, they brought him to action, and dispersed his force. They then rejoined Lord Essex's army upon its entry into Worcester.†

The war had by this time assumed a more determinate object and system, and its operations were conducted on a

---

* Viccars—Parl. Chron.   † Special Passages, Sept. 23 and 24.

larger scale. Hitherto, ignorant of the amount of each other's strength, doubtful of the extent of each other's views, and irresolute as to their own, and each looking daily for some decisive proposal of accommodation to be made from the adverse side,—both parties had contented themselves with uncombined enterprises and encounters, which had, for the most part, sprung from local causes rather than from any which could materially expedite the great issue of the conflict. But the natural consequences of these uncombined enterprises and encounters now began to appear. Neighbouring posts were strengthened and multiplied, in order to give support to the scattered parties in the field. Extensive lines of communication were formed, and the armies on both sides drew in their detachments to move on points. The King, who had now advanced from Shrewsbury and Ludlow, having manœuvred for some days with skill and success in the neighbourhood of Worcester, was enabled, suddenly putting himself in march to the eastward, to effect a junction with Lord Northampton's division. It was now about the middle of October. His army was collected in a body of near twenty thousand men, and a large part of it on Essex's flank was actually covering one of the main roads to the metropolis, where the Parliament sat protected only by the train-bands of the city, and by some half-formed and undisciplined levies which still remained to guard the stores of the midland counties, and which might have been either forced or passed. The flanking roads on both sides were circuitous and bad. Essex's communications extended from Worcester, through part of Oxfordshire, into Buckinghamshire, Bedfordshire, Hertfordshire, and Middlesex. But the line was too much extended; it was weak, and easy to be broken through in almost any part. The King's were complete, from Ludlow and Shrewsbury, northward, to the furthest extremity of Cheshire, and, westward, through Wales to Cornwall, Devonshire, and Somersetshire, where Hopton, Grenvil, and Slanning, were daily increasing their powers. The King had succeeded in placing himself nearly two days' march in advance of the main army of the Parliament, on the way to London. The Parliament had already dispatched peremptory orders to Lord Essex to proceed, by forced marches, on the Warwickshire road, in order to menace, and, if possible, turn, the King's right flank; but, this failing, at all hazards to bring him to action. Lord Essex had a double motive for wishing to force a battle;—first, to prove his troops, and, if possible, give the impression of a victory; and, secondly, to delay the King, and endeavour to break through his army, and thus resume that defensive position, with his back upon London, of which the King had so dexterously deprived him. Charles had every interest in avoiding a battle. If successful, it would not have very materially advanced his operations, further than by the name of a victory; for he could not have pursued a beaten enemy without removing farther from his main object—London. On the other hand, defeat would have been to him irretrievable ruin. His troops, confident in their better discipline, and in the skill of their experienced generals, did not require to be convinced of their superiority over their enemy. At all events, there was nothing to justify such a risk. They already took it for granted that they could conquer whenever they should have occasion to fight.

And now Coventry was again threatened by Prince Rupert. His summons was treated with contempt by the gallant citizens; intelligence of which being dispatched to Charles, propositions were sent under the sign-manual, ordering the surrender of the town to the Prince, and promising in return, ' on the faith ' of a King,' protection from plunder, and an act of entire oblivion. To this message, after a general council of the inhabitants, the Mayor and Aldermen sent an answer, conceived in the most respectful terms, but expressing their determination not to surrender their city to any armed force or person coming in the name of the King, without the concurrent authority of the Parliament; having, as they said, had experience of the robberies and cruelties of the cavaliers in divers parts of the kingdom. ' All which being seriously considered,' they declared themselves bound in conscience to God, in loyalty to his Majesty, and in regard for their own safety and honour, and the safety and honour of all who were the dearest to them, ' to deny his Majesty's desires, and to oppose all those that ' might in any way endeavour, under pretence of his Majesty's ' commands legally given, to disturb the peace of the kingdom.' And that, ' having with all humility presented these lines, as ' the perfect copy of their intentions,' they betake themselves, ' every man to his charge, leaving these particulars to his ' Majesty's consideration.' *

---

* His Majesty's Declaration and Proposition, and Answer thereto. Printed for T. West, October 22, 1642.

The garrison accordingly prepared themselves for the worst. But, the second day after their last defiance had been dispatched, their spirits were raised and confirmed by the intelligence of Denzil Holles having, on the 18th, obliged Lord Digby, at the head of a very superior force, to retire from the neighbourhood of Wolverhampton, after a severe skirmish in which many had fallen on each side. The Parliament's reports magnify this into a great victory against incredible odds, giving an equally incredible account of the killed of Lord Digby's party; while the King's press, by passing the whole event in silence, confirms the general fact that the issue was unfavourable to the cavaliers. All that is certain, besides this, is that Digby's brigade in those parts was composed of three regiments; that he endeavoured to force the main road, which was held by Holles's regiment only, and that, after a sharp encounter, he retired upon the King's quarters at Leicester.

Meanwhile, the armies were rapidly approaching, and a general engagement was evidently at hand. The joint terrors of the King's name and Rupert's presence having failed to alarm Coventry into an instant surrender, no more time was to be lost by the King. He accordingly abandoned all further attempt upon that city, and left it in his rear, little being to be feared from any annoyance to be attempted by a weak garrison of undisciplined citizens.

The different divisions of the Parliament's army, meanwhile, moved in a converging line with that of the King's march. Moreover, being less encumbered with useless followers, and with forage and provisions, (the country being generally friendly, and bringing in these things from all sides for their daily consumption,) they advanced with a rapidity which induced the King to abandon the less obstructed course by St. Alban's, and to take, with both columns, the more westerly direction of Southam, in order to avoid the risk of his right flank being gained or passed. And of this there was some danger; for Stratford on Avon, with its bridge, was already occupied by the Parliamentarians. Hampden and Brook had entered it on the 18th; and, on the next morning, with the assistance of the townsmen, had repulsed a severe attack made by two brigades, and had secured the passage of the river. On the 20th the King's advanced guard was before Banbury.[*]

[*] Lord Essex's Relation.

A little before midnight, on the 21st of October, from the road which traverses the brow of Edge Hill, the fires of the Parliament's pickets were descried in the Vale of Redhorse, and at dawn the main body of its army was seen moving in a direction parallel with the King's rear-guard, from the town of Keinton, which it had entered the night before. Here Rupert halted, and sent instant intelligence to the King. Soon after daybreak, Charles was on the heights. He pitched his tent on the eastern extremity of the range, resting his right on the Burton Dassett and Wormleighton Hills, his centre posted over Radway, and his left on a steep road leading down from a lone inn, then called, as now, the 'Sun Rising.' That flank was further protected by the difficult country in front of Lord Northampton's house at Compton Wynyate. A stronger position cannot easily be imagined. Here, then, the Parliament army, already fatigued and harassed by forced marches through a deep country; under orders, at all risks, to stop the King's passage to London, and having, by its late movements, staked its reputation upon this object; found itself suddenly checked.

A feeling of military pride made it, doubtless, desirable to Charles, having a full view of the enemy in order of battle, not to pursue what might have been miscalled a retreating march upon the metropolis. Still, it was apparent that he might, without avoiding a conflict, have waited, with great advantage, the attack of troops who had no choice left them in the selection of ground, and whose whole purpose would be impeded until they might have been able to force him from those commanding heights. Regiment after regiment was seen coming up on the Parliament's side and forming in front of the town of Keinton, in three lines. Their force in that field, ready to engage, consisted of ten regiments of foot, forty-two troops of regular horse, and about seven hundred dragoons; in all, between twelve and thirteen thousand men. A detachment of their guns took post on their right, among the enclosures on a rising ground to the westward of the town, and a little in advance of it, and commanding that part of the field, then open, which is still known by the name of 'the two Battle Farms.' The rest of their small park of artillery was on their extreme left. But this was very inferior in force to the artillery of the King; for the greater part of the Parliament's train had been left behind unprovided with draught horses, by the negligence of M. de Boys, their French engineer. They were now brought on, with great exertion and difficulty, but still nearly a day's march in the rear, under the command of Hampden, who, with a brigade, consisting of his own regiment, Colonel Grantham's, Colonel Barkham's, and Lord Rochford's, in all about three thousand infantry, had been appointed to guard them.

A hasty council of war was now called by the King. His army was superior in numbers to that of his enemy, by at least two thousand infantry, and sixteen troops of horse, and in sight of a plain where cavalry might act with eminent advantage. His soldiers were high in spirit, eager to engage, and impatient of delay with an adversary whom they despised. In addition to this, he knew from his scouts that the main body of the Parliament's guns, with a whole brigade, could not be brought into action that day, but might, if he were to waste many hours more, be made available against him. To all these tempting incentives to a battle there was no consideration to oppose, save that of the absolute uselessness of fighting at all, and the great importance of not delaying the march of at least a portion of his force upon London. But Prince Rupert's temper was peremptory and unmanageable. He commanded the cavalry; on them the greater share of the day's glory in the plain of Keinton was likely to rest; and Prince Rupert's was a brilliant, but ever a selfish, enthusiasm. He had, only a few days before, received with great contumely a message delivered by Lord Falkland, and had declared that he would acknowledge no orders, in march or in battle, but from the King himself. This, as an insult upon Falkland's office, was treated by him in a tone of sharp but courteous sarcasm, well befitting the lofty spirit of a well-bred gentleman, who keenly resented the Prince's petulance, yet would not allow it to interfere with his own duties, or the public service.* It forced the King, however, on a new and very inconvenient arrangement.† The Earl of Lindsey, the King's Lieutenant-General, saw that the Prince had thus disclaimed his control also. To allow the line to be commanded by that headstrong young man, (and somebody must command it in chief,) was impossible. A sort of compromise was therefore attempted. The King proposed that the order of battle should

---

* Clarendon—Hist. Reb.
† Clarendon—Hist. Reb. Bulstrode's Memoirs.

be formed by General Ruthven, who had long served under the Princes Maurice and Henry of Orange in the Netherlands, and for some time in the same army with Rupert himself in Germany. To this Lindsey consented, putting himself, on foot, at the head of the King's Guards, in the centre of the first line; there remaining answerable for the fate of an army drawn out by another, and the whole right wing of which was commanded by a rash man, who would take no orders from him.

The adventurous courage of Rupert gave him an influence over the mind of the King which he had no other quality to justify. Against the counsel of Lindsey, and of several other experienced officers, it was determined not to await the battle in position, but to push forward the two first lines, and meet the attack half-way. The morning was bright and cold. The main body of the King's troops had been on the hills all night: the King had joined them in person, from Sir William Chancie's, at Ratott Bridge; and Prince Rupert from the Lord Spencer's, at Wormleighton, where he had rested for a few hours. The army advanced in great pomp; the King himself, having first ridden along the lines, clad in steel, and wearing his Star and George on a black velvet mantle over his armour, and a steel cap, covered with velvet, on his head.* He had already addressed his principal officers in his tent, in a brave and eloquent harangue. 'If this day shine prosperous unto 'us,' said he, 'we shall all be happy in a glorious victory. 'Your King is both your cause, your quarrel, and your 'captain. The foe is in sight. Now show yourselves no 'malignant parties, but with your swords declare what courage 'and fidelity is within you. I have written and declared that 'I intended always to maintain and defend the Protestant 'Religion, the rights and privileges of Parliament, and the 'liberty of the subject; and now I must prove my words by 'the convincing argument of the sword. Let Heaven show 'his power by this day's victory, to declare me just, and as a 'lawful, so a loving, King, to my subjects. The best encour-'agement I can give you is this; that come life or death, your 'King will bear you company, and ever keep this field, this 'place, and this day's service, in his grateful remembrance.'

He spoke twice at the head of his troops. His speech to his soldiers, immediately before the battle, was thus given out in print.

* Bulstrode's Memoirs.

' Friends and soldiers,—I look upon you with joy to behold so
' great an army as ever King of England had in these later times,
' standing with high resolutions to defend your King, the Parlia-
' ment, and all my loyal subjects. I thank your loves, offered to
' your King, with a desire to hazard your lives and fortunes with
' me and in my cause, freely offered, and that in my urgent necessity,
' I see by you that no father can relinquish and leave his son—no
' subject his lawful King; but I attribute this to the justness of
' my cause. *He that made us a King will protect us.* We have
' marched so long in hopes to meet no enemy; we knowing none
' at whose hands we deserve any opposition. Nor can our sun,
' shining through the clouds of malignant envy, suffer such an
' obscurity, but that some influence of my royal authority, *derived*
' *from God, whose substitute and supreme governor under Christ I am,*
' hath begotten in you a confidence in my intentions. But matters
' are now not to be declared by words, but by swords. You all
' think our thoughts. Endeavour to defend our person, while
' I reign over your affections as well as your persons. Now, there-
' fore, know my resolution is to try the doubtful chance of war,
' which, with much grief, I must stand to, and endure the hazard.
' I desire not the effusion of blood; but, since Heaven hath so
' declared that so much preparation hath been made, we must needs
' accept of this present occasion and opportunity of gaining an
' honourable victory, and some addition of glory to our crown;
' since reputation is that which doth gild over the richest gold, and
' shall ever be the endeavour of our whole reign. The present
' action of this battle makes me speak briefly, and yet lovingly
' and loyally towards you, our loyal army. I put not my confidence
' in your strength or number, but confide that, though your King
' speaks to you, and that with as much love and affection as ever
' King of England did to his army, yet God, and the justness
' of our cause, together with the love I bear to the whole kingdom,
' must give you the best encouragement. In a word, your King
' bids you all be courageous, and Heaven make you victorious.' *

At about two o'clock in the afternoon they advanced. The order in which they descended from the hill was this:—Prince Rupert, at the head of the Prince of Wales's regiment, led the cavalry of the right wing, and Lord Byron the reserve, on the extreme right of which Colonel Washington's dragoons, supported by six hundred regular horse, took possession of some bushes and enclosures. On his left were eight regiments of

---

* Colonel Weston's Letter. Printed for Richard Johnson, 1642. In Mr. Staunton's collection.

infantry. The infantry of the centre, in column of six lines, was led by General Ruthven and Sir Jacob Astley; Lord Lindsey, with his son Lord Willoughby, at the head of the royal foot guards, the red coats; and Sir Edmund Verney, carrying the standard, which had been displayed, all the morning, from the hill. Behind these, and a little to the right, the King took post with his guard of pensioners. The cavalry of the left wing was commanded by Lord Wilmot, and consisted of the regiments of Lord Goring and Lord Fielding.* These were supported by Lord Carnarvon, at the head of six hundred pikemen and a small body of musqueteers. The reserve was commanded by Lord Digby; and Sir George Lisle's and Colonel Ennis's dragoons lined the hedges and broken ground in advance of the extreme left, as Washington's had done on the right. In the rear of these were the ill-armed and almost undisciplined levies from Wales.

The brave Sir Jacob Astley's prayer, immediately before the advance, was short and fervent. 'Oh, Lord, thou knowest 'how busy I must be this day. If I forget thee, do not thou 'forget me. March on, boys!' †

The Parliamentarians were drawn up in three brigades. The right wing was composed of three regiments of horse, under the orders of Sir John Meldrum, Sir Philip Stapleton, and Sir William Balfore, with Colonel Richard Fielding's regiment, and some guns in reserve, and supported by musqueteers lining a long hedge, at a right angle with their front. Next to these were the Lord Roberts's and Sir William Constable's infantry. In the centre were the Lord-General's own regiment, and Colonel Ballard's, and Lord Brook's, with Holles's, also infantry, in reserve. The left wing consisted of five regiments of infantry; Lord Wharton's, Lord Mandeville's, Colonel Cholmley's, and Colonel Charles Essex's, with Sir William Fairfax's in reserve. On the extreme flank were a few guns, with twenty-four troops of horse, commanded by Sir James Ramsay, a Scot. Ministers of the Word were seen riding along the ranks as they formed, exhorting the men to do their duty, and fight valiantly.‡

The action was commenced by the Parliament's guns, which

---

* George Baron Fielding, second son to William Earl of Denbigh, who likewise bore arms for the King, and was in the field as a volunteer that day. Basil Viscount Fielding, elder brother to George, had taken part with the Parliament, but was not with the army at Edge Hill.
† Sir Philip Warwick's Memoirs.   ‡ Viccars's Parl. Chron.

opened from their right flank, and were instantly answered by the whole park of the King's artillery from the centre; the cannonade continuing briskly for some time. The first charge was made by the King's cavalry from his left, which was repulsed; the musqueteers who supported them being also driven back to take refuge behind the second line of pikes. But, on the other wing, their success was very different. The Parliament's line had been weakened here, by extending itself to avoid being outflanked. And, at the commencement of the conflict on this part, Sir Faithful Fortescue, an Irishman, (very unworthy of either of his honourable names,) who commanded a squadron of the Parliament's horse, ordered his men to fire their pistols into the ground, and then galloped with them into Prince Rupert's lines; where, however, accident gave them the punishment they deserved: for, being mistaken for enemies by those to whom they were deserting, they received a fire which instantly laid twenty-five of them dead.*

And now Prince Rupert, charging with the whole of the cavalry of the King's right wing, broke through, and entirely routed, Sir James Ramsay's horse; who, enfeebled and dismayed, were making an irresolute attempt to gain the advantage of the hill. Even Colonel Essex's regiment, who had moved up to support them, also broke and fled. The battle, on that part, soon became a chase; though Essex did all that he could to rally the flying troops, and Holles and Ballard advanced gallantly from their right to cover their ground. The side of the hill, and, soon afterwards, the plain beneath it, were covered with nearly the whole of the Parliament's left wing in complete disorder, and Rupert's horse in close and unsparing pursuit. 'The Lord Mandeville's men,' says an eye witness, 'would not 'stand the field; though his Lordship beseeched, nay cudgelled, 'them. No, nor yet the Lord Wharton's men. Sir William 'Fairfax, his regiment, except some eighty of them, used their 'heeles.'† Nor did Cholmley's behave better. Cavalry endeavouring to force their flight through the infantry who were ordered to support them, the infantry scarcely better disposed to stand, but unable to fly before the rapid torrent of Rupert's charge,—all were in one confused mass, and not a face of a private soldier fronted that of his enemy, except Lord Brook's purple

---

* Clarendon—Hist. Reb. Mrs. Hutchinson's Memoirs.
† Speciall Newes from the Army at Warwicke since the fight; sent from a minister of good note. In Mr. Staunton's Collection.

coats, Colonel Ballard's grey coats, and Denzil Holles's gallant red coats, who, again opposed to superior numbers, and under the severer trial of witnessing the cowardice of their comrades, had nobly rushed across the advancing enemy. But the King's cavalry had already swept by with an impetuosity which infantry, forming hastily, and from a flank, could not withstand. But these brave regiments, though overborne, rallied, and at once engaged and checked the whole infantry of the King's right and centre. Meanwhile, the pursuit lasted across the open fields for three miles, up to Keinton itself, with tremendous slaughter. But here Rupert's triumph ended; and he incurred the reproach of allowing himself to be detained in an inglorious work of plunder for upwards of an hour, while the King's infantry was engaged, and worsted for lack of his support. The principal part of the baggage of the Parliament's army was lying in waggons in the streets of Keinton. Few were left to guard it, and the horses had been all moved forward to assist with the artillery, which was in action. The pillage of these now wholly fixed the attention of the Prince, who thus delayed his return to the battle, and gave his soldiers an example of insubordination which it was one of his most urgent duties to discountenance and repress.* The alarm was given to him, while thus employed, that the enemy was again forming, reinforced by fresh troops, on the outskirts of the town. The ground on which he rallied and drew up his cavalry to charge them again, is still known as ' Prince Rupert's ' Head-land,' and gives its name to a farm about a mile to the north-eastward of Keinton. But it was now too late. Hampden, who had left Stratford-on-Avon the evening before, had pushed on with Colonel Grantham's regiment, and his own green coats, and five guns, with which the men had, all night, toiled through the deep roads, leaving behind Colonel Barkham's and Lord Rochford's regiments to bring up the rest of the artillery and great store of ammunition, which did not arrive till the day after. And now the two regiments, led by Hampden, were seen hastening across the enclosures to support the mangled squadrons of flying horse. Dragging their guns out of the lanes along which they had advanced, they formed

---

* It is said of the Prince, that, on his return to the field of battle, finding the royal army in confusion, and the King himself in great danger, he told him that he 'could give a good account of the enemy's horse.' ' Ay, by G—d,' exclaimed a cavalier, ' and of their carts too !'

between the pursued and the pursuers, and opened their fire upon Rupert, killing several of his men and horses, and, though unable to pursue, obliging him, in his turn, to recross the plain in great confusion.

Rupert, on his return, found the King's battle wearing a very different aspect from that under which he had left it. Holles's, and Ballard's, and Brook's regiments, having made good the ground abandoned by the fugitives, had now poured in from the flank upon the main body of the King, which, at the same time, was charged in front by the rest of the Parliament's infantry, headed by the Earl of Essex in person. The gentlemen and officers of the cavalry, instead of flying with their men, had joined to strengthen the centre. And Colonel Charles Essex, having striven in vain to rally his craven regiment, returned to die bravely as a volunteer in more honourable company. He, and the Lord St. John, met their death in this charge.

The Lord-General's life-guard of gentlemen, to whom these gallant persons had joined themselves, first broke the King's guards, who were afterwards 'abundantly smitten down by the 'orange coats, by Sir William Constable's blue coats, the Lord 'Roberts's red coats, and the Lord Say's blue coats, led by Sir 'John Meldrum.' And the cavalry from the Parliament's right, under Balfore, Stapleton, and the Lord Willoughby of Parham, and composed of the troops of Hazlerigge, Lord Brook, Lord Grey, Gunter, Draper, Temple, Long, Fiennes, Luke, Cromwell, Hunt, and Urrey, now rushed in furiously. At this time was slain Sir Edmund Verney, and the royal standard, which he bore, was taken by Mr. Young, one of Sir William Constable's ensigns, and delivered by Lord Essex to his own secretary, Chambers, who rode by his side. Elated by the prize, the secretary rode about, more proudly than wisely, waving it round his head. Whereupon, in the confusion, one of the King's officers, Captain Smith of the Lord John Stewart's troop, seeing the standard captured, threw round him the orange scarf of a fallen Parliamentarian, and, riding in among the lines of his enemies, told the secretary that ' it 'were shame that so honourable a trophy of war should be 'borne by a penman.' To which suggestion the credulous guardian of this honourable trophy consenting surrendered it to the disguised cavalier, who galloped back with it amain, and, before evening, received knighthood under its shadow.

And now the royal army was so severely pressed in front and on its left, being menaced also on its right by a body of horse which had regained that rising ground from which Ramsay's brigade had, early in the fight, been driven, that Charles was vehemently importuned to leave the field. But this, his ardent courage, and the pledge which he had given to his troops, to abide with them for life or death, would not permit. He would have charged in person with his reserves of two regiments and his band of pensioners, were it not that his household officers withheld him. But now the evening was setting in, and, as the authorised narrative on the King's part says, the darkness made it difficult to distinguish friends from foes.* No one of the accounts published by authority on either side is throughout true, either as to the details, or as to the general result, of this famous battle. To believe them on both sides would be to conclude that an hour more of daylight would have blessed both armies with a sure and signal victory. The truth appears to be that both had already suffered too severely, and that the condition of each was too perilous, for either to be eager to renew the conflict. The King's officers were dismayed at the sudden and unexpected chance which had placed the safety of the whole army in hazard, after they had seen nearly one-half of the host of their enemies routed, and had firmly and surely believed the day to be already their own. Rupert's men and horses were too much fatigued for another charge. On the other side, what remained together of the Parliament's cavalry were weak in numbers, and equally spent with the exertion of a long march and a hard and doubtful contest, and with the effects of exposure for many nights to wet and cold. Moreover, they felt only the extent of their own disadvantage; they knew not that their enemy's plight was no less severe; and they looked with distrust towards the issue of another attack on the part of the more numerous, better-disciplined, and, perhaps, more confident, troops of the Prince. But the reinforcement of the two regiments had now come up with Hampden. Lord Essex saw that the higher ground was still in the King's hands. He called a council of his principal

---

* The account of the battle is taken from Clarendon, Viccars, Bulstrode, Warwick, Whitelocke, Heath's Chronicle, Ludlow's Memoirs, Charles Pym's and Nathaniel Fiennes's Letters, other published tracts and letters, principally in Mr. Staunton's collection, the Parliament's Diurnals, and the Oxford Intelligencers.

officers, and he listened mainly, as he had ever done, to the advice of the cautious Dalbier. A general who, during an unfinished battle, puts to a council the question of again advancing or not, may be presumed to have a leaning of opinion towards the less adventurous course. Resolute under difficulty and repulse, it was when success was to be improved that Essex was timid and indecisive. In vain did Hampden, Grantham, Holles, and Brook, urge him to renew the attack. Hampden was for instantly pressing forward, and endeavouring to force the King's position; and so to relieve Banbury, and throw himself at once on the contested line of the great London road. And Ludlow and Whitelocke assert, and Warwick and Clarendon confess, that if this course had been adopted, the King's condition might have become hazardous in the extreme.

Of the loss of men on either side no truth is to be gained from any of the authorised statements taken separately. According to one of the accounts sent to the Parliament, and published 'to prevent false informations,' the King lost in slain about three thousand, the Parliament three hundred. According to that which issued from the King's press at Oxford, the amount of the King's loss is doubtful, but, 'this 'is certain, that the royal army slew five Parliamentarians for 'every one slain of theirs.' To attempt to balance these would be misspent labour. The Parliamentarians seem to have lost rather more in private soldiers, the King certainly more in persons of distinction. Of these, besides Sir Edmund Verney, was slain the Lord Aubigny. Among a number of prisoners of note, the brave old General, Lord Lindsey, was taken, but mortally wounded. His son, the Lord Willoughby, in vain rushed to the rescue. He had only the sad comfort of performing the last filial duties. Lindsey died in the Lord-General's coach, on the way to Warwick Castle, under whose portcullis his corpse entered side by side with that of his youthful and gallant enemy, Charles Essex.*

* In the Appendix is subjoined a reprint of a scarce and curious tract in Mr. Staunton's collection. It is not altogether uninteresting to speculate on the causes and extent of human credulity, the more remarkable always when not excited by the conflicts of political or religious prejudice. The world abounds with histories of præternatural appearances the most utterly incredible, supported by testimony the most undeniable. Here is a ghost story of the most preposterous sort. Two great armies of ghosts, for the mere purpose, as it seems, of making night hideous to the innocent and

A tolerably correct judgment is to be formed of the conduct and issue of the Edge Hill fight, only by comparing together the conflicting accounts, which are abundant. On the whole, the fairest, and the most consistent with each other, and with probability, are Nathaniel Fiennes's, (which, written at the time, deserves credit for its moderation,) and Edmund Ludlow's and Sir Philip Warwick's, which have the best chance of being dispassionate, having been written many years after the event, and not, as it appears, in a spirit violently disposed to favour either party. Clarendon's, if compared with the others, or even with the map, will be found to be, in parts, extremely incorrect.

Seldom has ill success been left so nearly balanced between two conflicting armies after so great a battle, ' Victor uterque ' fuit, victus uterque fuit,' says Sir Richard Bulstrode. And, therefore, both returned solemn thanks to God as for a victory. Both lost guns, stores, and colours. The one remained master of the field of battle, and the other kept the London road, the gaining or retaining possession of which had been the only reasonable motive for fighting at all. And, eventually, both retreated; the one forgetting that the way to the metropolis was open to his enemy, and the other, before whom it was open, neglecting to march upon it. Of this neglect on the King's part there appears to be but one probable solution: of which hereafter.

In the original papers of James II., collected by Carte, it is

scared townsmen of Keinton, fighting over again the battle of Edge Hill, which had been decided, as far as their mortal efforts could decide it, more than two months before. Yet is this story attested upon the oath of three officers, men of honour and discretion, and of 'three other gentlemen of ' credit,' selected by the King as commissioners to report upon these prodigies, and to tranquillise and disabuse the alarms of a country town; adding, moreover, in confirmation, their testimony to the identity of several of the illustrious dead, as seen among the unearthly combatants who had been well known to them, and who had fallen in the battle. A well supported imposture, or a stormy night on the hill-side, might have acted on the weakness of a peasantry in whose remembrance the terrors of the Edge Hill fight were still fresh; but it is difficult to imagine how the minds of officers, sent there to correct the illusion, could have been so imposed upon. It will also be observed, that no inference is attempted by the witnesses to assist any notion of a judgment or warning favourable to the interests or passions of their own party. It is a pure inexplicable working of fancy upon the minds of shrewd and well-educated men, in support of ' the superstitions of timid and vulgar ones, who had, for several nights, been brought to consent to the same belief. For the story, see Appendix H. The solution of it must be left to the ingenuity of the reader.

thus stated. 'It was of fatal consequence that he did not 'march to London, which, in the fright, would not have cost 'him a stroke. Ruthven, the day after the battle, desired the 'King to send him with most of the horse and three thousand 'foot to London, where he would get before Essex, seize 'Westminster, drive away the rebel part of the Parliament, 'and maintain it till the King came up with the rest of the 'army. But this was opposed by the advice of many of the 'council. They were afraid that the King should return by 'conquest; and said so openly. They persuaded the King to 'advance so slowly to London, that Essex got there before 'him; and the Parliament, ready before to fly, took heart.' Of the King's officers, (besides the Lord Willoughby,) Colonels Lunsford, Vavasour, Stradling, Rodney, and Munro, were taken prisoners. The roads were covered with the wounded of both armies. 'It would be a charitable worke,' says 'a 'minister of good note,' in his letter to the Lord Mayor of London,* 'if some rich citizen would drop the silver oyle 'of his purse into the wounds of the sick and maimed 'souldiers who have soe freely hazarded theire lives for the 'gospell.'

The King marched back with a great part of his army, the evening after the battle, to the position from which he had that·day descended; and, from thence, further up, to the Wormleighton Hills, lying out, that night, in a hard and piercing frost. The main body of the Parliamentarians also retired from the bleak plain to the 'warmer quarter' of Keinton, but leaving a brigade of observation on the advanced position which they had won on the eastern extremity of the battle. 'This gave Essex,' says Sir Philip Warwick, 'a title 'unto the victory of that day.' On the next morning both armies remained for several hours opposed in order of battle, as if again to engage; but neither was disposed to begin the attack. Charles sent a flag of truce, borne by Clarencieux King at Arms, with a proclamation, dated 'from our Court on 'Edge Hill,' offering to Lord Essex, and to such of his army as should surrender, a free pardon. To this, the General, after strictly prohibiting the herald from tampering with the soldiers, returned for answer, that he should take the instructions of Parliament on his Majesty's gracious offer. About sunset,

* Mr. Staunton's Collection.

'for what reason,' says Ludlow, 'I know not,' and indeed without any apparent motive, he began a retreat on Warwick. Again Hampden interposed with a remonstrance, and strongly advised a rapid advance, to harass the retiring King, to restore the spirits of the midland counties, and save London. He volunteered to lead the advance himself, with his fresh and eager brigade. But Dalbier, in whom the methodical system of the German science was grafted upon what is supposed to be the characteristic caution of his native land, supported Essex's inclination to be content with the fame of a doubtful victory.

Had the King's position been forced, and his army in consequence driven to a precipitate retreat, it would have been extremely difficult for him to save even a remnant of his army. He had no point on which he could have safely retired. Oxford was wholly unfortified. Banbury lay in his way, with a garrison, which, though powerless against his army when together and unembarrassed with any other enemy, would have been a formidable obstacle to him in retreat; and the nearer he approached to London, the more unfriendly was the country through which he must have passed. The extreme west of England would have been the only secure refuge open to his troops; and so long a retreat, encumbered as he was with so much of the useless equipage of royal pomp, would have been difficult and hazardous.

His ministers and servants of state, with their followers of all sorts, above twelve hundred in number, accompanied him,—not bearing arms, but making larger demands for subsistence and conveniences than any number of military officers of the highest rank.

Sir William Dugdale was present in the action, as Norroy King at Arms, at the head of a numerous body of heralds, with each of whom was a retinue of pursuivants and horse-boys. The Prince of Wales and the Duke of York, then twelve and ten years old, were on the hill. They were placed under the care of Dr. William Harvey, afterwards so famous for his discoveries concerning the circulation of the blood, and then Physician in Ordinary to the King. During the action, forgetful both of his position and of his charge, and too sensible of the value of time to a philosophic mind to be cognisant of bodily danger, he took out a book, and sat him down on the grass to read, till, warned by the sound of the bullets that grazed and whistled round him, he rose, and withdrew the Princes to a securer distance.*

The first notice received in London of the Edge Hill fight was a very doubtful one. Beacons had been established along the line of communication between the Parliament and its army. In the alarm of the King's advance from Shrewsbury, Essex had received orders from the two Houses to give intelligence by firing the nearest beacon, whenever he might overtake the King and arrest his progress. The light by night, or the smoke by day, was to be the signal of his success in having brought the King to action, which the country people, on the different heights, up to London itself, were by proclamation directed to repeat. When the darkness had set in upon the hostile armies, and the fight was at an end, a small party of the Parliament's troops, who had gained the summit of the Beacon Hill, near Burton Dasset, gave the signal. Tradition says that some shepherds, on a part of the high ridge over Ivinghoe, on the borders of Buckinghamshire and Hertfordshire, and at a distance of at least thirty miles in a direct line from Edge Hill, saw a twinkling light to the northward, and, upon communication with their minister, a ' godly and well-affected person,' fired the beacon there also, which was seen at Harrow on the Hill, and from thence at once carried on to London; and that thus the news was given along a line of more than sixty miles, by the assistance of only two intermediate fires. But this mode of communication told the story very imperfectly, and most disastrous rumours soon followed. Fear is a fleet messenger. A party of the routed cavalry from the Parliament's left, contriving in the confusion to slip past the opposite flank of the King's army, fled forward through Banbury. They were accompanied by Ramsay, their commander, whose published defence delivered before a court-martial, (to the injury of his memory a very imperfect one,) is among the collection of broadsheets preserved in the British Museum.

These fugitives, offering in their haste and panic but a sorry sample of the condition of the Parliament's army, spread the news of an entire defeat as rapidly and as far as their own and their horses' speed would serve. This unhappy report that the battle was irretrievably lost reached London on the 24th,

---

* Aubrey's Letters and Lives of Eminent Men.

not many hours after the first intelligence by signal, of the encounter. It was not till the day after that Lord Wharton and Strode arrived at the doors of the two Houses where the Parliament was sitting; and almost at the same time came another official statement from Holles, Stapleton, Ballard, Balfore, Meldrum, and Charles Pym, to refresh the drooping confidence of the Parliament and the citizens with intelligence of a complete victory; modestly and well written, as to the account of the battle; but as to the claim of a victory, only one degree less untrue than the alarm had been of an entire defeat.

But the fact of the King being between Lord Essex's army and the metropolis was one which no 'special relation' had the power to disguise. The dismay of the citizens was intense. But their preparations for defence were rapid, vigorous, and resolute. The shops were shut up. The people thronged forth into the streets to close the barricades; everywhere the train-bands beat to arms, and mustered in Finsbury Fields, Hyde Park, and the village of Pancras, to take their orders to occupy the posts before their city, or to put themselves in march to oppose the King on his road. Directions the most positive were dispatched by repeated expresses to the Lord-General to endeavour, at all hazards, whether forcing his way by a second battle, or turning the King's flank by manœuvre, to throw himself across the main road, or, if that were impracticable, into London itself.*

Fortunately for the Parliament, the King's movements now became as disconnected and as dilatory as those of his adversary had been. He trifled away his time in taking and occupying several small places, such as Banbury and Broughton Castle, the last of which held out for a whole day with a garrison of only one troop of horse, and consumed another day in settling articles of capitulation; and after passing some few days more at Oxford, he moved onwards, resting his right flank, which was not menaced, on the Thames, and leaving his left, on which Essex was marching, uncovered, with two great roads open. It is impossible to believe that this could have been oversight. Charles himself had military talents of no mean order. He had begun to display them before the battle of Edge Hill, and he gave very decisive proofs of them in his conduct on many subsequent occasions during the war. He was besides

* Speciall Passages.

surrounded by experienced officers. The only probable mode of accounting for it must be by referring it to the political difficulties which were uppermost in the minds of some of his advisers. All who had interests of their own to serve with the adverse party, or terms to make with the King for such of their friends as had engaged themselves in it,—all who feared the lengths to which, in sudden and decisive success, the King might be led by passions which they had not influence enough over him to control; those too who vainly thought that a more reasonable accommodation might be come to by treaty while the issue of the war was yet in part uncertain; the timid and the temporising, were all alarmed at the prospect of their master obtaining at once the power of dictating peace upon his own terms.

Nor is it improbable that Falkland himself may have deprecated such success. For his well established favour with Charles was yet incapable of standing against such counsel as Rupert's or Digby's would have been, if given among such scenes as must have followed the triumphal entry into London, or the forcing of her defences by storm. This, indeed, is hinted intelligibly enough by several contemporary writers, among whom is Clarendon himself.

But whatever was the cause of Charles's conduct at this crisis, the energy and genius of Essex were roused equally by the reproaches of the Parliament and of some of his own officers, and by the inactivity of the King. He suddenly advanced upon Northampton, engaging the King's attention by threatening his flank with a detached force in the country about Brackly and Aynho; Hampden, and his friend and colleague Arthur Goodwyn, leading the advanced guard.

The Lieutenants of Buckinghamshire, who were raising and marshalling the volunteers of that county, received this letter from the Lord Wharton:*

'GENTLEMEN.—It greeues my heart thatt your County should
'be putt into soe g^t distraction. My L^{ds} haue considered of your
'letter, and are very desirous to doe any thing for the preseruation
'of your county. They conceaue itt most for the seruice of the
'county and the safety of yourselfes and the forces now raysed
'thatt you retire a little neerer to Uxbridge, which is appoynted to
'bee the rendezvous for a conuoy of g^t strength to bee sent downe

* Among Mr. Grenvil's papers.

'with diuerse things to my L^d of Essex; with which if you thinke
' good to fall in, and to joyne unto my L^d of Essex his army, the
' state will entertayne you, and allow such pay as all other officers
' and soldiers haue.

' My L^{ds} doe butt propound all this to your consideration, leauing
' you in euery part of itt to resolue of whatt you finde more fitt
' for your occasion to your owne judgement. I haue spouke to my
' L^d of Warwicke for some officers for you, and ame in hope to
' preuayle therein,

'I ame
' Your most affectionate frend
' to serve you,
' P. WHARTON.

' 30 *Octob.* 1642. LONDON.
' For Collonell Bullstrood and the
' rest of the deputy lieutennants
' of the county of Bucks
' att Amersham.'

During the march, Hampden wrote thus from Northampton to encourage them:

' To my noble friends, Colonel Bulstrode, Captain Grenvil, Captain
' Tyrell, Captain West, or any of them.

' GENTLEMEN.—The army is now at Northampton, moving
' every day nearer to you. If you disband not, we may be a
' mutual succour to each other; but if you disperse, you make
' yourselves and your country a prey.
' You shall hear daily from
' Your servant,
' JOHN HAMPDEN.

' NORTHAMPTON, *Oct.* 31.'

' I wrote this enclosed letter yesterday, and thought it would
' have come to you then; but the messenger had occasion to stay
' till this morning. We cannot be ready to march till to-morrow;
' and then, I believe, we shall. I desire you will be pleased to send
' to me again, as soon as you can, to the army, that we may know
' what posture you are in, and then you will hear which way we go.
' You shall do me a favour to certify me what you hear of the
' King's forces; for I believe your intelligence is better from Oxford
' and those parts than ours can be.
' Your humble servant,
' JOHN HAMPDEN.

' NORTHAMPTON, *Nov.* 1, 1642.'

One of Mr. Grenvil's informants, just returned from

Oxford, where he had lately witnessed, with some discomfort, the execution of a spy, writes to him thus:

'Right Wor^{full}.—Upon the motion of your man Cherry, I give
'you to understand that I, beinge at Oxon, 9^{ber} 2^d, warned by a
'warrant from his Matie amongst all ministers, freeholders, trades-
'men, and men of estate in Oxon shire, sawe his Matie sitting in
'Christ chch hall; prince Robert was gone before to Abingdon with
'510 men. The Kinge intends for London wth all speede. Redinge
'must be inhumanly plundered. One Blake, or Blakewell, I know
'not whether, was this day hanged, drawen, and quartered, in
'Oxon, for rec^g 50^{lb} a weeke from ye Parl^t for intelligence, he
'beinge Priuy Chamberlayne to Prince Robt. Wee were in Oxon
'streets under pole-axes, the cavaliers soe out-braved it. The K'^s
'horse are their, with 7000 dragooners. The foote I knowe not,
'saue that Colonell Salisbury, (my countryman,) hath 1200 poore
'Welch vermins, the offscowringe of the nation. Dr. Hood
'remembers his best respects to you; * but groanes for rent. He
'is much afraid of your safety. He prayes for you. Oxonshire
'was sent for to contribute to his Maties necessity. Little helpe
'(God knowes). They pillage extreamely about Oxon. Whole
'teames taken away, euen of ye E. of - - - -'s man Bigge of
'Staunton. Soe much happines to your wors^p, as to
                    'Your oblidged seruant,
                                'ROB. EVANS.
'WOOTTON, 9^{ber} 3rd, 1642.
'To the Right Wor^{full} Rich. Grenvil,
  'Esq., High Sheriffe of Bucks,
  'these present.'

On the day on which Hampden's letter was written to the Buckinghamshire Lieutenancy, encouraging them with the assurance of speedy support, and exhorting them to hold out manfully for the defence of their county until the succour should arrive, a severe skirmish took place at Aylesbury, in which a part of his own regiment and Colonel Grantham's, supported by six troops of horse under Sir William Balfore, repulsed a very superior force led by Prince Rupert in person. Strong parties had been sent forth from Banbury and Oxford to collect forage and drive in cattle for the King's army, to watch the march of Essex's army, to hover on his flank, and hinder his communications with the metropolis. The small garrison of

---

* Warden of New College. Mr. Grenvil held some large farms, near Wotton, under that college.

new-raised militia at Aylesbury had been moved to some quarter which was more closely threatened; and the town, and the rich pastures of the vale which surrounds it, were left unprotected. Thither Prince Rupert marched with a force of some thousands of horse and foot, and, after some days passed in securing for the King's use much of the produce of the vale, and despoiling and laying waste much more than he secured, entered and possessed himself of the town. Here, after one day more of free-quarter in Aylesbury, during which the inhabitants were made to suffer all sorts of outrage from his soldiers, he received intelligence of the approach of a brigade of the Parliament's troops from Stony Stratford. Rupert, probably afraid of attempting a defence within the walls of a place, however well adapted by its situation for defence, where the townsmen were all his enemies, and having in his front a country over which his cavalry could act with great advantage, left there but a troop of horse and two companies of foot, and marched out with all the rest of his force to meet the advancing enemy. But he had not gone farther than the brook about half-a-mile to the northward of the town, where there was then no passage but a bad ford, swollen by the rains, when he found himself checked by Balfore's horse and foot, in column, on the opposite bank. After the first volley or two, Rupert charged across the ford, and breaking through Balfore's two first lines of infantry, plunged into the centre of his horse, who were flanked on the right by Charles Pym's troop. And here a sharp and desperate conflict began. Sir Lewis Dives came up with the Prince's reserve, and Captain Herbert Blanchard with Balfore's; the musketry of the foot, the carbines and petronels of the cavalry, swords, and pole-axes, all doing the work of death, and the soldiers of all arms mixed and fighting in one close and furious throng. It lasted thus but a few minutes. The King's troops were driven back across the stream, and Rupert rallied on the other side, only to lose more men from the fire, and to receive a charge in return, which drove him back in confusion towards the town. In vain did the troops hurry down to his support. The townsmen rushed forth upon their rear, with whatever arms haste and fury could supply to them, and Rupert began his retreat towards Thame, before the mingled troops and populace, who, however, after slaughtering the hindmost for above a mile, did not venture further to pursue among the enclosures a force still superior to their own. In this action some hundreds of Rupert's men fell, and of the Parliamentarians above ninety, according to the confession of the report published in London.*

In a letter from Woburn on the 4th of November, the Lord-General desired the Deputy-Lieutenants of Buckinghamshire to march all their train-bands, horse and foot, to St. Albans, to join his army there on the next day, promising protection if the King should traverse their county, but calling upon them to strengthen his force for the defence of London, if his march should be pursued in that direction.†

It was soon evident, however, that London was the King's object. The advanced guard, under Prince Rupert, was quartered at Maidenhead, and a strong picket at Colnbrook. With all dispatch, therefore, Lord Essex proceeded to the metropolis, which he entered two days after. There he was received with every mark of gratitude and honour, the thanks of the two Houses being voted to him, and a sum of £5,000, in testimony of approbation of his conduct at Edge Hill.‡

Holles, with his regiment, was quartered at Brentford, and Hampden in the neighbourhood of Uxbridge. Meanwhile, two ships of war were brought up the Thames as high as the bridge, and a division of gun-boats moored off Westminster.§

And now the Houses voted that the Earls of Northumberland and Pembroke, and four members of the Commons, should act as commissioners to treat with the King for peace.

On the morning of Thursday the 10th of November, the commissioners set forth, and, at Colnbrook, were met by Sir Peter Killegrew, with news that the King was on horseback coming into the town with his artillery from Maidenhead. In Colnbrook they waited to receive him. Having read the petition the King bespoke them courteously. He said that they could not expect a present answer to a petition of so great importance; yet that he would deliver it in part the next day,

---

* Good and joyfull newes out of Buckinghamshire—Dr. Mundell's Letter. Some of the remains of this skirmish were discovered, a few years ago, by the labourers who were digging pits for gravel, in a field at Holman's Bridge, near the old ford. More than two hundred skeletons were found buried in the small space which was opened; among which, many appeared, from the manner in which they were laid, to have been those of officers. [Lord Nugent might have added, that by his care these remains of so many gallant Englishmen were transferred to a grave in Hardwicke church-yard, where a suitable tomb, with a touching inscription written by himself, was placed over them.]

† Mr. Grenvil's papers.   ‡ Speciall Passages.   § Ibid.

and send it by a special messenger to Parliament. On Friday morning, both Houses met, and, having received the report of their commissioners, resolved to sit that afternoon to await the signification of his Majesty's further pleasure. The promised message arrived not, but, instead, reports of hasty warrants by the King, violently enforced, requiring the inhabitants of the country round Maidenhead instantly to supply means of transport for guns and stores, and horses for a remount to his cavalry. On Saturday, however, the answer was brought by the Earl of Northumberland, in which the King called God to witness his great desire of peace, and, in order to avoid further blood-shedding, offered to treat at Windsor, or wherever else he might be. This was received with great demonstrations of joy. It was considered as no less than saving London from the attempt of an infuriated army to carry it by storm, and as a sure earnest of the King's disposition to grant fair terms of peace. But, on that very morning, while the King's answer was before the Houses, he was in full march to the execution of a foul and cruel act of treachery. He marched during a treaty, and while the other party were actually reading his message of readiness to listen to terms of peace. Vainly does Clarendon essay to clear Charles of this ineffaceable charge. He states him to have sent, some days after, a vindication of himself in a message to Parliament, in which he told them of the ' Earl of Essex's
' drawing out his forces towards him, and possessing those
' quarters about him, and almost hemming him in after the
' time that the Commissioners were sent to him with the
' Petition.' * But Clarendon himself shows that this advance of Essex's, with which, by a confusion of dates, the King artfully reproaches the Parliament, took place after the attack had been made on the Parliament's quarters at Brentford; and he moreover admits that ' the Houses were so well satisfied
' with the answer their committee had brought from the
' King, and with their report of his Majesty's clemency and
' gracious reception of them, that they had sent order to their
' forces "that they should not exercise any act of hostility
' towards the King's forces;" and at the same time despatched
' a messenger to acquaint his Majesty therewith, and to
' desire " that there might be the like forbearance on his
' part." ' †

* Clarendon—Hist. Reb. † Ibid.

At day-break, the morning being unusually misty, and the Parliament's pickets reposing under the security of a flag of truce which had passed their lines, eight regiments of the King's foot, and twenty troops of horse, with six guns, were dispatched from Colnbrook to Sion, and, finding only Holles's regiment in the town of Brentford, broke in upon their quarters. For three hours the fight was maintained by this small unsupported force, occupying the houses and disputing each street; until Brook and Hampden came in from their cantonments to the sound of the firing. The contest became more general, though still against fearful odds. Five times did Brook and Hampden charge the streets, to endeavour to open a retreat for this brave and suffering regiment who had so desperately maintained themselves. But the King's troops, having, in part, made good their advance through the town, now invested it, attacking on all sides with horse, foot, and artillery. No hope remained but to hold out till succour might arrive from London. Towards evening, Lord Essex was seen advancing from that direction with the train-bands of the City in brave array, having received the news of the struggle which was going on as they were assembled for exercise in Chelsea Fields. Still, the brigade under the Parliamentary colonels within the town remained surrounded. They maintained the fight in the streets, having held the post obstinately till the arrival of Essex; and now oppressed by numbers, and their ammunition spent, the remnant of this gallant little force threw themselves into the Thames, where many were drowned; but the greater part were enabled, some by the help of boats and barges, and some by swimming down the stream, to rejoin their friends, who covered the bank. Supported by the Earl and the train-bands, they again advanced, and in sufficient strength to beat the King's troops through the town, who had occupied it for some hours, and to pursue them for several miles in the dark, as long as they could see the glimmer of the matches.*

During this action, the King was at Hounslow, sending orders to his regiments, from time to time, to push on at all risks, and without delay, to London.†

---

* Speciall Passages. England's Memorable Accidents. Clarendon—Hist. Reb. Ludlow's Mem. Mrs. Hutchinson.

† In this action, John Lilburne was taken, among other prisoners, by the King, and being removed to Oxford, was tried before Judge Heath for his life. The manner of his defence of himself at law upon his trial, was

On the next morning the whole army of the Parliament, having arrived from London, joined their train-bands and other troops who had been engaged the evening before, and took up their ground on Turnham Green, in force about twenty-four thousand horse and foot. Orders were given that two regiments of horse, and four of foot, should march by Acton and Osterley Park towards Hounslow to the rear of the King's army, which had now moved from its different quarters about Kingston, and was drawn up on the heaths; while Essex, with the three great divisions that remained, was to attack them in front.

Hampden was detached to lead the van of the infantry, next to the horse. But he had not proceeded above a mile, when, in consequence of one of those changes of counsel so often fatal to Essex's success in the moment of advantage, the whole plan was abandoned, and Hampden was recalled.

The troops remained under arms for many hours, facing the King's lines, and occasionally advancing towards them. While the general was debating in another council of war whether he should fall on, the King drew off his ordnance and tumbrils, and began to retire. Lord Essex, (whether it was owing to his besetting vice of over-caution when rapid and resolute action was required, or whether he was deceived by false information respecting those troops of the King who had been on the Surrey side the day before,) had sent three thousand men across a bridge of boats between Battersea and Fulham to dislodge the cavaliers, after they had already passed over at Kingston to join their main army.*

Thus weakened, and made aware of his mistake by the increasing length of the lines opposed to him, he paused. The Earl of Holland, a man of neither courage nor fidelity, busied himself at this moment to work upon Lord Essex's irresolution, exaggerating to him the amount of the King's force, and advising him not to fight until the wing which had crossed the river should return. Dalbier again was at his side. Again Hampden's urgent remonstrance was over-ruled. Skippon, who, at the head of his London train-bands, and jealous of

in accordance with his deportment on other occasions. It was resolute and fearless. But his death was resolved upon, till delayed by a message from Lord Essex, who threatened the execution of three prisoners in the hands of the Parliament, for every one of the Parliament's officers executed by the King.

* Speciall Passages, &c. from 8th to 15th November.

their fame, thirsted for the occasion of leading them forward, now to their first encounter, joined eagerly with Hampden in imploring Essex at once to rush on upon the King, and, if they should fail to rout him at the first onset, to hang upon his march to enter every town in action with his rear guard, and not to quit him till they had destroyed his army, and thus brought the war to a conclusion, or at least had so weakened him as to put beyond question his further projects for that winter. Instead of this, not a blow was struck. For the second time, the great occasion of decisive success was lost; and the King was allowed, unmolested, to retreat on Colnbrook, and having passed two days at Hampton Court, from thence, by the way of Reading, to Oxford.*

* Whitelocke's Memorials. Warwick's and Ludlow's Memoirs. Perfect Diurnal. Continuation of Speciall and Remarkable Occurrences. England's Memorable Accidents. Mrs. Hutchinson's Memoirs. Clarendon—Hist. Reb.

PART THE TENTH.

FROM 1642 TO 1643.

Hampden and Urrie take Reading by assault—Hampden arranges the plan of union of the six associated counties—Parliament's troops press upon the King's quarters at Oxford—Lord Wentworth attacks High Wycombe, and is repulsed—Essex retires—King's successes in divers parts—Queen lands in England—Reading re-entered by the King's troops—Hampden and Mr. Richard Grenvil repulsed from Brill—Sir Bevill Grenvil in Cornwall—Bradock Down, and Stratton Hill—Lansdown—Trelawney's letter to the Lady Grace Grenvil, announcing Sir Bevill's death—Siege of Lichfield—Lord Brook slain—Warder Castle twice taken—Overtures of peace, and cessation of arms—Broken off—Reading besieged by Lord Essex—Surrenders—Defections from the Parliament's cause—Waller's Plot—Rupert's expeditions against the Parliament's quarters—Attacks Chinnor and Postcombe—Chalgrove fight—Hampden wounded—His last moments and death—Conclusion of the Memorials.

THE King had failed in his attempt to seize the metropolis while a treaty was pending. This act had exasperated and united against him those in London who had been divided, disheartened and reduced to ask for peace upon almost any terms that might secure their city from assault and plunder. The contributions had begun to come in slowly from the city, and the army were clamouring for pay. A new levy of customs had been made, and Lord Brook, Lord Say, and Sir Harry Vane, had been deputed to meet the citizens in Guildhall. They had urged with all their eloquence and power, enforced with all the topics which the necessity of the times suggested, a speedy and vigorous supply. But the propositions had been coldly received. Great meetings of idlers, under the name of 'the Apprentices,' had been called together, in Covent Garden and other open spaces, to petition the

Houses for peace and accommodation, and symptoms of tumult had appeared among the soldiers assembling at the Globe Tavern and divers other places of public resort, which it required the presence of some of the most popular of the leaders to allay. But the general cry of perfidy against the King now reconciled all differences and armed all spirits to improve the late advantage. Even his friends endeavoured but faintly and confusedly to apologise for the circumstances of his late enterprise. Success sometimes covers over the iniquity of an act, which, in failure only, is branded with appropriate disgrace; and, against the exultations of a triumphant party, the reproach of bad faith can seldom gain an attentive or patient hearing. But Charles's retreat was as inglorious as his advance had been morally shameful. Yet, through the criminal indecision of Essex, the repulse of the King became as little signal, and the result of it substantially as little beneficial to the Parliament, as, under the circumstances, it could be. He who had been the 'darling of the sword-men' still maintained all that frankness of manner with the soldiers which, joined to personal bravery, makes a leader beloved of them. He had, besides, the nobler quality of a quick and lofty sense of military honour. But his weak fondness for hereditary distinction, ill-disguised in converse with his equals; his cautious reserve on all points relating to the great principles of that cause, on which he had entered rather, as was suspected, from disappointed ambition than from any attachment to popular doctrines; and his frigid reluctance at all times to seize the fruits of prosperity, so as to turn them to instant and important account; began to disgust the principal persons both in the Parliament and in the army, and to make it seen that he was but an ineffective champion in a revolutionary conflict. Distrustful of the consequences, even before the achievement was complete, and alarmed as much at the decisive character of the persons with whom, as of the times in which he had to act, his first care always was to control rather than advance the tide of success, and his besetting fear was that of doing too much. This was continually and fatally inclining him to secret compromises, which, in the end, made him well nigh faithless to the cause with which he was entrusted, because he had undertaken it without reconciling himself to all that it might in its course demand. His example chilled the spirit of his troops, and disturbed the cordiality of their leaders. He saw not the necessity of exciting in his ranks an enthusiasm which might cope with the chivalrous sentiment cultivated throughout those of the King, and the constitution of the Parliamentary army became justly liable to the criticism passed upon it by Cromwell in conversation with Hampden.* Hampden's duty in the field was to obey.—It was mortifying to his genius. But his modesty and public virtue rendered, in his mind, the dangers of disunion paramount over all other dangers. He sometimes remonstrated, but, when overruled, always did his best to make even those counsels prosper which he disapproved. His conduct in detached command ever formed a striking contrast with that of his dilatory chief. This was a practical reproach which Hampden could not spare him. Hampden was ever prompt, and, generally, successful.

After the King's retreat, Essex, by order of the Parliament, advanced upon Windsor, and, crossing the Thames at Marlow, drove Rupert out of that town and Henley. He placed a garrison in both, and made good the whole country on the right bank of the Thames. Hampden had pressed forward with his own brigade to Reading; and a small body of cavalry had been sent from Henley, under Urrie, to second him. With this reinforcement, he endeavoured to place himself between Prince Rupert and Oxford. The Prince, however, on his approach, to avoid being cut off, hastened his own retreat, leaving all the baggage of his division in Reading, with a garrison of about fifteen hundred men, commanded by Colonel Lewis Kirke, the father of him who, in after times, was so infamously notorious for his cruelties in the west of England. Reading had been, about a month before, abandoned to the King's troops, in a manner not very reputable, by Henry Marten. It was a place of importance to an army advancing either towards or from London, being capable of holding a large garrison, and having four roads open to it. Upon this town Hampden marched, having captured some straggling parties of the cavaliers; and, sitting down before it, opened trenches, and threw up a redoubt, on the rising ground to the north-west. He then sent in a gentleman of quality, with a flag of truce and a trumpet, offering as terms an entire indemnity to all who were not included in the Parliament's proclamation, with full liberty to depart when the town should have

---

* See Burton's Diary, Appendix, vol. ii., p. 501, 2.

surrendered. To this an arrogant answer was returned by Kirke.* He confided not a little in Hampden's reluctance to open batteries upon a town full of inhabitants who were generally well affected to the Parliamentary cause, and some of whom probably were connected in friendly habits with the neighbouring family of the Vachells of Coley. Accordingly, though commanding a view of almost every street, Hampden fired few shot into the town, except what were necessary to cover his approaches within a distance at which he might drive the troops from the walls with musquetry. Kirke, in the meanwhile, pressed the town's people to serve, not only in working parties, but also in the defence. On the second night, he attempted several sallies to destroy the Parliament's works, but was repulsed at each time with loss. At day-break on the third morning, Hampden and Urrie seeing all quiet within, and judging the garrison to be fatigued and dispirited with the unsuccessful enterprises of the night, determined to try if, with some companies of their best and most resolute soldiers, they could force and carry the walls by assault. In the grey twilight of the morning, advancing silently from the trenches with four hundred chosen men, Hampden passed the outer and second ditch, and, mounting the rampart, threw himself into the northernmost bastion. The townsmen, who formed part of the guard, at once laid down their arms; but the regular troops, falling back upon the second line of batteries, though hotly pursued, were well supported by the main garrison of the place, and made a stout stand. ·Here the success of the attack became very doubtful; the cavaliers rallying bravely, and beating back the assailants into the ditches, where, scattering grenades among them, a fearful slaughter began. But Hampden, calling forward the reserves, placed himself at the head of a second attack, and, again struggling up the walls with fresh men, renewed the fight on the crest of the main work. It was then that, Kirke drawing out nearly the whole garrison from the body of the place, the conflict came to push of pike, chief to chief, each at the head of his party. and each cheering his men by his presence and example. Several of the officers on both sides rushing to the front were slain, and Hampden could not long have maintained himself

---

* A true relation of the proceedings of His Excellency the Earl of Essex, with the taking of Reading by Colonel Hampden and Colonel Hurry.—King's Collection. Brit. Mus.

against the superior force now crowding out upon him, and supported by the fire from the body of the place, had not Urrie, who had been detached to the right, pushed between the cavaliers and the town. Instantly the inhabitants within ceased their fire. It was not till after four hour's fighting, and till above four hundred of the garrison had been laid dead, and the Parliamentarians had planted their ensigns on the top of the work, that Colonel Kirke abandoned the defence. Escaping with a few of his followers through a sally-port on the left into the town, he got to his horses, and fled to Oxford, leaving Hampden master of Reading, the stores and baggage which had been left there, and a great number of prisoners.*

Meanwhile Lord Essex, who remained at Henley, had sent some forces from Kingston-upon-Thames to make head against the Cavaliers' levies in Sussex, which, under Lord Thanet and the high sheriff, Ford, were committing great havoc in that county. They were advancing upon Lewes, between which town and Cuckfield, on Hawood Heath, they were met by the Parliament's detachments, defeated, and beaten back upon Chichester, which was fortified, and held for the King.

The King's garrison of Farnham Castle, commanded by Sir John Denham, was also attacked and reduced, after a very slight and bad defence, and little loss on the Parliament's side, excepting that of Colonel Fane, son to the Earl of Westmorland, who was shot through the cheek, and died a few days after. Sir John Denham was more eminent as poet, gamester, and wit, than soldier. When George Wither was, shortly after this time, brought prisoner to Oxford, and was in some jeopardy, having been taken in arms against the King, Sir John Denham begged the King not to hang him, for that ' while Wither lives, Denham will not be the worst poet in ' England.'† This good-natured epigram contributed to save Wither's life, and was afterwards also the means of restoring to Denham some of his property in Surrey, which had been confiscated by Parliament and given to Wither. But it would be unfair to refer a kind and gentle act to an interested motive.

These were not the only successes now obtained by the detachments of the Parliament's army in the midland districts of England. The King had scarcely established his head

---

* A True Relation, &c. Kingdom's Weekly Intelligencer.
† Wood.—Ath. Oxon.

quarters at Oxford when Prince Rupert resumed his incursions on the country between that city and the Parliament's lines. Hampden was almost daily on the road between the advanced posts of the army and London. With prodigious activity did he appear fulfilling at almost the same time the double duties of command in the field, and counsel in the Close Committee; reporting to the House on the state of the army from the head quarters, and of the nation from the Committee; and then, without stay of time or purpose, posting down to take command of his brigade in action, or to strengthen the garrison of some menaced town.* Nor were these the sum of his various, unceasing, and important labours. From Aylesbury he began to form the union of the six associated midland counties of Bucks, Hertford, Bedford, Huntingdon, Cambridge, and Northampton. He conducted the correspondence, he arranged the details, he allayed the jealousies, which beset the first formation of a plan in conformity with which different districts, threatened by one common danger, yet unaccustomed to act under one common chief, were called upon to contribute out of a common fund of money and men to each other's necessities, when each felt only its own weakness and poverty. In concert with Lord Say and Lord Kimbolton, he gradually brought all the materials which these counties could separately supply, to act as one compacted machine, full of vigour and alacrity. He lived not indeed to see this engine working with all the power which belonged to it; but, before his death, it began to be adopted as a model in other parts of England, and, afterwards, furnished Cromwell with the means which his great genius and energy made successful.

Lord Essex, meanwhile, strongly urged by messages from the two Houses, proceeded, though slowly, towards the great object of the war. On the 5th of December, he put the main body of his army in motion, with the design of investing

---

* See Perfect Diurnal, Sept. 12, 19, 26.—Oct. 3. Nov. 16, 28. Dec. 5. Continuation of certain Speciall and Remarkable Passages. &c. Nov. 23. Dec. 8, 15. Denham thus describes it, in his lampoon on Hampden, entitled 'A Speech Against Peace, at the Close Committee.'

> ' Have I so often passed between
> ' Windsor and Westminster, unseen,
> ' And did myself divide,
> ' To keep His Excellency in awe,
> ' And give the Parliament the law?
> ' For they knew none beside.'

Oxford. This had never been a favourite enterprise of his own, nor is it probable that he would have undertaken it now, had he not known that an impression of his inactivity was daily sinking deeper into the minds of the army and of the Parliament. Hampden's influence in the Close Committee, which in truth had the supreme direction of the war, made his position with Lord Essex, under whom he was acting as a colonel in the field, one of great difficulty. His advice, from the beginning of the King's retreat, had always been, as we have seen, the bolder one of an instant advance upon Oxford, in order to bring the King to terms which he should afterwards have neither the temptation nor power to break through. Peremptory directions were now sent to the Lord General to make a forward movement. He could no longer find a pretext for remaining on his ground in the south of Berkshire and Buckinghamshire, when the country was open before him. . He therefore chose the least enterprising course which was allowed him. He determined to narrow his distance from Oxford, and to begin the forms of a regular investment, when he ought to have marched his army into the town. On his advance, he had a successful skirmish at Stoken Church with a brigade of the King's troops, who retired before him; and, a few days after, having fortified Tedstock, about ten miles from Oxford, he sent forward Arthur Goodwyn with his regiment of foot and five troops of horse to possess themselves of Abingdon, where they lay within a mile of the advanced pickets of the King. Meanwhile, Sir John Meldrum and Colonel Langham, with their two regiments of infantry, seven troops of horse, and nine heavy guns and four small drakes, had passed by the westward without opposition beyond Oxford, and had entrenched themselves near Woodstock. The country to the eastward alone remained open to the operations of the King's troops. To be tempted into action with the Parliamentarians on either of the other two sides might have weakened the King's powers too much by dividing them, and would have taken them away from the main object of London. It would besides have left Oxford exposed to a sudden assault from any one of the small parties which had now approached so near on three sides. Something it was necessary that the King should do to prevent the investment from becoming complete. He conceived the project of turning the whole of Essex's right flank, and again throwing a body of troops in the rear of it upon the eastern road to London. Prince Rupert was sent to besiege Cirencester, in order to prevent the Parliament's garrison there from interfering with this enterprise. A strong body of horse, near five thousand, with artillery, now proceeded, under the command of the young Lord Wentworth, Lord Strafford's son, by the way of Thame, to menace Aylesbury and Wycombe. The King had forces on the Cambridgeshire and Bedfordshire side who were to overrun those counties, and so possess themselves of the Hertfordshire road. But the Association had been active in Cambridgeshire. They had collected their levies with great rapidity upon these points, and appeared in such force, that to attack them would have materially delayed the King's object, and to leave them in the rear would have been unsafe. The detachments which had moved into Hertfordshire had no better success. They were checked at Watford; and, finding themselves opposed in front, and threatened on their right by the militias of the six counties, they were fain to retreat by the same road along which they had advanced.*

Wentworth made a more promising attempt. Finding Aylesbury well fortified to the northward and westward by strong batteries, and to the east by a redoubt on the rising ground towards Bierton, and not wishing to waste time in a siege, he suddenly left it, moving rapidly by the lanes across the Chilterns, and coming down through the Woodlands upon Wycombe.

There he took post on the two high hills towards the side of Wycombe Heath and the Penn Woods. To such as know the appearance of Wycombe from either of those heights it would seem that the assailants would not have required artillery, nay, hardly more than the fire-arms of the dragoons, to render it untenable. But Lord Wentworth 'sounded his 'trumpets and made a glorious show,' and then, descending into the valley, endeavoured to enter the town from the side of the Rye. Here he was taken in flank by about four thousand pike-men, volunteers raised in the neighbourhood, and opposed in front by the small garrison of regular troops commanded by Captain Hayes, who were supported by some guns. After several hours' fighting, Lord Wentworth retired, himself wounded, having lost near nine hundred of his men,

* Speciall Passages.

and with no other success than the having slain about three hundred of the Parliamentarians.*

The purpose of these enterprises having failed, and Lord Essex having now so nearly succeeded in investing Oxford, Charles was urgently advised by some to betake himself to the North; the rather, as his army in those parts, now hard pressed by the Fairfaxes and Hothams, might receive countenance from their sovereign's presence, and that he, by a personal view of their necessities, might be induced to spare to them, from his magazines in the South, supplies of ammunition and other stores, which, by the vigilance of Lord Warwick's cruisers, they had failed to obtain from abroad. These supplies, timely obtained, might, it was hoped, enable them to reduce Hull and convert it into an important place of arms for his service. The Earl of Essex being made aware of this intention, instantly dispatched orders to the forces in the Committees of Northampton, Warwick, Derby, and the neighbourhood of Worcester, and to Lord Stamford in Hertfordshire, to collect with all possible speed all their strength, to intercept the King's progress to the North, and to oppose Lord Digby, who was marching to the Westward in great force for the purpose of diverting them from watching the King. Lord Essex also set forward with an advanced guard of infantry and artillery, now near Oxford, in pursuit. Thus prosperously looked the affairs of the Parliament in this quarter, when a sudden combination of active and successful movements in various parts of England, assisted by other circumstances of good fortune, turned the whole aspect of the campaign in favour of the King, and closed that year with giving him a very decisive advantage. Cirencester was taken by Prince Rupert, who committed the most dreadful severities, putting a great part of the garrison and numbers of the townspeople to the sword. ' It yielded,' says Clarendon, 'much ' plunder, from which the undistinguishing soldier could not ' be kept, but was equally injurious to friend and foe;' so that many who had been imprisoned by the Parliament, ' found ' themselves at liberty, and undone, together.' Rupert, instantly after, scoured the borders of North Wales, giving support and confidence to the King's friends in those districts,

---

* Captain Hayes's and Goodwyn's Letters.—A most glorious and happy victory obtained of the Lord Wentworth by the Buckingham &c. Volunteers, 7th December, 1642. King's Collect. Brit. Mus.

and receiving only a slight check at Gloucester, where he was stopped and beaten off by the gallantry of General Massey.

The Queen had about this time arrived from Holland, making good her landing at Burlington, though pursued by the Parliament's fleet. She brought three ships laden with ammunition, arms, and stores of all sorts, and a large sum of money, which, together, enabled the Earl of Newcastle to put into activity the powers of an association which he had formed for the King in the four northern counties, and to which he now gave the name of the Queen's army. Thus supported and reinforced he cleared the whole country to the north of the Humber, and laid siege to Hull. A great body of the principal gentry of the West had now taken the field in the King's behalf, supported by a numerous army, and opposed only by General Ruthen and General James Chudleigh, who had to carry on the operations of the campaign in a district the people of which were generally hostile to the Parliament's cause. Exeter was besieged by Hopton and Sir Bevill Grenvil, who, though more than once repulsed, ceased not to threaten that city, and impede the supplies coming up to it from the sea.

Marlborough also was entered, and held by a powerful garrison under the Lords Wilmot, Grandison, and Digby.

These advantages on the King's part were scarcely counterbalanced by the taking of Winchester, Hereford, and Monmouth, by Sir William Waller, and shortly after, of Leeds, by Sir Thomas Fairfax, who also, in the course of the next month, gave the Earl of Newcastle a signal defeat at Wakefield.*

The Earl of Essex saw the necessity of detaching a part of his own army to succour the cause in the West, and Prince Rupert was now on his return to strengthen that of the King. Instead, then, of the long and often demanded attack on Oxford (for which all things were ripe, and which could hardly have failed in the execution, and the success of which would have probably gone near to end the war), the Lord General preferred to concentrate his force by abandoning that neighbourhood and drawing nearer to London.

Oxford could not have withstood a two days' siege. Besides the natural disadvantages of its position, its inhabitants, though loud for the King while he was present and the

---

* Heath's Chronicle.

enemy at a distance, were not to be depended on. The University, during the advance of the Parliament's army upon Worcester, in the preceding autumn, had petitioned the Earl of Pembroke, their Chancellor, for his protection; to which a scornful answer had been returned by the Earl, telling the Vice-Chancellor, that the open course of hostility which that body had adopted against the authority of Parliament, not only by the raising of supplies of plate and money for the King, but by enrolling the gownsmen in troops, had deprived them of all claim to favour, except such as the laws of war granted to garrisons submitting at discretion. Lord Say and Hampden, however, on their entry, had not

'Lifted their spear against the Muses' bower.'

Oxford had not been subject to plunder or to any of the other extremities of war.

Reading was now for the second time abandoned to be garrisoned for the King, and Maidenhead became an advanced post of the Parliament's army, again reduced to a defensive position before London.

In this posture were the two armies at the beginning of 1643. Proposals of peace were again voted by Parliament; but they were still grounded upon the assumption that the King had, under the control of evil advisers, levied war upon his Parliament, and the basis of accommmodation was the stipulation that he should return to London. A cessation of arms, however, was agreed to, during which commissioners might meet to negotiate terms. But hitherto the various successes on both sides had left the issue of the war as doubtful as it had been before the Edge-Hill fight. The armies were in their winter-quarters, without any immediate prospect of a forward movement on either side that could lead to any decisive advantage, and the sanguine temperament of the King, daily flattering him with the expectation of favourable news from the North and from the West, made him reject all overtures of treaty.

On the 1st of January appeared at Oxford the first number of the 'Mercurius Aulicus.' Journals of occurrences had been for some time published weekly by the Parliament, and proclamations and intelligences issued on the King's part, generally in the shape of single broad sheets printed by authority. Dr. Heylin now undertook the business of the press, and he worked it with an activity and virulence, and with a disregard of fact in his statements, which even more than rivalled the exaggerations of those sent forth by the weekly writers of the Parliament's party. Indeed, it requires great care, in referring to such authority on either side at about this time, not to be grossly deceived as to the reality as well as the character of many of the events which are recorded. We find battles announced as won by the Earl of Newcastle and Lord Northampton which never were fought, and 'Cer-'taine intelligence of great and signal victories obtained by 'the Earl of Essex,' or 'joyfull newes from the West, with a 'greate defeate of the Malignants under Hopton,' with more than once a 'confident belief' that Prince Rupert was slain. It is difficult to say on which side the balance of untruth preponderated. More newspapers were published by the Parliament;—six in London alone. For the King there were the Mercurius Aulicus published at Oxford, and the Belgicus at the Hague for distribution on the English coast, besides proclamations and other intelligences. But Dr. Heylin was eminent above all other men in the compounding of what, in modern phrase, would be called a bulletin from the army. If, on the one hand, Essex forbore from occupying a town or village which would have made a strong post in advance against the King, and a picket of Rupert's entered it at night, the transaction was next week magnified by Dr. Heylin into a triumphant routing of the runaway roundheads, or a signal and providential argument of the unanimity of the country round in favour of the royal cause. It must, however, be admitted that, if Heylin equalled, and sometimes surpassed, the Parliament's journalists in exaggeration, the Mercurius Aulicus was written with great ability, and had much the advantage over the other papers of those times in its powers of sarcasm and invective, and in the ingenuity of its misrepresentations. On the whole, it is seldom safe to state a fact of any importance to the characters of those engaged in it on contemporary evidence, when it is not vouched by the concurrent testimony of both parties.

On the morning of the 1st of January there was a sharp skirmish in the town of Burford, between some of the Parliament's dragoons and Sir John Byron, who, with his regiment, was escorting ammunition to the Marquis of Hertford. At about midnight of the 31st, Byron and his men having retired to their quarters, their sentinels descried four horsemen by the light of their matches, the advanced guard of a troop entering the town from the Cirencester road, and, before the alarm could be well given, about two hundred dragoons were in the market-place. The conflict began about the White Hart, an inn at the town's end, from which a lane led to the market-cross. Byron, taking possession of the cross and the houses about it, opened a fire of musquetry on the Parliamentarians, who, as little expecting to find an enemy in Burford as they had been expected by them, were thrown into some confusion. A fierce struggle ensued, in the course of which Sir John was wounded in the face with a pole-axe; but at last he succeeded in clearing the town, pursuing the dragoons near six miles, beyond which it was unsafe to advance, the moon not having risen, and the road not having been reconnoitred by him.*

On the night of the 5th Hampden's regiment was doing duty on the outposts near Brackly. The pickets were attacked by a strong body of horse, sent out by the Earl of Northampton to surprise them. The Parliamentarians were on the alert, and repulsed the assailants with loss, pursuing them for several hours after day-break with two regiments of dragoons, whom Hampden, suspecting or having intelligence of their design, had brought into the town, from the Buckingham side, after dark on the evening before. On the first conflict, however, Wagstaffe, who had, from the beginning, served under Hampden as lieutenant-colonel of his regiment, was taken; and, being a prisoner of some note, was hurried off with a few troopers to Oxford. Wagstaffe had been for some years in the service of the French king, and actively employed in his wars.† Like some of the other soldiers of fortune, the nature and condition of his engagement had left him, in his own estimation, at liberty to change his party and cause with great facility of conscience. Wagstaffe no sooner arrived at the head-quarters of the King than he engaged his services to him with the same eagerness with which they had before been given to the Parliament. And, to make them more available, he was thenceforward usually employed in enterprises in which he would be most likely to be opposed personally against the troops and against the skill of his old master, whose habits of

---

* Mercurius Aulicus. Continuation of Speciall Passages.
† Mercurius Aulicus.

warfare and whose troops he well knew, and under whom he had become well acquainted with those parts of the country in which they were likely to meet. Accordingly at Brill we find him, almost immediately afterwards, acting with the garrison, by which an enterprise of Hampden's 'was defeated, and, shortly after, at Stratford-on-Avon, commanding the party which was beaten by him.

In the course of the late operations, Lord Essex had neglected a post of great strength and importance between Aylesbury and Thame;—of great importance as lying directly upon his principal line of communication, and affording a place of refuge and support for the parties employed from Oxford to harass the Parliament's lines, and naturally of great and commanding strength. Brill-Hill is the highest of a small steep range on the borders of Oxfordshire and Buckinghamshire, and is backed by a deep mass of woodland on the side towards Aylesbury, through which large bodies of men might move in that direction for several miles, unobserved. This position was allowed without opposition to be occupied by the cavaliers, who established a garrison there, and strengthened it with a large redoubt and lines of defence on all sides. Sir Gilbert Gerrard, a brave and good officer, held it for the King with a force of about six hundred men. It was not till the full effects of this oversight began to be felt by Lord Essex, in the interruption which this garrison gave to all his arrangements in that quarter, that he turned his attention to repossessing himself of it. Arthur Goodwyn had made a successful attack by night upon the neighbouring quarters at Piddington, and had carried off three troops of horse with their officers.* But the fortress still remained unassailed and threatening. Suddenly, Mr. Grenvil, the high-sheriff, planned an assault upon this formidable and commanding post. He marched the volunteers from Aylesbury, and sent for Hampden with his regiment from Wycombe to assist him. But the enterprise entirely failed. The King had reinforced the garrison the day before the attack, and Hampden had been unable, from the bad state of the roads, to bring up any artillery, except a few small sakers. After three several attempts to carry the lines by storm, in each of which they were repulsed by the steadiness of Gerrard's troops

---

* Continuation of Certain Speciall and Remarkable Passages, &c. From Thursday 19th January, to Thursday 26th.

and the great strength of the place, the Parliamentarians were forced to retire, covering their retreat as well as they could, pursued, however, by the cavalry of the garrison, and suffering the loss of many men and horses among the deep lanes and woods and marshes. In this action, Mr. Grenvil received a dangerous wound from a musquet shot, and from this time it does not appear that the high sheriff was tempted to take the field in person.* Meanwhile, his kinsman, on the opposite party, pursued in Cornwall a gallant and eager course of service, generally distinguished by success.

On the 19th of January was fought the fight of Bradock Down, in which the King's troops, commanded in chief by Sir Ralph Hopton, obtained a signal advantage. This action was of the more importance, as being the first which restored the King's affairs in those parts, after the failure and retreat of the Marquis of Hertford, Lieutenant General of the Western Association. A fresh army had been raised in a marvellously short time by the efforts of Hopton, Sir Nicholas Slanning, and Sir Bevill Grenvil.† The Lord Mohun, too, having, since the beginning of the civil war, kept himself in close retirement upon his estate at Boconnock, now joined the rising party, and showed himself in arms for the first time in this battle, within sight of his own house. The Parliamentarians, encouraged by their former success, were threatening Liskeard, the capture of which would have opened to them a line of communication along nearly the whole of the western coast. It was within a few miles from this town that the two armies met. Heath and Clarendon describe the unexpected opening of a masked battery of two small drakes as mainly instrumental in the issue of this encounter; one of the instances of the effect of a very small force of artillery in times when the use was so little known of that engine of war in the field. The victory was complete. The Parliamentarians were checked and routed, and 1250 prisoners taken; and, on the same evening, Hopton entered Liskeard in triumph.

The following letter was sent by Sir Bevill to his wife, who was then at his house at Stow, about thirty miles from the place of action. It describes with warm and hurried energy the achievement in which he had that day borne a very forward part, and was written before he had put off the armour he had

* Mercurius Aulicus. † Heath's Chronicle.

worn in the fight.* Nothing that is natural to a frank and gallant man's feelings is ungraceful in the expression; nor is it dishonouring to Sir Bevill that something of the spirit of self-commendation, which on that night swelled his heart, should have been poured forth in a letter to his 'best friend,' to whom he knew that his fame was dear and precious as his safety.

'For the Lady Grace Grenvil,
 'at Stow.
 'The messenger is paid,
'Yet give him a shilling more.

'MY DEARE LOVE,—It hath pleased God to give us a happy
'victory on this present Thursday, being the 19th of January, for
'wch pray joyne wth me in giving God thanks. We advanced
'yesterday from Bodmyn to finde the Enemy wch we heard was
'abrode, or, if we missed him in the field, we were resolved to
'unhouse them in Liskeard, or leave our boddies in the high way.
'We were not above 3 mile from Bodmyn when we had viewe of
'two troopes of theire horse to whom we sent some of our's w^{ch}
'chasd them out of the field, while our foote marchd after our
'horse. But night coming on, we could march no farther then
'Boconnock Parke, where, (upon my Lo: Mohun's kinde motion,)
'we quartered all our army that night by good fires under the
'hedges. The next morning, (being this day) we marched forth,
'and, about noone, came in full view of the enemie's whole army
'uppon a faire heath between Bocon: and Braddock church. They
'were in horse much stronger than we, but, in foote, we were
'superior as I thinke. They were possest of a pritty rising ground
'wch was in the way towards Liskerd: and we planted ourselves
'upon such another against them wthin musket shott; and we
'saluted each other wth bulletts about two howers or more, each
'side being willing to keepe their ground of advantage and to
'have the other to come over to his prejudice. But after so long
'delay, they standing still firme, and being obstinate to hould their
'advantage, S^r Ra: Hopton resolved to march over to them, and
'to leave all to the mercy of God and valour of our side. I had
'the van, and so, after sollemne prayers at the head of every
'devision, I ledd my part away, who followed me wth so great
'courage both downe the one hill and up the other, that it strooke
'a terror in them, while the seconds came up gallantly after me,
'and the winges of horse charged on both sides. But their courage
'so faild as they stood not the first charge of the foote, but fledd
'in great disorder; and we chast them diverse miles. Many are

* In Lord Carteret's Collection.

'not slaine, because of their quick disordering. But we have
'taken above 600 prisoners, and more are still brought in by the
'soldiers. Much armes they have lost; 8 collours we have won,
'and 4 pieces of ordinance from them; and w^{th}out rest we marchd
'to Liskerd, and tooke it w^{th}out delaye, all theire men flying from
'itt before we came; and so I hope we are now againe in the way
'to settle the countrey in peace. All our Cornish Grandies were
'present at the battell, wth the Scotch Generall Ruthven, the
'Somersett Collonells, and the Horse Captaines Pim and Tomson,
'and, but for their horses' speed, had been all in our hands. Lett
'my sister, my cossens of Clovelly, wth y^{r} other friends, understand
'of gods mercy to us; and we lost not a man. So I rest

'Y^{rs} ever,
'BEVILL GRENVIL.

'Liskerd, July 19, 1642.'

But the Parliamentarians, thus beaten at Bradock, and driven in confusion through Liskeard, were not prevented from again rallying in force further to the westward. The little experience of both parties in the art of war, the want of combination, and the difficulties which the country presented all over England owing to the fewness and badness of the roads, gave on all occasions great advantages to beaten armies. Assurances were sent to them of powerful assistances. It was promised that Sir William Waller, with a large and better disciplined force, should soon be on the march to support them from the neighbourhood of Gloucester. They were thus encouraged to make head as long and as obstinately as they could, and to harass as much as possible the King's force by dividing their own and acting upon their flanks, until this expected assistance might arrive. Accordingly we find from Sir Bevill's letters,* that, as soon as the beginning of February, the Royalists, having advanced upon the main body of the Parliamentarians who had retreated on Plymouth, were again distracted by fresh powers gathering in their rear in the country round Tavistock. A large body of the King's army was detached to Okehampton, where they found themselves opposed by near 5000 men, who, retreating on Chagford, were attacked without success. The approaches to the town being difficult, and the King's cavalry too far in advance of their infantry, 'our men,' says Sir Bevill, 'were

* Letter to Lady Grace, dated Okehampton: Feb. 9.—In Lord Carteret's possession.

'forced to retire againe after they were in; and one loss we
'have sustained that is unvalluable, to witt, Sydney Godolphin
'is slaine in the attempt, who was as gallant a gent: as the
'world had.'

Saltash was next attacked and forced by Sir Ralph Hopton, where he took many cannon and prisoners and a ship of war;* Ruthen escaping in an open boat to Plymouth.†

But Hopton was now in great difficulties. Placed between the force near Tavistock and the garrison of Plymouth, and unable to reduce the latter place, or to clear the country to the eastward of him without directing his whole power on that point, contrary to the advice of Sir Bevill, he divided his army, occupying himself for near a fortnight in a hopeless siege of Plymouth, the garrison of which could scarcely have ventured to move out, and allowing the Parliamentarians in other parts adjacent to gather strength and spirits. On the 25th of February, however, the siege of Plymouth was abandoned, 'which,' says Sir Bevill, 'for my part, I never expected could 'be successfull: yet, in submission to better judgement, I 'gave way. And we are now at Tavistock, united again in 'one boddy. The party of our's wch was at Modbury indured 'a cruell assault for 12 howers against many thousand men, 'and killd many of them, with the losse of fewe and some 'hurt. But our's at last were forced to retire to Plympton 'for want of ammunition, having spent all their stock. We 'are still threatned, but I hope god's favour will not for-'sake us.'‡

During this sharp campaign in the West, while Ruthen, General Chudleigh, and the Earl of Stamford, commanded jointly for the Parliament, the Earl of Stamford, whether from jealousy or some more dishonouring motive, appears to have failed in giving the support which was demanded from him by the other two. They were active, enterprising, and indefatigable. Stamford had rarely the good fortune to be with his division, where the danger and exigency of the business in hand the most urgently required his presence in the field. At Bradock·Down his absence was the more remarkable, inasmuch as Ruthen had halted for two days for him to come up from a distance of only about twenty miles, and when his additional numbers could hardly have failed of securing an

---

* Heath's Chronicle.   † Clarendon, Hist. Reb.
‡ From a letter ' To the Lady Grace at Stow, Feb. 25.'

important advantage. It seems as if nothing but the danger of offending a person of his rank and connections, and the deserved popularity of his son the brave Lord Gray of Groby, can account for so bad a soldier as Lord Stamford having been left in command of troops, or even having escaped censure from the Parliament. But the difficulties which the close committee had in these respects to encounter, among the religious jealousies of the Independents and the Presbyterians, and the political jealousies of the nobles and the levellers engaged together in this cause, having often to balance the disadvantage of retaining incompetent leaders against that of disgusting their party by removing them, may easily be conceived, but will probably never be known in all the various and complicated details.

The state of Devonshire, strongly against the King, and of Cornwall doubtful, disposed him,—and the character of their leaders in the West and the important business nearer home induced the Parliament,—to conclude an armistice that was soon broken also by common consent.

The defeat of Stratton Hill was that which determined the Parliament to place the western army under one leader in whose acknowledged abilities and claims for supreme command they might have confidence, and to turn their attention much more seriously to the war in that important quarter. Here Chudleigh commanded for the Parliament, supported by Sir Richard Buller and Sir Alexander Carew;* and Hopton, and under him Grenvil, and Slanning, John Arundell, Sir John Berkeley, John Ashburnham, and John Trevanion, for the King. Lord Stamford, as usual, had neglected to join in the position which the Parliament's army had taken up, and the whole of its cavalry had been detached, a few miles off to Bodmin, under the command of Sir George Chudleigh, the general's father, to disperse or capture a force which had assembled there to recruit for the royal cause under the commission of array. Availing himself of the advantage of this moment, Hopton pushed forward his whole army by a forced march of two days, and, on his arrival in sight of the enemy, instantly attacked. Sir Bevill led the advance with his musqueteers and pikemen, supported by Sir John Berkeley's brigade, and, for some time, drew the whole power of the

* Clarendon, Hist. Reb.

enemy's troops on the hill to that part, where, from the steepness of the ascent and the stubbornness of the defence, the assailants met with great difficulty and loss. At length, after several hours of severe fighting, relieved from some of the stress of the action by three other divisions coming up to the attack on the three other sides, the Cornish leaders, finding the ammunition nearly spent, a defect which they agreed, says Clarendon, 'could only be supplied by courage,' determined to push forward at once for the plain on the summit. There the four parties met, and overthrew the Parliamentarians, who, unfurnished with cavalry to protect their flanks, although behaving with the utmost courage, and their officers doing all that skill and soldiership could do, were entirely routed and driven down in great disorder, leaving General Chudleigh and seventeen hundred other prisoners, thirteen pieces of cannon, and all their baggage and stores, in the hands of the victors. The success of this battle reduced all that part of the West country to submit to the King, excepting Plymouth, which still held out, protected by the strength of its citadel, and receiving its supplies, unmolested, by sea. On Sir Ralph Hopton, in memory of the victory, was conferred the title of Baron Hopton of Stratton.

These events had gradually raised the war in the West into greater importance with both parties. The Parliament saw itself daily losing ground in those parts, and at length determined to send thither Sir William Waller to the supreme command, supported with a small additional force, and with all the reputation which he had derived from his military experience abroad, increased by his late services and successes in Surrey, Hampshire, Gloster, and Hereford. No sooner had the Commonwealth party received this reinforcement of means and of system than Prince Maurice and Lord Hertford were detached thither by the King. This led to a course of alternate successes and defeats which kept the issue of the war in balance for nearly two years, the cause of the Parliament appearing more than once nearly extinguished there, but at length prevailing. The history of these events would carry us wide of the main subject of these memorials, and, in respect of dates, far beyond it. Lansdown was, on the whole, a victory for Waller; but, at the battle of Roundway Down, which followed soon after, he received a complete and signal overthrow. He returned to London, unfortunate, but with the well-deserved glory of having conducted himself, though unsuccessfully, with skill, determination, and valour, against a combination of circumstances beyond his control; ill-supplied with means, and cruelly thwarted by the jealousy of Essex. But, on his return, he was met by both Houses with a vote of thanks, honourable to them as to him, like that of the Roman senate to their consul after Cannæ.—' Quo in tempore, adeo ' magno animo civitas fuit, ut consuli, ex tantâ clade redeunti, et ' obviam itum frequenter ab omnibus ordinibus sit, et gratiæ actæ, ' quod de republicâ non desperasset.' * Cornwall, Devonshire, and Somersetshire, afterwards became the principal scene of the war, Essex and Fairfax leading on the one part, and the King in person on the other: and it ceased not until the entire abandonment of the West by the King, owing mainly to the carelessness, the excesses, the cowardice, and, perhaps, treachery, of Goring, who commanded his cavalry. But the fight at Lansdown closed the brave and honourable life of Sir Bevill Grenvil. Waller had retired into Bath upon some reinforcements of cavalry, lately arrived from London. There he knew that Maurice and the Marquis of Hertford must attack him, or lose all the fruits of what had been done in Cornwall, and leave that country and Devonshire to be brought again under the undisputed dominion of the Parliament by the reduction of the few small garrisons held for the King, and by the power of Lord Warwick's fleet upon the coast. The King's army advanced from Wells and Frome by Bradford. But, finding Waller strongly posted on Lansdown, his artillery flanking the main road and covered by fascines and stone walls, they retired to Marsfield, where they were charged by Haselrigge's regiment of cuirassiers, 'the Lobsters,' with great execution. Here, however, rallying with their whole force of cavalry, under Maurice and the Earl of Carnarvon, and the Cornish musqueteers under Sir Nicholas Slanning, they again beat back the cuirassiers to the foot of the hill. And now Sir Bevill Grenvil's troops on the right becoming impatient at the sight of the batteries and breastworks on the hill, 'cried out that they might have leave to ' fetch off those cannon.' † Sir Bevill himself headed this gallant attack, flanked by a party of horse on his right, his own regiment of musqueteers on the left, himself on horseback

---

* Tit. Liv., lib. xxii. ad fin.   † Clarendon, Hist. Reb.

leading up his pikes midway, in the face of the cannon, and meeting a strong body of the King's routed and pursued by the Parliament's cavalry. In vain did the cannon and musquetry from the brow of the hill play fast and thick upon the resolute Cornishmen, who, pressing forward and 'scritching like their own wild sea-mows,'* bore up against two charges of cavalry on their ascent. But, on the third charge, Sir Bevill's horse was killed, and this gallant gentleman fell to rise no more, covered with wounds, and his head cloven with the blow of a poll-axe. The troops retired, further disordered by the blowing up of a magazine among them; and Clarendon, though he unaccountably claims the victory for the King, admits that Waller quartered that night again in the city of Bath, at the foot of the disputed hill; while Hopton was borne off the field severely wounded, many of his officers slain, and his army retreating towards Oxford by the way of Devizes. In this town they were for some days enclosed by Waller, till they were relieved by the other army under the Earl of Hertford and Prince Maurice.† I have been led beyond the proper date of these memorials to pursue the short and bright career of Sir Bevill to its honourable close. But I trust that the subject and the feeling of the following letter, written by his faithful friend Trelawney, announcing his death to that high-minded and amiable woman, Lady Grace, may excuse this violation of the unity of time in my narrative.

'HONORABLE LADY,—How cann I containe myselfe or longer conceale my sorrow for ye Death of y^t excellent Man y^r most deare Husband, and my noble Freind. Bee pleased wth y^r wisdome to consider of the events of warr wch is seldom or never constant, but as full of mutability as hazard. And seeing it hath pleased God to take him from y^r La^{pp}, yet this may something appease y^r greate flux of teares, that hee died an Honorable Death, wch all his enemies will envy, fighting wth invincible valour and Loyalty ye Battle of his God, his King, and Country. A greater honour then this noe Man living can enioy. But God hath cal'd him unto himselfe to crowne him (I doubt not) wth immortall Glory for his noble constancye in this blessed Cause. It is too true (most noble Lady) that God hath made you drinke of a bitter Cupp, yett, if you please to submit unto his Devine Will and pleasure by kissing his rodd patiently, God (noe doubt) hath a staff of Consolation for to comfort you in this greate affliction

---

* Western Tragedy. † Clarendon, Hist. Reb. Ludlow's Memoirs.

' and tryall. Hee will wipe y^r eyes, drie up the flowing springe of
' y^r Teares, and make y^r Bedd easye, and by y^r patience overcome
' God's Justice by his retourning Mercie. Maddam, hee is gone
' his Journey but a little before us, wee must march after when it
' shall please God, for your La^pp knows y^t none fall without his
' Providence, wch is as greate in the thickest showre of Bulletts,
' as in ye Bedd. I beseeche you (deare Lady) to pardon this
' my trouble and boldness, and ye God of Heaven blesse you and
' comfort you and all my noble Cosens in this y^r greate visitation,
' which shal bee the unfayned Prayers of him that is, Most noble
' Lady,
     ' Your Ladishipps honerer
      ' and humble Servant
       ' JOHN TRELAWNE.
' Trelawne, 20th July, 1643.'

We now return to the affairs of the midland counties as we left them about the end of February.

The town of Lichfield had throughout been steady in its adherence to the Parliament's cause; but its garrison had been for some time withdrawn, and detached to other parts which appeared to be more urgently menaced. Suddenly, in furtherance of a design long laid in secret by Lord Chesterfield and a party of the gentry of the surrounding country, the Cathedral Close was seized and fortified for the King. Provisions and ammunition had been collected in a house within this precinct, and the position of the place, and the double wall which surrounded it, rendered it strong, according to the means and rules then known for defence and for attack. Lord Brook, from Warwickshire, assisted by Sir John Gell, from the neighbourhood of Derby, undertook to reduce it. Although the Earl of Northampton was moving from Banbury to support the party which occupied the Close, it capitulated upon mere quarter after three days' siege. But, on the second day of the attack, Lord Brook, who was directing from a window the advance of a body of troops up a street leading towards the Close, was slain by a musket shot, fired from the Cathedral tower. It was on the 2nd of March, the calendar day of St. Chad, a Mercian bishop, the founder of Lichfield Cathedral; a coincidence which did not escape being dealt with by the court writers as a visible judgment, in which it is difficult to suppose that they themselves could have been believers. Clarendon, as usual, does not disdain to countenance, by insinuation, the observations made by others on this childish augury. Dr. Heylin very gravely remarks that Lord Brook, when he left Coventry, had desired his chaplain to preach upon this text from Esther, 'If I perish— 'I perish;' and that 'it is on credible testimony, that before 'his entry into Lichfield, he was heard to wish, if the cause 'he was in were not right and just, he might be presently 'cut off; which, being compared with the event, may serve 'sufficiently to convince the conscience of those, who have 'been hitherto seduced unto a good opinion of so fowle a 'cause, that it is neither justifiable in itself nor acceptable 'unto God.' 'These things,' says he, 'should be heartily con- 'sidered of.'* It is asserted by Dugdale, and repeated on his authority by Carte, that Brook, ' seeing the consequences 'of the cause he had espoused, was inclined to change his 'side, when he lost his life at Lichfield.' This is shown to be untrue by every part of his character and conduct to the last. One even of less high and scrupulous honour than Lord Brook would hardly have stooped to the treachery of planning, and conducting a voluntary enterprise against those whom, at the same time, he was 'inclining' to join. It would be moreover something contradictory to Dr. Heylin's theory of visible judgments, that one whose life was spared through a long and dangerous career of service to the Parliament should be cut off by a special providence at the time when, repenting his former courses, he was about to devote himself to the cause of the King. He was, indeed, of a spirit so pure, pious, and brave, that, while he was revered by the Parliamentarians as one whose reputation added glory and power to their cause, his enemies could find no ground of censure against his motives. 'They who were acquainted with him,' says Lord Clarendon, 'believed him to be well natured and just.'

Lord Chesterfield, and the party in the Close, surrendered; and the Earl of Northampton, retiring, took up his quarters in Stafford. On the fifteenth was fought, near this town, the battle of Hopton Heath; the division of the Parliamentarians from Lichfield having advanced under Sir William Gell, and joined itself to that of Sir William Brereton, coming from the north. Here, within a few days after his great rival and opponent, Lord Brook, had been carried to his grave, the Earl

---

* Mercurius Aulicus. Tuesday, March 14.

BLANCH SOMERSET
BARONESS ARUNDEL OF WARDOUR.
OB. 1649.

of Northampton lost his life, fighting with desperate valour, and, even when unhorsed and surrounded, refusing quarter.

As the evening closed upon these troops, the cavalry of both sides equally were prevented by the coal-pits from pursuing any casual advantage in a manner which might have determined the success. After a bloody, but indecisive day, both armies retreated at nightfall; the Parliament's to some rising ground southward, and the King's into Stafford. And, as was the custom on all like occasions, both parties took to themselves the credit of a victory.*

Meanwhile, Lord Herbert's small and newly-raised army was surrounded and entirely destroyed by Sir William Waller, who, shortly after, reduced Hereford also, and Tewkesbury. While these places were won and lost alternately by King and Parliament in the midland counties, and while a great campaign was preparing in the extreme West of England, the intermediate county of Wilts was the scene of no less active operations; but these were carried on by parties inconsiderable in number, and unconnected in position. The castle of Warder, small and unimportant for any object that could have influence on the fate of the war, was, in the course of a few months, twice besieged, and twice taken; once by Sir Edward Hungerford and Strode, for the Parliament, and again retaken by the Lord Arundell, Colonel Barnes and Sir Francis Doddington from Edmund Ludlow, who had been left in command and had assisted in the first siege. The last of these defences was remarkable for the obstinate bravery with which Ludlow, for several months, maintained against a very superior force an edifice weakened by the lapse of many centuries, originally constructed to resist only the attacks of archery and such other powerless machines of ancient warfare, and surrounded on three sides by a steep woody hill in the possession of the enemy. It was at last taken by the explosion of a mine, which laid a great part of one of the flanking towers open, and grievously damaged the main body of the castle. The first defence, which had lasted little more than a week, was rendered memorable as having been conducted by the courage and fidelity of two noble ladies; these were the aged Lady Blanch, wife of Thomas Lord Arundell, and her

---

* Clarendon, Hist. Reb. Kingdome's Weekly Intelligencer. Speciall Passages, &c.

son's wife, the Lady Cecily, daughter of Sir Henry Compton, of Brambletye in Sussex. They held the castle, in the absence of their husbands, with a garrison consisting of little more than their menial servants. The firing of a mine on one side of the building so weakened the remaining means of resistance, that, on the besiegers threatening to spring another on the other side, and then to storm the castle, if it were not delivered up before an hour-glass should have run out, a surrender was proposed on an honourable capitulation, the terms of which were signed by Hungerford and the Lady Blanch.*

By these successive sieges this antique mansion was brought nearly to the condition of a ruin. The ponds were drained, the deer parks destroyed, the gardens and terraces dismantled, and the walls shattered almost to their foundations. A great part of the outer wall, inner court, and two towers, still stand, a monument of the ancient glories and greatness of a noble house, beautiful and venerable in the bareness in which war and time have left it.

A cessation of arms in Oxfordshire and Buckinghamshire had been proposed by the King, and assented to by Parliament, on the first of March; and grounds of treaty were discussed by Commissioners, at Oxford, with the King in person. It was agreed that, during the cessation, the King's forces in Oxfordshire should advance no nearer to Windsor than Wheatley, and, in Buckinghamshire, no nearer to Aylesbury than Brill; the Parliament's in Oxfordshire, no nearer to Oxford than Henley, and, in Buckinghamshire, no nearer than Aylesbury. And the King's troops, soon after, retired from before Gloucester, which, after Waller had left those parts, had been maintained with the utmost resolution and skill by General Massey, for several weeks, against the vigorous and unremitting attacks of a large army.†

But, at Oxford, from beginning to end of the long-protracted negotiations, the insincere and inconstant temper of the King cast endless difficulties in the way of the treaty, and often marred the prospect when it seemed the most promising of success. Whitelocke, who was present with the Commissioners, and acted as their clerk at the conferences, ascribes this mainly to the influence of certain others, 'some of the

---

* Ludlow's Memoirs. Clarendon, Hist. Reb, Mercurius Rusticus. Original MS. terms of capitulation, preserved at Warder.

† Viccars's Parl, Chron. Mercurius Rusticus. Clarendon, Hist. Reb,

'bed-chamber and higher,' whose weaker judgments it was the King's misfortune to have permitted to sway his own.*

He received the commissioners with courtesy; he feasted them in his Court at Christ Church; he occasionally even condescended to share the entertainment of the Earl of Northumberland, who kept a magnificent and costly table for the Commissioners, and to accept presents of wine and other dainties from them.† But, early in the armistice, he essayed to amend the terms of cessation, in order to keep his communications open with London; and the Earl of Newport was taken at Coventry, coming from the Queen, without a pass from Sir Thomas Fairfax, and contrary to the stipulations agreed upon.‡ These attempts were strongly resisted by the Parliament's Commissioners. But the Close Committee in Westminster were not inclined, any more than the King, that these disputes should abruptly end the negotiation. For they had a great and difficult work in hand elsewhere, which required time, and which, in case of the King proving insincere in his professed desire for peace, it was of the utmost importance to them to conclude.

Hitherto, from the breaking out of the war, Scotland had preserved a careful neutrality. She had been content that the dispute should be waged by others, though not insensible of the deep interest which she had in the result. From the struggle into which she had entered for the security of her National Church she had been relieved only by the events which had turned the King's whole attention to what was going on nearer home. She dreaded lest any issue, either of treaty or of arms, disadvantageous to the Parliament, might be followed by a renewed attempt on the King's part to extinguish that spark of the Genevan discipline and doctrine in his northern kingdom which had kindled and spread through the South among the materials with which he had vainly endeavoured to smother it up. Argyle was for an open junction with the cause of the English Parliament. But most of the other Covenanters, having parted with the King on such good terms, and having, since that time, received no provocation of a strictly national sort, and moreover being neutralised by the influence of the Marquis of Hamilton, did not choose to risk anything by joining in the general cause

---

* Whitelocke's Memorials. † Ibid.
‡ Weekly Intelligencer.

with the Parliamentary leaders of England. They had therefore coldly met all the overtures made to them for assistance. But the time was now come when Scotland saw her interest in bearing a share in the arrangement of the treaty. Henderson, whose abilities and favour with the King marked him as a fit person to conduct such a conference on her behalf, was now therefore despatched, at the head of a deputation of Ministers of the Kirk to Oxford. Their propositions, however, were strictly confined to the project of a settlement of Ecclesiastical affairs; in which, they contended, the Kirk should take part. Meanwhile the King's proposals to the Parliament's Commissioners varied almost daily, and soon took a shape which gave little reason to expect a peaceful issue. He stipulated for a surrender, at the outset, of all the forts, magazines, towns, ships, and revenue, into his own hands, and that 'all 'illegal power claimed or acted by orders of Parliament be 'disclaimed.' This was no less than proposing to the Parliament to disarm and deprive themselves of all further power to raise troops or money, promising in return to 'execute all 'laws concerning Popery or Reformation,' and afterwards ' to 'try *per pares* all persons excepted against in the treaty.' *

Yet did these hopeless conferences endure for more than a month; the King manifesting, says Whitelocke, ' his great ' parts and abilities, strength of reason, and quickness of ' apprehension, with much patience in hearing what was ' objected against him, wherein he allowed all freedom, and ' would himself sum up the arguments, and give a most clear ' judgment upon them.' Upon the great subject of difficulty, respecting the Parliament's not giving away the means of defence until the other terms should have been carried into effect, the King at length 'said he was fully satisfied, and ' promised to give the Commissioners his answer in writing ' according to their desire; but, because it was then past ' midnight, he would have it drawn up the next morning, as it ' was now agreed upon.' They returned to their lodgings 'full ' of joyful hopes.' ' But, instead of that answer which they ' expected and were promised, the King gave them a paper ' quite contrary to what was concluded the night before, and ' very much tending to the breach of the treaty. They did ' humbly expostulate this with his Majesty, and pressed him

* Whitelocke's Memorials.

'upon his royal word, and the ill consequences which they
'feared would follow upon this his new paper. But the King
'told them he had altered his mind, and that this paper which
'he now gave them was his answer which he was now resolved to
'make upon their last debate.' * This answer was that, as
soon as he should be satisfied in his first proposition, namely,
the surrender of the forts, towns, magazines, navy, and
revenue, and as soon as the members of both Houses should
be restored, and he and they 'secured from tumultuous
'assemblies, (which he conceived could not be otherwise done
'but by adjourning the Parliament to some place twenty
'miles from London, such as the Houses should agree upon,)
'he would consent to the disbanding of the armies, and would
'return speedily to his Parliament. This being intimated to
'the Commissioners, they dissuaded the sending of it, as
'fearing it might break off the treaty, and the improbability
'that the Houses would adjourn and leave the city of London,
'their best friends and strength, and put a discontent upon
'them.' Such is the account of this unhappy transaction,
written after the Restoration, by Whitelocke, who was himself
the witness of what he relates.

Thus, then, was the last cherished chance of peace destroyed, and, on the 15th of April, the Commissioners left Oxford in obedience to a peremptory order of recall. But, while the last negotiations were proceeding, Prince Rupert had recommenced his incursions into Buckinghamshire with a large force. On Monday morning, the 13th of March, he again appeared with 6000 men and the King's life guard, and the black regiment, at the village of Stone, within two miles of Aylesbury. But the news of the intended enterprise having reached the Parliament the day before, Hampden and Stapleton had 'posted away to their charges.' † With their regiments, and those of Goodwyn and Homestead, which lay at Wycombe, in all about 3000 horse and foot, they set forth to reinforce Colonel Bulstrode, who commanded at Aylesbury. They were joined on their march by Colonel Mills, with a regiment of dragoons from Beaconsfield; so that, early on the morning of Prince Rupert's intended attack, the town was found thronged with a powerful force for its defence. It now became their duty to endeavour to protect the country round

* Whitelocke's Memorials. † Kingdome's Weekly Intelligencer.

from pillage which had already commenced. The Prince had begun to retire, but had detached Lord Carnarvon to his right, who entered the town of Wendover, and, having plundered it, proceeded towards Chesham, where he met a few of the Parliament's horse, whom he routed and forced back into Missenden. On rejoining Rupert that night he found him in full retreat, laying waste, as he passed, the villages which lay on his road to Oxford. But towards the morning, the Prince hastened his retreat by Brill, his rear-guard severely harassed by repeated charges, and, moreover, having received the alarm that Lord Essex was moving to intercept him at Thame. On the 24th he resumed his enterprise with an increased power, and ten pieces of ordnance—but with no better success. The disposition of the Parliament's troops was now complete; the country people all along this line of march on the alert; a large force in position before Aylesbury; and Hampden's brigade joined with the main body under the Earl of Essex, on his flank near Thame and menacing Oxford, in the event of his further advance.*

Before the Commissioners had left Oxford, and while the King was still anxious to avoid making such a movement as must fix upon him in person the reproach of having broken the armistice in those parts, Rupert traversed the whole of Northamptonshire and Warwickshire with his cavalry, and, putting himself at the head of that army which had remained inactive since the Earl of Northampton's death, on Easter Monday he took Birmingham by assault. Of all his acts of cruelty and rapacity, none are a fouler stain upon his memory than those which, without provocation or excuse, he perpetrated against this town after all resistance was at an end. There had been nothing done by the defenders of Birmingham which justified any extraordinary severity. The inhabitants, it is true, had strongly and uniformly attached themselves to the party and fortunes of Lord Brook. They had twice gallantly defended their town; but, in those defences, they had shown no spirit and done no act contrary to the acknowledged usages of war. On this occasion, they had been left defenceless, at the mercy of a powerful army. But mercy there was none. The town was sacked and pillaged, and, the night after it was

---

* Whitelocke's Memorials. Perfect Diurnall, from March 6th to 27th. Speciall and Remarkable Passages, from March 16th to 23d.

entered, nearly one half was burned to the ground by the furious soldiery. Without delay, moving into Staffordshire, the Prince laid siege to Lichfield, and took that place also. But Lichfield was saved from a like vengeance by a peremptory letter dispatched by the King, with a postscript from Secretary Nicholas; both of which, though written in terms which might not offend the Prince or discredit him with the army, sufficiently mark, in the way of advice, what Charles felt of the wanton violence of his nephew's conduct.*

And now the judges' sessions of Oyer and Terminer were suspended by message from the Houses, 'untill it should 'please God to end these distractions between King and 'people.' This consequence of civil war, long deprecated, long delayed, had become inevitable. The course of the common law was stopped through the land. It had hitherto been wondrously maintained in a country beset by fighting armies. But the Great Seal was in the King's hands, and, under the guise of general justice, commissions had for some time been issued only to such judges as were with the King or of his party; and the cases brought before them bore relation all to state matters. Moreover, the King now issued a proclamation for holding the Easter term at Oxford instead of Westminster, and requiring all the judges to attend him there.† For some time after the commencement of the war the power of the law had been preserved, respected, and duly administered, on both sides. The judges had gone their circuits, passing with flags of truce through the districts held by opposite armies, and holding their courts with sheriffs who at other times headed the levies of their respective counties in the field. And it is remarkable and memorable to all posterity, and glorious to the character of our country, that, throughout this great struggle, from first to last, there is no instance on record of private assassination or popular massacre, nor of plunder except under the orders of war. 'Non inter- ' necinum inter cives fuisse bellum ; de dignitate atque imperio

---

* 'A Message with a Letter from his Majesty to Prince Rupert at or ' before the time of the taking of Lichfield and the Close ; willing and ' commanding Prince Rupert not to use any cruelty upon the inhabitants ' of the aforesaid city,' &c., with a postscript from Sec. Nicholas, concerning ' His Majesty's reall intentions how your princely thoughts ought to be ' steered in your resolutions and all your warlike affairs and enterprizes. ' April 18.'—In Mr. Staunton's Collection.

† Continuation of Speciall Passages, from 13th to 20th of April.

'certasse.'* Doubtless, on both sides, as must ever be when interests lie deep and rising passions overflow, and where the war is carried on by small detached parties of ill disciplined troops, often acting under feelings of local feud,—the work of spoliation was carried on with more eagerness and severity where there was a spirit of personal or family animosity to be gratified. There were confiscations, there was free quarter occasionally allowed, but much oftener restrained; and private pillage there was none. What very strongly marks this is the loud complaining, by the journalists on both sides, of the enormities done by the troops, but which, when specified, even with all the exaggeration of party recitals of events then fresh, appear to have been few, and, with one or two great exceptions, trifling. These accounts are full of petty inflated details of such atrocities as those committed upon the furniture and wine-cellars of Sir Robert Minshull's house at Bourton,† or of Lord Say's at Broughton;‡ a minister of the gospel led astride upon a bear,§ or bed-tickings and curtains cut to pieces and household stuff destroyed at Brentford;|| now and then recounting, in terms of deep horror or of vast commendation, a practical jest like that of the Parliament's soldiers eating up the batch of apple-pies which Mrs. Armitage, the wife of the clergyman of Wendover, had baked for Prince Rupert's troopers. ¶

The instances of sanguinary cruelty which find their place among the stories of these wars were of acts done in military execution: no secret murder, no bands of freebooters assembling for spoil between the quarters of the armies or among the villages deserted by their fighting men, no savage outbreak of a licentious rabble, disfigured the grave severity of this mighty conflict. An honourable memorial of the comportment of the English people in those unhappy times.

The suspension of commissions of Oyer and Terminer did not last beyond a few months. No sooner had the Parliament resolved to make a Great Seal of its own than the common law courts again sat throughout the realm; and Hutton and Davenport, assisted by Maynard, Glyn, Wylde, and Rolls, for the Parliament, and Chief Justice Heath and Ryves for the

---

* Tit. Liv. † Mercurius Rusticus. ‡ Viccars's Parl. Chron.
§ Mercurius Rusticus. || Speciall Passages.
¶ A Perfect Diurnall of the Passages in Parliament, Tuesday 21st of March.

King, tried causes under the authority of the two seals of England; the King's being in the hands of the Lord Keeper Littleton, and Whitelocke being appointed by the Parliament to hold theirs.

On the 15th of April, the day on which the treaty was formally declared by both parties to be at an end, the Earl of Essex marched his whole army to besiege Reading. Reading had been carefully fortified, and the three entrances, by Forbury, Harrison's barn, and Pangbourne-lane, covered with works; some reliefs had been sent in by water, but still there was a great want both of provisions and ammunition. Hampden, commanding the advance guard, broke ground within a short distance of the town during that night, taking advantage of the hedges and banks to shelter his working parties. On the afternoon of the next day, the army being strengthened by three regiments of foot coming up by Sonning and Caversham with Lord Grey, the cannonade was opened from the trenches and batteries hastily thrown up to the south between the Thames and Kennett, and was briskly answered from the town. Towards the evening, Sir Arthur Aston, the governour, having received a grievous blow on the head from a falling tile, was disabled from further duty, and the command of the garrison devolved on Colonel Fielding.* The King, having made preparation to relieve the town, set forward early on the morning of the 24th to Wallingford. Two days before, an attempt of the same sort had been made by Vavasour, which was defeated with great slaughter by Colonel Middleton.

In the collection of manuscripts at Stowe is a journal of these transactions, written by Sir Edward Deering, who was present with the King during the attempted relief. Charles established his head-quarters at Wallingford; and, after dining at Mr. Molyn's house, went round the fortifications, and passed that evening in preparations for his attack. He took up the ground for his army about two miles before Wallingford, and gave orders that all should be in readiness for moving at five in the morning. At day-break, having slept the night before in the governor's apartments at the castle, he mounted, having his household, heralds, and guard of gentlemen-pensioners, in attendance; and with him went

---

* Letter to the Speaker, from Hampden, Stapleton, and Goodwyn, King's Collect., Brit. Mus.

forth his own troop of horse, consisting of a great number of persons of high quality, commanded by the Lord Bernard Stuart, brother to the Duke of Richmond. Another troop followed, composed of their servants, under the command of Sir William Killigrew, with the baggage of the King and of his retinue. The army, being forty-five troops of horse, and nine regiments of foot, besides dragoons and artillery, now marched in two divisions; the one, with General Ruthven, straight upon the town of Reading; the other, commanded by the King in person, upon a road to the left, towards Caversham, where the two divisions again met, with the intention of surprising the besiegers' quarters, and taking their works in reverse. Here the fight began and soon became general,— the Parliamentarians having enclosed the rear of their works, and turning a great part of their battering train upon the King's troops as they advanced, at the same time filling the hedgerows on the flanks with musquetry, and having two regiments of infantry (Colonel Barclay's and Lord Roberts's) within the lines opposite, ready to act on any point. The King's troops, however, received no effectual check until they reached Caversham bridge, which General Ruthven endeavoured to force with his whole power, under cover of his guns, 'some of which were so large,' says Dr. Coates, 'that they 'discharged balls of twenty-four pounds weight,' a calibre of artillery scarcely ever before used in the field. But repulsed here, after a long and bloody struggle, the Cavaliers retired upon Wallingford, making no further attack.

And, this enterprise having failed, the town surrendered. For, unknown to the King, on the morning on which he moved to the relief, the garrison had hung out a white flag from the walls, had sounded a parley, and were actually treating, hostages having been exchanged, and commissioners from both sides sitting at Sir Francis Knowles's house, while the armies were engaged.

On the next day, the capitulation was signed; by which, on the morning of the 27th, the garrison marched out with the honours of war, but leaving ten pieces of ordnance, their stores, and prisoners, in the town, and engaging to retire directly to Oxford, without committing any hostilities in their way. Hampden and Skippon were instantly sent in alone, with a few soldiers and a working party, to view the town, an alarm having been spread that some of the works were mined and slow matches left burning: but, in the evening, the Earl of Essex, with his whole army, entered. The recent conduct of Prince Rupert at Birmingham had so inflamed the anger of the Parliament's troops, that it was by the utmost exertions of their officers that they could be restrained from outrage. It was with difficulty that they were held from violating the treaty, and attacking the King's troops marching out, their rage being increased by seeing the waggons of the retiring cavaliers laden with much more than they were entitled by the capitulation to carry away;—'much unlawful baggage,' says the Mercurius Bellicus, 'besides of women, great, though not 'good, store.' The conduct of the Earl of Essex, and the other officers, was scrupulously honourable and just; and, by an issue of twelve shillings to each man, from the military chest, in lieu of plunder, the threatened disorders were stayed. It was not, however, till the Sunday following that discipline was quite restored. On that day, public thanksgivings were offered up through the town; all the churches were thronged with the soldiery, and the preachers effectually quenched the flame which the leaders had had only power enough to restrain.*

Colonel Fielding was instantly brought before a Council of War at Oxford to answer for the surrender. The indignation of the King, the court, and the whole army, was intense against him who had delivered up a place to an enemy in face of a royal army fighting to relieve it, when, as it was urged, the King depended on his seconding the attempted relief by a vigorous sally of the whole garrison. With such feelings arrayed against him, Fielding was not likely to have his case fairly judged. It was in vain he pleaded that the negotiations had been begun before he had any knowledge of his Majesty's intended enterprise; that, before the action, the treaty was in progress, and that his honour was engaged to the enemy, not at such a moment to 'defy them, to break off.' Those who had advanced on Brentford during a treaty, and harassed the country round Oxford for weeks during an armistice, were little disposed to listen to a justification of the surrender of Reading upon the

---

* These details of the siege and surrender are taken from Dr. Coates's papers; 'Mercurius Bellicus, being the fourth intelligence from Reading, April the last;' 'Joyful Intelligence from our Camp at Reading, John Alexander, April 27th;' and Hampden's, Stapleton's, and Goodwyn's letter to the Speaker; all in the King's Coll. Brit. Mus.: likewise from the Mercurius Aulicus; and Sir Edward Deering's Journal, in the MS. Coll. at Stowe.

plea of faith to be kept with rebels. In vain did Hampden, Stapleton, and Skippon, offer, if safe conduct might be given them, to come before the Council as witnesses in Fielding's behalf that the negotiation was justified in the beginning by dearth of food and stores, and the surrender demanded in the end by engagement; and thus a brave and faithful officer, distinguished by many forepast services to the King's cause, was found guilty on a mixed charge of cowardice and treason, and sentenced to an ignominious death. Charles reprieved him at the last moment, when the soldiers were under arms in Oxford streets, and the crowd assembled round the scaffold. But the revenge of the court was fully wreaked upon Fielding in the destruction of his character.

The occupation of Reading was of great importance to the Parliament's interest. But the immediate result of it was a great calamity in their army. The unhealthy state in which the town had been left by the former garrison, and the closely crowded lodgement of the victors for some weeks after their entry, produced a fever and ague among their ranks, the effects of which were scarcely mitigated by the withdrawal of the greater part of them to quarters round, in a country now left unusually damp by heavy rains. Sickness, and many other causes of discontent, raised a mutinous spirit, and, on orders being given for marching to the cantonments near Reading, some regiments refused to put themselves under arms. Among these was Hampden's. Their leader was absent at Westminster. He instantly hastened to subdue the storm by his presence, and it was by his courage, address, and popularity, that the mutineers were again reduced to discipline and duty.*

But more serious discontents even than these, and in higher quarters, distracted the affairs of the Parliament. Up to this time, and from that of the Edge Hill fight, the Close Committee had seen the genius and the resolution of Hampden in conflict with the timorous counsels of Essex, in all his latter views of state policy, and in most of his operations of war. The evil influence of the Lord General's inactive temper was shown in the unresisted advantages reaped by the Royal party. In Staffordshire and Northamptonshire, cities were taken, within reach of support, yet unsupported. The Queen's forces had increased and become formidable in the North,

---

* Dr. Coates's Papers, May 26. Mercurius Civicus.

where Fairfax was cramped by his orders. Waller, in Herefordshire, had been unable to profit by his successes; and the campaign in the west was starved for want of necessary supplies. And all this because no decisive movement was made by the army covering London, to occupy the King's attention, by which, if it had failed to bring the war to an instant close, it might at least have obliged the King to fall back from Oxford, and have afforded succour to the cause in other parts. The disheartening aspect of things had its effect upon the politics of many of the party. The less courageous, and the less faithful, were endeavouring to make what terms they could with the King for their own safety. The fruit of those opportunities which the long-protracted conferences at Oxford had afforded to the King, for detaching many powerful persons, some of the Commissioners themselves, from their engagements to the Parliament, had now become manifest. The Earls of Northumberland and Holland made their submission and joined the Court; the latter of these, under circumstances of humiliation so mortifying to his spirit that, before long, his wounded pride again led him back to rejoin the cause to which he had not virtue enough to cleave in its adversity. Edmund Waller, who had also been on that commission, was detected, with Tomkins his brother-in-law, Chaloner, and a few other subordinate agents, in their wild and treacherous plot to deliver over their party to destruction. During the treaty of Oxford, the King's friends in the city, among whom was Sir Nicholas Crispe, a rash but brave partisan of the Royal cause, had engaged to seize the Parliament and the Metropolis. The commission of array, under which they were to act when the scheme should be ripe for action, was entrusted to the care of the Lady Aubigny, who came up to London with a pass from the Parliament under the pretext of family affairs. The conspiracy was discovered to Pym by a servant of Tomkins. Among those apprehended and tried, was Mr. Alexander Hampden; a name which, probably out of reverence to the memory of his illustrious kinsman, is kept out of sight by almost all the Parliamentarian writers in their narratives of this transaction. 'Ne in tali facinore optimi hujusce nominis ulla fieret mentio.'

'Waller, a member of the House of Commons, Tomkins, 'Chaloner, *and others*,' says Whitelocke; '*those* who were

'engaged in this conspiracy, of which Mr. Tomkins and
'Mr. Chaloner were found guilty and executed for it,' says
Edmund Ludlow. 'One plot,' says Mrs. Hutchinson, who
disguises nothing for interest or fear, 'conducted by Mr.
'Waller, and carried on by many disaffected persons in the
'cittie, was now taking effect, to the utter subversion of the
'Parliament and People; but that God, by his providence,
'brought it timely to light, and the authours were condemned
'and some executed. But Waller, for being more a knave
'than the rest, and peaching his complices, was permitted to
'buy his life for 10,000*l.*' Of those who had sided with the
Parliament, all are silent respecting the name of Alexander
Hampden, except Rushworth, who details everything.
'May 19:' says Dugdale in his Diary, 'Mr. Hampden sent
'with a message for treaty, and stayed.' He was apprehended
on the 21st.

Alexander Hampden had indeed always been about the
Court and person of the King, and against him there is but
this mitigated reproach that, for the advancement of a cause
to which he had throughout attached himself, he, under pretence of negotiation, became a party in a plot which, both on
account of the means and the associates employed in it, a high
sense of honour should have bid him shun. But no baseness
can be conceived greater than Edmund Waller's. Formerly,
officious in his services to the Parliamentary leaders, he had
distinguished himself by the virulence of his invective against
those who were then sinking under the power of the House of
Commons; now, forward in the design to deliver up to ruin
and destruction the cause in which he had engaged and the
friends and kindred who had trusted him, he was cowardly
and begged their mercy when the peril recoiled upon himself.

The following letter is in Lord Wharton's papers in the
Bodleian. In it he meanly prays the favour of Arthur
Goodwyn to save him, in regard to the memory of John
Hampden, who was among those whom the plot was to have
delivered up prisoners to the King.

'SIR,—If you will be pleased to remember what your poore
'neighbour hath been, or did knowe what his hearte now is, you
'might perhaps be inclined to contribute something to his preser-
'vation. I hearde of your late being in towne, but am so closelye
'confined that I knowe not how to present my humble serviss unto

'you. Alas, Sir, what should I say for myself? Unless your
' owne good nature and proneness to compassion encline you to-
' wards me, I can use no argument, having deserved so ill. And
' yet 'tis possible you may remember I have heretofore done some-
' thing better, when God blest me so as to take you and my deare
' cosen, (your late friend now with God,) for my example. Sir, as
' you succeede him in the general hopes of your country, so do
' you likewise in my particular hope. I knowe you would not
' willingly have let that fall oute, which he, (if alive,) would have
' wisht otherwise. Be not offended, (I beseech you,) if I put you
' in minde what you were plesed to say to your servant, when the
' life of that worthye person was, in danger in a noble cause as
' anye is now in the country. You asked me then if I were content
' my kinsman's bloode should be spilt; and truly I thinke you
' found not by my words onely, but my actions also, my earnest
' desire to preserve and defend him, having had the honour to be
' employed among those who persuaded the Shreeves with the
' trayned bands to protect him and the rest in the same danger
' to the House. As then you were plesed to remember I was of
' his bloode, so I beseech you forgett it not now ; and then I shall
' have some hopes of your favour. Sir, my first request is, that
' you will be nobly plesed to use your interest with Dr. Dorislaus
' to shew me what lawful favour he may in the tryall; and, if I
' am forfeited to justice, that you will plese to encline my Lord
' General to grant me his pardon. Your interest, both with his
' Excellence and in the House, is very great; but, I will not direct
' your wisdome which way to favour me ; onely give me leave to
' assure you that, (God with his grace assisting the resolution he
' has given me,) you shall never have cause to repent the saving a
' life, which I shall make haste to render you again in the cause
' you maintain, and express myself during all the life you shall
' lengthen,

'SIR,
' Your most humble, faithfull and
' obedient Servant,
'EDMUND WALLER.'

Waller's was but one, the most important, and the last, of
a train of conspiracies and defections, which, exploding
separately, were dealt with, and their mischiefs repaired, in
detail; but which, if they had all taken effect together, would
probably have shaken the power of the Parliament to its
foundations. Sir Hugh Cholmeley, who commanded a brigade
in the North, went over to the Queen; but of his whole force
he could prevail on only twenty troopers to accompany him

in his desertion. Cheshire, his native county, was strong for the King; but Lancashire, where he had raised the principal part of his force, was equally so for the Parliament. Manchester was already beginning to be an important trading town. 'It had declared, magisterially,' says Lord Clarendon, ' for the Parliament:' and Lord Derby, with all his chivalrous fidelity to the King, was, by disposition, indolent, and unable to cope with the vigorous and earnest spirit of that county.

Sir John Hotham and his son had, for some time, been lukewarm in the discharge of their appointed duty, and, whether from jealousy of the ascendancy of the Fairfaxes, or hopeless of the issue of the war, had remained motionless within the walls of Hull. They were now discovered in a conspiracy, with some of the other officers, to deliver up that place to the Queen. It was detected by Moyer and Ripley, two captains of merchantmen lying in the river, who, instantly mustering the crews of all the ships, seized the three blockhouses by surprise, and proceeding to the castle, harangued the troops, got possession of the main guard and magazine, and put Captain Hotham, with such of the conspirators as they found there, into irons. Sir John Hotham fled to Beverley; where Colonel Boynton, his cousin, upon intelligence from Hull, went out to meet him, and took his horse by the bridle, saying,—' Sir John, you are my kinsman, and one ' whom I have much honoured; but I must now waive all ' this, and arrest you as a traitor to the kingdom.' And the conspirators were sent up prisoners to London, to expiate their treachery on the scaffold.* By these prompt and decisive acts the great position of Hull, with all its important garrison and stores, was saved to the Parliament; and a plot, which would have given all Yorkshire, to the South of the Humber, into the Queen's hands, was at once defeated and undone.

Almost at the same time an enterprise of the same sort failed at Lincoln. It had been undertaken by two of Hotham's captains, who were to have opened the gates of that town to a detachment of the Queen's troops. They were seized, together with about sixty cavaliers, who had already entered the city in disguise, by the mayor, who, taking command of the garrison and batteries, opened their fire on the

---

* Viccars—Parl. Chron.

assailants advancing in force on the Gainsborough side from Newark, and obliged them to retire.

From the central army, even from the head-quarters of the Lord General himself, desertions were not unfrequent. Among others who went over at this time was Urrie, of whom it may be truly said that, though his services proved of great advantage to the King, his character had been long so odious that his example rather did benefit than injury to the Parliament's cause, as deterring any man who had a care for honourable reputation from being seen to follow him in his course. Failing of promotion with Lord Essex, he fled to Oxford, giving to Prince Rupert an able and active assistant in all the business of partisan warfare, and carrying with him information and experience of the disposition and strength of all the quarters lying between Oxford and the capital.*

Hampden incessantly, but in vain, endeavoured to promote some great enterprise which might restore the cause and give heart to its supporters. But, failing in this, he served to the last under Essex, with a zeal as obedient as if those means had been adopted which his superiour mind clearly saw were necessary for the success and credit of their arms.

Reading having surrendered, the troops who had been engaged in that siege were not directed to any forward movement; they were not effectually removed from the neighbourhood of contagious disease, nor was the position turned to account as the base of any new set of operations. To prevent the sickness spreading, as well as to cover the country which principally produced his supplies, Essex extended his quarters greatly, but still continued to act on the defensive; thus imposing on himself the necessity of protecting a lengthened and more vulnerable line, while the enemy was left unembarrassed and at leisure to choose both the time and point of attack. Whenever Rupert wanted cattle or any other provisions for his troops, he seized them from some part of these feeble and ill-connected lines. The remonstrances of the troops could no longer be suppressed, and Hampden was

---

* Lord Clarendon, endeavouring to apologize for Urrie's treachery, states that he had, for some time before, withdrawn himself from the active service of the Parliament. This is, however, clearly contradicted by several of the Parliament's papers printed just before his desertion, which recount skirmishes in which he bore an active part in command of parties of Lord Essex's horse.

again loudly named to the Parliament as the fit person to place at their head. To remove from himself all suspicion of a querulous or selfish ambition, and to exhibit to murmuring spirits a great example of patient subordination, he placed himself in constant and personal intercourse with the chief whose plans he disapproved, and many of whose qualities he held in disesteem. Meanwhile, the distant cantonments in the country round Thame and Wycombe, worn by fierce and wasteful sickness, by inglorious suffering, and deep discontent, were nightly harassed by the enemy. Rupert's zeal was unremitting : while Essex slumbered at his post, and while that sullen recklessness of its own fate which soon shows through an army distrustful of its chief was spread from end to end of the Parliament's long line, the King's troopers were ever alert, and generally successful in their enterprises, and therefore always hopeful, and always formidable. Not a week, scarcely a night, passed, but they were heard laying waste some defenceless district,—worse than defenceless, because occupied by the wearied and the disheartened, inviting attack, and never prepared to repel it. The country round suited well the activity of the young Prince and his cavalry. The gorges of the hills, lined with deep tracts of beech woods, shrouded his stealthy march through the night, upon the flank or rear of his sleeping enemy; and at daybreak would he pour forth his squadrons sparkling like a torrent on the plain which lay before him open for the manœuvre or the charge. Often would a village many a mile from the King's country suddenly wake to a dreadful irruption of horsemen who came thundering in from the side opposite to that of his distant lines; the track of the night march marked from afar by the blaze of burning houses and the tumults of posts surprised, and the morning retreat by the dust of columns returning to Oxford and leaving behind them a region of desolation and panic.

In these expeditions the renegade Urrie was eminently qualified to bear his part. His knowledge of the country, and of the points occupied, as well as his address and experience in that sort of service, especially recommended him to the Prince and his council of war. It was only the opinion which all men had of the baseness of his motives, and the hazard which there must always be in employing such agents where a second treachery might produce the utmost mischief, that could make the cavaliers distrustful of their new partisan. But these considerations added to Urrie's eagerness for early action. Nor was it many days before he found the occasion he wished for. He planned the expedition which ended in the memorable fight at Chalgrove; an enterprise not very important in its promise, nor in its success, otherwise than that the skirmish to which it led was fatal to Hampden, at the time when his powers were in their fullest vigour, when his military abilities were ripening by experience of war, and when prospects were daily opening to him for exercising them on a scale of larger responsibility.

A detachment of Essex's troops had, two days before, made a feeble show of attack upon one of the King's outposts at Islip. These small disconnected enterprises were always dangerous for them to undertake; the King's troops acting from a centre, and being able to bring a powerful body, from within or near the walls of Oxford, to any point that was menaced. The Parliamentarians, meeting with a larger force than they had expected, had retreated without coming to action. On Saturday, the 17th of June, about four o'clock in the afternoon, Rupert's trumpets sounded through the streets of Oxford, and the cavalry were called to general muster and parade. In less than half an hour the column had passed Magdalen Bridge, and were in march for the Parliament's country, joined, as they went, by the infantry, who had been sent on, the day before, from the rendezvous at Islip, to different stations from which they might fall in upon the line of the cavalry's advance.

Forming a body of about two thousand, they proceeded cautiously towards the Chilterns, crossing the Cherwell at Chiselhampton Bridge, and leaving Thame, where Essex lay, but two or three miles on their left. Then, burying themselves in the Woodlands, somewhere about Stoken Church, they proceeded to the left, nearly opposite to the hamlets of Postcombe and Lewknor.* It was now too late to reach Wycombe. Some delays with the infantry had made that night's expedition longer than they had intended. They began their attack, at about three in the morning, upon Postcombe. Here was only a troop of horse, who, mounting,

---

* 'His Highnesse Prince Rupert's late beating up the rebels' quarters, '&c., and his victory in Chalgrove-field, on Sunday morning, June 18.' Printed at Oxford, by Leonard Lichfield, printer to the University, 1643.

as the dragoons appeared at the street's end, after a slight skirmish retired in good order, leaving only a few prisoners behind. But Rupert pursued the work of havock rapidly. At Chinnor, about two miles off, there lay, according to Urric's information, a stronger party. Thither Rupert hastened with his whole force of cavalry, and, sweeping off the picket as he galloped in, instantly dismounted his headmost regiment of four squadrons. He entered the quarters, slaughtering and capturing all within; while the mounted carabineers who lined the village street and the backs of the houses and barns where the Parliament's soldiers lay, shot down those who attempted escape. They then set fire to Chinnor, and left it. In this place, according to the account published at Oxford, about fifty were killed and about six score prisoners were dragged away half naked at the horses' sides to the infantry who were in full march, under the ledge of hills to the left, to secure the main road back to Oxford. Here they narrowly escaped taking a rich prize of money on its way to the Earl of Essex; but those who were with it drove the carts into a wood, and escaped. The sun had now risen, the alarm had spread, and a party of the Parliament's horse appeared on the side of the Beacon-hill.* Hampden had very lately and strongly remonstrated upon the loose and defenceless condition in which the pickets were spread out over a wide and difficult country. He had, the day before, visited Major Gunter's cavalry in and about Tetsworth. With the foresight of an active spirit, he had established a chain of communication between the principal posts to the eastward, and, the day before, had despatched his own lieutenant to Lord Essex, to urge the strengthening of the line by calling in the remote pickets from Wycombe, and from those very villages which were now suffering from Rupert's attack. Had this advice been adopted when it was given, that morning's disaster at Chinnor would have been spared, and a force would have been collected on the main line of the Stoken Church road, sufficient to have stopped and defeated Rupert on his advance, or effectually cut off all possibility of his retreat.

Hampden had obtained, in early life, from the habits of the chase, a thorough knowledge of the passes of this country. It

* 'His Highnesse Prince Rupert's late beating up,' &c. &c.

is intersected in the upper parts with woods and deep chalky hollows, and in the vales with brooks and green lanes; the only clear roads along the foot of the hills, from east to west, and these not very good, being the two ancient Roman highways called the upper and lower Ickenild way. Over this district he had expected that some great operation would be attempted on the King's part, to force the posts round Thame, and turn the whole eastern flank of the army. To this neighbourhood he had, the evening before, repaired, and had lain that night in Watlington.* On the first alarm of Rupert's irruption, he sent off a trooper to the Lord General at Thame, to advise moving a force of infantry and cavalry to Chiselhampton Bridge, the only point at which Rupert could recross the river. Some of his friends would have dissuaded him from adventuring his person with the cavalry on a service which did not properly belong to him, wishing him rather to leave it to those officers of lesser note under whose immediate command the pickets were. But, wherever danger was and hope of service to the cause, there Hampden ever felt that his duty lay. He instantly mounted, with a troop of Captain Sheffield's horse, who volunteered to follow him, and, being joined by some of Gunter's dragoons, endeavoured by several charges, to harass and impede the retreat, untill Lord Essex should have had time to make his dispositions at the river. Towards this point, however, Rupert hastened, through Tetsworth, his rear guard skirmishing the whole way. On Chalgrove Field, the Prince overtook a regiment of his infantry, and here, among the standing corn, which covered a plain of several hundred acres, (then as now, unenclosed,) he drew up in order of battle. Gunter, now joining three troops of horse and one of dragoons who were advancing from Easington and Thame, over Golden Hill, came down among the enclosures facing the right of the Prince's line, along a hedgerow which still forms the boundary on that side of Chalgrove Field.

---

* It is traditionarily said, that a military chest of money was left at the house of one Robert Parslow, where Hampden lay that night, and that it was never called for after; by which means, Parslow was enabled to bequeath a liberal legacy to the poor of that parish. On every anniversary of his funeral, Nov. 19th, a bell tolls in Watlington, from morning till sunset, and twenty poor men are provided with coats. These particulars I derive from the intelligent Mr. John Badcock, for forty years a resident at Pyrton and its neighbourhood, but now of St. Helen's, who wrote, in 1816, a very ingenious little History of Watlington.

The Prince with his life guards and some dragoons being in their front, the fight began with several fierce charges. And now Colonel Neale, and General Percy coming up, with the Prince's left wing, on their flank, Gunter was slain and his party gave way. Yet, every moment, they expected the main body, with Lord Essex, to appear. Meanwhile, Hampden, with the two troops of Sheffield and Cross, having come round the right of the cavaliers, from the enclosures by Wapsgrove House, advanced to rally and support the beaten horse. Every effort was to be made to keep Rupert hotly engaged till the reinforcements should arrive from Thame. Hampden put himself at the head of the attack; but, in the first charge, he received his death. He was struck in the shoulder with two carabine balls, which, breaking the bone, entered his body, and his arm hung powerless and shattered by his side. Sheffield was severely wounded, and fell into the hands of the enemy. Overwhelmed by numbers, their best officers killed or taken, the great leader of their hopes and of their cause thus dying among them, and the day absolutely lost, the Parliamentarians no longer kept their ground. Essex came up too late; and Rupert, though unable to pursue, made good his retreat across the river to Oxford.*

* These details have been taken from the account printed, by Leonard Lichfield, at the university press at Oxford, for the King; also, from Mercurius Aulicus, from Lord Essex's two letters, from 'The Parliament 'Scout,' from 'A True Relation of a Great Fight between the King's Forces 'and the Parliament's at Chinnor, near Thame,' &c., and 'Certaine 'Intelligences from different Parts of the Kingdom,' printed for the Parliament in London. There is a groundless story told, upon the authority of a nameless paper, by Horace Walpole, and by Echard, of Hampden having received a wound from the bursting of one of his own pistols. All the contemporary accounts, diurnals, letters, and memoirs, state the details as I have given them. In the Common-Place Book of Henry James Pye, late poet laureate, now in the possession of his son, the lineal descendant of Sir Robert Pye, son-in-law to Hampden, I find the following entry:—
' In the St. James's Chronicle for the year 1761, there is an account of the
' death of Mr. Hampden, different from that given by Lord Clarendon. The
' account is, that Sir Robert Pye, being at supper at Farringdom House
' with two of the Harleys and one of the Foleys, related the death of
' Hampden as follows:—That, at Chalgrove Field, his pistol burst, and
' shattered his hand in a terrible manner; that, when dying, he sent for
' Sir Robert Pye, his son-in-law, and told him he was in some degree
' accessary to his death, as he had the pistols from him. Sir Robert
' assured him he bought them in France of an eminent maker, and tried
' them himself. It appeared, on examining the other pistol, that it was
' loaded to the top with several supernumerary charges, owing to the
negligence of his servant.' Mr. Pye adds these words, which discredit the

Thus ended the fight of that fatal morning when Hampden shed his blood; closing the great work of his toilsome life with a brilliant reputation and an honourable death; crowned, not, as some happier men, with the renown of victory, but with a testimony, not less glorious, of fidelity to the sinking fortunes of a conflict which his genius might have more prosperously guided, and to a better issue.

> 'Disce ... virtutem ex hoc, verumque laborem,
> 'Fortunam ex aliis.'——

His head bending down, and his hands resting on his horse's neck, he was seen riding off the field before the action was done,—'a thing,' says Lord Clarendon, 'he never used to 'do, and from which it was concluded he was hurt.' It is a tradition, that he was seen first moving in the direction of his father-in-law's (Simeon's) house at Pyrton. There he had in youth married the first wife of his love, and thither he would have gone to die. But Rupert's cavalry were covering the plain between. Turning his horse, therefore, he rode back across the grounds of Hazeley in his way to Thame.* At the brook, which divides the parishes, he paused awhile; but, it being impossible for him, in his wounded state, to remount, if he had alighted to turn his horse over, he suddenly summoned his strength, clapped spurs, and cleared the leap. In great pain, and almost fainting, he reached Thame,† and was conducted to the house of one Ezekiel Browne,‡ where, his wounds being dressed, the surgeons would, for a while, have given him hopes of life. But he felt that his hurt was mortal, and, indulging no weak expectations of recovery, occupied the few days that remained to him in despatching letters of counsel to the Parliament, in prosecution of his

---

whole of this anonymous account :—' My father, on reading this account, ' sent to enquire of Baldwin, the printer of the paper, how he met with the ' anecdote, who informed him, that it was found written on a loose sheet of ' paper in a book that he, or some friend of his, bought out of Lord ' Oxford's family. My father always questioned the authenticity of it, as ' my grandfather was bred up and lived with Sir Robert Pye till he was ' eighteen years old, and he never mentioned any such circumstance.'

* Todd, upon the authority of Mr. Blackall, of Great Hazeley, by his grandson, to the Earl of Macclesfield.

† Parliament's Scout.

‡ 'A True and Faithfull Narrative of the Death of Master Hampden, &c., by Edward Clough, 1643.'

favourite plan. While the irresolute and lazy spirit which had directed the army in the field should continue to preside in the counsel of war, Hampden had reason to despair of the great forward movement to which he had throughout looked for the success of the cause. And now the reinforcements which were pouring into Oxford from the North, and the weakened condition of the Parliament, made the issue of this more doubtful. His last urgent advice was to concentrate the position of the army covering the London road, and provide well for the threatened safety of the metropolis,—and thus to rouse the troops from the mortifying remembrance of their late disasters to vigorous preparations, which yet might lead, by a happier fortune, in turn, to a successful attack.—This was his last message;—like that from the dying Consul, after Cannæ, to the senate of his country:—' Abi, nuncia patribus ' urbem muniant, ac, priusquam hostis victor adveniat, præsi-' diis firment. . . . . . Me, in hac strage meorum patere expirare, ' ne aut reus e consulatu sim, aut accusator collegæ existam, ' ut alieno crimine innocentiam meam protegam.'*

After nearly six days of cruel suffering, his bodily powers no longer sufficed to pursue or conclude the business of his earthly work. About seven hours before his death he received the Sacrament of the Lord's Supper; declaring, that 'though ' he could not away with the governance of the church by ' bishops, and did utterly abominate the scandalous lives of ' some clergymen, he thought its doctrine in the greater part ' primitive and conformable to God's word, as in Holy Scrip-' ture revealed.' He was attended by Dr. Giles, the rector of Chinnor, with whom he had lived in habits of close friendship, and by Dr. Spurstow, an independent minister, the chaplain of his regiment.† At length, being well nigh spent, and labouring for breath, he turned himself to die in prayer. ' O Lord God of Hosts,' said he, ' great is thy mercy, just and ' holy are thy dealings unto us sinful men. Save me, O Lord, ' if it be thy good will, from the jaws of death. Pardon my ' manifold transgressions. O Lord, save my bleeding country. ' Have these realms in thy special keeping. Confound and ' level in the dust those who would rob the people of their ' liberty and lawful prerogative. Let the King see his error, ' and turn the hearts of his wicked counsellours from the malice

---

* Tit. Liv. lib. xxii. † Baxter's Life.

'and wickedness of their designs. Lord Jesu, receive my
'soul!' He then mournfully uttered, 'O Lord, save my
'country—O Lord be merciful to . . . . . .' and here his
speech failed him. He fell back in the bed, and expired.*

It was thus that Hampden died; justifying, by the courage, patience, piety, and strong love of country, which marked the closing moments of his life, the reputation for all those qualities which had, even more than his great abilities, drawn to him the confidence and affections of his own party, and the respect of all. Never, in the memory of those times, had there been so general a consternation and sorrow at any one man's death as that with which the tidings were received in London, and by the friends of the Parliament all over the land.† Well was it said, in the Weekly Intelligencer of the next week, 'The loss of Colonel Hampden goeth near the heart
' of every man that loves the good of his King and country,
' and makes some conceive little content to be at the army
' now that he is gone . . . . The memory of this deceased
' colonel is such that in no age to come but it will more and
' more be had in honour and esteem; a man so religious, and
' of that prudence, judgment, temper, valour, and integrity,
' that he hath left few his like behind him.'‡

All the troops that could be spared from the quarters round joined to escort the honoured corpse to its last resting place, once his beloved abode, among the hills and woods of the Chilterns. They followed him to his grave in the parish church close adjoining his mansion, their arms reversed, their drums and ensigns muffled, and their heads uncovered. Thus they marched, singing the 90th Psalm as they proceeded to the funeral, and the 43rd as they returned.§

Nor was it the Parliament, and its army, and the friends of its cause, only, that deplored his fall. 'The King,' says Sir Philip Warwick, 'being informed of Mr. Hampden's being
' wounded, would have sent him over any chirurgeon of his

---

* Clough's Narrative, &c. In the Ashmole Museum is a locket of plain cornelian, which, it is said, was worn upon his breast. On the silver rim in which the stone is set these words are inscribed:

> ' Against my king I never fight,
> ' But for my king, and country's right.'

† Clarendon—Hist. Reb.

‡ The Kingdome's Weekly Intelligencer. From Tuesday the 27th of June to Tuesday the 4th of July, 1643.   § Clough's Narrative.

'if he had been wanting; for he looked upon his interest, if
'he could gain his affection, as a powerful means of begetting
'a right understanding between him and the two Houses.'

The rancour, with which, after his death, his name and character were instantly assailed by the heated and servile diurnals of the Court party, was the appropriate tribute of the base to the memory of the great and good. But Charles and such of his public servants as were better acquainted with the probable motives of Hampden, and the objects which he pursued, were silent. While Hampden lived, the King had in the camp of his enemies the most powerful and popular man in the country, whose views were bounded by an honourable and publick-minded object; which, gained, would at any time, through his influence, have concluded the war. To this the King always looked with confidence, in the event of his being himself obliged by some reverse of fortune to make terms with his Parliament. Hampden's counsels and conduct as a soldier, tended, through vigorous measures, to a decisive issue. But the object was peace, and security for liberty, and the restoration of monarchy under such limitations as might be a guarantee for both. His demand for the militia to be placed for a time at the disposal of a popular body was as a provision which had been made necessary for protecting the Houses in their debates; not as a final scheme of settled government. His measures for the putting down of Episcopacy were the immediate consequences of a rash vote of the Lords in maintenance of the political power of an order who had, in those days, formed themselves into an obstinate faction to impede and punish the efforts which were making for publick freedom. His death left no man on the Parliament's side who had influence enough to command, or, perhaps, discretion enough to direct, terms of accommodation. To Falkland no man remained, in the party opposed to the Court, with whom to treat as an equal in virtue, wisdom, and moderaon of purpose. What might have been the result if these two great men, over both of whom the grave closed in the course of the same campaign, had lived, must be matter of mere speculation. But the remarkable coincidence, in one important respect, of Falkland's views, as described by Lord Clarendon, with Hampden's, as witnessed by his comportment, and by the sorrow with which the King received the news of his fate, leaves it matter of probability that this design at least they had in common, that, on whichever side the victory had fallen, a final settlement should be secured by that year's conflict. 'Et, in luctu, Bellum inter remedia fuit,' says Lord Clarendon, in his immortal character of his friend.

To his own party, the loss of Hampden was irreparable. It left Lord Essex uncontrolled, unexcited by the example and ascendency of a greater mind than his own. The events which followed justified Hampden's prognostics, his policy, and advice. Essex failed to advance the great object of the war one step. Fairfax wanted firmness as a statesman to improve his military successes. Cromwell pursued in his wars the active course which Hampden had recommended; but Cromwell's ambition, or the varied circumstances under which he was left to act, had changed the stake for which he contended, and overthrew that monarchy which Hampden only laboured to bring back within the measured limits of the English constitution.

Of Hampden's character, it would be presumptuous to say more than what his acts tell. The words are good in which it is shortly comprised in an inscription remembered by me, on many accounts, with many feelings of affection. 'With great
' courage, and consummate abilities, he began a noble opposi-
' tion to an arbitrary court, in defence of the liberties of his
' country; supported them in Parliament, and died for them
' in the field.'*

If, in the imperfect outline, now concluded, of the principal passages of Hampden's life, it has been shewn that his motives and conduct have been by the passions of some writers unfairly traduced, and that his great qualities were never exerted but in such manner as may beseem a virtuous and honourable man labouring for a great public end, I have done all that I proposed, and the object of these memorials has been answered.

* Such was the inscription over the bust of Hampden in the Temple of British Worthies at Stowe.

APPENDIX.

A.

(See page 44.)

WHEREAS his Matie. as well for his brotherly respect and correspondencie w^{h.} the Ffrench King, as for other reasons to him knowne, hath been pleased at ye. motion of his Ambassado^{re.} to fitt out for his service ye. Vantguarde (a principall shipp of his owne Navy royall) ande further to permitt an agreement to bee made wth. you the Captaines, Masters, and owners of the goode Shipps called the Neptune, the Industrie, the Perle, the Marygold, the Loyaltie, the Guift, the Peter and John, for the like employm^{t.} in the said King's Service upon such Articles as are interchangeably sealed betwixt the saide Ambassado^{re.} and ye. Comissioners for the Navy on his Ma^{ts.} behalf, ande yo^u (the said Masters & Owners), for yo^rselves. And his Ma^{ts.} pleasure hath been sufficiently signified for the putting in readines of all the saide Shippes, wch. hee doubts not is accordingly performed, the occasion of the said King's Service requiring all convenient expedicion. Theis are therefore to will and require yo^{u.} and every of yo^{u.} forthw^{th.} to call the Companies aboarde wch. have been raised and fitted to every Shipp, *according to former instructions* in that behalf. And then to take the first opportunitie of winde ande weather to proceede on yor. voyage to such a Porte in the Dominions of Ffraunce as the Ambassador^{re} shall direct and there to attende the further directions y^{t.} such principall person as shall bee appoynted Admirall of the ffleete prepared for the service of the saide ffrench King, Requiring further all Viceadmiralls and Officers of the Admiraltie, Captaines of Castells and fforts, Captaines, Masters and owners of Shippes, Mair^{s.} Sheriffes, Justices of the Peace, Bayliffes, Constables, and all other his M^{ts.} Officers, Minis^{rs.} & lovving Subjects & every of them to giue yo^{u.} all assistaunce and furtheraunce, not to hinder or interrupt yo^{u.} or any of yor. Shippes or Company in the due performaunce of the Service aforesaid as they will answere the contrary at their perills. ffrom Whitehall 8 May 1625.

(Signed)

BUCKINGHAM.

To my very loving friends Captaynes Pennington, Cap^{n.} of his Ma^{ts.} Shipp the Vantguarde, & to ye. Captaines & Masters of ye seven Shipps apointed for the Services of the ffrench King, & to every of them, and to all others whome it maie concerne.

His Majestie's express pleasure is that yo^u take knowledge that hee hath left the comaund of his Shipps under your chardge unto his deare brother the most Christian Kinge, and that therefore yo^u receive into these Shipps so many persons as that Kinge shall bee pleased to put into them: and to be continued there dureing ye tyme of the contract:. and this yo^u are to obey intirely with the greatest moderation & discretion yo^u can: this beinge that I have in chardge from his Majestie, I recòmend it to yo^u as you^r warrant & remayne

Your assured frend to
Serve you,
EDWARD CONWAY.

Hampton Courte,
Julie the 10th 1625.

Aboard the good Shipp the Neptune this 28^t
July 1625. stilo anglie.

I AM sent hither by my Lord and Maister the Duke of Buckingham (Lord High Admirall of England) to see the execution & performaunce of his Ma$^{ties.}$ pleasure (signified by letters from my Lord Conway). And doe crave answer in wrighting under your hands whether you will (according to my Lord Conwaie's L$^{rs.}$ & uppon the caution and securitie w$^{ch.}$ was agreed one and paraffited at Rochester by the three Lords Ambassado$^{rs.}$ off France and by them delivered to my lord who remitted it to mee as the securitie I was to take) deliver over your Shipps to bee disposed off by the Most Xian Ma$^{tie.}$ or noe, & if you will perfourme this I will procure you a suficient discharge to your contentment.

Signed   EDW. NICHOLAS.

CAROLUS REX.

PENNINGTON these are to charge and command you immediately upon sight hereof that without all difficulty & delay you put our former commandment in execution for ye consigning of your Ship under your chardge called the Vantgard into the hande of the Marquis D'effiiatt with all her equipage artillery & munition assuring the officers of the saide Ship whome it may concerne y^t we will provide for their indemnity & we farther chardge & command you that you also require the seaven Marchants Ships in our name to put themselves into the Service of our deare Brother the French King according to the promise we have made unto him & in case of backwardnesse or refusall we commande you to use all possible meanes in yor power to compell them thereunto even unto their sinking & in these severall charges see you faile not as you will answer to the contrary at the uttermost perill & this shal be your sufficient Warrant. Given at our Court at Richmond the 28th of July, 1625.

To our trusty and wellbeloved Jn°· Pennington, Capt. of our Ship called the Vantgard.

B.

(See page 49.)

At Whitehall, March, 1627.

PRESENT THE KING'S MAJESTY.

Lord Treasurer.	Lord Viscount Conway.
Lord President.	Lord Bp of Durham.
Lord Admiral.	Lord Bp of Bath and Wells.
Lord Steward.	Mr. Treasurer.
Lord Chamberlain.	Mr. Comptroller.
Earl of Suffolk.	Master of the Wards.
Earl of Dorset.	Mr. Secretary Cook.
Earl of Salisbury.	Mr. Chancellor of the Exchequer.
Earl of Morton.	Mr. Chancellor of the Dutchy.

It is this day ordered by his Majesty, being present in Council, That the several persons hereunder written shall, from henceforth, be discharged and set at liberty from any restraint heretofore put upon them by his Majesty's commandment. And hereof all sheriffs and officers are to take notice.

Sir John Strangeways.
Sir Thomas Grantham.
Sir William Armyn.
Sir William Massam.
Sir William Willmore.
Sir Erasmus Drailton.
Sir Edward Aiscough.
Sir Nath. Bernardiston.
Sir Robert Pointz.
Sir Beauchamp St. John. } Knights.
Sir Oliver Luke.
Sir Maurice Berkeley.
Sir Thomas Wentworth.
Sir John Wray.
Sir William Constable.
Sir John Hotham.
Sir John Pickering.
Sir Francis Barrington.
Sir William Chancey.

William Anderson.
Terringham Norwood.
John Trigonwell.
Thomas Godfrey.
Richard Knightley.
Thomas Nicholas.
John Hampden. } Esquires.
George Ratcliffe.
John Dalton.
Henry Poole.
Nathaniel Coxwell.
Robert Hatley.
Thomas Elmes.

Thomas Wood.
John Wilkinson.
William Allen. } Gents.
Thomas Holyhead.

All these remained confined to several counties.

370   APPENDIX.

Sir Walter Earl.
Sir Thomas Darnel.   } Knights.
Sir Harbottle Grimston.

Sir John Corbet.
Sir John Eliot.   } Knights.

William Coriton.
George Catesby.   } Esquires.

Edward Hooker.
George Bassett.
James Wooldrond.   } Londoners.
Henry Sanders.

John Stevens.
Thomas Deacon.   } Londoners.
John Potter.

All Prisoners in the Fleet.   *In the Gatehouse.*

Sir John Heveningham,   Knight.
Samuel Vassal.   } Londoners.
William Angel.

William Savage.
Nathaniel Mansty.

In the Marshalsey.   *In the New Prison.*

Robert Lever.
John Peacock.
Edward Ridge.
John Oclabury.
Andrew Stone.
William Spurstow.   } Londoners.
Roger Hughes.
John Pope.
James Bunch.
Thomas Garris.
James Waldron.
John Bennet.

Ambrose Aylot.
Thomas Sharp.
Thomas Hotham.
Augustine Brabrooke.
Robert Payne.
Edward Talstone.
John Whiting.
Thomas Webb.
John Ferry.

All in the custody of a Messenger. *

* See Rushworth, i., 472.

C.

(See page 95.)

Distribution of Shipps to the several Shires of England and Wales, with their Tonnage, Number of Men, and charge, and the summs sett on the Corporation Townes in each County.—From Sir Peter Temple's MS. Papers—Stowe.

	Tons	Men	£	s.	d.
BERKSHIRE—One Shipp of	320	128	4000	0	0
Towne of Windsor			100	0	0
Burrough of Newberry			100	0	0
Burrough of Reading			220	0	0
Burrough of Abingdon			100	0	0
Burrough of Towne Wallingford			020	0	0
BUCKINGHAMS.—One Shipp of	360	144	4500	0	0
Burrough and Parish of Buckingham			70	0	0
Burrough of Chipping Wicombe			50	0	0

APPENDIX. 371

	Tons	Men	£	s.	d.
BEDFORDSHIRE—One Shipp of . . .	240	096	3000	0	0
Towne of Bedford			120	0	0
BRISTOL—One Shipp of	064	026	0800	0	0
CORNWALL—One Ship of	440	176	5500	0	0
Burrough of Saltash.			40	0	0
Burrough of Portbiham als. Westlowe			13	0	0
Burrough of Eastlowe			30	0	0
Burrough of Truroe			70	0	0
Burrough of Penryn			48	0	0
Towne of Penzance			28	0	0
Burrough of Padstowe			70	0	0
Burrough of Liskird			40	0	0
Burrough of Leastwithell			20	0	0
Burrough of Cullington als. Kellington			20	0	0
Burrough of Tregonney			33	0	0
Burrough of Granporte and Creede			29	0	0
Burrough of Dunnevid als. Launceston			80	0	0
Towne of Helstone			40	0	0
Burrough of Bossenna			36	0	0
Burrough of St. Mawes			10	0	0
Burrough of Camelford . . . - . .			10	0	0
CAMBRIDGSH.—One Shipp of . . .	280	112	3500	0	0
Burrough of Cambridg			100	0	0
CUMBERLAND ⎰ One Shipp of . . .	112	045	3500	0	0
and ⎱ Burrough of Kirkby Kendal			15	0	0
WESTMORELAND Burrough of Apulby			05	0	0
CHESHIRE—One Shipp of	240	096	3000	0	0
Citty of Chester			260	0	0
DEVONSHIRE—One Shipp of . . .	720	288	9000	0	0
Citty and County of Exeter			350	0	0
Burrough of Clifton Dartmouth als. Hardness . . .			80	0	0
Burrough of Totnes			120	0	0
Burrough of Plimpton			35	0	0
Burrough of Plimouth			190	0	0
Towne and Parish of Tiverton			130	0	0
Burrough of Bideford			40	0	0
Burrough and Parish of Barnstaple			150	0	0
Burrough of Torrington			60	0	0
Burrough and Towne of Oakehampton			30	0	0
Burrough of Bradminton			50	0	0
Burrough of South Moulton			45	0	0
DERBYSHIRE—One Shipp of . . .	280	112	3500	0	0
Burrough of Darby			175	0	0
Burrough of Chesterfield			50	0	0
DORSETSHIRE—One Shipp of . . .	400	160	3000	0	0
Towne and County of Poole			30	0	0
Burrough of Dorchester			45	0	0
Burrough of Wareham			25	0	0
Towne of Weymouth and Melcombe Regis . . .			40	0	0
Burrough of Brideport, cum Membris			20	0	0
Burrough of Corffe			40	0	0

B B 2

APPENDIX.

	Tons	Men	£	s.	d.
Burrough of Shaftesbury			35	0	0
Burrough of Blandford Forum			25	0	0
DURHAM—One Shipp of	160	064	2000	0	0
Citty of Durham and Framwelgate			150	0	0
ESSEX—One Shipp of	640	256	8000	0	0
Burrough of Thaxted			40	0	0
Towne and Parish of Walden			80	0	0
Towne of Colchester			400	0	0
Burrough of Malden			80	0	0
Burrough of Harwich			20	0	0
GLOUCESTERSH.—One Shipp of	440	176	5500	0	0
Citty of Gloucester and County thereof			300	0	0
Burrough of Tewkesbury			60	0	0
Burrough of Chipping Campden			20	0	0
HAMPSHIRE—One Shipp of	480	192	6000	0	0
Burrough of Portsmouth			060	0	0
Towne of Southampton			195	0	0
Citty of Winchester, besides the Close			150	0	0
Burrough of Andover			50	0	0
Towne of Romsey			30	0	0
Towne of Basingstoake			60	0	0
HERTFORDSH.—One Shipp of	320	128	4000	0	0
Burrough of Hertford			055	0	0
Burrough of St. Albans			122	0	0
Burrough of Barkhamsted			025	0	0
HEREFORDSH.—One Shipp of	280	112	3600	0	0
Citty of Hereford			220	0	0
Burrough or Towne of Leomster			044	0	0
HUNTINGDONSH.—One Shipp of	160	064	2000	0	0
Burrough of Huntingdon			040	0	0
Burrough of Godmanchester			074	0	0
KENT, and CINQUE PORTS in KENT—					
One Shipp of	640	250	8000	0	0
Citty of Canterbury, besides the Church and Members thereof			280	0	0
Towne and Port of Dover, and Members thereof			330	0	0
Port and Town of Sandwich, and Members thereof, in the County of Kent			250	0	0
Towne and Port of Hithe			040	0	0
Towne and Port of New Romney and Members			180	0	0
Oswalston and Tenderden			090	0	0
Burrough of Queenborough			010	0	0
Towne and Parish of Maidstone			150	0	9
Towne of Gravesend, together with Milton			035	0	0
Citty of Rochester			070	0	0
LANCASTER—One Shipp of	320	128	4000	0	0
Burrough or Towne of Preston			40	0	0
Towne of Lancaster			30	0	0
Towne of Liverpoole			25	0	0
Burrough of Clidrowe			07	10	0
Towne of Newton			07	10	0

APPENDIX. 373

	Tons	Men	£	s.	d.
LEICESTERSH.—One Shipp of	360	144	4500	0	0
Burrough of Leicester			200	0	0
LINCOLNSH.—One Shipp of	640	256	8000	0	0
Citty of Lincoln and Liberties			193	6	8
Burrough of Boston			70	0	0
Burrough of Great Grimsby			15	0	0
Towne and Burrough of Stamford			60	0	0
Towne or Burrough of Grantham, with the Soke			200	0	0
LONDON—Two Shippes of	1120	448	14000	0	0
MIDDLESEX—One Shipp of	400	160	5000	0	0
MONMOUTH—One Shipp of	120	048	1500	0	0
Burrough of Monmouth			40	0	0
Burrough of Newport			23	0	0
NORTH.TONSH.—One Shipp of	480	192	6000	0	0
Towne of Northampton			200	0	0
Burrough or Parish of Higham Ferrers			36	0	0
Citty of Peterborough			120	0	0
Burrough of Daventry			50	0	0
Burrough of Brackley			50	0	0
NORTHUMB.—One Shipp of	168	068	2100	0	0
Towne of Newcastle-upon-Tyne			700	0	0
Burrough of Barwicke-upon-Tweede			20	0	0
Towne of Morpeth			20	0	0
NOTTINGHAMS.—One Shipp of	280	112	3500	0	0
Towne of Nottingham			200	0	0
Towne of Newarke-upon-Trent			120	0	0
Towne of East Retford			30	0	0
NORFOLK—One Shipp of	624	233	7800	0	0
Citty of Norwich			400	0	0
Burrough of King's Linne			200	0	0
Burrough of Great Yarmouth			220	0	0
Burrough of Thetford			030	0	0
Burrough of Castle Rising			014	0	0
OXFORDSHIRE.—One Shipp of	280	112	3500	0	0
Citty of Oxforde			100	0	0
Towne of Burforde			40	0	0
Burrough and Parish of Banbury			40	0	0
Burrough or Towne of Chipping Norton			30	0	0
Towne of Henley-upon-Thames			60	0	0
Burrough of Woodstoke			20	0	0
RUTLANDSH.—One Shipp of	062	026	800	0	0
SOMERSETSH.—One Shipp of	640	256	8000	0	0
Citty of Bath			70	0	0
Burrough of Bridgewater			70	0	0
Citty or Burrough of Wells			60	0	0
Burrough of Axbridg			30	0	0
Towne of Yeovill			30	0	0
SURREY.—One Shipp of	280	112	3500	0	0
Towne of Guildeforde			53	0	0

374   APPENDIX.

	Tons	Men	£	s.	d.
Burrough of Southwarke			350	0	0
Towne of Kingston-upon-Thames			088	0	0
SUSSEX—One Shipp of	400	160	5000	0	0
Towne and Port of Hastinges, with the Members thereof in Sussex			250	0	0
Citty of Chichester besides the Close			77	7	8
Burrough of Arundel			18	0	0
Burrough of Shoreham			08	0	0
SUFFOLKE—One Shipp of	640	256	8000	0	0
Towne of Ipswiche			240	0	0
Burrough of Oxforde			12	0	0
Burrough of Aldborough			08	16	0
Towne of Dunwiche			04	0	0
Towne of Southwolde			08	0	0
Towne of Hadleigh			64	9	4
Towne and Burrough of Eye			30	12	3
Burrough of St. Edmondsbury			206	5	4
Burrough of Sudbury			66	3	4
STAFFORDSH.—One Shipp of	240	096	3000	0	0
Citty of Lichfield, besides the Close			150	0	0
Burrough of Stafforde			30	0	0
Burrough of Newcastle-upon-Tyne			24	0	0
Burrough of Walsall			32	0	0
SHROPSHIRE—One Shipp of	360	144	4500	0	0
Towne of Shrewsbury			376	0	0
Towne of Bridgenorth, als. Bruges			060	0	0
Burrough of Ludlowe			102	0	0
Burrough of Bishopp's Castle			015	10	0
Burrough of Oswestry			037	0	0
Towne Burrough or Liberty of Wenloke			300	0	0
Citty of Carlisle			020	0	0
WARWICKSH.—One Shipp of	320	128	4000	0	0
Citty of Coventrie			266	0	0
Towne of Colefield			080	0	0
Burrough of Stratford-upon-Avon			050	0	0
WORCESTERSH.—One Shipp of	280	112	3500	0	0
Citty of Worcester			233	0	0
Burrough of Evesham			074	0	0
Burrough of Droitwiche			062	0	0
Towne or Burrough of Kidderminster			027	0	0
WILTSHIRE—One Shipp of	560	224	7000	0	0
Citty of New Sarum, besides the Close			192	0	0
Burrough or Towne of Marleborough			060	0	0
Burrough of Devizes			050	0	0
Burrough of Chippenham			030	0	0
Burrough of Wilton			005	0	0
YORKSHIRE—Two Shipps of	960	384	12000	0	0
Citty of Yorke, with the Ansty			520	0	0
Burrough of Rippon			040	0	0
Burrough of Doncaster			100	0	0
Burrough or Towne of Pontfract			060	0	0

APPENDIX. 375

	Tons	Men	£	s.	d.
Burrough of Richmonde			050	0	0
Burrough of Leeds			200	0	0
Towne of Headon			020	0	0
Towne of Beaverly			057	0	0
Towne of Scarrborough			030	0	0
Towne of Kingstone-upon-Hull			140	0	0
NORTH WALES—One Shipp of	320	128	4000	0	0
Anglesey			448	0	0
Burrough of Beaumaris			14	0	0
Caernarvon			575	0	0
Towne and Burrough of Caernarvon			12	0	0
Denbighshire			1122	0	0
Burrough of Denbigh			32	0	0
Towne of Ruthyn			19	4	0
Towne of Holte			10	0	0
Flintshire			575	0	0
Towne of Flint			4	0	0
Montgomeryshire			864	0	0
Burrough of Montgomery			94	6	0
Merioneth			416	0	0
SOUTH WALES—One Shipp of	400	160	500	0	0
Brecknockshire			933	0	0
Burrough of Brecknock			54	0	0
Cardigan			654	0	0
Towne of Cardigan			10	0	0
Caermarthen			790	0	0
Burrough of Caermarthen			30	0	0
Burrough of Kidwelly			10	0	0
Glamorganshire			1449	0	0
Citty of Llandaffe			13	0	0
Towne of Cardiffe			60	0	0
Pembrokeshire			683	10	0
Burrough of Pembroke			12	0	0
Towne of Haverforde West			34	0	0
Radnorshire			490	10	0
Burrough of New Radnor			42	0	0
Towne of Presteigne			12	8	10

D.

(See page 99.)

AFTER our hearty comendations, whereas his Majestie and his boarde havinge taken into consideration ye short time wch now remaineth for ye furnishinge out of ye fleete, beinge a service of g^t importance for ye safetie of ye state, and y^t ye same may admitt of noe delay. And for y^t his Majestie hath now appointed new Sheriffes for ye severall Counties of England and Wales. Wee have therefore thought fitt, (according to his Maties expresse comands,) hereby straightly to charge and require as well you ye Sheriffe of y^e

Countie for ye yeare past, forthwith to sende up all such monies as you have receaved for ye businesse of Shipp Mony, unto Sr Wm Russell, K^{nt} & Bar^{nt}, Treas^r of ye Navy, and to give unto y^r Successor as memorialls of all ye monies you have levied by vertue of his Maties Writt, and what remayneth behinde of ye whole assessment, and to sende ye like memorialls to this boarde. And also to deliver unto ye new Sheriffe ye writt itselfe, with all such letters, directions, warrants, and returnes, or other writinges as you have in your handes, or authentique copies of the same, touching this businesse, with an information of your doinges and proceedinges therein, for his better direction and furtheraunce in ye perfectinge of ye worke. As also you ye s^d new Sheriffe to applie your best indeavours and diligence in ye execution of his Maties writts, and former directions of this Boarde for suche parte of this Service as is nott yett finished by y^r predecessors, whereof his Matie and this Boarde will expect a good account from you. And soe wee bid you heartily farewell—from Whytehall, the 25th of January, 1635.

        Y^r lovinge friends,

W. CANT,	H. MANCHESTER,
THO. COVENTRYE, C^s.	DORSETT,
THEO. SUFFOLKE,	E. NEWBURGH,
J. BRIDGWATER,	FRANC. WINDEBANKE,
WILMOT,	WILL. BAKER.

To our lovinge friends Sr Peter Temple, B^t. late High Sheriffe, and Heneage Proby, Esq., now appointed High Sheriffe of the County of Bucks.

We greet yo^u well. Whereas there is especiall cause of yor personall attendance upon us for some matters concerning the bussines of the Shipping. These are therefore to will and command you, all delayes and exeuses set apart, to give your attendance upon the Boarde, at his Ma^{ts} Court at Oatlands upon Sunday morning next, the third of July. And hereof wee require yo^u not to fayle, as yo^u will answere the contrary at yor perill. Dated at the Court at Hampton Court, the 24 of June, 1636.

 W. CANT.   THO. COVENTRYE, C^s.   GUIL. LONDON.
                       H. MANCHESTER.
            WENTWORTH.
                       FRA. COTTINGTON.
        H. VANE, S.   FRANC. WINDEBANKE.
        T. EDMONDE.

To Sr Peter Temple.

E.

(See page 173.)

The proceedings of this committee are given at length in the journal of Sir Ralph Verney, who was one of its members. The remonstrance being read, the grievances were divided under nineteen heads, the principal of which relate to the inequality of benefices ; the amount of burthen on the public ; the claim set up by the hierarchy of a divine institution ; civil jurisdiction ; pluralities ; power to delay or withhold probates of wills, to refuse rites of marriage, and to compel subscription by penalties ; the abuse of commendams in the hands of bishops ; and lastly the scandalous lives of the higher clergy. The committee then took into consideration the challenge of divine right made in the Lord Archbishop's speech in the Star Chamber, and in Bishop Downham's and the Bishop of Exeter's Books, and also their claim of ' a superiority in ' sole ordination and sole jurisdiction, not warranted by Scripture ' or antiquity, by virtue of a distinct order superior to a Presbyter.' ' Yeates his mistery of the Gentiles,' (proceeds the journal) ' saies ' Bishopps are *as immediately from God as Kinges.* Swan, in ' fourteen pages of his sermon, calls them that deny the hierarchy ' of the church, The Bane of Religion.'—' Resolved on question that ' the third article (the bishops assuming sole power of ordination ' and jurisdiction) is a material head, and fit to be presented to the ' house to be considered of.' The journal then proceeds with the charges of the committee from day to day against books and speeches which claim divine institution and jurisdiction for the hierarchy, and next enters into an elaborate and learned citation of the authorities set forth by the committee from the practice and writings of the fathers of the church, and doctrines of the early councils, to shew that (as among the Independents) the power of ordination was given to and exercised by the clergy at large, and that bishops did not hold jurisdiction alone. It was then voted by the committee that ' the challenge of Episcop^{le} jure divino, which is ' the sole power assumed by bishopps in ordination and jurisdiction ' by vertue of a distinct order superiour to a Presbyter, is a ' materiall head and fitt to bee presented to the house.' The next day was employed by the committee in the same manner, in references to fathers and councils of the church, and then to passages in Scripture to support their citation of Augustine, Civit. Dei, to the doctrine that ' bish^{pp} is a name of duty and not of dignity,' and that the jurisdiction ' is not in bish^{pps}, but the presbiters were equall ' to them in all things.' ' Those that have the same name and y^e ' same offices in Scripture are all one. But Bish^{pps} and Presbiters ' have the same name and office ; ergo they are all one. First ' named in 20 Actes, 28 verse; 1 Phil. 1 verse ; 1 Pet. 5. verse 1 and ' 2 ; 1 Titus, 5, 6, 7 ; 1 Tim. 3 at ye beginninge of ye chapter ; 16 ' Matthew, 19 ; the key of doctrine the key of power or discipline ; ' 20 John 22, 23 ; 1 Thes. 5. 12 ; Heb. 13. 17 ; 1 Tim. 4. 14 ; 2 Tim.

'1. 6. Mr. Selden desiers to know what is meant by the sole power
'of ordination and jurisdiction that the bish^{pps} nowe claime; over
'persoñs, places, and thinges, or causes; and what power the
'presbiters had in ye primitive times in these 3 thinges. On these
'matters the committee next examine Dr. Burgis.'
They then proceed to the 'largenesse of bish^{pps} dioces, the incon-
'veniences of it. Ministers are put to great charge and travell, and
'bish^{pps} courts are multiplied thereby. They cañot dispatch soe
'much businesse themselves,' and 'delegatinge their power to unmeet
'persons.' The same vote respecting these. Next, abuses of confirmation. 'The B^p. Glocester forbids to marry any that are not
'first confirmed. B. of Eli the like. The rubrick makes little lesse
'than a sacriment of it.' Next 'Bish^{pps} claime sole probats of wills.
'If a legacy bee given to a silenced minister hee is not capable of it
'by the bish^{pps} lawe. Bish^{pps} had noe power in this in ye primitive
'times. Venables gave 1000l. to divers ministers. Mr. Jones gave
'much money to ye same purpose; but ye Archb^{pp} of Caut. would
'not suffer it to bee given to them but to other beneficed ministers.'
Next, 'bish^{pps} consecrate churches, &c., and make it necessary. The
'forme of consecratinge is not allowed by lawe. Consecration is not
'necessarye, but 'tis very chargeable. Noe humain institution can
'putt any inherent holinesse into any thinge.' Next, 'bish^{pps} inhibit
'marriage at divers times of ye yeare, at least a third parte. And
'this makes some thinke these times are more holy than others, and
'it is a great charge to buy licences.' Next, 'bish^{pps} compose formes
'of publique prayer containinge matters of state; as at fasts, and
'ye prayers agst the honest Scotts. Two ministers, Wilson and
'Bright, were suspended for not readinge it.' Next, 'bish^{pps} impose
'oathes as of canonicall obedience, ex officio, &c. agst lawe. B^{pp}. of
'Chichester sweares men to obey the Kinge's edicts, &c., oath, de
'stando juri et parando mandatis ecclesiæ.' Next, 'subscription,
'they extend this beyond ye articles of religion—many hundreds
'deprived for not subscribinge to the cañons made about 2° Jacob.'
Next, 'they hold comendams, and never come att them.—B^{pp} of
'St. Davids and B^{pp} of Chester hold 2 of 1100l. per ann.' Next,
'b^{pps} charge at theire consecration; but they observe itt not.' The
next article is 'scandalous bishopps,' in which certain bishops are
charged with speeches and quotations from Scripture in drinking
healths, cited at length; they are in a strain of impiety very unfit
to appear in any form more currently legible than the cramped
penmanship of Sir Ralph. The last and 19th article is of 'The
'burdens of B^{pps} officers and dependents and servants, &c., being
'above 10,000l.' These were the principal heads of the report of
this laborious committee.

APPENDIX. 379

F.

(See page 237.)

Original draft of Ordinance of both Houses, establishing the Committee of Lieutenancy, &c. In the handwriting of Mr. Richard Grenvil.

For the better mannaginge of the affaires of the County of Buck^m, the more effectuall execution of the orders and ordinances of Parliam^t, and the better payinge of Soldyirs belonginge to the Garrison at Aylesbury, bee it ordained by the Lords and Comons in Parliam^t assembled, that Sir Peeter Temple,[1] of Stowe, Baronett, Sir Richard Ingoldsby,[2] Sir Ralph Verney,[3] Sir Alexander Denton,[4] Sir William Andrewes,[5] Sir Thomas Sanders,[6] Sir Richard Pigott,[7] Knights, Sir John Lawrence,[8] Baronett, Sir Heneage Proby,[9] Knight, Sir William Drake,[10] Baronett, The Gouernor of Aylesbury for ye time beinge,[11] Thomas Tyrrill,[12] Boulstrod Whitlocke,[13] Richard Winwood,[14] Thomas Fountaine,[15] Edmunde West,[16] Richard Grenvill,[17] Thomas Tirringham[18] of Netherwinchenden, Thomas Bulstroode,[19] Thomas Archdall,[20] Thomas Lane,[21] Henry Beale,[22] Richard Seriant,[23] Raines Low,[24] Edm: Waller of Gregory,[25] Esquires, Xrofer Egleton,[26] Anthonie Carpenter,[27] Peeter Dormer,[28] Thomas Theed, of Leborne,[29] John Deuerell ye younger, of Swanbourne,[30] Russill, Gent.,[31] John Lane, Gent,[32] shalbee, and are hereby appoynted to bee comittees of the Countie of Bucks; and they or any fiue of them shall dispose the affaires of that countie, and shall put in execution all and euery the ordinances and comands of either or both houses of Parliam^t. And to that purpose the said comittee shall soe diuide themselues that fiue of them at the least may be continually resident at Aylesbury during the space of three weekes, and then other fiue to come in theire places, et sic alternis vicibus; and whosoeuer shall neglect or refuse after notice hereof giuen to be psent and execute theire authority hereby giuen when his turn cometh, shalbee taken for a delinquent, and his estate sequestered.

This comittee shall with all conuenient speede (either by themselues or by some other pson chosen by any fiue or more of them for that purpose) take perforce accounts of all such moneys and other goods and profitts as haue bin taken and seised wthin the said countye by uertue of any order or ordinnance of either or both houses of Parliam^t, and likewise of such moneyes as haue been or shalbee allowed out of any other Countye for the mayntenance of the garrison at Aylesbury, soe that their maie bee a pfect account giuen thereof when it shallbee called for, and to that end the said comittee or other pson by them chosen shall haue power to send for parties, witnesses, and writinges.

This comittee, or any fiue or more of them, shall wth all conuenient speede make choise of one able and sufficient person whoe hath a real responsible estate in the said countye of Buck to be Treasurer of ye said Countye, unto whom all mony collected in the said countye, and allsoe the money allowed out of any other countyes for the mayntenance of the said garrison, shallbee paid and deliuered. Said Treasurer shall not issue out any of ye said money wthout warrante in writing under the hands of fiue or more of the said comittee.

This comittee shall, either by themselues or by such person as they or any fiue or more of them shall appointe, viewe and muster at least once euerie month, and oftener if they thinke it expedient, all ye souldiers belonginge to the garrison of Aylesbury, wch are to be paid out of the countie of Buck, and out of the mony allowed out of anie other countyes for the maynetenance of the gard and garrison; and they are to take especiall care that the said souldiers be duly paid. All and sundrie the officers and souldiers belonging to the garrison at Aylesbury shallbee aydinge and assistinge to the said comittee, to compel obedience, if neede require, to the orders and comands of Parliam^t, and to leuy and receiue for them all such sumes of mony as any fiue or more of the said comittee shall under theire hands giue warrante for and estreate out unto them. Alsoe the said comittee shall be aydinge and assistinge to the governor of the said garrison, as oft as neede shall require, in raysinge and summoninge the countye for strengtheninge the garrison.

It is the true intent and meaninge of this ordinance that nothinge shallbee altered by this comittee, unlesse fiue of them att the least be present att the debate thereof at Aylesbury.

G.

(See page 237.)

By the King.

A Proclamation, by his Majestie, requiring the Aid and Assistance of all His Subjects on the North-side *Trent*, and within twenty Miles Southward thereof, for the suppressing of the Rebels, now marching against Him.

WHEREAS divers Persons, bearing an inward Hatred and Malice against Our Person and Government, and ambitious of Rule and places of Preferment and Command, have raised an Army, and are now trayterously and rebelliously, (though under the specious pretence of Our Royall Name and Authority, and of the defence of Our Person and Parliament,) marching in Battell Array, against Us their Liege Lord and Soveraign, contrary to their Duty and

Allegiance, whereby the common Peace is like to be wholly destroyed, and this flourishing Kingdom in danger to perish under the miseries of a Civill War, if the Malice and Rage of these Persons be not instantly resisted : And as we do, and must relie on Almighty God (the Protector and Defender of his Anointed) to defend Us, and Our good People, against the Malice and Pernicious designes of these men, tending to the utter ruine of our Person, the true Protestant Religion, the Laws established, the Property and Liberty of the Subject, and the very Being of Parliaments ; So we doubt not but Our good People will in this necessity Contribute unto Us, with all Alacrity and Cheerfulnesse, their assistance in their Persons, Servants, and Money, for the suppression of the same Rebellion : And therein We cannot but with much contentment of heart acknowledge the Love and Affection of Our Subjects of Our County of *York*, and divers other Counties, in their free and ready assistance of Us, which We shall never forget; and Our Posterity will, as We hope, ever remember, for their good.

Neverthelesse, in this our extream necessitie, though we have been most unwilling, We are now inforced, for Our most just and necessary Defence, again to call and invite them, and all other Our Subjects of the true Protestant Religion, reciding on the North-side of *Trent*, or within twenty Miles Southward thereof, whose hearts God Almighty shall touch with a true sence and apprehension of Our sufferings, and of the ill use, which the Contrivers and Fomenters of this Rebellion have made of Our Clemency, and desire of Peace, That according to their Allegiance, and as they tender the safety of Our Person, the Property of their Estates, their just Liberties, the true Protestant Religion, and Priviledges of Parliament, and indeed the very Being of Parliaments, they attend Our Person upon Munday, the two and twentieth day of this instant *August*, at Our Town of *Nottingham*, Where, and when We intend to erect Our Standard Royall, in Our just and necessary Defence, and whence We resolve to advance forward for the suppression of the said Rebellion, and the Protection of Our good Subjects amongst them, from the burthen of the Slavery and Insolence, under which they cannot but groan, till they be relieved by Us.

And We likewise call, and invite all Our Subjects, of the true Protestant Religion, in the remoter parts of this Our Kingdom, to whom notice of this Our Proclamation cannot so soon arive, That with all speed possible, as they tender the forenamed Considerations, they attend Our Person in such Place as we shall then happen to Encamp ; And such of Our said Subjects, as shall come unto Us (either to Our said Town of *Nottingham*, or to any other place, where We shall happen to Encamp) Armed, and Arrayed, with Horse, Pistolls, Muskets, Pikes, Corslets, Horses for Dragoons, or other fitting Arms and Furniture, We shall take them into Our Pay, (such of them excepted, who shall be willing, as Volontiers, to serve Us in this Our necessity without Pay.) And whosoever shall, in this Our Danger and Necessity, supply Us either by Guift, or Loan of Money, or Plate, for this Our necessary Defence (wherein they also are so neerly concerned) We shall, as soon as God shall enable Us, repay whatsoever is so lent, and upon all Occasions Remember, and Reward those Our good Subjects, according to the measure of their Love, and Affections to Us and their Countrey.

Given at Our Court at York the twelfth day of August, in the eighteenth yeer of Our Reign, 1642.

H.

(See page 301.)

A Great Wonder in Heaven, shewing the late Apparitions and 'Prodigious Noyses of War and Battels, seen on Edge-Hill, 'neere Keinton in Northamptonshire.—Certified under the 'Hands of WILLIAM WOOD, Esquire, and Justice for the Peace 'in the said Countie, SAMUEL MARSHALL, Preacher of GODS 'Word in Keinton, and other Persons of Qualitie.—London: 'Printed for Thomas Jackson, Jan. 23, Anno Dom. 1642.

'THAT there hath beene, and ever will be, Laruæ, Spectra, and such 'like apparitions, namely, Ghosts and Goblins, hath beene the 'opinion of all the famousest Divines of the Primitive Church, and 'is, (though oppugned by some,) the received Doctrine of divers 'learned men at this day; their opinion being, indeed, ratified and 'confirmed by divers Texts of Scripture, as the Divells possessing 'the Swine, and the men possessed with Divells, in the Acts of the 'Apostles, that came out of them, and beat the Exorcists, by which 'it is evidently confirmed that those legions of erring angels that 'fell with their great Master Lucifer, are not all confined to the 'locall Hell, but live scattered, here and there, dispersed in the 'empty regions of the ayre, as thicke as motes in the Sunne; and 'those are the things which our too superstitious ancestors called 'Elves, and Goblins, Furies, and the like, such as were those who 'appeared to Macbeth, the after King of Scotland, and foretold him 'of his fortunes both in life and death. It is evident, besides, that 'the Divell can condense the ayre into any shape he pleaseth, as hee 'is a subtill spirit, thin and open, and rancke himselfe into any forme 'or likenesse, as Saint Augustin, Prudentius, Hieronimus, Cyril, 'Saint Basil the Great, and none better than our late Soveraigne 'King James, of ever-living memory, in his Treatise de Demonologia, 'hath sufficiently proved. But, to omit circumstance and preamble; 'no man that thinkes hee hath a soule, but will verily and con- 'fidently believe that there are divells; and so, consequently, such 'divells as appeare either in premonstrance of Gods Judgements, or 'as fatall Embassadours to declare the message of mortality and 'destruction to offending nations, and hath, in Germany and other 'places, afflicted afterwards with the horror of a civill and forraigne 'warres, notoriously manifested.

'But to our purpose. Edge-Hill, in the very confines of Warwick- 'shire, neere unto Keynton in Northamptonshire, a place, as

' appeares by the sequele, destined for civill warres and battells ;
' as where King John fought a battell with his Barons, and where,
' in defence of the Kingdomes lawes and libertie, was fought a
' bloody conflict between his Majesties and the Parliaments forces ;
' at this Edge-Hill, in the very place where the battell was strucken,
' have since, and doth appeare, strange and portentuous Apparitions
' of two jarring and contrary Armies, as I shall in order deliver, it
' being certified by the men of most credit in those parts, as William
' Wood, Esquire, Samuel Marshall, Minister, and others, on Saturday,
' which was in Christmas time, as if the Saviour of the world, who
' died to redeem mankinde, had beene angry that so much Christian
' blood was there spilt, and so had permitted these infernall Armies
' to appeare where the corporeall Armies had shed so much blood;
' —between twelve and one of the clock in the morning was heard
' by some sheepherds, and other countrey-men, and travellers, first
' the sound of drummes afar off, and the noyse of soulders, as it were,
' giving out their last groanes ; at which they were much amazed, and
' amazed stood still, till it seemed, by the neerenesse of the noyse, to
' approach them ; at which too much affrighted, they sought to
' withdraw as fast as possibly they could ; but then, on the sudden,
' whilest they were in these cogitations, appeared in the ayre the
' same incorporeall souldiers that made those clamours, and imme-
' diately, with Ensignes display'd, Drummes beating, Musquets
' going off, Cannons discharged, Horses neyghing, which also to these
' men were visible, the alarum or entrance to this game of death
' was strucke up, one Army, which gave the first charge, having the
' Kings colours, and the other the Parliaments, in their head or
' front of the battells, and so pell mell to it they went ; the battell
' that appeared to the Kings forces seeming at first to have the best,
' but afterwards to be put into apparent rout ; but till two or three
' in the morning in equall scale continued this dreadful fight, the
' clattering of Armes, noyse of Cannons, cries of souldiers, so amazing
' and terrifying the poore men, that they could not believe they were
' mortall, or give credit to their eares and eyes ; runne away they
' durst not, for feare of being made a prey to these infernall souldiers,
' and so they, with much feare and affright, stayed to behold the
' successe of the businesse, which at last suited to this effect : after
' some three houres fight, that Army which carryed the Kings
' colours withdrew, or rather appeared to flie ; the other remaining,
' as it were, masters of the field, stayed a good space triumphing, and
' expressing all the signes of joy and conquest, and then, with all
' their Drummes, Trumpets, Ordnance, and Souldiers, vanished ; the
' poore men glad they were gone, that had so long staid them there
' against their wils, made with all haste to Keinton, and there
' knocking up Mr. Wood, a Justice of Peace, who called up his
' neighbour, Mr. Marshall, the Minister, they gave them an account
' of the whole passage, and averred it upon their oaths to be true.
' At which affirmation of theirs, being much amazed, they should
' hardly have given credit to it, but would have conjectured the
' men to have been either mad or drunk, had they not knowne some
' of them to have been of approved integritie : and so, suspending
' their judgments till the next night about the same houre, they, with

'the same men, and all the substantiall Inhabitants of that and the
'neighbouring parishes, drew thither; where, about halfe an houre
'after their arrivall, on Sunday, being Christmas night, appeared in
'the same tumultuous warlike manner, the same two adverse Armies,
'fighting with as much spite and spleen as formerly: and so departed
'the Gentlemen and all the spectatours, much terrified with these
'visions of horror, withdrew themselves to their houses, beseeching
'God to defend them from those hellish and prodigious enemies.
'The next night they appeared not, nor all that week, so that the
'dwellers thereabout were in good hope they had for ever departed;
'but on the ensuing Saturday night, in the same place, and at the
'same houre, they were again seene with far greater tumult, fighting
'in the manner afore-mentioned for foure houres, or verie neere, and
'then vanished, appearing againe on Sunday night, and performing
'the same actions of hostilitie and bloudshed; so that both Mr.
'Wood and others, whose faith, it should seeme, was not strong
'enough to carrie them out against these delusions, forsook their
'habitations thereabout, and retired themselves to other more secure
'dwellings; but Mr. Marshall stayed, and some other; and so
'successively the next Saturday and Sunday the same tumults and
'prodigious sights and actions were put in the state and condition
'they were formerly. The rumour whereof comming to his
'Majestie at Oxford, he immediately dispatched thither Colonell
'Lewis Kirke, Captaine Dudley, Captaine Wainman, and three
'other Gentlemen of credit, to take the full view and notice of the
'said businesse, who, first hearing the true attestation and relation
'of Mr. Marshall and others, staid there till Saturday night follow-
'ing, wherein they heard and saw the fore-mentioned prodigies, and
'so on Sunday, distinctly knowing divers of the apparitions or
'incorporeall substances by their faces, as that of Sir Edmund
'Varney, and others that were there slaine; of which upon oath
'they made testimony to his Majestie. What this does portend
'God only knoweth, and time perhaps will discover; but doubtlessly
'it is a signe of his wrath against this Land, for these civill wars,
'which He in his good time finish, and send a sudden peace between
'his Majestie and Parliament.—FINIS.'

THE END.

INDEX.

A.

ABBOTT, Archbishop, suspended by Charles I., 49
Abingdon held by Arthur Goodwyn for Parliament, 321
Ancestry of Hampden, 5
Antipædobaptists, a sect of Independents, 113
Apparitions in the air after the battle of Edgehill (App. H), 382
Arguelles, the Spanish patriot, his friendship for, and letters to, Lord Nugent, xxxi., xxxiv.
Argyle, Earl of, his conduct in the Scottish war, 206
Arminians and Calvinists in 1635, 84
Arms, their rude and ancient character during the Civil War, 241
—— of the Parliamentary troops, 254
Army, the, its origin and progress in England, 11, 36, 50; its disaffection during the second Scotch War, 142
Army Plot, participation of Charles I. and his queen in it, 193, 197; measures of Parliament defeating it, 195
Array, commissions of, issued by Charles I., 234, 260
Art encouraged by Charles I., 35
Arundell, Lady, her heroic defence of Wardour Castle, 339
Ascot, Bucks, the Earl of Berkshire and others captured there by Hampden, 260

Ashmolean Museum, Hampden's locket preserved there, 363
Astley, Sir Jacob, his prayer before the battle of Edgehill, 295
Attainder of the Earl of Strafford, 157
Aylesbury, Lord Nugent member for, xvi., xxviii., xlii., li., lxviii.; gunpowder stored there by a Committee of Parliament, 236; declares in favour of Parliament, 261; Hampden defeats Royalists at, 287; Prince Rupert repulsed at, 308; skeletons of the killed lately discovered, 310; threatened by Prince Rupert, 343; defended by Bulstrode and Hampden, ib.

B.

Bacon, Lord, his fall and punishment, 23
Bamford, Samuel, his patriotism and political persecution, xx.
Banbury plundered of arms by Lord Northampton, 276; taken by the Royalists, 305
Base money proposed as a source of revenue to Charles I., 135
Bastwick and Burton imprisoned, 81, 108; released and compensated, 148
Beacons lighted to announce to Parliament the result of the battle of Edgehill, 304
Benevolences exacted by Charles I., 48

C C

Berkeley, Judge, apprehended by order of Parliament, 190

Berkshire, Earl of, and other Royalists captured by Hampden, 260

Berwick, treaty of, 120

Bill of attainder against Strafford, 157

Birmingham taken and pillaged by Prince Rupert, 344

Bishops, their servility to Charles I., 166, 169; their power restrained by the Long Parliament, 169, 231, 273

Book of Canons, or "Anti-Covenant," issued by Convocation, 134

Bossuet, his panegyric on Queen Henrietta, 36

Brackley, Royalists repulsed by Hampden at, 327

Bradock Down, near Liskeard, Royalist victory at, 329

Bramston, Chief Justice, held to bail by Parliament, 190

Brentford, Holles's regiment there, 310; Hampden's bravery at the battle of, 312

Brill-Hill, Oxfordshire, Hampden defeated at, 328

Brook of Warwick, Lord, his resistance to ship money, 105; founder of Saybrook, Connecticut, 109; his patriotism, 144; defends Coventry against the King's army, 264; his defence of Warwick, 265; his bold refusal to surrender, 266; defeats the Royalists at Southam, 268; his speech at Warwick Castle to the Parliamentary officers, 273; repulses the Royalists at Stratford on Avon, 290; at Edgehill, 295; at the battle of Brentford, 312; killed in the attack on Lichfield, 337

Brooke, Lord, his "Five Years of King James," 10, 17

Broughton Castle, Oxon, conferences of Puritans and Scotch Covenanters at, 140; taken by the Royalists, 305

Buckingham, Villiers Duke of, his character, 26; his influence with Prince Charles, 27; charged with poisoning James I., 30; impeached by the House of Commons, 45; elected Chancellor of Cambridge University, ib.; his assassination, 55; his order for English ships to join the French fleet (App. A), 367

———— Marquis of, father of Lord Nugent, ix., xiv., xvi., xvii., xxiv.

———— and Chandos, Richard Duke of, his political differences with Lord Nugent, xxv., xxvi., xxviii., xxxii.

Buckinghamshire represented by Hampden in the "Short Parliament," 122; and the "Long Parliament," 146; county deputation with petition to the king in favour of Hampden; his answer, 229; its offer to raise troops to defend Parliament, 230; its offer of 30,000*l.* in aid of Parliament, 256; Hampden's letter to the Deputy Lieutenants of, urging resistance, 307; ordinance of Parliament appointing Deputy Lieutenants (App. F), 379

"Buckinghamshire Petition" presented to Parliament, 228

Bulstrode, Colonel, and other Deputy Lieutenants of Bucks, Hampden's letter to, 307; his services at Aylesbury, 343

Burford, victory of the Royalists at, 326

Burton and Bastwick tortured as Puritans, 81, 108; released and compensated, 148

C.

Caldecot Manor-house, its heroic defence, its surrender to Prince Rupert, 278

Calvinists and Arminians in 1635, 84

Canning George, his speech on Lord Nugent's support of the Spanish war, xxxvi.; his subsequent views thereon, xxxiv.

Capel, Lord, his devotion to the royal cause, 286

Capital punishments, Lord Nugent's views on, xxii., lxx.

Catholic emancipation, supported by Lord Nugent, xviii., xlv.

Cavaliers, their temptations to the royal cause, 246

Cavalry during the Civil War, 282

Chambers, Richard, his refusal to pay ship money, 93

Chalgrove, muster of troops there under Hampden, 260

——————— Field, Hampden mortally wounded at, 360

Chaloner, executed for participation in Waller's plot, 352

Chandoys, Lord, compelled to leave Sudeley Castle to join the king, 261

Chinnor, Bucks, attacked by Rupert, 358

Church Government, committee on, Hampden a member of it, 173; Sir R. Verney's account of its proceedings (App. E), 377

Cirencester declares in favour of the Parliament, 261; taken by Rupert, 323

Clarendon, Edward Hyde, Earl of, his remarks on ship money, 91; on the Army Plot, 193; his political conduct in the Short Parliament, 122, 127, 132, 133; on the trial of Strafford, 149, 162, 163; joins the Royalists, 178; opposes the "General Remonstrance," 218; and replies on behalf of the king, 219; declared a traitor by Parliament, 272; his characters of Sir Beville Grenvil, 69-252; of Dr. Hales, 84; of Pym, 98; of Lord Say, 175, 176, of Nathaniel Fiennes, 175; of Montrose, 207; his general eulogy of Hampden, 107; his misrepresentations respecting Hampden's conduct and motives, 165, 175, 185, 195

Clergy, their corruption and servility to Charles I., 169; bill to restrain them from secular offices, 168; passed, 231

"Close Committee," Hampden's activity on it, 320

"Coat and conduct money" for the militia imposed by Charles I. as a source of revenue, 78, 135

Coke, Sir Edward, his early association with Hampden, 22

Colepeper, one of the king's council, 219; made Chancellor of the Exchequer for life, 230

"Commission of Superiority and Tythes" in Scotland, its oppressive operation, 114

Commissioners sent by the Long Parliament to Edinburgh, 205; their return to London, 210

"Commissions of Array" issued by Charles I., 234, 260

Committee of Privileges in defence of the Five Members, 226; its exertions in appealing to the citizens, 227

——————— on Church Government, Sir R. Verney's account of its proceedings (App. E), 377

Common Prayer Book, its use in Scotland resisted, 114

Compton, Lord, at the siege of Warwick Castle, 277

Compulsory knighthood fees, as a source of revenue, 78

——————— loans (see Forced loans)

Connecticut, emigration to by Puritans, 76, 109

Convocation, its operations under Archbishop Laud, 134

Conway, Lord, defeated by the

c c 2

Presbyterians, 135; reproved by Strafford, 136
Cornwall, the civil war in, 329
"Court of Wards," its oppressive character, 80; sacrificed by Charles I. to the people, 192
"Covenant," the Scottish, its origin, 114, 115; its terms accepted by Charles I., 206
Covenanters, their insurrection and its results, 116; their communications with the Puritans, 138; their stipulations with Charles I., 143; propitiated by Charles I., to awe the Parliament, 204
Coventry besieged by the Royalists, 263; their defeat, 264; again refuses to surrender, 290
Cozens, Dr., Dean of Durham, his persecution of Smart, 173
Crawford, Earl of, his participation in the "Scottish Incident," 209
Crawley, Judge, held to bail by Parliament, 190
Croke, Justice, his judgment against ship money, 104
Cromwell, Oliver, his relationship to Hampden, 89; his intended emigration said to have been prohibited by Charles I., 109; represented Cambridge in the Long Parliament, 146; his character; Hampden's prophecy of his future greatness, 182; his regiment termed "Ironsides," 254; his judgment in warfare, 271
Curran, J. P., Lord Nugent's friendship for him, xvii.
Customs placed under control of Parliament, 192; rearrangement under Parliament, 203

D.

Dalbier supports Essex's cautious policy at Edgehill, 300, 303; his weakness at the battle of Brentford, 313

Davenant, his participation in the army plot, 195
Davenport, Chief Baron, his judgment against ship money, 105; held to bail by Parliament, 190
Davila's "Civil Wars of France" the favourite study of Hampden, 77, 88
Declaration by Charles I. on the outbreak of the Civil War, 235, (App. G) 380
———— of Parliament against the king, 259
Deering, Sir Edward, a coadjutor of Hampden, his character, 181; his journal of the surrender of Reading to Essex, 347
Demand by Charles I. for the surrender of Hampden and other members of Parliament, 220, 225
Denham, Justice, his judgment against ship money, 105
———— Sir John, his inefficient defence of Farnham Castle; his intercession for the poet Wither, 319; his lampoon on Hampden, 320
Denman, Lord, his co-operation with Lord Nugent in erecting the monument to Hampden on Chalgrove Field, lxiii.
Derby, Earl of, besieges Manchester, 271; his defeat, 272
Digby, Lord, his treachery in the trial of Strafford, 160; joins the party of Charles I., 178; his attempt to coerce Parliament, 230; his betrayal of the queen's foreign negotiations, 232; defeated at Wolverhampton, 290; at Edgehill, 295
Digges and Eliot, committed by Charles I. on charges of treason, 45
D'Israeli's "Commentaries on the Life of Charles I.;" the author's imputations on Hampden and Sir John Eliot refuted, 65, 97
Dorset, Earl of, in charge of the

guard for the protection of Parliament, 216
Dugdale, Sir Wm., present at the battle of Edgehill, 303

E.

Eachard, his misrepresentation of Hampden, 145
Edgehill, battle of, 290; supposed apparitions in the air after the battle (App. H), 382
Education of Hampden, 7
Eliot, Sir John, his imprisonment by Charles I.; Mr. D'Israeli's imputations on his character refuted, 64, 65; his death and burial in the Tower, 68, 77; his private and public character, 69; letters from Hampden to him and to his son, 70-72, 74; Hampden's care for his sons, 71
Elizabeth, Queen, her visit to Hampden, Bucks, 6
Emigration of Puritans prohibited, 110
Episcopacy attacked by the Puritans in the Long Parliament, 172; its abolition "root and branch" proposed,175;"Bishops' Votes" bill passed, 231
Episcopal war in Scotland, 116
Episcopalian persecution in Scotland, 113
Essex, Earl of, leader of the Parliamentary army, 253; his motto "Cave, adsum" ridiculed, 254; joins the Parliamentary army, 259; his reply to Prince Rupert's challenge, 279; his advance to Worcester, his address to his army, 280; refused access to the king with proposals for peace, 286; at Edgehill, 298; his advance upon Northampton with Hampden, 306; his progress to London, 310; rewarded by Parliament, 310; drives Rupert from Windsor and Henley, 317; abandons the siege of Oxford, 324; his siege and capture at Reading, 348; his indecision of character, 270, 300, 313, 316, 350, 355
Excise duties oppressively enforced by Charles I. (see Tonnage and Poundage)
Execution of a spy at Oxford, 308

F.

Fairfax, Sir Thomas, his commission in the Parliamentary army, 253
—— Lord, commands the Parliamentary troops in Yorkshire, 271; his proposed neutrality overruled, 272
Falkland, Lord, his speech concerning episcopacy, 83; his conduct in the Short Parliament,127; a supporter of the attainder of Strafford, 162; his views on restraining episcopal power, 175; his conduct as to the "Grand Remonstrance," on public grievances, 219; on the demand for the surrender of the five members, 223; on the reply to the electors of Bucks, 230; made chief secretary of state, 230; his moderation at the outbreak of the civil war, 240; his motives compared with those of Hampden, 241; his integrity and fidelity to the royal cause, 248; delivers a conciliatory message from the king to the Parliament, 259; declared a traitor by Parliament, 272; at the battle of Edgehill, 292; his policy after the battle, 292
Family of Hampden, its antiquity, 56
Farnham Castle, taken by the Parliament, 319
Fasts directed by Parliament to be observed, 273
Fawsley, Northamptonshire, Puritans' and Covenanters' conferences at, 140

Female heroism, during the Civil War, 278, 339
Fielding, Colonel, his surrender of Reading to Essex, 349; tried, sentenced, and reprieved, 350
Fiennes, Nathaniel, a supporter of the abolition of episcopacy, 175; his character, 176, 179; Clarendon's opinion of him, 176; one of the commissioners to Charles I., at Edinburgh, 205; his valour at Powick Bridge, 282
Finch, Speaker of the House of Commons, supports the exactions of Charles I., 61, 62; made chief justice, advises the enforcement of ship money, 91; appointed Lord Keeper; his further enforcement of ship money, 122; arraigned by the Long Parliament, 149; impeached; his flight to France, 189
Finsbury Fields, muster of train bands against the royal army in, 305
Forced loans a source of public revenue, 43, 117, 135; Hampden imprisoned for non-compliance, 47; order for his release (App. B), 369
Forest laws, enforced by Charles I.; as a source of revenue, 78
Fortescue, Sir Faithful, his desertion to the Royalists at Edgehill, 296
Funeral of Hampden, 363

G.

General commitment claimed as a right by Charles I., 51, 52
Gerrard, Sir Gilbert, repulses the Puritans at Brill Hill, 328
Glanville, Serjeant, his committee on Parliamentary elections, 40; draws up the impeachment of Buckingham, 44; Speaker in the Short Parliament, 132
Godolphin, Sydney, killed at Okehampton, 332

Goodwin, Arthur, Hampden's colleague in Parliament, 122; his regiment of Parliamentary cavalry, 254; its services at Ascot, 260; at Aylesbury, 343; occupies Abingdon, 321
Goring, his connexion with the army plot, his treachery, 196; ordered to hold Portsmouth for "King and Parliament," 231; his weak defence of Portsmouth, 263; the town capitulates to Parliament, ib.; his escape to Holland, ib.; his treachery in the west of England, 335.
Grampound represented in Parliament by Hampden, 20
"Grand Committee" of the Short Parliament on public grievances, 123
——————— of the Long Parliament, 147
"Grand Remonstrance" on public grievances submitted to Charles I., 217; the king's reply drawn up by Clarendon, 219
Great Hampden, Bucks, the seat of Hampden's family, 5; Hampden's mansion at, 124; his supposed coffin opened, xlvii.
Great Seal made for the Parliament, Whitelocke appointed keeper, 347
Greek war of independence supported by Lord Nugent, xl.
Grenvil, Richard, High Sheriff of Bucks, his correspondence at Stow, 3; report to him of the execution of a spy at Oxford, 308; wounded at Brill Hill, 329; his draft ordinance appointing Deputy-Lieutenants of Bucks (App. F), 379
———, Sir Bevill, his friendship for Sir John Eliot, 69; his conduct in the Short Parliament, 127; on the attainder of Strafford, 164; his chivalrous attachment to the royal cause, 250; his letter to Sir John Tre-

lawney, 251; Clarendon's character of him, 252; his letter to Lady Grenvil on the victory at Liskeard, 330; killed at the battle of Lansdowne, 335; letter announcing his death to Lady Grenvil, 336

Guard for the protection of Parliament, placed under the Earl of Dorset, 216

Gun-boats moored at Westminster to defend the Parliament, 310

H.

Habeas Corpus Suspension Act opposed by Lord Nugent, xxii.

Hakewill, Hampden's law and Parliamentary agent, 41

Hales, Dr., his opposition to the High Church faction, 83; Clarendon's character of him, 84

Hamilton, Marquis of, his character, 115; his conduct in the Scotch War, 206; his enmity to Montrose, ib.

Hampden, Sybil, nurse to Edward VI., 6

————, Elizabeth, mother of John Hampden, her desire for a peerage for her son, 20

———————— first wife of Hampden, 8; her death and monument, 89

————, Letitia, Hampden's second wife, 128

Harvey, Dr. William, entrusted with the care of the Prince of Wales and Duke of York at the battle of Edgehill, 303

Haydon, B. R., his notice of Lord Nugent, lii.

Hazelrigge, his support of Hampden's measures, 181; his surrender demanded of Parliament by Charles I., 220; proceedings thereon, 221; his speech in his defence, 223; his regiment termed "Lobsters" from their armour, 254

Heath, Sir Robert, his opposition to the Petition of Rights, 51

Heber, Bishop, his friendship for Lord Nugent, xii.

Henley, Prince Rupert, driven from the town by Essex, 317

Henrietta, Queen of Charles I., her influence on the king's character, 33; on religious controversy, 171; her participation in the Army Plot, 193; her perception of the danger of Parliamentary ordinances, 217; her departure for Holland, 231; her return, 324

Hertford, Marquis of, summons Poole to surrender to the king, 262

Heylin, Dr. Peter, his support of the High Church faction, 85; his exaggerations in the "Mercurius Aulicus," 326

High Church corruption and servility of the clergy, 169

"High Commission Court," its arbitrary power, 87, 113, 149

Holbourne, Robert, counsel for Hampden on the illegality of ship money, 103; elected to the Long Parliament, 146

Holland, its support to the royal cause, 233, 269, 334

————, Lord, his remarks on Prince Polignac, xlix.; on Lord Nugent's administration of the Ionian Islands and his neglect by Ministers, lx.

Holles, Denzil, member of the secret committee on Strafford's impeachment, 149; his surrender demanded of Parliament by Charles I., 220; proceedings thereon, 221; defeats Royalists near Aylesbury, 287; at Wolverhampton, 290; at Edgehill, 295; and at the battle of Brentford, 310, 312

Hopton, Sir Ralph, defeats the Puritans at Bradock Down, 329; at Saltash, 332; his fruitless siege of Portsmouth, 332; his victory at Stratton Hill, 334; created Baron Hopton of Stratton, 332

Hopton Heath, battle at, Earl of Northampton slain, 338

Hotham, Sir John, ordered to hold Hull for "King and Parliament," 231; advances against the Royalists, 271; takes Doncaster, Selby, and Cawood Castle, 273; his treachery to Parliament, capture and execution, 354

Hounslow, Charles II. at, 312

Hull, garrisoned by Sir J. Hotham for the Parliament, 231; the king's ineffectual attempt to enter the town, 233; Hotham's conspiracy to surrender it detected; his execution, 354

Hutton, Justice, his judgment against ship money, 105

Hyde, Edward, afterwards Earl of Clarendon (see Clarendon)

Hyde Park, muster of train bands against the royal army, 305

I.

Impeachment of the Earl of Strafford, 149

Imprisonment of Members of Parliament claimed by Charles I. as royal prerogative, 45, 49, 51, 52, 63

"Incident," the Scottish, a plot to enable Charles I. to dissolve the Long Parliament, 208

Independents, their origin and characteristics; distinguished from the Presbyterians, 112; separation of the two sects, 139

Insurrection of Roman Catholics in Ireland, 211

Ionian Islands, Lord Nugent appointed Lord High Commissioner, lii; his policy and administration, liv, lix

Ireland, insurrection of Roman Catholics against the English Parliament, 211; alleged connivance of Charles I., 212

Irish Parliament, its opposition to Strafford on his trial, 152

"Ironsides," Cromwell's regiment so called from their armour, 254

Islington fortified against the royal forces, 305

J.

James I., his character, 12; his policy the cause of the Parliamentary war, 14; his disputes with Parliament, 16; suspicions as to his death by poison, 30

Journals of the House of Commons, their occasional errors, 3

Judges, their operations suspended, 345

"Junto," the, Hampden's party in the Long Parliament so called, 189

Juxon, Bishop, his fidelity to Charles I., 192

K.

Kerr, Henry, his defiance to Hamilton, and submission to the Scotch Parliament, 208

Kimbolton, Lord, a supporter of the abolition of episcopacy, 175; his character, 177; his surrender demanded of Parliament by Charles I., 220

"King and Parliament" associated by the Puritans at the outbreak of the Civil War, 245

Kirke, Colonel Lewis, his ineffectual defence of Reading, 319

Knighthood sold by Charles I., 36, 90

Knightley, Richard, of Fawsley, a colleague of Hampden, 89, 140

————, Mrs., daughter of Hampden; her death, 239

L.

Lansdown (Bath), battle of, 335

Laud, Archbishop, his character

INDEX.

and policy, 79; his persecution of the Scotch Presbyterians, 115, 117; his enforcement of ship money, 122, 134, 144; his flight from the populace after the dissolution of the Short Parliament, 135; impeached by the Long Parliament and committed to the Tower, 149

Leaders of the Parliamentary Army, 255

Leicester, the royal army at, 263, 269

Leighton, author of "Sion's Plea," persecuted as a Puritan, 80; released and compensated, 148

Lenthall, Speaker, his resistance to the king's demand for the surrender of the five members, 225

Lichfield, fortified for the King, is assailed, and capitulates, 337

Lilburne, John, prosecuted by Court, Parliament, Prelates, and Presbyterians, 81, 108; released and compensated, 148

Lilies, the seat of Lord Nugent, his library there, xi., xv., xxiv., liii., lxiv.

Lindsey, Lord, killed at Edgehill, 300

Liskeard taken by the Royalists, 329

Littleton, Sir Edward, appointed Lord Keeper; his character, 190; a supporter of the Militia Bill, 216; sends the Great Seal to the king on the outbreak of the Civil War, 236

"Lobsters," Hazelrigge's regiment, so called from their armour, 254

London resists the payment of ship money, 93; Charles I. received by the citizens on his return from Scotland, 214; the City adheres to Parliament, 214, 247; Charles I.'s appeal to, 227; civic loans in aid of the Parliament, 255; popular contributions of jewels and plate, 256; fortified against the king, 273; preparations for its defence after the battle of Edgehill, 305

"Long Parliament," its constitution, character, and proceedings, 144, 147

Lord's Day sports opposed by the Puritans, 82

Loudon, Lord, imprisoned by Charles I., 121

Lunsford, Colonel, the Tower and the Mint placed in his charge, 216; his attempt to coerce Parliament, 230

M.

Mackintosh, Sir James, his friendship for Lord Nugent, xlii.

Maidenhead, Charles I. and Rupert at, 310; Parliamentary troops at, 325

Mary of Medici, mother of Queen Henrietta Maria, her visit to England, 171

Maurice, Prince, at the battle of Lansdown, 335

Meadley, Mr., his collections for the life of Hampden, 2

Meetings to petition Parliament, their origin, 123

Members of Parliament imprisoned by Charles I., 45, 49, 64, 134

Merchants' goods seized by Charles I., 54

"Mercurius Aulicus" first published at Oxford, 325

Militia, bill to place it under Parliamentary Commissioners, 216

Mohun, Lord, joins the Royalists, 329

Monopolies a source of revenue to the Crown, 43, 78, 79, 110

Montague, Bishop, encouraged by Charles I., 54

Montrose, his treachery to the Presbyterian cause, 137; his conduct in the Scotch war, 206; his imprisonment and intrigues with Charles I., 207; his connexion with the "Scottish Incident," 209

Monument to Hampden at Chalgrove Field, lxiii

Moore, Roger, the instigator of the Irish rebellion, 212

Morley, Bishop of Winchester, his opposition to the High Church faction, 83, 85

Mottoes of the Parliamentary leaders, 254

N.

"National Covenant" of Scotland, its origin, 115

Navy, its condition in England under James I. and Charles I., 56; popular government essential to its prosperity, 57; its support of the Parliamentary cause, 257

Newcastle taken by the Presbyterians, 136

———, Marquis of, raises levies for the king, 231

———, Earl of, his exertions in the north, 324; defeated at Wakefield, 324

New England, emigration of Puritans to, 109

Newspapers in 1643, 326

Northampton declares for the Parliament, 261; fortified by the people, 269

——— ———, Earl of, a supporter of the Royal cause, 261; his narrow escape at Coventry, 264; besieges Warwick Castle, but is defeated, 277; killed at Hopton Heath, 338

Northumberland, Earl of, Lord High Admiral, his retirement at the outbreak of the Civil War, 257; treats for peace with the king at Colnbrook, 310; deserts the cause of Parliament, 351

Nottingham, the royal standard raised at, 237, 245

Noy (Attorney-General), his secession to the Court party, 61; his character, 90; a supporter of ship money, 91

Nugent, George Grenville, Lord, author of "Memorials of Hampden," Memoir of, ix., lxxii.; his Essay on Duelling, xi.; his preface to the "Memorials of Hampden," 1

———, Lady, her taste and accomplishments, xvii., lxiv.; her death, lxix.

———, Lady Mary, mother of Lord Nugent, ix.; her character, xiv., xv.

Nuncios from Rome received by Charles I., 171

O.

Oaths in the Customs and Excise abolished by Lord Nugent, li.

Ordinance to marshal the Buckinghamshire militia; its publication by Hampden, 240

"Ordinances" of Parliament first passed without the royal assent, 213; their effect anticipated by Charles I. and his queen, 217

Ordinances for arming the kingdom, 261

"Oxford Commissioners" captured by Hampden, 260

Oxford, Hampden attacks Lord Byron at, 287; Charles I. at Christ Church Hall, 308, 320; invested by Essex, 321; the siege abandoned, 324; negotiations for peace, 340; broken off, 343

P.

Paget, Lord, his flight from Buckinghamshire to Charles I. at York, 236

Pancras, St., musters of train bands against the royal army, 305

Panzani received by Charles I. as nuncio from Rome, 171

Parliament, extension of the representation, temp. Henry VIII. to Charles I., 41; declared indissoluble, save by its own consent, 187

Parliaments of James I., 18, 19, 29; of Charles I., 38, 44, 49, 61; the "Short Parliament," 122; the "Long Parliament," 144

Payment of members of Parliament, 39

Peace proposals by the Parliament rejected by the king, 286, 325

Pennington, Admiral, his protest against serving in the siege of Rochelle, 44; orders to him by Charles I. and Buckingham to join the French fleet (App. A), 367

Percy and Wilmot, participators in the Army Plot, 195, 196

Père d'Orleans, his errors as to the policy of the elder Vane, 131

Perth, Assembly of, 113

Petition of Right, prepared by Coke and Seldon, 51; opposed by Charles I.; 58; discussed and carried, 52

Peto, Sir Edward, defends Warwick Castle against the Royalists, 277

Pierce, Bishop, his episcopalian practices, 173

Plymouth unsuccessfully besieged by the Royalists, 332

Polignac, Prince, remarks on, by Lord Holland and the Duke of Wellington, xlix.

Poll-tax imposed by Charles I., 196

Pomfret Castle held by the Royalists, 271

Poole, Dorsetshire, declares for the Parliament, and refuses to surrender, 262

Popish influence at the Court of Charles I., 171

Portsmouth held for the king, by Goring; its capitulation, 262

"Portugal," a poem, by Lord Nugent, xiii.

Postcombe, Bucks, attacked by Rupert, 357

Powick Bridge, near Worcester, battle at, 282

"Precisians," a term applied to the Puritans, 109

Presbyterians, their characteristics, as distinct from the Independents; separation of the two sects, 111, 112; persecuted in Scotland, 115

———— (Scotch), their assistance sought by Charles I. and Parliament, 205

Proclamation by Parliament of the objects of the war, 273; by Charles I. in declaration of war, (App. G) 380

"Protestation" of Parliament, 1621, 25

Prynne persecuted and tortured as a Puritan, 80, 81, 108; released and compensated, 148

Purefoy, Mrs., her defence of Caldecot, 278

Puritans, their sufferings under Charles I., 80; restrained from emigrating, 110; their communications with the Scotch Covenanters, 138; their division into "Religious" and "Political" sects, 185

Pye, Sir Robert, son-in-law of Hampden, 360

Pym, his association with Hampden, 22; his advocacy of the Petition of Rights, 51; his reproof to Strafford on his secession to the Court party, 60; his exertions in the elections for the Long Parliament, 144; elected in Long Parliament, 146; his conduct on Strafford's impeachment, 147, 149, 152, 160; conferences at his lodgings in Gray's Inn-lane, 178; character of, 183; his knowledge of the Army Plot, 194;

his surrender demanded of Parliament by Charles I., 220; proceedings thereon, 221

R.

Reading, besieged and taken by Hampden and Urrie, 317; again garrisoned for the king, 325; besieged, surrendered to Essex, 347; Hampden commands the advanced guard, 347
Reform of Parliament, Lord Nugent's views on, xxii., xli.
Religious controvery in 1635, 84
"Remonstrance, Grand," on public grievances submitted to Charles I., 217; the king's reply drawn up by Clarendon, 219
Repeal of the Corn Laws, Lord Nugent's views on, lxviii.
Rochelle, siege of, aided by English ships, 43; second expedition and its failure, 55; third expedition, ib.
Rohan, Governor of Rochelle, his accusation of treachery against Charles I., 55
Romish influence at the Court of Charles I., 171
Rosetti received by Charles I. as nuncio from Rome, 171
Rupert, Prince, in arms at Leicester, 237; his attack on Caldecott Manor-house, 278; his challenge to the Earl of Essex, 279; at the skirmish at Powickbridge, 282; threatens Coventry, 290; his conduct at Edgehill, 292; repulsed at Aylesbury, 308; his retreat to Thame, 309; proceeds to Maidenhead, 310; driven by Essex from Windsor and Henley, 317; takes Cirencester, 323; his advance to and retreat from Aylesbury, 343; Birmingham assaulted by him, taken and pillaged, 344; threatens Lichfield, is restrained by the king, 345; his expedition from Oxford to Chalgrovefield, 358; Hampden mortally wounded there, 360; Rupert's severity in warfare, 285, 323, 344, 358
Russell, Lord John, his friendship for Lord Nugent, his speech on the Spanish War, xxiii., lxvi.
———, Sir Robert Greenhill, materials in his library for the history of the Civil War, 3, 53
Ruthven, General, at Edgehill, 293

S.

St. Albans declares for Parliament, 261
St. John, Oliver, his association with Hampden, 22; his opposition to ship money, 95; counsel for Hampden, 103; his reputation increased by his arguments, 107; his conduct on Strafford's impeachment, 149, 152, 160; appointed Solicitor-General, 165
———, Lord, killed at Edgehill, 298
Salisbury, Earl, his desertion of the royal cause, 236
Saltash taken by the Royalists, 332
Saville, his rivalry with Strafford, his secession to the Court party, 59; his forged invitation to the Scotch War, 203
Say and Sele, Lord, his resistance to ship money, 99, 105; founder of Saybrook, Connecticut, 109; his resistance to the Court party, 140, 144, 320; his opposition to the bill for the attainder of Strafford, 161; a supporter of the abolition of Episcopacy, 175; Clarendon's opinion of him, 176
Saybrook, Connecticut, founded by Lords Say and Brook, 109
"Scandalous Ministers' Committee," Hampden a member of it, 53
Scotland, persecutions by the Episcopalians, 113; the Book of

INDEX. 397

Common Prayer rejected by the Presbyterians, 114; insurrection and first Episcopal War, 116; treaty of Berwick, Parliament called, 119; second Episcopal War, 135; communications between Covenanters and Puritans, 138; treaty of Rippon, 142; the Scotch compensated for their losses by Parliament, 187; the Scotch army assisted by Parliament, 195; Charles I.'s visit to Edinburgh, 203-204; position of the Scotch and English armies, 203; the army propitiated, and Scottish nobles honoured by the King, 204; the "Scottish Incident," a plot to enable Charles I. to dissolve Parliament, 208; Charles I.'s intrigues with Montrose; failure of the "Scottish Incident;" the king's return to London, 204-211; its assistance to Parliament in suppressing the Irish rebellion, 256

"Scottish Incident," a plot to enable Charles I. to dissolve the Long Parliament, 208; its history and failure, 209

Selden, his association with Hampden, 22; opposes the exactions of Charles I., 61; and imprisonment of M.P.s, 64; his controversy with Grotius on the freedom of the seas, 90; his conduct on Strafford's impeachment, 149; his votes on the powers of the bishops, 174; opposes the bill to place the militia under Parliament, 216

Sheriffs appointed by Charles I. for political purposes, 86

Ship money the direct cause of the civil war; issue of the first writ, 91; resolutely opposed, 93; extended to inland places, 94; promoted by the Star Chamber and the Judges, ib.; its arbitrary and illegal character, 95; large amount collected, ib.; Hampden's opposition to it, ib.; writ addressed to Sir Peter Temple, High Sheriff of Bucks, 96; motive of Hampden's opposition defended, 97; return by the assessors of Great Kimble, Bucks, with Hampden's refusal of payment, 99; opinion of the judges in favour of its legality, 100; dissent of Croke and Hutton, 101; Strafford's approval of it, ib., 107; increased opposition, 102; legal proceedings against Hampden, ib.; ultimate decision against him, 105; its continued enforcement, 122; Hampden's case reported by the short Parliament as a grievance; the king's offers of concession, 123, 131; declared illegal, 192; compensation to sufferers, 203; decision of the courts reversed, 214; schedule of the distribution of ships and charges made on each county and town (App. C), 370; warrants to sheriff of Bucks for its collection (App. D), 375; and to account for arrears (App. D), 376

"Short Parliament," its constitution and proceedings, 127, 130

Shrewsbury, Prince Rupert at, 279; Charles I. at, 269

Smart, prebendary of Durham, imprisoned, released, and compersated, 190

Smith, Sydney, his description of Lord Nugent as "a political flugelman," lxxi.

Southam, Hampden, defeats the Parliamentary forces at, 267, 268

Spanish War, Lord Nugent's cooperation with the patriotic party, xxx.

Speeches of Charles I. to his army at Edgehill, 293

Stage plays, suppressed by Parliament, 273

Stamford, Earl of, his inefficiency as a Parliamentary general, 332
Star Chamber, its arbitrary proceedings, 63, 81, 87, 109, 128, 135, 141, 148; abolished, 192
"Statute of Improvements," enforced by Charles I. against the Parliamentary party, 79
Stoke Mandeville, Bucks, Hampden's assessment there for ship money, 102
Strafford, Lord, his early association with Hampden, 22; imprisoned by Charles I., 46; his secession to the royal party, 59; his rivalry to Saville, ib.; his approval of ship money, 101. 122, 142, 144; his government of Ireland, 120; his reproof of Lord Conway, 136; impeached by the Long Parliament, and committed, 149; his protracted trial, 150; his able defence, 152, 160; separate proceedings by bill of attainder, 156; that proceeding objectionable, 159; not supported by Hampden, 161, 163
Stratford-on-Avon, Hampden repulses the Royalists at, 290
Stratten Hill, Royalist victory at, 334
Strode, a supporter of Hampden in the Long Parliament, 181; Charles I. demands his surrender, 220; proceedings thereon, 225
Suckling, his participation in the Army Plot, 195

T.

Temple, Sir Peter, his papers at Stow, 2; writ for levying ship money addressed to him, 96; summoned to answer for arrears from Hampden and others, 99
Thame, Hampden taken there after his death-wound, 361

Theatres, suppressed by Parliament, 273
Tomkins executed for his participation in Waller's plot, 352
Tonnage and poundage imposed by Charles I., 48; its obnoxious character, 54; Charles I. attempt to enforce it, 61; resistance of the House of Commons, 61, 62; the king's offer to modify the impost, 123
Train bands mustered in London against the Royal army, 305
Treaties of Berwick, 120; and Rippon, 142
Trelawney, John, his letter to Lady Grenvil on the death of Sir Bevill, 336
Triennial Bill passed by the Long Parliament, 169
Turpin, Joseph, Lord Nugent's favourite servant, liii.

U.

"Undertakers" to influence elections, temp. James I., 18, 39
Uniforms of the Parliamentary army, 254
Urrie, Colonel, Reading besieged and taken by him and Hampden, 317; his desertion to the Royalists, 355-356; plans the expedition to Chalgrove, 357; Hampden mortally wounded there, 360
Uxbridge, Hampden's regiment at, 310

V.

Vane, Sir Henry, the elder, his policy during the Short Parliament, 131, 133
————— —————, the younger, a supporter of the abolition of episcopacy, 175; his character, 180
Verney, Sir Edmund, the Royal standard-bearer, his character,

250; killed at Edgehill, 295, 298
Verney, Sir Ralph, his account of the proceedings of the Committee on Church Government (App. E), 377
Villiers, Duke of Buckingham (see Buckingham)
Voluntary loans in aid of the Parliament, 255, 256

W.

Wagstaffe, Hampden's lieutenant-colonel, taken prisoner, enters the king's army, 327; brought into conflict with Hampden, 328
Waller, Edmund, his relationship to Hampden, 89; member for St. Ives, in the Long Parliament, 146; his plot to betray the Puritans, 351; fined 10,000*l*., his letter for mercy to Arthur Goodwyn, 352
Waller, Sir William, commands the Parliamentary forces in the west, 334; his honourable failure, 335; the battle of Lansdown, ib.; his success at Hereford and Tewksbury, 339
Wardour Castle, Wilts, bravely defended by Lady Arundell, taken by the Parliament, defended by Ludlow, retaken by the Royalists, 339
Warwick in favour of the Parliament, 261; threatened by the Royalists, 266; its refusal to surrender, ib.; assembly of Parliamentary officers, 273; Lord Brook's speech to them, 274; the castle defended by Sir J. Peto, 276
Warwick, Earl of, Lord High Admiral for the Parliament, 257
Watlington, Hampden at, the night before his death, 359
Wellington, Arthur, Duke of, on Lord Nugent's poem of "Portugal," xiv; on Prince Polignac, l.
Wellington, Salop, Charles I. at, 269
Wendover represented by Hampden, 38, 44; its right to representation restored by him, 40; Hampden elected for, and also for Buckinghamshire, 146
Wentworth, Sir Thomas, afterwards Earl of Strafford (see Strafford)
————— Lord (son of the Earl of Strafford), defeated at Wycombe, 322
Wharton, Lord, appointed Lord Lieutenant of Bucks, 236; his letter to the deputy-lieutenants of Bucks, 307
White Leaf Cross, Bucks, a Saxon memorial, 124
Whitelocke, Bulstrode, his opposition to ship money, 95; Keeper of the Great Seal for Parliament, 347
Wilberforce, his friendship for Lord Nugent, xli.
Williams, Bishop, persecuted and imprisoned by Charles I., 49, 128; seeks the assistance of Hampden, 129; his restoration and forbearance to his persecutors, 129, 130; his assent to the execution of Strafford, 166; a supporter of episcopal power, 175, 186
Wilmot and Percy, participators in the Army Plot, 195, 196
Wilson, Sir Robert, his views on the Spanish war, xxx., xxxv.
Wiltshire, the Civil War in, 339
Windebanke, Secretary Sir F., arraigned by Parliament; his escape to Holland, 189
Windsor, Prince Rupert driven from the town by Essex, 317
Wolverhampton, Royalists defeated at, 290

Worcester held by the Earl of Essex, 280; his address to his army, 285; skirmish near the city, 282

Wren, Bishop of Ely, his cause opposed by Hampden, 173

Wycombe, Lord Wentworth defeated at, 322

Y.

York, Williams, Archbishop of (see Williams).

THE END.

BOHN'S CLASSICAL LIBRARY.

A SERIES OF LITERAL PROSE TRANSLATIONS OF THE GREEK AND LATIN CLASSICS WITH NOTES AND INDEXES.

Uniform with the STANDARD LIBRARY, 5s. *each (except Thucydides, Æschylus, Virgil, Horace, Cicero's Offices, Demosthenes, Appendix to Æschylus, Aristotle's Organon, all of which are 3s. 6d. each volume).*

1. HERODOTUS. By the REV. HENRY CARY, M.A. *Frontispiece.*
2 & 3. THUCYDIDES. By the REV. H. DALE. In 2 Vols. (3s. 6d. each). *Frontispiece.*
4. PLATO. Vol. I. By CARY. [The Apology of Socrates, Crito Phædo, Gorgias, Protagoras, Phædrus, Theætetus, Euthyphron, Lysis.] *Frontis. &c.*
5. LIVY'S HISTORY OF ROME, literally translated. Vol. I., Books 1 to 8.
6. PLATO. Vol. II. By DAVIS. [The Republic, Timæus, and Critias.]
7. LIVY'S HISTORY OF ROME. Vol. II., Books 9 to 26.
8. SOPHOCLES. The Oxford Translation, revised.
9. ÆSCHYLUS, literally translated. By an OXONIAN. (Price 3s. 6d.)
9* ———— Appendix to, containing the new readings given in Hermann's posthumous edition of Æschylus, translated and edited by G. BURGES, M.A. (3s. 6d.).
10. ARISTOTLE'S RHETORIC AND POETIC. With Examination Questions.
11. LIVY'S HISTORY OF ROME. Vol. III., Books 27 to 36.
12 & 14. EURIPIDES, literally translated. From the Text of Dindorf. In 2 Vols.
13. VIRGIL. By DAVIDSON. New Edition, Revised. (Price 3s. 6d.) *Frontispiece.*
15. HORACE. By SMART. New Edition, Revised. (Price 3s. 6d.) *Frontispiece.*
16. ARISTOTLE'S ETHICS. By PROF. R. W. BROWNE, of King's College.
17. CICERO'S OFFICES. [Old Age, Friendship, Scipio's Dream, Paradoxes, &c.]
18. PLATO. Vol. III. By G. BURGES, M.A. [Euthydemus, Symposium, Sophistes, Politicus, Laches, Parmenides, Cratylus, and Meno]
19. LIVY'S HISTORY OF ROME. Vol. IV. (which completes the work).
20. CÆSAR AND HIRTIUS. With Index.
21. HOMER'S ILIAD, in prose, literally translated. *Frontispiece.*
22. HOMER'S ODYSSEY, HYMNS, EPIGRAMS, AND BATTLE OF THE FROGS AND MICE.
23. PLATO. Vol. IV. By G. BURGES, M.A. [Philebus, Charmides, Laches, The Two Alcibiades, and Ten other Dialogues.]
24, 25, & 32. OVID. By H. T. RILEY, B.A. Complete in 3 Vols. *Frontispieces.*
26. LUCRETIUS. By the REV. J. S. WATSON. With the Metrical Version of J. M. GOOD.
27, 30, 31, & 34. CICERO'S ORATIONS. By C. D. YONGE. Complete in 4 Vols. (Vol. 4 contains also the Rhetorical Pieces.)
28. PINDAR. By DAWSON W. TURNER. With the Metrical Version of MOORE. *Front.*
29. PLATO. Vol. V. By G. BURGES, M.A. [The Laws.]
33 & 36. THE COMEDIES OF PLAUTUS, By H. T. RILEY, B.A. In 2 Vols.
35. JUVENAL, PERSIUS, &c. By the REV. L. EVANS, M.A. With the Metrical Version of GIFFORD. *Frontispiece.*
37. THE GREEK ANTHOLOGY, translated chiefly by G. BURGES, A.M., with Metrical Versions by various Authors.
38. DEMOSTHENES. The Olynthiac, Philippic, and other Public Orations, with Notes, Appendices, &c., by C. RANN KENNEDY. (3s. 6d.)

39. SALLUST, FLORUS, and VELLEIUS PATERCULUS, with copious Notes, Biographical Notices, and Index, by the Rev. J. S. Watson, M.A.

40. LUCAN'S PHARSALIA, with copious Notes, by H. T. Riley, B.A.

41. THEOCRITUS, BION, MOSCHUS and TYRTÆUS, by the Rev. J. Banks, M.A. With the Metrical Versions of Chapman. *Frontispiece.*

42. CICERO'S ACADEMICS, DE FINIBUS and TUSCULAN QUESTIONS, by C. D. Yonge, B A. With Sketch of the Greek Philosophy.

43. ARISTOTLE'S POLITICS AND ECONOMICS, by E. Walford, M.A., with Notes, Analyses, Life, Introduction, and Index.

44. DIOGENES LAERTIUS. LIVES AND OPINIONS OF THE ANCIENT PHILOSOPHERS, with Notes by C. D. Yonge, B.A.

45. TERENCE and PHÆDRUS, by H. T. Riley. To which is added Smart's Metrical Version of Phædrus. *Frontispiece.*

46 & 47. ARISTOTLE'S ORGANON, or, Logical Treatises, and the Introduction of Porphyry, with Notes, Analysis, Introduction and Index, by the Rev. O. F. Owen, M.A. 2 Vols., 3s. 6d. per Vol.

48 & 49. ARISTOPHANES, with Notes and Extracts from the best Metrical Versions, by W. J. Hickie, in 2 Vols. *Frontispiece.*

50. CICERO ON THE NATURE OF THE GODS, DIVINATION, FATE, LAWS, REPUBLIC, &c, translated by C. D. Yonge, B.A.

51. APULEIUS. [The Golden Ass, Death of Socrates, Florida, and Defence or Discourse on Magic]. To which is added a Metrical Version of Cupid and Psyche; and Mrs. Tighe's Psyche. *Frontispiece.*

52. JUSTIN, CORNELIUS NEPOS and EUTROPIUS, with Notes and a General Index, by the Rev. J. S. Watson, M.A.

53 & 58. TACITUS. Vol 1. The Annals. Vol. II. The History, Germania, Agricola, &c. With Index.

54. PLATO. Vol VI., completing the work, and containing Epinomis, Axiochus, Eryxias, on Virtue, on Justice, sisyphus, Demodocus, and Definitions; the Treatise of Timæus Locrus on the Soul of the World and Nature; the Lives of Plato by Diogenes Laertius, Hesychius, and Olympiodorus; and the Introductions to his Doctrines by Alcinous and Albinus; Apuleius on the Doctrines of Plato, and Remarks on Plato's Writings by the Poet Gray. Edited, with Notes, by G. Burges, M.A., Trin. Coll., Camb. With general Index to the 6 Volumes.

55, 56, 57. ATHENÆUS. The Deipnosophists, or the Banquet of the Learned, translated by C. D. Yonge, B.A., with an Appendix of Poetical Fragments rendered into English verse by various Authors, and a general Index. Complete in 3 Vols.

59. CATULLUS, TIBULLUS, and the VIGIL OF VENUS. A literal prose translation. To which are added Metrical Versions by Lamb, Grainger, and others. *Frontispiece.*

60. PROPERTIUS, Petronius Arbiter, and Johannes Secundus, literally translated, and accompanied by Poetical Versions, from various sources; to which are added the Love Epistles of Aristænetus. Edited by W. K. Kelly.

61, 74, & 82 THE GEOGRAPHY OF STRABO. translated, with copious Notes, by W. Falconer, M.A., and H. C. Hamilton, Esq. In 3 vols., and Index.

62. XENOPHON'S ANABASIS, or Expedition of Cyrus, and MEMORABILIA, or Memoirs of Socrates, translated by the Rev. J. S. Watson, with a Geographical Commentary by W. F. Ainsworth. *Frontispiece.*

63. ———— Cyropædia and Hellenics, by the Rev. H. Dale, and the Rev. J. S. Watson.

BOHN'S CLASSICAL LIBRARY.

64, 67, 69, 72, 78, & 81. PLINY'S NATURAL HISTORY, with copious Notes, by Dr. BOSTOCK and T. H. RILEY. In 6 volumes. Vols. I., II., III., IV., V. and VI.

65. SUETONIUS. Lives of the Cæsars, and other Works. THOMSON'S Translation revised by T. FORESTER.

66. DEMOSTHENES ON THE CROWN, AND EMBASSY, by C. RANN KENNEDY.

58. CICERO ON ORATORY AND ORATORS, by the Rev. J. S. WATSON, M.A.
*** This volume completes the Classical Library edition of Cicero.

70. GREEK ROMANCES. Heliodorus, Longus, and Achilles Tatius.

71 & 76. QUINTILIAN'S INSTITUTES OF ORATORY. By the Rev. J. S. WATSON, M.A. Complete, with Notes, Index, and Biographical Notice. 2 volumes.

73. HESIOD, CALLIMACHUS, AND THEOGNIS, in Prose, by BANKS, with the Metrical Versions of ELTON, TYTLER, and FRERE.

75. DICTIONARY OF LATIN QUOTATIONS with the Quantities marked and English Translations; including Proverbs, Maxims, Mottoes, Law Terms and Phrases; with a Collection of above 500 GREEK QUOTATIONS.

77. DEMOSTHENES AGAINST LEPTINES, MIDIAS, ANDROTION, AND ARISTOCRATES. By CHARLES RANN KENNEDY.

79. XENOPHON'S MINOR WORKS; translated by the Rev. J. S. WATSON.

80. ARISTOTLE'S METAPHYSICS, literally translated, with Notes, Analysis, Examination Questions and Index, by the Rev. JOHN H. M'MAHON. M.A.

81. MARTIAL'S EPIGRAMS, literally translated; with Imitations in Verse.

BOHN'S ANTIQUARIAN LIBRARY.

Uniform with the STANDARD LIBRARY, *price* 5s.,

1. BEDE'S ECCLESIASTICAL HISTORY, & THE ANGLO-SAXON CHRONICLE.

2. MALLET'S NORTHERN ANTIQUITIES. By BISHOP PERCY. With Abstract of the Erbyggia Saga, by SIR WALTER SCOTT. Edited by J. A. BLACKWELL.

3. WILLIAM OF MALMESBURY'S CHRONICLE OF THE KINGS OF ENGLAND.

4. SIX OLD ENGLISH CHRONICLES: viz., Asser's Life of Alfred; the Chronicles of Ethelwerd, Gildas, Nennius, Geoffry of Monmouth, and Richard of Cirencester.

5. ELLIS'S EARLY ENGLISH METRICAL ROMANCES. Revised by J. ORCHARD HALLIWELL. Complete in one vol., *Illuminated Frontispiece.*

6. CHRONICLES OF THE CRUSADERS: Richard of Devizes. Geoffrey de Vinsauf. Lord de Joinville. Complete in 1 volume. *Frontispiece.*

7. EARLY TRAVELS IN PALESTINE. Willibald, Sæwulf, Benjamin of Tudela, Mandeville, La Brocquiere, and Maundrell. In one volume. *With Map.*

8, 10, & 12. BRAND'S POPULAR ANTIQUITIES OF GREAT BRITAIN. By SIR HENRY ELLIS. In 3 Vols.

9 & 11. ROGER OF WENDOVER'S FLOWERS OF HISTORY (formerly ascribed to Matthew Paris.) In 2 Vols.

13. KEIGHTLEY'S FAIRY MYTHOLOGY. Enlarged. *Frontispiece* by CRUIKSHANK.

14, 15, & 16. SIR THOMAS BROWNE'S WORKS. Edited by SIMON WILKIN. *Portrait.* In 3 Vols. With Index.

17, 19, & 31. MATTHEW PARIS'S CHRONICLE, containing the History of England from 1235, with Index to the whole, including the portion published under the name of ROGER OF WENDOVER, in 3 Vols. (See 9 and 11). *Portrait.*

18. YULE-TIDE STORIES. A collection of Scandinavian Tales and Traditions, edited by B. THORPE, Esq.

20 & 23. ROGER DE HOVEDEN'S ANNALS OF ENGLISH HISTORY, from A.D. 732 to A.D. 1201. Translated by H. T. RILEY, Esq., B.A. In 2 Vols.

21. HENRY OF HUNTINGDON'S HISTORY OF THE ENGLISH, from the Roman Invasion to Henry II.; with The Acts of King Stephen, &c.

BOHN'S ANTIQUARIAN LIBRARY.

22. **PAULI'S LIFE OF ALFRED THE GREAT.** To which is appended ALFRED'S ANGLO-SAXON VERSION OF OROSIUS, with a literal translation. Notes, and an Anglo-Saxon Grammar and Glossary, by B. THORPE, Esq.

24 & 25. **MATTHEW OF WESTMINSTER'S FLOWERS OF HISTORY,** especially such as relate to the affairs of Britain, from the beginning of the world to A.D. 1307. Translated by C. D. YONGE, B.A. In 2 Vols.

26. **LEPSIUS'S LETTERS FROM EGYPT, ETHIOPIA,** and the PENINSULA OF SINAI. Revised by the Author. Translated by LEONORA and JOANNA B. HORNER. With Maps and Coloured View of Mount Barkal.

27, 28, 30 & 36. **ORDERICUS VITALIS.** His Ecclesiastical History of England and Normandy, translated, with Notes, the Introduction of Guizot, Critical Notice by M. Delille, and very copious Index, by T. FORESTER, M.A. In 4 Vols.

29. **INGULPH'S CHRONICLE OF THE ABBEY OF CROYLAND,** with the Continuations by Peter of Blois and other Writers. Translated, with Notes and an Index, by H. T. RILEY, B.A.

32. **LAMB'S SPECIMENS OF ENGLISH DRAMATIC POETS** of the time of Elizabeth; including his Selections from the Garrick Plays.

33. **MARCO POLO'S TRAVELS,** the translation of Marsden, edited, with Notes and Introduction, by T. WRIGHT, M.A., F.S.A., &c.

34. **FLORENCE OF WORCESTER'S CHRONICLE,** with the Two Continuations; comprising Annals of English History, from the Departure of the Romans to the Reign of Edward I. Translated, with Notes, by T. FORESTER, Esq.

35. **HAND-BOOK OF PROVERBS,** comprising the whole of Ray's Collection, and a complete Alphabetical Index, in which are introduced large Additions collected by HENRY G. BOHN.

37. **CHRONICLES OF THE TOMBS:** a select Collection of Epitaphs; with Essay on Monumental Inscriptions, &c., by T. J. PETTIGREW, F.R.S., F.S.A.

38. **A POLYGLOT OF FOREIGN PROVERBS;** comprising French, Italian, German, Dutch, Spanish, Portuguese & Danish. With English Translations, & General Index.

BOHN'S HISTORICAL LIBRARY,
Uniform with the STANDARD LIBRARY, price 5s. per Volume.

1, 2 & 3. **JESSE'S MEMOIRS OF THE COURT OF ENGLAND DURING THE REIGN OF THE STUARTS,** including the PROTECTORATE. In 3 vols., with General Index, and upwards of 40 Portraits engraved on steel.

4. **JESSE'S MEMOIRS OF THE PRETENDERS AND THEIR ADHERENTS.** New edition, complete in 1 vol., with Index and Six Portraits after original Pictures.

5, 6, 7 & 8. **PEPY'S DIARY AND CORRESPONDENCE,** edited by LORD BRAYBROOKE. New and Improved Edition, with Additions. Complete in 4 Volumes. Illustrated with Portraits and plates.

9, 10, 11 & 12. **EVELYN'S DIARY AND CORRESPONDENCE,** with the Private Correspondence of Charles I. New edition, considerably enlarged, from the original Papers (by JOHN FORSTER, Esq.) In 4 vols. Portraits and plates.

BOHN'S LIBRARY OF FRENCH MEMOIRS.
Uniform with the STANDARD LIBRARY, price 3s. 6d. per Volume.

1 & 2. **MEMOIRS OF PHILIP DE COMMINES,** containing the Histories of Louis XI. and Charles VIII., Kings of France, and of Charles the Bold, Duke of Burgundy. To which is added, The Scandalous Chronicle. In 2 volumes. *Portraits.*

3, 4, 5, & 6. **MEMOIRS OF THE DUKE OF SULLY,** Prime Minister to Henry the Great. With Notes, and an Historical Introduction by SIR WALTER SCOTT. In 4 vols. With a General Index. *Portraits.*

BOHN'S BRITISH CLASSICS.

Uniform with the STANDARD LIBRARY, *price 3s. 6d. per Volume.*

1, 3, 5, 8, 11, 14 & 20. GIBBON'S ROMAN EMPIRE; Complete and Unabridged, with variorum Notes; including, in addition to all the Author's own, those of Guizot, Wenck, Niebuhr, Hugo, Neander, and other foreign scholars. Edited by an ENGLISH CHURCHMAN, with a very elaborate Index.

2, 4, 6, 10, 24 & 25. ADDISON'S WORKS, with the Notes of BISHOP HURD, and large additions collated and edited by Henry G. Bohn. *With Portrait and Engravings on steel.*

7. DEFOE'S WORKS. Edited by SIR WALTER SCOTT. Vol 1. Containing the Life, Adventure, and Piracies of Captain Singleton, and the Life of Colonel Jack. *Portrait of Defoe.*

9. DEFOE'S WORKS, Vol. 2. Containing Memoirs of a Cavalier, Adventures of Captain Carleton, Dickory Cronke, &c.

10. PRIOR'S LIFE OF BURKE, (forming the 1st Volume of BURKE'S WORKS), new Edition, revised by the Author. *Portrait.*

12. BURKE'S WORKS, Vol 1, containing his Vindication of Natural Society, Essay on the Sublime and Beautiful, and various Political Miscellanies.

13. DEFOE'S WORKS, Edited by SIR WALTER SCOTT. Vol. 3. Containing the Life of Moll Flanders, and the History of the Devil.

15. BURKE'S WORKS. Vol. 2, containing Essay on the French Revolution, Political Letters and Speeches.

17. DEFOE'S WORKS, Vol. 4. Roxana, or the Fortunate Mistress; and Life and Adventures of Mother Ross.

18. BURKE'S WORKS, Vol. 3. Appeal from the New to the Old Whigs, &c., &c.

19. BURKE'S WORKS, Vol. 4, containing his Report on the Affairs of India, and Articles against Warren Hastings.

21. DEFOE'S WORKS, Vol. 5, containing the History of the Great Plague of London, 1665; the Fire of London, 1666 (by an anonymous writer); the Storm; and the True Born Englishman.

22 & 23. BURKE'S WORKS (in Six Volumes). Vols. 5 & 6.

26. DEFOE'S WORKS, edited by SIR WALTER SCOTT. Vol. 6. Containing Life and Adventures of Duncan Campbell; Voyage Round the World; and Tracts relating to the Hanoverian Accession.

27 & 28. BURKE'S SPEECHES on the IMPEACHMENT of WARREN HASTINGS; with a Selection of his Letters, and a General Index. 2 vols. (Also forming vols. 7 and 8 of Burke's Works, which they complete.)

BOHN'S ECCLESIASTICAL LIBRARY.

Uniform with the STANDARD LIBRARY, *price 5s. per Volume.*

1. EUSEBIUS' ECCLESIASTICAL HISTORY, Translated from the Greek, with Notes.

2. SOCRATES' ECCLESIASTICAL HISTORY, in continuation of EUSEBIUS, with the Notes of VALESIUS.

3. THEODORET AND EVAGRIUS. Ecclesiastical Historics, from A.D. 332 to A.D. 427, and from A.D. 431 to A.D. 544. Translated from the Greek, with General Index.

4. THE WORKS OF PHILO JUDÆUS, translated from the Greek by C. D. YONGE, B.A. Vol. 1.

5. PHILO JUDÆUS, Vol. 2.

6. SOZOMEN'S ECCLESIASTICAL HISTORY from A.D. 324-440; and the Ecclesiastical History of PHILOSTORGIUS, translated from the Greek, with a Memoir of the Author, by E. WALFORD, M.A.

7 & 8. PHILO JUDÆUS, Vols. 3 & 4, with general Index.

BOHN'S SHILLING SERIES.

Those marked *, being Double Volumes, are 1s. 6d.

ON'S REPRESENTATIVE MEN.
'S LIFE OF MAHOMET.*
ENUINE AUTOBIOGRAPHY OF BENJAMIN FRANKLIN.
'S PEOPLE I HAVE MET.*
'S SUCCESSORS OF MAHOMET *
— LIFE OF GOLDSMITH.*
— SKETCH-BOOK.*
— TALES OF A TRAVELLER.*
— TOUR ON THE PRAIRIES.
— CONQUESTS OF GRANADA AND SPAIN. 2 Vols.*
— LIFE OF COLUMBUS. 2 Vols.*
— COMPANIONS OF COLUMBUS.*
AYLOR'S EL DORADO; or, Pictures of the Gold Region. 2 Vols.
'S ADVENTURES OF CAPTAIN BONNEVILLE.*
— KNICKERBOCKER.*
— TALES OF THE ALHAMBRA.*
— CONQUEST OF FLORIDA.*
— ABBOTSFORD AND NEWSTEAD.
— SALMAGUNDI.*
— BRACEBRIDGE HALL.*
— ASTORIA (*Portrait of the Author*). 2 Vols. in 1. 2s.
RTINE'S GENEVIEVE; or, The History of a Servant Girl. Translated
SCOBLE.
'S BERBER; or, The Mountaineer of the Atlas. A Tale of Morocco.
'S LIFE HERE AND THERE; or, Sketches of Society and Adventure.
T'S LIFE OF MONK, with Appendix and *Portrait*.*
CAPE AND THE KAFFIRS: A Diary of Five Years' Residence,
e to Emigrants. By H. WARD. *Plate and Map of the Seat of War.* 2s.
'S HURRY-GRAPHS; or, Sketches of Scenery, Celebrities, and Soc
from Life.*
HORNE'S HOUSE OF THE SEVEN GABLES. A Romance.
N AND ITS ENVIRONS; with Historical and Descriptive Sketch of
Exhibition. By CYRUS REDDING. *Numerous Illustrations.* 2s.
RTINE'S STONEMASON OF SAINT POINT.*
T'S MONK'S CONTEMPORARIES. A Series of Biographic Studies
nglish Revolution. *Portrait of Edward Lord Clarendon.*
HORNE'S TWICE-TOLD TALES.
——— The same, Second Series.
——— SNOW IMAGE, and other Tales.
——— SCARLET LETTER.
ON'S ORATIONS AND LECTURES.
TOM'S CABIN; or, Life among the Lowly; with Introductory Rem
REV. J. SHERMAN.
'HITE SLAVE. A new picture of American Slave Life.
OF BATTLE; or, Quatre Bras and Waterloo. By an ENGLISHWOM
nt at Brussels in June, 1815, (author of Rome in the Nineteenth Century

DA   Nugent, George Nugent
396   Grenville, Baron
H18N8   Memorials of John Hampden
1860   4th ed.

PLEASE DO NOT REMOVE
CARDS OR SLIPS FROM THIS POCKET

UNIVERSITY OF TORONTO LIBRARY

www.ingramcontent.com/pod-product-compliance
Lightning Source LLC
Chambersburg PA
CBHW051200300426
44116CB00006B/384